Lecture Notes in Artificial Intelligence 10483

Subseries of Lecture Notes in Computer Science

More information about this series at http://www.springer.com/series/1244

Clare Dixon · Marcelo Finger (Eds.)

Frontiers of Combining Systems

11th International Symposium, FroCoS 2017
Brasília, Brazil, September 27–29, 2017
Proceedings

Springer

Editors
Clare Dixon
University of Liverpool
Liverpool
UK

Marcelo Finger
University of Sao Paulo
Sao Paulo
Brazil

ISSN 0302-9743 ISSN 1611-3349 (electronic)
Lecture Notes in Artificial Intelligence
ISBN 978-3-319-66166-7 ISBN 978-3-319-66167-4 (eBook)
DOI 10.1007/978-3-319-66167-4

Library of Congress Control Number: 2017950044

LNCS Sublibrary: SL7 – Artificial Intelligence

Printed on acid-free paper

This Springer imprint is published by Springer Nature
The registered company is Springer International Publishing AG
The registered company address is: Gewerbestrasse 11, 6330 Cham, Switzerland

Preface

The 11th International Symposium on Frontiers of Combining Systems (FroCoS) was held 27–29th September 2017 at the University of Brasília, Brazil. It was co-located with the 26th International Conference on Automated Reasoning with Analytic Tableaux and Related Methods (Tableaux) and the 8th International Conference on Interactive Theorem Proving (ITP). The symposium included both invited speakers and contributed papers and the three co-located events shared a poster session and were preceded by a number of workshops and tutorials.

The first FroCoS symposium was held in Munich, Germany, in 1996. Initially held every two years, since 2004 it has been organised annually with alternate years forming part of IJCAR. Like previous events in the FroCoS series, FroCoS 2017 offered a forum for research in the general area of combination, modularisation, and integration of systems, with an emphasis on logic-based ones and on their practical use. The development of techniques and methods for the combination and integration of dedicated formal systems, as well as for their modularisation and analysis, is crucial to the development of systems in logic, computation, program development and verification, artificial intelligence, knowledge representation, and automated reasoning.

FroCoS 2017 received 26 full paper submissions, with authors from 16 different countries. These were reviewed and discussed by the Programme Committee and each paper received at least three reviews. From these, 17 papers were selected for presentation at the symposium and publication. Their topics include description and temporal logics, decision procedures, decidability and verification, SAT, SMT and automated theorem proving, term rewriting, and properties and combinations of logics. The proceedings also include papers from two of our invited speakers.

The FroCoS programme included two invited speakers:

- Cesare Tinelli (University of Iowa, USA) Designing Extensible Theory Solvers
- Renata Wassermann (University of São Paulo, Brazil) Revising System Specifications in Temporal Logic

with three additional invited speakers being shared between all conferences:

- Katalin Bimbó (University of Alberta, Canada) The Perimeter of Decidability (with Sequent Calculi on the Inside)
- Jasmin Blanchette (Vrije Universiteit Amsterdam, The Netherlands) Foundational (Co)datatypes and (Co)recursion for Higher-Order Logic
- Cezary Kaliszyk (University of Innsbruck, Austria) Locally Abstract, Globally Concrete Semantics of Concurrent Programming Languages

We would like to thank all the people who worked hard to make the 2017 symposium a success. In particular, we thank the invited speakers for their inspirational talks and contributed papers, authors for submitting, revising and presenting their work, and all the attendees for contributing to the symposium discussion. We also extend our thanks to the Program Committee and external reviewers for their prompt, careful reviewing and discussion of the submissions.

Finally we convey our gratitude and appreciation to everybody who contributed to the organisation of the event, in particular to Cláudia Nalon, Daniele Nantes Sobrinho, Elaine Pimentel, João Marcos and their team for taking care of all the local organisation so expertly and making our life as co-chairs much easier. Particular thanks go to Cláudia Nalon for bringing the symposium and co-located events to Brazil and for her thorough organisation, enthusiasm, leadership and patience.

We acknowledge and thank a number of organisations for supporting the symposium. The Association for Automated Reasoning (AAR), the European Association for Computer Science Logic (EACSL), and the Association for Symbolic Logic (ASL) provided scientific support. We received financial support from the National Council for Scientific and Technological Development (CNPq, ARC 03/2016). The University of Brasília and the Federal University of Rio Grande do Norte have both contributed to the organisation. We thank Springer for their continuing support with publishing the proceedings and to EasyChair for allowing us to use their conference management system. We are grateful for the support of all these organisations.

September 2017

Clare Dixon
Marcelo Finger

Organisation

Conference Chairs

Clare Dixon	University of Liverpool, UK
Marcelo Finger	University of São Paulo, Brazil

Local Organisation

Cláudia Nalon	University of Brasília, Brazil
Daniele Nantes Sobrinho	University of Brasília, Brazil
Elaine Pimentel	Federal University of Rio Grande do Norte, Brazil
João Marcos	Federal University of Rio Grande do Norte, Brazil

FroCoS Steering Committee

Franz Baader (President)	TU Dresden, Germany
Silvio Ghilardi	Università degli Studi di Milano, Italy
Pascal Fontaine	Université de Lorraine, France
Silvio Ranise	Fondazione Bruno Kessler, Italy
Renate Schmidt	University of Manchester, UK
Viorica Sofronie-Stokkermans	Universität Koblenz-Landau, Germany
Cesare Tinelli	University of Iowa, USA

Program Committee

Carlos Areces	FaMAF - Universidad Nacional de Córdoba, Argentina
Alessandro Artale	Free University of Bolzano-Bozen, Italy
Mauricio Ayala-Rincon	Universidade de Brasilia, Brazil
Franz Baader	TU Dresden, Germany
Peter Baumgartner	National ICT Australia
Christoph Benzmüller	Freie Universität Berlin, Germany
Thomas Bolander	Technical University of Denmark
Marcelo Coniglio	University of Campinas, Brazil
Clare Dixon	University of Liverpool, UK
François Fages	Inria Paris-Rocquencourt, France
Marcelo Finger	Universidade de Sao Paulo, Brazil
Pascal Fontaine	Loria, Inria, University of Lorraine, France
Didier Galmiche	Université de Lorraine - Loria, France
Vijay Ganesh	University of Waterloo, Canada
Silvio Ghilardi	Università degli Studi di Milano, Italy
Jürgen Giesl	RWTH Aachen, Germany

Laura Giordano	DISIT, Università del Piemonte Orientale, Italy
Agi Kurucz	King's College London, UK
Till Mossakowski	Otto-von-Guericke-University Magdeburg, Germany
Cláudia Nalon	University of Brasília, Brazil
Elaine Pimentel	Federal University of Rio Grande do Norte, Brazil
Silvio Ranise	FBK-Irst, Italy
Christophe Ringeissen	Loria-Inria, France
Uli Sattler	University of Manchester, UK
Roberto Sebastiani	DISI, University of Trento, Italy
Guillermo Simari	Universidad del Sur in Bahia Blanca, Argentina
Viorica Sofronie-Stokkermans	University Koblenz-Landau, Germany
Andrzej Szalas	University of Warsaw, Poland
René Thiemann	University of Innsbruck, Austria
Ashish Tiwari	SRI International, USA
Christoph Weidenbach	Max Planck Institute for Informatics, Germany

Additional Reviewers

Abraham, Erika
Almeida, Ariane Alves
Berzish, Murphy
Felgenhauer, Bertram
Flores-Montoya, Antonio
Gabbay, Murdoch
Gianola, Alessandro
Hutter, Dieter
Kaliszyk, Cezary
Khan, Muhammad
Kovtunova, Alisa
Kutsia, Temur
Kutz, Oliver
Kuznets, Roman
Li, Ian
Li, Yuan-Fang
Martelli, Alberto
Moyen, Jean-Yves
Nantes-Sobrinho, Daniele
Roland, Jérémie
Schmidt-Schauss, Manfred

Contents

SAT, SMT and Automated Theorem Proving

Decision Procedures, Decidability and Verification

Properties and Combinations of Logic

Invited Talks

Foundational (Co)datatypes and (Co)recursion for Higher-Order Logic

Julian Biendarra[1], Jasmin Christian Blanchette[2,3(✉)], Aymeric Bouzy[4], Martin Desharnais[5], Mathias Fleury[3], Johannes Hölzl[6], Ondřej Kunčar[1], Andreas Lochbihler[7], Fabian Meier[8], Lorenz Panny[9], Andrei Popescu[10,11], Christian Sternagel[12], René Thiemann[12], and Dmitriy Traytel[7]

[1] Fakultät für Informatik, Technische Universität München, Munich, Germany
[2] Vrije Universiteit Amsterdam, Amsterdam, The Netherlands
j.c.blanchette@vu.nl
[3] Max-Planck-Institut für Informatik, Saarland Informatics Campus, Saarbrücken, Germany
[4] InstantJob, Paris, France
[5] Ludwig-Maximilians-Universität München, Munich, Germany
[6] Carnegie Mellon University, Pittsburgh, USA
[7] Institute of Information Security, Department of Computer Science, ETH Zürich, Zurich, Switzerland
[8] Google, Zurich, Switzerland
[9] Technische Universiteit Eindhoven, Eindhoven, The Netherlands
[10] Middlesex University London, London, UK
[11] Institute of Mathematics Simion Stoilow of the Romanian Academy, Bucharest, Romania
[12] Universität Innsbruck, Innsbruck, Austria

Abstract. We describe a line of work that started in 2011 towards enriching Isabelle/HOL's language with coinductive datatypes, which allow infinite values, and with a more expressive notion of inductive datatype than previously supported by any system based on higher-order logic. These (co)datatypes are complemented by definitional principles for (co)recursive functions and reasoning principles for (co)induction. In contrast with other systems offering codatatypes, no additional axioms or logic extensions are necessary with our approach.

1 Introduction

Rich specification mechanisms are crucial to the usability of proof assistants—in particular, mechanisms for defining inductive datatypes, recursive functions, and inductive predicates. Datatypes and recursive functions are inspired by typed functional programming languages from the ML family. Inductive predicates are reminiscent of Prolog.

Coinductive methods are becoming increasingly widespread in computer science. Coinductive datatypes, corecursive functions, and coinductive predicates are useful to represent potentially infinite data and processes and to

C. Dixon and M. Finger (Eds.): FroCoS 2017, LNCS 10483, pp. 3–21, 2017.
DOI: 10.1007/978-3-319-66167-4_1

reason about them. Coinductive datatypes, or *codatatypes*, are freely generated by their constructors, but in contrast to datatypes, infinite constructor terms are also legitimate values for codatatypes. Corecursion makes it possible to build such values. A simple example is the "lazy" (or coinductive) list $\mathsf{LCons}\ 0\ (\mathsf{LCons}\ 1\ (\mathsf{LCons}\ 2\ \ldots))$ that enumerates the natural numbers. It can be specified via the corecursive equation $\mathsf{enum}\ n = \mathsf{LCons}\ n\ (\mathsf{enum}\ (n+1))$.

In 2011, we started an effort to enrich the Isabelle/HOL proof assistant with definitional mechanisms for codatatypes and corecursion. Until then, Isabelle/HOL and the other main systems based on higher-order logic (HOL4, HOL Light, and ProofPower–HOL) provided at most (inductive) datatypes, recursive functions, and (co)inductive predicates. Our aim was to support formalizations such as Lochbihler's verified compiler for a Java-like language [32] and his mathematization of the Java memory model [33], both of which rely on codatatypes to represent infinite traces.

Creating a monolithic codatatype package to supplement Isabelle/HOL's existing datatype package [4] was not an attractive prospect, because many applications need to mix datatypes and codatatypes, as in the following nested (co)recursive specification:

datatype $\alpha\ \mathit{list} = \mathsf{Nil} \mid \mathsf{Cons}\ \alpha\ (\alpha\ \mathit{list})$
codatatype $\alpha\ \mathit{ltree} = \mathsf{LNode}\ \alpha\ ((\alpha\ \mathit{ltree})\ \mathit{list})$

The first command introduces a polymorphic type of finite lists over an element type α, freely generated by the constructors $\mathsf{Nil} : \alpha\ \mathit{list}$ and $\mathsf{Cons} : \alpha \to \alpha\ \mathit{list} \to \alpha\ \mathit{list}$. The second command introduces a type of finitely branching trees of possibly infinite depth. For example, the infinite tree $\mathsf{LNode}\ 0\ (\mathsf{Cons}\ (\mathsf{LNode}\ 0\ (\mathsf{Cons}\ \ldots\ \mathsf{Nil}))\ \mathsf{Nil})$ specified by $t = \mathsf{LNode}\ 0\ (\mathsf{Cons}\ t\ \mathsf{Nil})$ is valid. Ideally, (co)datatypes should also be allowed to (co)recurse through well-behaved nonfree type constructors, such as the finite set constructor *fset*:

codatatype $\alpha\ \mathit{ltree}_{\mathsf{fs}} = \mathsf{LNode}_{\mathsf{fs}}\ \alpha\ ((\alpha\ \mathit{ltree}_{\mathsf{fs}})\ \mathit{fset})$

In this paper, we present the various new definitional packages for (co)datatypes and (co)recursive functions that today support Isabelle users with their formalizations. The theoretical cornerstone underlying these is a semantic criterion we call *bounded natural functors* (BNF, Sect. 3). The criterion is met by construction for a large class of datatypes and codatatypes (such as *list*, *ltree*, and $\mathit{ltree}_{\mathsf{fs}}$) and by bounded sets and bounded multisets. On the right-hand side of a **datatype** or **codatatype** command, recursion is allowed under arbitrary type constructors that are BNFs. This flexibility is not available in other proof assistants.

The **datatype** and **codatatype** commands construct a type as a solution to a fixpoint equation (Sect. 4). For example, $\alpha\ \mathit{list}$ is the solution for β in the equation $\beta \cong \mathit{unit} + \alpha \times \beta$, where *unit* is a singleton type, whereas $+$ and $\times$ are the type constructors for sum (disjoint union) and product (pairs), respectively. To ensure that the new types are nonempty, the commands must also synthesize a witness (Sect. 5).

The above mechanisms are complemented by commands for defining primitively (co)recursive functions over (co)datatypes (Sect. 6). But primitive (co)recursion is very restrictive in practice. For general (nonprimitive) well-founded recursion, Isabelle/HOL already provided the **fun** and **function** commands [29]; our new datatypes work well with them. For nonprimitive corecursion, we designed and implemented a definitional mechanism based on the notion of corecursion up to "friendly" operations (Sect. 7).

In *nonuniform* datatypes, the type arguments may vary recursively. They arise in the implementation of efficient functional data structures. We designed commands that reduce a large class of nonuniform datatypes, and nonuniform codatatypes, to their uniform counterparts (Sect. 8).

We integrated the new (co)datatypes with various Isabelle tools, including the Lifting and Transfer tools, which transfer definitions and theorems across isomorphisms, the Nitpick counterexample generator, and the Sledgehammer proof tool (Sect. 9). The new (co)datatypes are widely used, including in our own work—codatatypes for their convenience, and the new datatypes for their flexibility and scalability (Sect. 10).

Crucially, all our specification mechanisms follow the *definitional approach*, as is typical in Isabelle/HOL and the HOL family of systems. This means that the desired types and terms are explicitly constructed and introduced using more primitive mechanisms and their characteristic properties are derived as theorems. This guarantees that they introduce no inconsistencies, reducing the amount of code that must be trusted. The main drawback of this approach is that it puts a heavy burden on the mechanisms' designers and implementers. For example, the (**co**)**datatype** commands explicitly construct solutions to fixpoint equations and nonemptiness witnesses, and the constructions must be performed efficiently. Other approaches—such as the intrinsic approach, where the specification mechanism is built directly into the logic, and the axiomatic approach, where types and terms are added to the signature and characterized by axioms—require less work but do not guard against inconsistencies [4, Sect. 1].

The work described in this paper was first presented in conference and journal publications between 2012 and 2017 [7,9,10,12,13,15–18,46,50,51]. The current text is partly based on these papers. The source code consists of about 29 000 lines of Standard ML distributed as part of Isabelle and the *Archive of Formal Proofs* [47]. It is complemented by Isabelle lemma libraries necessary for the constructions, notably a theory of cardinals [15]. We refer to our earlier papers [10,13,18,51] for discussions of related work.

2 Isabelle/HOL

Isabelle [39] is a generic proof assistant whose metalogic is an intuitionistic fragment of polymorphic higher-order logic. The types τ are built from type variables α, β, ... and type constructors, written infix or postfix (e.g., $\to$, *list*). All types are inhabited. Terms t, u are built from variables x, constants c, abstractions $\lambda x.\ t$, and applications $t\ u$. Types are usually left implicit. Constants may be functions. A formula is a term of type *prop*. The metalogical operators are $\bigwedge$, $\Longrightarrow$, and $\equiv$, for universal quantification, implication, and equality. The notation $\bigwedge x.\ t$ abbreviates $\bigwedge (\lambda x.\ t)$. Internally, λ is the only binder.

Isabelle/HOL is the instantiation of Isabelle with classical higher-order logic (HOL) extended with type classes as its object logic, complete with a Boolean type *bool*, an equality predicate ($=$), the usual connectives ($\neg$, $\wedge$, $\vee$, $\longrightarrow$, $\longleftrightarrow$) and quantifiers ($\forall$, $\exists$), and Hilbert's choice operator. HOL formulas, of type *bool*, are embedded in the metalogic. The distinction between *prop* and *bool* is not essential to understand this paper.

Isabelle/HOL offers two primitive definitional mechanisms: The **typedef** command introduces a type that is isomorphic to a nonempty subset of an existing type, and the **definition** command introduces a constant as equal to an existing term. Other commands, such as **datatype** and **function**, build on these primitives.

Proofs are expressed either as a sequence of low-level *tactics* that manipulate the proof state directly or in a declarative format called Isar [53]. Basic tactics rely on resolution and higher-order unification. Other useful tactics include the *simplifier*, which rewrites terms using conditional oriented equations, and the *classical reasoner*, which applies introduction and elimination rules in the style of natural deduction. Specialized tactics can be written in Standard ML, Isabelle's main implementation language.

3 Bounded Natural Functors

An n-ary *bounded natural functor* (BNF) [12,51,52] is an $(n+k)$-ary type constructor equipped with a map function (or functorial action), a relator, n set functions (natural transformations), and a cardinal bound that satisfy certain properties. For example, *list* is a unary BNF. Its relator $\mathsf{rel} : (\alpha \to \beta \to bool) \to \alpha\ list \to \beta\ list \to bool$ extends binary predicates over elements to binary predicates over parallel lists: $\mathsf{rel}\ R\ xs\ ys$ is true if and only if the lists xs and ys have the same length and the elements of the two lists are elementwise related by R. Moreover, the cardinal bound bd constrains the number of elements returned by the set function set; it cannot depend on α's cardinality. To prove that *list* is a BNF, the **datatype** command discharges the following proof obligations:

$$\mathsf{map\ id} = \mathsf{id} \qquad \mathsf{map}\ (f \circ g) = \mathsf{map}\ f \circ \mathsf{map}\ g \qquad \frac{\bigwedge x.\ x \in \mathsf{set}\ xs \Longrightarrow f\ x = g\ x}{\mathsf{map}\ f\ xs = \mathsf{map}\ g\ xs}$$

$$|\mathsf{set}\ xs| \leq_o \mathsf{bd} \qquad \mathsf{set} \circ \mathsf{map}\ f = \mathsf{image}\ f \circ \mathsf{set}$$

$$\aleph_0 \leq_o \mathsf{bd} \qquad \mathsf{rel}\ R \circ\circ \mathsf{rel}\ S \sqsubseteq \mathsf{rel}\ (R \circ\circ S)$$

$$\mathsf{rel}\ R\ xs\ ys \longleftrightarrow \exists ps.\ \mathsf{set}\ ps \subseteq \{(xs, ys).\ R\ xs\ ys\} \wedge \mathsf{map\ fst}\ ps = xs \wedge \mathsf{map\ snd}\ ps = ys$$

The operator $\leq_o$ is a well-order on ordinals [15], $\sqsubseteq$ denotes implication lifted to binary predicates, $\circ\circ$ denotes the relational composition of binary predicates, fst and snd denote the left and right pair projections, and the horizontal bar denotes implication ($\Longrightarrow$).

The class of BNFs is closed under composition, initial algebra (for datatypes), and final coalgebra (for codatatypes). The last two operations correspond to least and greatest fixpoints, respectively. Given an n-ary BNF, the n type variables associated with set functions, and on which the map function acts, are *live*; the remaining k type variables are *dead*. For example, the function type $\alpha \to \beta$ is a unary BNF on β; the variable α is dead. Nested (co)recursion can only take place through live variables.

Composition of functors is widely perceived as being trivial. Nevertheless, the implementation must perform a carefully orchestrated sequence of steps to construct BNFs and discharge the emerging proof obligations for the types occurring on the right-hand sides of fixpoint equations. This is achieved by four operations: Composition proper works on normalized BNFs that share the same live variables, whereas the other three operations achieve this normalization by adding, killing, or permuting live variables.

4 Datatypes and Codatatypes

The **datatype** and **codatatype** commands [12] state and solve fixpoint equations. Then they define the constructor, discriminator, and selector constants and derive various theorems involving the constructors. The command for introducing lazy lists follows:

codatatype α *llist* = lnull: LNil | LCons (lhd: α) (ltl: α *list*)

The constructors are LNil and LCons. The discriminator lnull tests whether a lazy list is LNil. The selectors lhd and ltl return the head or tail of a non-LNil lazy list.

The **datatype** command also introduces a *recursor*, which can be used to define primitively recursive functions. The list recursor has type $\beta \to (\alpha \to \alpha\ \mathit{list} \times \beta \to \beta) \to \alpha\ \mathit{list} \to \beta$ and is characterized by the following theorems:

$$\mathsf{rec}\ n\ c\ \mathsf{Nil} = n \qquad \mathsf{rec}\ n\ c\ (\mathsf{Cons}\ x\ xs) = c\ x\ (xs,\ \mathsf{rec}\ n\ c\ xs)$$

In general, for a datatype equipped with m constructors, the recursor takes one argument corresponding to each constructor, followed by a datatype value, and returns a value of an arbitrary type β. The corresponding induction principle has one hypothesis per constructor. For example, for lists it is as follows:

$$\frac{P\ \mathsf{Nil} \quad \bigwedge x\ xs.\ P\ xs \Longrightarrow P\ (\mathsf{Cons}\ x\ xs)}{P\ t}$$

Recursive functions *consume* datatype values, peeling off constructors as they proceed. In contrast, corecursive functions *produce* codatatype values, consisting of finitely or infinitely many constructors, one constructor at a time. For each codatatype, a corresponding *corecursor* embodies this principle. It works as follows: Given a codatatype τ with m constructors, $m - 1$ predicates sequentially determine which constructor to produce. Moreover, for each argument to each constructor, a function specifies how to construct it from an abstract value of type α that captures the tuple of arguments given to the corecursive function.

For corecursive constructor arguments, the function has type $\alpha \to \tau + \alpha$ and returns either a value (τ) that stops the corecursion or a tuple of arguments (α) to a corecursive call. Thus, the corecursor for lazy lists has type

$$(\alpha \to \mathit{bool}) \to (\alpha \to \beta) \to (\alpha \to \beta\ \mathit{llist} + \alpha) \to \alpha \to \beta\ \mathit{llist}$$

and is characterized as follows, where Inl and Inr are the injections into the sum type:

$$n\ a \Longrightarrow \mathsf{corec}\ n\ h\ t\ a = \mathsf{LNil}$$
$$\neg\ n\ a \Longrightarrow \mathsf{corec}\ n\ h\ t\ a = \mathsf{LCons}\ (h\ a)\ (\mathsf{case}\ t\ a\ \mathsf{of}\ \mathsf{Inl}\ xs \Rightarrow xs \mid \mathsf{Inr}\ a' \Rightarrow \mathsf{corec}\ n\ h\ t\ a')$$

The coinduction principle can be used to prove equalities $l = r$. It is parameterized by a relation R that relates l and r and is closed under application of destructors. Such a relation is called a *bisimulation*. For lazy lists, we have the following principle:

$$\frac{R\ xs\ ys \qquad \bigwedge xs\ ys.\ R\ xs\ ys \Longrightarrow \mathsf{lnull}\ xs \longleftrightarrow \mathsf{lnull}\ ys \wedge (\neg\ \mathsf{lnull}\ xs \wedge \neg\ \mathsf{lnull}\ ys \longrightarrow \mathsf{lhd}\ xs = \mathsf{lhd}\ ys \wedge R\ (\mathsf{ltl}\ xs)\ (\mathsf{ltl}\ ys))}{xs = ys}$$

5 Nonemptiness Witnesses

The **typedef** primitive requires a nonemptiness witnesses before it introduces the desired type in HOL. Thus, the **datatype** and **codatatype** commands, which build on **typedef**, must provide such a witness [18]. For **datatype**, this is nontrivial. For example, the following inductive specification of "finite streams" must be rejected because it would lead to an empty datatype, one without a nonemptiness witness:

datatype α *fstream* = $\mathsf{FSCons}\ \alpha\ (\alpha\ \mathit{fstream})$

If we substituted **codatatype** for **datatype**, the infinite value $\mathsf{FSCons}\ x\ (\mathsf{FSCons}\ x\ \ldots)$ would be a suitable witness, given a value x of type α.

While checking nonemptiness appears to be an easy reachability test, nested recursion complicates the picture, as shown by this attempt to define infinitely branching trees with finite branches by nested recursion via a codatatype of (infinite) streams:

codatatype α *stream* = $\mathsf{SCons}\ \alpha\ (\alpha\ \mathit{stream})$
datatype α *tree* = $\mathsf{Node}\ \alpha\ ((\alpha\ \mathit{tree})\ \mathit{stream})$

The second definition should fail: To get a witness for α *tree*, we would need a witness for (α *tree*) *stream*, and vice versa. Replacing streams with finite lists should make the definition acceptable because the empty list stops the recursion. So even though codatatype specifications are never empty, here the datatype provides a better witness (the empty list) than the codatatype (which requires an α *tree* to build an (α *tree*) *stream*).

Mutual, nested datatype specifications and their nonemptiness witnesses can be arbitrarily complex. Consider the following commands:

datatype (α, β) *tree* $=$ Leaf β | Branch $((\alpha + (\alpha, \beta)\ \mathit{tree})\ \mathit{stream})$
codatatype (α, β) *ltree* $=$ LNode β $((\alpha + (\alpha, \beta)\ \mathit{ltree})\ \mathit{stream})$
datatype
$t_1 = \mathsf{T}_{11}\ (((t_1, t_2)\ \mathit{ltree})\ \mathit{stream}) \mid \mathsf{T}_{12}\ (t_1 \times (t_2 + t_3)\ \mathit{stream})$ **and**
$t_2 = \mathsf{T}_2\ ((t_1 \times t_2)\ \mathit{list})$ **and**
$t_3 = \mathsf{T}_3\ ((t_1, (t_3, t_3)\ \mathit{tree})\ \mathit{tree})$

The definitions are legitimate, but the last group of mutually recursive datatypes should be rejected if t_2 is replaced by t_3 in the constructor T_{11}.

What makes the problem interesting is the open-ended nature of our setting. BNFs form a *semantic* class that is not syntactically predetermined. In particular, they are not restricted to polynomial functors (sums of products); the user can register new type constructors as BNFs after discharging the BNF proof obligations.

Our solution exploits the package's abstract, functorial view of types. Each (co)datatype, and more generally each functor (type constructor) that participates in a definition, carries its own witnesses. Operations such as functorial composition, initial algebra, and final coalgebra derive their witnesses from those of the operands. Each computational step performed by the package is certified in HOL.

The solution is complete: Given precise information about the functors participating in a definition, all nonempty datatypes are identified as such. A corollary is that the nonemptiness of open-ended, mutual, nested (co)datatypes is decidable. The proof relies on a notion of possibly infinite derivation trees, which can be captured formally as a codatatype. We proved the key results in Isabelle/HOL for an arbitrary unary functor, using the **datatype** and **codatatype** commands to formalize their own metatheory.

6 Primitive Recursion and Corecursion

Primitively recursive functions can be defined by providing suitable arguments to the relevant recursor, and similarly for corecursive functions. The **primrec** and **primcorec** commands automate this process: From the recursive equations specified by the user, they synthesize a (co)recursor-based definition [12, 41]. For example, the command

primrec length : $\alpha\ \mathit{list} \to \mathit{nat}$ **where**
length Nil $= 0$
| length (Cons $x\ xs$) $= 1 +$ length xs

synthesizes the definition length $=$ rec 0 $(\lambda x\, xs\, n.\ 1 + n)$ and derives the specified equations as theorems, exploiting the recursor's characteristic theorems (Sect. 4).

To qualify as primitive, recursive calls must be directly applied to constructor arguments (e.g., xs in the second equation for length). Dually, primitive corecursive calls must occur under exactly one constructor—and possibly some 'if–then–else', 'case', and 'let' constructs—as in the next example:

primcorec $\mathsf{lappend} : \alpha\ \mathit{llist} \to \alpha\ \mathit{llist} \to \alpha\ \mathit{llist}$ **where**
$\mathsf{lappend}\ xs\ ys = (\mathsf{case}\ xs\ \mathsf{of}\ \mathsf{LNil} \Rightarrow ys \mid \mathsf{LCons}\ x\ xs \Rightarrow \mathsf{LCons}\ x\ (\mathsf{lappend}\ xs\ ys))$

With both **primrec** and **primcorec**, an interesting scenario arises for types defined by (co)recursion through a BNF. The (co)recursive calls must then appear inside the map function associated with the BNF. For example:

primrec $\mathsf{height\_tree_{fs}} : \alpha\ \mathit{tree}_{\mathsf{fs}} \to \mathit{nat}$ **where**
$\mathsf{height\_tree_{fs}}\ (\mathsf{Node_{fs}}\ x\ T) = 1 + \bigsqcup(\mathsf{fimage}\ \mathsf{height\_tree_{fs}}\ T)$

Here, $\alpha\ \mathit{tree}_{\mathsf{fs}}$ is the datatype constructed by $\mathsf{Node_{fs}} : \alpha \to (\alpha\ \mathit{tree}_{\mathsf{fs}})\ \mathit{fset} \to \alpha\ \mathit{tree}_{\mathsf{fs}}$, $\bigsqcup N$ stands for the maximum of N, and the map function fimage gives the image of a finite set under a function. From the specified equation, the command synthesizes the definition $\mathsf{height\_tree_{fs}} = \mathsf{rec\_tree_{fs}}\ (\lambda x\ TN.\ 1 + \bigsqcup(\mathsf{fimage}\ \mathsf{snd}\ TN))$. From this definition and $\mathit{tree}_{\mathsf{fs}}$'s recursor theorems, it derives the original equation as a theorem. Notice how the argument $T : (\alpha\ \mathit{tree}_{\mathsf{fs}})\ \mathit{fset}$ becomes $TN : (\alpha\ \mathit{tree}_{\mathsf{fs}} \times \mathit{nat})\ \mathit{fset}$, where the second pair components (extracted by snd) store the result of the corresponding recursive calls.

7 Corecursion up to Friendly Operations

Primitive corecursion is very restrictive. To work around this, Lochbihler and Hölzl dedicated an entire paper [35] to ad hoc techniques for defining operations on lazy lists; and when formalizing formal languages coinductively, Traytel [50] needed to recast the nonprimitive specifications of concatenation and iteration into specifications that can be processed by the **primcorec** command.

Consider the codatatype of streams (infinite lazy lists), with the constructor SCons and the selectors shd and stl:

codatatype $\alpha\ \mathit{stream} = \mathsf{SCons}\ (\mathsf{shd}{:}\ \alpha)\ (\mathsf{stl}{:}\ \alpha\ \mathit{stream})$

Primitive corecursion is expressive enough to define operations such as the componentwise addition of two streams of numbers:

primcorec $\oplus : \mathit{nat\ stream} \to \mathit{nat\ stream} \to \mathit{nat\ stream}$ **where**
$xs \oplus ys = \underline{\mathsf{SCons}}\ (\mathsf{shd}\ xs + \mathsf{shd}\ ys)\ (\mathsf{stl}\ xs \oplus \mathsf{stl}\ ys)$

Intuitively, the evaluation of $\oplus$ makes some progress with each corecursive call, since the call occurs directly under the constructor, which acts as a *guard* (shown underlined). The specification is *productive* and unambiguously characterizes a function. Moreover, it is primitively corecursive, because the topmost symbol on the right-hand side is a constructor and the corecursive call appears directly as an argument to it.

Although these syntactic restrictions can be relaxed to allow conditional statements and 'let' expressions, primitive corecursion remains hopelessly primitive. The syntactic criterion for admissible corecursive definitions in Coq [5] is more permissive in that it allows for an arbitrary number of constructors to guard the corecursive calls, as in the following definition: oneTwos = SCons 1 (SCons 2 oneTwos).

We designed and implemented a framework, code-named AmiCo, that can be used to define such functions and reason about them [10,17]. It achieves the same result as Coq by registering SCons as a *friendly* operation, or a *friend*. Intuitively, a friend needs to destruct at most one constructor of input to produce one constructor of output. For streams, such an operation may inspect the head and the tail (but not the tail's tail)—i.e., it may explore at most one layer of its arguments before producing an SCons. Because the operation preserves productivity, it can safely surround the guarding constructor.

But how can we formally express that operators such as SCons and $\oplus$ only explore at most one layer? Inspired by "up to" techniques in category theory [1,37], we require that the corecursor argument is a composition of an optional destructor and a "surface" function that does not explore its codatatype argument. Formally, the surface must be polymorphic and relationally parametric [43] in that argument.

Our **corec** command generalizes **primcorec** to allow corecursion under friendly operations. The codatatype constructors are automatically registered as friends. Other operations can be registered as friends either after their definition—using the dedicated **friend_of_corec** command, which takes as input either their definition or another proved equation—or at definition time, by passing the **friend** option to **corec**:

corec (**friend**) $\oplus$: *nat stream* → *nat stream* → *nat stream* **where**
  $xs \oplus ys$ = SCons (shd xs + shd ys) (stl $xs \oplus$ stl ys)

The command synthesizes the corecursor argument and surface functions, defines $\oplus$ in terms of the corecursor, and derives the user's equation as a theorem. It additionally checks that $\oplus$ meets the criteria on friends and registers it as such.

After registering friends, the corecursor becomes more expressive, allowing corecursive calls surrounded by any combinations of friends. In other words, the corecursor gradually grows to recognize more friends, going well beyond the syntactic criterion implemented in Coq and other systems. For example, the shuffle product $\otimes$ of two streams is defined in terms of $\oplus$, and already goes beyond the corecursive definition capabilities of Coq. Shuffle product being itself friendly, we can employ it to define stream exponentiation, which is also friendly:

corec (**friend**) $\otimes$: *nat stream* → *nat stream* → *nat stream* **where**
  $xs \otimes ys$ = SCons (shd xs × shd ys) (($xs \otimes$ stl ys) $\oplus$ (stl $xs \otimes ys$))
corec (**friend**) exp : *nat stream* → *nat stream* **where**
  exp xs = SCons (2 ^ shd xs) (stl $xs \otimes$ exp xs)

Friends also form a basis for soundly combining recursion with corecursion. The following definition exhibits both recursion on the naturals and corecursion on streams:

corec $\mathsf{cat} : \mathit{nat} \to \mathit{nat\ stream}$ **where**
$\mathsf{cat}\,n = (\text{if}\, n > 0\, \text{then}\, \mathsf{cat}\,(n-1) \oplus \underline{\mathsf{SCons}}\,0(\mathsf{cat}(n+1))$
$\quad \text{else}\, \underline{\mathsf{SCons}}\ 1\ (\mathsf{cat}\ 1))$

The call $\mathsf{cat}\ 1$ computes the stream $C_1, C_2, \ldots$ of Catalan numbers, where $C_n = \frac{1}{n+1}\binom{2n}{n}$. The first self-call, $\mathsf{cat}\ (n-1)$, is recursive, whereas the others are corecursive. Both recursive and corecursive calls are required to appear in friendly contexts, whereas only the corecursive calls are required to be guarded. In exchange, the recursive calls should be terminating: They should eventually lead to either a base case or a corecursive call. AmiCo automatically marks unguarded calls as recursive and attempts to prove their termination using Isabelle/HOL's termination prover [19]. Users also have the option to discharge the proof obligation manually.

8 Nonuniform Datatypes and Codatatypes

Nonuniform (co)datatypes are recursively defined types in which the type arguments vary recursively. Powerlists and powerstreams are prominent specimens:

nonuniform_datatype $\alpha\ \mathit{plist} = \mathsf{Nil} \mid \mathsf{Cons}\ \alpha\ ((\alpha \times \alpha)\ \mathit{plist})$
nonuniform_codatatype $\alpha\ \mathit{pstream} = \mathsf{SCons}\ \alpha\ ((\alpha \times \alpha)\ \mathit{pstream})$

The type $\alpha\ \mathit{plist}$ is freely generated by $\mathsf{Nil} : \alpha\ \mathit{plist}$ and $\mathsf{Cons} : \alpha \to (\alpha \times \alpha)\ \mathit{plist} \to \alpha\ \mathit{plist}$. When Cons is applied several times, the product type constructors $(\times)$ accumulate to create pairs, pairs of pairs, and so on. Thus, any powerlist of length 3 will have the form

$$\mathsf{Cons}\ a\ (\mathsf{Cons}\ (b_1, b_2)\ (\mathsf{Cons}\ ((c_{11}, c_{12}), (c_{21}, c_{22}))\ \mathsf{Nil}))$$

Similarly, the type *pstream* contains only infinite values of the form

$$\mathsf{SCons}\ a\ (\mathsf{SCons}\ (b_1, b_2)\ (\mathsf{SCons}\ ((c_{11}, c_{12}), (c_{21}, c_{22}))\ \ldots))$$

Nonuniform datatypes arise in the implementation of efficient functional data structures such as finger trees [23], and they underlie Okasaki's bootstrapping and implicit recursive slowdown optimization techniques [40]. Agda, Coq, Lean, and Matita allow nonuniform definitions, but these are built into the logic, with all the risks and limitations that this entails [17, Sect. 1]. For systems based on HOL, until recently no dedicated support existed for nonuniform types, probably because they were widely believed to lie beyond the logic's simple polymorphism. Building on the BNF infrastructure, we disproved this folklore belief by showing how to define a large class of nonuniform datatypes by reduction to their uniform counterparts within HOL [13,36].

Our constructions allow variations along several axes for both datatypes and codatatypes. They allow multiple recursive occurrences, with different type arguments:

nonuniform_datatype $\alpha\ \mathit{plist}' = \mathsf{Nil} \mid \mathsf{Cons}_1\ \alpha\ (\alpha\ \mathit{plist}') \mid \mathsf{Cons}_2\ \alpha\ ((\alpha \times \alpha)\ \mathit{plist}')$

They allow multiple type arguments, which may all vary independently of the others. Moreover, they allow the presence of uniform or nonuniform (co)datatypes and other BNFs both around the type arguments and around the recursive type occurrences:

$$\textbf{nonuniform\_datatype}\ \alpha\ \mathit{crazy} = \mathsf{Node}\ \alpha\ (((((\alpha\ \mathit{pstream})\ \mathit{fset})\ \mathit{crazy})\ \mathit{fset})\ \mathit{list})$$

Once a nonuniform datatype has been introduced, users want to define functions that recurse on it and carry out proofs by induction involving these functions—and similarly for codatatypes. A uniform datatype definition generates an induction theorem and a recursor. Nonuniform datatypes pose a challenge, because neither the induction theorem nor the recursor can be expressed in HOL, due to its limited polymorphism. For example, the induction principle for *plist* should look like this:

$$\bigwedge Q.\ Q\ \mathsf{Nil} \wedge (\bigwedge x\ xs.\ Q\ xs \Longrightarrow Q\ (\mathsf{Cons}\ x\ xs)) \Longrightarrow \bigwedge ys.\ Q\ ys$$

However, this formula is not typable in HOL, because the second and third occurrences of the variable Q need different types: $(\alpha \times \alpha)\ \mathit{plist} \to \mathit{bool}$ versus $\alpha\ \mathit{plist} \to \mathit{bool}$. Our solution is to replace the theorem by a procedure parameterized by a polymorphic property $\varphi_\alpha : \alpha\ \mathit{plist} \to \mathit{bool}$. For *plist*, the procedure transforms a proof goal of the form $\varphi_\alpha\ ys$ into two subgoals $\varphi_\alpha\ \mathsf{Nil}$ and $\bigwedge x\ xs.\ \varphi_{\alpha\times\alpha}\ xs \Longrightarrow \varphi_\alpha\ (\mathsf{Cons}\ x\ xs)$. A weak form of parametricity is needed to recursively transfer properties about φ_α to properties about $\varphi_{\alpha\times\alpha}$. Our approach to (co)recursion is similar.

9 Tool Integration

Lifting and Transfer. Isabelle/HOL's Lifting and Transfer tools [26] provide automation for working with type abstractions introduced via the **typedef** command. Lifting defines constants on the newly introduced abstract type from constants on the original raw type. Transfer reduces proof goals about the abstract type to goals about the raw type. Both tools are centered around parametricity and relators.

The BNF infrastructure serves as an abundant supply of relator constants, their properties, and parametricity theorems about the constructors, 'case' combinators, recursors, and the BNF map, set, and relator constants. The interaction between Lifting, Transfer, and the BNF and (co)datatype databases is implemented using Isabelle's plugin mechanism. Plugins are callbacks that are executed upon every update to the BNF or (co)datatype database, as well as for all existing database entries at the moment of the registration of the plugin. The Lifting and Transfer plugins derive and register properties in the format accepted by those tools from the corresponding properties in the BNF and (co)datatype databases.

To enable nested recursion through types introduced by **typedef**, we must register the types as BNFs. The BNF structure can often be lifted from the raw type to the abstract type in a canonical way. The command **lift_bnf** automates this lifting based on a few properties of the carved-out subset: Essentially, the subset must be closed under map f for any f, where map is the map function of the raw type's BNF. If the carved out subset is the entire type, the **copy_bnf** command performs the trivial lifting of the BNF structure. This command is particularly useful to register types defined via Isabelle/HOL's **record** command, which are type copies of some product type, as BNFs.

Size, Countability, Comparators, Show, and Hash. For each finitary datatype τ, the size plugin generates a function size : $\tau \rightarrow$ *nat*. The **fun** and **function** commands [29] rely on size to prove termination of recursive functions on datatypes.

The *countable_datatype* tactic can be used to prove the countability of many datatypes, building on the countability of the types appearing in their definitions.

The **derive** command [46], provided by the *Archive of Formal Proofs* [47], automatically generates comparators, show functions, and hash functions for a specified datatype and can be extended to generate other operations. The mechanism is inspired by Haskell's **deriving** mechanism, with the important difference that it also provides theorems about the operations it introduces.

Nitpick and Sledgehammer. Nitpick [6,8] is a counterexample generator for Isabelle/HOL that builds on Kodkod [49], a SAT-based first-order relational model finder. Nitpick supported codatatypes even before the introduction of a **codatatype** command. Users could define custom codatatypes from first principles and tell Nitpick to employ its efficient first-order relational axiomatization of ω-regular values (e.g., cyclic values).

Sledgehammer integrates automatic theorem provers in Isabelle/HOL to provide one-click proof automation. Some automatic provers have native support for datatypes [28,38,42]; for these, Sledgehammer generates native definitions, which are often more efficient and complete than first-order axiomatizations. Blanchette also collaborated with the developers of the SMT solver CVC4 to add codatatypes to their solver [42].

10 Applications

Coinductive. Lochbihler's Coinductive library [31] defines general-purpose codatatypes, notably extended natural numbers ($\mathbb{N} \uplus \{\infty\}$), lazy lists, and streams. It also provides related functions and a large collection of lemmas about these. Back in 2010, every codatatype was constructed manually—including its constructors and corecursor—and operations were defined directly in terms of the corecursor. Today, the codatatypes are defined with **codatatype** and most functions with **primcorec**, leading to considerably shorter definitions and proofs [12]. The library is used in several applications, including in Hölzl's formalization of Markov chains and processes [24,25] and in Lochbihler's JinjaThreads project to verify a Java compiler and formalize the Java memory model [30,32,33].

Coinductive Languages. Rutten [44] views formal languages as infinite tries—i.e., prefix trees branching over the alphabet with Boolean labels at the nodes indicating whether the path from the root denotes a word in the language. Traytel [50] formalized these tries in Isabelle as

codatatype α *lang* = Lang *bool* ($\alpha \rightarrow \alpha$ *lang*)

a type that nests corecursion through the right-hand side of the function space arrow ($\rightarrow$). He also defined regular operations on them as corecursive functions and proved by coinduction that the defined operations form a Kleene algebra.

Completeness of First-Order Logic. Gödel's completeness theorem [21] is a central result about first-order logic. Blanchette, Popescu, and Traytel [9,14,16] formalized a Beth–Hintikka-style proof [27] in Isabelle/HOL. It depends on a Gentzen or tableau system and performs a search that builds either a finite deduction tree yielding a proof (or refutation, depending on the system) or an infinite tree from which a countermodel (or model) can be extracted.

Even in the most formalistic textbooks, potentially infinite trees are defined rigorously (e.g., as prefix-closed sets), but the reasoning is performed informally, disregarding the definition and relying on the intuitive notion of trees. By contrast, the formalization relies on α $\mathit{ltree}_{\mathsf{fs}}$ (Sect. 1), a codatatype of finitely branching, possibly infinite trees with nodes labeled by elements in a set α of inference rules. One could argue that trees are intuitive and do not need a formal treatment, but the same holds for the syntax of formulas, which is treated very rigorously in most textbooks.

The core of the proof establishes an abstract property of possibly infinite derivation trees, independently of the concrete syntax or inference rules. This separation of concerns simplifies the presentation. The abstract proof can be instantiated for a wide range of Gentzen and tableau systems as well as variants of first-order logic.

IsaFoR and CeTA. The IsaFoR (Isabelle Formalization of Rewriting) formal library, developed by Sternagel, Thiemann, and their colleagues, is a collection of abstract results and concrete techniques from the term rewriting literature. It forms the basis of the CeTA (Certified Termination Analysis) certifier [48] for proofs of (non)termination, (non)confluence, and other properties of term rewriting systems. Termination proofs are represented by complicated mutually and nested recursive datatypes.

One of the benefits of the modular, BNF-based approach is its scalability. The previous approach [4,22] implemented in Isabelle/HOL consisted in reducing specifications with nested recursion to mutually recursive specifications, which scales poorly (and only allows nesting through datatypes). After the introduction of the new **datatype** command in 2014, Thiemann observed that the IsaFoR session *Proof-Checker* compiled in 10 minutes on his computer, compared with 50 minutes previously.

Generative Probabilistic Values. Lochbihler [34] proposed generative probabilistic values (GPVs) as a semantic domain for probabilistic input–output systems, which he uses to formalize and verify cryptographic algorithms. Conceptually, each GPV chooses probabilistically between failing, terminating with a result of type α, and continuing by producing an output γ and transitioning into a reactive probabilistic value, which waits for a response ρ of the environment before moving to the generative successor state. Lochbihler modeled GPVs as a codatatype (α, γ, ρ) *gpv* and defined a monadic language on GPVs similar to a coroutine monad:

$$\textbf{codatatype}\ (\alpha, \gamma, \rho)\ \mathit{gpv} = \mathsf{GPV}\ (\mathsf{unGPV}\colon (\alpha + \gamma \times (\rho \to (\alpha, \gamma, \rho)\ \mathit{gpv}))\ \mathit{spmf})$$

This codatatype definition exploits the full generality that BNFs provide as it corecurses through the nonfree type constructor *spmf* of discrete subprobability distributions and through the function space $(\to)$, products $(\times)$, and sums $(+)$.

The definition of the 'while' loop corecurses through the monadic sequencing operator $\gg\!=_{gpv}$ and is accepted by **corec** after $\gg\!=_{gpv}$ has been registered as a friend (Sect. 7):

$$\begin{array}{l}\textbf{corec}\ \mathsf{while} : (\sigma \to \mathit{bool}) \to (\sigma \to (\sigma, \gamma, \rho)\ \mathit{gpv}) \to \sigma \to (\sigma, \gamma, \rho)\ \mathit{gpv}\ \textbf{where}\\ \quad \mathsf{while}\ g\ b\ s =\\ \quad \mathsf{GPV}\ (\mathsf{map}_{\mathit{spmf}}\ (\mathsf{map}_{+}\ \mathsf{id}\ (\mathsf{map}_{\times}\ \mathsf{id}\ (\lambda x\ r.\ x\ r \gg\!=_{gpv} \mathsf{while}\ g\ b)))\ (\mathsf{search}\ g\ b\ s))\end{array}$$

The auxiliary operation $\mathsf{search}\ g\ b\ s$ iterates the loop body b starting from state s until the loop guard g is falsified or the first interaction is found. It is defined as the least fixpoint of the recursive specification in the *spmf* monad below. The search is needed to expose the constructor guard in while's definition. The recursion in search must be manually separated from the corecursion as the recursion is not well founded, so search is not the only solution—e.g., it is unspecified for $g\ s = \mathsf{True}$ and $b\ s = \mathsf{GPV}\ (\mathsf{return}_{\mathit{spmf}}\ (\mathsf{Inl}\ s))$.

$$\begin{array}{l}\mathsf{search}\ g\ b\ s = (\text{if}\ g\ s\ \text{then}\\ \qquad \mathsf{unGPV}\ (b\ s) \gg\!=_{\mathit{spmf}} (\lambda x.\ \text{case}\ x\ \text{of}\ \mathsf{Inl}\ s' \Rightarrow \mathsf{search}\ g\ b\ s' \mid \_ \Rightarrow \mathsf{return}_{\mathit{spmf}}\ x)\\ \quad \text{else}\ \mathsf{return}_{\mathit{spmf}}\ (\mathsf{Inl}\ s))\end{array}$$

Nested and Hereditary Multisets. Blanchette, Fleury, and Traytel [7,11] formalized a collection of results about (finite) nested multisets, as a case study for BNFs. Nested multisets can be defined simply, exploiting the BNF structure of *multiset*:

$$\textbf{datatype}\ \alpha\ \mathit{nmultiset} = \mathsf{Elem}\ \alpha \mid \mathsf{MSet}\ ((\alpha\ \mathit{nmultiset})\ \mathit{multiset})$$

This type forms the basis of their formalization of Dershowitz and Manna's nested multiset order [20]. If we omit the Elem case, we obtain the hereditary multisets instead:

$$\textbf{datatype}\ \mathit{hmultiset} = \mathsf{HMSet}\ (\mathit{hmultiset}\ \mathit{multiset})$$

This type is similar to hereditarily finite sets, a model of set theory without the axiom of infinity, but with multisets instead of finite sets. Indeed, we can replace *multiset* with *fset* to obtain the hereditarily finite sets.

It is easy to embed *hmultiset* in α *nmultiset*, and using the Lifting and Transfer tools, we can lift definitions and results from the larger type to the smaller type, such as the definition of the nested multiset order. Hereditary multisets offer a convenient syntactic representation for ordinals below ϵ_0, which can be expressed in Cantor normal form:

$$\alpha ::= \omega^{\alpha_1} \cdot c_1 + \cdots + \omega^{\alpha_n} \cdot c_n$$

where $c_i \in \mathbb{N}^{>0}$ and $\alpha_1 > \cdots > \alpha_n$. The correspondence with hereditary multisets is straightforward:

$$\alpha ::= \{\underbrace{\alpha_1, \ldots, \alpha_1}_{c_1 \text{ occurrences}}, \ldots, \underbrace{\alpha_n, \ldots, \alpha_n}_{c_n \text{ occurrences}}\}$$

The coefficients c_i are represented by multiset multiplicities, and the ω exponents are the multiset's members. Thus, $\{\} = 0$; $\{0\} = \{\{\}\} = \omega^0 = 1$; $\{0,0,0\} = \{\{\},\{\},\{\}\} = \omega^0 \cdot 3 = 3$; $\{1\} = \{\{\{\}\}\} = \omega^1 = \omega$; and $\{\omega\} = \{\{\{\{\}\}\}\} = \omega^\omega$.

The hereditary multisets were used to represent syntactic ordinals in a proof of Goodstein's theorem [7,11], in an ongoing proof of the decidability of unary PCF (programming computable functions) [7,11], and in a formalization of transfinite Knuth–Bendix orders [2,3].

11 Conclusion

It is widely recognized that proof automation is important for usability of a proof assistant, but it is not the only factor. Many formalizations depend on an expressive specification language. The axiomatic approach, which is favored in some subcommunities, is considered unreliable in others. Extending the logic is also a problematic option: Not only must the metatheory be extended, but the existing tools must be adapted. Moreover, the developers and users of the system must be convinced of the correctness and necessity of the extension.

Our challenge was to combine specification mechanisms that are both expressive and trustworthy, without introducing new axioms or changing the logic. We believe we have succeeded as far as (co)datatypes and (co)recursion are concerned, but more could be done, notably for nonfree datatypes [45]. Our new commands, based on the notion of a bounded natural functor, probably constitute the largest definitional package to have been implemented in a proof assistant. Makarius Wenzel [54], Isabelle's lead developer, jocularly called it "one of the greatest engineering projects since Stonehenge!"

Acknowledgments. We first want to acknowledge the support and encouragement of past and current bosses: David Basin, Wan Fokkink, Stephan Merz, Aart Middeldorp, Tobias Nipkow, and Christoph Weidenbach. We are grateful to the FroCoS 2017 program chairs, Clare Dixon and Marcelo Finger, and to the program committee for giving us this opportunity to present our research. We are also indebted to Andreas Abel, Stefan Berghofer, Sascha Böhme, Lukas Bulwahn, Elsa Gunter, Florian

Haftmann, Martin Hofmann, Brian Huffman, Lars Hupel, Alexander Krauss, Peter Lammich, Rustan Leino, Stefan Milius, Lutz Schröder, Mark Summerfield, Christian Urban, Daniel Wand, and Makarius Wenzel, and to dozens of anonymous reviewers (including those who rejected our manuscript "Witnessing (co)datatypes" [18] six times).

Blanchette was supported by the Deutsche Forschungsgemeinschaft (DFG) projects "Quis Custodiet" (NI 491/11-2) and "Den Hammer härten" (NI 491/14-1). He also received funding from the European Research Council under the European Union's Horizon 2020 research and innovation program (grant agreement No. 713999, Matryoshka). Hölzl was supported by the DFG project "Verifikation probabilistischer Modelle in interaktiven Theorembeweisern" (NI 491/15-1). Kunčar and Popescu were supported by the DFG project "Security Type Systems and Deduction" (NI 491/13-2 and NI 491/13-3) as part of the program Reliably Secure Software Systems (RS^3, priority program 1496). Kunčar was also supported by the DFG project "Integration der Logik HOL mit den Programmiersprachen ML und Haskell" (NI 491/10-2). Lochbihler was supported by the Swiss National Science Foundation (SNSF) grant "Formalising Computational Soundness for Protocol Implementations" (153217). Popescu was supported by the UK Engineering and Physical Sciences Research Council (EPSRC) starting grant "VOWS: Verification of Web-based Systems" (EP/N019547/1). Sternagel and Thiemann were supported by the Austrian Science Fund (FWF): P27502 and Y757. Traytel was supported by the DFG program "Programm- und Modell-Analyse" (PUMA, doctorate program 1480). The authors are listed alphabetically.

References

1. Bartels, F.: Generalised coinduction. Math. Struct. Comput. Sci. **13**(2), 321–348 (2003)
2. Becker, H., Blanchette, J.C., Waldmann, U., Wand, D.: Formalization of Knuth–Bendix orders for lambda-free higher-order terms. Archive of Formal Proofs (2016). Formal proof development. http://isa-afp.org/entries/Lambda_Free_KBOs.shtml
3. Becker, H., Blanchette, J.C., Waldmann, U., Wand, D.: A transfinite Knuth–Bendix order for lambda-free higher-order terms. In: de Moura, L. (ed.) CADE-26. LNCS, vol. 10395, pp. 432–453. Springer, Cham (2017). doi:10.1007/978-3-319-63046-5_27
4. Berghofer, S., Wenzel, M.: Inductive datatypes in HOL—lessons learned in formal-logic engineering. In: Bertot, Y., Dowek, G., Théry, L., Hirschowitz, A., Paulin, C. (eds.) TPHOLs 1999. LNCS, vol. 1690, pp. 19–36. Springer, Heidelberg (1999). doi:10.1007/3-540-48256-3_3
5. Bertot, Y., Casteran, P.: Interactive Theorem Proving and Program Development–Coq'Art: The Calculus of Inductive Constructions. Texts in Theoretical Computer Science. Springer, Heidelberg (2004). doi:10.1007/978-3-662-07964-5
6. Blanchette, J.C.: Relational analysis of (co)inductive predicates, (co)inductive datatypes, and (co)recursive functions. Softw. Qual. J. **21**(1), 101–126 (2013)
7. Blanchette, J.C., Fleury, M., Traytel, D.: Nested multisets, hereditary multisets, and syntactic ordinals in Isabelle/HOL. In: Miller, D. (ed.) FSCD 2017. LIPIcs, vol. 84, pp. 11:1–11:17 (2017). Schloss Dagstuhl—Leibniz-Zentrum für Informatik
8. Blanchette, J.C., Nipkow, T.: Nitpick: a counterexample generator for higher-order logic based on a relational model finder. In: Kaufmann, M., Paulson, L.C. (eds.) ITP 2010. LNCS, vol. 6172, pp. 131–146. Springer, Heidelberg (2010). doi:10.1007/978-3-642-14052-5_11

9. Blanchette, J.C., Popescu, A., Traytel, D.: Soundness and completeness proofs by coinductive methods. J. Autom. Reason. **58**(1), 149–179 (2017)
10. Blanchette, J.C., Bouzy, A., Lochbihler, A., Popescu, A., Traytel, D.: Friends with benefits. In: Yang, H. (ed.) ESOP 2017. LNCS, vol. 10201, pp. 111–140. Springer, Heidelberg (2017). doi:10.1007/978-3-662-54434-1_5
11. Blanchette, J.C., Fleury, M., Traytel, D.: Formalization of nested multisets, hereditary multisets, and syntactic ordinals. Archive of Formal Proofs (2016). Formal proof development. http://isa-afp.org/entries/Nested_Multisets_Ordinals.shtml
12. Blanchette, J.C., Hölzl, J., Lochbihler, A., Panny, L., Popescu, A., Traytel, D.: Truly modular (co)datatypes for Isabelle/HOL. In: Klein, G., Gamboa, R. (eds.) ITP 2014. LNCS, vol. 8558, pp. 93–110. Springer, Cham (2014). doi:10.1007/978-3-319-08970-6_7
13. Blanchette, J.C., Meier, F., Popescu, A., Traytel, D.: Foundational nonuniform (co)datatypes for higher-order logic. In: Ouaknine, J. (ed.) LICS 2017. IEEE Computer Society (2017)
14. Blanchette, J.C., Popescu, A., Traytel, D.: Abstract completeness. Archive of Formal Proofs (2014). Formal proof development. http://isa-afp.org/entries/Abstract_Completeness.shtml
15. Blanchette, J.C., Popescu, A., Traytel, D.: Cardinals in Isabelle/HOL. In: Klein, G., Gamboa, R. (eds.) ITP 2014. LNCS, vol. 8558, pp. 111–127. Springer, Cham (2014). doi:10.1007/978-3-319-08970-6_8
16. Blanchette, J.C., Popescu, A., Traytel, D.: Unified classical logic completeness. In: Demri, S., Kapur, D., Weidenbach, C. (eds.) IJCAR 2014. LNCS (LNAI), vol. 8562, pp. 46–60. Springer, Cham (2014). doi:10.1007/978-3-319-08587-6_4
17. Blanchette, J.C., Popescu, A., Traytel, D.: Foundational extensible corecursion–a proof assistant perspective. In: Fisher, K., Reppy, J.H. (eds.) ICFP 2015, pp. 192–204. ACM (2015)
18. Blanchette, J.C., Popescu, A., Traytel, D.: Witnessing (co)datatypes. In: Vitek, J. (ed.) ESOP 2015. LNCS, vol. 9032, pp. 359–382. Springer, Heidelberg (2015). doi:10.1007/978-3-662-46669-8_15
19. Bulwahn, L., Krauss, A., Nipkow, T.: Finding lexicographic orders for termination proofs in Isabelle/HOL. In: Schneider, K., Brandt, J. (eds.) TPHOLs 2007. LNCS, vol. 4732, pp. 38–53. Springer, Heidelberg (2007). doi:10.1007/978-3-540-74591-4_5
20. Dershowitz, N., Manna, Z.: Proving termination with multiset orderings. In: Maurer, H.A. (ed.) ICALP 1979. LNCS, vol. 71, pp. 188–202. Springer, Heidelberg (1979). doi:10.1007/3-540-09510-1_15
21. Gödel, K.: Über die Vollständigkeit des Logikkalküls. Ph.D. thesis, Universität Wien (1929)
22. Gunter, E.L.: Why we can't have SML-style `datatype` declarations in HOL. In: TPHOLs 1992. IFIP Transactions, vol. A-20, pp. 561–568. North-Holland/Elsevier (1993)
23. Hinze, R., Paterson, R.: Finger trees: a simple general-purpose data structure. J. Funct. Program. **16**(2), 197–217 (2006)
24. Hölzl, J.: Markov chains and Markov decision processes in Isabelle/HOL. J. Autom. Reason. doi:10.1007/s10817-016-9401-5
25. Hölzl, J.: Markov processes in Isabelle/HOL. In: Bertot, Y., Vafeiadis, V. (eds.) CPP 2017, pp. 100–111. ACM (2017)
26. Huffman, B., Kunčar, O.: Lifting and transfer: a modular design for quotients in Isabelle/HOL. In: Gonthier, G., Norrish, M. (eds.) CPP 2013. LNCS, vol. 8307, pp. 131–146. Springer, Cham (2013). doi:10.1007/978-3-319-03545-1_9

27. Kleene, S.C.: Mathematical Logic. Wiley, New York (1967)
28. Kovács, L., Robillard, S., Voronkov, A.: Coming to terms with quantified reasoning. In: Castagna, G., Gordon, A.D. (eds.) POPL 2017, pp. 260–270. ACM (2017)
29. Krauss, A.: Partial recursive functions in higher-order logic. In: Furbach, U., Shankar, N. (eds.) IJCAR 2006. LNCS (LNAI), vol. 4130, pp. 589–603. Springer, Heidelberg (2006). doi:10.1007/11814771_48
30. Lochbihler, A.: Jinja with threads. Archive of Formal Proofs (2007). Formal proof development. http://isa-afp.org/entries/JinjaThreads.shtml
31. Lochbihler, A.: Coinductive. Archive of Formal Proofs (2010). Formal proof development. http://afp.sf.net/entries/Coinductive.shtml
32. Lochbihler, A.: Verifying a compiler for Java threads. In: Gordon, A.D. (ed.) ESOP 2010. LNCS, vol. 6012, pp. 427–447. Springer, Heidelberg (2010). doi:10.1007/978-3-642-11957-6_23
33. Lochbihler, A.: Making the Java memory model safe. ACM Trans. Program. Lang. Syst. **35**(4), 12:1–12:65 (2014)
34. Lochbihler, A.: Probabilistic functions and cryptographic oracles in higher order logic. In: Thiemann, P. (ed.) ESOP 2016. LNCS, vol. 9632, pp. 503–531. Springer, Heidelberg (2016). doi:10.1007/978-3-662-49498-1_20
35. Lochbihler, A., Hölzl, J.: Recursive functions on lazy lists via domains and topologies. In: Klein, G., Gamboa, R. (eds.) ITP 2014. LNCS, vol. 8558, pp. 341–357. Springer, Cham (2014). doi:10.1007/978-3-319-08970-6_22
36. Meier, F.: Non-uniform datatypes in Isabelle/HOL. M.Sc. thesis, ETH Zürich (2016)
37. Milius, S., Moss, L.S., Schwencke, D.: Abstract GSOS rules and a modular treatment of recursive definitions. Log. Methods Comput. Sci. **9**(3), 1–52 (2013)
38. Moura, L., Bjørner, N.: Z3: an efficient SMT solver. In: Ramakrishnan, C.R., Rehof, J. (eds.) TACAS 2008. LNCS, vol. 4963, pp. 337–340. Springer, Heidelberg (2008). doi:10.1007/978-3-540-78800-3_24
39. Nipkow, T., Wenzel, M., Paulson, L.C. (eds.): Isabelle/HOL: A Proof Assistant for Higher-Order Logic. LNCS, vol. 2283. Springer, Heidelberg (2002). doi:10.1007/3-540-45949-9
40. Okasaki, C.: Purely Functional Data Structures. Cambridge University Press, Cambridge (1999)
41. Panny, L.: Primitively (co)recursive function definitions for Isabelle/HOL. B.Sc. thesis, Technische Universität München (2014)
42. Reynolds, A., Blanchette, J.C.: A decision procedure for (co)datatypes in SMT solvers. J. Autom. Reason. **58**(3), 341–362 (2017)
43. Reynolds, J.C.: Types, abstraction and parametric polymorphism. In: IFIP 1983, pp. 513–523 (1983)
44. Rutten, J.J.M.M.: Automata and coinduction (an exercise in coalgebra). In: Sangiorgi, D., Simone, R. (eds.) CONCUR 1998. LNCS, vol. 1466, pp. 194–218. Springer, Heidelberg (1998). doi:10.1007/BFb0055624
45. Schropp, A., Popescu, A.: Nonfree datatypes in Isabelle/HOL. In: Gonthier, G., Norrish, M. (eds.) CPP 2013. LNCS, vol. 8307, pp. 114–130. Springer, Cham (2013). doi:10.1007/978-3-319-03545-1_8
46. Sternagel, C., Thiemann, R.: Deriving comparators and show functions in Isabelle/HOL. In: Urban, C., Zhang, X. (eds.) ITP 2015. LNCS, vol. 9236, pp. 421–437. Springer, Cham (2015). doi:10.1007/978-3-319-22102-1_28
47. Sternagel, C., Thiemann, R.: Deriving class instances for datatypes. Archive of Formal Proofs (2015). Formal proof development. http://isa-afp.org/entries/Deriving.shtml

48. Thiemann, R., Sternagel, C.: Certification of termination proofs using CeTA. In: Berghofer, S., Nipkow, T., Urban, C., Wenzel, M. (eds.) TPHOLs 2009. LNCS, vol. 5674, pp. 452–468. Springer, Heidelberg (2009). doi:10.1007/978-3-642-03359-9_31
49. Torlak, E., Jackson, D.: Kodkod: a relational model finder. In: Grumberg, O., Huth, M. (eds.) TACAS 2007. LNCS, vol. 4424, pp. 632–647. Springer, Heidelberg (2007). doi:10.1007/978-3-540-71209-1_49
50. Traytel, D.: Formal languages, formally and coinductively. In: Kesner, D., Pientka, B. (eds.) FSCD 2016. LIPIcs, vol. 52, pp. 31:1–31:17 (2016). Schloss Dagstuhl—Leibniz-Zentrum für Informatik
51. Traytel, D., Popescu, A., Blanchette, J.C.: Foundational, compositional (co)datatypes for higher-order logic—category theory applied to theorem proving. In: LICS 2012, pp. 596–605. IEEE Computer Society (2012)
52. Traytel, D.: A category theory based (co)datatype package for Isabelle/HOL. M.Sc. thesis, Technische Universität München (2012)
53. Wenzel, M.: Isabelle/Isar—a generic framework for human-readable proof documents. From Insight to Proof: Festschrift in Honour of Andrzej Trybulec, Studies in Logic, Grammar, and Rhetoric **10**(23), 277–298 (2007). Uniwersytet w Białymstoku
54. Wenzel, M.: Re: [isabelle] "Unfolding" the sum-of-products encoding of datatypes (2015). https://lists.cam.ac.uk/pipermail/cl-isabelle-users/2015-November/msg00082.html

Designing Theory Solvers with Extensions

Andrew Reynolds[1], Cesare Tinelli[1(✉)], Dejan Jovanović[1,3], and Clark Barrett[2]

[1] Department of Computer Science, The University of Iowa, Iowa, USA
cesare-tinelli@uiowa.edu
[2] Department of Computer Science, Stanford University, Stanford, USA
[3] SRI International, Menlo Park, USA

Abstract. Satisfiability Modulo Theories (SMT) solvers have been developed to natively support a wide range of theories, including linear arithmetic, bit-vectors, strings, algebraic datatypes and finite sets. They handle constraints in these theories using specialized theory solvers. In this paper, we overview the design of these solvers, specifically focusing on theories whose function symbols are partitioned into a base signature and an extended signature. We introduce generic techniques that can be used in solvers for extended theories, including a new context-dependent simplification technique and model-based refinement techniques. We provide case studies showing our techniques can be leveraged for reasoning in an extended theory of strings, for bit-vector approaches that rely on lazy bit-blasting and for new approaches to non-linear arithmetic.

1 Introduction

A growing number of formal methods applications leverage SMT solvers as reasoning engines. To accommodate the unique requirements of these applications, a number of new theories are now natively supported by SMT solvers, including unbounded strings with length constraints [31,39], algebraic datatypes [33], finite sets [5], and floating-point arithmetic [13]. Solvers for these theories share functionalities, such as reporting conflicts and propagations based on theory reasoning. From both a formal and an engineering perspective, there is a need to express the common features in these solvers.

This paper focuses on theories whose function symbols can be partitioned into a *base* signature Σ^{b} and an *extension* signature Σ^{e}. We will refer to such theories as *extended* theories. The motivation for considering extended theories is two-fold:

1. Assume we have developed a constraint solving procedure for some Σ^{b}-theory, and say we want to extend this procedure to handle additional symbols in some signature Σ^{e}. Can we reuse our procedure for Σ^{b}-constraints in part to develop a procedure for $\Sigma^{\mathrm{b}} \cup \Sigma^{\mathrm{e}}$-constraints?
2. Assume we want to optimize a procedure for Σ-constraints. One way is to partition its signature Σ into $\Sigma^{\mathrm{b}} \cup \Sigma^{\mathrm{e}}$, where Σ^{b} contains the symbols that are easier to reason about. Can we use a stratified approach that first uses our existing procedure on Σ^{b}-constraints and reasons about Σ^{e}-constraints only when needed?

C. Dixon and M. Finger (Eds.): FroCoS 2017, LNCS 10483, pp. 22–40, 2017.
DOI: 10.1007/978-3-319-66167-4_2

We develop an approach for handling extended theories can be used for answering both of these questions. This paper observes that the design of many theory solvers for extended theories follows a similar pattern. First, we observe that it is often possible to reduce extended constraints to basic ones by reasoning modulo the equalities entailed by the current assignment. As a simple example, in the context where $y \approx 2$ is entailed by the current assignment, the non-linear constraint $x \times y + y > 5$ can be simplified to a linear one $2 \times x > 3$. We refer to this technique as *context-dependent simplification*. Constraints that are not reducible in this way can be handled by techniques that follow the common paradigm of model-based abstraction refinement, where basic constraints can be used to refine the abstraction of extended terms. The latter is an approach followed used by several recent approaches to SMT solving [15,17].

In previous work, we showed that techniques based on simplification can significantly improve the performance of DPLL(T)-based string solvers [34]. In this work: we formalize the design of theory solvers with extensions, specifically:

- we introduce a generic technique, which we call *context-dependent simplification*, which can reduce extended constraints to basic ones and propagate equalities between extended terms;
- we define a generic approach for extended theories that leverages this technique and others to implement modular extensions for the theories of strings, linear arithmetic and bit-vectors, showing that:
  - context-dependent simplification techniques significantly improve the performance and precision of our solver for an extended theory of strings;
  - lightweight techniques based on context-dependent simplification and model-based refinement can extend DPLL(T) linear arithmetic solvers to handle non-linear arithmetic and have some advantages over state-of-the-art solvers; and
  - the performance of bit-vector solvers can be improved by delaying bit-blasting of certain functions that require sophisticated propositional encodings.

1.1 Formal Preliminaries

We assume the reader is familiar with the following notions from many-sorted logic with equality: (sorted) signature, term, literal, formula, clause, free variable, interpretation, and satisfiability of a formula in an interpretation (see, e.g., [11] for more details). We consider only signatures Σ that contain an (infix) logical symbol $\approx$ for equality. We write $t \not\approx s$ as shorthand for $\neg t \approx s$. We write $\mathcal{L}it(\varphi)$ to denote the set of literals of formula φ. We extend these notations to tuples and sets of terms or formulas as expected.

If φ is a Σ-formula and $\mathcal{I}$ a Σ-interpretation, we write $\mathcal{I} \models \varphi$ if $\mathcal{I}$ satisfies φ. If t is a term, we denote by $\mathcal{I}(t)$ the value of t in $\mathcal{I}$. A *theory* is a pair $T = (\Sigma, \mathbf{I})$ where Σ is a signature and $\mathbf{I}$ is a class of Σ-interpretations, the *models* of T, that is closed under variable reassignment (i.e., every Σ-interpretation that differs from one in **I** only in how it interprets the variables is also in **I**). A Σ-formula φ is *satisfiable* (resp., *unsatisfiable*) *in* T if it is satisfied by some (resp., no) interpretation in **I**. A set Γ of Σ-formulas *entails in* T a Σ-formula φ, written $\Gamma \models_T \varphi$, if every interpretation in **I** that satisfies all formulas in Γ satisfies φ as well. Two Σ-formulas are *equisatisfiable in* T if for every model $\mathcal{A}$ of T that satisfies one, there is a model of T that satisfies the other and differs from $\mathcal{A}$ at most over the free variables not shared by the two formulas. We say that Γ *propositionally entails* φ, written $\Gamma \models_{\mathrm{p}} \varphi$, if Γ entails φ when considering all atoms as propositional variables.

2 Theory Solvers

In this paper, we are interested in the design of *theory solvers*. At an abstract level, a theory solver for a Σ-theory T is a terminating procedure specialized in determining the satisfiability of sets of T-literals, interpreted conjunctively. For our purposes, we summarize the interface for a theory solver in Fig. 1. We view a theory solver as a procedure Solve_T that takes as input a set of T-literals M, which we will call a *context*, and outputs a value of the following algebraic datatype

$$\mathsf{type}\ \mathit{Response} = \mathsf{Learn\ of}\ \mathit{Clause} \mid \mathsf{Infer\ of}\ \mathit{Literal} \mid \mathsf{Sat\ of}\ \mathit{Model} \mid \mathsf{Unknown}$$

where *Clause*, *Literal* and *Model* are types respectively for representing clauses, literals and interpretations. If $\mathsf{Solve}_T(\mathsf{M}) = \mathsf{Sat}(\mathcal{M})$ then $\mathcal{M}$ is a finitary representation of a model of T that satisfies M, hence we will identity the two in the rest of the paper. We assume that no input context contains both a literal and its negation.

The value returned by Solve_T can be used in various ways depending on the overall search procedure. In most SMT solvers, this search procedure is based on variants of the DPLL(T) procedure [32] where a theory solver for T is used in combination with a CDCL propositional satisfiability (SAT) solver to determine the satisfiability in T of quantifier-free formulas. In a nutshell, given a quantifier-free formula φ, this procedure maintains a set of Σ-clauses F equisatisfiable in T with φ, and tries to construct a context M that is satisfiable in T and propositionally entails F. Such context, if it exists, is a witness of the satisfiability of φ in T. Constructing M and checking its satisfiability in T is done with the aid of a theory solver Solve_T.

$\mathsf{Solve}_T(\mathsf{M})$: Return one of the following:
- $\mathsf{Learn}(\varphi)$ where $\varphi = \ell_1 \vee \ldots \vee \ell_n,\ \ell_1, \ldots, \ell_n \subseteq \mathcal{L},\ \emptyset \models_T \varphi$, and $\mathsf{M} \not\models_{\mathrm{p}} \varphi$
- $\mathsf{Infer}(\ell)$ where $\mathsf{M} \models_T \ell,\ \ell \notin \mathsf{M}$, and $\ell \in \mathcal{L}$
- $\mathsf{Sat}(\mathcal{M})$ where $\mathcal{M} \models \mathsf{M}$
- $\mathsf{Unknown}$

Fig. 1. Basic functionality of a theory solver.

As indicated in Fig. 1, calling a theory solver on a set M of literal may produce one of four results. In the first case (Learn), the theory solver returns a *lemma*, clause φ that is valid in T and not propositionally entailed by M. This clause may consist of complements of literals in M, indicating that M is unsatisfiable in T, or may contain atoms not in M, indicating to the rest of the DPLL(T) procedure that M needs to be extended further. In the second case (Infer), the theory solver returns a literal ℓ that is entailed by the current context M. We assume here that the literals returned by these calls are taken from a set $\mathcal{L}$ of T-literals that ultimately depends on the original input formula φ. In DPLL(T), this typically includes all literals over the atoms occurring in F, but may include additional ones, for instance, for theory solvers that implement the splitting-on-demand paradigm [10]. In the third case (Sat), the procedure returns a (finitary representation) of a model of T that satisfies M. In the last case, the theory solver simply returns $\mathsf{Unknown}$, indicating that it is unable to determine the satisfiability of M or suggest further extensions.

Using previous results on DPLL(T) [10,32], it can be shown that a DPLL(T) procedure invoking a theory solver Solve_T based on this interface is:

- refutation-sound (i.e., it says an input formula is unsatisfiable in T only if it is so),
- model-sound (i.e., it says an input formula is satisfiable in T only if it is so),
- refutation-complete (i.e., it says an input formula is unsatisfiable in T whenever it is so) if Solve_T never returns $\mathsf{Unknown}$, and
- terminating if $\mathcal{L}$ is a finite set.

3 Theory Solvers with Extensions

In this section, we consider a Σ-theory T whose signature Σ is the union $\Sigma^{\mathrm{b}} \cup \Sigma^{\mathrm{e}}$ of a basic signature Σ^{b} and an extention signature Σ^{e} where Σ^{b} and Σ^{e} have the same sort symbols and share no function symbols. We will refer to the function symbols in Σ^{b} as *basic* function symbols, and to those in Σ^{e} as *extension* function symbols.

We are interested in developing a procedure for the T-satisfiability of a set F of Σ-clauses based on the availability of a theory solver $\mathsf{Solve}^{\mathrm{b}}_T$, which implements the interface from Fig. 1, for contexts M consisting of Σ^{b}-literals only. For the purposes of the presentation, we assume that the variables in F are from some infinite set X and we associate to every Σ-term t over X a unique variable z_t not from X which we call *the purification variable for t*. If e is a Σ-term or formula possibly containing purification variables, we denote by $\mathsf{X}(e)$ the set $\{z_t \approx t \mid z_t$ is a purification variable in $e\}$; we write $\lceil e \rceil$ to denote the expression $e\sigma$ where σ is the substitution $\{z_t \mapsto t \mid x_t \approx t \in \mathsf{X}(e)\}$. We extend these notations to sets of terms or formulas as expected.

Without loss of generality, we assume every extension function symbol f in F occurs only in terms of the form $f(x_1, \ldots, x_n)$ where $x_1, \ldots, x_n$ are variables from X. We let $\lfloor \mathsf{F} \rfloor$ be the result of replacing every term t of this form in F

by its purification variable z_t. It is not difficult to show that $\lfloor \mathsf{F} \rfloor \cup \mathsf{X}(\lfloor \mathsf{F} \rfloor)$ is equisatisfiable with F in T.

Example 1. Assume $f \in \Sigma^{\mathrm{e}}$. Let F be the set $\{f(x_5, x_3) \approx x_4, x_5 \approx f(x_1, x_2)\}$. After replacing $f(x_5, x_3)$ and $f(x_1, x_2)$ with their respective purification variables z_1 and z_2, say, we get $\lfloor \mathsf{F} \rfloor = \{z_1 \approx x_4, x_5 \approx z_2\}$ and $\mathsf{X}(\lfloor \mathsf{F} \rfloor) = \{z_1 \approx f(x_5, x_3), z_2 \approx f(x_1, x_2)\}$. Note that $\lceil \lfloor \mathsf{F} \rfloor \rceil = \mathsf{F}$. □

We are interested in developing *extended theory solvers* which take as input *extended contexts*, that is, sets of literals of the form $\mathsf{M} \cup \mathsf{X}(\mathsf{M})$, where M a given set of Σ-literals possibly with purification variables (coming from the purification process for F). We discuss in the following two generic classes of techniques: context-dependent simplification and model-based refinement that can be used to develop extended theory solvers on top of a basic solver.

3.1 Context-Dependent Simplification

We first observe that many theory solvers already have several features of interest handling extended contexts $\mathsf{M} \cup \mathsf{X}(\mathsf{M})$, namely they:

1. Compute an equivalence relation over terms $\mathcal{T}(\mathsf{M})$, where t_1 and t_2 are in the same equivalence class if and only if $\mathsf{M} \models_T t_1 \approx t_2$, and
2. Make use of *simplified* forms $t\!\downarrow$ of Σ-terms t, where $\emptyset \models_T t \approx t\!\downarrow$.

Regarding the first point, a number of theory solvers [5,26,31,33] are developed as modular extensions of the standard congruence closure algorithm, which builds equivalence classes over the terms in the current context.

Regarding the second point, computing simplified forms for T-literals is advantageous since it reduces the number of cases that must be handled by the procedure for T. Moreover, it reduces the number of unique theory literals for a given input, which is highly beneficial for the performance of DPLL(T)-based solvers since it allows the underlying SAT solver to abstract multiple T-literals as the same propositional (Boolean) variable. For example, assuming $(x \times 2 > 8)\!\downarrow$ is $x > 4$, the set $\{x \times 2 > 8, \neg(x > 4)\}$ can be simplified to $\{x > 4, \neg(x > 4)\}$, which is already unsatisfiable at the propositional level. In most SMT solvers, this is determined by simplification and does not require invoking a theory solver that implements a procedure for arithmetic.

We argue that it is helpful to apply the same simplification technique while taking into account the equalities that are entailed by M. In detail, let $\boldsymbol{y}$ be a tuple of variables and $\boldsymbol{s}$ be a tuple of terms from $\mathcal{T}(\mathsf{M})$ where $\mathsf{M} \models_T \boldsymbol{y} \approx \boldsymbol{s}$. Let σ be the substitution $\{\boldsymbol{y} \mapsto \boldsymbol{s}\}$ which we will refer to as a *derivable substitution (in* M*)*. For any term t, we have that $\mathsf{M} \models_T t \approx (t\sigma)\!\downarrow$ by definition of simplifications and derivable substitutions.

Reducing Extended Terms to Basic Terms. We may derive equalities between extended terms and basic ones based on simplification. In particular, consider an equality $x \approx t$ from the $\mathsf{X}(\mathsf{M})$ component of our context, recalling that t is a Σ^{e}-term. If $(t\sigma)\downarrow$ is a Σ^{b}-term, then it must be that $\mathsf{M} \models_T (x \approx t) \Leftrightarrow (x \approx (t\sigma)\downarrow)$. Hence, we may discard $x \approx t$ and handle $x \approx (t\sigma)\downarrow$ using the basic procedure.

Example 2. Consider the extended theory A of (integer or rational) arithmetic, whose basic signature $\Sigma^{\mathrm{b}}_{\mathsf{A}}$ contains the symbols of linear arithmetic and whose extension signature $\Sigma^{\mathrm{e}}_{\mathsf{A}}$ contains the multiplication symbol $\times$. Let $\mathsf{M} = \{z \approx x,\, y \approx w + 2,\, w \approx 1\}$ and $\mathsf{X}(\mathsf{M}) = \{x \approx y \times y\}$. Since $\mathsf{M} \models_{\mathsf{A}} y \approx 3$, the substitution $\sigma = \{y \mapsto 3\}$ is a derivable substitution in M. Assuming the simplified form *linearizes* multiplication by constants, we have that $(y \times y)\sigma\downarrow = (3 \times 3)\downarrow = 9$ where, observe, 9 is a $\Sigma^{\mathrm{b}}_{\mathsf{A}}$-term. Thus, we may infer the (basic) equality $x \approx 9$ which is entailed by M. □

Inferring Equivalence of Extended Terms. If two extended terms t_1 and t_2 can be simplified to the same term under a derivable substitution, we can conclude that they must be equivalent. This is regardless of whether their simplified form is a basic term or not.

Example 3. Let $\mathsf{M} = \{x_1 \not\approx x_2,\, w \approx 4 \cdot z,\, y \approx 2 \cdot z\}$ and $\mathsf{X}(\mathsf{M}) = \{x_1 \approx y \times y,\, x_2 \approx w \times z\}$ where $\cdot$ denotes linear multiplication (i.e., $2 \cdot z$ is equivalent to $z + z$ in A). We have that $\sigma = \{w \mapsto 4 \cdot z,\, y \mapsto 2 \cdot z\}$ is a derivable substitution in M. Moreover, $(y \times y)\sigma\downarrow = ((2 \cdot z) \times (2 \cdot z))\downarrow = 4 \cdot (z \times z) = ((4 \cdot z) \times z)\downarrow = (w \times z)\sigma\downarrow$. Thus, we may infer that $x_1 \approx x_2$ is entailed by M (which shows that M is unsatisfiable in A). □

We call this class of techniques *context-dependent simplification.* For theory solvers that build an equivalence relation over terms, a simple method for constructing a derivable substitution is to map every variable in $\mathcal{T}(\mathsf{M})$ to the representative of its equivalence class in the congruence closure of M. However, more sophisticated methods for constructing derivable substitutions are possible, which we will describe later.

3.2 Model-Based Refinement

Note that $\lfloor \mathsf{F} \rfloor$ is effectively a conservative abstraction of F. A complementary approach to context-dependent simplification involves then refining this abstraction as needed to determine the satisfiability of F in T. We do that based on the model that the basic solver finds for a context M, which consists of literals from F. Generally speaking, other SMT theory approaches already rely on some form of model-based refinement [15,17]. This section defines this notion according to the terminology used here.

Consider an extended context $\mathsf{M} \cup \mathsf{X}(\mathsf{M})$ where context-dependent simplification does not apply, and moreover the basic theory solver has found that M is satisfied by some model $\mathcal{M}$ of T. If $\mathcal{M} \models \mathsf{X}(\mathsf{M})$, then it is a model of our context. On the other hand, if $\mathcal{M} \not\models \mathsf{X}(\mathsf{M})$, then the extended solver may be instrumented to return a clause that when added to F refines the abstraction by eliminating the *spurious* model $\mathcal{M}$. We generate such clauses from *refinement lemmas*.

Definition 1. *Let* $\mathsf{M} \cup \mathsf{X}(\mathsf{M})$ *be an extended context and let* $\mathcal{M}$ *be a model of* T *satisfying* M. *A refinement lemma for* $(\mathsf{M}, \mathsf{X}(\mathsf{M}), \mathcal{M})$ *is a* Σ^{b}*-clause* φ *such that* $\mathsf{X}(\mathsf{M}) \models_T \varphi$ *and* $\mathcal{M} \not\models \varphi$. □

Example 4. Let M be the set $\{x \not\approx 0\}$ and $\mathsf{X}(\mathsf{M})$ be $\{x \approx y \times y\}$. Let $\mathcal{M}$ be a model A satisfying M with $\mathcal{M}(x) = -1$. A refinement lemma for $(\mathsf{M}, \mathsf{X}(\mathsf{M}), \mathcal{M})$ is $x \geq 0$. Observe that $\lceil x \geq 0 \rceil = y \times y \geq 0$ is valid in T. □

An extended solver that constructs a refinement lemma φ for an input context $\mathsf{M} \cup \mathsf{X}(\mathsf{M})$ may return clause $\lceil \varphi \rceil$ which by construction is valid in T, as one can show.

The following definition will be useful when discussing how refinement lemmas are constructed for specific theories.

Definition 2. *Let* $\mathcal{M}$ *be a model of* T, *let* M *a set of basic constraints. The set:*

$$\mathcal{I}^{\mathsf{X}}_{\mathcal{M}}(\mathsf{M}) = \{x \approx t \mid x \approx t \in \mathsf{X}(\mathsf{M}),\ \ell \in \mathsf{M},\ x \in \mathcal{V}(\ell),\ \mathcal{M} \not\models \lceil \ell \rceil\}$$

is the relevant inconsistent subset of $\mathsf{X}(\mathsf{M})$ with respect to $\mathcal{M}$. □

To compute the relevant inconsistent subset of $\mathsf{X}(\mathsf{M})$ with respect to $\mathcal{M}$, we consider each literal $\ell \in \mathsf{M}$, and check whether $\lceil \ell \rceil$ is satisfied by $\mathcal{M}$. For such literal $\ell\sigma$, $\mathcal{I}^{\mathsf{X}}_{\mathcal{M}}(\mathsf{M})$ contains the equalities $x \approx t$ for purification variables x that occur the free variables of ℓ. Relevant inconsistent subsets are useful because they tell us which variables should likely appear in refinement lemmas.

Example 5. Let $\mathsf{M} = \{x \geq 0, y \geq 0, z \geq 0\}$, $\mathsf{X}(\mathsf{M}) = \{x \approx y \times z\}$, and let $\mathcal{M}$ be the model of T satisfying M where $\mathcal{M}(x) = 3$, $\mathcal{M}(y) = 2$, and $\mathcal{M}(z) = 1$. We have that $\mathcal{I}^{\mathsf{X}}_{\mathcal{M}}(\mathsf{M}) = \emptyset$ since $\lceil x \geq 0 \rceil = y \times z \geq 0$, which is satisfied by $\mathcal{M}$. On the other hand, if M is the set $\{x \geq 3, y \geq 0, z \geq 0\}$, then $\mathcal{I}^{\mathsf{X}}_{\mathcal{M}}(\mathsf{M}) = \{x \approx y \times z\}$ since $\lceil x \geq 3 \rceil = y \times z \geq 3$ which is not satisfied by $\mathcal{M}$. Intuitively, this means the value of x should be refined based on its definition in $\mathsf{X}(\mathsf{M})$, which is $y \times z$. A possible refinement lemma for $(\mathsf{M}, \mathsf{X}(\mathsf{M}), \mathcal{M})$ is then $(y < 3 \wedge z \approx 1) \Rightarrow x < 3$. □

We will see examples of how refinement lemmas are constructed in Sects. 4 through 6, each of which learn Σ^{b}-formulas that state properties of extended terms that appear in the relevant inconsistent subset of the current context.

3.3 A Strategy for Extended Theory Solvers

We summarize a strategy, given by $\mathsf{Solve}^{\mathsf{e}}_T$ in Fig. 2, for designing a solver to handle an extended theory. It first tries to apply context-dependent simplification techniques based on the two kinds of inferences in Sect. 3.1. Otherwise,

$\mathsf{Solve}^{\mathsf{e}}_{\mathcal{T}}(\mathsf{M} \cup \mathsf{X}(\mathsf{M}))$: Perform the following steps.

1. **(Context-Dependent Simplification)** Let $\boldsymbol{y}, \boldsymbol{s}$ be terms in $\mathcal{T}(\mathsf{M})$ such that $\mathsf{M} \models_{\mathcal{T}} \boldsymbol{y} \approx \boldsymbol{s}$. Let σ be the substitution $\{\boldsymbol{y} \mapsto \boldsymbol{s}\}$.
   (a) **(Ext-Reduce)** If there exists a $x \approx t \in \mathsf{X}(\mathsf{M})$ such that $s = (t\sigma)\downarrow$ is a Σ^{b}-term and $x \approx s \in \mathcal{L}$, return $\mathsf{Infer}(x \approx s)$.
   (b) **(Ext-Equal)** If there exists $x_1 \approx t_1, x_2 \approx t_2 \in \mathsf{X}(\mathsf{M})$ such that $(t_1\sigma)\downarrow = (t_2\sigma)\downarrow$ and $x_1 \approx x_2 \in \mathcal{L}$, return $\mathsf{Infer}(x_1 \approx x_2)$.
2. **(Basic Procedure)** Let $\mathsf{r} = \mathsf{Solve}^{\mathsf{b}}_{\mathcal{T}}(\mathsf{M})$. If $\mathsf{r} \neq \mathsf{Sat}(\_)$, return r.
3. **(Model-Based Refinement)** If $\mathsf{r} = \mathsf{Sat}(\mathcal{M})$, either:
   (a) **(Check)** return r if $\mathcal{M} \models \mathsf{X}(\mathsf{M})$,
   (b) **(Refine)** return $\mathsf{Learn}(\lceil\varphi\rceil)$ for some Σ^{b}-clause φ such that $\mathsf{X}(\mathsf{M}) \models_{\mathcal{T}} \varphi$, $\mathcal{M} \not\models \varphi$, and $\mathcal{L}it(\varphi) \subseteq \mathcal{L}$
   (c) **(Unknown)** return Unknown

Fig. 2. A strategy for an extended theory solver.

it invokes the basic procedure $\mathsf{Solve}^{\mathsf{b}}_{T}$ on the basic portion M of our context. If this determines that M is satisfied by model $\mathcal{M}$, it uses model-based refinement techniques, as described in Sect. 3.2. This will either determine that $\mathcal{M}$ is also a model of X(M) in which case it returns $\mathsf{Sat}(\mathcal{M})$, construct a refinement lemma for $(\mathsf{M}, \mathsf{X}(\mathsf{M}), \mathcal{M})$, or return Unknown. As mentioned, implementations of model-based refinement vary significantly from theory to theory, and hence our definition of how refinement lemmas are chosen is intentionally left underspecified here.

The next three sections considers examples of DPLL(T) theory solvers that are designed according to Fig. 2. In each section, we provide details on how the steps in $\mathsf{Solve}^{\mathsf{e}}_{T}$ are specifically implemented for that theory. We consider an extended theory of strings, a theory of bit-vectors with a partitioned signature, and the theory of linear arithmetic extended with multiplication.

4 An Efficient Solver for an Extended Theory of Strings

Recently, SMT solvers have been extended with native support for the theory unbounded strings and regular expressions. Implementations of these solvers have significant improved in both performance and reliability in the past several years [1,31,39]. This support has enabled a number of applications in security analysis, including symbolic execution approaches that reason about strings as a built-in type [34].

Consider the extended theory of strings whose signature Σ_{S} contains a sort Str for character strings and a sort Int for integers. We partition the function symbols of this signature in two parts. The base signature $\Sigma^{\mathsf{b}}_{\mathsf{S}}$ contains the standard symbols of linear integer arithmetic, words constructed from a finite alphabet $\mathcal{A}$, string concatenation con and string length len. The extension signature $\Sigma_{\mathsf{S}}^{\mathsf{e}}$ contains four function symbols whose semantics are as follows in every model of the theory. For all x, y, z, n, m, the term $\mathsf{substr}(x, n, m)$ is interpreted as the maximal substring of x starting at position n with length at most m, or the empty string if n is an invalid position; $\mathsf{contains}(x, y)$ is interpreted as true if and only if string x contains string y; $\mathsf{idof}(x, y, n)$ is interpreted as the position of the first occurrence of y in x starting from position n, or -1 if y is empty, n is an invalid position, or if no such occurrence exists; $\mathsf{repl}(x, y, z)$ is interpreted as the result of replacing the first occurrence in x of y by z, or x if x does not contain y.

We describe our approach for this extended theory of strings in terms of the three steps outlined in Fig. 2.

Procedure for $\Sigma_{\mathsf{S}}^{\mathsf{b}}$-constraints. In previous work [31], we developed an efficient calculus for the satisfiability of quantifier-free strings with length constraints. The calculus handles $\Sigma_{\mathsf{S}}^{\mathsf{b}}$-constraints (but not $\Sigma_{\mathsf{S}}^{\mathsf{e}}$-constraints), and also includes partial support for regular expressions. The calculus is implemented as a theory solver in CVC4. At a high level, this solver infers equalities between string variables based on a form of unification (e.g., it infers $x \approx z$ when $\mathsf{con}(x, y) \approx \mathsf{con}(z, w)$ and $\mathsf{len}\, x \approx \mathsf{len}\, z$ are both in M), returns splitting lemmas based on the lengths of string terms and derives conflicts for instance when it can infer an equality between distinct character strings. The decidability of strings constraints, even in the basic signature that includes length constraints, is an open problem [24]. Nevertheless, the calculus from [31] is sound with respect to models and refutations, and terminates often for constraints that occur in applications.

Context-Dependent Simplification. Functions in the extended signature of strings are a clear target for context-dependent simplification, due to the complexity of their semantics and the multitude of simplifications that can be applied to extended string terms. Examples of non-trivial simplifications for extended string terms include:

$$\mathsf{contains}(\mathsf{con}(y, x, \mathsf{abc}), \mathsf{con}(x, \mathsf{a}))\!\downarrow\, = \top \qquad \mathsf{contains}(\mathsf{abcde}, \mathsf{con}(\mathsf{d}, x, \mathsf{a}))\!\downarrow\, = \bot$$
$$\mathsf{contains}(\mathsf{con}(\mathsf{a}, x), \mathsf{con}(\mathsf{b}, x, \mathsf{a}))\!\downarrow\, = \bot \qquad \mathsf{repl}(\mathsf{con}(\mathsf{a}, x), \mathsf{b}, \mathsf{c})\!\downarrow\, = \mathsf{con}(\mathsf{a}, \mathsf{repl}(x, \mathsf{b}, \mathsf{c}))$$
$$\mathsf{idof}(\mathsf{con}(\mathsf{A}, x, \mathsf{b}), \mathsf{b}, 0)\!\downarrow\, = 1 + \mathsf{idof}(x, \mathsf{B}, 0) \qquad \mathsf{repl}(x, \mathsf{a}, \mathsf{a})\!\downarrow\, = x$$

The method for computing the simplified form of extended string terms is around 2000 lines of C++ code in the CVC4 code base.[1] Despite the complexity of the simplifier, computing simplified forms often leads to significant performance benefits, as we discuss later. In addition to using aggressive rewriting techniques for extended string terms, it is often advantageous to use methods for constructing derivable substitutions based on flattening sequences of equalities that involve string concatenation terms. For instance, if M contains $x \approx \mathsf{con}(\mathsf{ab}, y)$, $y \approx \mathsf{con}(\mathsf{c}, z)$ and $z \approx \mathsf{con}(\mathsf{de}, u)$, where ab, c and de are string constants, then our implementation computes $\{x \mapsto \mathsf{con}(\mathsf{abcde}, u)\}$ as a derivable substitution in M.

[1] See [34] for more details.

$$
\begin{aligned}
[\![x \approx \mathsf{substr}(y,n,m)]\!] &\equiv \mathsf{ite}(\ 0 \leq n < \mathsf{len}\, y \wedge 0 < m,\\
&\qquad y \approx \mathsf{con}(z_1,x,z_2) \wedge \mathsf{len}\, z_1 \approx n \wedge \mathsf{len}\, z_2 \approx \mathsf{len}\, y \dot{-} m, x \approx \epsilon)\\
[\![x \approx \mathsf{contains}(y,z)]\!] &\equiv (x \not\approx \top) \Leftrightarrow \textstyle\bigwedge_{n=0}^{K} n \leq \mathsf{len}\, y - \mathsf{len}\, z \Rightarrow \neg[\![z \approx \mathsf{substr}(y,n,\mathsf{len}\, z)]\!]\\
[\![x \approx \mathsf{idof}(y,z,n)]\!] &\equiv [\![z_1 \approx \mathsf{substr}(y,n,\mathsf{len}\, y - n)]\!] \wedge\\
&\qquad \mathsf{ite}(\ 0 \leq n \wedge z \not\approx \epsilon \wedge [\![\top \approx \mathsf{contains}(z_1,z)]\!],\\
&\qquad [\![z \approx \mathsf{substr}(z_1, x-n, \mathsf{len}\, z)]\!] \wedge\\
&\qquad [\![\bot \approx \mathsf{contains}(\mathsf{substr}(y',0,x+\mathsf{len}\, z - (n+1)), z)]\!], x \approx -1\ )\\
[\![x \approx \mathsf{repl}(y,z,w)]\!] &\equiv \mathsf{ite}(\ z \not\approx \epsilon \wedge [\![\top \approx \mathsf{contains}(y,z)]\!],\\
&\qquad x \approx \mathsf{con}(z_1,w,z_2) \wedge y \approx \mathsf{con}(z_1,z,z_2) \wedge [\![\mathsf{len}\, z_1 \approx \mathsf{idof}(y,z,0)]\!],\\
&\qquad x \approx y\ )
\end{aligned}
$$

Fig. 3. Reduction of Σ_{S}-constraints to $\Sigma_{\mathsf{S}}^{\mathsf{b}}$-constraints for bounded length K, where z_1, z_2 are fresh variables. The operation $n_1 \dot{-} n_2$ denotes the maximum of $n_1 - n_2$ and 0.

Model-Based Refinement. If all string variables are known to have length bounded above by some concrete natural number K, then reasoning about constraints in the full signature Σ_{S} of the extended theory of strings can be reduced to reasoning about $\Sigma_{\mathsf{S}}^{\mathsf{b}}$-constraints. Concretely, for any equality of the form $x \approx f(x_1, \ldots, x_n)$ where $f \in \Sigma_{\mathsf{S}}^{\mathsf{e}}$, we write $[\![x \approx f(x_1, \ldots, x_n)]\!]$ to denote a formula equivalent to $x \approx f(x_1, \ldots, x_n)$ based on the recursive definition in Fig. 3. The size of $[\![x \approx f(x_1, \ldots, x_n)]\!]$ is finite since the reduction replaces extended terms with simpler ones based on a well-founded ordering over extended string functions. Our model-based refinement for the extended theory of strings chooses some $x \approx t$ in the relevant inconsistent subset $\mathcal{I}_{\mathcal{M}}^{\mathsf{X}}(\mathsf{M})$ and returns a lemma of the form $(x \approx t) \Leftrightarrow [\![x \approx t]\!]$. The lemmas we learn by this form require us to fix a bound K on the length of strings. Although not shown here, this can be done in an incremental fashion by reasoning about bounded integer quantified formulas, that is formulas of the form $\forall k. 0 \leq k \leq t \Rightarrow \varphi$, where t does not contain k and φ is quantifier-free. Such formulas can be handled in an incomplete way by guessing upper bounds on the value of t, and subsequently applying finite instantiation as needed [34].

Similar techniques are used in a number of approaches to the extended theory of strings [12], which perform this reduction to basic constraints eagerly. In contrast to those approaches, we perform this reduction in a model-based manner, and only when reasoning by context-dependent simplification does not suffice.

Example 6. Let M be $\{x \approx \bot, y \approx \mathsf{abc}, z \approx \mathsf{con}(\mathsf{b}, w, \mathsf{a})\}$ and $\mathsf{X}(\mathsf{M})$ be $\{x \approx \mathsf{contains}(y, z)\}$, where a, b and abc are string constants. The substitution $\sigma = \{y \mapsto \mathsf{abc}, z \approx \mathsf{con}(\mathsf{b}, w, \mathsf{b})\}$ is a derivable substitution in M. Moreover, $\mathsf{contains}(y, z)\sigma\!\downarrow\, = \mathsf{contains}(\mathsf{abc}, \mathsf{con}(\mathsf{b}, w, \mathsf{b}))\!\downarrow\, = \bot$ with $\bot$ a basic term. Thus, using context-dependent simplification, we may infer that $x \approx \mathsf{contains}(y, z)$ is equivalent to $x \approx \bot$ in this context. This allows us to avoid constructing the refinement lemma $x \approx \mathsf{contains}(y, z) \Leftrightarrow [\![x \approx \mathsf{contains}(y, z)]\!]$ according to Fig. 3. □

Evaluation. We considered 25,386 benchmarks generated by PyEx, an SMT-based symbolic execution engine for Python programs which is a recent extension of PyExZ3 [4]. These benchmarks heavily involve string functions in the extended

	PyEx-c (5557)		**PyEx-z3** (8399)		**PyEx-z32** (11430)		**Total** (25386)	
Solver	#	time	#	time	#	time	#	time
cvc4+sm	**5485**	52m	**11298**	2h33m	**7019**	1h43m	**23802**	5h8m
cvc4+m	5377	1h8m	10355	2h29m	6879	3h6m	22611	6h44m
z3	4695	2h44m	8415	5h18m	6258	3h30m	19368	11h33m
z3str2	3291	3h47m	5908	7h24m	4136	4h48m	13335	16h1m

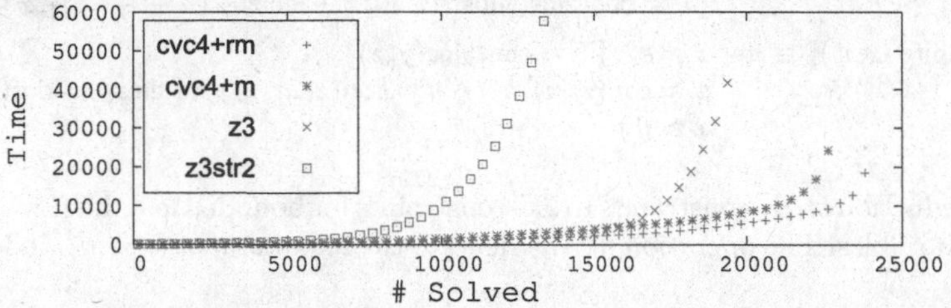

Fig. 4. Table of results of running each solver over benchmarks generated by PyEx, where all benchmarks were run with a 30 s timeout. The cactus plot shows the cumulative runtime taken by each of the four configurations over all benchmarks from the three sets.

signature. We compare our implementation in the SMT solver CVC4 [7] against Z3-STR [39] and Z3 [19], both of which use eager reductions to handle extended string functions. We tested two configurations of CVC4. The first, **cvc4+m** uses model-based refinement techniques (**m**) for reducing constraints over extended string terms to basic ones. The second, **cvc4+sm** additionally uses context-dependent simplification techniques (**s**) which, following Fig. 2, are applied with higher priority than the model-based refinement techniques.[2]

The results are shown in Fig. 4 for three sets of benchmarks, **PyEx-c**, **PyEx-z3** and **PyEx-z32**. These benchmarks were generated by PyEx on functions sampled from popular Python packages (httplib2, pip, pymongo, requests) using CVC4, Z3 and Z3-STR as a backend solver respectively. The results show that **cvc4+sm** has better overall performance than the other solvers, solving 23,802 benchmarks while taking a total of 5 h and 38 min on benchmarks it solves. This is 1,193 more benchmarks that CVC4 with context-dependent simplification disabled, indicating that context-dependent rewriting is a highly effective technique for this set. With respect to its nearest competitor Z3, which took 11 h and 33 min on the 19,368 benchmarks its solves, **cvc4+sm** solved its first 19,368 benchmarks in 1 h and 23 min, and overall solves a total of 4,434 more benchmarks.

5 Lightweight Techniques for Non-linear Arithmetic

In this section, we consider an extended theory of (real or integer) arithmetic A whose signature Σ_{A} is partitioned so that $\Sigma_{\mathsf{A}}^{\mathrm{b}}$ contains the basic symbols of linear arithmetic, and $\Sigma_{\mathsf{A}}^{\mathrm{e}}$ contains the variadic multiplication symbol $\times$. In the

[2] For details on our experiments, see http://cvc4.stanford.edu/papers/FroCoS2017-ext.

following, a *monomial* refers to a flattened application of multiplication $x_1 \times \ldots \times x_n$, where $x_1, \ldots, x_n$ are (not necessarily distinct) variables. The obvious motivation for this partitioning is that SMT solvers implement efficient decision procedures for linear arithmetic, but their support for non-linear arithmetic is limited (and is necessarily incomplete for integer arithmetic). We outline our approach according to the steps in Fig. 2.

Basic Procedure for $\Sigma^{\mathsf{b}}_{\mathsf{A}}$-constraints. Many efficient solvers for linear arithmetic in DPLL(T)-based SMT solvers are based on work by de Moura and Dutertre [22]. Approaches for linear arithmetic in our solver CVC4 are described in King's thesis [29].

Context-Dependent Simplification. For arithmetic, context-dependent simplification allows us to "linearize" non-linear terms by straightforward evaluation of constant factors. To start, all literals are normalized to atoms of the form $p \sim 0$ where $\sim$ is a relational operator and p is a sum of terms of the form $c \cdot x_1 \times \ldots \times x_n$ with c a concrete integer or rational constant and $x_1 \times \ldots \times x_n$ a monomial. Note a term in this sum is a basic if $m \leq 1$. To construct derivable substitutions for a given set of linear equalities M, we use a technique inspired by Gaussian elimination that finds a set of variables that are entailed to be equal to constants based on the equalities in M. For example, if M contains $x + y \approx 4$ and $y \approx 3$, then $\{x \mapsto 1, y \mapsto 3\}$ is a derivable substitution in M.

Model-Based Refinement. Differently from the theory strings, there is no finite reduction from extended constraints to basic ones for the theory of arithmetic. Instead, our approach for model-based refinement technique for equalities $x \approx t$ in our relevant inconsistent subset of $\mathsf{X}(\mathsf{M})$, where t is a monomial, adds lemmas that help refine the value of x in future models by stating various properties of multiplication. We see t as decomposed into the product $t_1 \times t_2$ of two monomials. Figure 5 lists three basic templates we use for generating refinement lemmas based on $x \approx t_1 \times t_2$. This list is not comprehensive, but represents the three most commonly used lemma templates in our implementation.

Suppose we have a model $\mathcal{M}$ for our set of basic constraints M. Let φ be a formula that is an instance of one of the templates in Fig. 5, meets the side conditions in the figure (if any), and is such that $\lceil \varphi \rceil = \varphi\{x \mapsto t_1 \times t_2\}$ is a valid formula in theory A. Notice that φ is a refinement lemma for $(\mathsf{M}, \mathsf{X}(\mathsf{M}), \mathcal{M})$ if $\mathcal{M} \not\models \varphi$. For the first two lemmas, φ is equivalent to a formula whose literals are either of the form $u_1 \sim u_2$, where $\sim$ is one of $\{\approx, >, <, \leq, \geq\}$, and for $i = 1, 2$, the term u_i is either

(Sign)	$t_1 \sim_1 0 \wedge t_2 \sim_2 0 \Rightarrow x \sim 0$	
(Magnitude)	$\lvert t_1 \rvert \sim_1 \lvert s_1 \rvert \wedge \lvert t_2 \rvert \sim_2 \lvert s_2 \rvert \Rightarrow \lvert x \rvert \sim \lvert (s_1 \times s_2) \rvert$	**where** $(s_1 \times s_2)\!\downarrow\, \in \mathcal{T}(\mathsf{X}(\mathsf{M}))$
(Multiply)	$t_1 \sim_1 p \wedge t_2 \sim_2 0 \Rightarrow x \sim (t_2 \times p)$	**where** $\mathsf{deg}(t_1) \geq \mathsf{deg}(p)$ **and** $(t_1 \sim_1 p)\!\downarrow\, \in \mathsf{M}$

Fig. 5. Templates for model-based refinement lemmas for $x \approx t_1 \times t_2$, where t_1, t_2, s_1, s_2 are monomials, p is a polynomial, $\sim_1, \sim_2, \sim \in \{\approx, >, <, \leq, \geq\}$, $|t|$ is shorthand for the if-then-else term $\mathsf{ite}(t > 0, t, -t)$, and $\mathsf{deg}(t)$ denotes the degree of t.

0, or a monomial of the form $x_1 \times \ldots \times x_n$, where for each $j = 1, \ldots, n$, x_j is a variable from $\mathcal{V}(\mathsf{X}(\mathsf{M}))$. Only a finite number of literals of this form exist. Thus, all refinement lemmas generated using the first two templates are built from a finite set of literals $\mathcal{L}$. A more detailed argument can show that lemmas generated from the third template are built from a finite set of literals as well. This fact suffices to argue that our extended solver will generate only a finite number of refinement lemmas for a given context M which is enough for termination in DPLL(T). However, it is not enough for refutation completeness in A since one may need refinement lemmas that are not an instance of these templates.

Example 7. Let $\mathsf{M} = \{x < 0, y > z\}$ and $\mathsf{X}(\mathsf{M}) = \{x \approx y \times z\}$. Let $\mathcal{M}$ be a model of M where $\mathcal{M}(x) = -1$, $\mathcal{M}(y) = 3$ and $\mathcal{M}(z) = 2$. The relevant inconsistent subset $\mathcal{I}^{\mathsf{X}}_{\mathcal{M}}(\mathsf{M})$ contains $x \approx y \times z$. The formula $\varphi = (y > 0 \wedge z > 0) \Rightarrow x > 0$ is an instance of first template in Fig. 5, and $\lceil \varphi \rceil = (y > 0 \wedge z > 0) \Rightarrow y \times z > 0$ is valid in A. Since $\mathcal{M} \models y > 0 \wedge z > 0$ but $\mathcal{M} \not\models x > 0$, we have that φ is a refinement lemma for $(\mathsf{M}, \mathsf{X}(\mathsf{M}), \mathcal{M})$. Returning $\lceil \varphi \rceil$ as a learned clause has the effect of ruling out a class of models that includes $\mathcal{M}$ in subsequent states. □

Example 8. Let $\mathsf{M} = \{y > 3, x > y, x < 3 \cdot z - 1\}$ and $\mathsf{X}(\mathsf{M}) = \{x \approx y \times z\}$. Let $\mathcal{M}$ be a model of M where $\mathcal{M}(y) = 4$, $\mathcal{M}(x) = 5$ and $\mathcal{M}(z) = 3$, where again $(x \approx y \times z) \in \mathcal{I}^{\mathsf{X}}_{\mathcal{M}}(\mathsf{M})$. The formula $\varphi = (y > 3 \wedge z > 0) \Rightarrow x > 3 \cdot z$ is an instance of the third template in Fig. 5, and $\lceil \varphi \rceil = (y > 3 \wedge z > 0) \Rightarrow y \times z > 3 \cdot z$ is valid in A. Since $\mathcal{M} \models y > 3 \wedge z > 0$ but $\mathcal{M} \not\models x > 3 \cdot z$, we have that φ is a refinement lemma for $(\mathsf{M}, \mathsf{X}(\mathsf{M}), \mathcal{M})$. Returning $\lceil \varphi \rceil$ as a learned clause suffices to show this context is unsatisfiable. □

Evaluation. We considered all benchmarks of the SMT-LIB library [9] that contain non-linear real (QF_NRA) and non-linear integer (QF_NIA) quantifier-free problems. We evaluated two configurations of CVC4: **cvc4+sm** and **cvc4+m**. The first configuration implements both context-dependent simplification (based on linearizing variables that are entailed to be equal to constants), and model-based refinement lemmas (Fig. 5), whereas the second implements model-based refinement only.

The results are presented in Fig. 6. On the QF_NRA problems, we compared CVC4 with Z3, YICES2 [21], and RASAT [37]. RASAT is an incomplete interval based solver, while both Z3 and YICES2 are complete solvers based on NLSAT [28] (with YICES2 relying on the more recent variant called MCSAT [20]). Note that NLSAT and the underlying algorithms are highly non-trivial and not based on DPLL(T), making integration with DPLL(T)-based solvers such as CVC4 impossible.

Although our method is incomplete, overall CVC4 solves an impressive fraction of SMT-LIB problems. The first interesting observation is that CVC4 solves all instances in the **hong** problem set. These are problems that are know to be hard for the methods underlying Z3 and YICES2, but easy for solvers based on interval reasoning such as RASAT. Note that CVC4 does not directly employ any interval reasoning, and the extra deductive power comes as a side-effect of model-based refinement. Another positive result is that CVC4 solves most problems in the **lranker** [30] and **uauto** problem sets. CVC's performance on these

QF_NIA	aprove		calypto		lranker		lctes		leipzig		mcm		uauto		ulranker		Total	
	#	time	#	time	#	time	#	time	#	time	#	time	#	time	#	time	#	time
yices	**8706**	1761	**173**	83	98	102	0	0	92	30	4	32	**7**	0	**32**	11	**9112**	2021
z3	8253	7636	172	146	93	767	0	0	157	173	**16**	180	**7**	0	32	43	8730	8947
cvc4+m	8234	4799	164	43	**111**	52	**1**	0	69	589	0	0	6	0	32	84	8617	5569
cvc4+sm	8190	3723	170	61	108	57	**1**	0	68	375	3	107	7	1	32	86	8579	4413
AProVE	8028	3819	72	110	3	2	0	0	**157**	169	0	0	0	0	6	4	8266	4106

QF_NRA	hong		hycomp		kissing		lranker		mtarski		uauto		zankl		Total	
	#	time	#	time	#	time	#	time	#	time	#	time	#	time	#	time
z3	9	16	**2442**	3903	**27**	443	235	1165	**7707**	370	**60**	175	87	23	**10567**	6098
yices	7	59	2379	594	10	0	213	3110	7640	707	50	210	**91**	61	10390	4744
raSat	20	1	1933	409	12	32	0	0	6998	504	0	0	54	52	9017	999
cvc4+sm	**20**	0	2246	718	5	0	**623**	8375	5434	3711	11	31	33	36	8372	12874
cvc4+m	**20**	0	2236	491	6	0	603	6677	5440	3532	10	33	31	25	8346	10761

Fig. 6. Results for benchmarks in the QF_NIA and QF_NRA logics of SMT-LIB. All experiments are run with a 60 s timeout. Time columns give cumulative seconds on solved benchmarks.

problems which come from invariant generation [18], show that our proposed methods work well on practical problems. An example of a class of benchmarks where CVC4 does not perform well are the **mtarski** benchmarks [2]. These benchmarks come from the analysis of elementary real functions and, due to their high degrees, solving them requires full support for algebraic reasoning. The results show that our new method is positioned between the incomplete interval-based methods like those implemented in RASAT, and the complete methods like those implemented in Z3 and YICES2, while performing well on practical problems.

On the QF_NIA problems, we compare CVC4 with Z3, YICES2, and APROVE [25]. The APROVE solver relies on bit-blasting [23], Z3 relies on bit-blasting aided with linear and interval reasoning, while YICES2 extends NLSAT with branch-and-bound [27]. Both versions of CVC4 perform well, especially considering that we do not rely on bit-blasting or sophisticated non-linear reasoning. Again, on the **lranker** and **ulranker** problem sets the new method in CVC4 excels, solving the highest number of problems. Overall, **cvc4+m** proves 812 problems unsatisfiable, and **cvc4+sm** proves 825 problems unsatisfiable, while YICES2, Z3, and APROVE can show 975, 485 and 0 problems unsatisfiable, respectively. Focusing on unsatisfiable problems, our results show that the new method is positioned between the incomplete bit-blasting-based solvers like APROVE, and more sophisticated solvers like YICES2.

6 Lazy Bit-Blasting for Bit-Vector Constraints

In this section, we present our preliminary work on a stratified approach for solving bit-vector constraints. We consider the theory of fixed-width bit-vectors whose signature contains a bit-vector sort BV_n for each $n > 0$, and a variety of functions that are used to encode bit-level arithmetic and other operations [8].

A common method for constraints in this theory is to eagerly reduce bit-vector constraints to propositional ones, where this method is often called *bit-blasting*. However, certain bit-vector functions require fairly sophisticated propositional encodings which may degrade the performance of the SAT solver that reasons about the bit-blasted form of the problem. Thus, we consider a theory of bit-vectors whose signature is partitioned such that its extended signature contains the symbols for bit-vector multiplication (bvmul), unsigned and signed division (bvudiv and bvsdiv), unsigned and signed remainder (bvurem and bvsrem), and signed modulus (bvsmod). All other symbols are assumed to be in the basic signature.

Procedure for $\Sigma^{\mathsf{b}}_{\mathsf{BV}}$*-constraints.* In previous work [26], Hadarean et al. developed lazy techniques for a theory of fixed width bit-vectors. In their approach, the solver resorts to bit-blasting only when algebraic approaches do not suffice to establish satisfiability. The solver may use algebraic reasoning to infer additional equalities, for instance based on specialized reasoning about inequalities, bit-shifting, or concatenation and extraction. If M is still satisfiable, then the solver resorts to bit-blasting. In other words, for each $\ell \in \mathsf{M} \cap \mathcal{L}$, the solver learns the formula $\ell \Leftrightarrow \mathcal{B}(\ell)$, where $\mathcal{B}(\ell)$ is the propositional encoding of bit-vector literal ℓ.

Context-Dependent Simplification. Competitive modern solvers including CVC4 use aggressive simplification techniques for the theory of bit-vectors which we leverage in the first step of Fig. 2. Our technique for constructing derivable substitutions is based on mapping variables x to bit-vector constants that occur in the same equivalence class as x in the congruence closure of M.

Model-Based Refinement. Our model-based refinement techniques chooses a $x \approx t$ in $\mathcal{I}^{\mathsf{X}}_{\mathcal{M}}(\mathsf{M})$ and learns $x \approx t \Leftrightarrow \mathcal{B}(x \approx t)$, where $\mathcal{B}(x \approx t)$ is the propositional encoding of $x \approx t$. In other words, we bit-blast constraints from $\mathsf{X}(\mathsf{M})$ at lower priority than constraints in M, and only if they appear in our relevant inconsistent subset.

Evaluation. We provide a preliminary evaluation of a new version **cvc4+sm** whose signature is partitioned according to this section and that implements both context-dependent simplification and model-based refinement techniques, and compared this with the default configuration of CVC4 with lazy bit-blasting from [26] that does not consider the partitioned signature. We ran both on the **sage2** family of benchmarks from the QF_BV division of SMT LIB [9]. Overall, **cvc4+sm** solved 11415 benchmarks compared to 11256 solved by **cvc4**. While these results are not competitive with state-of-the-art eager bit-blasting techniques such as those in Boolector [14] which solves 13549, we believe these results are encouraging due to the simplicity of the implementation and orthogonality with eager bit-blasting approaches, as **cvc4+sm** solved 2171 benchmarks in this set not solved by Boolector.

7 Related Work

A common way to support extensions of theories is to provide first-order axiomatizations of additional symbols in the signature of the extension. One can show decision procedures for theory extensions exist, given a finite instantiation strategy [6,35]. In contrast, the approaches we develop are specialized to particular extensions, and thus have specific advantages over an axiomatic approach in practice.

The idea of using inconsistent (partial) models that guide the learning of new facts is not new. For example, the CDCL algorithm of modern SAT solvers learns clauses to eliminate inconsistent assignments; branch-and-bound in integer programming learns lemmas to eliminate real solutions; and the decision procedure for the theory of arrays [15] generates expensive array lemmas based on the current model. The MCSAT approach to SMT, as another example, [20] is based entirely on the interplay of models and lemmas that refute them. Although our approach is similar in spirit, our goals are different. All mentioned approaches are targeting concrete theories where saturation with lemmas is complete and the models are used to guide control the saturation. Our approach, on the other hand, targets generic theories where a decision procedure is either not available or incompatible with DPLL(T). The advantage of the presented framework is that reasoning in complex theories can be achieved by relying on existing DPLL(T) technology supported by the majority of existing SMT solvers (solving the base theory, relying on equality reasoning and simplification), and very little additional engineering effort to generate relevant refinement lemmas.

A number of SMT solvers support string reasoning [1,31,36,39]. Techniques for extended string constraints [12,36,39] rely on eager reductions to a core language of basic constraints. To our knowledge, no other string solvers leverage context-dependent simplification. Recent lightweight approaches for non-linear arithmetic constraints have been explored in [3,17]. Current state-of-the-art approaches for bit-vectors rely on eager bit-blasting techniques with approaches. An earlier approach for lazy bit-blasting was proposed by Bruttomesso et al. [16]. A recent approach for bit-vectors uses lazy bit-blasting based on the MCSAT framework is given by Zeljic et al. [38].

8 Conclusion and Future Work

We have presented new approaches for handling constraints in the theories of strings, bit-vectors, and non-linear arithmetic. The common thread in each of these approaches is to partition the signatures of these signatures into a basic and extended parts, and treat constraints in the extended signature using context-dependent simplification and model-based refinement techniques. Our evaluation indicates that these techniques are highly effective for an extended theory of strings and give CVC4 some advantages with the state-of-the-art for non-linear arithmetic. Our preliminary results suggest the approach may be promosing for bit-vectors as well.

We plan use these techniques in part to develop further theory extensions that would be useful to support in SMT solvers. Other extensions of interest worth pursuing include a stratified approach for floating-point constraints, commonly used type conversion functions (e.g. bv_to_int, int_to_str), and transcendental functions.

Acknowledgments. We would like to thank Liana Hadarean and Martin Brain for helpful discussion about bit-vectors, and Tim King for his support for arithmetic in cvc4.

References

1. Abdulla, P.A., Atig, M.F., Chen, Y.-F., Holík, L., Rezine, A., Rümmer, P., Stenman, J.: Norn: an SMT solver for string constraints. In: Kroening, D., Păsăreanu, C.S. (eds.) CAV 2015. LNCS, vol. 9206, pp. 462–469. Springer, Cham (2015). doi:10.1007/978-3-319-21690-4_29
2. Akbarpour, B., Paulson, L.C.: Metitarski: an automatic theorem prover for real-valued special functions. J. Autom. Reason. **44**(3), 175–205 (2010)
3. Avigad, J., Lewis, R.Y., Roux, C.: A heuristic prover for real inequalities. J. Autom. Reason. **56**(3), 367–386 (2016)
4. Ball, T., Daniel, J.: Deconstructing dynamic symbolic execution. In: Proceedings of the 2014 Marktoberdorf Summer School on Dependable Software Systems Engineering. IOS Press (2014)
5. Bansal, K., Reynolds, A., Barrett, C., Tinelli, C.: A new decision procedure for finite sets and cardinality constraints in SMT. In: Olivetti, N., Tiwari, A. (eds.) IJCAR 2016. LNCS (LNAI), vol. 9706, pp. 82–98. Springer, Cham (2016). doi:10.1007/978-3-319-40229-1_7
6. Bansal, K., Reynolds, A., King, T., Barrett, C., Wies, T.: Deciding local theory extensions via e-matching. In: Kroening, D., Păsăreanu, C.S. (eds.) CAV 2015. LNCS, vol. 9207, pp. 87–105. Springer, Cham (2015). doi:10.1007/978-3-319-21668-3_6
7. Barrett, C., Conway, C.L., Deters, M., Hadarean, L., Jovanović, D., King, T., Reynolds, A., Tinelli, C.: CVC4. In: Gopalakrishnan, G., Qadeer, S. (eds.) CAV 2011. LNCS, vol. 6806, pp. 171–177. Springer, Heidelberg (2011). doi:10.1007/978-3-642-22110-1_14
8. Barrett, C., Fontaine, P., Tinelli, C.: The SMT-LIB Standard: version 2.5. Technical report, Department of Computer Science, The University of Iowa (2015). www.SMT-LIB.org
9. Barrett, C., Fontaine, P., Tinelli, C.: The satisfiability modulo theories library (SMT-LIB) (2016). www.SMT-LIB.org
10. Barrett, C., Nieuwenhuis, R., Oliveras, A., Tinelli, C.: Splitting on demand in SAT modulo theories. In: Hermann, M., Voronkov, A. (eds.) LPAR 2006. LNCS (LNAI), vol. 4246, pp. 512–526. Springer, Heidelberg (2006). doi:10.1007/11916277_35
11. Barrett, C., Sebastiani, R., Seshia, S., Tinelli, C.: Satisfiability modulo theories. In: Biere, A., Heule, M.J.H., van Maaren, H., Walsh, T. (eds.) Handbook of Satisfiability, Chap. 26, vol. 185, pp. 825–885. IOS Press, February 2009
12. Bjørner, N., Tillmann, N., Voronkov, A.: Path feasibility analysis for string-manipulating programs. In: Kowalewski, S., Philippou, A. (eds.) TACAS 2009. LNCS, vol. 5505, pp. 307–321. Springer, Heidelberg (2009). doi:10.1007/978-3-642-00768-2_27

13. Brain, M., D'Silva, V., Griggio, A., Haller, L., Kroening, D.: Deciding floating-point logic with abstract conflict driven clause learning. Form. Methods Syst. Des. **45**, 213 (2014)
14. Brummayer, R., Biere, A.: Boolector: an efficient SMT solver for bit-vectors and arrays. In: Kowalewski, S., Philippou, A. (eds.) TACAS 2009. LNCS, vol. 5505, pp. 174–177. Springer, Heidelberg (2009). doi:10.1007/978-3-642-00768-2_16
15. Brummayer, R., Biere, A.: Lemmas on demand for the extensional theory of arrays. J. Satisf. Boolean Model. Comput. **6**, 165–201 (2009)
16. Bruttomesso, R., et al.: A lazy and layered SMT($\mathcal{BV}$) solver for hard industrial verification problems. In: Damm, W., Hermanns, H. (eds.) CAV 2007. LNCS, vol. 4590, pp. 547–560. Springer, Heidelberg (2007). doi:10.1007/978-3-540-73368-3_54
17. Cimatti, A., Griggio, A., Irfan, A., Roveri, M., Sebastiani, R.: Invariant checking of NRA transition systems via incremental reduction to LRA with EUF. In: Legay, A., Margaria, T. (eds.) TACAS 2017. LNCS, vol. 10205, pp. 58–75. Springer, Heidelberg (2017). doi:10.1007/978-3-662-54577-5_4
18. Colón, M.A., Sankaranarayanan, S., Sipma, H.B.: Linear invariant generation using non-linear constraint solving. In: Hunt, W.A., Somenzi, F. (eds.) CAV 2003. LNCS, vol. 2725, pp. 420–432. Springer, Heidelberg (2003). doi:10.1007/978-3-540-45069-6_39
19. Moura, L., Bjørner, N.: Z3: an efficient SMT solver. In: Ramakrishnan, C.R., Rehof, J. (eds.) TACAS 2008. LNCS, vol. 4963, pp. 337–340. Springer, Heidelberg (2008). doi:10.1007/978-3-540-78800-3_24
20. Moura, L., Jovanović, D.: A model-constructing satisfiability calculus. In: Giacobazzi, R., Berdine, J., Mastroeni, I. (eds.) VMCAI 2013. LNCS, vol. 7737, pp. 1–12. Springer, Heidelberg (2013). doi:10.1007/978-3-642-35873-9_1
21. Dutertre, B.: Yices 2.2. In: Biere, A., Bloem, R. (eds.) CAV 2014. LNCS, vol. 8559, pp. 737–744. Springer, Cham (2014). doi:10.1007/978-3-319-08867-9_49
22. Dutertre, B., Moura, L.: A fast linear-arithmetic solver for DPLL(T). In: Ball, T., Jones, R.B. (eds.) CAV 2006. LNCS, vol. 4144, pp. 81–94. Springer, Heidelberg (2006). doi:10.1007/11817963_11
23. Fuhs, C., Giesl, J., Middeldorp, A., Schneider-Kamp, P., Thiemann, R., Zankl, H.: SAT solving for termination analysis with polynomial interpretations. In: Marques-Silva, J., Sakallah, K.A. (eds.) SAT 2007. LNCS, vol. 4501, pp. 340–354. Springer, Heidelberg (2007). doi:10.1007/978-3-540-72788-0_33
24. Ganesh, V., Minnes, M., Solar-Lezama, A., Rinard, M.: Word equations with length constraints: what's decidable? In: Biere, A., Nahir, A., Vos, T. (eds.) HVC 2012. LNCS, vol. 7857, pp. 209–226. Springer, Heidelberg (2013). doi:10.1007/978-3-642-39611-3_21
25. Giesl, J., Brockschmidt, M., Emmes, F., Frohn, F., Fuhs, C., Otto, C., Plücker, M., Schneider-Kamp, P., Ströder, T., Swiderski, S., Thiemann, R.: Proving termination of programs automatically with AProVE. In: Demri, S., Kapur, D., Weidenbach, C. (eds.) IJCAR 2014. LNCS (LNAI), vol. 8562, pp. 184–191. Springer, Cham (2014). doi:10.1007/978-3-319-08587-6_13
26. Hadarean, L., Bansal, K., Jovanović, D., Barrett, C., Tinelli, C.: A tale of two solvers: eager and lazy approaches to bit-vectors. In: Biere, A., Bloem, R. (eds.) CAV 2014. LNCS, vol. 8559, pp. 680–695. Springer, Cham (2014). doi:10.1007/978-3-319-08867-9_45
27. Jovanović, D.: Solving nonlinear integer arithmetic with MCSAT. In: Bouajjani, A., Monniaux, D. (eds.) VMCAI 2017. LNCS, vol. 10145, pp. 330–346. Springer, Cham (2017). doi:10.1007/978-3-319-52234-0_18

28. Jovanović, D., Moura, L.: Solving non-linear arithmetic. In: Gramlich, B., Miller, D., Sattler, U. (eds.) IJCAR 2012. LNCS, vol. 7364, pp. 339–354. Springer, Heidelberg (2012). doi:10.1007/978-3-642-31365-3_27
29. King, T.: Effective algorithms for the satisfiability of quantifier-free formulas over linear real and integer arithmetic. Ph.D. thesis, Courant Institute of Mathematical Sciences New York (2014)
30. Leike, J., Heizmann, M.: Ranking templates for linear loops. In: Ábrahám, E., Havelund, K. (eds.) TACAS 2014. LNCS, vol. 8413, pp. 172–186. Springer, Heidelberg (2014). doi:10.1007/978-3-642-54862-8_12
31. Liang, T., Reynolds, A., Tinelli, C., Barrett, C., Deters, M.: A DPLL(T) theory solver for a theory of strings and regular expressions. In: Biere, A., Bloem, R. (eds.) CAV 2014. LNCS, vol. 8559, pp. 646–662. Springer, Cham (2014). doi:10.1007/978-3-319-08867-9_43
32. Nieuwenhuis, R., Oliveras, A., Tinelli, C.: Solving SAT and SAT modulo theories: from an abstract Davis-Putnam-Logemann-Loveland Procedure to DPLL(T). J. ACM **53**(6), 937–977 (2006)
33. Reynolds, A., Blanchette, J.C.: A decision procedure for (co)datatypes in SMT solvers. In: Felty, A.P., Middeldorp, A. (eds.) CADE 2015. LNCS (LNAI), vol. 9195, pp. 197–213. Springer, Cham (2015). doi:10.1007/978-3-319-21401-6_13
34. Reynolds, A., Woo, M., Barrett, C., Brumley, D., Liang, T., Tinelli, C.: Scaling up DPLL(T) string solvers using context-dependent simplification. In: Majumdar, R., Kunčak, V. (eds.) CAV 2017. LNCS, vol. 10427. Springer, Cham (2017). doi:10.1007/978-3-319-63390-9_24
35. Sofronie-Stokkermans, V.: Hierarchic reasoning in local theory extensions. In: Nieuwenhuis, R. (ed.) CADE 2005. LNCS (LNAI), vol. 3632, pp. 219–234. Springer, Heidelberg (2005). doi:10.1007/11532231_16
36. Trinh, M.-T., Chu, D.-H., Jaffar, J.: S3: a symbolic string solver for vulnerability detection in web applications. In: Yung, M., Li, N. (eds.) Proceedings of the 21st ACM Conference on Computer and Communications Security (2014)
37. Van Khanh, T., Ogawa, M.: SMT for polynomial constraints on real numbers. Electron. Notes Theor. Comput. Sci. **289**, 27–40 (2012)
38. Zeljić, A., Wintersteiger, C.M., Rümmer, P.: Deciding bit-vector formulas with mcSAT. In: Creignou, N., Le Berre, D. (eds.) SAT 2016. LNCS, vol. 9710, pp. 249–266. Springer, Cham (2016). doi:10.1007/978-3-319-40970-2_16
39. Zheng, Y., Zhang, X., Ganesh, V.: Z3-str: a z3-based string solver for web application analysis. In: Foundations of Software Engineering, ESEC/FSE 2013 (2013)

Description and Temporal Logics

A New Description Logic with Set Constraints and Cardinality Constraints on Role Successors

Franz Baader(✉)

Theoretical Computer Science, TU Dresden, Dresden, Germany
franz.baader@tu-dresden.de

Abstract. We introduce a new description logic that extends the well-known logic $\mathcal{ALCQ}$ by allowing the statement of constraints on role successors that are more general than the qualified number restrictions of $\mathcal{ALCQ}$. To formulate these constraints, we use the quantifier-free fragment of Boolean Algebra with Presburger Arithmetic (QFBAPA), in which one can express Boolean combinations of set constraints and numerical constraints on the cardinalities of sets. Though our new logic is considerably more expressive than $\mathcal{ALCQ}$, we are able to show that the complexity of reasoning in it is the same as in $\mathcal{ALCQ}$, both without and with TBoxes.

1 Introduction

Description Logics (DLs) [2] are a well-investigated family of logic-based knowledge representation languages, which are frequently used to formalize ontologies for application domains such as biology and medicine [9]. To define the important notions of such an application domain as formal concepts, DLs state necessary and sufficient conditions for an individual to belong to a concept. These conditions can be Boolean combinations of atomic properties required for the individual (expressed by concept names) or properties that refer to relationships with other individuals and their properties (expressed as role restrictions). For example, the concept of a man (i.e., a non-female human) that has a wife and only daughters can be formalized by the concept description

$$Human \sqcap \neg Female \sqcap \exists spouse.Female \sqcap \forall child.Female,$$

which uses the concept names *Human* and *Female* and the role names *spouse* and *child* as well as the concept constructors conjunction ($\sqcap$), negation ($\neg$), value restriction ($\forall r.C$), and existential restriction ($\exists r.C$). Number restrictions can express to how many individuals, possibly with certain properties, an element of the concept is related to for a given role. For example, the concept of a woman that has two daughters, three sons, and no other children can be formalized as

$$Human \sqcap Female \sqcap (\geqslant 2\ child.Female) \sqcap (\geqslant 3\ child.\neg Female) \sqcap (\leqslant 5\ child).$$

Partially supported by DFG within the Research Unit 1513 Hybris.

C. Dixon and M. Finger (Eds.): FroCoS 2017, LNCS 10483, pp. 43–59, 2017.
DOI: 10.1007/978-3-319-66167-4_3

The first two number restrictions in this concept description are called *qualified* since they restrict the number of role successors belonging to certain concepts, whereas the last number restriction is *unqualified* since it is concerned with all role successors. Number restrictions have been used as concept constructors for DLs for a long time, but first only in the unqualified variant [4,11]. Qualified number restrictions were first introduced and investigated in [10], but it took almost a decade before the exact complexity of reasoning in the DL $\mathcal{ALCQ}$, which has all the concept constructors introduced in the above examples, could be determined [18]. In fact, the tableau-algorithm for deciding the satisfiability of an $\mathcal{ALCQ}$ concept described in [10] generates n new individuals to satisfy a qualified at-least restriction $\geqslant n\, r.C$. If we assume binary rather than unary representation of numbers (i.e., the size of n in a number restriction is assumed to be $\log n$ rather than n), then this clearly generates exponentially many individuals, and thus the algorithm needs exponential space. The PSpace algorithm described in [18] does not keep n successors in memory at the same time. Instead, it uses appropriate book-keeping of the number of successors (represented in binary) and comparisons of numbers to determine a clash between at-least and at-most restrictions. In order to improve the performance of reasoners for DLs with qualified number restrictions, also more sophisticated numerical reasoning approaches (such as linear integer programming) have been employed (see, e.g., [5,7,8]).

More expressive number restrictions have been introduced in [3]. On the one hand, that paper considers number restrictions on complex roles, i.e., roles that are constructed from role names using operations on binary relations such as intersection and composition. For example, using role intersection within a number restriction, one can describe presidents that employ at least one relative:

$$\mathit{President} \sqcap (\geqslant 1\, \mathit{related} \sqcap \mathit{employs}).$$

On the other hand, the paper introduces symbolic number restrictions, in which variables can be used in place of explicit numbers. This allows one to express, e.g., that someone has more daughters than sons without specifying the actual number of them:

$$\mathit{Human} \sqcap {\downarrow}\alpha((\geqslant \alpha\, \mathit{child}.\mathit{Female}) \sqcap \neg(\geqslant \alpha\, \mathit{child}.\neg \mathit{Female})),$$

where ${\downarrow}\alpha$ says that there must exist such a cardinality α. Unfortunately, both extensions on their own already lead to undecidability of reasoning if they are added to a DL that is closed under all Boolean operations.

In the present paper, we propose a new DL strictly extending $\mathcal{ALCQ}$, which we call $\mathcal{ALCSCC}$.[1] Among other things, this DL can describe some of the concepts expressible in the DLs introduced [3], but not in $\mathcal{ALCQ}$. Nevertheless, reasoning in our new DL is not only decidable, but of the same complexity as reasoning in $\mathcal{ALCQ}$. The basic idea underlying the definition of this logic is the following. A DL concept expresses under what conditions an individual d belongs to the

[1] The name $\mathcal{ALCSCC}$ for our new DL indicates that it extends the basic DL $\mathcal{ALC}$ with set and cardinality constraints rather than just qualified number restrictions.

concept. On the one hand, these conditions refer to concept names to which d must or must not belong. On the other hand, they state conditions on the individuals that are related to d via some role. For example, the value restrictions $\forall r.C$ says that the set of r-successors of d is contained in the set of elements of C. Thus, such a value restriction states an inclusion constraint between sets. Number restrictions enforce cardinality constraints on sets. For example, the qualified number restriction $\geqslant n\, r.C$ says that the cardinality of the set obtained by intersecting the set of r-successors of d with the set of elements of C has cardinality at least n. We now integrate into our DL a logic that can express set constraints (such as inclusion constraints) and numerical constraints regarding the cardinality of sets. This logic is called QFBAPA, which stands for the quantifier-free fragment of Boolean Algebra with Presburger Arithmetic. Basically, the Boolean algebra part of this logic can be used to build set expressions and the Presburger arithmetic part can state numerical constraints. Both parts are linked by the cardinality function. It has been shown in [12] that satisfiability of QFBAPA formulae is an NP-complete problem. Our PSpace algorithm for deciding the satisfiability of $\mathcal{ALCSCC}$ concept descriptions (see Sect. 5) and our ExpTime algorithm for deciding satisfiability in $\mathcal{ALCSCC}$ w.r.t. TBoxes (see Sect. 6) use the NP decision procedure for satisfiability of QFBAPA formulae as subprocedure.

Ohlbach and Koehler [13] have introduced a DL that also allows for Boolean set terms and arithmetic constraints on the cardinality of role successors. The expressiveness of their logic is somewhat different from ours (see Sect. 7). The major difference to our work is, however, that Ohlbach and Koehler give only decidability results and no complexity results. In addition, they only consider satisfiability of concept descriptions, whereas we also consider satisfiability w.r.t. TBoxes consisting of general concept inclusions (GCIs). In fact, we show in Sect. 6 that also w.r.t. GCIs the complexity of the satisfiability problem in $\mathcal{ALCSCC}$ is the same as in $\mathcal{ALCQ}$, i.e., ExpTime-complete.

2 Preliminaries

Before defining $\mathcal{ALCSCC}$ in Sect. 3, we briefly introduce $\mathcal{ALCQ}$ and QFBAPA.

Given disjoint finite sets N_C and N_R of concept names and role names, respectively, the set of $\mathcal{ALCQ}$ concept descriptions is defined inductively:

- all concept names are $\mathcal{ALCQ}$ concept descriptions;
- if C, D are $\mathcal{ALCQ}$ concept descriptions, $r \in N_R$, and n is a non-negative integer, then $\neg C$ (negation), $C \sqcup D$ (disjunction), $C \sqcap D$ (conjunction), $\geqslant n\, r.C$ and $\leqslant n\, r.C$ (qualified number restrictions) are $\mathcal{ALCQ}$ concept descriptions.

An $\mathcal{ALCQ}$ GCI is of the form $C \sqsubseteq D$ where C, D are $\mathcal{ALCQ}$ concept descriptions. An $\mathcal{ALCQ}$ TBox is a finite set of $\mathcal{ALCQ}$ GCIs.

The semantics of $\mathcal{ALCQ}$ is defined using the notion of an interpretation. An *interpretation* is a pair $\mathcal{I} = (\Delta^{\mathcal{I}}, \cdot^{\mathcal{I}})$ where the *domain* $\Delta^{\mathcal{I}}$ is a non-empty set, and $\cdot^{\mathcal{I}}$ is a function that assigns to every concept name A a set $A^{\mathcal{I}} \subseteq \Delta^{\mathcal{I}}$ and to every role name r a binary relation $r^{\mathcal{I}} \subseteq \Delta^{\mathcal{I}} \times \Delta^{\mathcal{I}}$. This function is extended to $\mathcal{ALCQ}$ concept descriptions as follows:

- $(C \sqcap D)^{\mathcal{I}} = C^{\mathcal{I}} \cap D^{\mathcal{I}}, (C \sqcup D)^{\mathcal{I}} = C^{\mathcal{I}} \cup D^{\mathcal{I}}, (\neg C)^{\mathcal{I}} = \Delta^{\mathcal{I}} \setminus C^{\mathcal{I}}$;
- $(\geqslant n\, r.C)^{\mathcal{I}} = \{x \in \Delta^{\mathcal{I}} \mid$ there are at least n $y \in \Delta^{\mathcal{I}}$ with $(x, y) \in r^{\mathcal{I}}$ and $y \in C^{\mathcal{I}}\}$;
- $(\leqslant n\, r.C)^{\mathcal{I}} = \{x \in \Delta^{\mathcal{I}} \mid$ there are at most n $y \in \Delta^{\mathcal{I}}$ with $(x, y) \in r^{\mathcal{I}}$ and $y \in C^{\mathcal{I}}\}$.

The interpretation $\mathcal{I}$ is a *model* of a TBox $\mathcal{T}$ if it satisfies $C^{\mathcal{I}} \subseteq D^{\mathcal{I}}$ for all GCIs $C \sqsubseteq D \in \mathcal{T}$. Given an $\mathcal{ALCQ}$ concept description C, we say that C is *satisfiable* if there is an interpretation $\mathcal{I}$ such that $C^{\mathcal{I}} \neq \emptyset$. Analogously, C is *satisfiable w.r.t. the TBox $\mathcal{T}$* if there is a *model* $\mathcal{I}$ of $\mathcal{T}$ such that $C^{\mathcal{I}} \neq \emptyset$. Two $\mathcal{ALCQ}$ concept descriptions C, D are *equivalent* (written $C \equiv D$) if $C^{\mathcal{I}} = D^{\mathcal{I}}$ holds for all interpretations $\mathcal{I}$. Other inference problems such as subsumption can be reduced to satisfiability, which is why we concentrate on it. The introduced notions (GCI, TBox, model, satisfiability, and equivalence) can of course also be used for DLs other than $\mathcal{ALCQ}$, and in particular for the DL $\mathcal{ALCSCC}$ introduced in the next section.

The DL $\mathcal{ALC}$ differs from $\mathcal{ALCQ}$ in that it has existential restrictions $(\exists r.C)$ and value restrictions $(\forall r.C)$ as constructors in place of qualified number restrictions. It is a sublogic of $\mathcal{ALCQ}$ since these two constructors can be expressed using qualified number restrictions: $\exists r.C \equiv \geqslant 1\, r.C$ and $\forall r.C \equiv \leqslant 0\, r.\neg C$.

Let us now briefly introduce the logic *QFBAPA* (more details can be found in [12]). In this logic one can build *set terms* by applying Boolean operations (intersection, union, and complement) to set variables as well as the constants $\emptyset$ and $\mathcal{U}$. Set terms s, t can then be used to state inclusion and equality constraints $(s = t, s \subseteq t)$ between sets. *Presburger Arithmetic (PA) expressions* are built from integer variables, integer constants, and set cardinalities $|s|$ using addition as well as multiplication with an integer constant. They can be used to form numerical constraints of the form $k = \ell, k < \ell, N \,\mathsf{dvd}\, \ell$, where k, ℓ are PA expressions, N is an integer constant, and dvd stands for divisibility. A *QFBAPA formula* is a Boolean combination of set and numerical constraints.

A *solution* σ of a QFBAPA formula ϕ assigns a finite set $\sigma(\mathcal{U})$ to $\mathcal{U}$, subsets of $\sigma(\mathcal{U})$ to set variables, and integers to integer variables such that ϕ is satisfied by this assignment. The evaluation of set terms, PA expressions, and set and numerical constraints w.r.t. σ is defined in the obvious way. For example, σ satisfies the numerical constraint $|s \cup t| = |s| + |t|$ for set variables s, t if the cardinality of the union of the sets $\sigma(s)$ and $\sigma(t)$ is the same as the sum of the cardinalities of these sets. Note that this is the case iff $\sigma(s)$ and $\sigma(t)$ are disjoint, which we could also have expressed using the set constraint $s \cap t \subseteq \emptyset$. A QFBAPA formula ϕ is *satisfiable* if it has a solution.

3 Syntax and Semantics of $\mathcal{ALCSCC}$

Basically, the DL $\mathcal{ALCSCC}$ has all Boolean operations as concept constructors and can state constraints on role successors using the expressiveness of QFBAPA.

Given a finite set of set symbols T with $\{\emptyset, \mathcal{U}\} \cap T = \emptyset$, *set terms* over T are defined inductively as follows:

- the symbols $\emptyset$ and $\mathcal{U}$ are set terms;
- every set symbol is a set term;
- if s, t are set terms, then so are $s \cup t$, $s \cap t$, and s^c.

Cardinality terms over T are also defined inductively:[2]

- every non-negative integer N is a cardinality term;
- if s is a set term, then $|s|$ is a cardinality term;
- if k, ℓ are cardinality terms, then so are $k + \ell$ and $N \cdot \ell$ for every non-negative integer N.

Set constraints over T are of the form $s = t, s \subseteq t$ or their negation for set terms s, t. *Cardinality constraints* over T are of the form $k = \ell$, $k < \ell$, $k \leq \ell$, $N \,\mathsf{dvd}\, \ell$ or their negation for cardinality terms k, ℓ and a non-negative integer $N > 0$.

Given a set $\Delta^\mathcal{I}$ and a mapping $\cdot^\mathcal{I}$ that maps

- $\emptyset$ to $\emptyset^\mathcal{I} = \emptyset$,
- $\mathcal{U}$ to a *finite* subset $\mathcal{U}^\mathcal{I}$ of $\Delta^\mathcal{I}$, and
- every symbol σ in T to a subset $\sigma^\mathcal{I}$ of $\mathcal{U}^\mathcal{I}$,

we extend this mapping to set terms and cardinality terms as follows:

- $(s \cup t)^\mathcal{I} = s^\mathcal{I} \cup t^\mathcal{I}$, $(s \cap t)^\mathcal{I} = s^\mathcal{I} \cap t^\mathcal{I}$, and $(s^c)^\mathcal{I} = \mathcal{U}^\mathcal{I} \setminus s^\mathcal{I}$,
- $|s|^\mathcal{I} = |s^\mathcal{I}|$,
- $(k + \ell)^\mathcal{I} = k^\mathcal{I} + \ell^\mathcal{I}$ and $(N \cdot \ell)^\mathcal{I} = N \cdot \ell^\mathcal{I}$.

This mapping satisfies

- the set constraint $s = t$ if $s^\mathcal{I} = t^\mathcal{I}$, and its negation if $s^\mathcal{I} \neq t^\mathcal{I}$,
- the set constraint $s \subseteq t$ if $s^\mathcal{I} \subseteq t^\mathcal{I}$, and its negation if $s^\mathcal{I} \not\subseteq t^\mathcal{I}$,
- the cardinality constraint $k = \ell$ if $k^\mathcal{I} = \ell^\mathcal{I}$, and its negation if $k^\mathcal{I} \neq \ell^\mathcal{I}$,
- the cardinality constraint $k < \ell$ if $k^\mathcal{I} < \ell^\mathcal{I}$, and its negation if $k^\mathcal{I} \geq \ell^\mathcal{I}$,
- the cardinality constraint $k \leq \ell$ if $k^\mathcal{I} \leq \ell^\mathcal{I}$, and its negation if $k^\mathcal{I} > \ell^\mathcal{I}$,
- the cardinality constraint $N \,\mathsf{dvd}\, \ell$ if there is a non-negative integer M such that $N \cdot M = \ell^\mathcal{I}$, and its negation if there is no such M.

Given disjoint *finite* sets N_C and N_R of concept names and role names, respectively, we define the set of $\mathcal{ALCSCC}$ concept descriptions by induction:

[2] In contrast to PA expressions, we do not have integer variables here and numerical constants must be non-negative.

- every concept name is an $\mathcal{ALCSCC}$ concept description;
- if C, D are $\mathcal{ALCSCC}$ concept descriptions, then so are $C \sqcap D, C \sqcup D, \neg C$;
- if c is a set constraint or a cardinality constraint over a finite set of symbols consisting of role names and $\mathcal{ALCSCC}$ concept descriptions, then $succ(c)$ is an $\mathcal{ALCSCC}$ concept description.

As usual, we will use $\top$ (top) and $\bot$ (bottom) as abbreviations for $A \sqcup \neg A$ and $A \sqcap \neg A$, respectively.

An *interpretation* of N_C and N_R consists of a non-empty set $\Delta^{\mathcal{I}}$ and a mapping $\cdot^{\mathcal{I}}$ that maps

- every concept name $A \in N_C$ to a subset $A^{\mathcal{I}}$ of $\Delta^{\mathcal{I}}$;
- every role name $r \in N_R$ to a binary relation $r^{\mathcal{I}}$ over $\Delta^{\mathcal{I}}$ such that every element of $\Delta^{\mathcal{I}}$ has only finitely many r-successors, i.e., the set

$$r^{\mathcal{I}}(d) := \{e \in \Delta^{\mathcal{I}} \mid (d, e) \in r^{\mathcal{I}}\}$$

is finite for all $d \in \Delta^{\mathcal{I}}$.

The interpretation function $\cdot^{\mathcal{I}}$ is inductively extended to $\mathcal{ALCSCC}$ concept descriptions as follows:

- $(C \sqcup D)^{\mathcal{I}} := C^{\mathcal{I}} \cup D^{\mathcal{I}}$, $(C \sqcap D)^{\mathcal{I}} := C^{\mathcal{I}} \cap D^{\mathcal{I}}$, and $(\neg C)^{\mathcal{I}} = \Delta^{\mathcal{I}} \setminus C^{\mathcal{I}}$;
- $succ(c)^{\mathcal{I}} := \{d \in \Delta^{\mathcal{I}} \mid \text{the mapping } \cdot^{\mathcal{I}_d} \text{ satisfies } c\}$,
where $\cdot^{\mathcal{I}_d}$ maps $\emptyset$ to $\emptyset^{\mathcal{I}} = \emptyset$, $\mathcal{U}$ to $\mathcal{U}^{\mathcal{I}} = rs^{\mathcal{I}}(d)$, where

$$rs^{\mathcal{I}}(d) := \bigcup_{r \in N_R} r^{\mathcal{I}}(d),$$

and the concept descriptions and role names occurring in c to subsets of $\mathcal{U}^{\mathcal{I}}$ as follows: $C^{\mathcal{I}_d} := C^{\mathcal{I}} \cap rs^{\mathcal{I}}(d)$ for concept descriptions C occurring in c and $r^{\mathcal{I}_d} := r^{\mathcal{I}}(d)$.

Note that $\cdot^{\mathcal{I}_d}$ is well-defined since we can assume by induction that $C^{\mathcal{I}}$ is already defined for concept descriptions C occurring in c. In addition, it indeed maps $\mathcal{U}$ to a *finite* set since $rs^{\mathcal{I}}(d)$ is finite due to the facts that (i) N_R is finite, and (ii) every element of $\Delta^{\mathcal{I}}$ has only finitely many r-successors for all role names $r \in N_R$.

Also note that top and bottom are interpreted as the whole interpretation domain and the empty set, respectively, i.e. $\top^{\mathcal{I}} = \Delta^{\mathcal{I}}$ and $\bot^{\mathcal{I}} = \emptyset$.

4 Expressive Power

We claim that $\mathcal{ALCSCC}$ has the description logic $\mathcal{ALCQ}$ [10, 18] as sublogic. For this it is sufficient to show that qualified number restrictions $\geqslant n\, r.C$ and $\leqslant n\, r.C$ can be expressed in $\mathcal{ALCSCC}$.

Lemma 1. *For all interpretations $\mathcal{I}$ we have*

$$(\geqslant n\, r.C)^{\mathcal{I}} = succ(|C \cap r| \geq n)^{\mathcal{I}} \ \text{ and } \ (\leqslant n\, r.C)^{\mathcal{I}} = succ(|C \cap r| \leq n)^{\mathcal{I}}.$$

As an easy consequence we obtain that reasoning (e.g., subsumption, satisfiability) in $\mathcal{ALCSCC}$ is at least as complex as reasoning in $\mathcal{ALCQ}$, i.e., PSpace-hard without a TBox and ExpTime-hard w.r.t. a TBox. The only thing to take care of here is that the notion of interpretation defined above is more restrictive than the one used for $\mathcal{ALCQ}$ since in $\mathcal{ALCQ}$ individuals are not required to have only finitely many role successors. However, due to the fact that $\mathcal{ALCQ}$ has the finite model property, we can assume without loss of generality that interpretations of $\mathcal{ALCQ}$ satisfy the finite-role-successors property required in this paper for interpretations.

We can, however, express things in $\mathcal{ALCSCC}$ that cannot be expressed in $\mathcal{ALCQ}$. For example, we can define the persons that have the same number of sons as daughter by writing $\mathit{Person} \sqcap succ(|\mathit{child} \cap \mathit{Male}| = |\mathit{child} \cap \mathit{Female}|)$. Description Logics that can express such restrictions have been introduced in [3], but due to the use of explicit variables for cardinalities of sets of role successors in the logic defined in [3], this logic becomes undecidable.

In [3], also number restrictions on complex role expressions are considered, but again the high expressiveness of the corresponding logics introduced in [3] often leads to undecidability. We can express weaker versions of such restrictions in $\mathcal{ALCSCC}$. For example, $\mathit{Employer} \sqcap succ(|\mathit{related} \cap \mathit{employs}| \leq 1)$ describes employers that employ at most one relative, and

$$\mathit{Employer} \sqcap succ(2 \cdot |\mathit{related} \cap \mathit{employs}| < |\mathit{employs}|)$$

describes employers that employ more no-relatives than relatives. Using divisibility cardinality constraints, we can for example express creatures that have an even number of legs as $\mathit{Creature} \sqcap succ(2 \,\mathsf{dvd}\, |\mathit{has\text{-}limb} \cap \mathit{Leg}|)$, without having to specify how man legs the respective creature actually has.

As an example for an inexpressibility proof in $\mathcal{ALCQ}$, we consider a simplified version of our first example.

Lemma 2. *The $\mathcal{ALCSCC}$ concept description $succ(|r| = |s|)$ for distinct role names r, s cannot be expressed in $\mathcal{ALCQ}$.*

Proof. Assume that C is an $\mathcal{ALCQ}$ concept description such that, for all interpretations $\mathcal{I}$, we have $C^{\mathcal{I}} = succ(|r| = |s|)^{\mathcal{I}}$. Let n be a non-negative integer that is larger than the largest number occurring in a number restriction in C. Consider an interpretation $\mathcal{I}$ with $\Delta^{\mathcal{I}} = \{0, 1, 2, \ldots\}$ such that

$$r^{\mathcal{I}} = \{(0, i) \mid 1 \leq i \leq n\} \text{ and } s^{\mathcal{I}} = \{(0, n+i) \mid 1 \leq i \leq n\}.$$

Then $0 \in succ(|r| = |s|)^{\mathcal{I}}$ and thus $0 \in C^{\mathcal{I}}$. We change $\mathcal{I}$ to $\mathcal{I}'$ by giving 0 an additional s-successor, i.e., $\Delta^{\mathcal{I}'} = \Delta^{\mathcal{I}}$, $r^{\mathcal{I}'} = r^{\mathcal{I}}$, and $s^{\mathcal{I}'} = s^{\mathcal{I}} \cup \{(0, 2n+1)\}$. Then $0 \notin succ(|r| = |s|)^{\mathcal{I}'}$. However, since all the numbers occurring in number restrictions in C are smaller than n, changing the number of s-successors of 0 from n to $n+1$ has no impact on whether 0 belongs to C or not. Consequently, we have $0 \in C^{\mathcal{I}'}$, and thus $C^{\mathcal{I}'} \neq \mathit{succ}(|r| = |s|)^{\mathcal{I}'}$, which yields a contradiction to our assumption that C expresses $\mathit{succ}(|r| = |s|)$. □

5 Satisfiability of $\mathcal{ALCSCC}$ Concept Descriptions

Recall that the $\mathcal{ALCSCC}$ concept description C is satisfiable if there is an interpretation $\mathcal{I}$ and an element $d \in \Delta^{\mathcal{I}}$ such that $d \in C^{\mathcal{I}}$. We call $\mathcal{I}$ a *model* of C and d a *witness* for the satisfaction of C in $\mathcal{I}$.

Since $\mathcal{ALCSCC}$ can express $\mathcal{ALCQ}$ and thus also $\mathcal{ALC}$, the satisfiability problem for $\mathcal{ALCSCC}$ concept descriptions is PSpace-hard [17]. In this section, we use the ideas underlying the proof that satisfiability in QFBAPA is in NP [12] to show a matching upper bound (assuming binary representation of numbers). For $\mathcal{ALCQ}$ such an upper bound was first shown in [18].

A given $\mathcal{ALCSCC}$ concept description is a Boolean combination of *atoms*, i.e., concept names A and successor constraints $\mathit{succ}(c)$ for set or cardinality constraints c. Viewing these atoms as propositional variables, we first guess which of them are true and which are false. In case the guessed assignment does not satisfy the propositional formula corresponding to C, we fail. Otherwise, the assignment tells us that there is a way to assign concept names to an individual such that the part of C that concerns atoms that are concept names is satisfied. It remains to see whether such an individual can receive role successors such that the part of C that concerns atoms that are successors constraints can be satisfied as well. Before showing how this can be done in general, let us consider a simple example.

Example 1. Let $C := (\neg A \sqcup \neg \mathit{succ}(2\,\mathsf{dvd}\,|r|)) \sqcap (\neg B \sqcup \mathit{succ}(|r| = 2 \cdot |s|))$.
If we guess that the atoms A and B should be true, then we need to guess that the atom $\mathit{succ}(2\,\mathsf{dvd}\,|r|)$ is false and the atom $\mathit{succ}(|r| = 2 \cdot |s|)$ is true since otherwise the propositional formula corresponding to C would become false, leading to failure. Consequently, we need an individual that belongs to A and B and whose role successors satisfy the constraints $\neg(2\,\mathsf{dvd}\,|r|)$ and $|r| = 2 \cdot |s|$. If we replace the role names r and s in these constraints by set variables X_r and X_s, respectively, then we obtain the QFBAPA formula $\neg(2\,\mathsf{dvd}\,|X_r|) \wedge |X_r| = 2 \cdot |X_s|$. Obviously, this formula is not satisfiable since the second conjunct requires $|X_r|$ to be even, whereas the first one forbids this.

Now assume that we have guessed that the atom A is false and the atoms B, $\mathit{succ}(2\,\mathsf{dvd}\,|r|)$, and $\mathit{succ}(|r| = 2 \cdot |s|)$ are true. This yields the QFBAPA formula $2\,\mathsf{dvd}\,|X_r| \wedge |X_r| = 2 \cdot |X_s|$, which can be satisfied by assigning the set $\{d_1, d_2\}$ to X_r and the set $\{d_2\}$ to X_s. Thus, if we build the interpretation $\mathcal{I}$ with domain $\{d_0, d_1, d_2\}$ where d_0 belongs to B, but not to A, and where d_1, d_2 are the $r^{\mathcal{I}}$-successors of d_0 and d_2 is the only $s^{\mathcal{I}}$-successors of d_0, then we have $d_0 \in C^{\mathcal{I}}$.

When building the QFBAPA formula corresponding to an assignment, we need to take the semantics of $\mathcal{ALCSCC}$ into account, which says that, when evaluating the successors constraints of a given individual d, the set $\mathcal{U}$ must consist of exactly the role successors of this individual. Consequently, in addition to the conjuncts induced by the successor constraints on the top-level of C, the QFBAPA formula must contain the conjunct $X_{r_1} \cup \ldots \cup X_{r_n} = \mathcal{U}$, where $N_R = \{r_1, \ldots, r_n\}$. In the above example, the presence of this conjunct is irrelevant. The following example shows why it is in general necessary to add this conjunct.

Example 2. Let $C := succ(|\mathcal{U}| \geq 1) \sqcap succ(r \subseteq \emptyset) \sqcap succ(|s| = 0)$, where $N_R = \{r, s\}$. Then C is unsatisfiable according to our semantics, but the QFBAPA formula $|\mathcal{U}| \geq 1 \wedge X_r \subseteq \emptyset \wedge |X_s| = 0$ is satisfiable. However, this QFBAPA formula becomes unsatisfiable if we add the conjunct $X_r \cup X_s = \mathcal{U}$.

Until now, we have considered examples where the successor constraints do not contain (possibly complex) concept descriptions. If this is the case, an additional problem needs to be solved, as illustrated by the next example, which is obtained by modifying Example 1.

Example 3. Let $C := (\neg A \sqcup \neg succ(2\,\mathsf{dvd}\,|D|)) \sqcap (\neg B \sqcup succ(|D| = 2 \cdot |E|))$, where D, E are (possibly complex) $\mathcal{ALCSCC}$ concept descriptions. Guessing that the atom A is false and the atoms B, $succ(2\,\mathsf{dvd}\,|D|)$, and $succ(|D| = 2 \cdot |E|)$ are true, we obtain the QFBAPA formula $2\,\mathsf{dvd}\,|X_D| \wedge |X_D| = 2 \cdot |X_E| \wedge \bigcup_{r \in N_R} X_r = \mathcal{U}$. One solution of this formula is the one that assigns $\{d_1, d_2\}$ to X_D, $\{d_2\}$ to X_E, and $\{d_1, d_2\}$ to all the variables X_r for $r \in N_R$.

In contrast to the case considered in Example 1, the existence of such a solution does not yet show that C is satisfiable. In fact, this solution requires d_1 to belong to D, but not to E, whereas d_2 must belong to both D and E. This is only possible if the concept descriptions $D \sqcap \neg E$ and $D \sqcap E$ are satisfiable. Thus, we need recursive calls of the satisfiability procedures for $\mathcal{ALCSCC}$ for these two inputs. This recursion is well-founded (with a linear recursion depth) since the nesting depth of successor constraints in D and E (and thus in $D \sqcap \neg E$ and $D \sqcap E$) is by at least one smaller than the nesting depth in C.

Now assume that these recursive calls yield the result that $D \sqcap \neg E$ is satisfiable, but $D \sqcap E$ is not. This does not mean that C is unsatisfiable. In fact, there is also a solution of the above QFBAPA formula that assigns $\{d_1, d_2\}$ to X_D, $\{d_3\}$ to X_E, and $\{d_1, d_2, d_3\}$ to all the variables X_r for $r \in N_R$. This solution requires $D \sqcap \neg E$ and $\neg D \sqcap E$ to be satisfiable. Assuming that this is the case also for the latter concept description, we can construct an interpretation $\mathcal{I}$ containing an element d_0 that has the individuals d_1, d_2, d_3 as role successors for all roles $r \in N_R$. The rest of $\mathcal{I}$ is a disjoint union of two models of $D \sqcap \neg E$ with a model of $\neg D \sqcap E$, where the respective witnesses are identified with d_1, d_2, and d_3. By construction, this yields a model of C with witness d_0.

Summing up, we have illustrated by the above examples that a guessed assignment for the top-level atoms of C either leads to failure (if the propositional formula corresponding to C is not satisfied by the assignment) or it yields a QFBAPA formula corresponding to the successor constraints under this assignment. Unsatisfiability of this QFBAPA formula again leads to failure. A solution for the QFBAPA formula creates recursive calls of the satisfiability procedure, where the inputs have a smaller nesting depth of successor constraints than C. In case one of these recursive calls returns "unsatisfiable," we cannot conclude that C is unsatisfiable. In fact, it may be the case that another solution of the QFBAPA formula creates other recursive calls, which may all yield "satisfiable." The remaining question is now how to find such a solution in case one exists.

A naive idea could be to add the information that a certain combination of concepts (i.e., a conjunction of concepts and negated concepts) is unsatisfiable to the QFBAPA formula. In Example 3, after finding out that $D \sqcap E$ is unsatisfiable, we could have added the conjunct $|X_D \cap X_E| = 0$ to ensure that the next solution does not require $D \sqcap E$ to be satisfiable. The problem with this approach is that the next solution may create another recursive call returning "unsatisfiable," and thus an additional conjunct needs to be added (e.g., if $\neg D \sqcap \neg E$ turns out to be unsatisfiable, we need to add $|X_D^c \cap X_E^c| = 0$), etc. If the top-level successor constraints of C contain k concept descriptions, then in the worst case a number of conjuncts that is exponential in k may need to be added to the QFBAPA formula. Since satisfiability of QFBAPA formulae is NP-complete, testing the resulting exponentially large QFBAPA formula for satisfiability would require non-deterministic exponential time and representing the formula would need exponential space.

In order to stay within PSpace, we use a result from [12], which is the main tool used there to show that satisfiability in QFBAPA is in NP. Assume that ϕ is a QFBAPA formula containing the set variables $X_1, \ldots, X_k$. A *Venn region* is of the form $X_1^{p_1} \cap \ldots \cap X_k^{p_k}$, where $p_i \in \{0, 1\}$ for $i = 1, \ldots, k$ and $X_i^0 = X_i^c$ and $X_i^1 = X_i$. It is shown in [12] that, given ϕ, one can easily compute a number N whose value is polynomial in the size of ϕ such that the following holds: ϕ is satisfiable iff it has a solution in which $\leq N$ Venn regions are interpreted by non-empty sets. In [1] it is shown that this result can actually be strengthened as follows.

Lemma 3. *For every QFBAPA formula ϕ, one can compute in polynomial time a number N whose value is polynomial in the size of ϕ such that the following holds for every solution σ of ϕ: there is a solution σ' of ϕ such that*

- $|\{v \mid v \text{ Venn region and } \sigma'(v) \neq \emptyset\}| \leq N$, *and*
- $\{v \mid v \text{ Venn region and } \sigma'(v) \neq \emptyset\} \subseteq \{v \mid v \text{ Venn region and } \sigma(v) \neq \emptyset\}$.

We can now continue with the description of our approach. Given a QFBAPA formula ϕ induced by our assignment for the top-level atoms of C, we compute the corresponding number N and then guess $\leq N$ Venn regions to be interpreted as non-empty sets. For each of these Venn regions $X_1^{p_1} \cap \ldots \cap X_k^{p_k}$, we add the conjunct $|X_1^{p_1} \cap \ldots \cap X_k^{p_k}| \geq 1$ to ϕ. In addition, we add the conjunct that states that the union of the guessed Venn regions is equal to $\mathcal{U}$, and thus that all other Venn regions are empty. The resulting QFBAPA formula ψ has a size that is polynomial in the size of ϕ, and thus of C. We then

1. test whether ψ is satisfiable using the NP satisfiability algorithm for QFBAPA;
2. for every guessed Venn region, we consider the part that consists of set variables corresponding to concept descriptions, and recursively test the induced concept descriptions for satisfiability.

If ϕ is satisfiable, then there is a solution in which $\leq N$ Venn regions are interpreted by non-empty sets, and thus the first test is successful for one of the guessed sets of Venn regions. Due to the construction of ψ, the corresponding solution interprets all other Venn regions as empty sets. Consequently, it is sufficient to test the concept descriptions considered in 2. for satisfiability. If all tests are successful then we can construct a model of C as illustrated in Example 3. Basically, this model has a witness d_0 whose role successors w.r.t. all roles in N_R are determined by the solutions for the set variables corresponding to roles. These successors are witnesses for the concept descriptions considered in 2., where the respective models are made disjoint and reproduced as many times as needed.

Theorem 1. *Satisfiability of $\mathcal{ALCSCC}$ concept descriptions is PSpace-complete.*

Proof. Given an $\mathcal{ALCSCC}$ concept description C, the algorithm sketched above proceeds as follows:

1. It views the atoms (concept names and successor constraints) on the top level of C (i.e., atoms that are not nested within successor constraints) as propositional variables, guesses a truth assignment for these variables, and then checks whether this assignment satisfies the propositional formula corresponding to C (where the atoms are replaced by propositional variables). If this test is negative, then this run of the algorithm *fails*. Otherwise, it continues with the next step.
2. The truth assignment for the variables corresponding to successor constraints induces a QFBAPA formula ϕ, as described above. We conjoin to this formula the set constraint $X_{r_1} \cup \ldots \cup X_{r_n} = \mathcal{U}$, where $N_R = \{r_1, \ldots, r_n\}$. For the resulting formula ϕ', we compute the number N that bounds the number of Venn regions that need to be non-empty in a solution of ϕ' (see Lemma 3). Then we guess $\leq N$ Venn regions. For each of these Venn regions $X_1^{p_1} \cap \ldots \cap X_k^{p_k}$, we add the conjunct $|X_1^{p_1} \cap \ldots \cap X_k^{p_k}| \geq 1$ to ϕ'. In addition, we add the conjunct that states that the union of the guessed Venn regions is equal to $\mathcal{U}$. For the resulting formula ψ, we test whether ψ is satisfiable using the NP satisfiability algorithm for QFBAPA. If this test is negative, then this run of the algorithm *fails*. Otherwise, it continues with the next step.
3. For every guessed Venn region v, we consider the part that consists of set variables X_D corresponding to concept descriptions D. We then build a concept description C_v that contains a conjunct for every set variable X_D occurring in v, where this conjunct is D in case v contains X_D and it is $\neg D$ in case v contains X_D^c. We then apply the algorithm recursively to C_v for each of the guessed Venn regions v. If one of these applications *fails*, then this run of the algorithm *fails*. Otherwise, this run of the algorithm *succeeds*.

This algorithm indeed runs *in PSpace* since

- guessing is harmless due to Savitch's theorem, which says that PSpace is equal to NPSpace [6];
- the recursion stack for the recursive calls has linear depth since the nesting of successor restrictions decreases with each call, and for each concept to be tested, only polynomially many such calls are creates (since the values of the numbers N are polynomial in the size of the tested concepts);
- the satisfiability test for QFBAPA formulae is in NP and applied to formulae of polynomial size.

Regarding *soundness* (i.e., if the algorithm succeeds, then the input concept C is indeed satisfiable), we have already sketched above how a model of C can be obtained from a successful run. Indeed, if Step 1 of the algorithm succeeds, then we create a witness d_0. The truth assignment for the propositional variables corresponding to concept names tells us, for every concept name A, whether d_0 needs to belong to A or not. Regarding the role successors of d_0, we consider the solution for the QFBAPA formula ψ found in Step 2 of the algorithm. Assume that this solution assigns the finite set $\{d_1, \ldots, d_m\}$ to the set term $\mathcal{U}$. Then d_0 receives the role successors $d_1, \ldots, d_m$, where the assignments for the set variables X_r for $r \in N_R$ tell us which roles connect d_0 with these new individuals. Finally, each d_i belongs to one of the guessed non-empty Venn regions v, and the recursive call of the algorithm with input C_v was successful. By induction, we can assume that this implies the existence of a model $\mathcal{I}_v$ of C_v with a witness e_v. We create a disjoint copy of $\mathcal{I}_v$ where the witness is replaced by d_i. Our interpretation $\mathcal{I}$ consists of the disjoint union of these copies, for $i = 1, \ldots, m$, together with d_0, where d_0 is linked by roles to the witnesses $d_1, \ldots, d_m$ as described above. A simple induction proof over the nesting depth of successor restrictions in C can be used to show that $\mathcal{I}$ is a model of C with witness d_0.

To show *completeness* (i.e., if C is satisfiable, then the algorithm succeeds), assume that $\mathcal{I}$ is a model of C with witness d_0. Then the membership and non-membership of d_0 in the top-level atoms of C provides us with a truth assignment that satisfies the propositional formula corresponding to C. Thus, the first step of the algorithm succeeds if we guess this assignment. Let $d_1, \ldots, d_m$ be the finitely many role successors of d_0 in $\mathcal{I}$. We can use the membership of these successors in $r^{\mathcal{I}}(d_0)$ for $r \in N_R$ and in $D^{\mathcal{I}}$ for concept descriptions D occurring in successor restrictions on the top-level of C to obtain assignments of subsets of $\{d_1, \ldots, d_m\}$ to the set variables X_r and X_D. The fact that $d_0 \in C^{\mathcal{I}}$ implies that the resulting assignment is a solution of the QFBAPA formula ϕ' constructed in Step 2 of the algorithm. However, this solution is not necessarily a solution of one of the formulae ψ extending ϕ' corresponding to the guesses of $\leq N$ non-empty Venn regions. In fact, the assignment induced by $\mathcal{I}$ may make more than N Venn regions non-empty. In this case, it cannot solve any of the formulae ψ constructed in Step 2 of the algorithm. However, since ϕ' is solvable, by Lemma 3 it also has a solution that (i) makes $\leq N$ Venn regions non-empty, and (ii) only makes Venn regions non-empty that are also non-empty w.r.t. the solution induced by $\mathcal{I}$. Thus, we can guess the set of Venn regions that are non-empty in such a solution. This ensures that the corresponding formula ψ has a solution. Because of (ii), each of the guessed Venn regions v has a satisfiable concept C_v since these Venn regions (and the corresponding concepts) are actually populated by one of the elements $d_1, \ldots, d_m$ of $\mathcal{I}$. □

6 Satisfiability in $\mathcal{ALCSCC}$ w.r.t. GCIs

Recall that the $\mathcal{ALCSCC}$ concept description C is satisfiable w.r.t. a TBox $\mathcal{T}$ if there is a model $\mathcal{I}$ of $\mathcal{T}$ and an element $d \in \Delta^{\mathcal{I}}$ such that $d \in C^{\mathcal{I}}$. We call $\mathcal{I}$ a *model* of C w.r.t. $\mathcal{T}$ and d a *witness* for the satisfaction of C w.r.t. $\mathcal{T}$ in $\mathcal{I}$. ExpTime-hardness of satisfiability in $\mathcal{ALCSCC}$ w.r.t. a TBox is an obvious consequence of the fact that satisfiability w.r.t. a TBox in the sublogic $\mathcal{ALC}$ of $\mathcal{ALCSCC}$ is already ExpTime-complete [16]. Thus, it is sufficient to show that satisfiability w.r.t. a TBox can be decided using only exponential time.

It is well-known that one can assume without loss of generality that the TBox consists of a single GCI of the form $\top \sqsubseteq D$. In fact, the TBox $\{C_1 \sqsubseteq D_1, \ldots, C_n \sqsubseteq D_n\}$ has obviously the same models as the TBox $\{\top \sqsubseteq (\neg C_1 \sqcup D_1) \sqcap \ldots \sqcap (\neg C_n \sqcup D_n)\}$. Thus, in the following we assume that C_0 is an $\mathcal{ALCSCC}$ concept description and $\mathcal{T} = \{\top \sqsubseteq D_0\}$ an $\mathcal{ALCSCC}$ TBox. We want to test whether C_0 is satisfiable w.r.t. $\mathcal{T}$.

A simple approach for showing that the satisfiability problem w.r.t. a TBox in a given DL is in ExpTime is *type elimination* [14,15]. Basically, given a set of concept descriptions $\mathcal{S}$, the *type* of an individual in an interpretation consists of the elements of $\mathcal{S}$ to which the individual belongs. If the set $\mathcal{S}$ contains the concept descriptions C_0, D_0, then the type of any individual in a model of $\mathcal{T}$ must contain D_0. In addition, any witness for the satisfaction of C_0 w.r.t. $\mathcal{T}$ must contain C_0 in its type. Finally successor constraints occurring in the type of an individual imply that there exist other individuals whose types satisfy these constraints. For example, if there is an individual whose type contains the constraint $succ(|r \cap C| > 0)$, which corresponds to the existential restriction $\exists r.C$, then there must be an individual in the interpretation whose type contains C. Type elimination tries to find a collection of types that are exactly the types of a model $\mathcal{I}$ of C_0 w.r.t. $\mathcal{T}$ by starting with all possible types and eliminating those that contain successor constraints that cannot be satisfied by the still available types. For this to work correctly, the set $\mathcal{S}$ must contain sufficiently many concept descriptions. We assume in the following, that $\mathcal{S}$ contains *all subdescriptions* of C_0 and D_0 as well as the *negations of these subdescriptions.*

Definition 1. A subset t of $\mathcal{S}$ is a *type* for C_0 and $\mathcal{T}$ if it satisfies the following properties:

- $D_0 \in t$;
- for every concept description $\neg C \in \mathcal{S}$, either C or $\neg C$ belongs to t;
- for every concept description $C \sqcap D \in \mathcal{S}$, we have that $C \sqcap D \in t$ iff $C \in t$ and $D \in t$;

– for every concept description $C \sqcup D \in \mathcal{S}$, we have that $C \sqcup D \in t$ iff $C \in t$ or $D \in t$.

Given a model $\mathcal{I}$ of $\mathcal{T}$ and an individual $d \in \Delta^{\mathcal{I}}$, the *type of* d is the set

$$t_{\mathcal{I}}(d) := \{C \in \mathcal{S} \mid d \in C^{\mathcal{I}}\}.$$

It is easy to show that the type of an individual in a model of $\mathcal{T}$ really satisfies the conditions stated in the definition of a type.

Intuitively, these conditions take care of the TBox and of the semantics of the Boolean operation. However, we must also take the successor constraints into account. Given a type t, the (possibly negated) successor constraints in t induce a QFBAPA formula ϕ_t in the obvious way.[3] Obviously, if $t = t_{\mathcal{I}}(d)$ for an individual in a model of $\mathcal{T}$, then the corresponding QFBAPA formula ϕ_t has a solution in which the universal set $\mathcal{U}$ consists of all the role successors of d, and the other set variables are assigned sets according to the interpretations of roles and concept descriptions in the model. In order to do type elimination, however, we also need to know which are the non-empty Venn regions in this solution. Again, it is sufficient to look at solutions for which only a polynomial number of Venn regions are non-empty.

To be more precise, given a type t, we consider the corresponding QFBAPA formula ϕ_t, and conjoin to this formula the set constraint $X_{r_1} \cup \ldots \cup X_{r_n} = \mathcal{U}$, where $N_R = \{r_1, \ldots, r_n\}$. For the resulting formula ϕ'_t, we compute the number N_t that bounds the number of Venn regions that need to be non-empty in a solution of ϕ'_t (see Lemma 3).

Definition 2. An *augmented type* (t, V) for C_0 and $\mathcal{T}$ consists of a type t for C_0 and $\mathcal{T}$ together with a set of Venn region V such that $|V| \leq N_t$ and the formula ϕ'_t has a solution in which exactly the Venn regions in V are non-empty.

The existence of a solution of ϕ'_t in which exactly the Venn regions in V are non-empty can obviously be checked (within NP) by adding to ϕ'_t conjuncts that state non-emptiness of the Venn regions in V and the fact that the union of these Venn regions is the universal set (see the description of the PSpace algorithm in the proof of Theorem 1). Another easy to show observation is that there are only exponentially many augmented types (see [1] for a proof of the following lemma).

Lemma 4. *The set of augmented types for C_0 and $\mathcal{T}$ contains at most exponentially many elements in the size of C_0 and D_0 and it can be computed in exponential time.*

Basically, type elimination starts with the set of all augmented types, and then successively eliminates augmented types whose Venn regions are not realized by the currently available augmented types. To make this more precise,

[3] This is just like the QFBAPA formula ϕ obtained from a Boolean valuation in our PSpace algorithm in the previous section.

assume that $\mathcal{A}$ is a set of augmented types and that v is a Venn region. The Venn region v yields a concept description C_v (see the description of the PSpace algorithm in the proof of Theorem 1), and it is easy to see that C_v is actually a conjunction of elements of $\mathcal{S}$ (modulo removal of double negation). We say that v is *realized by* $\mathcal{A}$ if there is an augmented type $(t, V) \in \mathcal{A}$ such that every conjunct of C_v is an element of t.

Theorem 2. *Satisfiability of $\mathcal{ALCSCC}$ concept descriptions w.r.t. a TBox is ExpTime-complete.*

Proof. Given an $\mathcal{ALCSCC}$ concept description C_0 and a TBox $\mathcal{T} = \{\top \sqsubseteq D_0\}$, the type elimination algorithm for deciding satisfiability of C_0 w.r.t. $\mathcal{T}$ proceeds as follows:

1. Compute the set $\mathcal{S}$ consisting of all subdescriptions of C_0 and D_0 as well as the negations of these subdescriptions, and continue with the next step.
2. Based on $\mathcal{S}$, compute the set $\mathcal{A}$ of all augmented types for C_0 and $\mathcal{T}$, and continue with the next step.
3. If the current set $\mathcal{A}$ of augmented types is empty, then the algorithm *fails*. Otherwise, check whether $\mathcal{A}$ contains an element (t, V) such that not all the Venn regions in V are realized by $\mathcal{A}$. If there is no such element (t, V) in $\mathcal{A}$, then continue with the next step. Otherwise, let (t, V) be such an element, and set $\mathcal{A} := \mathcal{A} \setminus \{(t, V)\}$. Continue with this step, but now using the new current set of augmented types.
4. If $\mathcal{A}$ contains an augmented type (t, V) such that $C_0 \in t$, then the algorithm *succeeds*. Otherwise, the algorithm *fails*.

This algorithm indeed runs *in exponential time* since

- Step 1 can obviously be performed in polynomial time;
- according to Lemma 4, Step 2 can be performed in exponential time;
- Step 3 can be iterated only an exponentially number of times since each time one augmented type is removed, and there are only exponentially many to start with. Every single execution of Step 3 takes exponential time since at most exponentially many augmented types and Venn regions need to be considered when testing whether every Venn region occurring in an augmented type of $\mathcal{A}$ is realized in $\mathcal{A}$;
- in Step 4, at most exponentially many augmented types need to be checked as to whether their first component contains C_0.

Due to space constraints we cannot prove *soundness* and *completeness* of the algorithm here. Complete proofs can be found in [1]. □

7 Related Work and Future Work

The work most closely related to ours is the one by Ohlbach and Koehler [13], which also allows for Boolean set terms and arithmetic constraints on the cardinality of role successors. On the one hand, this work is more general than ours in that the authors allow also for bridging functions other than cardinality from successors sets into the arithmetic domain. Actually, while the authors of [13] use the cardinality function in most of their examples, the formal problem specification (Definition 4 in [13]) only requires the bridging functions to satisfy an additivity axiom (Definition 3 in [13]), which in the case of cardinality says:

$$\text{If } x \cap y = \emptyset \text{ then } |x \cup y| = |x| + |y|.$$

It is not clear whether reasoning is done w.r.t. all possible bridging functions satisfying the additivity axiom or w.r.t. specific bridging functions such as cardinality.

On the other hand, the set expressions in [13] can only contain roles and not complex concept descriptions. However, a combination of value restrictions on subroles and cardinality constraints on these subroles can simulate this expressiveness. For example, as pointed out in [13], a qualified number restriction such as $\geqslant n\, r.C$ can be expressed as $succ(r' \subseteq C) \sqcap succ(r' \subseteq r) \sqcap succ(|r'| \geq n)$, where r' is a newly introduced role name.[4] Similarly, $\leqslant n\, r.C$ can be expressed as $succ(r' \subseteq C) \sqcap succ(r \cap r'^c \subseteq \neg C) \sqcap succ(r' \subseteq r) \sqcap succ(|r'| \leq n)$. More generally, one can replace the concept description C within a successor constraint by the new role name r' if one conjoins $r' \subseteq C$ and $r'^c \subseteq \neg C$ to this constraint.

The major difference to our work is, however, that Ohlbach and Koehler [13] give only decidability results and no complexity results. Due to the fact that they consider all Venn regions and also resolve Boolean reasoning on the Description Logic side using disjunctive normal form, the complexity of their decision procedures is considerably higher than the upper bounds we show. In addition, they do not consider GCIs in their work. Even without GCIs, the complexity of the unoptimized procedure in [13] is probably non-deterministic-exponential since an NP procedure solving the arithmetic constraints is applied to a potentially exponentially large constraint system.

The emphasis of the current paper was on showing worst-case optimal complexity results, and thus the algorithms as described here cannot directly be used for implementation purposes. To make the PSpace algorithm more practical, guessing would need to be replaced by SAT solving. Such an algorithm would need to combine (similarly to SMT solvers) an efficient SAT solver with a solver for QFBAPA and with a recursive application of itself. Type elimination is exponential also in the best case since it first computes an exponential number of (augmented) types and only then starts the elimination process. Instead, one could use an algorithm similar to the practically more efficient version of the PSpace algorithm just sketched. However, due to the presence of GCIs, the recursion depth of recursive calls is no longer bounded. Thus, one would need to ensure termination by an appropriate blocking strategy, similar to what tableau-based algorithms use. One could also try to design tablau-based satisfiability algorithms, but then needs to be very careful to avoid the problems caused by the "naive idea" sketched below Example 3 when backtracking.

---

[4] Note that [13] actually uses a different syntax for cardinality restrictions on role successors. To avoid having to introduce another syntax, we have translated this into our syntax. The constraint $succ(r' \subseteq C)$ expresses the value restriction $\forall r'.C$.

Acknowledgment. The author thanks Viktor Kuncak for helpful discussions regarding the proof of Lemma 3.

References

1. Baader, F.: Concept descriptions with set constraints and cardinality constraints. LTCS-Report 17–02, Chair for Automata Theory, Institute for Theoretical Computer Science, TU Dresden, Germany, 2017. http://lat.inf.tu-dresden.de/research/reports.html
2. Baader, F., Calvanese, D., McGuinness, D., Nardi, D., Patel-Schneider, P.F. (eds.): The Description Logic Handbook: Theory, Implementation, and Applications. Cambridge University Press, New York (2003)
3. Baader, F., Sattler, U.: Expressive number restrictions in description logics. J. Logic Comput. **9**(3), 319–350 (1999)
4. Borgida, A., Brachman, R.J., McGuinness, D.L., Alperin Resnick, L.: CLASSIC: a structural data model for objects. In: Proceedings of the ACM SIGMOD International Conference on Management of Data, pp. 59–67 (1989)
5. Faddoul, J., Haarslev, V.: Algebraic tableau reasoning for the description logic SHOQ. J. Appl. Logic **8**(4), 334–355 (2010)
6. Garey, M.R., Johnson, D.S.: Computers and Intractability – A guide to NP-Completeness. W.H. Freeman and Company, San Francisco (1979)
7. Haarslev, V., Sebastiani, R., Vescovi, M.: Automated reasoning in $\mathcal{ALCQ}$ via SMT. In: Bjørner, N., Sofronie-Stokkermans, V. (eds.) CADE 2011. LNCS, vol. 6803, pp. 283–298. Springer, Heidelberg (2011). doi:10.1007/978-3-642-22438-6_22
8. Haarslev, V., Timmann, M., Möller, R.: Combining tableaux and algebraic methods for reasoning with qualified number restrictions. In: Proceedings of DL 2001, CEUR Workshop Proceedings, vol. 49. CEUR-WS.org (2001)
9. Hoehndorf, R., Schofield, P.N., Gkoutos, G.V.: The role of ontologies in biological and biomedical research: a functional perspective. Brief. Bioinform. **16**(6), 1069–1080 (2015)
10. Hollunder, B., Baader, F.: Qualifying number restrictions in concept languages. In: Proceedings of KR 1991, pp. 335–346 (1991)
11. Hollunder, B., Nutt, W., Schmidt-Schauß, M.: Subsumption algorithms for concept description languages. In: Proceedings of ECAI 1990, pp. 348–353. Pitman, London (United Kingdom) (1990)
12. Kuncak, V., Rinard, M.: Towards efficient satisfiability checking for boolean algebra with presburger arithmetic. In: Pfenning, F. (ed.) CADE 2007. LNCS (LNAI), vol. 4603, pp. 215–230. Springer, Heidelberg (2007). doi:10.1007/978-3-540-73595-3_15
13. Ohlbach, H.J., Koehler, J.: Modal logics, description logics and arithmetic reasoning. Artif. Intell. **109**(1–2), 1–31 (1999)
14. Pratt, V.R.: Models of program logic. In: Proceedings of FOCS 1979, pp. 115–122 (1979)
15. Rudolph, S., Krötzsch, M., Hitzler, P.: Type-elimination-based reasoning for the description logic $\mathcal{SHIQ}\mathrm{b}_s$ using decision diagrams and disjunctive datalog. Logical Methods Comput. Sci. **8**(1), 1–38 (2012)
16. Schild, K.: A correspondence theory for terminological logics: preliminary report. In: Proceedings of IJCAI 1991, pp. 466–471 (1991)
17. Schmidt-Schauß, M., Smolka, G.: Attributive concept descriptions with complements. Artif. Intell. **48**(1), 1–26 (1991)
18. Tobies, S.: A PSpace algorithm for graded modal logic. CADE 1999. LNCS, vol. 1632, pp. 52–66. Springer, Heidelberg (1999). doi:10.1007/3-540-48660-7_4

Metric Temporal Description Logics with Interval-Rigid Names

Franz Baader, Stefan Borgwardt, Patrick Koopmann, Ana Ozaki(✉), and Veronika Thost

Institute of Theoretical Computer Science and cfaed, TU Dresden, Dresden, Germany
{franz.baader,stefan.borgwardt,patrick.koopmann, ana.ozaki,veronika.thost}@tu-dresden.de

Abstract. In contrast to qualitative linear temporal logics, which can be used to state that some property will eventually be satisfied, metric temporal logics allow to formulate constraints on how long it may take until the property is satisfied. While most of the work on combining Description Logics (DLs) with temporal logics has concentrated on qualitative temporal logics, there has recently been a growing interest in extending this work to the quantitative case. In this paper, we complement existing results on the combination of DLs with metric temporal logics over the natural numbers by introducing interval-rigid names. This allows to state that elements in the extension of certain names stay in this extension for at least some specified amount of time.

1 Introduction

Description Logics [8] are a well-investigated family of logic-based knowledge representation languages, which provide the formal basis for the Web Ontology Language OWL.[1] As a consequence, DL-based ontologies are employed in many application areas, but they are particularly successful in the medical domain (see, e.g., the medical ontologies Galen and SNOMED CT[2]). For example, the concept of a patient with a concussion can formally be expressed in DLs as $\mathsf{Patient} \sqcap \exists \mathsf{finding}.\mathsf{Concussion}$, which is built from the concept names (i.e., unary predicates) Patient and Concussion and the role name (i.e., binary predicate) finding using the concept constructors conjunction ($\sqcap$) and existential restriction ($\exists r.C$). Concepts and roles can then be used within terminological and assertional axioms to state facts about the application domain, such as that concussion is a disease ($\mathsf{Concussion} \sqsubseteq \mathsf{Disease}$) and that patient Bob has a concussion ($\mathsf{Patient}(\mathsf{BOB}), \mathsf{finding}(\mathsf{BOB}, \mathsf{F1}), \mathsf{Concussion}(\mathsf{F1})$).

This example, taken from [9], can also be used to illustrate a shortcoming of pure DLs. For a doctor, it is important to know whether the concussed

Supported by DFG in the CRC 912 (HAEC), the project BA 1122/19-1 (GoAsQ) and the Cluster of Excellence "Center for Advancing Electronics Dresden" (cfaed).

[1] https://www.w3.org/TR/2009/WD-owl2-overview-20090327/.

[2] See http://www.opengalen.org/ and http://www.snomed.org/.

C. Dixon and M. Finger (Eds.): FroCoS 2017, LNCS 10483, pp. 60–76, 2017.
DOI: 10.1007/978-3-319-66167-4_4

patient has lost consciousness, which is the reason why SNOMED CT contains a concept for "concussion with no loss of consciousness" [19]. However, the temporal pattern inherent in this concept (after the concussion, the patient remained conscious until the examination) cannot be modeled in the DL used for SNOMED CT.

To overcome the problem that pure DLs are not able to express such temporal patterns, a great variety of temporal extensions of DLs have been investigated in the literature.[3] In the present paper, we concentrate on the DL $\mathcal{ALC}$ and combine it with linear temporal logic (LTL), a point-based temporal logic whose semantics assumes a linear flow of time. But even if these two logics are fixed, there are several other design decisions to be made. One can either apply temporal operators only to axioms [9] or also use them within concepts [15,20]. With the latter, one can then formalize "concussion with no loss of consciousness" by the (temporal) concept

$$\exists \mathsf{finding}.\mathsf{Concussion} \sqcap (\mathsf{Conscious}\ \mathcal{U}\ \exists \mathsf{procedure}.\mathsf{Examination}),$$

where $\mathcal{U}$ is the *until*-operator of LTL. With the logic of [9], one cannot formulate temporal concepts, but could express that a particular patient, e.g., Bob, had a concussion and did not lose consciousness until he was examined. Another decision to be made is whether to allow for *rigid concepts and roles*, whose interpretation does not vary over time. For example, concepts like Human and roles like hasFather are clearly rigid, whereas Conscious and finding are flexible, i.e., not rigid. If temporal operators can be used within concepts, rigid concepts can be expressed using terminological axioms, but rigid roles cannot. In fact, they usually render the combined logic undecidable [15, Proposition 3.34]. In contrast, in the setting considered in [9], rigid roles do not cause undecidability, but adding rigidity leads to an increase in complexity.

In this paper, we address a shortcoming of the purely qualitative temporal description logics mentioned until now. The qualitative until-operator in our example does not say anything about how long after the concussion that examination happened. However, the above definition of "concussion with no loss of consciousness" is only sensible in case the examination took place in temporal proximity to the concussion. Otherwise, an intermediate loss of consciousness could also have been due to other causes. As another example, when formulating eligibility criteria for clinical trials, one needs to express quantitative temporal patterns [12] like the following: patients that had a treatment causing a reaction between 45 and 180 days after the treatment, and had no additional treatment before the reaction:

$$\mathsf{Treatment} \sqcap \bigcirc\big((\neg \mathsf{Treatment})\, \mathcal{U}_{[45,180]}\, \mathsf{Reaction}\big),$$

where $\bigcirc$ is the *next*-operator. On the temporal logic side, extensions of LTL by such intervals have been investigated in detail [1,2,16]. Using the next-operator of LTL as well as disjunction, their effect can actually be simulated within qualitative LTL, but if the interval boundaries are encoded in binary, this leads to

[3] We refer the reader to [15,17] for an overview of the field of temporal DLs.

an exponential blowup. The complexity results in [1] imply that this blowup can in general not be avoided, but in [16] it is shown that using intervals of a restricted form (where the lower bound is 0) does not increase the complexity compared to the qualitative case. In [13], the combination of the DL $\mathcal{ALC}$ with a metric extension of LTL is investigated. The paper considers both the case where temporal operators are applied only within concepts and the case where they are applied both within concepts and outside of terminological axioms. In Sect. 2, we basically recall some of the results obtained in [13], but show that they also hold if additionally temporalized assertional axioms are available.

In Sect. 3, we extend the logic $\mathrm{LTL}^{\mathsf{bin}}_{\mathcal{ALC}}$ of Sect. 2 with *interval-rigid* names, a means of expressiveness that has not been considered before. Basically, this allows one to state that elements belonging to a concept need to belong to that concept for at least k consecutive time points, and similarly for roles. For example, according to the WHO, patients with paucibacillary leprosy should receive MDT as treatment for 6 consecutive months,[4] which can be expressed by making the role $\mathsf{getMDTagainstPB}$ rigid for 6 time points (assuming that each time point represents one month). In Sect. 4, we consider the effect of adding interval-rigid concepts and roles as well as metric temporal operators to the logic $\mathcal{ALC}$-LTL of [9], where temporal operators can only be applied to axioms. Interestingly, in the presence of rigid roles, interval-rigid concepts actually cause undecidability. Without rigid roles, the addition of interval-rigid concepts and roles leaves the logic decidable, but in some cases increases the complexity (see Table 2). Finally, in Sect. 5 we investigate the complexity of this logic without interval-rigid names, which extends the analysis from [9] to quantitative temporal operators (see Table 3). An overview of the logics considered and their relations is shown in Fig. 1. Detailed proofs of all results can be found in [7].

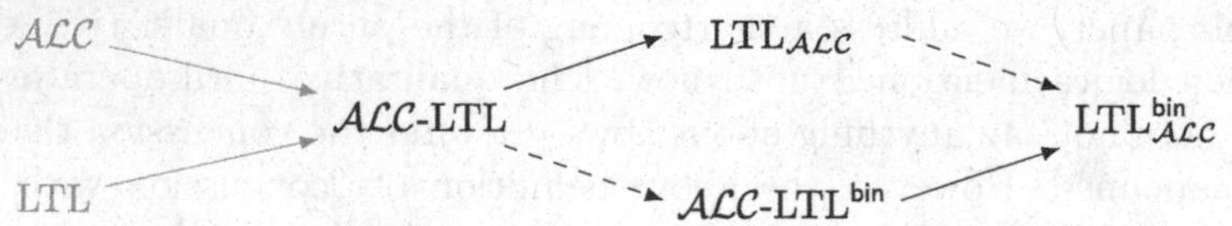

Fig. 1. Language inclusions, with languages investigated in this paper highlighted. Dashed arrows indicate same expressivity.

Related Work. Apart from the above references, we want to point out work on combining DLs with Halpern and Shoham's interval logic [3,4]. This setting is quite different from ours, since it uses intervals (rather than time points) as the basic time units. In [6], the authors combine $\mathcal{ALC}$ concepts with the (qualitative) operators $\Diamond$ ('at some time point') and $\Box$ ('at all time points') on roles, but do not consider quantitative variants. Recently, an interesting metric temporal extension of Datalog over the reals was proposed, which however cannot express interval-rigid names nor existential restrictions [11].

[4] See http://www.who.int/lep/mdt/duration/en/.

2 The Temporal Description Logic $\mathrm{LTL}^{\mathsf{bin}}_{\mathcal{ALC}}$

We first introduce the description logic $\mathcal{ALC}$ and its metric temporal extension $\mathrm{LTL}^{\mathsf{bin}}_{\mathcal{ALC}}$ [13], which augments $\mathcal{ALC}$ by allowing metric temporal logic operators [1] both within $\mathcal{ALC}$ axioms and to combine these axioms. We actually consider a slight extension of $\mathrm{LTL}^{\mathsf{bin}}_{\mathcal{ALC}}$ by assertional axioms, and show that this does not change the complexity of reasoning compared to the results of [13].

Syntax. Let $\mathsf{N_C}$, $\mathsf{N_R}$ and $\mathsf{N_I}$ be countably infinite sets of *concept names*, *role names*, and *individual names*, respectively. An $\mathcal{ALC}$ *concept* is an expression given by

$$C, D ::= A \mid \top \mid \neg C \mid C \sqcap D \mid \exists r.C,$$

where $A \in \mathsf{N_C}$ and $r \in \mathsf{N_R}$. $\mathrm{LTL}^{\mathsf{bin}}_{\mathcal{ALC}}$ *concepts* extend $\mathcal{ALC}$ concepts with the constructors $\bigcirc C$ and $C\,\mathcal{U}_I D$, where I is an interval of the form $[c_1, c_2]$ or $[c_1, \infty)$ with $c_1, c_2 \in \mathbb{N}$, $c_1 \leq c_2$, given in *binary*. We may use $[c_1, c_2)$ to abbreviate $[c_1, c_2 - 1]$, and similarly for the left endpoint. For example, $A\,\mathcal{U}_{[2,5)} B \sqcap \exists r.\bigcirc A$ is an $\mathrm{LTL}^{\mathsf{bin}}_{\mathcal{ALC}}$ concept.

An $\mathrm{LTL}^{\mathsf{bin}}_{\mathcal{ALC}}$ *axiom* is either a *general concept inclusion (GCI)* of the form $C \sqsubseteq D$, or an *assertion* of the form $C(a)$ or $r(a, b)$, where C, D are $\mathrm{LTL}^{\mathsf{bin}}_{\mathcal{ALC}}$ concepts, $r \in \mathsf{N_R}$, and $a, b \in \mathsf{N_I}$. $\mathrm{LTL}^{\mathsf{bin}}_{\mathcal{ALC}}$ *formulae* are expressions of the form

$$\phi, \psi ::= \alpha \mid \top \mid \neg\phi \mid \phi \wedge \psi \mid \bigcirc\phi \mid \phi\,\mathcal{U}_I \psi,$$

where α is an $\mathrm{LTL}^{\mathsf{bin}}_{\mathcal{ALC}}$ axiom.

Semantics. A DL *interpretation* $\mathcal{I} = (\Delta^{\mathcal{I}}, \cdot^{\mathcal{I}})$ over a non-empty set $\Delta^{\mathcal{I}}$, called the *domain*, defines an *interpretation function* $\cdot^{\mathcal{I}}$ that maps each concept name $A \in \mathsf{N_C}$ to a subset $A^{\mathcal{I}}$ of $\Delta^{\mathcal{I}}$, each role name $r \in \mathsf{N_R}$ to a binary relation $r^{\mathcal{I}}$ on $\Delta^{\mathcal{I}}$ and each individual name $a \in \mathsf{N_I}$ to an element $a^{\mathcal{I}}$ of $\Delta^{\mathcal{I}}$, such that $a^{\mathcal{I}_i} \neq b^{\mathcal{I}_i}$ whenever $a \neq b$, $a, b \in \mathsf{N_I}$ (*unique name assumption*). As usual, we extend the mapping $\cdot^{\mathcal{I}}$ from concept names to $\mathcal{ALC}$ concepts as follows:

$$\top^{\mathcal{I}_i} := \Delta^{\mathfrak{I}}, \qquad (\neg C)^{\mathcal{I}_i} := \Delta^{\mathfrak{I}} \setminus C^{\mathcal{I}_i}, \qquad (C \sqcap D)^{\mathcal{I}_i} := C^{\mathcal{I}_i} \cap D^{\mathcal{I}_i},$$
$$(\exists r.C)^{\mathcal{I}_i} := \{d \in \Delta^{\mathfrak{I}} \mid \exists e \in C^{\mathcal{I}_i} : (d, e) \in r^{\mathcal{I}_i}\}.$$

A *(temporal DL) interpretation* is a structure $\mathfrak{I} = (\Delta^{\mathfrak{I}}, (\mathcal{I}_i)_{i \in \mathbb{N}})$, where each $\mathcal{I}_i = (\Delta^{\mathfrak{I}}, \cdot^{\mathcal{I}_i})$, $i \in \mathbb{N}$, is a DL interpretation over $\Delta^{\mathfrak{I}}$ (*constant domain assumption*) and $a^{\mathcal{I}_i} = a^{\mathcal{I}_j}$ for all $a \in \mathsf{N_I}$ and $i, j \in \mathbb{N}$, i.e., the interpretation of individual names is fixed. The mappings $\cdot^{\mathcal{I}_i}$ are extended to $\mathrm{LTL}^{\mathsf{bin}}_{\mathcal{ALC}}$ concepts as follows:

$$(\bigcirc C)^{\mathcal{I}_i} := \{d \in \Delta^{\mathfrak{I}} \mid d \in C^{\mathcal{I}_{i+1}}\},$$
$$(C\,\mathcal{U}_I D)^{\mathcal{I}_i} := \{d \in \Delta^{\mathfrak{I}} \mid \exists k\colon k - i \in I,\ d \in D^{\mathcal{I}_k},\ \text{and}\ \forall j \in [i, k)\colon d \in C^{\mathcal{I}_j}\}.$$

The concept $C\,\mathcal{U}_I D$ requires D to be satisfied at some point in the interval I, and C to hold at all time points before that.

The *validity* of an $\mathrm{LTL}^{\mathsf{bin}}_{\mathcal{ALC}}$ formula ϕ in $\mathfrak{I}$ at time point $i \in \mathbb{N}$ (written $\mathfrak{I}, i \models \phi$) is inductively defined as follows:

$\mathfrak{I}, i \models C \sqsubseteq D$	iff $C^{\mathcal{I}_i} \subseteq D^{\mathcal{I}_i}$	$\mathfrak{I}, i \models \phi \wedge \psi$	iff $\mathfrak{I}, i \models \phi$ and $\mathfrak{I}, i \models \psi$
$\mathfrak{I}, i \models C(a)$	iff $a^{\mathcal{I}_i} \in C^{\mathcal{I}_i}$	$\mathfrak{I}, i \models \bigcirc\phi$	iff $\mathfrak{I}, i+1 \models \phi$
$\mathfrak{I}, i \models r(a,b)$	iff $(a^{\mathcal{I}_i}, b^{\mathcal{I}_i}) \in r^{\mathcal{I}_i}$	$\mathfrak{I}, i \models \phi \mathcal{U}_I \psi$	iff $\exists k\colon k - i \in I,\ \mathfrak{I}, k \models \psi,$
$\mathfrak{I}, i \models \neg\phi$	iff not $\mathfrak{I}, i \models \phi$		and $\forall j \in [i,k)\colon \mathfrak{I}, j \models \phi.$

As usual, we define $\bot := \neg\top$, $C \sqcup D := \neg(\neg C \sqcap \neg D)$, $\forall r.C := \neg(\exists r.\neg C)$, $\phi \vee \psi := \neg(\neg\phi \wedge \neg\psi)$, $\alpha\mathcal{U}\beta := \alpha\mathcal{U}_{[0,\infty)}\beta$, $\Diamond_I\alpha := \top\mathcal{U}_I\alpha$, $\Box_I\alpha := \neg\Diamond_I\neg\alpha$, $\Diamond\alpha := \top\mathcal{U}\alpha$, and $\Box\alpha := \neg\Diamond\neg\alpha$, where α, β are either concepts or formulae [8,15]. Note that, given the semantics of $\mathrm{LTL}^{\mathsf{bin}}_{\mathcal{ALC}}$, $\bigcirc\alpha$ is equivalent to $\Diamond_{[1,1]}\alpha$.

Relation to $\mathrm{LTL}_{\mathcal{ALC}}$. The notation $\cdot^{\mathsf{bin}}$ refers to the fact that the endpoints of the intervals are given in binary. However, this does not increase the expressivity compared to $\mathrm{LTL}_{\mathcal{ALC}}$ [17], where only the qualitative $\mathcal{U}$ operator is allowed. In fact, one can expand any formula $\phi\mathcal{U}_{[c_1,c_2]}\psi$ to $\bigvee_{c_1 \le i \le c_2}(\bigcirc^i\psi \wedge \bigwedge_{0 \le j < i}\bigcirc^j\phi)$, where $\bigcirc^i$ denotes i nested $\bigcirc$ operators, and similarly for concepts. Likewise, $\phi\mathcal{U}_{[c_1,\infty)}\psi$ is equivalent to $\left(\bigwedge_{0 \le i < c_1}\bigcirc^i\phi\right) \wedge \bigcirc^{c_1}\phi\mathcal{U}\psi$. If this transformation is recursively applied to subformulae, then the size of the resulting formula is exponential: ignoring the nested $\bigcirc$ operators, its syntax tree has polynomial depth and an exponential branching factor; and the $\bigcirc^i$ formulae have exponential depth, but introduce no branching. This blowup cannot be avoided in general [1,13].

Reasoning. We are interested in the complexity of the *satisfiability* problem in $\mathrm{LTL}^{\mathsf{bin}}_{\mathcal{ALC}}$, i.e., deciding whether there exists an interpretation $\mathfrak{I}$ such that $\mathfrak{I}, 0 \models \phi$ holds for a given $\mathrm{LTL}^{\mathsf{bin}}_{\mathcal{ALC}}$ formula ϕ. We also consider a syntactic restriction from [9]: we say that ϕ is an $\mathrm{LTL}^{\mathsf{bin}}_{\mathcal{ALC}}$ *formula with global GCIs* if it is of the form $\Box\mathcal{T} \wedge \varphi$, where $\mathcal{T}$ is a conjunction of GCIs and φ is an $\mathrm{LTL}^{\mathsf{bin}}_{\mathcal{ALC}}$ formula that does not contain GCIs. By *satisfiability w.r.t. global GCIs* we refer to the satisfiability problem restricted to such formulae.

First Results. The papers [13,17] consider the reasoning problems of concept satisfiability in $\mathrm{LTL}^{\mathsf{bin}}_{\mathcal{ALC}}$ w.r.t. *TBoxes* (corresponding to formulae with global GCIs and without assertions) and satisfiability of $\mathrm{LTL}^{\mathsf{bin}}_{\mathcal{ALC}}$ *temporal TBoxes* (formulae without assertions). However, these results from [13,17] can be extended to our setting by incorporating *named types* into their quasimodel construction to deal with assertions (see also [20], our Sect. 3, and [15, Theorem 2.27]).

Theorem 1. *Satisfiability in* $\mathrm{LTL}^{\mathsf{bin}}_{\mathcal{ALC}}$ *is* 2-ExpSpace-*complete, and* ExpSpace-*complete w.r.t. global GCIs. In* $\mathrm{LTL}_{\mathcal{ALC}}$*, this problem is* ExpSpace-*complete, and* ExpTime-*complete w.r.t. global GCIs.*

Note that ExpSpace-completeness for $\mathrm{LTL}_{\mathcal{ALC}}$ with assertions has already been shown in [20]; we only state it here for completeness. In [13], also the intermediate logic $\mathrm{LTL}^{0,\infty}_{\mathcal{ALC}}$ was investigated, where only intervals of the form $[0,c]$ and $[c,\infty)$ are allowed. However, in [16], it was shown for a branching temporal logic that $\mathcal{U}_{[0,c]}$ can be simulated by the classical $\mathcal{U}$ operator, while only increasing the size of the formula by a polynomial factor. We extend this result to intervals of the form $[c, \infty)$, and apply it to $\mathrm{LTL}^{0,\infty}_{\mathcal{ALC}}$.

Theorem 2. *Any* $\mathrm{LTL}^{0,\infty}_{\mathcal{ALC}}$ *formula can be translated in polynomial time into an equisatisfiable* $\mathrm{LTL}_{\mathcal{ALC}}$ *formula.*

This reduction is quite modular; for example, if the formula has only global GCIs, then this is still the case after the reduction. In fact, the reduction applies to all sublogics of $\mathrm{LTL}^{\mathsf{bin}}_{\mathcal{ALC}}$ that we consider in this paper. Hence, in the following we do not explicitly consider logics with the superscript $\cdot^{0,\infty}$, knowing that they have the same complexity as the corresponding temporal DLs using only $\mathcal{U}$.

3 $\mathrm{LTL}^{\mathsf{bin}}_{\mathcal{ALC}}$ with Interval-Rigid Names

In many temporal DLs, so-called *rigid* names are considered, whose interpretation is not allowed to change over time. To formally define this notion, we fix a finite set $\mathsf{N_{Rig}} \subseteq \mathsf{N_C} \cup \mathsf{N_R}$ of *rigid* concept and role names, and require interpretations $\mathfrak{I} = (\Delta^{\mathfrak{I}}, (\mathcal{I}_i)_{i\in\mathbb{N}})$ to *respect* these names, in the sense that $X^{\mathcal{I}_i} = X^{\mathcal{I}_j}$ should hold for all $X \in \mathsf{N_{Rig}}$ and $i, j \in \mathbb{N}$. It turns out that $\mathrm{LTL}^{\mathsf{bin}}_{\mathcal{ALC}}$ can already express rigid concepts via the (global) GCIs $C \sqsubseteq \bigcirc C$ and $\neg C \sqsubseteq \bigcirc\neg C$. The same does not hold for rigid roles, which lead to undecidability even in $\mathrm{LTL}_{\mathcal{ALC}}$ [15, Theorem 11.1]. Hence, it is not fruitful to consider rigid names in $\mathrm{LTL}^{\mathsf{bin}}_{\mathcal{ALC}}$ (they will become meaningful later, when we look at other logics).

To augment the expressivity of temporal DLs while avoiding undecidability, we propose *interval-rigid* names. In contrast to rigid names, interval-rigid names only need to remain rigid for a limited period of time. Formally, we take a finite set $\mathsf{N_{IRig}} \subseteq (\mathsf{N_C} \cup \mathsf{N_R})\setminus\mathsf{N_{Rig}}$ of *interval-rigid names*, and a function $\mathsf{iRig}\colon \mathsf{N_{IRig}} \to \mathbb{N}_{\geq 2}$. An interpretation $\mathfrak{I} = (\Delta^{\mathfrak{I}}, (\mathcal{I}_i)_{i\in\mathbb{N}})$ *respects* the interval-rigid names if the following holds for all $X \in \mathsf{N_{IRig}}$ with $\mathsf{iRig}(X) = k$, and $i \in \mathbb{N}$:

> For each $d \in X^{\mathcal{I}_i}$, there is a time point $j \in \mathbb{N}$ such that $i \in [j, j+k)$ and $d \in X^{\mathcal{I}_\ell}$ for all $\ell \in [j, j+k)$.

Intuitively, any element (or pair of elements) in the interpretation of an interval-rigid name must be in that interpretation for at least k consecutive time points. We call such a name *k-rigid.* The names in $(\mathsf{N_C} \cup \mathsf{N_R})\setminus(\mathsf{N_{Rig}} \cup \mathsf{N_{IRig}})$ are called *flexible.* For simplicity, we assume that iRig assigns 1 to all flexible names.

We investigate the complexity of *satisfiability w.r.t. (interval-)rigid names* (or *(interval-)rigid concepts* if $\mathsf{N_{IRig}} \subseteq \mathsf{N_C}$ / $\mathsf{N_{Rig}} \subseteq \mathsf{N_C}$), which is defined as before, but considers only interpretations that respect (interval-)rigid names. Note that (interval-)rigid roles can be used to simulate (interval-)rigid concepts via existential restrictions $\exists r.\top$ (e.g., see [9]). Therefore, it is not necessary to consider the case where only role names can be (interval-)rigid. The fact that $\mathsf{N_{Rig}}$ and $\mathsf{N_{IRig}}$ are finite is not a restriction, as formulae can only use finitely many names. We assume that the values of iRig are given in binary.

Table 1 summarizes our results for $\mathrm{LTL}^{\mathsf{bin}}_{\mathcal{ALC}}$. Since interval-rigid concepts A can be simulated by conjuncts of the form

$$(A \sqsubseteq \Box_{[0,k)} A) \wedge \Box(\neg A \sqsubseteq \bigcirc(\neg A \sqcup \Box_{[0,k)} A)),$$

Theorem 1 directly yields the complexity results in the right column (again, for sublogics of $\mathrm{LTL}^{\mathsf{bin}}_{\mathcal{ALC}}$ this is not always so easy). The GCI $A \sqsubseteq \Box_{[0,k)} A$ that applies only to the first time point does not affect the complexity results, even if we restrict all other GCIs to be global.

Table 1. Complexity of satisfiability in $\mathrm{LTL}^{\mathsf{bin}}_{\mathcal{ALC}}$ w.r.t. interval-rigid names. For (*), we have 2-ExpTime-completeness for the temporal semantics based on $\mathbb{Z}$ (Theorem 5).

	$\mathsf{N_{IRig}} \subseteq \mathsf{N_C} \cup \mathsf{N_R}$	$\mathsf{N_{IRig}} \subseteq \mathsf{N_C}$
$\mathrm{LTL}^{\mathsf{bin}}_{\mathcal{ALC}}$	2-ExpSpace $\leq$ [Theorem 4]	2-ExpSpace $\geq$ [13]
$\mathrm{LTL}^{\mathsf{bin}}_{\mathcal{ALC}}$, global GCIs	2-ExpTime-hard (*)	ExpSpace $\geq$ [2], $\leq$ [Theorem 1]
$\mathrm{LTL}_{\mathcal{ALC}}$	2-ExpTime-hard	ExpSpace $\geq$ [15], $\leq$ [20]
$\mathrm{LTL}_{\mathcal{ALC}}$, global GCIs	2-ExpTime-hard [Theorem 7]	ExpTime $\geq$ [18], $\leq$ [Theorem 1]

The complexity of $\mathrm{LTL}^{\mathsf{bin}}_{\mathcal{ALC}}$ with interval-rigid roles is harder to establish. We first show in Sect. 3.1 that the general upper bound of 2-ExpSpace still holds, by a novel quasimodel construction. For global GCIs, we show 2-ExpTime-hardness in Sect. 4, by an easy adaption of a reduction from [9]. We show 2-ExpTime-completeness if we modify the temporal semantics to be infinite in both directions, i.e., replace $\mathbb{N}$ by $\mathbb{Z}$ in the definition of interpretations (see Sect. 3.2). We leave the case for the semantics based on $\mathbb{N}$ as future work. To simplify the proofs of the upper bounds, we usually assume that $\mathsf{N_{IRig}} \subseteq \mathsf{N_R}$ since interval-rigid concepts can be simulated. Moreover, for this section we assume that $\mathsf{N_{Rig}}$ is empty, as rigid concepts do not affect the complexity of $\mathrm{LTL}^{\mathsf{bin}}_{\mathcal{ALC}}$, and rigid roles make satisfiability undecidable.

3.1 Satisfiability Is in 2-ExpSpace

For the 2-ExpSpace upper bound, we extend the notion of *quasimodels* from [13]. In [13], quasimodels are abstractions of interpretations in which each time point is represented by a *quasistate*, which contains *types*. Each type describes the interpretation for a single domain element, while a quasistate collects the information about all domain elements at a single time point. Central for the complexity results in [13] is that every satisfiable formula has a quasimodel of a certain regular form, which can be guessed and checked in double exponential space. To handle interval-rigid roles, we extend this approach so that each quasistate additionally provides information about the temporal evolution of domain elements over a window of fixed width, and show that under this extended notion, satisfiability is still captured by the existence of regular quasimodels.

We now formalize this intuition. Let φ be an $\mathrm{LTL}^{\mathsf{bin}}_{\mathcal{ALC}}$ formula. Denote by $\mathsf{csub}(\varphi)/\mathsf{fsub}(\varphi)/\mathsf{ind}(\varphi)/\mathsf{rol}(\varphi)$ the set of all concepts/formulae/individuals/roles occurring in φ, by $\mathsf{cl}^{\mathsf{c}}(\varphi)$ the closure of $\mathsf{csub}(\varphi) \cup \{C\mathcal{U}D \mid C\mathcal{U}_{[c,\infty)}D \in \mathsf{csub}(\varphi)\}$ under single negations, and likewise for $\mathsf{cl}^{\mathsf{f}}(\varphi)$ and $\mathsf{fsub}(\phi)$. A *concept type for* φ is any subset t of $\mathsf{cl}^{\mathsf{c}}(\varphi) \cup \mathsf{ind}(\varphi)$ such that

T1 $\neg C \in t$ iff $C \notin t$, for all $\neg C \in \mathsf{cl}^{\mathsf{c}}(\varphi)$;
T2 $C \sqcap D \in t$ iff $C, D \in t$, for all $C \sqcap D \in \mathsf{cl}^{\mathsf{c}}(\varphi)$; and
T3 t contains at most one individual name.

Similarly, we define *formula types* $t \subseteq \mathsf{cl}^{\mathsf{f}}(\varphi)$ by the following conditions:

T1' $\neg\alpha \in t$ iff $\alpha \notin t$, for all $\neg\alpha \in \mathsf{cl}^{\mathsf{f}}(\varphi)$; and
T2' $\alpha \wedge \beta \in t$ iff $\alpha, \beta \in t$, for all $\alpha \wedge \beta \in \mathsf{cl}^{\mathsf{f}}(\varphi)$.

Intuitively, a concept type describes one domain element at a single time point, while a formula type expresses constraints on all domain elements. If $a \in t \cap \mathsf{ind}(\varphi)$, then t describes an named element, and we call it a *named type*.

To put an upper bound on the time window we have to look at, we consider the largest number occurring in φ and iRig, and denote it by ℓ_φ. Then, a *(concept/formula) run segment* for φ is a sequence $\sigma = \sigma(0)\ldots\sigma(\ell_\varphi)$ composed exclusively of concept or formula types, respectively, such that

R1 $\bigcirc\alpha \in \sigma(0)$ iff $\alpha \in \sigma(1)$, for all $\bigcirc\alpha \in \mathsf{cl}^*(\varphi)$;
R2 for all $a \in \mathsf{ind}(\varphi)$ an $n \in (0, \ell_\varphi]$, we have $a \in \sigma(0)$ iff $a \in \sigma(n)$;
R3 for all $\alpha\mathcal{U}_I\beta \in \mathsf{cl}^*(\varphi)$, we have $\alpha\mathcal{U}_I\beta \in \sigma(0)$ iff (a) there is $j \in I \cap [0, \ell_\varphi]$ such that $\beta \in \sigma(j)$ and $\alpha \in \sigma(i)$ for all $i \in [0, j)$, or (b) I is of the form $[c, \infty)$ and $\alpha, \alpha\mathcal{U}\beta \in \sigma(i)$ for all $i \in [0, \ell_\varphi]$,

where cl^* is either cl^{c} or cl^{f} (as appropriate), and **R2** does not apply to formula run segments. A concept run segment captures the evolution of a domain element over a sequence of $\ell_\varphi+1$ time points, and a formula run segment describes general constraints on the interpretation over a sequence of $\ell_\varphi + 1$ time points.

The evolution over the complete time line is captured by *(concept/formula) runs* for φ, which are infinite sequences $r = r(0)r(1)\ldots$ such that each subsequence of length $\ell_\varphi + 1$ is a (concept/formula) run segment, and additionally

R4 $\alpha\mathcal{U}_{[c,\infty)}\beta \in r(n)$ implies that there is $j \geq n + c$ such that $\beta \in r(j)$ and $\alpha \in r(i)$ for all $i \in [n, j)$.

A concept run (segment) is *named* if it contains only (equivalently, any) named types. We may write r_a (σ_a) to denote a run (segment) that contains an individual name a. For a run (segment) σ, we write $\sigma^{>i}$ for the subsequence of σ starting at $i+1$, $\sigma^{<i}$ for the one stopping at $i-1$, and $\sigma^{[i,j]}$ for $\sigma(i)\ldots\sigma(j)$.

Since we cannot explicitly represent infinite runs, we use run segments to construct them step-by-step. For this, it is important that a set of concept runs (segments) can actually be composed into a coherent model. In particular, we have to take care of (interval-rigid) role connections between elements. A *role constraint* for φ is a tuple (σ, σ', s, k), where σ, σ' are concept run segments, $s \in \mathsf{rol}(\varphi)$, and $k \in [1, \mathsf{iRig}(s)]$, such that

C1 $\{\neg C \mid \neg\exists s.C \in \sigma(0)\} \subseteq \sigma'(0)$; and
C2 if σ' is named, then σ is also named.

We write $\sigma \overset{s}{\underset{k}{\rightsquigarrow}} \sigma'$ as a shorthand for the role constraint (σ, σ', s, k). Intuitively, $\sigma \overset{s}{\underset{k}{\rightsquigarrow}} \sigma'$ means that the domain elements described by $\sigma(0), \sigma'(0)$ are connected by the role s at the current time point, and also at the $k-1$ previous time points. In this case, we need to ensure that these elements stay connected for at least the following $\mathsf{iRig}(s) - k$ time points. Condition **C1** ensures that, if $\sigma(0)$ cannot have any s-successors that satisfy C, then $\sigma'(0)$ does not satisfy C.

We can now describe the behaviour of a whole interpretation and its elements at a single time point, together with some bounded information about the future (up to ℓ_φ time points). A *quasistate* for φ is a pair $Q = (\mathcal{R}_Q, \mathcal{C}_Q)$, where $\mathcal{R}_Q$ is a set of run segments and $\mathcal{C}_Q$ a set of role constraints over $\mathcal{R}_Q$ such that

Q1 $\mathcal{R}_Q$ contains exactly one formula run segment σ_Q;
Q2 $\mathcal{R}_Q$ contains exactly one named run segment σ_a for each $a \in \mathsf{ind}(\varphi)$;
Q3 for all $C \sqsubseteq D \in \mathsf{cl}^\mathsf{f}(\varphi)$, we have $C \sqsubseteq D \in \sigma_Q(0)$ iff $C \in \sigma(0)$ implies $D \in \sigma(0)$ for all concept run segments $\sigma \in \mathcal{R}_Q$;
Q4 for all $C(a) \in \mathsf{cl}^\mathsf{f}(\varphi)$, we have $C(a) \in \sigma_Q(0)$ iff $C \in \sigma_a(0)$;
Q5 for all $s(a,b) \in \mathsf{cl}^\mathsf{f}(\varphi)$, we have $s(a,b) \in \sigma_Q(0)$ iff $\sigma_a \overset{s}{\underset{k}{\rightsquigarrow}} \sigma_b \in \mathcal{C}_Q$ for some $k \in [1, \mathsf{iRig}(s)]$; and
Q6 for all $\sigma \in \mathcal{R}_Q$ and $\exists s.D \in \sigma(0)$, there is $\sigma \overset{s}{\underset{k}{\rightsquigarrow}} \sigma' \in \mathcal{C}_Q$ with $D \in \sigma'(0)$ and $k \in [1, \mathsf{iRig}(s)]$.

We next capture when quasistates can be connected coherently to an infinite sequence. A pair (Q, Q') of quasistates is *compatible* if there is a *compatibility relation* $\pi \subseteq \mathcal{R}_Q \times \mathcal{R}_{Q'}$ such that

C3 every run segment in $\mathcal{R}_Q$ and $\mathcal{R}_{Q'}$ occurs at least once in the domain and range of π, respectively;
C4 each pair $(\sigma, \sigma') \in \pi$ satisfies $\sigma^{>0} = \sigma'^{<\ell_\varphi}$;
C5 for all $(\sigma_1, \sigma_1') \in \pi$ and $\sigma_1 \overset{s}{\underset{k}{\rightsquigarrow}} \sigma_2 \in Q$ with $k < \mathsf{iRig}(s)$, there is $\sigma_1' \overset{s}{\underset{k+1}{\rightsquigarrow}} \sigma_2' \in Q'$ with $(\sigma_2, \sigma_2') \in \pi$; and
C6 for all $(\sigma_1, \sigma_1') \in \pi$ and $\sigma_1' \overset{s}{\underset{k+1}{\rightsquigarrow}} \sigma_2' \in Q'$ with $k > 1$, there is $\sigma_1 \overset{s}{\underset{k}{\rightsquigarrow}} \sigma_2 \in Q$ with $(\sigma_2, \sigma_2') \in \pi$.

Such a relation makes sure that we can combine run segments of consecutive quasistates such that the interval-rigid roles are respected. Note that the unique formula run segments must be matched to each other, and likewise for the named run segments. Moreover, the set of all compatibility relations for a pair of quasistates (Q, Q') is closed under union, which means that compatible quasistates always have a unique maximal compatibility relation (w.r.t. set inclusion).

To illustrate this, consider Fig. 2, showing a sequence of pairwise compatible quasistates, each containing two run segments. Here, $\ell_\varphi = \mathsf{iRig}(s) = 3$. The relations π_0, π_1, and π_2 satisfy Conditions **C3**–**C6**, which, together with **C1** and **C2**, ensure that a run going through the types t_1, t_2, t_3, and t_4 can be connected to another run via the role s for at least 3 consecutive time points.

Finally, a *quasimodel* for φ is a pair $(S, \mathfrak{R})$, where S is an infinite sequence of compatible quasistates $S(0)S(1)\ldots$ and $\mathfrak{R}$ is a non-empty set of runs, such that

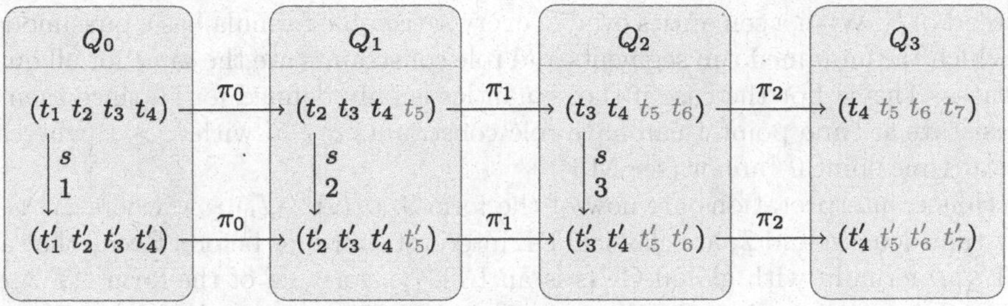

Fig. 2. Illustration of role constraints and compatibility relations.

M1 the runs in $\mathfrak{R}$ are of the form $\sigma_0(0)\sigma_1(0)\sigma_2(0)\ldots$ such that, for every $i \in \mathbb{N}$, we have $(\sigma_i, \sigma_{i+1}) \in \pi_i$, where π_i is the maximal compatibility relation for the pair $(S(i), S(i+1))$;
M2 for every $\sigma \in \mathcal{R}_{S(i)}$, there exists a run $r \in \mathfrak{R}$ with $r^{[i,i+\ell_\varphi]} = \sigma$;
M3 every role constraint in $S(0)$ is of the form $\sigma_1 \overset{s}{\underset{1}{\S}} \sigma_2$; and
M4 $\varphi \in \sigma_{S(0)}(0)$.

By **M1**, the runs $\sigma_0(0)\sigma_1(0)\sigma_2(0)\ldots$ always contain the whole run segments $\sigma_0, \sigma_1, \sigma_2, \ldots$, since we have $\sigma_1(0) = \sigma_0(1)$, $\sigma_2(0) = \sigma_0(2)$, and so on. Moreover, $\mathfrak{R}$ always contains exactly one formula run and one named run for each $a \in \mathsf{ind}(\varphi)$.

We can show that every quasimodel describes a satisfying interpretation for φ and, conversely, that every such interpretation can be abstracted to a quasimodel. Moreover, one can always find a quasimodel of a regular shape.

Lemma 3. *An* $\mathrm{LTL}^{\mathsf{bin}}_{\mathcal{ALC}}$ *formula* φ *is satisfiable w.r.t. interval-rigid names iff* φ *has a quasimodel* $(S, \mathfrak{R})$ *in which* S *is of the form*

$$S(0)\ldots S(n)(S(n+1)\ldots S(n+m))^\omega,$$

where n *and* m *are bounded triple exponentially in the size of* φ *and* iRig.

This allows us to devise a non-deterministic 2-ExpSpace algorithm that decides satisfiability of a given $\mathrm{LTL}^{\mathsf{bin}}_{\mathcal{ALC}}$ formula. Namely, we first guess n and m, and then the quasistates $S(0), \ldots, S(n+m)$ one after the other. To show that this sequence corresponds to a quasimodel as in Lemma 3, note that only three quasistates have to be kept in memory at any time, the sizes of which are double exponentially bounded in the size of the input: the current quasistate, the next quasistate, and the first repeating quasistate $S(n+1)$. 2-ExpSpace-hardness holds already for the case without interval-rigid names or assertions [13].

Theorem 4. *Satisfiability in* $\mathrm{LTL}^{\mathsf{bin}}_{\mathcal{ALC}}$ *with respect to interval-rigid names is 2-*ExpSpace*-complete.*

3.2 Global GCIs

For $\mathrm{LTL}^{\mathsf{bin}}_{\mathcal{ALC}}$ formulae with global GCIs, we can show a tight (2-ExpTime) complexity bound only if we consider a modified temporal semantics that uses $\mathbb{Z}$

instead of $\mathbb{N}$. With a semantics over $\mathbb{Z}$, every satisfiable formula has a quasimodel in which the unnamed run segments and role constraints are the same for all quasistates. This is not the case if the semantics is only defined for $\mathbb{N}$, since then a quasistate at time point 1 can have role constraints $\sigma \overset{s}{\underset{k}{\,}} \sigma'$ with $k > 1$, whereas one at time point 0 cannot (see **M3**).

Hence, interpretations are now of the form $\mathfrak{I} = (\Delta^{\mathfrak{I}}, (\mathcal{I}_i)_{i \in \mathbb{Z}})$, where $\Delta^{\mathfrak{I}}$ is a constant domain and $\mathcal{I}_i$ are classical DL interpretations, as before. Recall that an $\mathrm{LTL}^{\mathsf{bin}}_{\mathcal{ALC}}$ formula with global GCIs is an $\mathrm{LTL}^{\mathsf{bin}}_{\mathcal{ALC}}$ formula of the form $\Box\mathcal{T} \wedge \phi$, where $\mathcal{T}$ is a conjunction of GCIs and ϕ is an $\mathrm{LTL}^{\mathsf{bin}}_{\mathcal{ALC}}$ formula that does not contain GCIs. In order to enforce our GCIs on the whole time line (including the time points before 0), we replace $\Box\mathcal{T}$ with $\Box^-_+$ in that definition, where $\Box^-_+\mathcal{T}$ expresses that in all models $\mathfrak{I}$, $\mathfrak{I}, i \models \mathcal{T}$ for all $i \in \mathbb{Z}$. We furthermore slightly adapt some of the notions introduced in Sect. 3.1. First, to ensure that GCIs hold on the whole time line, we require (in addition to **T1'** and **T2'**) that all formula types contain all GCIs from $\mathcal{T}$. Additionally, we adapt the notions of runs $\ldots r(-1)r(0)r(1)\ldots$ and sequences $\ldots S(-1)S(0)S(1)\ldots$ of quasistates to be infinite in both directions. Hence, we can now drop Condition **M3**, reflecting the fact that, over $\mathbb{Z}$, role connections can exist before time point 0. All other definitions remain unchanged.

The complexity proof follows a similar idea as in the last section. We first show that every formula is satisfiable iff it has a quasimodel of a regular shape, which now is also constant in its unnamed part, in the sense that, if unnamed run segments and role constraints occur in $S(i)$, then they also occur in $S(j)$, for all $i, j \in \mathbb{Z}$. This allows us to devise an elimination procedure (in the spirit of [17, Theorem 3] and [13, Theorem 2]), with the difference that we eliminate run segments and role constraints instead of types, which gives us a 2-ExpTime upper bound. The matching lower bound can be shown similarly to Theorem 7 in Sect. 4.

Theorem 5. *Satisfiability in* $\mathrm{LTL}^{\mathsf{bin}}_{\mathcal{ALC}}$ *w.r.t. interval-rigid names and global GCIs over* $\mathbb{Z}$ *is* 2-ExpTime*-complete.*

4 $\mathcal{ALC}$-LTL^{bin} with Interval-Rigid Names

After the very expressive DL $\mathrm{LTL}^{\mathsf{bin}}_{\mathcal{ALC}}$, we now focus on its sublogic $\mathcal{ALC}$-LTL^{bin}, which does not allow temporal operators within concepts (cf. [9]). That is, an $\mathcal{ALC}$-LTL^{bin} *formula* is an $\mathrm{LTL}^{\mathsf{bin}}_{\mathcal{ALC}}$ formula in which all concepts are $\mathcal{ALC}$ concepts. Recall that $\mathcal{ALC}$-LTL, which has been investigated in [9] (though not with interval-rigid names), restricts $\mathcal{ALC}$-LTL^{bin} to intervals of the form $[0, \infty)$. In this section, we show several complexity lower bounds that already hold for $\mathcal{ALC}$-LTL with interval-rigid names. As done in [9], for brevity, we distinguish here the variants with global GCIs by the subscript $\cdot_{|gGCI}$. In contrast to $\mathrm{LTL}^{\mathsf{bin}}_{\mathcal{ALC}}$, in $\mathcal{ALC}$-LTL rigid concepts cannot be simulated by GCIs and rigid roles do not lead to undecidability [9]. Hence, we investigate here also the settings with rigid concepts and/or roles.

The results of this section are summarized in Table 2. Central to our hardness proofs is the insight that interval-rigid concepts can express the operator $\bigcirc$

on the concept level. In particular, we show that the combination of rigid roles with interval-rigid concepts already leads to undecidability, by a reduction from a tiling problem. If rigid names are disallowed, but we have interval-rigid names, we can only show 2-ExpTime-hardness. If only interval-rigid concepts are allowed, then satisfiability is ExpSpace-hard. All of these hardness results already hold for $\mathcal{ALC}$-LTL, and some of them even with global GCIs.

Table 2. Complexity of satisfiability in $\mathcal{ALC}$-LTL^{bin} w.r.t. (interval-)rigid names.

	$\mathsf{N_{IRig}} \subseteq \mathsf{N_C}$, $\mathsf{N_{Rig}} \subseteq \mathsf{N_C} \cup \mathsf{N_R}$	$\mathsf{N_{IRig}} \subseteq \mathsf{N_C} \cup \mathsf{N_R}$, $\mathsf{N_{Rig}} \subseteq \mathsf{N_C}$ or $\mathsf{N_{Rig}} = \emptyset$	$\mathsf{N_{IRig}} \subseteq \mathsf{N_C}$, $\mathsf{N_{Rig}} \subseteq \mathsf{N_C}$ or $\mathsf{N_{Rig}} = \emptyset$
$\mathcal{ALC}$-LTL^{bin}	Undec.	2-ExpTime-hard	ExpSpace $\leq$ [Theorem 1]
$\mathcal{ALC}$-LTL$^{\mathsf{bin}}_{\lvert gGCI}$	Undec.	2-ExpTime-hard	ExpSpace = [2]
$\mathcal{ALC}$-LTL	Undec.	2-ExpTime-hard	ExpSpace $\geq$ [Theorem 8]
$\mathcal{ALC}$-LTL$_{\lvert gGCI}$	Undec. [Theorem 6]	2-ExpTime-hard [Theorem 7]	ExpTime $\geq$ [18], $\leq$ [Theorem 1]

4.1 Rigid Roles and Interval-Rigid Concepts

We show that satisfiability of $\mathcal{ALC}$-LTL with rigid roles and interval-rigid concepts is undecidable, even if we only allow global GCIs. Our proof is by a reduction from the following tiling problem.

> Given a finite set of tile types T with horizontal and vertical compatibility relations H and V, respectively, and $t_0 \in T$, decide whether one can tile $\mathbb{N} \times \mathbb{N}$ with t_0 appearing infinitely often in the first row.

We define an $\mathcal{ALC}$-LTL$_{\lvert gGCI}$ formula ϕ_T that expresses this property. In our encoding, we use the following names:

- a rigid role name r to encode the vertical dimension of the $\mathbb{N} \times \mathbb{N}$ grid;
- flexible concept names A^0, A^1, A^2 to encode the progression along the horizontal (temporal) dimension; for convenience, we consider all superscripts modulo 3, i.e., we have $A^3 = A^0$ and $A^{-1} = A^2$;
- flexible concept names P_t, $t \in T$, to denote the current tile type;
- 2-rigid concept names N_t^0, N_t^1, N_t^2, for the horizontally adjacent tile type;
- an individual name a denotes the first row of the grid.

We define ϕ_T as the conjunction of the following $\mathcal{ALC}$-LTL$_{\lvert gGCI}$ formulae. First, every domain element must have exactly one tile type:

$$\Box\Big(\top \sqsubseteq \bigsqcup_{t \in T}\Big(P_t \sqcap \bigsqcap_{t' \in T,\, t \neq t'} \neg P_{t'}\Big)\Big)$$

For the vertical dimension, we enforce an infinite rigid r-chain starting from a, and restrict adjacent tile types to be compatible:

$$\Box(\top \sqsubseteq \exists r.\top), \quad \Box\Big(P_t \sqsubseteq \bigsqcup_{(t,t')\in V} \forall r.P_{t'}\Big)$$

For each time point i, we mark all individuals along the r-chain with the concept name $A^{(i \bmod 3)}$, by using the following formulae, for $0 \leq i \leq 2$:

$$A^0(a), \quad \Box(A^i(a) \rightarrow \bigcirc A^{i+1}(a)), \quad \Box(A^i \sqsubseteq \neg A^{i+1} \sqcap \forall r.A^i)$$

To encode the compatibility of horizontally adjacent tiles, we add the following formulae, for $0 \leq i \leq 2$ and $t \in T$:

$$\Box\Big(P_t \sqcap A^i \sqsubseteq \bigsqcup_{(t,t')\in H} N^i_{t'}\Big), \quad \Box(N^i_t \sqcap A^{i+1} \sqsubseteq P_t), \quad \Box(A^{i-1} \sqsubseteq \neg N^i_t)$$

These express that any domain element with tile type t (expressed by P_t) at a time point marked with A^i must have a compatible type t' at the next time point (expressed by $N^i_{t'}$). Since all $N^i_{t'}$ are false at the previous time point (designated by A^{i-1}) and $\mathsf{iRig}(N^i_{t'}) = 2$, any $N^i_{t'}$ that holds at the current time point is still active at the next time point (described by A^{i+1}), where it then implies $P_{t'}$.

Finally, we express the condition on t_0 via the formula $\Box\Diamond P_{t_0}(a)$. We now obtain the claimed undecidability from known results about the tiling problem [14].

Theorem 6. *Satisfiability in $\mathcal{ALC}$-$LTL_{|gGCI}$ w.r.t. rigid roles and interval-rigid concepts is Σ^1_1-hard, and thus not even recursively enumerable.*

4.2 Interval-Rigid Roles

Since rigid roles cause undecidability, we consider the case where instead only interval-rigid roles (and concepts) are allowed, and obtain 2-ExpTime-hardness by an easy adaptation of a result for $\mathcal{ALC}$-LTL$_{|gGCI}$ with rigid roles from [9].

Theorem 7. *Satisfiability in $\mathcal{ALC}$-$LTL_{|gGCI}$ with respect to interval-rigid names is* 2-ExpTime*-hard.*

4.3 Rigid and Interval-Rigid Concepts

As the last setting, we consider the case where only concept names can be rigid or interval-rigid, and show ExpSpace-completeness. For the upper bound, recall from Sect. 3 that rigid concepts and interval-rigid concepts are expressible in $\mathrm{LTL}^{0,\infty}_{\mathcal{ALC}}$ via global GCIs, so that we can apply Theorem 1. The same observation yields an ExpTime upper bound for satisfiability in $\mathcal{ALC}$-LTL w.r.t. global GCIs, which is tight since satisfiability in ordinary $\mathcal{ALC}$ is already ExpTime-hard [18].

We show the ExpSpace lower bound by a reduction from satisfiability of $\mathcal{ALC}$-LTL$^{\bigcirc}$, the extension of $\mathcal{ALC}$-LTL in which $\bigcirc$ can be applied to concepts, to satisfiability of $\mathcal{ALC}$-LTL w.r.t. interval-rigid concepts. It is shown in [15, Theorem 11.33] that satisfiability in (a syntactic variant of) $\mathcal{ALC}$-LTL$^{\bigcirc}$ is ExpSpace-hard. To simulate $\bigcirc$ using interval-rigid concept names, we use a similar construction as in Sect. 4.1, where we mark all individuals at time point i with $A^{(i \bmod 3)}$, and use 2-rigid concept names to transfer information between time points. More precisely, we first define an $\mathcal{ALC}$-LTL formula ψ as the conjunction of the following formulae, where $0 \leq i \leq 2$:

$$(\top \sqsubseteq A^0), \quad \Box((\top \sqsubseteq A^i) \rightarrow \bigcirc(\top \sqsubseteq A^{i+1})), \quad \Box(A^i \sqsubseteq \neg A^{i+1})$$

We now simulate concepts of the form $\bigcirc C$ via fresh, 2-rigid concept names $A^i_{\bigcirc C}$, $0 \leq i \leq 2$. Given any $\mathcal{ALC}$-LTL$^{\bigcirc}$ formula α (resp., $\mathcal{ALC}$-LTL$^{\bigcirc}$ concept D), we denote by $\alpha^{\bigcirc}$ (resp., $D^{\bigcirc}$) the result of replacing each outermost concept of the form $\bigcirc C$ in α (resp., D) by

$$\bigsqcup_{0 \leq i \leq 2} (A^i_{\bigcirc C} \sqcap A^i).$$

To express the semantics of $\bigcirc C$, we use the conjunction $\psi_{\bigcirc C}$ of the following formulae (where the replacement operator $\cdot^{\bigcirc}$ is applied to the inner concept C):

$$\Box(A^i_{\bigcirc C} \sqcap A^{i+1} \sqsubseteq C^{\bigcirc}), \quad \Box(C^{\bigcirc} \sqcap A^{i+1} \sqsubseteq A^i_{\bigcirc C}), \quad \Box(A^{i-1} \sqsubseteq \neg A^i_{\bigcirc C})$$

As in Sect. 4.1, $A^i_{\bigcirc C}$ must either be satisfied at both time points designated by A^i and A^{i+1}, or at neither of them. Furthermore, an individual satisfies $\bigcirc C$ iff it satisfies $A^i_{\bigcirc C} \sqcap A^i$ for some i, $0 \leq i \leq 2$. One can show that an $\mathcal{ALC}$-LTL$^{\bigcirc}$ formula ϕ is satisfiable iff the $\mathcal{ALC}$-LTL formula $\phi^{\bigcirc} \wedge \psi \wedge \bigwedge_{\bigcirc C \in \mathsf{csub}(\phi)} \psi_{\bigcirc C}$ is satisfiable.

Theorem 8. *Satisfiability in $\mathcal{ALC}$-LTL with respect to interval-rigid concepts is* ExpSpace*-hard.*

5 $\mathcal{ALC}$-LTL^{bin} Without Interval-Rigid Names

To conclude our investigation of metric temporal DLs, we consider the setting of $\mathcal{ALC}$-LTL^{bin} without interval-rigid names. Table 3 summarizes the results of this section, where we also include the known results about $\mathcal{ALC}$-LTL for comparison [9]. Observe that all lower bounds follow from known results. In particular, ExpSpace-hardness for $\mathcal{ALC}$-LTL$^{\mathsf{bin}}_{|gGCI}$ is inherited from LTL^{bin} [1,2], while rigid role names increase the complexity to 2-ExpTime in $\mathcal{ALC}$-LTL$_{|gGCI}$ [9].

The upper bounds can be shown using a unified approach that was first proposed in [9]. The idea is to split the satisfiability test into two parts: one for the temporal and one for the DL dimension. In what follows, let ϕ be an $\mathcal{ALC}$-LTL^{bin} formula. The *propositional abstraction* ϕ^{p} is the propositional LTL^{bin} formula obtained from ϕ by replacing every $\mathcal{ALC}$ axiom by a propositional variable

Table 3. Complexity of satisfiability in $\mathcal{ALC}$-LTL^{bin} without interval-rigid names.

	$\mathsf{N_{Rig}} \subseteq \mathsf{N_C} \cup \mathsf{N_R}$	$\mathsf{N_{Rig}} \subseteq \mathsf{N_C}$	$\mathsf{N_{Rig}} = \emptyset$
$\mathcal{ALC}$-LTL^{bin}	2-ExpTime $\leq$ [Theorem 10]	ExpSpace $\leq$ [Theorem 10]	ExpSpace
$\mathcal{ALC}$-LTL$^{\mathsf{bin}}_{\vert gGCI}$	2-ExpTime	ExpSpace	ExpSpace $\geq$ [1]
$\mathcal{ALC}$-LTL	2-ExpTime	NExpTime [9]	ExpTime $\leq$ [9]
$\mathcal{ALC}$-LTL$_{\vert gGCI}$	2-ExpTime $\geq$ [9]	ExpTime $\leq$ [9]	ExpTime $\geq$ [18]

in such a way that there is a 1:1 relationship between the $\mathcal{ALC}$ axioms $\alpha_1, \ldots, \alpha_m$ occurring in ϕ and the propositional variables $p_1, \ldots, p_m$ in ϕ^{p}.

The goal is to try to find a model of ϕ^{p} and then use it to construct a model of ϕ (if such a model exists). While satisfiability of ϕ implies that ϕ^{p} is also satisfiable, the converse is not true. For example, the propositional abstraction $p \wedge q \wedge \neg r$ of $\phi = A \sqsubseteq B \wedge A(a) \wedge \neg B(a)$ is satisfiable, while ϕ is not. To rule out such cases, we collect the propositional worlds occurring in a model of ϕ^{p} into a (non-empty) set $\mathcal{W} \subseteq 2^{\{p_1,\ldots,p_m\}}$, which is then used to check the satisfiability of the original formula (w.r.t. rigid names). This is captured by the LTL^{bin} formula $\phi^{\mathsf{p}}_{\mathcal{W}} := \phi^{\mathsf{p}} \wedge \phi_{\mathcal{W}}$, where $\phi_{\mathcal{W}}$ is the (exponential) LTL formula

$$\Box \bigvee_{W \in \mathcal{W}} \left(\bigwedge_{p \in W} p \wedge \bigwedge_{p \in \overline{W}} \neg p \right)$$

in which $\overline{W} := \{p_1, \ldots, p_m\} \setminus W$ denotes the complement of W. The formula $\phi^{\mathsf{p}}_{\mathcal{W}}$ states that, when looking for a propositional model of ϕ^{p}, we are only allowed to use worlds from $\mathcal{W}$.

Since satisfiability of ϕ implies satisfiability of $\phi^{\mathsf{p}}_{\mathcal{W}}$ for some $\mathcal{W}$, we can proceed as follows: choose a set of worlds $\mathcal{W}$, test whether $\phi^{\mathsf{p}}_{\mathcal{W}}$ is satisfiable, and then check whether a model with worlds from $\mathcal{W}$ can indeed be lifted to a temporal DL interpretation (respecting rigid names). To check the latter, we consider the conjunction $\bigwedge_{p_j \in W} \alpha_j \wedge \bigwedge_{p_j \in \overline{W}} \neg\alpha_j$ for every $W \in \mathcal{W}$. However, the rigid names require that all these conjunctions are *simultaneously* checked for satisfiability. To tell apart the *flexible* names X occurring in different elements of $\mathcal{W} = \{W_1, \ldots, W_k\}$, we introduce copies $X^{(i)}$ for all $i \in [1, k]$. The axioms $\alpha_j^{(i)}$ are obtained from α_j by replacing every flexible name X by $X^{(i)}$, which yields the following conjunction of exponential size:

$$\chi_{\mathcal{W}} := \bigwedge_{i=1}^{k} \Big(\bigwedge_{p_j \in W_i} \alpha_j^{(i)} \wedge \bigwedge_{p_j \in \overline{W_i}} \neg\alpha_j^{(i)} \Big).$$

The following characterization from [9] can be easily adapted to our setting:

Lemma 9 (Adaptation of [9]). *An $\mathcal{ALC}$-LTL^{bin} formula ϕ is satisfiable w.r.t. rigid names iff a set $\mathcal{W} \subseteq 2^{\{p_1,\ldots,p_m\}}$ exists so that $\phi^{\mathsf{p}}_{\mathcal{W}}$ and $\chi_{\mathcal{W}}$ are both satisfiable.*

To obtain the upper bounds in Table 3, recall from Sect. 2 that there is an exponentially larger LTL formula $\phi^{\mathsf{p}\prime}$ that is equivalent to the $\text{LTL}^{\mathsf{bin}}$ formula ϕ^{p}. Since $\phi_{\mathcal{W}}$ is also an LTL formula of exponential size, satisfiability of the conjunction $\phi^{\mathsf{p}\prime} \wedge \phi_{\mathcal{W}}$ can be checked in ExpSpace. Since the complexity of the satisfiability problem for $\chi_{\mathcal{W}}$ remains the same as in the case of $\mathcal{ALC}$-LTL, we obtain the claimed upper bounds from the techniques in [9]. This means that, in most cases, the complexity of the DL part is dominated by the ExpSpace complexity of the temporal part. The only exception is the 2-ExpTime-bound for $\mathcal{ALC}\text{-LTL}^{\mathsf{bin}}$ with rigid names.

Theorem 10. *Satisfiability in $\mathcal{ALC}\text{-LTL}^{\mathsf{bin}}$ is in* 2-ExpTime *w.r.t. rigid names, and in* ExpSpace *w.r.t. rigid concepts.*

6 Conclusions

We investigated a series of extensions of $\text{LTL}_{\mathcal{ALC}}$ and $\mathcal{ALC}$-LTL with interval-rigid names and metric temporal operators, with complexity results ranging from ExpTime to 2-ExpSpace. Some cases were left open, such as the precise complexity of $\text{LTL}^{\mathsf{bin}}_{\mathcal{ALC}}$ with global GCIs, for which we have a partial result for the temporal semantics based on $\mathbb{Z}$. Nevertheless, this paper provides a comprehensive guide to the complexities faced by applications that want to combine ontological reasoning with quantitative temporal logics.

In principle, the arguments for $\mathcal{ALC}\text{-LTL}^{\mathsf{bin}}$ in Sect. 5 are also applicable if we replace $\mathcal{ALC}$ by the light-weight DLs *DL-Lite* or $\mathcal{EL}$, yielding tight complexity bounds based on the known results from [5,10]. It would be interesting to investigate temporal DLs based on *DL-Lite* and $\mathcal{EL}$ with interval-rigid roles and metric operators.

References

1. Alur, R., Henzinger, T.A.: Real-time logics: complexity and expressiveness. Inf. Comput. **104**(1), 35–77 (1993)
2. Alur, R., Henzinger, T.A.: A really temporal logic. J. ACM **41**(1), 181–204 (1994)
3. Artale, A., Bresolin, D., Montanari, A., Sciavicco, G., Ryzhikov, V.: DL-lite and interval temporal logics: a marriage proposal. In: Proceedings of the 21st European Conference on Artificial Intelligence (ECAI 2014), pp. 957–958. IOS Press (2014)
4. Artale, A., Kontchakov, R., Ryzhikov, V., Zakharyaschev, M.: Tractable interval temporal propositional and description logics. In: Proceedings of the 29th AAAI Conference on Artificial Intelligence (AAAI 2015), pp. 1417–1423. AAAI Press (2015)
5. Artale, A., Kontchakov, R., Lutz, C., Wolter, F., Zakharyaschev, M.: Temporalising tractable description logics. In: Proceedings of the 14th International Symposium on Temporal Representation and Reasoning (TIME 2007), pp. 11–22. IEEE Press (2007)
6. Artale, A., Lutz, C., Toman, D.: A description logic of change. In: Proceedings of the 20th International Joint Conference Artificial Intelligence (IJCAI 2007), pp. 218–223 (2007)

7. Baader, F., Borgwardt, S., Koopmann, P., Ozaki, A., Thost, V.: Metric temporal description logics with interval-rigid names (extended version). LTCS-Report 17-03 (2017). https://lat.inf.tu-dresden.de/research/reports.html
8. Baader, F., Calvanese, D., McGuinness, D.L., Nardi, D., Patel-Schneider, P.F. (eds.): The Description Logic Handbook: Theory, Implementation, and Applications, 2nd edn. Cambridge University Press, Cambridge (2007)
9. Baader, F., Ghilardi, S., Lutz, C.: LTL over description logic axioms. ACM Trans. Comput. Log. **13**(3), 21:1–21:32 (2012)
10. Borgwardt, S., Thost, V.: Temporal query answering in the description logic $\mathcal{EL}$. In: Proceedings of the 24th International Joint Conference on Artificial Intelligence (IJCAI 2015), pp. 2819–2825. AAAI Press (2015)
11. Brandt, S., Kalaycı, E.G., Kontchakov, R., Ryzhikov, V., Xiao, G., Zakharyaschev, M.: Ontology-based data access with a horn fragment of metric temporal logic. In: Proceedings of the 31st AAAI Conference on Artificial Intelligence (AAAI 2017), pp. 1070–1076. AAAI Press (2017)
12. Crowe, C.L., Tao, C.: Designing ontology-based patterns for the representation of the time-relevant eligibility criteria of clinical protocols. In: AMIA Summits on Translational Science Proceedings 2015, pp. 173–177 (2015)
13. Gutiérrez-Basulto, V., Jung, J.C., Ozaki, A.: On metric temporal description logics. In: Proceedings of the 22nd European Conference on Artificial Intelligence (ECAI 2016), pp. 837–845. IOS Press (2016)
14. Harel, D.: Effective transformations on infinite trees, with applications to high undecidability, dominoes, and fairness. J. ACM **33**(1), 224–248 (1986)
15. Kurucz, A., Wolter, F., Zakharyaschev, M., Gabbay, D.M.: Many-dimensional modal logics: theory and applications. Gulf Professional Publishing (2003)
16. Lutz, C., Walther, D., Wolter, F.: Quantitative temporal logics over the reals: PSPACE and below. Inf. Comput. **205**(1), 99–123 (2007)
17. Lutz, C., Wolter, F., Zakharyaschev, M.: Temporal description logics: a survey. In: Proceedings of the 15th Symposium on Temporal Representation and Reasoning (TIME 2008), pp. 3–14. IEEE Press (2008)
18. Schild, K.: A correspondence theory for terminological logics: preliminary report. In: Proceedings of the 12th International Joint Conference on Artificial Intelligence (IJCAI 1991), pp. 466–471. Morgan Kaufmann (1991)
19. Schulz, S., Markó, K., Suntisrivaraporn, B.: Formal representation of complex SNOMED CT expressions. BMC Med. Inform. Decis. Mak. **8**(Suppl 1), S9 (2008)
20. Wolter, F., Zakharyaschev, M.: Temporalizing description logics. In: Frontiers of Combining Systems, vol. 2, pp. 379–402. Research Studies Press/Wiley (2000)

Using Ontologies to Query Probabilistic Numerical Data

Franz Baader(✉), Patrick Koopmann(✉), and Anni-Yasmin Turhan(✉)

Institute of Theoretical Computer Science,
Technische Universität Dresden, Dresden, Germany
{franz.baader,patrick.koopmann,anni-yasmin.turhan}@tu-dresden.de

Abstract. We consider ontology-based query answering in a setting where some of the data are numerical and of a probabilistic nature, such as data obtained from uncertain sensor readings. The uncertainty for such numerical values can be more precisely represented by continuous probability distributions than by discrete probabilities for numerical facts concerning exact values. For this reason, we extend existing approaches using discrete probability distributions over facts by continuous probability distributions over numerical values. We determine the exact (data and combined) complexity of query answering in extensions of the well-known description logics $\mathcal{EL}$ and $\mathcal{ALC}$ with numerical comparison operators in this probabilistic setting.

1 Introduction

Ontology-based query answering (OBQA) has recently attracted considerable attention since it dispenses with the closed world assumption of classical query answering in databases and thus can deal with incomplete data. In addition, background information stated in an appropriate ontology can be used to deduce more answers. OBQA is usually investigated in a setting where queries are (unions of) conjunctive queries and ontologies are expressed using an appropriate Description Logic (DL). Depending on the expressiveness of the DL, the complexity of query answering may vary considerably, starting with data complexity (i.e., complexity measured in the size of the data only) of AC^0 for members of the DL-Lite family [2,9] to P for DLs of the $\mathcal{EL}$ family [28], all the way up to intractable data complexity for expressive DLs such as $\mathcal{ALC}$ and beyond [15].

In many application scenarios for OBQA, however, querying just symbolic data is not sufficient. One also wants to be able to query numerical data. For example, in a health or fitness monitoring application, one may want to use concepts from a medical ontology such as SNOMED CT [14] or Galen [29] to express information about the health status of a patient, but also needs to store and refer to numerical values such as the blood pressure or heart rate of this patient. As an example, let us consider hypertension management using a smartphone app [21].

Supported by the DFG within the collaborative research center SFB 912 (HAEC) and the research unit FOR 1513 (HYBRIS).

C. Dixon and M. Finger (Eds.): FroCoS 2017, LNCS 10483, pp. 77–94, 2017.
DOI: 10.1007/978-3-319-66167-4_5

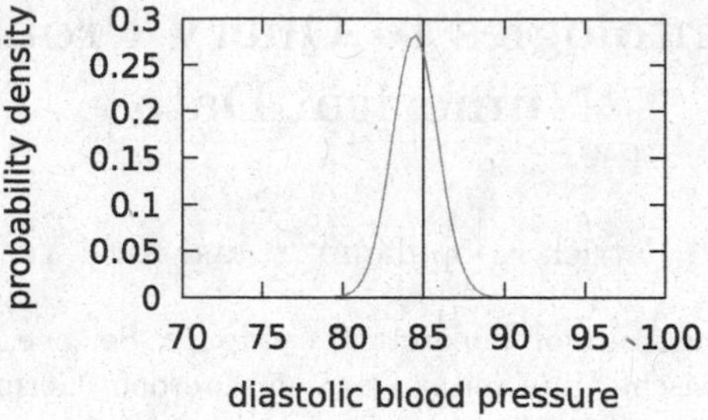

Fig. 1. Measured blood pressure as normal distribution.

What constitutes dangerously high blood pressure (HBP) depends on the measured values of the diastolic pressure, but also on other factors. For example, if a patient suffers from diabetes, a diastolic blood pressure above 85 may already be classified as too high, whereas under normal circumstances it is only considered to be too high above 90. This could, for example, be modelled as follows by an ontology:

$$\exists \mathsf{diastolicBloodPressure}.{>_{90}} \sqsubseteq \mathsf{PatientWithHBP} \quad (1)$$

$$\exists \mathsf{finding}.\mathsf{Diabetes} \sqcap \exists \mathsf{diastolicBloodPressure}.{>_{85}} \sqsubseteq \mathsf{PatientWithHBP} \quad (2)$$

Note that we have used a DL with concrete domains [6] to refer to numerical values and predicates on these values within concepts. While there has been quite some work on traditional reasoning (satisfiability, subsumption, instance) in DLs with concrete domains [24], there is scant work on OBQA for such DLs. To the best of our knowledge, the only work in this direction considers concrete domain extensions of members of the DL-Lite family [3,4,17,31], and develops query rewriting approaches. In contrast, we consider concrete domain extensions of $\mathcal{EL}$ and $\mathcal{ALC}$ and determine the (combined and data) complexity of query answering.

However, the main difference to previous work is that we do not assume the numerical values in the data to be exact. In fact, a value of 84.5 for the diastolic pressure given by a blood pressure sensor does not really mean that the pressure is precisely 84.5, but rather that it is around 84.5. The actual value follows a probability distribution—for example a normal distribution with expected value 84.5 and a variance of 2 as shown in Fig. 1—which is determined by the measured value and some known variance that is a characteristic of the employed sensor. We can represent this in the knowledge base for example as follows:

$$\mathsf{finding}(\mathsf{otto}, \mathsf{f1}) \qquad \mathsf{Diabetes}(\mathsf{f1}) \qquad \mathsf{diastolicBloodPressure}(\mathsf{otto}) \sim \mathsf{norm}(84.5, 2)$$

From this information, we can derive that the minimal probability for the patient Otto to have high blood pressure is slightly above 36%, which might be enough to issue a warning. In contrast, if instead of using a probability distribution we had asserted 84.5 as the exact value for Otto's diastolic blood pressure, we could not have inferred that Otto is in any danger.

Continuous probability distributions as used in this example also emerge in other potential applications of OBQA such as in robotics [34], tracking of object positions in video analytics [35], and mobile applications using probabilistic sensor data [12], to name a few. The interest in continuous probability distributions is also reflected in the development of database systems that support these [33].

In addition to using continuous probability distributions for sensor values, we also consider discrete probability distributions for facts. For example, it might be that the finding f1 for Otto is diabetes only with a certain probability. While OBQA for probabilistic data with discrete probability distributions has been considered before for DL-Lite and $\mathcal{EL}$ without concrete domains [19], OBQA for probabilistic data with both discrete and continuous probability distributions is investigated here for the first time. A rather expressive combination we consider is the DL $\mathcal{ALC}$ extended with a concrete domain in which real numbers can be compared using the (binary) predicates $>$ and $=$. A less expressive combination we consider is the DL $\mathcal{EL}$ extended with a concrete domain in which real numbers can be compared with a fixed number using the (unary) predicates $>_r$ for $r \in \mathbb{R}$. Since OBQA for classical knowledge bases (i.e., without probabilities) in these two DLs has not been investigated before, we first determine their (data and combined) complexity of query answering. When considering probabilistic KBs with continuous probability distributions (modelled as real-valued functions), the resulting probabilities may be numbers without a finite representation. To overcome this problem, we define probabilistic query entailment with respect to a given precision parameter. To allow a reasonable complexity analysis, we define a set of feasibility conditions for probability distributions, based on the complexity theory of real functions [20], which capture most typical probability distributions that appear in practical applications. For probabilistic KBs that satisfy these conditions, we give tight bounds on the complexity of probabilistic query answering w.r.t data and combined complexity for all considered DLs. Detailed proofs for all results can be found in the long version of the paper [7].

2 Description Logics with Numerical Domains

We recall basic DLs with concrete domains, as introduced in [6], and give complexity results for classical query answering.

A *concrete domain* is a tuple $\mathcal{D} = (\Delta_\mathcal{D}, \Phi_\mathcal{D})$, where $\Delta_\mathcal{D}$ contains objects of the domain, and $\Phi_\mathcal{D}$ contains predicates P_n with associated arity n and extension $P_n^\mathcal{D} \subseteq \Delta_\mathcal{D}^n$. Let N_c, N_r, N_{cF} and N_i be pair-wise disjoint sets of *names* for *concepts*, *roles*, *concrete features* and *individuals*, respectively. Let $N_{aF} \subseteq N_r$ be a set of *abstract feature names*. Concrete features are partial functions that map individuals to a value in the concrete domain. Abstract features are functional roles and their use in *feature paths* does not harm decidability [23]. A *feature path* is an expression of the form $u = s_1 s_2 \ldots s_n g$, where $s_i \in N_{aF}$, $1 \leq i \leq n$, and $g \in N_{cF}$. $\mathcal{ALC}(\mathcal{D})$ concepts are defined as follows, where $A \in N_c$, $s \in N_r$, u and u' are feature paths, $P_n \in \Phi_\mathcal{D}$ is a predicate of arity n, and C_1 and C_2 are $\mathcal{ALC}(\mathcal{D})$ concepts:

$$C := \top \mid A \mid \neg C_1 \mid C_1 \sqcap C_2 \mid \exists s.C_1 \mid \exists(u_1, \ldots, u_n).P_n \mid u\uparrow.$$

Additional concepts are defined as abbreviations: $C_1 \sqcup C_2 = \neg(\neg C_1 \sqcap \neg C_2)$, $\forall s.C = \neg\exists s.\neg C$, and $\bot = \neg\top$. If a concept uses only the constructors $\top$, A, $C_1 \sqcap C_2$, $\exists s.C_1$ and $\exists(u_1,\dots,u_n).P_n$ and no abstract features, it is an $\mathcal{EL}(\mathcal{D})$ concept. The restrictions for $\mathcal{EL}(\mathcal{D})$ concepts ensure polynomial time complexity for standard reasoning tasks. Specifically, as done in [5], we disallow abstract features, since axiom entailment in $\mathcal{EL}$ with functional roles is ExpTime-hard [5].

A *TBox* is a finite set of *general concept inclusion axioms* (GCIs), which are of the form $C \sqsubseteq D$, where C and D are concepts. A *classical ABox* is a finite set of *assertions*, which are of the forms $A(a)$, $s(a,b)$ and $g(a,d)$, where $a, b \in N_i$, $A \in N_c$, $s \in N_r$, $g \in N_{cF}$ and $d \in \Delta^{\mathcal{D}}$. We call GCIs and assertions collectively *axioms*. A *knowledge base* (KB) $\mathcal{K}$ is a pair $(\mathcal{T},\mathcal{A})$ of a TBox $\mathcal{T}$ and an ABox $\mathcal{A}$. Given a KB $\mathcal{K}$, we denote by $\text{sub}(\mathcal{K})$ the *subconcepts* occurring in $\mathcal{K}$. Let $\mathcal{L}$ be a DL, then a TBox/KB that uses only $\mathcal{L}$ concepts is a $\mathcal{L}$ TBox/$\mathcal{L}$ KB.

The semantics of $\mathcal{EL}(\mathcal{D})$ and $\mathcal{ALC}(\mathcal{D})$ is defined in terms of interpretations. An *interpretation* is a tuple $\mathcal{I} = (\Delta^{\mathcal{I}}, \cdot^{\mathcal{I}})$ consisting of a *set of domain elements* $\Delta^{\mathcal{I}}$ and an *interpretation function* $\cdot^{\mathcal{I}}$. The *interpretation function* $\cdot^{\mathcal{I}}$ maps individual names to elements of $\Delta^{\mathcal{I}}$, concept names to subsets of $\Delta^{\mathcal{I}}$, concrete features to partial functions $\Delta^{\mathcal{I}} \to \Delta^{\mathcal{D}}$, and role names to subsets of $\Delta^{\mathcal{I}} \times \Delta^{\mathcal{I}}$ s.t. for all $s \in N_{aF}$, $s^{\mathcal{I}}$ is a partial function. The extension of $\cdot^{\mathcal{I}}$ to feature paths is $(s_1 \dots s_n g)^{\mathcal{I}} = g^{\mathcal{I}} \circ s_n^{\mathcal{I}} \circ \dots \circ s_1^{\mathcal{I}}$, and to (complex) concepts is:

$$\top^{\mathcal{I}} = \Delta^{\mathcal{I}} \qquad (\neg C)^{\mathcal{I}} = \Delta^{\mathcal{I}} \setminus C^{\mathcal{I}} \qquad (C_1 \sqcap C_2)^{\mathcal{I}} = C_1^{\mathcal{I}} \cap C_2^{\mathcal{I}}$$

$$(\exists s.C)^{\mathcal{I}} = \{x \in \Delta^{\mathcal{I}} \mid \exists y \in \Delta^{\mathcal{I}} : (x,y) \in s^{\mathcal{I}} \wedge y \in C^{\mathcal{I}}\}$$

$$(\exists(u_1,\dots,u_n).P)^{\mathcal{I}} = \{x \in \Delta^{\mathcal{I}} \mid (u_1^{\mathcal{I}}(x),\dots,u_n^{\mathcal{I}}(x)) \text{ is defined and in } P^{\mathcal{D}}\}$$

$$(u\uparrow)^{\mathcal{I}} = \{x \in \Delta^{\mathcal{I}} \mid u^{\mathcal{I}}(x) \text{ is undefined}\}.$$

An axiom α is *true* in an interpretation $\mathcal{I}$, in symbols $\mathcal{I} \models \alpha$, if $\alpha = C \sqsubseteq D$ and $C^{\mathcal{I}} \subseteq D^{\mathcal{I}}$, $\alpha = C(a)$ and $a^{\mathcal{I}} \in C^{\mathcal{I}}$, $\alpha = s(a,b)$ and $(a^{\mathcal{I}}, b^{\mathcal{I}}) \in s^{\mathcal{I}}$, or $\alpha = g(a,n)$ and $g^{\mathcal{I}}(a) = n$. An interpretation $\mathcal{I}$ is a *model* of a TBox (an ABox), if all GCIs (assertions) in it are true in $\mathcal{I}$. An interpretation is a model of a KB $\mathcal{K} = (\mathcal{T},\mathcal{A})$, if it is a model of $\mathcal{T}$ and $\mathcal{A}$. A KB is satisfiable iff it has a model. Given a KB $\mathcal{K}$ and an axiom α, we say α *is entailed in* $\mathcal{K}$, in symbols $\mathcal{K} \models \alpha$, iff $\mathcal{I} \models \alpha$ in all models $\mathcal{I}$ of $\mathcal{K}$.

The particular concrete domain to be used needs to be selected carefully, in order to obtain a decidable logic with reasonable complexity bounds. Specifically, axiom entailment with TBoxes already becomes undecidable if $\Delta_{\mathcal{D}} = \mathbb{N}$ and $\Phi_{\mathcal{D}}$ can express incrementation, as well as equality between numbers and with 0 [25]. However, by restricting the predicates to basic comparison operators, decidability cannot only be retained, but an increase of complexity for common reasoning tasks can be avoided when adding such concrete domains to the logic. To pursue this as a goal, we concentrate on two concrete domains that allow for standard reasoning in P and ExpTime, respectively. The first concrete domain is $\mathsf{R} = \{\mathbb{R}, \Phi_{\mathsf{R}}\}$ investigated in [22], where Φ_{R} contains the binary predicates $\{<,=,>\}$ with the usual semantics, and the unary predicates $\{<_r, =_r, >_r \mid r \in \mathbb{R}\}$, where for $\oplus \in \{<,=,>\}$, the extension is defined as

$\oplus_r^{\mathsf{R}} = \{r' \in \mathbb{R} \mid r' \oplus r\}$. This concrete domain allows for axiom entailment in ExpTime, while even small extensions lead to undecidability [22]. The second concrete domain is $\mathsf{R}_> = \{\mathbb{R}, \Phi_{\mathsf{R}_>}\}$, where $\Phi_{\mathsf{R}_>} = \{>_r \mid r \in \mathbb{R}\}$. Since polynomial time reasoning requires the concrete domain to be *convex* [5], we consider this convex concrete domain.

Example 1. The axioms in the introduction only use predicates from $\mathsf{R}_>$ and are in the logic $\mathcal{EL}(\mathsf{R}_>)$. Feature paths and the more expressive concrete domain R allow to compare different values referred to by concrete features. The following more flexible definition of HBP patients compares their diastolic blood pressure (BP) with the maximal diastolic blood pressure assigned to their age group:

$$\exists(\mathsf{diastolicBP}, \mathsf{belongsToAgeGroup}\ \mathsf{maxDiastolicBP}).> \sqsubseteq \mathsf{PatientWithHBP}.$$

2.1 Queries

We recall atomic, conjunctive and unions of conjunctive queries. Let N_v be a set of variables disjoint from N_c, N_r, N_{cF} and N_i. An *atom* is of the form $C(x)$ or $s(x,y)$, where C is a concept, $s \in N_r$, $x, y \in N_v \cup N_i$. A *conjunctive query (CQ)* q is an expression of the form $\exists x_1, \ldots, x_n : a_1 \wedge \ldots \wedge a_m$, where $x_1, \ldots, x_n \in N_v$ and $a_1, \ldots, a_m$ are atoms. The variables $x_1, \ldots, x_n$ are the *existentially quantified variables in* q, the remaining variables in q are the *free variables in* q. If a CQ contains only one atom, it is an *atomic query* (AQ). A *union of conjunctive queries (UCQ)* is an expression of the form $q_1 \vee \ldots \vee q_n$, where $q_1, \ldots, q_n$ are CQs with pairwise-disjoint sets of variables. The existentially quantified/free variables of a UCQ are the existentially quantified/free variables of its disjuncts. We call AQs, CQs and UCQs collectively *queries.* A query is *Boolean* if it has no free variables.

Given an interpretation $\mathcal{I}$ and a Boolean CQ q, q is *true in* $\mathcal{I}$, in symbols $\mathcal{I} \models q$, iff there is a mapping π that maps variables in q to domain elements in $\mathcal{I}$ and each $a \in N_i$ to $a^{\mathcal{I}}$ such that for every atom $A(x)$ in q, $\pi(x) \in A^{\mathcal{I}}$, and for every atom $s(x,y)$ in q, $(\pi(x); \pi(y)) \in s^{\mathcal{I}}$. A Boolean UCQ is true in $\mathcal{I}$ iff one of its disjuncts is true in $\mathcal{I}$. Finally, given a KB $\mathcal{K} = (\mathcal{T}, \mathcal{A})$ and a Boolean query q, *q is entailed by* $\mathcal{K}$, in symbols $\mathcal{K} \models q$, if $\mathcal{I} \models q$ in every model of $\mathcal{K}$. The *query entailment problem* is to decide whether a given Boolean query is entailed by a given KB.

The *query answering* problem is to find a substitution from the free variables in the query to individual names such that the resulting Boolean query is entailed by the KB. Because this problem can be polynomially reduced to query entailment, it is typical to focus on the query entailment problem, which is a decision problem, when analysing computational complexity. We follow the same route in this paper.

Note that according to our definition, concrete features cannot be used outside of concepts in a query. Therefore, our queries can only express relations between concrete features that can be captured by a concept in our language. For example, the FOL formula

$$\exists y_1, y_2, z_1, z_2 : s_1(x, y_1) \wedge g_1(y_1, z_1) \wedge s_2(x, y_2) \wedge g_2(y_2, z_2) \wedge z_1 < z_2.$$

can be captured the query $\exists(s_1g_1, s_2g_2).<(x)$, but only given $s_1, s_2 \in N_{aF}$, $g_1, g_2 \in N_{cF}$, and $<$ is a predicate of the concrete domain.

Example 2. In a KB with patient records, the following query can be used to retrieve a list of doctors who diagnosed their patients with high blood pressure.

$$\exists y, z : \mathsf{hasPatient}(x, y) \wedge \mathsf{finding}(y, z) \wedge \mathsf{observed}(x, z) \wedge \mathsf{HighBloodPressure}(z)$$

2.2 Complexity of Classical Query Entailment

We give tight complexity bounds for query entailment for the introduced DLs. To the best of our knowledge, the complexity of query answering for the logics studied here has not been considered in the literature before. We focus on the DLs $\mathcal{EL}(\mathsf{R}_>)$ and $\mathcal{ALC}(\mathsf{R})$, since $\mathcal{EL}(\mathsf{R})$ has the same expressive power as $\mathcal{ALC}(\mathsf{R})$ [5], and $\mathcal{ALC}(\mathsf{R}_>)$ already has matching lower bounds from $\mathcal{ALC}$ to our upper bounds for $\mathcal{ALC}(\mathsf{R})$. We further assume values from the concrete domain to be represented in binary. Our complexity analysis only concerns knowledge bases that have a finite representation, which by this assumption are those in which each number can be represented with a finite number of bits. When analysing complexity of query entailment, we distinguish between *combined* and *data complexity*, where in combined complexity, the size of the complete input is taken into consideration, while for data complexity, everything but the ABox is fixed.

Table 1. Complexity of classical query entailment.

	$\mathcal{EL}(\mathsf{R}_>)$		$\mathcal{ALC}(\mathsf{R})$	
	AQs	UCQs	AQs	UCQs
Data complexity	P	P	coNP	coNP
Combined Complexity	P	NP	ExpTime	ExpTime

An overview of the complexities is shown in Table 1. Since the corresponding lower bounds are the same for CQs as for UCQs, we do not include CQs. Matching lower bounds are already known for the DLs $\mathcal{EL}$ and $\mathcal{ALC}$ [10,30,32], so that adding the respective concrete domains does not increase the complexity of query answering for these logics. We show in the extended version of the paper how to reduce query entailment in $\mathcal{EL}(\mathsf{R}_>)$ to query entailment of $\mathcal{EL}$ KBs, following a technique from [23, Sect. 2.4]. For $\mathcal{ALC}(\mathsf{R})$, the results are based on and match results from [22], [23, Sect. 6.2], and [26], which concern the combined complexities of $\mathcal{SHIQ}(\mathsf{R})$ TBox satisfiability and $\mathcal{ALC}(\mathsf{R})$ KB satisfiability, as well as the combined complexity of query entailment in $\mathcal{SHQ}^\cap$.

3 Probabilistic Knowledge Bases with Continuous Probability Distributions

We want to represent both, discrete probabilities of assertions and continuous probability distributions of values of concrete features. As we can simply assign a probability of 1 to assertions that are certain, there is no need to handle certain assertions separately. A *discrete probability assertion* assigns a minimal probability to a classical assertion. This corresponds to the approach taken by *tuple-independent probabilistic database systems* [11], where probabilities are assigned to database and to *ipABoxes* introduced in [19]. For example, the fact that "Otto has a finding that is Diabetes with a probability of at least 0.7" is expressed by the two assertions $\mathsf{finding}(\mathsf{otto}, \mathsf{f1}) : 1$ and $\mathsf{Diabetes}(\mathsf{f1}) : 0.7$.

Note that discrete probability assertions state a lower bound on the probability, rather than the actual probability, and that statistical independence is only assumed on this lower bound. This way, it is consistent to have the assertions $A(a) : 0.5$, $B(a) : 0.5$ together with the axiom $A \sqsubseteq B$ in the knowledge base. Under our semantics, the probability of $B(a)$ is then higher than 0.5, since this assertion can be entailed due to two different, statistically independent statements in the ABox. Namely, we would infer that the probability of $B(a)$ is at least 0.75 (compare also with [19]).

While for symbolic facts, assigning discrete probabilities is sufficient, for numerical values this is not necessarily the case. For example, if the blood pressure of a patient follows a continuous probability distribution, the probability of it to have any specific value is 0. For this reason, in a *continuous probability assertion*, we connect the value of a concrete feature with a probability density function. This way, the fact that "the diastolic blood pressure of Otto follows a normal distribution with an expected value of 84.5 and a variance of 2" can be expressed by the assertion $\mathsf{diastolicBloodPressure}(\mathsf{otto}) \sim \mathsf{norm}(84.5, 2)$. In addition to a concrete domain $\mathcal{D}$, the DLs introduced in this section are parametrised with a set $\mathcal{P}$ of *probability density functions* (*pdfs*), i.e., Lebesgue-integrable functions $f : A \to \mathbb{R}^+$, with $A \subseteq \mathbb{R}$ being Lebesgue-measurable, such that $\int_A f(x)\,\mathrm{d}x = 1$ [1].

Example 3. As a typical set of probability density functions [1], we define the set $\mathcal{P}_{ex}$ that contains the following functions, which are parametrised with the numerical constants $\mu, \omega, \lambda, a, b \in \mathbb{Q}$, with $\lambda > 0$ and $a > b$:

normal distribution with mean μ and variance ω:
$\mathsf{norm}(\mu, \omega) : \mathbb{R} \to \mathbb{R}^+,\ x \mapsto \frac{1}{\sqrt{2\pi\omega}} e^{-(x-\mu)^2/2\omega}$,
exponential distribution with mean λ:
$\mathsf{exp}(\lambda) : \mathbb{R}^+ \to \mathbb{R}^+, x \mapsto \lambda e^{-\lambda x}$,
uniform distribution between a and b:
$\mathsf{uniform}(a, b) : [a, b] \to \mathbb{R}^+, x \mapsto \frac{1}{b-a}$.

Next, we define probabilistic KBs, which consist of a classical TBox and a set of probability assertions.

Definition 1. *Let $\mathcal{L} \in \{\mathcal{EL}(\mathsf{R}_>), \mathcal{ALC}(\mathsf{R})\}$ and $\mathcal{P}$ be a set of pdfs. A* probabilistic $\mathcal{L}_\mathcal{P}$ ABox *is a finite set of expressions of the form $\alpha : p$ and $g(a) \sim f$, where α is an $\mathcal{L}$ assertion, $p \in [0, 1] \cap \mathbb{D}$,[1] $g \in N_{cF}$, $a \in N_i$, and $f \in \mathcal{P}$. A* probabilistic $\mathcal{L}_\mathcal{P}$

[1] Here, the set $\mathbb{D} \subseteq \mathbb{R}$ denotes the *dyadic rationals*, that is, the set of all real numbers that have a finite number of bits after the binary point.

KB *is a tuple* $\mathcal{K} = (\mathcal{T}, \mathcal{A})$, *where* $\mathcal{T}$ *is an* $\mathcal{L}$ *TBox and* $\mathcal{A}$ *is a probabilistic* $\mathcal{L}_\mathcal{P}$ *ABox. If* $\mathcal{P} = \emptyset$, $\mathcal{K}$ *and* $\mathcal{A}$ *are called* discrete, *and if* $\mathcal{P} \neq \emptyset$, *they are called* continuous.

3.1 Semantics of Probabilistic Knowledge Bases

As typical for probabilistic DLs and databases, we define the semantics using a *possible worlds semantics.* In probabilistic systems that only use discrete probabilities, the possible world semantics can be defined based on finite sets of non-probabilistic data sets, the possible worlds, each of which is assigned a probability [11,19,27]. The probability that a query q is entailed then corresponds to the sum of the probabilities of the possible worlds that entail q. If continuous probability distributions are used, this approach is insufficient. For example, if the KB contains the assertion $\mathsf{diastolicBP}(p) \sim \mathsf{norm}(84.5, 2)$, the probability of $\mathsf{diastolicBP}(p, x)$ should be 0 for every $x \in \mathbb{R}$. Therefore, we cannot obtain the probability of $\mathsf{diastolicBP}(p) > 85$ by just adding the probabilities of the possible worlds that entail $\mathsf{diastolicBP}(p, x)$ for some $x > 85$. To overcome this problem, we assign probabilities to (possibly uncountable) *sets* of possible worlds, rather than to single possible worlds. Specifically, we define the semantics using continuous probability measure spaces [1]. A *measure space* is a tuple $M = (\Omega, \Sigma, \mu)$ with $\Sigma \subseteq 2^\Omega$ and $\mu : \Sigma \to \mathbb{R}$ such that

1. $\Omega \in \Sigma$ and Σ is closed under complementation, countable unions and countable intersections,
2. $\mu(\emptyset) = 0$, and
3. $\mu(\bigcup_{E \in \Sigma'}) = \sum_{E \in \Sigma'} \mu(f)$ for every countable set $\Sigma' \subseteq \Sigma$ of pair-wise disjoint sets.

If additionally $\mu(\Omega) = 1$, M is a *probability measure space.*

We define a probability measure space $M_\mathcal{A} = (\Omega_\mathcal{A}, \Sigma_\mathcal{A}, \mu_\mathcal{A})$ that captures the relevant probabilities in a probabilistic ABox $\mathcal{A}$, similar to how it is done in [19] for discrete probabilistic ABoxes. For this, we introduce the three components $\Omega_\mathcal{A}$, $\Sigma_\mathcal{A}$ and $\mu_\mathcal{A}$ one after another. For simplicity, we assume all pdfs $f : A \to \mathbb{R} \in \mathcal{P}$ to be extended to the full real line by setting $f(x) = 0$ for all $x \in \mathbb{R} \setminus A$.

Given a probabilistic ABox $\mathcal{A}$, the set of *possible worlds for* $\mathcal{A}$, in symbols $\Omega_\mathcal{A}$, consists of all classical ABoxes w such that for every $g(a) \sim f \in \mathcal{A}$, w contains $g(a, x)$ for some $x \in \mathbb{R}$, and for every axiom $\alpha \in w$, either $\alpha : p \in \mathcal{A}$, or α is of the form $g(a, x)$ and $g(a) \sim f \in \mathcal{A}$. For $w \in \Omega_\mathcal{A}$, we write $w \models g(a) \oplus x$, $x \in \mathbb{R}$, $\oplus \in \{<, \leq, =, \geq, >\}$, iff $w \models g(a, y)$ and $y \oplus x$. We write $w \models g(a) \oplus h(b)$ iff $w \models g(a, y), h(b, z)$ and $y \oplus z$. We abbreviate $w \models g(a) \geq x, g(a) \leq y$ by $w \models g(a) \in [x, y]$. The *event space over* $\Omega_\mathcal{A}$, in symbols $\Sigma_\mathcal{A}$, is now the smallest subset $\Sigma_\mathcal{A} \subseteq 2^{\Omega_\mathcal{A}}$ that satisfies the following conditions:

1. $\Omega_\mathcal{A} \in \Sigma_\mathcal{A}$,
2. for every $\alpha : p \in \mathcal{A}$, $\{w \in \Omega_\mathcal{A} \mid \alpha \in w\} \in \Sigma_\mathcal{A}$,
3. for every $g(a) \sim f \in \mathcal{A}$, $x \in \mathbb{R}$, $\{w \in \Omega_\mathcal{A} \mid w \models g(a) < x\} \in \Sigma_\mathcal{A}$,

4. for every $g_1(a_1) \sim f_1, g_2(b) \sim f_2 \in \mathcal{A}$, $\{w \in \Omega_\mathcal{A} \mid w \models g_1(a) < g_2(b)\} \in \Sigma_\mathcal{A}$, and
5. $\Sigma_\mathcal{A}$ is closed under complementation, countable unions and countable intersections.

The conditions ensure that for every query q and TBox $\mathcal{T}$, the set of possible worlds w such that $(\mathcal{T}, w) \models q$ is included in $\Sigma_\mathcal{A}$. To complete the definition of the measure space, we now assign probabilities to these sets via the measure function $\mu_\mathcal{A}$. This function has to respect the probabilities expressed by the discrete and continuous probability assertions in $\mathcal{A}$, as well as the assumption that these probabilities are statistically independent. We define $\mu_\mathcal{A}$ explicitly for sets of possible worlds that are selected by the assertions in them, and by upper bounds on the concrete features occurring in continuous probability assertions. By additionally requiring that Condition 3 in the definition of measure spaces is satisfied for $\mu_\mathcal{A}$, this is sufficient to fix the probability for any set in $\Sigma_\mathcal{A}$.

Given a probabilistic ABox $\mathcal{A}$, we denote by $\text{cl-ass}(\mathcal{A}) = \{\alpha \mid \alpha : p \in \mathcal{A}\}$ the classical assertions occurring in $\mathcal{A}$. A *bound set for* $\mathcal{A}$ is a set $\mathbf{B}$ of inequations of the form $g(a) < x$, $x \in \mathbb{R}$, where $g(a) \sim f \in \mathcal{A}$ and every concrete feature $g(a)$ occurs at most once in $\mathbf{B}$. Given a set $\mathcal{E} \subseteq \text{cl-ass}(\mathcal{A})$ of assertions from $\mathcal{A}$ and a bound set $\mathbf{B}$ for $\mathcal{A}$, we define the corresponding set $\Omega_\mathcal{A}^{\mathcal{E},\mathbf{B}}$ of possible worlds in $\Omega_\mathcal{A}$ as

$$\Omega_\mathcal{A}^{\mathcal{E},\mathbf{B}} = \{w \in \Omega_\mathcal{A} \mid w \cap \text{cl-ass}(\mathcal{A}) = \mathcal{E}, w \models \mathbf{B}\}.$$

The probability measure space for $\mathcal{A}$ is now the probability measure space $M_\mathcal{A} = (\Omega_\mathcal{A}, \Sigma_\mathcal{A}, \mu_\mathcal{A})$, such that for every $\mathcal{E} \subseteq \text{cl-ass}(\mathcal{A})$ and every bound set $\mathbf{B}$ for $\mathcal{A}$,

$$\mu_\mathcal{A}(\Omega_\mathcal{A}^{\mathcal{E},\mathbf{B}}) = \prod_{\substack{\alpha:p\in\mathcal{A} \\ \alpha\in\mathcal{E}}} p \cdot \prod_{\substack{\alpha:p\in\mathcal{A} \\ \alpha\notin\mathcal{E}}} (1-p) \cdot \prod_{\substack{g(a)\sim f\in\mathcal{A} \\ g(a)<x\in\mathbf{B}}} \int_{-\infty}^{x} f(y)\,\mathrm{d}y.$$

As shown in the extended version of the paper, this definition uniquely determines $\mu_\mathcal{A}(W)$ for all $W \in \Sigma_\mathcal{A}$, including sets such as $W = \{w \in \Omega_\mathcal{A} \mid w \models g_1(a) < g_2(b)\}$. The above product is a generalisation of the corresponding definition in [19] for discrete probabilistic KBs, where in addition to discrete probabilities, we take into consideration the continuous probability distribution of the concrete features in $\mathcal{A}$. Recall that if a concrete feature $g(a)$ follows the pdf f, the integral $\int_{-\infty}^{x} f(y)\,\mathrm{d}y$ gives us the probability that $g(a) < x$.

Since we have now finished the formal definition of the semantics of probabilistic ABoxes, we can now define the central reasoning task studied in this paper. As in Sect. 2.1, we concentrate on probabilistic query entailment rather than on probabilistic query answering. The latter is a ranked search problem that can be polynomially reduced to probabilistic query entailment as in [19]. Based on the measure space $M_\mathcal{A}$, we define the *probability of a Boolean query* q in a probabilistic KB $\mathcal{K} = (\mathcal{T}, \mathcal{A})$ as $P_\mathcal{K}(q) = \mu_\mathcal{A}(\{w \in \Omega_\mathcal{A} \mid (\mathcal{T}, w) \models q\})$. Note that due to the open-world assumption, strictly speaking, $P_\mathcal{K}(q)$ corresponds to a lower bound on the probability of q, since additional facts may increase the value of $P_\mathcal{K}(q)$.

Different to [19] and classical approaches in probabilistic query answering, because $\mathcal{P}$ contains real functions, $P_{\mathcal{K}}(q)$ is in general a real number, and as such not finitely representable. In practice, it is typical and usually sufficient to compute approximations of real numbers. To capture this adequately, we take the required precision of the probability $P_{\mathcal{K}}(q)$ as additional input to the probabilistic query entailment problem. For a real number $x \in \mathbb{R}$ and $n \in \mathbb{N}$, we use the notation $\langle x \rangle_n$ to refer to an *n-bit approximation of* x, that is, a real number such that $|\langle x \rangle_n - x| < 2^{-n}$. Note that, while we do not enforce it, generally n bits after the binary point are sufficient to identify $\langle x \rangle_n$. We can now state the main reasoning problem studied in this paper.

Definition 2. *The* probabilistic query entailment problem *is the problem of computing, given a probabilistic KB $\mathcal{K}$, a Boolean query q and a natural number n in unary encoding, a number x s.t. $x = \langle P_{\mathcal{K}}(q) \rangle_n$.*

Since the precision parameter n determines the size of the result, we assume it in unary encoding. If we would represent it in binary, it would already take exponential time just to write the result down.

4 Feasibility Conditions for PDFs

Up to now, we did not put any restrictions on the set $\mathcal{P}$ of pdfs, so that a given set $\mathcal{P}$ could easily render probabilistic query entailment uncomputable. In this section, we define a set of feasibility conditions on pdfs that ensure that probabilistic query entailment is not computationally harder than when no continuous probability distributions are used. We know from results in probabilistic databases [11], that query-entailment over probabilistic data is #·P-hard. Note that integration of pdfs over bounded intervals can be reduced to probabilistic query answering. Namely, if $g(a) \sim f \in \mathcal{A}$, we have $P_{(\emptyset,\mathcal{A})}((\exists g.{>_r})(a)) = \int_r^\infty f(x)\,\mathrm{d}y$ for all $r \in \mathbb{R}$. Our feasibility conditions ensure that the complexity of approximating integrals does not dominate the overall complexity of probabilistic query entailment.

We first recall some notions from the complexity theory of real functions by Ker-I Ko [20], which identifies computability of real numbers $x \in \mathbb{R}$ and functions $f : A \to \mathbb{R}$, $A \subseteq \mathbb{R}$, with the computability of n-bit approximations $\langle x \rangle_n$ and $\langle f(x) \rangle_n$, where n is given in unary encoding. Since real function arguments have no finite representation in general, computable real functions are modelled as function oracle Turing machines $T^{\phi(x)}$, where the oracle $\phi(x)$ represents the function argument x and can be queried for n-bit approximations $\langle x \rangle_n$ in time linear in $c + n$, where c is the number of bits in x before the binary point. Given a precision n in unary encoding on the input tape, $T^{\phi(x)}$ then writes a number $\langle f(x) \rangle_n$ on the output tape. This formalism leads to a natural definition of computability and complexity of real numbers and real functions. Namely, a real number $x \in \mathbb{R}$ is P-*computable* iff there is a polynomial time Turing machine that computes a function $\phi : \mathbb{N} \mapsto \mathbb{D}$ s.t. $\phi(n) = \langle x \rangle_n$. A function $f : A \to \mathbb{R}$, $A \subseteq \mathbb{R}$, is P-computable iff there is a function oracle Turing machine $T^{\phi(x)}$ as above that computes for all $x \in A$ a function $\psi : \mathbb{N} \mapsto \mathbb{D}$ with $\psi(n) = \langle f(x) \rangle_n$ in time polynomial in n and the number of bits in x before the binary point.

An important property of P-computable functions f that we use in the next section is that they have a monotone and polynomial *modulus of continuity* (*modulus*), that is, a monotone, polynomial function $\omega_f : \mathbb{N} \to \mathbb{N}$ s.t. for all $n \in \mathbb{N}$ and $x, y \in [2^{-n}, 2^n]$, $|x - y| < 2^{-\omega_f(n)}$ implies $|f(x) - f(y)| < 2^{-n}$ [18,20, Chap. 3].

Approximating integrals $\int_0^1 f(x)\,\mathrm{d}x$ of P-computable functions $f : [0,1] \to \mathbb{R}$ is #·P-complete [20, Chap. 5]. To be able to integrate over unbounded integrals in #·P, we introduce an additional condition.

Definition 3. *A probability density function f is* #·P-admissible *iff it satisfies the following conditions:*

1. *f is* P*-computable, and*
2. *there is a monotone polynomial function $\delta_f : \mathbb{N} \to \mathbb{N}$ such that for all $n \in \mathbb{N}$:*

$$1 - \int_{-2^{\delta_f(n)}}^{2^{\delta_f(n)}} f(x)\,\mathrm{d}x < 2^{-n}.$$

Condition 2 allows us to reduce integration over *un*bounded integrals to integration over bounded integrals: to obtain a precision of n bits, it is sufficient to integrate inside the interval $[-2^{\delta_f(n)}, 2^{\delta_f(n)}]$. Note that as a consequence of Condition 1, there is also a polynomial $\rho_f : \mathbb{N} \to \mathbb{N}$ s.t. for all $x \in [-2^{\delta_f(n)}, 2^{\delta_f(n)}]$, $f(x) < 2^{\rho_f(n)}$. Otherwise, approximations of $f(x)$ would require a number of bits that is not polynomially bounded by the number of bits in x before the binary point, and could thus not be computed in polynomial time. We call δ_f and ρ_f respectively *bounding function* and *range function* of f. In the following, we assume that for any set $\mathcal{P}$ of #·P-admissible pdfs, their moduli, bounding functions and range functions are known.

The above properties are general enough to be satisfied by most common pdfs. Specifically, we have the following lemma for the set $\mathcal{P}_{\mathsf{ex}}$ defined in Example 3:

Lemma 1. *Every function in $\mathcal{P}_{\mathsf{ex}}$ is #·P-admissible.*

5 Complexity of Probabilistic Query Answering

We study the complexity of probabilistic query answering for KBs with #·P-admissible pdfs. As often in probabilistic reasoning, counting complexity classes play a central role in our study. However, strictly speaking, these are defined for computation problems for *natural numbers*. To get a characterisation for probabilistic query answering, we consider corresponding counting problems. Their solutions are obtained by, intuitively, shifting the binary point of an approximated query probability to the right to obtain a natural number. We first recall counting complexity classes following [16].

Definition 4. *Let $\mathcal{C}$ be a class of decision problems. Then, $\#{\cdot}\mathcal{C}$ describes the class of functions $f : A \rightarrow \mathbb{N}$ such that*

$$f(x) = \|\{y \mid R(x, y) \wedge |y| < p(|x|)\}\|$$

for some $\mathcal{C}$-decidable relation R and polynomial function p.

Relevant to this section are the counting complexity classes $\#{\cdot}\mathrm{P}$, $\#{\cdot}\mathrm{NP}$ and $\#{\cdot}\mathrm{coNP}$. The class $\#{\cdot}\mathrm{P}$ is also called $\#\mathrm{P}$. The following inclusions are known: $\#{\cdot}P \subseteq \#{\cdot}\mathrm{NP} \subseteq \#{\cdot}\mathrm{coNP} \subseteq \mathrm{FPSPACE}$ [16].

In order to characterise the complexity of probabilistic query answering using counting classes, we consider corresponding counting problems, inspired by [20, Chap. 5] and [11]. For a function $f : A \rightarrow \mathbb{D}$, we call $g : A \rightarrow \mathbb{N}$ a *corresponding counting problem* if $g(x) = 2^{p(x)} f(x)$ for all $x \in A$, where $p : A \rightarrow \mathbb{N}$ and p can be computed in unary in polynomial time.[2]

For discrete probabilistic KBs, the above definition allows us to give a complexity upper bound for a counting problem corresponding to probabilistic query entailment in a quite direct way. Without loss of generality, we assume that queries contain only concept names as concepts. If $\mathcal{K} = (\mathcal{T}, \mathcal{A})$ is discrete, the probability measure space $M_\mathcal{A}$ has only a finite set $\Omega_\mathcal{A}$ of possible worlds, and each possible world $w \in \Omega_\mathcal{A}$ has a probability $\mu_\mathcal{A}(\{w\})$ that can be represented with a number of bits polynomial in the size of the input. We use this to define a relation R as used in Definition 4. Let $b_\mathcal{K}$ be the maximal number of bits used by any probability $\mu_\mathcal{A}(\{w\})$, $w \in \Omega_\mathcal{A}$. Define the relation R by setting $R((\mathcal{K}, q, n), (w, d))$ for all $w \in \Omega_\mathcal{A}$, $d \in \mathbb{N}$ s.t. $(\mathcal{T}, w) \models q$ and $d < 2^{b_\mathcal{K}} \cdot \mu_\mathcal{A}(\{w\})$, where $\mathcal{K} = (\mathcal{T}, \mathcal{A})$. One easily establishes that $\langle P_\mathcal{K}(q)\rangle_n = 2^{-b_\mathcal{K}} \cdot \|\{y \mid R((\mathcal{K}, q, n), y)\}\|$ for any $n \in \mathbb{N}$. (Note that our "approximation" is always the precise answer in this case.) For discrete KBs, we thus obtain a complexity upper bound of $\#{\cdot}\mathcal{C}$ for the corresponding counting problem defined by $g(\mathcal{K}, q, n) = 2^{b_\mathcal{K}} \cdot P_\mathcal{K}(q)$, where $\mathcal{C}$ is the complexity of classical query entailment.

In order to transfer this approach to continuous probabilistic KBs, we define a discretisation of continuous probability measure spaces based on the precision parameter n and the TBox $\mathcal{T}$. Namely, given a probabilistic KB $\mathcal{K} = (\mathcal{T}, \mathcal{A})$ and a desired precision n, we step-wise modify the measure space $M_\mathcal{A}$ into an approximated measure space $M^a_{\mathcal{K},n} = (\Omega^a_{\mathcal{K},n}, \Sigma^a_{\mathcal{K},n}, \mu^a_{\mathcal{K},n})$ such that (i) the size of each possible world $w \in \Omega^a_{\mathcal{K},n}$ is polynomially bounded by $|\mathcal{K}| + n$, (ii) for each $w \in \Sigma^a_{\mathcal{K},n}$, $\mu^a_{\mathcal{K},n}(\{w\})$ can be computed precisely and in time polynomial in $|\mathcal{K}| + n$, and (iii) it holds $\mu^a_{\mathcal{K},n}(\{w \in \Omega^a_{\mathcal{K},n} \mid (\mathcal{T}, w) \models q\}) = \langle P_\mathcal{K}(q)\rangle_n$ for every query q. Real numbers occur in $M_\mathcal{A}$ in concrete feature values and in the range of $\mu_\mathcal{A}$, and have to be replaced by numbers with a polynomially bounded number of bits. We proceed in three steps: (1) we first reduce the number of bits that occur *before* the binary point in any concrete feature value, (2) we then reduce the number of bits that occur *after* the binary point in any concrete feature value, and (3) we finally reduce the number of bits in the range of $\mu_\mathcal{A}$.

[2] Note that the counting complexity classes considered here are all closed under this operation. To see this, consider f and g characterized by the relations R and R' s.t. $R' = \{(x, y\#z) \mid R(x, y), z \in \{0, 1\}^*, |z| = p(x)\}$. Clearly, $g(x) = 2^{p(x)} f(x)$.

We define $\mathbf{C} = \{g_i(a_i) \sim f_i \in \mathcal{A}\}$ as the set of continuous probability assertions in $\mathcal{K}$ and $\mathcal{F} = \{f_i \mid g_i(a_i) \sim f_i \in \mathbf{C}\}$ as the relevant pdfs in $\mathcal{K}$. We also set $n_v = \|\mathbf{C}\|$ and n_c as the number of unary concrete domain predicates in $\mathcal{K}$.

Step 1: Reduce the number of bits before the binary point. Because every function $f \in \mathcal{F}$ has a monotone polynomial bounding function, we can obtain a function $\delta : \mathbb{N} \to \mathbb{N}$ s.t. for every pdf $f \in \mathcal{F}$ and every $n' \in \mathbb{N}$, we have

$$1 - \int_{-2^{\delta(n')}}^{2^{\delta(n')}} f(x)\,\mathrm{d}x < 2^{-n'}.$$

The first step is to remove all possible worlds w in which for some $g(a) \sim f \in \mathbf{C}$, we have $w \not\models g(a) \in [-2^{\delta(n_v+n)}, 2^{\delta(n_v+n)}]$. Note that for each $g(a) \sim f \in \mathcal{A}$, the probability of $g(a)$ to lay outside this interval is 2^{-n_v-n}. Based on this, one can show that for the resulting measure space $M_1 = (\Omega_1, \Sigma_1, \mu_1)$, we have $|\mu_{\mathcal{A}}(\Omega_{\mathcal{A}}) - \mu_1(\Omega_1)| < 2^{-n-1}$. This restricts also the overall error on the probability of any query. Therefore, we have a remaining error of 2^{-n-1} that we can make in subsequent steps. Note that the number of bits before the binary point in any concrete feature value is now polynomially bounded by the input.

Step 2: Reduce the number of bits after the binary point. Intuitively, in this step we "replace" each possible world $w \in \Omega_1$ by a possible world w' that is obtained by "cutting off" in all concrete feature values all digits after a certain position after the binary point, preserving its probability. First, we specify the maximum number m of digits after the binary point we keep. Similar as for the bounding function δ, we can obtain a polynomial function ω that is a modulus of all functions $f \in \mathcal{F}$, and a polynomial function ρ that is a range function of all functions $f \in \mathcal{F}$. Let $k = \rho(n_v + n)$ be the highest number of bits before the binary point in the range of any pdf in the remaining interval $[-2^{\delta(n+n_v)}, 2^{\delta(n+n_v)}]$, and set $l = n_v + \delta(n_v + n) + 2 + n$. Based on k, l and ω, we define the maximal precision m by

$$m = \lceil \log_2(n_v(n_v + n_c)) + k + n + 3 + \omega(l) \rceil .$$

The motivation behind this definition will become clear in the following. For now, just notice that m is polynomially bounded by $|\mathcal{K}| + n$.

In the approximated measure space $M_2 = (\Omega_2, \Sigma_2, \mu_2)$, Ω_2 contains all worlds from Ω_1 in which each concrete feature value has at most m bits after the binary point. To preserve the probabilities, we define a function $\Omega_{2\to 1} : \Omega_2 \to 2^{\Omega_1}$ that maps each possible world $w \in \Omega_2$ to the possible worlds in Ω_1 that have been "replaced" by w. $\Omega_{1\to 2}$ is defined as

$$\begin{aligned}\Omega_{2\to 1}(w) = \{w' \in \Omega_1 \mid & w \cap \mathsf{cl\text{-}ass}(\mathcal{A}) = w' \cap \mathsf{cl\text{-}ass}(\mathcal{A}),\\ & \forall g(a,x) \in w, g(a) \sim f \in \mathbf{C} : w' \models g(a) \in [x, x + 2^{-m}]\}.\end{aligned}$$

The measure function μ_2 is now defined by

$$\mu_2(\{w\}) = \mu_1(\Omega_{2\to 1}(w)).$$

This transformation affects the probability of concepts such as $\exists(g_1, g_2).>$ and $\exists g.>_r$, because the probability that two concrete features have the same value, or that a concrete feature has a value occurring in some unary domain predicate, increases. One can show that this probability is bounded by $n_v(n_v+n_c) \cdot 2^{-m+k+1}$. By definition, $m > \log_2(n_v(n_v + n_c)) + k + n + 3$, so that the error created in this step is bounded by 2^{-n-2}.

Step 3: Reduce the number of bits in the probabilities. Each possible world M_2 can be finitely represented and has a size that is polynomially bounded in the size of the input. However, the probabilities for each possible world are still real numbers. We first explain how we approximate the probabilities for a single concrete feature. For an assertion $g_i(a_i) \sim f_i \in \mathbf{C}$, and a number $x \in \mathbb{R}$ with m bits after the binary point, we have $\mu_2(\{w \in \Omega_2 \mid w \models g(a) = x\}) = \int_x^{x+2^{-m}} f_i(y)\, \mathrm{d}y$. To discretise this probability, we make use of the modulus ω of the pdfs used in $\mathcal{K}$. Recall that, by the definition of a modulus, for any precision $n' \in \mathbb{N}$ and two real numbers $x, y \in [2^{-n'}, 2^{n'}]$, $|x - y| < 2^{-\omega(n')}$ implies $|f_i(x) - f_i(y)| < 2^{-n'}$. By construction, we have $m > \omega(l)$, and hence, for $x \in [2^{-l}, 2^{l}]$ and $y \in [x, x+2^{-m}]$, we have $|f_i(x) - f_i(y)| < 2^{-l}$. Consequently, the integral $\int_x^{x+2^{-m}} f_i(y)\, \mathrm{d}y$ can be approximated by the product $2^{-m} \cdot \langle f_i(x) \rangle_l$, and we have

$$\left| \int_x^{x+2^{-m}} f_i(y)\, \mathrm{d}y - 2^{-m} \cdot \langle f_i(x) \rangle_l \right| < 2^{-m-l}.$$

There are $2^{\delta(n_v+n)+1+m}$ different values per concrete feature in our measure space, so that an error of 2^{-m-l} per approximated interval introduces a maximal error of 2^{-n-n_v-1} for each concrete feature value (recall $l = n_v+\delta(n_v+n)+2+n$). If we approximate all pdfs this way, for similar reasons as in Step 1, we obtain a maximal additional error of 2^{-n-2} for any query.

Based on these observations, we define the final discretised measure space. Specifically, we define the measure space $M^a_{\mathcal{K},n} = (\Omega^a_{\mathcal{K},n}, \Sigma^a_{\mathcal{K},n}, \mu^a_{\mathcal{K},n})$, where $\Omega^a_{\mathcal{K},n} = \Omega_2$ and $\mu^a_{\mathcal{K},n}$ is specified by

$$\mu^a_{\mathcal{K},n}(\{w\}) = \prod_{\substack{\alpha:p \in \mathcal{A} \\ \alpha \in w}} p \cdot \prod_{\substack{\alpha:p \in \mathcal{A} \\ \alpha \notin w}} (1-p) \cdot \prod_{\substack{g(a) \sim f \in \mathcal{A} \\ g(a,x) \in w}} 2^{-m} \langle f(x) \rangle_l.$$

Note that $\mu^a_{\mathcal{K},n}(\{w\})$ can be evaluated in polynomial time, and can be represented with at most $2 + n_a \cdot n_b + n_v \cdot (m + l)$ bits, where n_a is the number of discrete probability assertions and n_b the maximal number of bits in a discrete probability assertion.

Given a probabilistic KB $\mathcal{K}$ and a precision $n \in \mathbb{N}$, we call the measure space $M^a_{\mathcal{K},n}$ constructed above the *n-approximated probability measure space* for $\mathcal{K}$. We have the following lemma.

Table 2. Complexities of counting problems corresponding to prob. query entailment.

	$\mathcal{EL}(\mathsf{R}_>)_\mathcal{P}$		$\mathcal{ALC}(\mathsf{R})_\mathcal{P}$	
	AQs	UCQs	AQs	UCQs
Data complexity	#·P	#·P	#·coNP	#·coNP
Combined Complexity	#·P	#·NP	ExpTime	ExpTime

Lemma 2. *Let* $\mathcal{K} = (\mathcal{T}, \mathcal{A})$ *be a probabilistic KB,* q *a query,* $n \in \mathbb{N}$ *and* $M^a_{\mathcal{K},n}$ *the* n*-approximated probability measure space for* $\mathcal{K}$*. Then,*

$$\mu^a_{\mathcal{K},n}(\{w \in \Omega^a_{\mathcal{K},n} \mid (\mathcal{T}, w) \models q\}) = \langle P_\mathcal{K}(q)\rangle_n.$$

Note that one can test in polynomial time whether a given possible world is in $\Omega^a_{\mathcal{K},n}$, and compute its probability in polynomial time. Using the observations from the beginning of this section, together with the complexity results in Table 1, we can establish the upper bounds for data and combined complexity shown in Table 2 on counting problems corresponding to probabilistic query answering, which already hold for discrete probabilistic KBs without concrete domain. To the best of our knowledge, only the data complexity for query answering in probabilistic $\mathcal{EL}$ has been considered in the literature before [19], while the other results are new. For the ExpTime upper bounds, note that the approximated measure space has at most exponentially many elements, and can thus be constructed and checked in exponential time.

Hardness for all complexities already holds for discrete probabilistic KBs, so that continuous, #·P-admissible probability distributions do not increase the complexity of probabilistic query answering. A general #·P-lower bound follows from the corresponding complexity of probabilistic query entailment in probabilistic databases [11], while for the combined complexities in $\mathcal{ALC}(\mathsf{R})_\mathcal{P}$, the lower bound follows from the non-probabilistic case. For the remaining complexities, we provide matching lower bounds for the corresponding counting problems in the extended version of the paper using appropriate reductions. Specifically, we show #·NP-hardness w.r.t. combined complexity under *subtractive reductions* in the case of UCQ entailment in $\mathcal{EL}$, and #·coNP-hardness w.r.t data complexity under *parsimonious reductions* in the case of AQ entailment in $\mathcal{ALC}$ [13].

6 Conclusion

When numerical data are of an uncertain nature, such as data obtained by sensor readings or video tracking, they can often be more precisely represented using continuous probability distributions than using discrete distributions. While there is work on OBQA for discrete probabilistic KBs in DL-Lite and $\mathcal{EL}$ [19], this is the first work that considers KBs with concrete domains and continuous probability distributions. For our complexity analysis, we devised a set of feasibility conditions for probability distributions based on the complexity theory of real functions, which captures most typical distributions one might encounter in realistic applications. We show that under these conditions, continuous probability distributions do not increase the complexity of probabilistic query entailment. Using a similar technique as in [20, Chap. 5], our results can likely be extended to a wider class of probability distributions, where the requirement of P-computability is weakened to *polynomial approximability.*

For light-weight description logics, it is often possible to rewrite queries w.r.t the ontology, so that they can be answered directly by a corresponding database system. As there are probabilistic database systems like Orion 2.0 that support continuous probability distributions [33], query rewriting techniques for continuous probabilistic KBs could be employed in our setting as well. For more expressive DLs, a practical implementation could be based on a less fine-grained representation of measure spaces, for which relevant intervals for each concrete feature value are determined based on the concrete domain predicates in the TBox. Probabilities could then be computed using standard algorithms for numerical integration. It might also be worth investigating whether Monte-Carlo approximations can be used for practical implementations. However, as observed in [19], this might be hard to accomplish already for discrete probabilistic $\mathcal{EL}$ KBs. Another basis for practical implementations could be approximation techniques developed for other logical frameworks involving continuous probability distributions, such as the one presented in [8].

References

1. Adams, M.R., Guillemin, V.: Measure Theory and Probability. Springer, Boston (1996)
2. Artale, A., Calvanese, D., Kontchakov, R., Zakharyaschev, M.: The DL-Lite family and relations. J. Artif. Intell. Res. **36**, 1–69 (2009)
3. Artale, A., Ryzhikov, V., Kontchakov, R.: DL-Lite with attributes and datatypes. In: Proceedings ECAI 2012, pp. 61–66. IOS Press (2012)
4. Baader, F., Borgwardt, S., Lippmann, M.: Query rewriting for DL-Lite with n-ary concrete domains. In: Proceedings IJCAI 2017 (2017, to appear)
5. Baader, F., Brandt, S., Lutz, C.: Pushing the $\mathcal{EL}$ envelope. In: Proceedings of IJCAI 2005, pp. 364–369. Professional Book Center (2005)
6. Baader, F., Hanschke, P.: A scheme for integrating concrete domains into concept languages. In: Proceedings of IJCAI 1991, pp. 452–457 (1991)
7. Baader, F., Koopmann, P., Turhan, A.Y.: Using ontologies to query probabilistic numerical data (extended version). LTCS-Report 17–05, Chair for Automata Theory, Technische Universität Dresden, Germany (2017). https://lat.inf.tu-dresden.de/research/reports.html
8. Belle, V., Van den Broeck, G., Passerini, A.: Hashing-based approximate probabilistic inference in hybrid domains: an abridged report. In: Proceedings of IJCAI 2016, pp. 4115–4119 (2016)
9. Calvanese, D., De Giacomo, G., Lembo, D., Lenzerini, M., Rosati, R.: Tractable reasoning and efficient query answering in description logics: the DL-Lite family. J. Autom. Reas. **39**(3), 385–429 (2007)
10. Calvanese, D., Giacomo, G.D., Lembo, D., Lenzerini, M., Rosati, R.: Data complexity of query answering in description logics. Artif. Intell. **195**, 335–360 (2013)

11. Dalvi, N., Suciu, D.: Management of probabilistic data: foundations and challenges. In: Proceedings of SIGMOD 2007, pp. 1–12. ACM (2007)
12. Dargie, W.: The role of probabilistic schemes in multisensor context-awareness. In: Proceedings of PerCom 2007, pp. 27–32. IEEE (2007)
13. Durand, A., Hermann, M., Kolaitis, P.G.: Subtractive reductions and complete problems for counting complexity classes. Theoret. Comput. Sci. **340**(3), 496–513 (2005)
14. Elkin, P.L., Brown, S.H., Husser, C.S., Bauer, B.A., Wahner-Roedler, D., Rosenbloom, S.T., Speroff, T.: Evaluation of the content coverage of SNOMED CT: ability of SNOMED clinical terms to represent clinical problem lists. Mayo Clin. Proc. **81**(6), 741–748 (2006)
15. Glimm, B., Lutz, C., Horrocks, I., Sattler, U.: Conjunctive query answering for the description logic $\mathcal{SHIQ}$. J. Artif. Intell. Res. (JAIR) **31**, 157–204 (2008)
16. Hemaspaandra, L.A., Vollmer, H.: The satanic notations: counting classes beyond $\#P$ and other definitional adventures. ACM SIGACT News **26**(1), 2–13 (1995)
17. Hernich, A., Lemos, J., Wolter, F.: Query answering in DL-Lite with datatypes: a non-uniform approach. In: Proceedings of AAAI 2017 (2017)
18. Hoover, H.J.: Feasible real functions and arithmetic circuits. SIAM J. Comput. **19**(1), 182–204 (1990)
19. Jung, J.C., Lutz, C.: Ontology-based access to probabilistic data with OWL QL. In: Cudré-Mauroux, P., et al. (eds.) ISWC 2012. LNCS, vol. 7649, pp. 182–197. Springer, Heidelberg (2012). doi:10.1007/978-3-642-35176-1_12
20. Ko, K.I.: Complexity Theory of Real Functions. Birkhäuser, Boston (1991)
21. Kumar, N., Khunger, M., Gupta, A., Garg, N.: A content analysis of smartphone-based applications for hypertension management. J. Am. Soc. Hypertens. **9**(2), 130–136 (2015)
22. Lutz, C.: Adding numbers to the $\mathcal{SHIQ}$ description logic–first results. In: Proceedings KR 2001, pp. 191–202. Citeseer (2001)
23. Lutz, C.: The complexity of description logics with concrete domains. Ph.D. thesis, RWTH Aachen (2002)
24. Lutz, C.: Description logics with concrete domains–a survey. In: Advances in Modal Logic 4, pp. 265–296. King's College Publications (2002)
25. Lutz, C.: NExpTime-complete description logics with concrete domains. ACM Trans. Comput. Logic (TOCL) **5**(4), 669–705 (2004)
26. Lutz, C.: The complexity of conjunctive query answering in expressive description logics. In: Armando, A., Baumgartner, P., Dowek, G. (eds.) IJCAR 2008. LNCS (LNAI), vol. 5195, pp. 179–193. Springer, Heidelberg (2008). doi:10.1007/978-3-540-71070-7_16
27. Lutz, C., Schröder, L.: Probabilistic description logics for subjective uncertainty. In: Proceedings of KR 2010, pp. 393–403. AAAI Press (2010)
28. Lutz, C., Toman, D., Wolter, F.: Conjunctive query answering in the description logic $\mathcal{EL}$ using a relational database system. In: Proceedings of IJCAI 2009, pp. 2070–2075. IJCAI/AAAI (2009)
29. Rector, A., Gangemi, A., Galeazzi, E., Glowinski, A., Rossi-Mori, A.: The GALEN CORE model schemata for anatomy: towards a re-usable application-independent model of medical concepts. In: Proceedings of MIE 1994, pp. 229–233 (1994)
30. Rosati, R.: On conjunctive query answering in $\mathcal{EL}$. In: Proceedings of DL 2007, pp. 451–458. CEUR-WS.org (2007)
31. Savković, O., Calvanese, D.: Introducing datatypes in DL-Lite. In: Proceedings of ECAI 2012, pp. 720–725 (2012)

32. Schild, K.: A correspondence theory for terminological logics: preliminary report. In: Mylopoulos, J., Reiter, R. (eds.) Proceedings of IJCAI 1991, pp. 466–471. Morgan Kaufmann (1991)
33. Singh, S., Mayfield, C., Mittal, S., Prabhakar, S., Hambrusch, S., Shah, R.: Orion 2.0: native support for uncertain data. In: Proceedings of SIGMOD 2008, pp. 1239–1242. ACM (2008)
34. Thrun, S., Burgard, W., Fox, D.: A probabilistic approach to concurrent mapping and localization for mobile robots. Auton. Robots **5**(3–4), 253–271 (1998)
35. Yilmaz, A., Javed, O., Shah, M.: Object tracking: a survey. ACM Comput. Surv. (CSUR) **38**(4), 13 (2006)

Pushing the Boundaries of Reasoning About Qualified Cardinality Restrictions

Jelena Vlasenko, Volker Haarslev(✉), and Brigitte Jaumard

Concordia University, Montreal, QC, Canada
haarslev@cse.concordia.ca

Abstract. We present a novel hybrid architecture for reasoning about description logics supporting role hierarchies and qualified cardinality restrictions (QCRs). Our reasoning architecture is based on saturation rules and integrates integer linear programming. Deciding the *numerical* satisfiability of a set of QCRs is reduced to solving a corresponding system of linear inequalities. If such a system is infeasible then the QCRs are unsatisfiable. Otherwise the numerical restrictions of the QCRs are satisfied but unknown entailments between qualifications can still lead to unsatisfiability. Our integer linear programming (ILP) approach is highly scalable due to integrating learned knowledge about concept subsumption and disjointness into a column generation model and a decomposition algorithm to solve it. Our experiments indicate that this hybrid architecture offers a better scalability for reasoning about QCRs than approaches combining both tableaux and ILP or applying traditional (hyper)tableau methods.

1 Introduction

The performance of the original $\mathcal{ALCQ}$ tableau algorithm [19] that is implemented by most description logic (DL) reasoners covering qualified cardinality restrictions[1] (QCRs) is not optimal. To perform a concept satisfiability test, the tableau algorithm creates role successors to satisfy at-least restrictions, e.g., $\geq 20\, R.C$. Given at-most restrictions, e.g., $\leq 10\, R.D$, $\leq 10\, R.E$, the algorithm resolves each R-successor as either D or $\neg D$, and E or $\neg E$. If an at-most restriction for R is violated ($\leq 10\, R.D$), the algorithm nondeterministically merges two R-successors that are instances of D. This uninformed process is highly inefficient, especially when the algorithm has to deal with larger cardinalities and/or large sets of related QCRs. In [11, Sect. 4.1.1] it was shown that if a set of QCRs contains p at-least ($\geq n_i\, R_i.C_i$) and q at-most restrictions ($\leq m_j\, R'_j.C'_j$), then roughly $2^{qN} \prod_{i=0}^{M-2} \binom{M-i}{2}/(M-1)!$ branches need to be explored in the worst case by the standard $\mathcal{ALCQ}$ algorithm (assuming that M R'_j-successors exist in C'_j with $M > m_j$ and $N = \sum_{i=1}^{p} n_i$).

In our previous work (inspired by [26]) we have shown that algebraic tableaux can improve reasoning on QCRs dramatically for DLs such as $\mathcal{SHQ}$ [11], $\mathcal{SHIQ}$

[1] Also known as graded modalities in modal logics.

C. Dixon and M. Finger (Eds.): FroCoS 2017, LNCS 10483, pp. 95–112, 2017.
DOI: 10.1007/978-3-319-66167-4_6

[28], and $\mathcal{SHOQ}$ [9,10]. The basic idea in these calculi is to transform a set of QCRs into a linear optimization problem that will be solved accordingly. These algorithms need to explore $2^{2^{p+q}}$ branches in the worst case but they are independent of N, M. If there is a feasible solution to the problem then the corresponding set of QCRs is satisfiable provided completion rules encounter no logical clashes for the returned solution. The prototypes implementing the above-mentioned approaches on algebraic tableaux [10,11,28] could demonstrate runtime improvements by several orders of magnitude for reasoning about QCRs (and nominals). However, we identified the following two disadvantageous characteristics.

(i) Given n QCRs (and nominals) the naive encoding of the corresponding system of inequalities requires n rows and 2^m columns, where m is the cardinality of the set P of all pairs of roles and their qualifications occurring in the n given QCRs. Let us illustrate this with a small example: $\geq 2R.C \sqcap \geq 2R.D \sqcap \leq 2R.E$. In this case, $P = \{R_C, R_D, R_E\}$, $n = 3$, $m = 3$. In order to represent the QCRs as inequalities we create $\sum x_{C_i} \geq 2$, $\sum x_{D_j} \geq 2$, and $\sum x_{E_k} \leq 2$. For instance, the variables x_{C_i} represent the cardinalities of all elements in the power set of P that contain R_C. The same holds for the other variables respectively. As an additional constraint we specify that all variables must have values in $\mathbb{N}$. Our objective function minimizes the sum of all variables. Intuitively speaking, the above-mentioned concept conjunction is feasible and also satisfiable in this trivial case if the given system of inequalities has a solution in $\mathbb{N}$. It is easy to see that the size of such an inequality system is exponential with respect to m. Furthermore, in order to ensure completeness, in our previous work we required a so-called choose rule that implements a semantic split that nondeterministically adds for each variable x either the inequality $x \leq 0$ or $x \geq 1$. Unfortunately, this uninformed choose-rule could fire 2^{2^m} times in the worst case and cause a severe performance degradation.

(ii) The employed integer linear programming (ILP) algorithms were best-case exponential in the number of occurring QCRs due to the explicit representation of 2^m variables. In [9,10] we developed an optimization technique called lazy partitioning that tries to delay the creation of ILP variables but it cannot avoid the creation of 2^m variables in case m QCRs are part of a concept model. Our experiments in [9–11] indicated that quite a few ILP solutions can cause clashes due to lack of knowledge about known subsumptions, disjointness, and unsatisfiability of concept conjunctions. This knowledge can help reducing the number of variables and eliminating ILP solutions that would fail logically. For instance, an ILP solution for the example presented in the previous paragraph might require to create an R-successor as an instance of $C \sqcap D$. However, if C and D are disjoint this ILP solution will cause a clash (and fail logically).

Characteristic (i) can be avoided by eliminating the choose-rule for variables. This does not sacrifice completeness because the algorithms implementing our ILP component are complete (and certainly sound) for deciding (in)feasibility. In case a system is feasible (or numerically satisfiable), dedicated saturation rules determine whether the returned solutions are logically satisfiable. In case of logical unsatisfiability a corresponding unsatisfiable concept conjunction is added to the input of the ILP component and therefore monotonically constrains the remaining feasibility space. Consequently, previously computed solutions that result in unsatisfiability are eliminated. For instance, the example above would be deemed as infeasible once ILP knows that C, D are subsumed by E and C, D are disjoint.

The avoidance of characteristic (ii) is motivated by the observation that only a small number of the 2^m variables will have non-zero values in the optimal solution of the linear relaxation, i.e., no more variables than the number of constraints following the characteristics of the optimal solution of a linear program, see, e.g., [6]. Moreover, in practice, only a limited number of variables have a non-zero value in the integer optimal solution. In addition, linear programming techniques such as column generation [7,13] can operate with as few variables as the set of so-called basic variables in linear programming techniques at each iteration, i.e., nonbasic variables can be eliminated and are not required for the guarantee of reaching the conclusion that a system of linear inequalities is infeasible, or for reaching an optimal LP solution. Although the required number of iterations varies from one case to another, it is usually extremely limited in practice, in the order of few times the number of constraints. The efficiency of the branch-and-price method, which is required in order to derive an optimal ILP solution, e.g., [3,23,31], depends on the quality of the integrality gap (i.e., how far the optimal linear programming solution is from the optimal ILP solution in case the system of inequalities is feasible, and on the level of infeasibility otherwise). Furthermore, our new ILP approach considers known subsumptions, disjointness, and unsatisfiability of concept conjunctions and uses a different encoding of inequalities that already incorporates the semantics of universal restrictions. We delegate the generation of inequalities completely to the ILP component.

To summarize, the novel features of our architecture are (i) saturation rules that do not backtrack to decide subsumption (and disjointness) [32]; (ii) feasibility of QCRs is decided by ILP (in contrast to [4]); (iii) our revised encoding of inequalities, which incorporates role hierarchies, the aggregation of information about subsumption, disjointness, and unsatisfiability of concept conjunctions, allows a more informed mapping of QCR satisfiability to feasibility and reduces the number of returned solutions that fail logically; (iv) the best-case time complexity of our ILP feasibility test is polynomial to the number of inequalities [24]. This work extends our previous research on the $\mathcal{ELQ}$ Avalanche reasoner [32].

2 Preliminaries

Description logics are a family of knowledge representation languages that form a basis for the Web Ontology Language (OWL). The DL $\mathcal{ALCHQ}$, which is a core subset of OWL, allows role hierarchies ($\mathcal{H}$) and the concept-forming constructors conjunction, disjunction, negation, at-least and at-most restriction ($\mathcal{Q}$). The semantics of $\mathcal{ALCHQ}$ concepts and roles is defined by an interpretation $\mathcal{I} = (\Delta^{\mathcal{I}}, \cdot^{\mathcal{I}})$ that maps a concept C to $C^{\mathcal{I}} \subseteq \Delta^{\mathcal{I}}$ and a role R to $R^{\mathcal{I}} \subseteq \Delta^{\mathcal{I}} \times \Delta^{\mathcal{I}}$. For convenience we use the concepts $\top$ and $\bot$ with $\top^{\mathcal{I}} = \Delta^{\mathcal{I}}$ and $\bot^{\mathcal{I}} = \emptyset$.

$\mathcal{ALCHQ}$ concepts are inductively defined from concept and role names using the constructors as follows ($n, m \in \mathbb{N}$, $n \geq 1$, $\|\cdot\|$ denotes set cardinality, $F^{R,C}(x) = \{y \in C^{\mathcal{I}} \mid (x,y) \in R^{\mathcal{I}}\}$): (i) $(C \sqcap D)^{\mathcal{I}} = C^{\mathcal{I}} \cap D^{\mathcal{I}}$; (ii) $(C \sqcup D)^{\mathcal{I}} = C^{\mathcal{I}} \cup D^{\mathcal{I}}$; (iii) $(\neg C)^{\mathcal{I}} = \Delta^{\mathcal{I}} \setminus C^{\mathcal{I}}$; (iv) $(\geq n R.C)^{\mathcal{I}} = \{x \mid \|F^{C,R}(x)\| \geq n\}$; (v) $(\leq m R.C)^{\mathcal{I}} = \{x \mid \|F^{C,R}(x)\| \leq m\}$. The latter two constructors are called QCRs. A concept C is satisfiable if there exists an $\mathcal{I}$ such that $C^{\mathcal{I}} \neq \emptyset$.

An $\mathcal{ALCHQ}$ Tbox $\mathcal{T}$ is defined as a finite set of axioms of the form $C \sqsubseteq D$ or $R \sqsubseteq S$, where C, D are concepts and R, S roles, and such axioms are satisfied by $\mathcal{I}$ if $C^{\mathcal{I}} \subseteq D^{\mathcal{I}}$ or $R^{\mathcal{I}} \subseteq S^{\mathcal{I}}$. We call $\mathcal{I}$ a model of $\mathcal{T}$ if it satisfies all axioms in $\mathcal{T}$. A Tbox $\mathcal{T}$ entails an axiom if all models of $\mathcal{T}$ satisfy that axiom.

One of the main tasks of a DL reasoner is to classify a Tbox by computing all subsumptions between named concepts. Tableau-based algorithms [2] are the most applied reasoning algorithms to date. Consequence-based or saturation-based algorithms [4,30] are algorithms that accumulate or *saturate* entailed knowledge in a bottom-up way while tableaux attempt to prove entailment in a goal-oriented or top-down way. The idea of saturating knowledge comes from the one-pass saturation algorithm for the DL $\mathcal{EL}^{++}$ [1]. $\mathcal{EL}$ only allows conjunction and existential value restriction ($\exists R.C \equiv \geq 1\, R.C$). Different optimization techniques exist for different types of tasks performed by DL reasoners. In this work, we are interested in applying linear optimization in order to handle qualified number restrictions [9–11] in ontologies expressed in $\mathcal{ELQ}$, which is a superset of $\mathcal{EL}$ that additionally allows QCRs. It is well-known that $\mathcal{ELQ}$ is a syntactic variant of $\mathcal{ALCQ}$ [1].

Atomic decomposition was initially proposed in [26] to reason about sets, however it can also be used to reason about role fillers of qualified number restrictions in description logics. This technique allows us to reduce the problem of deciding feasibility of qualified number restrictions to solving a linear program. The example below illustrates how to transform qualified number restrictions into inequalities. Let us assume the following three qualified number restrictions $\geq 3\, \mathit{hasColor.Blue}$, $\geq 4\, \mathit{hasColor.Red}$, $\leq 5\, \mathit{hasColor.Green}$. We denote the partition of the set $\{b, r, g\}$ ($b = \mathit{blue}$, $r = \mathit{red}$, $g = \mathit{green}$) as $\{b, r, g, br, bg, rg, brg\}$ where the absence of a letter indicate the implied presence of its negation, e.g., b stands for the intersection of blue, not red, not green. Then, we get the corresponding inequalities ($|.|$ denotes set cardinality).

$$|b| + |br| + |bg| + |brg| \geq 3$$
$$|r| + |br| + |rg| + |brg| \geq 4$$
$$|g| + |bg| + |rg| + |brg| \leq 5$$

In such a way we preserve the semantics of qualified number restrictions and reduce a satisfiability problem to a feasibility problem, i.e., whether a 0–1 linear program is feasible.

3 Column Generation and Branch-and-Price Methods

We discuss here how to check the feasibility of a 0–1 linear program with a column generation model, i.e., with an exponential number of variables. It consists in first checking whether its linear relaxation, a linear program with an exponential number of variables, is feasible. We next provide a brief overview of linear programming (LP for short) and column generation.

Linear Programming was recognized as one of the most important scientific achievements of the 20th century. It allows the solution of complicated problems that concern allocation of scarce resources with respect to various constraints in a minimum amount of time. There exist different approaches to solve linear programs. One of them is the simplex method that was proposed in 1947 by George B. Dantzig. Although the simplex method requires an exponential number of iterations in the worst case, it performs very well in practice. In 1979 the ellipsoid method was proposed by Leonid Khachiyan, and could solve linear programming problems in polynomial time. Nevertheless, the simplex method, despite being worst-case exponential is more efficient in practice than the ellipsoid method. The interior-point method is another polynomial-time algorithm that was proposed in 1984 by Narendra Karmarkar and its recent refinements [12] are competitive with the simplex algorithm.

The algorithms mentioned above have been integrated into different commercial and open source solvers, e.g., CPLEX, Gurobi, XPRESS. These solvers are capable of solving very large linear programming problems, i.e., with up to hundreds of thousands of variables. When it comes to millions of variables, their performance starts to deteriorate. We can then use the column generation method. The idea behind this method is that only a subset of all variables (columns) have non zero values in the optimal LP solution. Indeed, there are no more than the number of constraints, i.e., the number of so-called basic variables in linear programming. Numerous large-scale optimization problems are now using it [23].

Back to feasibility checking, column generation can easily detect infeasible linear programs. However, infeasible integer linear programs do not necessarily have an infeasible linear programming relaxation. In order to detect infeasibility in such cases, it is then required to use a branch-and-price algorithm [3] (i.e., a branch-and-bound algorithm [25] in which the linear relaxation is solved with a column generation method).

In the context of our work, we create very large integer linear programs with numerous variables. Therefore, we choose to solve the continuous relaxation with the column generation method to address scalability issues, following the success of using it for, e.g., deciding the consistency of a set of clauses in the context of probabilistic logic [17,20]. In order to produce integer solutions, column generation is combined with a branch-and-price algorithm [3] to either conclude that the model has no solution or to obtain an integer solution.

Column generation together with the branch-and-price method have been implemented into a system that we decided to call QMediator. QMediator is a middle layer or a mediator that facilitates communication between Avalanche and CPLEX. This process will be described in detail in Sect. 5. In short, whenever

Avalanche needs to process qualified number restrictions it calls QMediator. QMediator in turn creates a corresponding integer linear program based on the received information and solves it by means of column generation and branch-and-price methods. To actually solve the integer linear program QMediator calls CPLEX.

The example below illustrates how column generation works in practice, without the need of a branch-and-price method for this particular example.

Consider the axiom $D \sqsubseteq \geq 2\, R.A \sqcap \geq 3\, R.B \sqcap \leq 4\, R.C$. Initially we assume that there is no known subsumption relationship between the QCR qualifications A, B, C. Since we have only one role, we can ignore its name and only focus on $Q_D = Q_D^{\geq} \cup Q_D^{\leq}$, which is our base set for partitioning, with $Q_D^{\geq} = \{A, B\}$ and $Q_D^{\leq} = \{C\}$. The complete decomposition set (or partition) is $\mathcal{D}_D = \{\{A\}, \{B\}, \{C\}, \{A, B\}, \{A, C\}, \{B, C\}, \{A, B, C\}\}$ where each partition element p represents the intersection of p's elements plus the intersection of all $\neg e_i$ with $e_i \in Q_D \backslash p$. We denote the elements of $\mathcal{D}_D$ by the variables x_A, x_B, x_C, x_{AB}, x_{AC}, x_{BC}, x_{ABC}. In the context of the ILP model, note that each variable is associated with a column, so we may use either terms in the sequel.

First Example. The QCRs for concept D result in the following ILP problem.

$$\min \sum_{p \in \mathcal{D}_D} x_p \tag{1}$$

subject to:

$$x_A + 0x_B + 0x_C + x_{AB} + x_{AC} + 0x_{BC} + x_{ABC} \geq 2 \quad \rightsquigarrow \geq 2\, R.A \tag{2}$$

$$0x_A + x_B + 0x_C + x_{AB} + 0x_{AC} + x_{BC} + x_{ABC} \geq 3 \quad \rightsquigarrow \geq 3\, R.B \tag{3}$$

$$0x_A + 0x_B + x_C + 0x_{AB} + x_{AC} + x_{BC} + x_{ABC} \leq 4 \quad \rightsquigarrow \leq 4\, R.C \tag{4}$$

$$x_p \in \mathbb{N}, \qquad \text{for } p \in \mathcal{D}_D.$$

The optimal solution is $x_B = 1$, $x_{AB} = 2$, and all other variables are equal to zero.

However, since the size of $\mathcal{D}_D$ is exponential with respect to the size of Q_D, in general one cannot afford to enumerate all variables. In order to use a column generation modelling, model (1)–(4) is decomposed into a restricted master problem (RMP), made of a subset of columns, and the pricing problem (PP), which can be viewed as a column generator. The RMP contains the inequalities (rows) representing the QCRs, with a very restricted set of variables. Initially one can start with an empty set P of variables x_p, and a set of artificial variables h_q, one for each constraint, i.e., for each element in Q_D (here $n = 3$) using an arbitrarily large cost W (here $W = 10$). Those artificial variables define an initial artificial feasible solution, however, in order to be feasible, the QCR set must not use any of them in its solution.

The cost of a partition element p is defined as the number of elements it contains. Consequently, the objective function of the RMPs is defined as $\sum_{p \in P} \text{cost}_p x_p + W \sum_{i=1}^{n} h_i$. The choice of the cost is related to the selection of partition elements of smaller sizes and thus of less restricted solutions. Indeed, it promotes the reuse of nodes in Avalanche's saturation graph. The optimal solution[2] of (RMP 1) has a cost 50, and contains two non-zero artificial variables.

$$\text{Minimize } 10h_1 + 10h_2 + 10h_3 \text{ subject to} \qquad \text{(RMP 1)}$$
$$h_1 \geq 2$$
$$h_2 \geq 3$$
$$h_3 \leq 4$$
$$\text{Solution: cost} = 50;\ h_1 = 2, h_2 = 3;\ \text{Dual: } \pi_A = 10, \pi_B = 10$$

The objective of the PP is equal to the so-called reduced cost in linear programming (see, e.g., Chvatal [6] if not familiar with linear programming). It uses the dual price values as coefficients of the variables associated with a potential partition element, i.e., binary variables b_q, r_q ($q \in Q_D$) to ensure the description logics semantics of QCRs. The variables b_q indicate whether role successors must be an instance of q and r_q whether an R-successor that is an instance of q must exist. For each at-least QCR with a role and its qualification, P must contain a corresponding variable, e.g., for $\geq 2\,R.A$ if $r_A = 1$ a variable b containing A in its subscript must exist ($r_A - b_A \leq 0$). If P contains a qualification of an at-most QCR, then a corresponding variable must be present, e.g., if C occurs in P ($b_C = 1$), then a variable r containing C in its subscript must exist ($b_C - r_C \leq 0$). The objective function of the PP can then be written as

$$\sum_{q \in Q_D} b_q - \sum_{q \in Q_D^{\geq}} \pi_q r_q - \sum_{q \in Q_D^{\leq}} \omega_q r_q \qquad (5)$$

Based on this formula we can define (PP 1). In its objective function the only non-zero dual price values (coefficients) are π_A, π_B due to (RMP 1).

$$\text{Minimize } b_A + b_B + b_C - 10r_A - 10r_B \text{ subject to} \qquad \text{(PP 1)}$$
$$r_A - b_A \leq 0$$
$$r_B - b_B \leq 0 \qquad \text{(CPP1)}$$
$$b_C - r_C \leq 0$$
$$\text{Solution: } \mathit{cost} = -18, r_A = 1, r_B = 1, b_A = 1, b_B = 1.$$

Since the values of r_A, r_B are 1, we add the variable x_{AB} to the next RMP ($P = \{\{A, B\}\}$). The cost of its solutions is reduced, from 50 in (RMP 1) to 6 in (RMP 2).

$$\text{Minimize } 2x_{AB} + 10h_1 + 10h_2 + 10h_3 \text{ subject to:} \qquad \text{(RMP 2)}$$
$$x_{AB} + h_1 \geq 2$$
$$x_{AB} + h_2 \geq 3$$
$$h_3 \leq 4$$
$$\text{Solution: } \mathit{cost} = 6, x_{AB} = 3;\ \text{Dual: } \pi_B = 2$$

[2] The value of variables not listed in a solution are equal to zero.

In the objective of (PP 2) the only non-zero dual price value is π_B (see also (5)).

$$\text{Minimize } b_A + b_B + b_C - 2r_B \text{ subject to (CPP 1)} \qquad \text{(PP 2)}$$
$$\text{Solution: } cost = -1, r_B = 1, b_B = 1$$

Since the value of r_B is 1, we add the variable x_B to the next RMP ($P = \{\{B\}, \{A, B\}\}$), whose cost is further reduced, from 6 in (RMP 2) to 5 in (RMP 3).

$$\text{Minimize } x_B + 2x_{AB} + 10h_1 + 10h_2 + 10h_3 \text{ subject to} \qquad \text{(RMP 3)}$$
$$x_{AB} + h_1 \geq 2$$
$$x_B + x_{AB} + h_2 \geq 3$$
$$h_3 \leq 4$$
$$\text{Solution: } cost = 5, x_B = 1, x_{AB} = 2; \text{ Dual: } \pi_A = 1, \pi_B = 1$$

In the objective of (PP 2) the only non-zero dual price values are π_A, π_B.

$$\text{Minimize } b_A + b_B + b_C - r_A - r_B \text{ subject to (CPP 1)} \qquad \text{(PP 3)}$$
$$\text{Solution: } cost = 0$$

At this point all variables h_i in (RMP 3) and r_q in (PP 3) are zero indicating that we have reached a feasible solution. Moreover, since the reduced cost of the problem is always positive no "improving" column can be added. This allows us to conclude that we have reached the optimal solution of the LP. Lastly, as this LP optimal solution is integer, we can also claim that it defines the optimal set of partition elements. The inequality system (1) is feasible and the solution in (RMP 3) results in creating one R-successor that is an instance of B with cardinality 1 ($x_B = 1$) and one R-successor that is an instance of $A \sqcap B$ with cardinality 2 ($x_{AB} = 2$). Obviously, this solution satisfies the initial inequalities since the successor $A \sqcap B$ satisfies $\geq 2\, R.A$ and $\geq 2\, R.B$. Thus, the B successor together with the $A \sqcap B$ successor will satisfy $\geq 3\, R.B$.

Second Example. This example adds to the first example the axioms $A \sqsubseteq C$ and $B \sqsubseteq C$. The original inequality system (1) and (RMP 1) remain unchanged. The new pricing problem below accommodates the added subsumptions, e.g., $A \sqsubseteq C$ is modelled as $b_A \leq b_C \iff b_A - b_C \leq 0$.

$$\text{Minimize } b_A + b_B + b_C - 10r_A - 10r_B \text{ subject to} \qquad \text{(PP 4)}$$
$$r_A - b_A \leq 0$$
$$r_B - b_B \leq 0$$
$$b_C - r_C \leq 0 \qquad \text{(CPP4)}$$
$$b_A - b_C \leq 0$$
$$b_B - b_C \leq 0.$$
$$\text{Solution: } cost = -17, r_A = 1, r_B = 1, r_C = 1, b_A = 1, b_B = 1, b_C = 1.$$

Since the values of r_A, r_B, r_C are 1 we add the variable x_{ABC} to the next version of our RMP ($P = \{\{A, B, C\}\}$), which reduces the cost from 50 to 9 in (RMP 5).

$$\begin{aligned} &\text{Minimize } 3x_{ABC} + 10h_1 + 10h_2 + 10h_3 \text{ subject to} && \text{(RMP 5)}\\ &\quad x_{ABC} + h_1 \geq 2\\ &\quad x_{ABC} + h_2 \geq 3\\ &\quad x_{ABC} + h_3 \leq 4\\ &\text{Solution: } cost = 9, x_{ABC} = 3;\ \text{Dual: } \pi_B = 3 \end{aligned}$$

$$\begin{aligned} &\text{Minimize } b_A + b_B + b_C - 3r_B \text{ subject to (CPP 4)} && \text{(PP 5)}\\ &\text{Solution: } cost = -1, r_B = 1, r_C = 1, b_B = 1, b_C = 1 \end{aligned}$$

Since the values of r_B, r_C are 1 we add the variable x_{BC} to the next version of our RMP ($P = \{\{B, C\}, \{A, B, C\}\}$), which reduces the cost from 9 to 8 in (RMP 6).

$$\begin{aligned} &\text{Minimize } 2x_{BC} + 3x_{ABC} + 10h_1 + 10h_2 + 10h_3 \text{ subject to} && \text{(RMP 6)}\\ &\quad x_{ABC} + h_1 \geq 2\\ &\quad x_{BC} + x_{ABC} + h_2 \geq 3\\ &\quad x_{BC} + x_{ABC} + h_3 \leq 4\\ &\text{Solution: } cost = 8, x_{BC} = 1, x_{ABC} = 2;\ \text{Dual: } \pi_A = 1, \pi_B = 2 \end{aligned}$$

$$\begin{aligned} &\text{Minimize } b_A + b_B + b_C - r_A - 2r_B \text{ subject to (CPP 4)} && \text{(PP 6)}\\ &\text{Solution: } cost = 0 \end{aligned}$$

All variables r_q are zero, so, no variable can be added to minimize (RMP 6) further. The inequality system (1) is feasible and according to (RMP 6) we create an R-successor that is an instance of $B \sqcap C$ with cardinality 1 and an R-successor that is an instance of $A \sqcap B \sqcap C$ with cardinality 2. Since we have 3 R-successors that instances of C, the QCR $\leq 4\, R.C$ is satisfied.

Third Example. This example adds to the second example the axiom $A \sqcap B \sqsubseteq \bot$. The original inequality system (1) and (RMP 1) remain unchanged. The new pricing problem below accommodates the added disjointness, i.e., $A \sqcap B \sqsubseteq \bot$ is modelled as $b_A + b_B \leq 1$.

$$\begin{aligned}
&\text{Minimize } b_A + b_B + b_C - 10r_A - 10r_B \text{ subject to} && \text{(PP 7)}\\
&r_A - b_A \leq 0\\
&r_B - b_B \leq 0\\
&b_C - r_C \leq 0 && \text{(CPP7)}\\
&b_A - b_C \leq 0\\
&b_B - b_C \leq 0\\
&b_A + b_B \leq 1\\
&\text{Solution: } cost = -8, r_A = 1, r_C = 1, b_A = 1, b_C = 1
\end{aligned}$$

Since the values of r_A, r_C are 1 we add the variable x_{AC} to the next version of our RMP ($P = \{\{A, C\}\}$), which reduces the cost from 50 to 34 in (RMP 8).

$$\begin{aligned}
&\text{Minimize } 2x_{AC} + 10h_1 + 10h_2 + 10h_3 \text{ subject to} && \text{(RMP 8)}\\
&x_{AC} + h_1 \geq 2\\
&h_2 \geq 3\\
&x_{AC} + h_3 \leq 4\\
&\text{Solution: } cost = 34, x_{AC} = 2, h_2 = 3;\ \text{Dual: } \pi_A = 2, \pi_B = 10
\end{aligned}$$

$$\begin{aligned}
&\text{Minimize } b_A + b_B + b_C - 2r_A - 10r_B \text{ subject to (CPP 7)} && \text{(PP 8)}\\
&\text{Solution: } cost = -8, r_B = 1, r_C = 1, b_B = 1, b_C = 1
\end{aligned}$$

Since the values of r_B, r_C are 1 we add the variable x_{BC} to the next version of our RMP ($P = \{\{B, C\}, \{A, C\}\}$), which reduces the cost from 34 to 14 in (RMP 9).

$$\begin{aligned}
&\text{Minimize } 2x_{AC} + 2x_{BC} + 10h_1 + 10h_2 + 10h_3 \text{ subject to} && \text{(RMP 9)}\\
&x_{AC} + h_1 \geq 2\\
&x_{BC} + h_2 \geq 3\\
&x_{AC} + x_{BC} + h_3 \leq 4\\
&\text{Solution: } cost = 14, x_{BC} = 2, x_{AC} = 2, h_2 = 1;\ \text{Dual: } \pi_A = 8, \pi_B = 10,\\
&\omega_C = -8
\end{aligned}$$

$$\begin{aligned}
&\text{Minimize } b_A + b_B + b_C - 8r_A - 10r_B + 8r_C \text{ subject to (CPP 7)} && \text{(PP 9)}\\
&\text{Solution: } cost = 0
\end{aligned}$$

All variables r_q are zero, so, no variable can be added to minimize (RMP 9) further. However, the inequality system (1) is now infeasible because (RMP 9) still contains the non-zero artificial variable h_2. The infeasibility is caused by the disjointness between the QCR qualifications A and B.

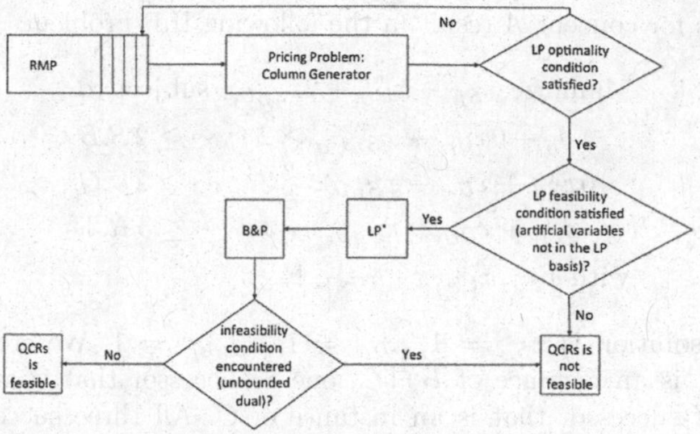

Fig. 1. Optimization chart

The process described above is summarized in Fig. 1. We first define RMP and apply column generation to produce new columns until we obtain an optimal solution. Then, if the solution is infeasible the submitted QCRs are infeasible as well. Otherwise, if the solution is feasible then we proceed with applying the branch-and-price method. If the problem is not feasible, then it will be detected at some iteration in the branch-and-price, while solving the linear relaxation with the column generation algorithm. Otherwise, if the problem is feasible, then the branch-and-price will output a feasible solution.

4 Role Hierarchies

Role hierarchies can easily be mapped to ILP. We illustrate the methodology first with a small example and later with one that entails role subsumption. However, please note that they have not yet been integrated in the current version of Avalanche.

Simple Example. Let $A \sqsubseteq \geq 2\,S.B \sqcap \geq 2\,U.C \sqcap \leq 3\,R.\top$ with S, U subroles of R. The concept A is satisfiable and its least constrained model must have at least one SU-successor that is an instance of $B \sqcap C$. Role hierarchies only need to be considered if an at-most QCR referring to a superrole (R) is restricting other QCRs referring to subroles (S, U) of R. The semantics of role hierarchies is encoded in the inequalities generated for the corresponding at-most QCRs.

We define $Q_A^{\geq} = \{S_B, U_C\}$ and $Q_A^{\leq} = \{R\}$. Since S, U are subroles of R, any partition element containing a subrole and its superrole can be simplified by removing the superrole because their intersection is equal to the subrole, e.g., $\{S_B, R\}$ is equal to $\{S_B\}$. Additionally, R can be removed from Q_A because no at-least QCR mentioning R exists. The complete decomposition set is $\mathcal{D}_A = \{\{S_B\}, \{U_C\}, \{S_B, U_C\}\}$. We denote these partition elements by the variables $x_{S_B}, x_{U_C}, x_{S_B U_C}$.

The QCRs for concept A result in the following ILP problem.

$$\begin{aligned} &\text{Minimize } x_{S_B} + x_{U_C} + 2x_{S_BU_C} \text{ subject to} \\ &x_{S_B} + 0x_{U_C} + x_{S_BU_C} \geq 2 \quad \rightsquigarrow \geq 2\, S.B \\ &0x_{S_B} + x_{U_C} + x_{S_BU_C} \geq 2 \quad \rightsquigarrow \geq 2\, U.C \\ &x_{S_B} + x_{U_C} + x_{S_BU_C} \leq 3 \quad \rightsquigarrow \leq 3\, R.\top \\ &\text{with } x_{S_B}, x_{U_C}, x_{S_BU_C} \in \mathbb{N} \end{aligned} \tag{6}$$

The optimal solution is $x_{S_B} = 1$, $x_{U_C} = 1$, $x_{S_BU_C} = 1$. We create one SU-successor that is an instance of $B \sqcap C$, one S-successor that is an instance of B, and one U-successor that is an instance of C. All three successors have a cardinality of 1.

Example with Entailed Role Subsumption. The combination of role hierarchies and QCRs can be used to entail role subsumptions. Let us assume a Tbox $\mathcal{T} = \{\top \sqsubseteq \leq 1\, R.\top, \geq 1\, S.\top \sqsubseteq C, C \sqsubseteq \geq 1\, U.\top, A \sqsubseteq \geq 1\, S.B \sqcap \leq 0\, U.B\}$ with S, U subroles of R. $\mathcal{T}$ entails that S is a subrole of U and thus $A \sqsubseteq \bot$. It is easy to see that A is subsumed by C via the role S. Thus the QCRs applicable to A are $\leq 1\, R.\top, \geq 1\, S.B, \leq 0\, U.B, \geq 1\, U.\top$.

We define $Q_A^{\geq} = \{S_B, U\}$ and $Q_A^{\leq} = \{R, U_B\}$. After applying the simplifications from above we get $\mathcal{D}_A = \{\{U\}, \{S_B\}, \{U_B\}, \{U, S_B\}, \{S_B, U_B\}\}$. We denote these partition elements by the variables $x_U, x_{S_B}, x_{U_B}, x_{US_B}, x_{S_BU_B}$.

The QCRs for concept A result in the following ILP problem.

$$\begin{aligned} &\text{Minimize } x_U + x_{S_B} + x_{U_B} + 2x_{US_B} + 2x_{S_BU_B} \text{ subject to} \\ &0x_U + x_{S_B} + 0x_{U_B} + x_{US_B} + x_{S_BU_B} \geq 1 \quad \rightsquigarrow \geq 1\, S.B \\ &x_U + 0x_{S_B} + x_{U_B} + x_{US_B} + x_{S_BU_B} \geq 1 \quad \rightsquigarrow \geq 1\, U.\top \\ &x_U + x_{S_B} + x_{U_B} + x_{US_B} + x_{S_BU_B} \leq 1 \quad \rightsquigarrow \leq 1\, R.\top \\ &0x_U + 0x_{S_B} + x_{U_B} + x_{US_B} + x_{S_BU_B} \leq 0 \quad \rightsquigarrow \leq 0\, U.B \\ &\text{with } x_U, x_{S_B}, x_{U_B}, x_{US_B}, x_{S_BU_B} \in \mathbb{N} \end{aligned} \tag{7}$$

The system's infeasibility is caused by the encoding of the entailed role subsumption $S \sqsubseteq U$ (first three inequalities) and $\leq 0\, U.B$ (fourth inequality). If any of these four inequalities is removed, the remaining system becomes feasible.

5 Communication of Avalanche with QMediator

Avalanche is a complex rule-based system that implements a consequence-based reasoning algorithm presented in [32]. The algorithm manages the application of rules to an input ontology by traversing the completion graph. A dedicated module QMediator is called when a rule needs to expand the underlying graph or when a clash has been detected in a node due to the presence of qualified number restrictions. With the help of the module we can reduce the problem of deciding satisfiability of qualified number restrictions to the feasibility of inequalities, which gives us a clear advantage over other existing systems. To avoid circular dependencies between the two systems (considered an anti-pattern in software design) QMediator cannot call or access any data from Avalanche. Avalanche in its turn cannot directly call CPLEX.

During the execution of the algorithm the rules are being applied to an input ontology and a directed completion graph is constructed to store the inferred information. There can be four types of nodes in the graph – identified nodes, anonymous nodes, auxiliary nodes, and two types of cloned nodes – a positive clone to test subsumption between concepts and a negative clone to test disjointness between concepts. If a positive/negative node becomes unsatisfiable then the subsumption/disjointness holds. Each node in a given completion graph is uniquely identified by its representative concept. A representative concept is either a concept (a concept name) declared in the original ontology or a concept created during the reasoning process. All nodes contain a set of subsumers and only identified nodes contain a set of possible subsumers. Subsumers are other concepts that subsume the representative concept of a node. Possible subsumers are collected by a dedicated rule and are needed for subsumption testing. As it can be guessed from their name, possible subsumers represent the subsumers that can possibly subsume the representative concept of a node. Thus, we can avoid performing unnecessary subsumption tests.

When a node is subsumed by qualified number restrictions it has to call the graph expansion rule. The rule in its turn will call QMediator and pass the corresponding information: the qualified number restrictions, the subsumers of the qualifications and their unsatisfiable concept conjunctions. After that, the mediator will transform this information into a linear program, and it will call CPLEX to solve it or in other words to find a model. The result of this call is returned to the rule. Thus, the rule will have all the necessary information to expand the graph or to make the node unsatisfiable by adding $\bot$ (bottom) to its

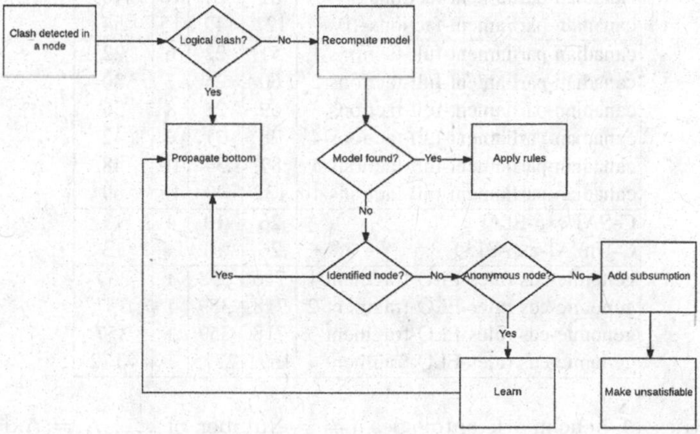

Fig. 2. Clash detection

subsumers. As a result, the expansion rule may create additional nodes in the graph - the anonymous nodes. An anonymous node represents a situation when a role filler is not a single concept (e.g., A) but rather an intersection of concepts ($A \sqcap B$).

In Fig. 2 we show how the call to QMediator is integrated into the clash detection process. If a node becomes unsatisfiable, then the cause of the unsatisfiability has to be identified. If there is a logical clash (e.g., A and $\neg A$ are present in the node) then the corresponding ancestors of the node will be made unsatisfiable. However, if the clash is due to the presence of qualified number restrictions then the mediator should be called and it should be asked to recompute a more constrained model. If a new model was computed, the rules can continue to be applied. If there is no model and the node is an identified node, then the corresponding ancestors of the node should be made unsatisfiable. If the node is an anonymous node this information will be recorded to avoid having the QMediator recompute the same model. Otherwise, the node in question must be a positive/negative cloned node. In this case it can be concluded that the subsumption/disjointness holds and the node will be marked as unsatisfiable.

6 Performance Evaluation

We extended the test suite that we used in our previous work to evaluate the performance of Avalanche [32]. The test suite is composed of three different collections of test ontologies that will be presented below. We chose these ontologies

Ontology Name	#A	#C	#R	#QCRs
canadian-parliament-factions-1	48	21	6	19
canadian-parliament-factions-2	56	24	7	25
canadian-parliament-factions-3	64	27	8	30
canadian-parliament-factions-4	72	30	9	35
canadian-parliament-factions-5	81	34	10	40
canadian-parliament-factions-10	121	49	15	54
canadian-parliament-full-factions-1	51	22	6	22
canadian-parliament-full-factions-2	60	25	7	30
canadian-parliament-full-factions-3	69	28	8	36
canadian-parliament-full-factions-4	78	31	9	42
canadian-parliament-full-factions-5	87	34	10	48
canadian-parliament-full-factions-10	132	49	15	69
C-SAT-exp-ELQ	26	10	4	13
C-UnSAT-exp-ELQ	26	10	4	13
genomic-cds rules-ELQ-fragment-1	716	358	1	357
genomic-cds rules-ELQ-fragment-2	718	359	1	357
genomic-cds rules-ELQ-fragment-3	718	359	1	357
genomic-cds rules-ELQ-fragment-4	1691	2775	1	8172

Fig. 3. Metrics of benchmark ontologies (# = Number of ..., A = Axioms, C = Concepts, R = Roles)

to be classified to stress test the performance of Avalanche with respect to different applications of qualified cardinality restrictions. Some metrics about the test ontologies are shown in Fig. 3. The ontologies differ by the number of axioms, concepts, roles, and qualified number restrictions.

The first test collection models the House of Commons of the Canadian parliament [5] (see top part of Fig. 4). It is our own collection of $\mathcal{ELQ}$ ontologies where we represent a real-world situation. There are two versions of this benchmark - short and full, each consisting of six variants. The variants differ by the number of included factions [5]. The only reasoners that can classify all variants of the simplest of these ontologies within the given time limit are Avalanche and Racer. Avalanche is the only reasoner that can classify all variants of these ontologies.

The second test collection (see middle part of Fig. 4) uses synthetic concept templates. The original $\mathcal{ALCQ}$ concepts are shown below the table. They were manually rewritten into normalized $\mathcal{ELQ}$. The concept templates use a variable n that is increased exponentially. The numbers used in the template are bounded by the value of $2n$. The first template is satisfiable and the second one is unsatisfiable. Only Avalanche and Racer can classify all variants of these small ontologies within the time limit.

The third test collection (see bottom part of Fig. 4) uses four $\mathcal{ELQ}$ fragments of a real world ontology, genomic-cds_rules [29], which was developed for pharmacogenetics and clinical decision support. It contains many concepts using QCRs of the form $= 2\, has.A_i$. However, in these fragments the concepts (A_i) occurring in the qualification of the QCRs do not interact with one another. This simplifies reasoning and all reasoners except Racer perform well. Avalanche (with the exception of the fourth fragment) and HermiT as well as FaCT++ and Konclude have similar runtimes. These fragments are interesting because the concept `<#human>` contains several hundred QCRs using the same role. This is one of the reasons why Racer times out for all fragments. At the moment we can classify only the above mentioned fragments of the ontology in question. Our ultimate goal is classify the entire ontology. As we know, no other reasoner can do it yet.

As compared to our previous work [32], the performance of Avalanche has already been greatly improved. However, we expect to achieve even better results in future. Avalanche's speed for the Canadian Parliament ontologies has been improved by several orders of magnitude. Previously it could not classify the version of Canadian Parliament with 10 factions within 10,000 s. The reason for such a change is mainly due to the improved communication with QMediator. Previously we delegated all computations that concerned qualified number restrictions to the dedicated module. After a scrupulous analysis of Avalanche's runtime we noticed that a lot of time is spent in the module to solve rather simple cases. It appears that Linear Programming methods are typically used to solve feasible problems. If a problem is infeasible then it should be considered as erroneous and it has to be remodelled. However, in our case we do not consider infeasible models to be erroneous. On the contrary, they help us to discover valuable knowledge about the ontology in question, e.g. subsumption or disjointness.

As a result, we identified several cases where feasibility/infeasibility information can be discovered without CPLEX. For example, we do not need to call QMediator when we have only at-least or only at-most restrictions. In the former case we simply connect with an edge the node that contains the number restrictions and the nodes that contain role fillers as their representative concepts. In the latter case we do not need to do anything because at-most inequalities do not require us to create successors (remember that 0 will satisfy $\leq 5R.C$). We have a special treatment when we have a set of at-least and at-most inequalities and all at-most inequalities are of cardinality 0. We also check if we can reduce all at-least inequalities and all at-most inequalities to only one inequality. For example, $\geq 3R.C$ and $\geq 5R.C$ could be replaced by $\geq 5R.C$. Similarly, $\leq 0R.C$ and $\leq 6R.C$ could be replaced by $\leq 0R.C$. Further, we have other ways to determine early infeasibility. For example, $\leq 3R.C$ and $\geq 1R.D$ would be infeasible if C is subsumed by D. Thus, QMediator is now called only when it cannot be avoided.

Although Racer can classify some of the test ontologies faster than Avalanche, we are not discouraged by this fact because we know exactly how we have to improve Avalanche in order to achieve comparable or even better results. In particular, we will be working on a reimplementation of the strategy that is used to apply rules to nodes.

Canadian Parliament										
	Factions only					Full				
#F	Ava	Fac	Her	Kon	Rac	Ava	Fac	Her	Kon	Rac
10	1.1	TO	TO	TO	0.12	1.4	TO	TO	TO	TO
5	0.56	TO	TO	TO	0.12	0.73	TO	TO	TO	TO
4	0.46	TO	TO	TO	0.11	0.58	TO	TO	TO	TO
3	0.36	TO	TO	TO	0.07	0.43	TO	TO	TO	TO
2	0.26	TO	TO	TO	0.07	0.33	TO	TO	TO	10.5
1	0.18	TO	TO	7.3	0.05	0.24	TO	TO	TO	0.44

	C-SAT-exp-ELQ					C-UnSAT-exp-ELQ				
n	Ava	Fac	Her	Kon	Rac	Ava	Fac	Her	Kon	Rac
40	1.3	TO	TO	TO	0.01	1.6	TO	TO	TO	0.01
20	1.3	TO	TO	TO	0.01	1.5	TO	TO	TO	0.01
10	1.2	TO	TO	TO	0.01	1.6	TO	TO	TO	0.01
5	0.95	6.3	4.4	0.91	0.01	1.8	TO	TO	784	0.01
3	1.1	0.17	0.18	0.33	0.01	1.6	0.25	1.15	1.18	0.01

Sat: $C \sqsubseteq (\leq n\,R.\neg A \sqcup \leq n-1\,R.\neg B) \sqcap \geq 2n\,R.\top \sqcap \leq n\,R.A \sqcap \leq n\,R.B$

Unsat: $C \sqsubseteq (\leq n-1\,R.\neg A \sqcup \leq n-1\,R.\neg B) \sqcap \geq 2n\,R.\top \sqcap \leq n\,R.A \sqcap \leq n\,R.B$

Satisfiability of concept <#human>					
Name	Ava	Fac	Her	Kon	Rac
genomic-cds_rules-ELQ-fragment-1	0.75	27.7	0.87	27.7	TO
genomic-cds_rules-ELQ-fragment-2	1.2	28.2	1.14	28.3	TO
genomic-cds_rules-ELQ-fragment-3	4.8	28.8	1.27	26.3	TO
genomic-cds_rules-ELQ-fragment-4	26.7	28.8	4.4	29.4	TO

Fig. 4. Benchmark runtimes in seconds with a timeout of 1000 s (TO = timeout, #F = Number of Factions, Ava = Avalanche, Fac = FaCT++, Her = HermiT, Kon = Konclude, Rac = Racer)

The experiments were performed on a MacBook Pro (2.6 GHz Intel Core i7 processor, 16 GB memory). The comparison results (average of 3 runs) are shown in Fig. 4. We compared Avalanche with major OWL reasoners: FaCT++ (1.6.4) [8], HermiT (1.3.8) [18], Konclude (0.6.2) [22], and Racer (3.0) [14,15,27]. In fact, Racer is the only other available OWL reasoner using an ILP component for reasoning about QCRs in contrast to [21] where ILP is used in the context of probabilistic reasoning. The algorithms implementing Racer's ILP component are in general best-case exponential with respect to the number of QCRs given for one concept. Another reasoning approach for $\mathcal{ALCQ}$ [16] used SMT with a theory that is a specific and computationally much cheaper subcase of Linear Arithmetic under the Integers but this approach suffers from inefficiencies for nested QCRs where reasoning involves backtracking. It would also not scale well for role hierarchies and its extension to inverse roles is an open problem.

7 Conclusion

In this work we presented a hybrid architecture for reasoning about description logics supporting role hierarchies and QCRs. It allows us to reduce the QCR satisfiability problem to a feasibility problem. We tested our system and identified ontologies that cannot be classified by other reasoners in a reasonable amount of time. We almost finished extending the architecture to cover $\mathcal{ALCHQ}$. Our ultimate goal is to extend our architecture to the DL $\mathcal{ALCHIQ}$ by adding inverse roles ($\mathcal{I}$).

References

1. Baader, F., Brandt, S., Lutz, C.: Pushing the $\mathcal{EL}$ envelope. In: Proceeding of IJCAI, pp. 364–369 (2005)
2. Baader, F., Sattler, U.: An overview of tableau algorithms for description logics. Stud. Logica. **69**(1), 5–40 (2001)
3. Barnhart, C., Johnson, E.L., Nemhauser, G.L., Savelsbergh, M.W.P., Vance, P.H.: Branch-and-price: column generation for solving huge integer programs. Oper. Res. **46**(3), 316–329 (1998)
4. Bate, A., Motik, B., Cuenca Grau, B., Simančík, F., Horrocks, I.: Extending consequence-based reasoning to $\mathcal{SRIQ}$. In: Proceeding of KR, pp. 187–196 (2016)
5. Canadian Parliament: https://en.wikipedia.org/wiki/House_of_Commons_of_Canada
6. Chvatal, V.: Linear Programming. Freeman, New York (1983)
7. Dantzig, G.B., Wolfe, P.: Decomposition principle for linear programs. Oper. Res. **8**(1), 101–111 (1960)
8. FaCT++: http://owl.cs.manchester.ac.uk/tools/fact/
9. Faddoul, J., Haarslev, V.: Algebraic tableau reasoning for the description logic $\mathcal{SHOQ}$. J. Appl. Logic **8**(4), 334–355 (2010)
10. Faddoul, J., Haarslev, V.: Optimizing algebraic tableau reasoning for $\mathcal{SHOQ}$: First experimental results. In: Proceeding of DL, pp. 161–172 (2010)

11. Farsiniamarj, N., Haarslev, V.: Practical reasoning with qualified number restrictions: a hybrid Abox calculus for the description logic $\mathcal{SHQ}$. AI Commun. **23**(2–3), 334–355 (2010)
12. Freund, R., Mizuno, S.: Interior point methods: current status and future directions. Optima **51**, 1–9 (1996)
13. Gilmore, P.C., Gomory, R.E.: A linear programming approach to the cutting-stock problem. Oper. Res. **9**(6), 849–859 (1961)
14. Haarslev, V., Hidde, K., Möller, R., Wessel, M.: The RacerPro knowledge representation and reasoning system. Semant. Web **3**(3), 267–277 (2012)
15. Haarslev, V., Möller, R.: RACER system description. In: Goré, R., Leitsch, A., Nipkow, T. (eds.) IJCAR 2001. LNCS, vol. 2083, pp. 701–705. Springer, Heidelberg (2001). doi:10.1007/3-540-45744-5_59
16. Haarslev, V., Sebastiani, R., Vescovi, M.: Automated reasoning in $\mathcal{ALCQ}$ via SMT. In: Proceeding of CADE, pp. 283–298 (2011)
17. Hansen, P., Jaumard, B., de Aragão, M.P., Chauny, F., Perron, S.: Probabilistic satisfiability with imprecise probability. Int. J. Approximate Reasoning **24**(2–3), 171–189 (2000)
18. HermiT: http://www.hermit-reasoner.com/download.html
19. Hollunder, B., Baader, F.: Qualifying number restrictions in concept languages. In: Proceeding of KR, pp. 335–346 (1991)
20. Jaumard, B., Hansen, P., de Aragão, M.P.: Column generation methods for probabilistic logic. ORSA J. Comput. **3**(2), 135–148 (1991)
21. Klinov, P., Parsia, B.: Pronto: a practical probabilistic description logic reasoner. In: Bobillo, F., Costa, P.C.G., d'Amato, C., Fanizzi, N., Laskey, K.B., Laskey, K.J., Lukasiewicz, T., Nickles, M., Pool, M. (eds.) UniDL/URSW 2008-2010. LNCS, vol. 7123, pp. 59–79. Springer, Heidelberg (2013). doi:10.1007/978-3-642-35975-0_4
22. Konclude: http://www.derivo.de/en/produkte/konclude/
23. Lübbecke, M., Desrosiers, J.: Selected topics in column generation. Oper. Res. **53**, 1007–1023 (2005)
24. Megiddo, N.: On the complexity of linear programming. In: Advances in Economic Theory, pp. 225–268. Cambridge University Press (1987)
25. Nemhauser, G.L., Wolsey, L.A.: Integer and Combinatorial Optimization. Wiley, New York (1988)
26. Ohlbach, H., Köhler, J.: Modal logics, description logics and arithmetic reasoning. Artif. Intell. **109**(1–2), 1–31 (1999)
27. Racer: https://www.ifis.uni-luebeck.de/index.php?id=385
28. Roosta Pour, L., Haarslev, V.: Algebraic reasoning for $\mathcal{SHIQ}$. In: Proceeding of DL, pp. 530–540 (2012)
29. Samwald, M.: Genomic CDS: an example of a complex ontology for pharmacogenetics and clinical decision support. In: 2nd OWL Reasoner Evaluation Workshop, pp. 128–133 (2013)
30. Simančík, F., Motik, B., Horrocks, I.: Consequence-based and fixed-parameter tractable reasoning in description logics. Artif. Intell. **209**, 29–77 (2014)
31. Vanderbeck, F.: Branching in branch-and-price: a generic scheme. Math. Program. **130**(2), 249–294 (2011)
32. Vlasenko, J., Daryalal, M., Haarslev, V., Jaumard, B.: A saturation-based algebraic reasoner for $\mathcal{ELQ}$. In: PAAR@IJCAR, Coimbra, Portugal, pp. 110–124 (2016)

Rewriting

Parallel Closure Theorem for Left-Linear Nominal Rewriting Systems

Kentaro Kikuchi[1(✉)], Takahito Aoto[2], and Yoshihito Toyama[1]

[1] RIEC, Tohoku University, Sendai, Japan
{kentaro,toyama}@nue.riec.tohoku.ac.jp
[2] Faculty of Engineering, Niigata University, Niigata, Japan
aoto@ie.niigata-u.ac.jp

Abstract. Nominal rewriting has been introduced as an extension of first-order term rewriting by a binding mechanism based on the nominal approach. In this paper, we extend Huet's parallel closure theorem and its generalisation on confluence of left-linear term rewriting systems to the case of nominal rewriting. The proof of the theorem follows a previous inductive confluence proof for orthogonal uniform nominal rewriting systems, but the presence of critical pairs requires a much more delicate argument. The results include confluence of left-linear uniform nominal rewriting systems that are not α-stable and thus are not represented by any systems in traditional higher-order rewriting frameworks.

1 Introduction

Variable binding is ubiquitous in many expressive formal systems such as systems of predicate logics, λ-calculi, process calculi, etc. Every language containing variable binding needs to deal with α-equivalence. Intuitively α-equivalence may be dealt with implicitly, but much effort is required in formal treatment. To overcome the difficulty, many studies have been made in the literature (e.g. [5,18]), among which the nominal approach [9,17] is a novel one—unlike other approaches, it incorporates permutations and freshness conditions on variables (atoms) as basic ingredients.

To deal with equational logics containing variable binding, various rewriting frameworks have been proposed (e.g. [12,13]). *Nominal rewriting* [8] has been introduced as a new rewriting framework based on the nominal approach. A distinctive feature of nominal rewriting is that α-conversion and capture-avoiding substitution are not relegated to the meta-level—they are explicitly dealt with at the object-level. In contrast, previous rewriting frameworks as in [12,13] employ some meta-level calculus (e.g. the simply-typed λ-calculus) and accomplish α-conversion and capture-avoiding substitution via the meta-level calculus.

Confluence and *critical pairs* are fundamental notions for systematic treatment of equational reasoning based on rewriting. Some basic confluence results such as Rosen's criterion (orthogonal systems are confluent) and Knuth-Bendix's criterion (terminating systems with joinable critical pairs are confluent) have been extended to the case of nominal rewriting [3,8,19,20].

C. Dixon and M. Finger (Eds.): FroCoS 2017, LNCS 10483, pp. 115–131, 2017.
DOI: 10.1007/978-3-319-66167-4_7

In the present paper, we are concerned with Huet's criterion [10] (left-linear systems with parallel closed critical pairs are confluent, which is known as the parallel closure theorem) in the setting of nominal rewriting. We are also aiming to obtain its generalisation analysing overlaps at the root as in the case of term rewriting [21]. These results extend the previous results of Rosen's criterion in the nominal rewriting setting [3,8,19], and include confluence of, in particular, weakly orthogonal nominal rewriting systems, i.e. left-linear nominal rewriting systems in which all critical pairs are α-equivalent.

The difficulties in proving confluence properties of nominal rewriting systems, compared to the case of ordinary term rewriting, are threefold. First, rewriting is performed via matching modulo α-equivalence, so that a redex is not necessarily an instance of the LHS of a rule but a term that is α-equivalent to it. This causes, among others, similar difficulties in proving the critical pair lemma to those for E-critical pairs [11]. Secondly, rewrite rules have freshness contexts (or constraints), and accordingly, critical pairs are also accompanied with freshness contexts. This is analogous to the case of term rewriting with certain constraints (e.g. [7]). Thirdly, as a characteristic feature of nominal rewriting, rewrite steps involve permutations, or, in terms of [8], the set of rewrite rules is closed under equivariance. Therefore, to keep finiteness of the representations, critical pairs need to be parametrised by permutations.

Due to these difficulties, it is not obvious in nominal rewriting that a peak with rewriting at a non-variable position of one of the rules is an instance of a critical pair. This property is necessary in the proof of Lemma 13, where we construct required permutations and substitutions using some lemmas and the property of the most general unifier occurring in the critical pair.

The parallel closure theorem for left-linear nominal rewriting systems has not been shown for years, while confluence by orthogonality and the critical pair lemma has already been discussed in [3,8,19,20]: [3,8,19] deal with left-linear systems without critical pairs, and [20] deals with terminating or left-and-right-linear systems. We give an example of a nominal rewriting system whose confluence is shown by our criterion but cannot be shown by any of the criteria given in the previous papers (see Example 1). Moreover, in the present paper, we do not particularly assume α-stability [19] of nominal rewriting systems. This is in contrast to [3,19,20] where confluence criteria are considered only for α-stable rewriting systems. We give an example of a nominal rewriting system that is not α-stable and that is shown to be confluent by our criterion (see Example 2).

The structure of our confluence proof follows the so-called inductive method for first-order orthogonal term rewriting systems as explained, e.g. in Chap. 9 of [4, pp. 208–211], but much more complicated than the first-order case by the above-mentioned difficulties. Our confluence proof also shows that such an inductive method can be adapted to cases with critical pairs.

The paper is organised as follows. In Sect. 2, we recall basic notions of nominal rewriting and critical pairs. In Sect. 3, we prove confluence for some classes of nominal rewriting systems via the parallel closure theorem and its generalisation. In Sect. 4, we conclude with discussion on related work.

2 Nominal Rewriting

Nominal rewriting [8] is a framework that extends first-order term rewriting by a binding mechanism. In this section, we recall basic definitions on nominal terms and nominal rewriting, following [19,20]. For further descriptions and examples, see [8,19,20].

2.1 Nominal Terms

A *nominal signature* Σ is a set of *function symbols* ranged over by $f, g, \ldots$. We fix a countably infinite set $\mathcal{X}$ of *variables* ranged over by $X, Y, Z, \ldots$, and a countably infinite set $\mathcal{A}$ of *atoms* ranged over by $a, b, c, \ldots$, and assume that Σ, $\mathcal{X}$ and $\mathcal{A}$ are pairwise disjoint. Unless otherwise stated, different meta-variables for objects in Σ, $\mathcal{X}$ or $\mathcal{A}$ denote different objects. A *swapping* is a pair of atoms, written $(a\ b)$. *Permutations* π are bijections on $\mathcal{A}$ such that the set of atoms for which $a \neq \pi(a)$ is finite. Permutations are represented by lists of swappings applied in the right-to-left order. For example, $((b\ c)(a\ b))(a) = c$, $((b\ c)(a\ b))(b) = a$, $((b\ c)(a\ b))(c) = b$. We write Id for the identity permutation, π^{-1} for the inverse of π, and $\pi \circ \pi'$ for the composition of π' and π, i.e., $(\pi \circ \pi')(a) = \pi(\pi'(a))$.

Nominal terms, or simply *terms*, are generated by the grammar

$$t, s ::= a \mid \pi{\cdot}X \mid [a]t \mid f\ t \mid \langle t_1, \ldots, t_n \rangle$$

and called, respectively, atoms, moderated variables, abstractions, function applications and tuples. We abbreviate $Id{\cdot}X$ as X if there is no ambiguity. $f\ \langle\rangle$ is abbreviated as f, and referred to as a *constant*. An abstraction $[a]t$ is intended to represent t with a bound. We write $V(t)(\subseteq \mathcal{X})$ for the set of variables occurring in t. A *linear* term is a term in which any variable occurs at most once.

Positions are finite sequences of positive integers. The empty sequence is denoted by ε. For positions p, q, we write $p \preceq q$ if there exists a position o such that $q = po$. We write $p \parallel q$ for $p \not\preceq q$ and $q \not\preceq p$. The set of positions in a term t, denoted by $Pos(t)$, is defined as follows: $Pos(a) = Pos(\pi{\cdot}X) = \{\varepsilon\}$; $Pos([a]t) = Pos(f\ t) = \{1p \mid p \in Pos(t)\} \cup \{\varepsilon\}$; $Pos(\langle t_1, \ldots, t_n \rangle) = \bigcup_i \{ip \mid p \in Pos(t_i)\} \cup \{\varepsilon\}$. The subterm of t at a position $p \in Pos(t)$ is written as $t|_p$. We write $s \subseteq t$ if s is a subterm occurrence of t, and write $s \subset t$ if $s \subseteq t$ and $s \neq t$. A position $p \in Pos(t)$ is a *variable position* in t if $t|_p$ is a moderated variable. The set of variable positions in t is denoted by $Pos_{\mathcal{X}}(t)$. The size $|t|$ of a term t is defined as the number of elements in $Pos(t)$.

Next, two kinds of permutation actions $\pi{\cdot}t$ and t^π, which operate on terms extending a permutation on atoms, are defined as follows:

$$\begin{array}{rlrl}
\pi{\cdot}a &= \pi(a) & a^\pi &= \pi(a) \\
\pi{\cdot}(\pi'{\cdot}X) &= (\pi \circ \pi'){\cdot}X & (\pi'{\cdot}X)^\pi &= (\pi \circ \pi' \circ \pi^{-1}){\cdot}X \\
\pi{\cdot}([a]t) &= [\pi{\cdot}a](\pi{\cdot}t) & ([a]t)^\pi &= [a^\pi]t^\pi \\
\pi{\cdot}(f\ t) &= f\ \pi{\cdot}t & (f\ t)^\pi &= f\ t^\pi \\
\pi{\cdot}\langle t_1, \ldots, t_n \rangle &= \langle \pi{\cdot}t_1, \ldots, \pi{\cdot}t_n \rangle & \langle t_1, \ldots, t_n \rangle^\pi &= \langle t_1^\pi, \ldots, t_n^\pi \rangle
\end{array}$$

The difference between the two consists in the clause for moderated variables. In particular, when $\pi' = Id$, π is suspended before X in the first action as $\pi\cdot(Id\cdot X) = (\pi \circ Id)\cdot X = \pi\cdot X$, while in the second action π has no effect as $(Id\cdot X)^{\pi} = (\pi \circ Id \circ \pi^{-1})\cdot X = Id\cdot X$. Note also that the permutation actions do not change the set of positions, i.e. $Pos(\pi\cdot t) = Pos(t^{\pi}) = Pos(t)$.

A *context* is a term in which a distinguished constant $\Box$ occurs. Contexts having precisely one $\Box$ are written as $C[\,]$. The term obtained from a context C by replacing each $\Box$ at positions p_i by terms t_i is written as $C[t_1,\ldots,t_n]_{p_1,\ldots,p_n}$ or simply $C[t_1,\ldots,t_n]$. Similarly, the term obtained from a term s by replacing each subterm at positions p_i by terms t_i is written as $s[t_1,\ldots,t_n]_{p_1,\ldots,p_n}$.

A *substitution* σ is a map from variables to terms. Substitutions act on variables, without avoiding capture of atoms, where substituting $\sigma(X)$ for X of a moderated variable $\pi\cdot X$ induces a permutation action $\pi\cdot(\sigma(X))$. The application of a substitution σ on a term t is written as $t\sigma$. For a permutation π and a substitution σ, we define the substitution $\pi\cdot\sigma$ by $(\pi\cdot\sigma)(X) = \pi\cdot(\sigma(X))$.

The following properties hold.

Proposition 1. *$\pi\cdot(\pi'\cdot t) = (\pi \circ \pi')\cdot t$ and $(t^{\pi})^{\pi'} = t^{\pi' \circ \pi}$.*

Proposition 2 ([8,22])**.** *$\pi\cdot(t\sigma) = (\pi\cdot t)\sigma$.*

Lemma 1. *$\pi\cdot(t\sigma) = t^{\pi}(\pi\cdot\sigma)$.*

2.2 Freshness Constraints and α-Equivalence

A pair $a\#t$ of an atom a and a term t is called a *freshness constraint.* A finite set $\nabla \subseteq \{a\#X \mid a \in \mathcal{A}, X \in \mathcal{X}\}$ is called a *freshness context.* For a freshness context ∇, we define $V(\nabla) = \{X \in \mathcal{X} \mid \exists a.\, a\#X \in \nabla\}$, $\nabla^{\pi} = \{a^{\pi}\#X \mid a\#X \in \nabla\}$ and $\nabla\sigma = \{a\#\sigma(X) \mid a\#X \in \nabla\}$.

The rules in Fig. 1 define the relation $\nabla \vdash a\#t$, which means that $a\#t$ is satisfied under the freshness context ∇.

$$\frac{}{\nabla \vdash a\#b} \qquad \frac{\nabla \vdash a\#t}{\nabla \vdash a\#f\ t} \qquad \frac{\nabla \vdash a\#t_1 \quad \cdots \quad \nabla \vdash a\#t_n}{\nabla \vdash a\#\langle t_1,\ldots,t_n\rangle}$$

$$\frac{}{\nabla \vdash a\#[a]t} \qquad \frac{\nabla \vdash a\#t}{\nabla \vdash a\#[b]t} \qquad \frac{\pi^{-1}\cdot a\#X \in \nabla}{\nabla \vdash a\#\pi\cdot X}$$

Fig. 1. Rules for freshness constraints

The rules in Fig. 2 define the relation $\nabla \vdash t \approx_{\alpha} s$, which means that t is α-equivalent to s under the freshness context ∇. $ds(\pi,\pi')$ in the last rule denotes the set $\{a \in \mathcal{A} \mid \pi\cdot a \neq \pi'\cdot a\}$. Note that if $\nabla \vdash t \approx_{\alpha} s$ then $Pos(t) = Pos(s)$.

The following properties are shown in [8,22].

$$\frac{}{\nabla \vdash a \approx_\alpha a} \qquad \frac{\nabla \vdash t \approx_\alpha s}{\nabla \vdash f\, t \approx_\alpha f\, s} \qquad \frac{\nabla \vdash t_1 \approx_\alpha s_1 \quad \cdots \quad \nabla \vdash t_n \approx_\alpha s_n}{\nabla \vdash \langle t_1, \ldots, t_n \rangle \approx_\alpha \langle s_1, \ldots, s_n \rangle}$$

$$\frac{\nabla \vdash t \approx_\alpha s}{\nabla \vdash [a]t \approx_\alpha [a]s} \qquad \frac{\nabla \vdash (a\ b){\cdot}t \approx_\alpha s \quad \nabla \vdash b\#t}{\nabla \vdash [a]t \approx_\alpha [b]s} \qquad \frac{\forall a \in ds(\pi, \pi').\ a\#X \in \nabla}{\nabla \vdash \pi{\cdot}X \approx_\alpha \pi'{\cdot}X}$$

Fig. 2. Rules for α-equivalence

Proposition 3. *1.* $\nabla \vdash a\#t$ *if and only if* $\nabla \vdash \pi{\cdot}a\#\pi{\cdot}t$.
2. $\nabla \vdash t \approx_\alpha s$ *if and only if* $\nabla \vdash \pi{\cdot}t \approx_\alpha \pi{\cdot}s$.
3. If $\nabla \vdash a\#t$ *and* $\nabla \vdash t \approx_\alpha s$ *then* $\nabla \vdash a\#s$.
4. $\forall a \in ds(\pi, \pi').\ \nabla \vdash a\#t$ *if and only if* $\nabla \vdash \pi{\cdot}t \approx_\alpha \pi'{\cdot}t$.

Proposition 4. *For any freshness context* ∇, *the binary relation* $\nabla \vdash - \approx_\alpha -$ *is a congruence (i.e. an equivalence relation that is closed under any context).*

In the sequel, $\vdash$ is extended to mean to hold for all members of a set (or a sequence) on the RHS.

2.3 Nominal Rewriting Systems

Nominal rewrite rules and nominal rewriting systems are defined as follows.

Definition 1 (Nominal rewrite rule). A *nominal rewrite rule*, or simply *rewrite rule*, is a triple of a freshness context ∇ and terms l and r such that $V(\nabla) \cup V(r) \subseteq V(l)$ and l is not a moderated variable. We write $\nabla \vdash l \to r$ for a rewrite rule, and identify rewrite rules modulo renaming of variables. A rewrite rule $\nabla \vdash l \to r$ is *left-linear* if l is linear. For a rewrite rule $R = \nabla \vdash l \to r$ and a permutation π, we define R^π as $\nabla^\pi \vdash l^\pi \to r^\pi$.

Definition 2 (Nominal rewriting system). A *nominal rewriting system*, or simply *rewriting system*, is a finite set of rewrite rules. A rewriting system is *left-linear* if so are all its rewrite rules.

Definition 3 (Rewrite relation). Let $R = \nabla \vdash l \to r$ be a rewrite rule. For a freshness context Δ and terms s and t, the *rewrite relation* is defined by

$$\Delta \vdash s \to_{\langle R,\pi,p,\sigma\rangle} t \stackrel{\text{def}}{\iff} \Delta \vdash \nabla^\pi\sigma,\ s = C[s']_p,\ \Delta \vdash s' \approx_\alpha l^\pi\sigma,\ t = C[r^\pi\sigma]_p$$

where $V(l) \cap (V(\Delta) \cup V(s)) = \emptyset$. We write $\Delta \vdash s \xrightarrow{p}_R t$ if there exist π and σ such that $\Delta \vdash s \to_{\langle R,\pi,p,\sigma\rangle} t$. We write $\Delta \vdash s \to_{\langle R,\pi\rangle} t$ if there exist p and σ such that $\Delta \vdash s \to_{\langle R,\pi,p,\sigma\rangle} t$. We write $\Delta \vdash s \to_R t$ if there exists π such that $\Delta \vdash s \to_{\langle R,\pi\rangle} t$. For a rewriting system $\mathcal{R}$, we write $\Delta \vdash s \to_{\mathcal{R}} t$ if there exists $R \in \mathcal{R}$ such that $\Delta \vdash s \to_R t$.

Lemma 2. *If* $\Delta \vdash s \to_{\langle R,\pi,p,\sigma\rangle} t$ *then* $\Delta \vdash \tau{\cdot}s \to_{\langle R,\tau\circ\pi,p,\tau{\cdot}\sigma\rangle} \tau{\cdot}t$.

In the following, a binary relation $\Delta \vdash - \bowtie -$ ($\bowtie$ is $\rightarrow_R$, $\approx_\alpha$, etc.) with a fixed freshness context Δ is called the relation $\bowtie$ under Δ or simply the relation $\bowtie$ if there is no ambiguity. If a relation $\bowtie$ is written using $\rightarrow$ then the inverse is written using $\leftarrow$. Also, we write $\bowtie^=$ for the reflexive closure and $\bowtie^*$ for the reflexive transitive closure. We use $\circ$ for the composition of relations. We write $\Delta \vdash s_1 \bowtie_1 s_2 \bowtie_2 \ldots \bowtie_{n-1} s_n$ for $\Delta \vdash s_i \bowtie_i s_{i+1}$ $(1 \leq i < n)$.

2.4 Basic Critical Pairs

In this subsection, we define our notion of critical pairs, following [20].

First, we recall unification of nominal terms. Let P be a set of equations and freshness constraints $\{s_1 \approx t_1, \ldots, s_m \approx t_m, a_1 \# u_1, \ldots, a_n \# u_n\}$ (where a_i and a_j may denote the same atom). Then, P is *unifiable* if there exist a freshness context Γ and a substitution θ such that $\Gamma \vdash s_1\theta \approx_\alpha t_1\theta, \ldots, s_m\theta \approx_\alpha t_m\theta, a_1\#u_1\theta, \ldots, a_n\#u_n\theta$; the pair $\langle \Gamma, \theta \rangle$ is called a *unifier* of P. It is shown in [22] that the unification problem for nominal terms is decidable. Moreover, if P is unifiable then there exists a *most general unifier* (*mgu* for short) of P, where an mgu of P is a unifier $\langle \Gamma, \theta \rangle$ of P such that for any unifier $\langle \Delta, \sigma \rangle$ of P, there exists a substitution δ such that $\Delta \vdash \Gamma\delta$ and $\Delta \vdash X\theta\delta \approx_\alpha X\sigma$ for any variable X.

Definition 4 (Basic critical pair). Let $R_i = \nabla_i \vdash l_i \rightarrow r_i$ $(i = 1, 2)$ be rewrite rules. We assume w.l.o.g. $V(l_1) \cap V(l_2) = \emptyset$. Let $\nabla_1 \cup \nabla_2^\pi \cup \{l_1 \approx l_2^\pi|_p\}$ be unifiable for some permutation π and a non-variable position p such that $l_2 = L[l_2|_p]_p$, and let $\langle \Gamma, \theta \rangle$ be an mgu. Then, $\Gamma \vdash \langle L^\pi\theta[r_1\theta]_p, r_2^\pi\theta \rangle$ is called a *basic critical pair* (*BCP* for short) of R_1 and R_2. $BCP(R_1, R_2)$ denotes the set of all BCPs of R_1 and R_2, and $BCP(\mathcal{R})$ denotes the set $\bigcup_{R_i, R_j \in \mathcal{R}} BCP(R_i, R_j)$.

We remark that any BCP $\Gamma \vdash \langle L^\pi\theta[r_1\theta]_p, r_2^\pi\theta \rangle$ of R_1 and R_2 forms a peak, i.e., we have $\Gamma \vdash L^\pi\theta[r_1\theta]_p \leftarrow_{\langle R_1, Id, p, \theta \rangle} L^\pi\theta[l_2^\pi|_p\theta]_p = (L[l_2|_p]_p)^\pi\theta = l_2^\pi\theta \rightarrow_{\langle R_2, \pi, \varepsilon, \theta \rangle} r_2^\pi\theta$.

2.5 Uniform Rewrite Rules

In the rest of the paper, we are concerned with confluence properties for particular classes of nominal rewriting systems. For this, we restrict rewriting systems by some conditions. First we consider the uniformity condition [8]. Intuitively, uniformity means that if an atom a is not free in s and s rewrites to t then a is not free in t.

Definition 5 (Uniformity). A rewrite rule $\nabla \vdash l \rightarrow r$ is *uniform* if for any atom a and any freshness context Δ, $\Delta \vdash \nabla$ and $\Delta \vdash a\#l$ imply $\Delta \vdash a\#r$. A rewriting system is *uniform* if so are all its rewrite rules.

The following properties of uniform rewrite rules are important and will be used in the sequel.

Proposition 5 ([8]). *Suppose $\Delta \vdash s \to_R t$ for a uniform rewrite rule R. Then, $\Delta \vdash a\#s$ implies $\Delta \vdash a\#t$.*

Lemma 3. *Let $\nabla \vdash l \to r$ be a uniform rewrite rule, and let $\Delta \vdash C[l^\pi \sigma]_p \approx_\alpha \hat{C}[u]_p$. Then there exists a permutation $\hat{\pi}$ such that $\Delta \vdash l^\pi \sigma \approx_\alpha \hat{\pi} \cdot u$ and $\Delta \vdash C[r^\pi \sigma]_p \approx_\alpha \hat{C}[\hat{\pi}^{-1} \cdot (r^\pi \sigma)]_p$.*

Proof. We prove the following generalised statement: if $\Delta \vdash \tau \cdot (C_1[u]_p) \approx_\alpha C_2[v]_p$ then there exists a permutation π satisfying

1. $\Delta \vdash (\pi \circ \tau) \cdot u \approx_\alpha v$.
2. Let u' and v' be terms such that (i) $\forall a \in \mathcal{A}.\ \Delta \vdash a\#u \Longrightarrow \Delta \vdash a\#u'$, and (ii) $\Delta \vdash (\pi \circ \tau) \cdot u' \approx_\alpha v'$. Then $\Delta \vdash \tau \cdot (C_1[u']_p) \approx_\alpha C_2[v']_p$. ((i) is equivalent to $\forall a \in \mathcal{A}.\ \Delta \vdash a\#v \Longrightarrow \Delta \vdash a\#v'$ under 1 and (ii).)

The lemma is obtained as a special case of this where $\tau = Id$, $C_1 = \hat{C}$, $C_2 = C$, $\pi = \hat{\pi}$, $v = l^\pi \sigma$, $v' = r^\pi \sigma$ and $u' = \hat{\pi}^{-1} \cdot (r^\pi \sigma)$. The proof of the above statement is by induction on the context $C_1[\,]$. □

Lemma 4. *Let R be a uniform rewrite rule. If $\Delta \vdash s' \approx_\alpha s \to_{\langle R,\pi,p,\sigma \rangle} t$, then there exist π', σ', t' such that $\Delta \vdash s' \to_{\langle R,\pi',p,\sigma' \rangle} t' \approx_\alpha t$.*

Proof. Noting that $\Delta \vdash s \approx_\alpha s'$ implies $Pos(s) = Pos(s')$, we obtain the lemma from Lemma 3 by taking $\pi' = \hat{\pi}^{-1} \circ \pi$ and $\sigma' = \hat{\pi}^{-1} \cdot \sigma$. □

3 Confluence of Left-Linear Nominal Rewriting Systems

In this section, we study confluence properties of left-linear nominal rewriting systems. Specifically, we prove a version of Huet's parallel closure theorem [10] in the setting of nominal rewriting. Huet's parallel closure theorem states that all left-linear parallel closed term rewriting systems are confluent, where a term rewriting system is parallel closed if all its critical pairs are joinable in one-step parallel reduction from left to right. (It is important to note that critical pairs are ordered.) We also prove a generalisation of the theorem, analysing overlaps at the root as in the case of term rewriting [21].

First we introduce, for precise treatment of α-equivalence, confluence properties modulo the equivalence relation $\approx_\alpha$ in terms of abstract reduction systems [14].

Definition 6. Let $\mathcal{R}$ be a nominal rewriting system.

1. s and t are *joinable modulo* $\approx_\alpha$ under a freshness context Δ, denoted by $\Delta \vdash s \downarrow_{\approx_\alpha} t$, iff $\Delta \vdash s\ (\to^*_\mathcal{R} \circ \approx_\alpha \circ \leftarrow^*_\mathcal{R})\ t$.
2. $\to_\mathcal{R}$ is *confluent modulo* $\approx_\alpha$ iff $\Delta \vdash s\ (\leftarrow^*_\mathcal{R} \circ \to^*_\mathcal{R})\ t$ implies $\Delta \vdash s \downarrow_{\approx_\alpha} t$.
3. $\to_\mathcal{R}$ is *Church-Rosser modulo* $\approx_\alpha$ iff $\Delta \vdash s\ (\leftarrow_\mathcal{R} \cup \to_\mathcal{R} \cup \approx_\alpha)^*\ t$ implies $\Delta \vdash s \downarrow_{\approx_\alpha} t$.
4. $\to_\mathcal{R}$ is *strongly locally confluent modulo* $\approx_\alpha$ iff $\Delta \vdash s\ (\leftarrow_\mathcal{R} \circ \to_\mathcal{R})\ t$ implies $\Delta \vdash s\ (\to^=_\mathcal{R} \circ \approx_\alpha \circ \leftarrow^*_\mathcal{R})\ t$.

5. $\to_\mathcal{R}$ is *strongly compatible with* $\approx_\alpha$ iff $\Delta \vdash s \ (\approx_\alpha \circ \to_\mathcal{R}) \ t$ implies $\Delta \vdash s \ (\to_\mathcal{R}^{=} \circ \approx_\alpha) \ t$.

It is known that Church-Rosser modulo an equivalence relation $\sim$ is a stronger property than confluence modulo $\sim$ [14]. So in the rest of this section we aim to show Church-Rosser modulo $\approx_\alpha$ for some class of left-linear uniform nominal rewriting systems through the theorems that can be seen as extensions of Huet's parallel closure theorem [10] and its generalisation [21].

3.1 Parallel Reduction

A key notion for proving confluence of left-linear rewriting systems is parallel reduction. Here we define it inductively, using a particular kind of contexts.

Definition 7. The *grammatical contexts*, ranged over by G, are the contexts defined by

$$G ::= a \mid \pi{\cdot}X \mid [a]\Box \mid f\ \Box \mid \langle \Box_1, \ldots, \Box_n \rangle$$

Let $\mathcal{R}$ be a nominal rewriting system. For a given freshness context Δ, we define the relation $\Delta \vdash - \twoheadrightarrow\!\!\!\!\!\!\,+\!\!\!\!+\ _\mathcal{R} -$ inductively by the following rules:

$$\frac{\Delta \vdash s_1 \mathrel{+\!\!\!\!+\!\!\!\!\rightarrow}_\mathcal{R} t_1 \quad \cdots \quad \Delta \vdash s_n \mathrel{+\!\!\!\!+\!\!\!\!\rightarrow}_\mathcal{R} t_n}{\Delta \vdash G[s_1, \ldots, s_n] \mathrel{+\!\!\!\!+\!\!\!\!\rightarrow}_\mathcal{R} G[t_1, \ldots, t_n]} \ (\mathsf{C}) \qquad \frac{\Delta \vdash s \to_{\langle R, \pi, \varepsilon, \sigma \rangle} t \quad R \in \mathcal{R}}{\Delta \vdash s \mathrel{+\!\!\!\!+\!\!\!\!\rightarrow}_\mathcal{R} t} \ (\mathsf{B})$$

where $n\,(\geq 0)$ depends on the form of G. We define $\Delta \vdash \sigma \mathrel{+\!\!\!\!+\!\!\!\!\rightarrow}_\mathcal{R} \delta$ by $\forall X \in \mathcal{X}.\ \Delta \vdash X\sigma \mathrel{+\!\!\!\!+\!\!\!\!\rightarrow}_\mathcal{R} X\delta$.

The relation $\Delta \vdash s \mathrel{+\!\!\!\!+\!\!\!\!\rightarrow}_\mathcal{R} t$ can also be defined by $\Delta \vdash C[s_1, \ldots, s_n]_{p_1,\ldots,p_n} \mathrel{+\!\!\!\!+\!\!\!\!\rightarrow}_\mathcal{R} C[t_1, \ldots, t_n]_{p_1,\ldots,p_n}$ for some context C, where $\Delta \vdash s_i \to_{R_i} t_i$ for some $R_i \in \mathcal{R}$, and $p_i \parallel p_j$ for $i \neq j$. In that case, we write $\Delta \vdash s \overset{P}{\mathrel{+\!\!\!\!+\!\!\!\!\rightarrow}}_\mathcal{R} t$ where $P = \{p_1, \cdots, p_n\}$ (P is uniquely determined from the derivation of $\Delta \vdash s \mathrel{+\!\!\!\!+\!\!\!\!\rightarrow}_\mathcal{R} t$).

Lemma 5. *1.* $\Delta \vdash s \mathrel{+\!\!\!\!+\!\!\!\!\rightarrow}_\mathcal{R} s$.
2. If $\Delta \vdash s \mathrel{+\!\!\!\!+\!\!\!\!\rightarrow}_\mathcal{R} t$ *then* $\Delta \vdash C[s] \mathrel{+\!\!\!\!+\!\!\!\!\rightarrow}_\mathcal{R} C[t]$.
3. If $\Delta \vdash s \to_{\langle R, \pi, p, \sigma \rangle} t$ *and* $R \in \mathcal{R}$ *then* $\Delta \vdash s \mathrel{+\!\!\!\!+\!\!\!\!\rightarrow}_\mathcal{R} t$.
4. If $\Delta \vdash s \mathrel{+\!\!\!\!+\!\!\!\!\rightarrow}_\mathcal{R} t$ *then* $\Delta \vdash s \to_\mathcal{R}^* t$.

Proof. 1. By induction on s.
2. By induction on the context $C[\,]$.
3. By 2 and the rule (B).
4. By induction on the derivation of $\Delta \vdash s \mathrel{+\!\!\!\!+\!\!\!\!\rightarrow}_\mathcal{R} t$. □

Lemma 6. *If* $\Delta \vdash s \mathrel{+\!\!\!\!+\!\!\!\!\rightarrow}_\mathcal{R} t$ *then* $\Delta \vdash \pi{\cdot}s \mathrel{+\!\!\!\!+\!\!\!\!\rightarrow}_\mathcal{R} \pi{\cdot}t$.

Proof. By induction on the derivation of $\Delta \vdash s \mathrel{+\!\!\!\!+\!\!\!\!\rightarrow}_\mathcal{R} t$. If the last applied rule in the derivation is (B), then we use Lemma 2. □

Lemma 7. *If* $\Delta \vdash \sigma \mathrel{+\!\!\!\!+\!\!\!\!\rightarrow}_\mathcal{R} \delta$ *then* $\Delta \vdash s\sigma \mathrel{+\!\!\!\!+\!\!\!\!\rightarrow}_\mathcal{R} s\delta$.

Proof. By induction on s. If $s = \pi{\cdot}X$, then we use Lemma 6. □

Lemma 8. *Let $\mathcal{R}$ be a uniform nominal rewriting system. If $\Delta \vdash a\#s$ and $\Delta \vdash s \twoheadrightarrow_{\mathcal{R}} t$ then $\Delta \vdash a\#t$.*

Proof. By Proposition 5 and Lemma 5(4). □

We define the notions in Definition 6 for $\twoheadrightarrow_{\mathcal{R}}$ as well. Our aim is to prove strong local confluence modulo $\approx_\alpha$ (Theorems 1 and 2), which together with strong compatibility with $\approx_\alpha$ (Lemma 9) yields Church-Rosser modulo $\approx_\alpha$ of $\twoheadrightarrow_{\mathcal{R}}$ (and hence of $\rightarrow_{\mathcal{R}}$).

Lemma 9 (Strong compatibility with $\approx_\alpha$). *Let $\mathcal{R}$ be a uniform rewriting system. If $\Delta \vdash s' \approx_\alpha s \twoheadrightarrow_{\mathcal{R}} t$ then there exists t' such that $\Delta \vdash s' \twoheadrightarrow_{\mathcal{R}} t' \approx_\alpha t$.*

Proof. By induction on the derivation of $\Delta \vdash s \twoheadrightarrow_{\mathcal{R}} t$. If the last applied rule in the derivation is (B), then the claim follows by Lemma 4. Among the other cases, we treat the case where $G = [a]\Box$. Then the last part of the derivation has the form

$$\frac{\Delta \vdash s_1 \twoheadrightarrow_{\mathcal{R}} t_1}{\Delta \vdash [a]s_1 \twoheadrightarrow_{\mathcal{R}} [a]t_1}\ (\mathsf{C})$$

where $[a]s_1 = s$ and $[a]t_1 = t$. Now we have two cases.

(a) $s' = [a]s'_1$ and $\Delta \vdash [a]s'_1 \approx_\alpha [a]s_1$.
Then $\Delta \vdash s'_1 \approx_\alpha s_1$, and so by the induction hypothesis, there exists t'_1 such that $\Delta \vdash s'_1 \twoheadrightarrow_{\mathcal{R}} t'_1 \approx_\alpha t_1$. Hence we have $\Delta \vdash [a]s'_1 \twoheadrightarrow_{\mathcal{R}} [a]t'_1 \approx_\alpha [a]t_1$.

(b) $s' = [b]s'_1$ and $\Delta \vdash [b]s'_1 \approx_\alpha [a]s_1$.
Then $\Delta \vdash s_1 \approx_\alpha (a\ b){\cdot}s'_1$ and $\Delta \vdash a\#s'_1$. So by the induction hypothesis, there exists t'_1 such that $\Delta \vdash (a\ b){\cdot}s'_1 \twoheadrightarrow_{\mathcal{R}} t'_1 \approx_\alpha t_1$. By taking $\pi = (a\ b)$ in Lemma 6, we have $\Delta \vdash s'_1 \twoheadrightarrow_{\mathcal{R}} (a\ b){\cdot}t'_1$, and by Lemma 8, we have $\Delta \vdash a\#(a\ b){\cdot}t'_1$. Hence, we obtain the following derivations, from which the claim follows.

$$\frac{\Delta \vdash t'_1 \approx_\alpha t_1 \qquad \Delta \vdash a\#(a\ b){\cdot}t'_1}{\Delta \vdash [b](a\ b){\cdot}t'_1 \approx_\alpha [a]t_1} \quad \text{and} \quad \frac{\Delta \vdash s'_1 \twoheadrightarrow_{\mathcal{R}} (a\ b){\cdot}t'_1}{\Delta \vdash [b]s'_1 \twoheadrightarrow_{\mathcal{R}} [b](a\ b){\cdot}t'_1}\ (\mathsf{C})$$

The cases where $G \neq [a]\Box$ are simpler. □

A key lemma to the parallel closure theorem is Lemma 11, which corresponds to Lemma 9.3.10 of [4] in the first-order case. Here we employ a version of the statement that can be adapted to cases where critical pairs exist. First we show a lemma to address the separated case of moderated variables.

Lemma 10. *Let $\mathcal{R}$ be a uniform rewriting system. Then, if $\Delta \vdash \nabla\sigma$, $\Delta \vdash s \approx_\alpha \pi{\cdot}X\sigma$ and $\Delta \vdash s \twoheadrightarrow_{\mathcal{R}} t$ then there exists δ such that $\Delta \vdash \nabla\delta$, $\Delta \vdash t \approx_\alpha \pi{\cdot}X\delta$, $\Delta \vdash \sigma \twoheadrightarrow_{\mathcal{R}} \delta$ and for any $Y \neq X$, $Y\sigma = Y\delta$.*

Proof. From $\Delta \vdash s \approx_\alpha \pi{\cdot}X\sigma$, we have $\Delta \vdash \pi^{-1}{\cdot}s \approx_\alpha X\sigma$, and from $\Delta \vdash s \twoheadrightarrow\!\!\!\!\!\!+\;_{\mathcal{R}} t$, we have $\Delta \vdash \pi^{-1}{\cdot}s \twoheadrightarrow_{\mathcal{R}} \pi^{-1}{\cdot}t$ by Lemma 6. Hence by Lemma 9, there exists t' such that $\Delta \vdash X\sigma \twoheadrightarrow_{\mathcal{R}} t' \approx_\alpha \pi^{-1}{\cdot}t$. We take δ defined by $X\delta = t'$ and $Y\delta = Y\sigma$ for any $Y \neq X$. Then we have $\Delta \vdash t \approx_\alpha \pi{\cdot}X\delta$ and $\Delta \vdash \sigma \twoheadrightarrow_{\mathcal{R}} \delta$. Since $\mathcal{R}$ is uniform, it follows from Lemma 8 that if $\Delta \vdash a\#X\sigma$ then $\Delta \vdash a\#t'(= X\delta)$. Hence, from $\Delta \vdash \nabla\sigma$, we have $\Delta \vdash \nabla\delta$. □

Lemma 11. *Let $\mathcal{R}$ be a uniform rewriting system. Then, for any linear term l, if $\Delta \vdash \nabla^\pi\sigma$, $\Delta \vdash s \approx_\alpha l\sigma$ and $\Delta \vdash s \overset{P}{\twoheadrightarrow}_{\mathcal{R}} t$ where $\forall p \in P. \exists o \in Pos_{\mathcal{X}}(l). o \preceq p$ then there exists δ such that $\Delta \vdash \nabla^\pi\delta$, $\Delta \vdash t \approx_\alpha l\delta$, $\Delta \vdash \sigma \twoheadrightarrow_{\mathcal{R}} \delta$ and for any $X \notin V(l)$, $X\sigma = X\delta$.*

Proof. By induction on l. The case where l is a moderated variable $\pi{\cdot}X$ follows from Lemma 10. For the other cases, since $\forall p \in P. \exists o \in Pos_{\mathcal{X}}(l). o \preceq p$, the last rule used in the derivation of $\Delta \vdash s \twoheadrightarrow_{\mathcal{R}} t$ must be (C). We proceed by case analysis according to the form of l. Here we consider the cases where $l = \langle l_1, \ldots, l_n\rangle$ and $l = [a]l_1$.

1. $l = \langle l_1, \ldots, l_n\rangle$. Since $\Delta \vdash s \approx_\alpha l\sigma$, s is of the form $\langle s_1, \ldots, s_n\rangle$. Then the last part of the derivation of $\Delta \vdash s \twoheadrightarrow_{\mathcal{R}} t$ has the form

$$\frac{\Delta \vdash s_1 \twoheadrightarrow_{\mathcal{R}} t_1 \quad \ldots \quad \Delta \vdash s_n \twoheadrightarrow_{\mathcal{R}} t_n}{\Delta \vdash \langle s_1, \ldots, s_n\rangle \twoheadrightarrow_{\mathcal{R}} \langle t_1, \ldots, t_n\rangle}\ (\mathsf{C})$$

and for each $i \in \{1, \ldots, n\}$, $\Delta \vdash s_i \approx_\alpha l_i\sigma$. By the induction hypothesis, there exist δ_i's such that $\Delta \vdash \nabla^\pi\delta_i$, $\Delta \vdash t_i \approx_\alpha l_i\delta_i$, $\Delta \vdash \sigma \twoheadrightarrow_{\mathcal{R}} \delta_i$ and $\forall X \notin V(l_i). X\sigma = X\delta_i$. Since l is linear, we can take δ such that if $X \in V(l_i)$ then $X\delta = X\delta_i$ and if $X \notin V(l)$ then $X\delta = X\sigma$. It is easy to check that this δ satisfies the required condition.

2. $l = [a]l_1$. Since $\Delta \vdash s \approx_\alpha [a]l_1\sigma$, we have two cases.
   (a) $s = [a]s_1$. Then $\Delta \vdash s_1 \approx_\alpha l_1\sigma$, and the last part of the derivation of $\Delta \vdash s \twoheadrightarrow_{\mathcal{R}} t$ has the form

$$\frac{\Delta \vdash s_1 \twoheadrightarrow_{\mathcal{R}} t_1}{\Delta \vdash [a]s_1 \twoheadrightarrow_{\mathcal{R}} [a]t_1}\ (\mathsf{C})$$

   Then by the induction hypothesis, there exists δ such that $\Delta \vdash \nabla^\pi\delta$, $\Delta \vdash t_1 \approx_\alpha l_1\delta$, $\Delta \vdash \sigma \twoheadrightarrow_{\mathcal{R}} \delta$ and $\forall X \notin V(l_1). X\sigma = X\delta$. By $\Delta \vdash t_1 \approx_\alpha l_1\delta$, we have $\Delta \vdash [a]t_1 \approx_\alpha [a]l_1\delta$. Since $V(l_1) = V(l)$, we have $\forall X \notin V(l). X\sigma = X\delta$. Thus we see that the claim holds.

   (b) $s = [b]s_1$. Then $\Delta \vdash (b\ a){\cdot}s_1 \approx_\alpha l_1\sigma$, $\Delta \vdash a\#s_1$, and the last part of the derivation of $\Delta \vdash s \twoheadrightarrow_{\mathcal{R}} t$ has the form

$$\frac{\Delta \vdash s_1 \twoheadrightarrow_{\mathcal{R}} t_1}{\Delta \vdash [b]s_1 \twoheadrightarrow_{\mathcal{R}} [b]t_1}\ (\mathsf{C})$$

   From $\Delta \vdash s_1 \twoheadrightarrow_{\mathcal{R}} t_1$, we have $\Delta \vdash (b\ a){\cdot}s_1 \twoheadrightarrow_{\mathcal{R}} (b\ a){\cdot}t_1$ by Lemma 6. Since $\mathcal{R}$ is uniform, it also follows $\Delta \vdash a\#t_1$ by Lemma 8. Hence $\Delta \vdash b\#(b\ a){\cdot}t_1$.

Thus, by the induction hypothesis, there exists δ such that $\Delta \vdash \nabla^\pi \delta$, $\Delta \vdash (b\ a) \cdot t_1 \approx_\alpha l_1 \delta$, $\Delta \vdash \sigma \twoheadrightarrow\!\!\!\!\!\!\!+\ _{\mathcal{R}} \delta$ and $\forall X \notin V(l_1). X\sigma = X\delta$. Then from $\Delta \vdash (b\ a) \cdot t_1 \approx_\alpha l_1 \delta$ and $\Delta \vdash a \# t_1$, it follows that $\Delta \vdash [b] t_1 \approx_\alpha [a] l_1 \delta$. Since $V(l_1) = V(l)$, we see that the claim holds. □

3.2 Confluence of Left-Linear Parallel Closed Rewriting Systems

In this subsection, we prove the main theorems of the paper: the parallel closure theorem (Theorem 1) and its generalisation (Theorem 2).

First, we state a lemma concerning substitutions.

Lemma 12 ([8]). *Let σ and σ' be substitutions such that $\forall X \in \mathcal{X}. \Delta \vdash X\sigma \approx_\alpha X\sigma'$. Then $\Delta \vdash t\sigma \approx_\alpha t\sigma'$ for any term t.*

The following can be seen as a critical pair lemma for left-linear systems.

Lemma 13. *Let $\mathcal{R}$ be a left-linear uniform rewriting system and let $R \in \mathcal{R}$. If $\Delta \vdash s_1 \overset{\varepsilon}{\leftarrow}_R s \overset{P}{\twoheadrightarrow\!\!\!\!\!\!+}_{\mathcal{R}} s_2$ then one of the following holds:*

1. *There exists a term t such that $\Delta \vdash s_1 \twoheadrightarrow\!\!\!\!\!\!+_{\mathcal{R}} t \leftarrow_R s_2$.*
2. *There exist $p \in P$, $R' \in \mathcal{R}$, $\Gamma \vdash \langle u, v \rangle \in BCP(R', R)$, s', π and θ such that $\Delta \vdash s \overset{p}{\rightarrow}_{R'} s' \overset{P \setminus \{p\}}{\twoheadrightarrow\!\!\!\!\!\!+}_{\mathcal{R}} s_2$, $\Delta \vdash \Gamma^\pi \theta$, $\Delta \vdash s' \approx_\alpha u^\pi \theta$ and $\Delta \vdash s_1 \approx_\alpha v^\pi \theta$.*

Proof. Let $R = \nabla \vdash l \to r \in \mathcal{R}$, and suppose $\Delta \vdash s_1 \leftarrow_{\langle R, \pi, \varepsilon, \sigma \rangle} s \overset{P}{\twoheadrightarrow\!\!\!\!\!\!+}_{\mathcal{R}} s_2$. Then by the definition of rewrite relation, we have $\Delta \vdash \nabla^\pi \sigma$, $\Delta \vdash s \approx_\alpha l^\pi \sigma$ and $s_1 = r^\pi \sigma$. Now we distinguish two cases.

- Case $\forall p \in P. \exists o \in Pos_{\mathcal{X}}(l). o \preceq p$.
  Then by Lemma 11, there exists δ such that $\Delta \vdash \nabla^\pi \delta$, $\Delta \vdash s_2 \approx_\alpha l^\pi \delta$ and $\Delta \vdash \sigma \twoheadrightarrow\!\!\!\!\!\!+_{\mathcal{R}} \delta$. Hence we have $\Delta \vdash s_2 \to_{\langle R, \pi, \varepsilon, \delta \rangle} r^\pi \delta$, and by Lemma 7, $\Delta \vdash r^\pi \sigma \twoheadrightarrow\!\!\!\!\!\!+_{\mathcal{R}} r^\pi \delta$. Thus, part 1 of the claim holds.
- Case $\exists p \in P. \neg \exists o \in Pos_{\mathcal{X}}(l). o \preceq p$.
  Then $p \in Pos(l) \setminus Pos_{\mathcal{X}}(l)$, and $\Delta \vdash s \to_{\langle R', \pi', p, \sigma' \rangle} s' \overset{P \setminus \{p\}}{\twoheadrightarrow\!\!\!\!\!\!+}_{\mathcal{R}} s_2$ for some $R' = \nabla' \vdash l' \to r' \in \mathcal{R}$, π', σ' and s'. Let L be the context with $l = L[l|_p]_p$. First we show claim I: the set $\nabla' \cup \nabla^{\breve{\pi}} \cup \{l' \approx l^{\breve{\pi}}|_p\}$ is unifiable for some $\breve{\pi}$.
  (Proof of claim I) By the definition of rewrite steps, we have $\Delta \vdash \nabla'^{\pi'} \sigma', \nabla^\pi \sigma, s|_p \approx_\alpha l'^{\pi'} \sigma', s \approx_\alpha l^\pi \sigma$. Thus, $\Delta \vdash s[l'^{\pi'} \sigma']_p \approx_\alpha s[s|_p]_p = s \approx_\alpha l^\pi \sigma$. Hence, $\Delta \vdash s[l'^{\pi'} \sigma']_p \approx_\alpha L^\pi \sigma [l^\pi|_p \sigma]_p$. Now, by Lemma 3, there exists $\hat{\pi}$ such that

$$\Delta \vdash l'^{\pi'} \sigma' \approx_\alpha \hat{\pi} \cdot (l^\pi|_p \sigma) \tag{3.1}$$

$$\Delta \vdash s[r'^{\pi'} \sigma']_p \approx_\alpha L^\pi \sigma [\hat{\pi}^{-1} \cdot (r'^{\pi'} \sigma')]_p \tag{3.2}$$

From $\Delta \vdash \nabla'^{\pi'} \sigma', \nabla^\pi \sigma$ and (3.1), we have

$$\Delta \vdash \nabla'(\pi'^{-1} \cdot \sigma'), \nabla^{\pi'^{-1} \circ \hat{\pi} \circ \pi}((\pi'^{-1} \circ \hat{\pi}) \cdot \sigma)$$

$$\Delta \vdash l'(\pi'^{-1} \cdot \sigma') \approx_\alpha l^{\pi'^{-1} \circ \hat{\pi} \circ \pi}|_p((\pi'^{-1} \circ \hat{\pi}) \cdot \sigma) \tag{3.3}$$

Now, let $\breve{\pi} = \pi'^{-1} \circ \hat{\pi} \circ \pi$ and let $\breve{\sigma}$ be the substitution such that $\breve{\sigma}(X) = (\pi'^{-1}{\cdot}\sigma')(X)$ for $X \in V(l')$, $\breve{\sigma}(X) = ((\pi'^{-1} \circ \hat{\pi}){\cdot}\sigma)(X)$ for $X \in V(l)$, and $\breve{\sigma}(X) = X$ otherwise, where we assume w.l.o.g. $V(l') \cap V(l) = \emptyset$. Then, the statement (3.3) equals $\Delta \vdash \nabla'\breve{\sigma}, \nabla^{\breve{\pi}}\breve{\sigma}, l'\breve{\sigma} \approx_\alpha l^{\breve{\pi}}|_p\breve{\sigma}$.

(End of the proof of claim I)

Thus, $\nabla' \cup \nabla^{\breve{\pi}} \cup \{l' \approx l^{\breve{\pi}}|_p\}$ is unifiable. Hence we have $\Gamma \vdash \langle L^{\breve{\pi}}\theta[r'\theta]_p, r^{\breve{\pi}}\theta\rangle \in BCP(R', R)$ where $\langle \Gamma, \theta\rangle$ is an mgu and so there is a substitution δ such that

$$\Delta \vdash \Gamma\delta \tag{3.4}$$

$$\forall X \in \mathcal{X}.\, \Delta \vdash X\theta\delta \approx_\alpha X\breve{\sigma} \tag{3.5}$$

Let $u = L^{\breve{\pi}}\theta[r'\theta]_p$ and $v = r^{\breve{\pi}}\theta$. In the following, we show claim II: with the BCP $\Gamma \vdash \langle u, v\rangle$, part 2 of the statement of the lemma holds.

(Proof of claim II) From the property (3.5) and Lemma 12, we have $\Delta \vdash r^{\breve{\pi}}\theta\delta \approx_\alpha r^{\breve{\pi}}\breve{\sigma}$. Hence $\Delta \vdash v\delta \approx_\alpha r^{\pi'^{-1}\circ\hat{\pi}\circ\pi}((\pi'^{-1} \circ \hat{\pi}){\cdot}\sigma)$, which means $\Delta \vdash v^{\hat{\pi}^{-1}\circ\pi'}((\hat{\pi}^{-1} \circ \pi'){\cdot}\delta) \approx_\alpha r^\pi\sigma$. Now, let $\hat{\pi}' = \hat{\pi}^{-1} \circ \pi'$ and $\delta' = (\hat{\pi}^{-1} \circ \pi'){\cdot}\delta$. Then we have $\Delta \vdash v^{\hat{\pi}'}\delta' \approx_\alpha r^\pi\sigma = s_1$. Also, from the property (3.4), we have $\Delta \vdash \Gamma^{\hat{\pi}'}\delta'$. It only remains to show $\Delta \vdash u^{\hat{\pi}'}\delta' \approx_\alpha s'$. Again, from the property (3.5) and Lemma 12, we have $\Delta \vdash L^{\breve{\pi}}[r']_p\theta\delta \approx_\alpha L^{\breve{\pi}}[r']_p\breve{\sigma}$. Hence $\Delta \vdash u\delta \approx_\alpha L^{\breve{\pi}}[r']_p\breve{\sigma} = L^{\breve{\pi}}\breve{\sigma}[r'\breve{\sigma}]_p = L^{\pi'^{-1}\circ\hat{\pi}\circ\pi}((\pi'^{-1} \circ \hat{\pi}){\cdot}\sigma)[r'(\pi'^{-1}{\cdot}\sigma')]_p$. Equivalently, $\Delta \vdash u^{\hat{\pi}^{-1}\circ\pi'}((\hat{\pi}^{-1} \circ \pi'){\cdot}\delta) \approx_\alpha L^\pi\sigma[\hat{\pi}^{-1}{\cdot}(r'^{\pi'}\sigma')]_p$. From this and (3.2), we have $\Delta \vdash u^{\hat{\pi}^{-1}\circ\pi'}((\hat{\pi}^{-1} \circ \pi'){\cdot}\delta) \approx_\alpha s[r'^{\pi'}\sigma']_p$, which means $\Delta \vdash u^{\hat{\pi}'}\delta' \approx_\alpha s[r'^{\pi'}\sigma']_p = s'$. (End of the proof of claim II) □

Before proceeding to Theorem 1, we state one more lemma.

Lemma 14. *1. If $\Gamma \vdash s \approx_\alpha t$ and $\Delta \vdash \Gamma^\pi\theta$ then $\Delta \vdash s^\pi\theta \approx_\alpha t^\pi\theta$.*
2. If $\Gamma \vdash s \to_R t$ and $\Delta \vdash \Gamma^\pi\theta$ then $\Delta \vdash s^\pi\theta \to_R t^\pi\theta$.
3. If $\Gamma \vdash s \mathrel{+\!\!\!\!\!\rightarrow}_{\mathcal{R}} t$ and $\Delta \vdash \Gamma^\pi\theta$ then $\Delta \vdash s^\pi\theta \mathrel{+\!\!\!\!\!\rightarrow}_{\mathcal{R}} t^\pi\theta$.

Now we show the parallel closure theorem which states that $\mathrel{+\!\!\!\!\!\rightarrow}_{\mathcal{R}}$ is strongly locally confluent modulo $\approx_\alpha$ for a class of left-linear nominal rewriting systems.

Definition 8. A nominal rewriting system $\mathcal{R}$ is *parallel closed* if for any $\Gamma \vdash \langle u, v\rangle \in BCP(\mathcal{R})$, $\Gamma \vdash u\ (\mathrel{+\!\!\!\!\!\rightarrow}_{\mathcal{R}} \circ \approx_\alpha)\ v$. A nominal rewriting system $\mathcal{R}$ is *weakly orthogonal* if it is left-linear and for any $\Gamma \vdash \langle u, v\rangle \in BCP(\mathcal{R})$, $\Gamma \vdash u \approx_\alpha v$.

Theorem 1 (Parallel closure theorem). *Let $\mathcal{R}$ be a left-linear parallel closed uniform rewriting system. If $\Delta \vdash t \mathrel{+\!\!\!\!\!\rightarrow}_{\mathcal{R}} t_1$ and $\Delta \vdash t \mathrel{+\!\!\!\!\!\rightarrow}_{\mathcal{R}} t_2$ then there exist t_1' and t_2' such that $\Delta \vdash t_1 \mathrel{+\!\!\!\!\!\rightarrow}_{\mathcal{R}} t_1'$, $\Delta \vdash t_2 \mathrel{+\!\!\!\!\!\rightarrow}_{\mathcal{R}} t_2'$ and $\Delta \vdash t_1' \approx_\alpha t_2'$.*

Proof. Suppose $\Delta \vdash t \overset{P_1}{\mathrel{+\!\!\!\!\!\rightarrow}}_{\mathcal{R}} t_1$ and $\Delta \vdash t \overset{P_2}{\mathrel{+\!\!\!\!\!\rightarrow}}_{\mathcal{R}} t_2$ where $P_1 = \{p_{11}, \ldots, p_{1m}\}$ and $P_2 = \{p_{21}, \ldots, p_{2n}\}$. We set subterm occurrences $\alpha_i = t|_{p_{1i}} (1 \leq i \leq m)$ and $\beta_j = t|_{p_{2j}} (1 \leq j \leq n)$, and let $Red_{in} = \{\alpha_i \mid \exists\beta_j.\, \alpha_i \subset \beta_j\} \cup \{\beta_j \mid \exists\alpha_i.\, \beta_j \subseteq \alpha_i\}$ and $Red_{out} = \{\alpha_i \mid \forall\beta_j.\, \alpha_i \not\subset \beta_j\} \cup \{\beta_j \mid \forall\alpha_i.\, \beta_j \not\subseteq \alpha_i\}$. We define $|Red_{in}|$ as $\sum_{\gamma \in Red_{in}} |\gamma|$. The proof of the claim is by induction on $|Red_{in}|$.

- Case $|Red_{in}| = 0$.
  Then we can write $t = C[s_{11}, \ldots, s_{1m}, s_{21}, \ldots, s_{2n}]_{p_{11},\ldots,p_{1m},p_{21},\ldots,p_{2n}}$, $t_1 = C[s'_{11}, \ldots, s'_{1m}, s_{21}, \ldots, s_{2n}]$ and $t_2 = C[s_{11}, \ldots, s_{1m}, s'_{21}, \ldots, s'_{2n}]$ where C is some context, $\Delta \vdash s_{1i} \rightarrow_{\mathcal{R}} s'_{1i} (1 \leq i \leq m)$ and $\Delta \vdash s_{2j} \rightarrow_{\mathcal{R}} s'_{2j} (1 \leq j \leq n)$. Hence, the claim follows by taking $t'_1 = t'_2 = C[s'_{11}, \ldots, s'_{1m}, s'_{21}, \ldots, s'_{2n}]$.
- Case $|Red_{in}| > 0$.
  Suppose $Red_{out} = \{s_1, \ldots, s_h\}$. Then we can write $t = C[s_1, \ldots, s_h]$, $t_1 = C[s_{11}, \ldots, s_{h1}]$ and $t_2 = C[s_{12}, \ldots, s_{h2}]$ where for each k with $1 \leq k \leq h$, $\Delta \vdash s_k \twoheadrightarrow_{\mathcal{R}} s_{k1}$, $\Delta \vdash s_k \twoheadrightarrow_{\mathcal{R}} s_{k2}$ and one of them is at the root. Now, to prove the claim, it is sufficient to show that for each k with $1 \leq k \leq h$, there exist s'_{k1} and s'_{k2} such that $\Delta \vdash s_{k1} \twoheadrightarrow_{\mathcal{R}} s'_{k1}$, $\Delta \vdash s_{k2} \twoheadrightarrow_{\mathcal{R}} s'_{k2}$ and $\Delta \vdash s'_{k1} \approx_\alpha s'_{k2}$.
  Let $1 \leq k \leq h$, and suppose $\Delta \vdash s_k \overset{\{\varepsilon\}}{\twoheadrightarrow}_{\mathcal{R}} s_{k1}$ and $\Delta \vdash s_k \overset{P}{\twoheadrightarrow}_{\mathcal{R}} s_{k2}$. (The symmetric case is proved similarly.) Then there exists $R \in \mathcal{R}$ such that $\Delta \vdash s_k \overset{\varepsilon}{\rightarrow}_R s_{k1}$. Hence by Lemma 13, one of the following holds:
  1. There exists a term $\hat{s}_k$ such that $\Delta \vdash s_{k1} \twoheadrightarrow_{\mathcal{R}} \hat{s}_k \leftarrow_R s_{k2}$.
  2. There exist $p \in P$, $R' \in \mathcal{R}$, $\Gamma \vdash \langle u, v \rangle \in BCP(R', R)$, s'_k, π and θ such that
  $\Delta \vdash s_k \overset{p}{\rightarrow}_{R'} s'_k \overset{P\setminus\{p\}}{\twoheadrightarrow}_{\mathcal{R}} s_{k2}$, $\Delta \vdash \Gamma^\pi\theta$, $\Delta \vdash s'_k \approx_\alpha u^\pi\theta$ and $\Delta \vdash s_{k1} \approx_\alpha v^\pi\theta$.

  If part 1 holds then the requirement is satisfied. So we treat the case where part 2 holds. Since $\mathcal{R}$ is parallel closed, there exists w such that $\Gamma \vdash u \twoheadrightarrow_{\mathcal{R}} w \approx_\alpha v$. Then by Lemma 14(1) and (3), we have $\Delta \vdash u^\pi\theta \twoheadrightarrow_{\mathcal{R}} w^\pi\theta \approx_\alpha v^\pi\theta \approx_\alpha s_{k1}$. Hence by Lemma 9, there exists $\hat{s}_{k1}$ such that $\Delta \vdash s'_k \twoheadrightarrow_{\mathcal{R}} \hat{s}_{k1} \approx_\alpha w^\pi\theta \approx_\alpha s_{k1}$.
  In the following, we intend to apply the induction hypothesis to the parallel peak $\Delta \vdash s'_k \overset{Q}{\twoheadrightarrow}_{\mathcal{R}} \hat{s}_{k1}$ and $\Delta \vdash s'_k \overset{P\setminus\{p\}}{\twoheadrightarrow}_{\mathcal{R}} s_{k2}$.
  Let $P \setminus \{p\} = \{p_1, \ldots, p_{n'-1}\}$ $(n' \geq 1)$. We are now considering a case where $s_k = \alpha_i$ for some i $(1 \leq i \leq m)$, and a set of occurrences $\{\beta_{j_1}, \ldots, \beta_{j_{n'}}\}$ as $\{\beta_j \mid \beta_j \subseteq \alpha_i\}$. Then, clearly $\sum_{l=1}^{n'} |\beta_{j_l}| \leq |Red_{in}|$. We also have $s_k|_p = \beta_{j_{l'}}$ for some l' $(1 \leq l' \leq n')$, and $\{s_k|_{p_1}, \ldots, s_k|_{p_{n'-1}}\} = \{s'_k|_{p_1}, \ldots, s'_k|_{p_{n'-1}}\} = \{\beta_{j_1}, \ldots, \beta_{j_{n'}}\} \setminus \{\beta_{j_{l'}}\}$. Now let $Q = \{q_1, \ldots, q_{m'}\}$. Let $\gamma_{i'} = s'_k|_{q_{i'}} (1 \leq i' \leq m')$ and $\rho_{j'} = s'_k|_{p_{j'}} (1 \leq j' \leq n' - 1)$, and let $Red'_{in} = \{\gamma_{i'} \mid \exists \rho_{j'}. \gamma_{i'} \subset \rho_{j'}\} \cup \{\rho_{j'} \mid \exists \gamma_{i'}. \rho_{j'} \subseteq \gamma_{i'}\}$. Then, $|Red'_{in}| \leq \sum_{j'=1}^{n'-1} |\rho_{j'}| < \sum_{j'=1}^{n'-1} |\rho_{j'}| + |\beta_{j_{l'}}| = \sum_{l=1}^{n'} |\beta_{j_l}|$. Hence we can apply the induction hypothesis to the parallel peak $\Delta \vdash s'_k \overset{Q}{\twoheadrightarrow}_{\mathcal{R}} \hat{s}_{k1}$ and $\Delta \vdash s'_k \overset{P\setminus\{p\}}{\twoheadrightarrow}_{\mathcal{R}} s_{k2}$, and obtain $\hat{s}'_{k1}$ and s'_{k2} such that $\Delta \vdash \hat{s}_{k1} \twoheadrightarrow_{\mathcal{R}} \hat{s}'_{k1}$, $\Delta \vdash s_{k2} \twoheadrightarrow_{\mathcal{R}} s'_{k2}$ and $\Delta \vdash \hat{s}'_{k1} \approx_\alpha s'_{k2}$. Since $\Delta \vdash \hat{s}_{k1} \approx_\alpha s_{k1}$, we have, by Lemma 9, some s'_{k1} such that $\Delta \vdash s_{k1} \twoheadrightarrow_{\mathcal{R}} s'_{k1} \approx_\alpha \hat{s}'_{k1} \approx_\alpha s'_{k2}$ as required.

□

We are now ready to show that $\rightarrow_{\mathcal{R}}$ is Church-Rosser modulo $\approx_\alpha$.

Corollary 1 (Church-Rosser modulo $\approx_\alpha$). *If $\mathcal{R}$ is a left-linear parallel closed uniform rewriting system, then $\rightarrow_{\mathcal{R}}$ is Church-Rosser modulo $\approx_\alpha$. In particular, if $\mathcal{R}$ is a weakly orthogonal uniform rewriting system, then $\rightarrow_{\mathcal{R}}$ is Church-Rosser modulo $\approx_\alpha$.*

Proof. By Lemma 9, $\twoheadrightarrow\!\!\!\!\!+_{\mathcal{R}}$ is strongly compatible with $\approx_\alpha$, and by Theorem 1, $\twoheadrightarrow\!\!\!\!\!+_{\mathcal{R}}$ is strongly locally confluent modulo $\approx_\alpha$. Hence by the results in [14] (see also [15, Sect. 2.5]), $\twoheadrightarrow\!\!\!\!\!+_{\mathcal{R}}$ is Church-Rosser modulo $\approx_\alpha$. Since $\to_{\mathcal{R}} \subseteq \twoheadrightarrow\!\!\!\!\!+_{\mathcal{R}} \subseteq \to^*_{\mathcal{R}}$ by Lemma 5, we see that $\to_{\mathcal{R}}$ is Church-Rosser modulo $\approx_\alpha$. □

As in the first-order term rewriting case [21], we can generalise the above result by analysing overlaps at the root in the proof of Theorem 1.

Theorem 2. *Suppose that $\mathcal{R}$ is a left-linear uniform rewriting system. Then, $\mathcal{R}$ is Church-Rosser modulo $\approx_\alpha$ if $\Gamma \vdash u\ (\twoheadrightarrow\!\!\!\!\!+_{\mathcal{R}} \circ \approx_\alpha)\ v$ for any $\Gamma \vdash \langle u, v\rangle \in BCP_{in}(\mathcal{R})$ and $\Gamma \vdash u\ (\twoheadrightarrow\!\!\!\!\!+_{\mathcal{R}} \circ \approx_\alpha \circ \leftarrow^*_{\mathcal{R}})\ v$ for any $\Gamma \vdash \langle u, v\rangle \in BCP_{out}(\mathcal{R})$, where $BCP_{in}(\mathcal{R})$ and $BCP_{out}(\mathcal{R})$ denote the sets of BCPs of $\mathcal{R}$ such that $p \neq \varepsilon$ and $p = \varepsilon$ in the definition of BCP (Definition 4), respectively.*

Proof. To show that $\twoheadrightarrow\!\!\!\!\!+_{\mathcal{R}}$ is strongly locally confluent modulo $\approx_\alpha$, we prove a modified statement of Theorem 1 with $\Delta \vdash t_2 \to^*_{\mathcal{R}} t_2'$ instead of $\Delta \vdash t_2 \twoheadrightarrow\!\!\!\!\!+_{\mathcal{R}} t_2'$. The proof proceeds in a similar way to that of Theorem 1. In the case where $\Gamma \vdash \langle u, v\rangle \in BCP(R', R)$ in part 2 is at the root, we use the assumption on $BCP_{out}(\mathcal{R})$. □

We demonstrate Theorem 2 on two examples.

Example 1. Consider a nominal signature with function symbols f and g. Let $\mathcal{R}_1$ be the following left-linear uniform rewriting system:

$$\mathcal{R}_1 = \begin{cases} \vdash \mathsf{f}\ \langle [a]X, Y\rangle \to \mathsf{f}\ \langle [a]X, [a]X\rangle & \text{(1-1)} \\ \vdash \mathsf{f}\ \langle [a]a, Y\rangle \to \mathsf{g} & \text{(1-2)} \end{cases}$$

In the following, we write down all patterns of the BCPs of $\mathcal{R}_1$ and check whether $\mathcal{R}_1$ satisfies the condition of Theorem 2.

First, consider BCPs induced by overlaps of (1-1) on its renamed variant, which arise from the unification problem $\{\mathsf{f}\ \langle [a]X, Y\rangle \approx (\mathsf{f}\ \langle [a]Z, W\rangle)^\pi|_\varepsilon (= \mathsf{f}\ \langle [\pi(a)]Z, W\rangle)\}$. If $\pi(a) = a$, then the BCP is $\vdash \langle \mathsf{f}\ \langle [a]Z, [a]Z\rangle, \mathsf{f}\ \langle [a]Z, [a]Z\rangle\rangle$, for which $\vdash \mathsf{f}\ \langle [a]Z, [a]Z\rangle \approx_\alpha \mathsf{f}\ \langle [a]Z, [a]Z\rangle$ holds. If $\pi(a) = b$, then the problem $\{\mathsf{f}\ \langle [a]X, Y\rangle \approx \mathsf{f}\ \langle [b]Z, W\rangle\}$ has an mgu $\langle \{a\#Z\}, \{X := (a\ b)\cdot Z,\ Y := W\}\rangle$. Hence, the BCP in this case is $a\#Z \vdash \langle \mathsf{f}\ \langle [a](a\ b)\cdot Z, [a](a\ b)\cdot Z\rangle, \mathsf{f}\ \langle [b]Z, [b]Z\rangle\rangle$, for which we have $a\#Z \vdash \mathsf{f}\ \langle [a](a\ b)\cdot Z, [a](a\ b)\cdot Z\rangle \approx_\alpha \mathsf{f}\ \langle [b]Z, [b]Z\rangle$.

The BCP induced by overlaps of (1-2) on its renamed variant is only $\vdash \langle \mathsf{g}, \mathsf{g}\rangle$, for which we have $\vdash \mathsf{g} \approx_\alpha \mathsf{g}$.

Next we consider BCPs induced by overlaps of (1-1) on (1-2) and vice versa. The former arise from the unification problem $\{\mathsf{f}\ \langle [a]X, Y\rangle \approx (\mathsf{f}\ \langle [a]a, Z\rangle)^\pi|_\varepsilon (= \mathsf{f}\ \langle [\pi(a)]\pi(a), Z\rangle)\}$. In either case of $\pi(a) = a$ and $\pi(a) = b$, the BCP is $\vdash \langle \mathsf{f}\ \langle [a]a, [a]a\rangle, \mathsf{g}\rangle$, for which we have $\vdash \mathsf{f}\ \langle [a]a, [a]a\rangle \twoheadrightarrow\!\!\!\!\!+_{\mathcal{R}_1} \mathsf{g}$. BCPs induced by overlaps of (1-2) on (1-1) arise from the unification problem $\{\mathsf{f}\ \langle [a]a, Y\rangle \approx (\mathsf{f}\ \langle [a]X, Z\rangle)^\pi|_\varepsilon (= \mathsf{f}\ \langle [\pi(a)]X, Z\rangle)\}$. If $\pi(a) = a$, then the problem has an mgu $\langle \emptyset, \{X := a,\ Y := Z\}\rangle$. Hence, the BCP in this case is $\vdash \langle \mathsf{g}, \mathsf{f}\ \langle [a]a, [a]a\rangle\rangle$, for which we have $\vdash \mathsf{g} \leftarrow^*_{\mathcal{R}_1} \mathsf{f}\ \langle [a]a, [a]a\rangle$. If $\pi(a) = b$, then the problem has an mgu

$\langle \emptyset, \{X := b, Y := Z\}\rangle$. Hence, the BCP in this case is $\vdash \langle \mathsf{g}, \mathsf{f}\ \langle [b]b, [b]b\rangle\rangle$, for which we have $\vdash \mathsf{g} \leftarrow^*_{\mathcal{R}_1} \mathsf{f}\ \langle [b]b, [b]b\rangle$.

We have seen that $\mathcal{R}_1$ satisfies the condition of Theorem 2. Thus we conclude that $\mathcal{R}_1$ is Church-Rosser modulo $\approx_\alpha$. □

The reader may wonder why the case analyses according to permutations in the above example are necessary. This is because there exist rewriting systems where choice of bound atoms in the same two rewrite rules can vary joinability of the induced critical pairs (cf. [20, Example 12]). That means that one has to check all combinations of atoms in the rules to guarantee confluence properties of nominal rewriting systems.

The next example demonstrates that our results can also be applied to nominal rewriting systems that are not α-stable [19] (i.e., applying the same rewrite step to two α-equivalent terms may result in terms that are not α-equivalent). A typical example of a non-α-stable rewriting system is found in [19, Example 19] (unconditional eta-expansion). See also [3, Example 4.3].

Example 2. Consider a nominal signature with function symbols f and g. Let $\mathcal{R}_2$ be the following left-linear uniform rewriting system:

$$\mathcal{R}_2 = \left\{ \begin{array}{ll} \vdash \mathsf{f}\ X \to \mathsf{f}\ [a]\langle X, X\rangle & \quad (2\text{-}1) \\ \vdash [a]X \to \mathsf{g} & \quad (2\text{-}2) \end{array} \right.$$

Since $\mathcal{R}_2$ is not α-stable, the confluence criterion by orthogonality in [19] cannot be applied. In the following, we write down all patterns of the BCPs of $\mathcal{R}_2$ and check whether $\mathcal{R}_2$ satisfies the condition of Theorem 2.

First, consider BCPs induced by overlaps of (2-1) on its renamed variant, which arise from the unification problem $\{\mathsf{f}\ X \approx (\mathsf{f}\ Y)^\pi|_\varepsilon (= \mathsf{f}\ Y)\}$. If $\pi(a) = a$, then the BCP is $\vdash \langle \mathsf{f}\ [a]\langle Y, Y\rangle, \mathsf{f}\ [a]\langle Y, Y\rangle\rangle$, for which we have $\vdash \mathsf{f}\ [a]\langle Y, Y\rangle \approx_\alpha \mathsf{f}\ [a]\langle Y, Y\rangle$. If $\pi(a) = b$, then the BCP is $\vdash \langle \mathsf{f}\ [a]\langle Y, Y\rangle, \mathsf{f}\ [b]\langle Y, Y\rangle\rangle$, for which we have $\vdash \mathsf{f}\ [a]\langle Y, Y\rangle \to_{\mathcal{R}_2} \mathsf{f}\ \mathsf{g} \leftarrow_{\mathcal{R}_2} \mathsf{f}\ [b]\langle Y, Y\rangle$.

Next we consider BCPs induced by overlaps of (2-2) on its renamed variant, which arise from the unification problem $\{[a]X \approx ([a]Y)^\pi|_\varepsilon (= [\pi(a)]Y)\}$. If $\pi(a) = a$, then the BCP is $\vdash \langle \mathsf{g}, \mathsf{g}\rangle$, for which we have $\vdash \mathsf{g} \approx_\alpha \mathsf{g}$. If $\pi(a) = b$, then the problem $\{[a]X \approx [b]Y\}$ has an mgu $\langle \{a\#Y\}, \{X := (a\ b)\cdot Y\}\rangle$. Hence, the BCP in this case is $a\#Y \vdash \langle \mathsf{g}, \mathsf{g}\rangle$, for which we have $a\#Y \vdash \mathsf{g} \approx_\alpha \mathsf{g}$.

We have seen that $\mathcal{R}_2$ satisfies the condition of Theorem 2. Thus we conclude that $\mathcal{R}_2$ is Church-Rosser modulo $\approx_\alpha$. □

4 Conclusion

We have presented proofs of Church-Rosser modulo $\approx_\alpha$ for some classes of left-linear uniform nominal rewriting systems, extending Huet's parallel closure theorem and its generalisation on confluence of left-linear term rewriting systems. In the presence of critical pairs, the proofs are more delicate than the previous proofs for orthogonal uniform nominal rewriting systems. Our theorems can be applied to nominal rewriting systems that are not α-stable, as we have seen in an example.

In traditional higher-order rewriting frameworks (e.g. [12,13]), α-equivalent terms are always identified in contrast to the framework of nominal rewriting. This makes effects on confluence in the two approaches rather different. In addition to the difference revealed in [20], we have seen that our results on the parallel closure theorem and its generalisation are incomparable with those in traditional higher-order rewriting formalisms, since nominal rewriting systems that are not α-stable cannot be represented by any systems in traditional rewriting formalisms. Also, it is known that under explicit α-equivalence, confluence of β-reduction in λ-calculus is already quite hard to show (cf. [23]). Up to our knowledge, there are no attempts to accomplish a similar effect in traditional higher-order rewriting frameworks.

On the other hand, it is known that in the case of traditional higher-order rewriting, results on confluence by parallel closed critical pairs can be extended to those by development closed critical pairs [16]. However, a rigorous proof of it becomes more complicated than the parallel case, and in the present paper, we have not tried that extension for the case of nominal rewriting. We expect that the extension is possible but it is not entirely an easy task.

Using the combination of all the methods of [19,20] and the present paper, we have implemented a confluence prover [1]. We use an equivariant unification algorithm [2,6] to check whether $\nabla_1 \cup \nabla_2^{\pi} \cup \{l_1 \approx l_2^{\pi}|_p\}$ is unifiable for some permutation π, for given $\nabla_1, \nabla_2, l_1, l_2|_p$. However, that is not enough to generate concrete critical pairs and check their joinability, parallel closedness, etc. It is necessary to instantiate atom variables and permutation variables from constraints obtained as the solutions of equivariant unification problems, and this process is not obvious. We refer to [1] for all details of the implementation and experiments.

Acknowledgements. We are grateful to the anonymous referees for valuable comments. This research was supported by JSPS KAKENHI Grant Numbers 15K00003 and 16K00091.

References

1. Aoto, T., Kikuchi, K.: Nominal confluence tool. In: Olivetti, N., Tiwari, A. (eds.) IJCAR 2016. LNCS (LNAI), vol. 9706, pp. 173–182. Springer, Cham (2016). doi:10.1007/978-3-319-40229-1_12
2. Aoto, T., Kikuchi, K.: A rule-based procedure for equivariant nominal unification. In: Proceedings of the 8th HOR (2016)
3. Ayala-Rincón, M., Fernández, M., Gabbay, M.J., Rocha-Oliveira, A.C.: Checking overlaps of nominal rewriting rules. Electron. Notes Theoret. Comput. Sci. **323**, 39–56 (2016)
4. Baader, F., Nipkow, T.: Term Rewriting and All That. Cambridge University Press, Cambridge (1998)

5. de Bruijn, N.G.: Lambda calculus notation with nameless dummies, a tool for automatic formula manipulation, with application to the Church-Rosser theorem. Indagationes Mathematicae **34**, 381–392 (1972)
6. Cheney, J.: Equivariant unification. J. Autom. Reasoning **45**, 267–300 (2010)
7. Comon, H.: Completion of rewritie systems with membership constraints. Part I: deduction rules. J. Symbolic Comput. **25**, 397–419 (1998)
8. Fernández, M., Gabbay, M.J.: Nominal rewriting. Inform. Comput. **205**, 917–965 (2007)
9. Gabbay, M.J., Pitts, A.M.: A new approach to abstract syntax with variable binding. Formal Aspects Comput. **13**, 341–363 (2002)
10. Huet, G.: Confluent reductions: abstract properties and applications to term rewriting systems. J. ACM **27**, 797–821 (1980)
11. Jounnaud, J.P., Kirchner, H.: Completion of a set of rules modulo a set of equations. SIAM J. Comput. **15**, 1155–1194 (1986)
12. Klop, J.W., van Oostrom, V., van Raamsdonk, F.: Combinatory reduction systems: introduction and survey. Theoret. Comput. Sci. **121**, 279–308 (1993)
13. Mayr, R., Nipkow, T.: Higher-order rewrite systems and their confluence. Theoret. Comput. Sci. **192**, 3–29 (1998)
14. Ohlebusch, E.: Church-Rosser theorems for abstract reduction modulo an equivalence relation. In: Nipkow, T. (ed.) RTA 1998. LNCS, vol. 1379, pp. 17–31. Springer, Heidelberg (1998). doi:10.1007/BFb0052358
15. Ohlebusch, E.: Advanced Topics in Term Rewriting. Springer, New York (2002). doi:10.1007/978-1-4757-3661-8
16. van Oostrom, V.: Developing developments. Theoret. Comput. Sci. **175**, 159–181 (1997)
17. Pitts, A.M.: Nominal logic, a first order theory of names and binding. Inform. Comput. **186**, 165–193 (2003)
18. Pollack, R., Sato, M., Ricciotti, W.: A canonical locally named representation of binding. J. Autom. Reasoning **49**, 185–207 (2012)
19. Suzuki, T., Kikuchi, K., Aoto, T., Toyama, Y.: Confluence of orthogonal nominal rewriting systems revisited. In: Proceedings of the 26th RTA, vol. 36. LIPIcs, pp. 301–317 (2015)
20. Suzuki, T., Kikuchi, K., Aoto, T., Toyama, Y.: Critical pair analysis in nominal rewriting. In: Proceedings of the 7th SCSS, vol. 39. EPiC, pp. 156–168. EasyChair (2016)
21. Toyama, Y.: Commutativity of term rewriting systems. In: Fuchi, K., Kott, L. (eds.) Programming of Future Generation Computers II, North-Holland, pp. 393–407 (1988)
22. Urban, C., Pitts, A.M., Gabbay, M.J.: Nominal unification. Theoret. Comput. Sci. **323**, 473–497 (2004)
23. Vestergaard, R., Brotherston, J.: A formalised first-order confluence proof for the λ-calculus using one-sorted variable names. Inform. Comput. **183**, 212–244 (2003)

Complexity Analysis for Term Rewriting by Integer Transition Systems

Matthias Naaf[1], Florian Frohn[1], Marc Brockschmidt[2], Carsten Fuhs[3], and Jürgen Giesl[1(✉)]

[1] LuFG Informatik 2, RWTH Aachen University, Aachen, Germany
matthias.naaf@rwth-aachen.de, florian.frohn@cs.rwth-aachen.de, giesl@informatik.rwth-aachen.de
[2] Microsoft Research, Cambridge, UK
mabrocks@microsoft.com
[3] Birkbeck, University of London, London, UK
carsten@dcs.bbk.ac.uk

Abstract. We present a new method to infer upper bounds on the innermost runtime complexity of term rewrite systems (TRSs), which benefits from recent advances on complexity analysis of integer transition systems (ITSs). To this end, we develop a transformation from TRSs to a generalized notion of ITSs with (possibly non-tail) recursion. To analyze their complexity, we introduce a modular technique which allows us to use existing tools for standard ITSs in order to infer complexity bounds for our generalized ITSs. The key idea of our technique is a summarization method that allows us to analyze components of the transition system independently. We implemented our contributions in the tool AProVE, and our experiments show that one can now infer bounds for significantly more TRSs than with previous state-of-the-art tools for term rewriting.

1 Introduction

There are many techniques for automatic complexity analysis of programs with integer (or natural) numbers, e.g., [1,2,4,11,13,14,16–18,23,26–28,34]. On the other hand, several techniques analyze complexity of *term rewrite systems* (TRSs), e.g., [7,8,12,19,20,24,29,32,36]. TRSs are a classical model for equational reasoning and evaluation with user-defined data structures and recursion [9].

Although the approaches for complexity analysis of term rewriting support modularity, they usually cannot completely remove rules from the TRS after having analyzed them. In contrast, approaches for integer programs may regard small program parts independently and combine the results for these parts to obtain a result for the overall program. In this work, we show how to obtain such a form of modularity also for complexity analysis of TRSs.

Supported by DFG grant GI 274/6-1 and the Air Force Research Laboratory (AFRL).

C. Dixon and M. Finger (Eds.): FroCoS 2017, LNCS 10483, pp. 132–150, 2017.
DOI: 10.1007/978-3-319-66167-4_8

After recapitulating TRSs and their complexity in Sect. 2, in Sect. 3 we introduce a transformation from TRSs into a variant of integer transition systems (ITSs) called *recursive natural transition systems* (RNTSs). In contrast to standard ITSs, RNTSs allow arbitrary recursion, and the variables only range over the natural numbers. We show that the innermost runtime complexity of the original TRS is bounded by the complexity of the resulting RNTS, i.e., one can now use any complexity tool for RNTSs to infer complexity bounds for TRSs.

Unfortunately, many existing techniques and tools for standard ITSs do not support the non-tail recursive calls that can occur in RNTSs. Therefore, in Sect. 4 we develop an approach to infer complexity bounds for RNTSs which can use arbitrary complexity tools for standard ITSs as a back-end. The approach from Sect. 4 is completely modular, as it repeatedly finds bounds for parts of the RNTS and combines them. In this way, our technique benefits from all advances of any ITS tools, irrespective of whether they support non-tail recursion (e.g., CoFloCo [16,17]) or not (e.g., KoAT [13]). As demonstrated by our implementation in AProVE [22], our contributions allow us to derive complexity bounds for many TRSs where state-of-the-art tools fail, cf. Sect. 5. All proofs can be found in [5].

2 Complexity of Term Rewriting

We assume basic knowledge of term rewriting [9] and recapitulate innermost (relative) term rewriting and its runtime complexity.

Definition 1 (Term Rewriting [8,9]**).** *We denote the set of* terms *over a finite signature Σ and the variables $\mathcal{V}$ by $\mathcal{T}(\Sigma, \mathcal{V})$. The* size *$|t|$ of a term t is defined as $|x| = 1$ if $x \in \mathcal{V}$ and $|f(t_1, \ldots, t_k)| = 1 + \sum_{i=1}^{k} |t_i|$. A* TRS *$\mathcal{R}$ is a set of rules $\{\ell_1 \to r_1, \ldots, \ell_n \to r_n\}$ with $\ell_i, r_i \in \mathcal{T}(\Sigma, \mathcal{V})$, $\ell_i \notin \mathcal{V}$, and $\mathcal{V}(r_i) \subseteq \mathcal{V}(\ell_i)$ for all $1 \leq i \leq n$. The* rewrite relation *is defined as $s \to_{\mathcal{R}} t$ iff there is a rule $\ell \to r \in \mathcal{R}$, a position $\pi \in \mathcal{P}os(s)$, and a substitution σ such that $s|_\pi = \ell\sigma$ and $t = s[r\sigma]_\pi$. Here, $\ell\sigma$ is called the* redex *of the rewrite step.*

For two TRSs $\mathcal{R}$ and $\mathcal{S}$, $\mathcal{R}/\mathcal{S}$ is a relative TRS, *and its* rewrite relation *$\to_{\mathcal{R}/\mathcal{S}}$ is $\to_{\mathcal{S}}^* \circ \to_{\mathcal{R}} \circ \to_{\mathcal{S}}^*$, i.e., it allows rewriting with $\mathcal{S}$ before and after each $\mathcal{R}$-step. We define the* innermost *rewrite relation as $s \xrightarrow{\mathsf{i}}_{\mathcal{R}/\mathcal{S}} t$ iff $s \to_{\mathcal{S}}^* s' \to_{\mathcal{R}} s'' \to_{\mathcal{S}}^* t$ for some terms s', s'', where the proper subterms of the redexes of each step with $\to_{\mathcal{S}}$ or $\to_{\mathcal{R}}$ are in normal form w.r.t. $\mathcal{R} \cup \mathcal{S}$. We write $\xrightarrow{\mathsf{i}}_{\mathcal{R}}$ instead of $\xrightarrow{\mathsf{i}}_{\mathcal{R}/\varnothing}$.*

$\Sigma_d^{\mathcal{R}\cup\mathcal{S}} = \{\mathrm{root}(\ell) \mid \ell \to r \in \mathcal{R} \cup \mathcal{S}\}$ and $\Sigma_c^{\mathcal{R}\cup\mathcal{S}} = \Sigma \setminus \Sigma_d^{\mathcal{R}\cup\mathcal{S}}$ are the defined *(resp.* constructor*) symbols of $\mathcal{R}/\mathcal{S}$. A term $f(t_1, \ldots, t_k)$ is* basic *iff $f \in \Sigma_d^{\mathcal{R}\cup\mathcal{S}}$ and $t_1, \ldots, t_k \in \mathcal{T}(\Sigma_c^{\mathcal{R}\cup\mathcal{S}}, \mathcal{V})$. $\mathcal{R}/\mathcal{S}$ is a* constructor system *iff ℓ is basic for all $\ell \to r \in \mathcal{R} \cup \mathcal{S}$.*

In this paper, we will restrict ourselves to the analysis of constructor systems.

Example 2. The following rules implement the insertion sort *algorithm.*

$$\mathsf{isort}(\mathsf{nil}, ys) \to ys \tag{1}$$
$$\mathsf{isort}(\mathsf{cons}(x, xs), ys) \to \mathsf{isort}(xs, \mathsf{ins}(x, ys)) \tag{2}$$
$$\mathsf{ins}(x, \mathsf{nil}) \to \mathsf{cons}(x, \mathsf{nil}) \tag{3}$$
$$\mathsf{ins}(x, \mathsf{cons}(y, ys)) \to \mathsf{if}(\mathsf{gt}(x, y), x, \mathsf{cons}(y, ys)) \tag{4}$$
$$\mathsf{if}(\mathsf{true}, x, \mathsf{cons}(y, ys)) \to \mathsf{cons}(y, \mathsf{ins}(x, ys)) \tag{5}$$
$$\mathsf{if}(\mathsf{false}, x, \mathsf{cons}(y, ys)) \to \mathsf{cons}(x, \mathsf{cons}(y, ys)) \tag{6}$$
$$\mathsf{gt}(\mathsf{0}, y) \to \mathsf{false} \tag{7}$$
$$\mathsf{gt}(\mathsf{s}(x), \mathsf{0}) \to \mathsf{true} \tag{8}$$
$$\mathsf{gt}(\mathsf{s}(x), \mathsf{s}(y)) \to \mathsf{gt}(x, y) \tag{9}$$

Relative rules are useful to model built-in operations in programming languages since applications of these rules are disregarded for the complexity of a TRS. For example, the translation from RAML *programs* [27] *to term rewriting in* [8] *uses relative rules to model the semantics of comparisons and similar operations on* RAML*'s primitive data types. Thus, we decompose the rules above into a relative TRS* $\mathcal{R}/\mathcal{S}$ *with* $\mathcal{R} = \{(1), \ldots, (6)\}$ *and* $\mathcal{S} = \{(7), (8), (9)\}$.[1]

In our example, we have $\Sigma_d^{\mathcal{R}\cup\mathcal{S}} = \{\mathsf{isort}, \mathsf{ins}, \mathsf{if}, \mathsf{gt}\}$ *and* $\Sigma_c^{\mathcal{R}\cup\mathcal{S}} = \{\mathsf{cons}, \mathsf{nil}, \mathsf{s}, \mathsf{0}, \mathsf{true}, \mathsf{false}\}$. *Since all left-hand sides are basic,* $\mathcal{R}/\mathcal{S}$ *is a constructor system. An example rewrite sequence to sort the list* [2, 0] *is*

$$\begin{array}{llll} t = & \mathsf{isort}(\mathsf{cons}(\mathsf{s}(\mathsf{s}(\mathsf{0})), \mathsf{cons}(\mathsf{0}, \mathsf{nil})), \mathsf{nil}) & \xrightarrow{\mathsf{i}}_{\mathcal{R}} \mathsf{isort}(\mathsf{cons}(\mathsf{0}, \mathsf{nil}), \mathsf{ins}(\mathsf{s}(\mathsf{s}(\mathsf{0})), \mathsf{nil})) & \xrightarrow{\mathsf{i}}_{\mathcal{R}} \\ & \mathsf{isort}(\mathsf{cons}(\mathsf{0}, \mathsf{nil}), \mathsf{cons}(\mathsf{s}(\mathsf{s}(\mathsf{0})), \mathsf{nil})) & \xrightarrow{\mathsf{i}}_{\mathcal{R}} \mathsf{isort}(\mathsf{nil}, \mathsf{ins}(\mathsf{0}, \mathsf{cons}(\mathsf{s}(\mathsf{s}(\mathsf{0})), \mathsf{nil}))) & \xrightarrow{\mathsf{i}}_{\mathcal{R}} \\ & \mathsf{isort}(\mathsf{nil}, \mathsf{if}(\mathsf{gt}(\mathsf{0}, \mathsf{s}(\mathsf{s}(\mathsf{0}))), \ldots, \ldots)) & \xrightarrow{\mathsf{i}}_{\mathcal{S}} \mathsf{isort}(\mathsf{nil}, \mathsf{if}(\mathsf{false}, \ldots, \ldots)) & \xrightarrow{\mathsf{i}}_{\mathcal{R}} \\ & \mathsf{isort}(\mathsf{nil}, \mathsf{cons}(\mathsf{0}, \mathsf{cons}(\mathsf{s}(\mathsf{s}(\mathsf{0})), \mathsf{nil}))) & \xrightarrow{\mathsf{i}}_{\mathcal{R}} \mathsf{cons}(\mathsf{0}, \mathsf{cons}(\mathsf{s}(\mathsf{s}(\mathsf{0})), \mathsf{nil})) & \end{array}$$

Note that ordinary TRSs are a special case of relative TRSs (where $\mathcal{S} = \varnothing$). We usually just write "TRSs" to denote "relative TRSs". We now define the *runtime complexity* of a TRS $\mathcal{R}/\mathcal{S}$. In Definition 3, ω is the smallest infinite ordinal, i.e., $\omega > e$ holds for all $e \in \mathbb{N}$, and for any $M \subseteq \mathbb{N} \cup \{\omega\}$, $\sup M$ is the least upper bound of M, where $\sup \varnothing = 0$.

Definition 3 (Innermost Runtime Complexity [24,25,32,36]**).** *The* derivation height *of a term* t *w.r.t. a relation* $\to$ *is the length of the longest sequence of* $\to$*-steps starting with* t, *i.e.,* $\mathrm{dh}(t, \to) = \sup\{e \mid \exists t' \in \mathcal{T}(\Sigma, \mathcal{V}).\ t \to^e t'\}$. *If* t *starts an infinite* $\to$*-sequence, this yields* $\mathrm{dh}(t, \to) = \omega$. *The* innermost runtime complexity *function* $\mathrm{irc}_{\mathcal{R}/\mathcal{S}}$ *maps any* $n \in \mathbb{N}$ *to the length of the longest sequence of* $\xrightarrow{\mathsf{i}}_{\mathcal{R}/\mathcal{S}}$*-steps starting with a basic term whose size is at most* n, *i.e.,* $\mathrm{irc}_{\mathcal{R}/\mathcal{S}}(n) = \sup\{\mathrm{dh}(t, \xrightarrow{\mathsf{i}}_{\mathcal{R}/\mathcal{S}}) \mid t$ *is basic,* $|t| \leq n\}$.

[1] In this way, the complexity of gt is 0, whereas comparisons have complexity 1 with the slightly more complicated encoding from [8]. Since this difference does not affect the asymptotic complexity of Example 2, we use the simpler encoding for the sake of readability.

Example 4. *The rewrite sequence for t in Example 2 is maximal, and thus, $\mathrm{dh}(t, \xrightarrow{\mathsf{i}}_{\mathcal{R}/\mathcal{S}}) = 6$. So the $\xrightarrow{\mathsf{i}}_{\mathcal{S}}$-step does not contribute to t's derivation height. As $|t| = 9$, this implies $\mathrm{irc}_{\mathcal{R}/\mathcal{S}}(9) \geq 6$. We will show how our new approach proves $\mathrm{irc}_{\mathcal{R}/\mathcal{S}}(n) \in \mathcal{O}(n^2)$ automatically.*

3 From TRSs to Recursive Natural Transition Systems

We now reduce complexity analysis of TRSs to complexity analysis of *recursive natural transition systems* (RNTSs). In contrast to term rewriting, RNTSs offer built-in support for arithmetic, but disallow pattern matching. To analyze TRSs, it suffices to regard RNTSs where all variables range over $\mathbb{N}$. We use the signature $\Sigma_{\mathsf{exp}} = \{+, \cdot\} \cup \mathbb{N}$ for arithmetic expressions and $\Sigma_{\mathsf{fml}} = \Sigma_{\mathsf{exp}} \cup \{\mathsf{true}, \mathsf{false}, <, \wedge\}$ for arithmetic formulas ("constraints"). We will also use relations like $=$ in constraints, but these are just syntactic sugar. To extend the rewrite relation with semantics for these symbols, let $[\![.]\!]$ evaluate all arithmetic and Boolean expressions in a term. So for example, $[\![\mathsf{gt}(1+2, 5+y)]\!] = \mathsf{gt}(3, 5+y)$ and $[\![3 > 5 \wedge \mathsf{true}]\!] = \mathsf{false}$. We allow substitutions with infinite domains and call σ a *natural substitution* iff $\sigma(x) \in \mathbb{N}$ for all $x \in \mathcal{V}$.

Definition 5 (Recursive Natural Transition System). *An* RNTS *over a finite signature Σ with $\Sigma \cap \Sigma_{\mathsf{fml}} = \varnothing$ is a set of rules $\mathcal{P} = \{\ell_1 \xrightarrow{w_1} r_1\ [\varphi_1], \ldots, \ell_n \xrightarrow{w_n} r_n\ [\varphi_n]\}$ with $\ell_i = f(x_1, \ldots, x_k)$ for $f \in \Sigma$ and pairwise different variables $x_1, \ldots, x_k$, $r_i \in \mathcal{T}(\Sigma \uplus \Sigma_{\mathsf{exp}}, \mathcal{V})$, constraints $\varphi_i \in \mathcal{T}(\Sigma_{\mathsf{fml}}, \mathcal{V})$, and weights $w_i \in \mathcal{T}(\Sigma_{\mathsf{exp}}, \mathcal{V})$. An RNTS $\mathcal{P}$ induces a rewrite relation $\xrightarrow{m}_{\mathcal{P}}$ on ground terms from $\mathcal{T}(\Sigma \uplus \Sigma_{\mathsf{exp}}, \varnothing)$, where $s \xrightarrow{m}_{\mathcal{P}} t$ iff there are $\ell \xrightarrow{w} r\ [\varphi] \in \mathcal{P}$, $\pi \in \mathcal{P}os(s)$, and a natural substitution σ such that $s|_\pi = \ell\sigma$, $[\![\varphi\sigma]\!] = \mathsf{true}$, $m = [\![w\sigma]\!] \in \mathbb{N}$, and $t = [\![s[r\sigma]_\pi]\!]$. We sometimes just write $s \to_{\mathcal{P}} t$ instead of $s \xrightarrow{m}_{\mathcal{P}} t$. Again, let $\Sigma_d^{\mathcal{P}} = \{\mathrm{root}(\ell) \mid \ell \xrightarrow{w} r\ [\varphi] \in \mathcal{P}\}$ and $\Sigma_c^{\mathcal{P}} = \Sigma \setminus \Sigma_d^{\mathcal{P}}$.*

A term $f(n_1, \ldots, n_k)$ with $f \in \Sigma$ and $n_1, \ldots, n_k \in \mathbb{N}$ is nat-basic, *and its size is $\|f(n_1, \ldots, n_k)\| = 1 + n_1 + \ldots + n_k$. To consider weights for derivation heights, we define $\mathrm{dhw}(t, \to_{\mathcal{P}})$ to be the maximum weight of any $\to_{\mathcal{P}}$-sequence starting with t, i.e., $\mathrm{dhw}(t_0, \to_{\mathcal{P}}) = \sup\{\sum_{i=1}^{e} m_i \mid \exists t_1, \ldots, t_e \in \mathcal{T}(\Sigma \cup \Sigma_{\mathsf{exp}}, \varnothing).\ t_0 \xrightarrow{m_1}_{\mathcal{P}} \ldots \xrightarrow{m_e}_{\mathcal{P}} t_e\}$. Then $\mathrm{irc}_{\mathcal{P}}$ maps $n \in \mathbb{N}$ to the maximum weight of any $\to_{\mathcal{P}}$-sequence starting with a nat-basic term whose size is at most n, i.e., $\mathrm{irc}_{\mathcal{P}}(n) = \sup\{\mathrm{dhw}(t, \to_{\mathcal{P}}) \mid t \text{ is nat-basic}, \|t\| \leq n\}$.*

Note that the rewrite relation for RNTSs is "innermost" by construction, as rules do not contain symbols from Σ below the root in left-hand sides, and they are only applicable if all variables are instantiated by numbers.

The crucial idea of our approach is to model the behavior of a TRS by a corresponding RNTS which results from abstracting constructor terms to their size. Thus, we use the following transformation $\wr\cdot\int$ from TRSs to RNTSs.

Definition 6 (Abstraction $\wr\cdot\wr$ from TRSs to RNTSs). *For a TRS $\mathcal{R}/\mathcal{S}$, the* size abstraction *$\wr t \wr$ of a term $t \in \mathcal{T}(\Sigma, \mathcal{V})$ is defined as follows:*

$$\begin{array}{rcll} \wr x \wr & = & x & \text{for } x \in \mathcal{V} \\ \wr f(t_1,\ldots,t_k) \wr & = & 1 + \wr t_1 \wr + \ldots + \wr t_k \wr & \text{if } f \in \Sigma_c^{\mathcal{R}\cup\mathcal{S}} \\ \wr f(t_1,\ldots,t_k) \wr & = & f(\wr t_1 \wr, \ldots, \wr t_k \wr) & \text{if } f \in \Sigma_d^{\mathcal{R}\cup\mathcal{S}} \end{array}$$

We lift $\wr\cdot\wr$ to rules with basic left-hand sides. For $\ell = f(t_1,\ldots,t_k)$ with $t_1,\ldots,t_k \in \mathcal{T}(\Sigma_c^{\mathcal{R}\cup\mathcal{S}}, \mathcal{V})$ and $w \in \mathcal{T}(\Sigma_{\mathsf{exp}}, \mathcal{V})$, we define

$$\wr \ell \to r \wr_w \quad = \quad f(x_1,\ldots,x_k) \xrightarrow{w} \wr r \wr \quad \left[\bigwedge\nolimits_{i=1}^{k} x_i = \wr t_i \wr \;\wedge\; \bigwedge\nolimits_{x \in \mathcal{V}(\ell)} x \geq 1 \right]$$

for pairwise different fresh variables $x_1,\ldots,x_k$. For a constructor system $\mathcal{R}/\mathcal{S}$, we define the RNTS $\wr \mathcal{R}/\mathcal{S} \wr = \{ \wr \ell \to r \wr_1 \mid \ell \to r \in \mathcal{R} \} \cup \{ \wr \ell \to r \wr_0 \mid \ell \to r \in \mathcal{S} \}$.

Example 7. For the TRS $\mathcal{R}/\mathcal{S}$ from Example 2, $\wr \mathcal{R}/\mathcal{S} \wr$ corresponds to the following RNTS.

$$\begin{array}{rll} \mathsf{isort}(xs, ys) \xrightarrow{1} ys & [xs \;= 1 \wedge \ldots] & (1') \\ \mathsf{isort}(xs', ys) \xrightarrow{1} \mathsf{isort}(xs, \mathsf{ins}(x, ys)) & [xs' = 1 + x + xs \wedge \ldots] & (2') \\ \mathsf{ins}(x, ys) \xrightarrow{1} 2 + x & [ys \;= 1 \wedge \ldots] & (3') \\ \mathsf{ins}(x, ys') \xrightarrow{1} \mathsf{if}(\mathsf{gt}(x, y), x, ys') & [ys' = 1 + y + ys \wedge \ldots] & (4') \\ \mathsf{if}(b, x, ys') \xrightarrow{1} 1 + y + \mathsf{ins}(x, ys) & [b = 1 \wedge ys' = 1 + y + ys \wedge \ldots] & (5') \\ \mathsf{if}(b, x, ys') \xrightarrow{1} 1 + x + ys' & [b = 1 \wedge ys' = 1 + y + ys \wedge \ldots] & (6') \\ \mathsf{gt}(x, y) \xrightarrow{0} 1 & [x \;= 1 \wedge \ldots] & (7') \\ \mathsf{gt}(x', y) \xrightarrow{0} 1 & [x' = 1 + x \wedge y = 1 \wedge \ldots] & (8') \\ \mathsf{gt}(x', y') \xrightarrow{0} \mathsf{gt}(x, y) & [x' = 1 + x \wedge y' = 1 + y \wedge \ldots] & (9') \end{array}$$

In these rules, "$\wedge \ldots$" stands for the constraint that all variables have to be instantiated with values ≥ 1. Note that we make use of fresh variables like x and xs on the right-hand side of $(2')$ to simulate matching of constructor terms. Using this RNTS, the rewrite steps in Example 2 can be simulated as follows.

$$\begin{array}{lll} t' \;=\; \mathsf{isort}(7, 1) & \xrightarrow{1} \mathsf{isort}(3, \mathsf{ins}(3, 1)) & \xrightarrow{1} \mathsf{isort}(3, 5) \\ \xrightarrow{1} \mathsf{isort}(1, \mathsf{ins}(1, 5)) & \xrightarrow{1} \mathsf{isort}(1, \mathsf{if}(\mathsf{gt}(1, 3), 1, 5)) & \xrightarrow{0} \mathsf{isort}(1, \mathsf{if}(1, 1, 5)) \\ \xrightarrow{1} \mathsf{isort}(1, 7) & \xrightarrow{1} 7 & \end{array}$$

For the nat-basic term t', we have $\|t'\| = 1 + 7 + 1 = 9$. So the above sequence proves $\mathrm{dhw}(t', \to_{\mathcal{P}}) \geq 6$ and hence, $\mathrm{irc}_{\mathcal{P}}(9) \geq 6$. Note that unlike Example 2, here rewriting nat-basic terms is non-deterministic as, e.g., we also have $\mathsf{isort}(7, 1) \xrightarrow{1} \mathsf{isort}(2, \mathsf{ins}(4, 1))$. The reason is that $\wr\cdot\wr$ is a blind abstraction *[10], which abstracts several different terms to the same number.*

$[\![\wr\cdot\wr]\!]$ maps basic ground terms to nat-basic terms, e.g., $[\![\wr \mathsf{ins}(\mathsf{s}(0),\mathsf{nil})\wr]\!] = [\![\mathsf{ins}(1+1,1)]\!] = \mathsf{ins}(2,1)$. We now show that under certain conditions, $\mathrm{dh}(t, \xrightarrow{\mathrm{i}}_{\mathcal{R}/\mathcal{S}}) \leq \mathrm{dhw}([\![\wr t\wr]\!], \to_{\wr\mathcal{R}/\mathcal{S}\wr})$ holds for all ground terms t, i.e., rewrite sequences of a TRS $\mathcal{R}/\mathcal{S}$ can be simulated in the RNTS $\wr\mathcal{R}/\mathcal{S}\wr$ resulting from its transformation. We would like to conclude that in these cases, we also have $\mathrm{irc}_{\mathcal{R}/\mathcal{S}}(n) \leq \mathrm{irc}_{\wr\mathcal{R}/\mathcal{S}\wr}(n)$. However, irc considers arbitrary (basic) terms, but the above connection between the derivation heights of t and $[\![\wr t\wr]\!]$ only holds for *ground* terms t. For *full* rewriting, we clearly have $\mathrm{dh}(t, \to_{\mathcal{R}}) \leq \mathrm{dh}(t\sigma, \to_{\mathcal{R}})$ for any substitution σ. However, this does not hold for *innermost* rewriting. For example, $\mathsf{f}(\mathsf{g}(x))$ has an infinite innermost reduction with the TRS $\{\mathsf{f}(\mathsf{g}(x)) \to \mathsf{f}(\mathsf{g}(x)), \mathsf{g}(\mathsf{a}) \to \mathsf{a}\}$, but $\mathsf{f}(\mathsf{g}(\mathsf{a}))$ is innermost terminating. Nevertheless, we show in Theorem 9 that for *constructor systems* $\mathcal{R}$, $\mathrm{dh}(t, \xrightarrow{\mathrm{i}}_{\mathcal{R}}) \leq \mathrm{dh}(t\sigma, \xrightarrow{\mathrm{i}}_{\mathcal{R}})$ holds for any ground substitution σ.

However, for *relative* rewriting with constructor systems $\mathcal{R}$ and $\mathcal{S}$, $\mathrm{dh}(t, \xrightarrow{\mathrm{i}}_{\mathcal{R}/\mathcal{S}}) \leq \mathrm{dh}(t\sigma, \xrightarrow{\mathrm{i}}_{\mathcal{R}/\mathcal{S}})$ does not necessarily hold if $\mathcal{S}$ is not innermost terminating. To see this, consider $\mathcal{R} = \{\mathsf{f}(x) \to \mathsf{f}(x)\}$ and $\mathcal{S} = \{\mathsf{g}(\mathsf{a}) \to \mathsf{g}(\mathsf{a})\}$. Now $\mathsf{f}(\mathsf{g}(x))$ has an infinite reduction w.r.t. $\xrightarrow{\mathrm{i}}_{\mathcal{R}/\mathcal{S}}$ since $\mathsf{g}(x)$ is a normal form w.r.t. $\mathcal{R} \cup \mathcal{S}$. However, its instance $\mathsf{f}(\mathsf{g}(\mathsf{a}))$ has the derivation height 0 w.r.t. $\xrightarrow{\mathrm{i}}_{\mathcal{R}/\mathcal{S}}$, as $\mathsf{g}(\mathsf{a})$ is not innermost terminating w.r.t. $\mathcal{S}$ and no rule of $\mathcal{R}$ can ever be applied. To solve this problem, we extend the TRS $\mathcal{S}$ by a *terminating variant* $\mathcal{N}$.

Definition 8 (Terminating Variant). *A TRS $\mathcal{N}$ is a* terminating variant *of $\mathcal{S}$ iff $\xrightarrow{\mathrm{i}}_{\mathcal{N}}$ terminates and every $\mathcal{N}$-normal form is also an $\mathcal{S}$-normal form.*

So if one can prove innermost termination of $\mathcal{S}$, then one can use $\mathcal{S}$ as a terminating variant of itself. For instance in Example 2, termination of $\mathcal{S} = \{(7), (8), (9)\}$ can easily be shown automatically by standard tools like AProVE [22]. Otherwise, one can for instance use a terminating variant $\{f(x_1, \ldots, x_k) \to t_f \mid f \in \Sigma_d^{\mathcal{S}}\}$ where for each f, we pick some constructor ground term $t_f \in \mathcal{T}(\Sigma_c^{\mathcal{R}\cup\mathcal{S}}, \varnothing)$. Now one can prove that for innermost (relative) rewriting, the derivation height of a term does not decrease when it is instantiated by a ground substitution.

Theorem 9 (Soundness of Instantiation and Terminating Variants). *Let $\mathcal{R}$, $\mathcal{S}$ be constructor systems and $\mathcal{N}$ be a terminating variant of $\mathcal{S}$. Then $\mathrm{dh}(t, \xrightarrow{\mathrm{i}}_{\mathcal{R}/\mathcal{S}}) \leq \mathrm{dh}(t\sigma, \xrightarrow{\mathrm{i}}_{\mathcal{R}/(\mathcal{S}\cup\mathcal{N})})$ holds for any term t where $t\sigma$ is ground.*

However, the restriction to ground terms t still does not ensure $\mathrm{dh}(t, \xrightarrow{\mathrm{i}}_{\mathcal{R}/\mathcal{S}}) \leq \mathrm{dhw}([\![\wr t\wr]\!], \to_{\wr\mathcal{R}/\mathcal{S}\wr})$. The problem is that $\xrightarrow{\mathrm{i}}_{\mathcal{R}/\mathcal{S}}$ can rewrite a term t at position π also if there is a defined symbol below $t|_\pi$ as long as no rule can be applied to that subterm. So for Example 2, we have $\mathsf{isort}(\mathsf{nil}, \mathsf{if}(\mathsf{true}, 0, \mathsf{nil})) \xrightarrow{\mathrm{i}}_{\mathcal{R}} \mathsf{if}(\mathsf{true}, 0, \mathsf{nil})$, but $\wr\mathcal{R}/\mathcal{S}\wr$ cannot rewrite $[\![\wr \mathsf{isort}(\mathsf{nil}, \mathsf{if}(\mathsf{true}, 0, \mathsf{nil}))\wr]\!] = \mathsf{isort}(1, \mathsf{if}(1,1,1))$ since the if-rules of $\wr\mathcal{R}/\mathcal{S}\wr$ may be applied only if the third argument is ≥ 3, and the variables in the isort-rule may be instantiated only by numbers (not by normal forms like $\mathsf{if}(1,1,1)$). This problem can be solved by requiring that $\mathcal{R}/\mathcal{S}$ is *completely defined*, i.e., that $\mathcal{R}\cup\mathcal{S}$ can rewrite every basic ground term. However, this is too restrictive as we, e.g., would like $\mathsf{gt}(\mathsf{true}, \mathsf{false})$ to be in normal form. Fortunately, (innermost) runtime complexity is *persistent* w.r.t. type introduction [6]. Thus, we only need to ensure that every *well-typed* basic ground term can be rewritten.

Definition 10 (Typed TRSs (cf. e.g. [21,37])). *In a many-sorted (first-order monomorphic) signature Σ over the set of types Ty, every symbol $f \in \Sigma$ has a type of the form $\tau_1 \times \ldots \times \tau_k \to \tau$ with $\tau_1, \ldots, \tau_k, \tau \in Ty$. Moreover, every variable has a type from Ty, and we assume that $\mathcal{V}$ contains infinitely many variables of every type in Ty. We call $t \in \mathcal{T}(\Sigma, \mathcal{V})$ a* well-typed *term of type τ iff either $t \in \mathcal{V}$ is a variable of type τ or $t = f(t_1, \ldots, t_k)$ where f has the type $\tau_1 \times \ldots \times \tau_k \to \tau$ and each t_i is a well-typed term of type τ_i.*

A rewrite rule $\ell \to r$ is well typed iff ℓ and r are well-typed terms of the same type. A TRS $\mathcal{R}/\mathcal{S}$ is well typed iff all rules of $\mathcal{R} \cup \mathcal{S}$ are well typed. (W.l.o.g., here one may rename the variables in every rule. Then it is not a problem if the variable x is used with type τ_1 in one rule and with type τ_2 in another rule.)

Example 11. For any TRS $\mathcal{R}/\mathcal{S}$, standard algorithms can compute a type assignment to make $\mathcal{R}/\mathcal{S}$ well typed (and to decompose the terms into as many types as possible). For the TRS from Example 2 we obtain the following type assignment. Note that for this type assignment the TRS is not completely defined since $\mathsf{if}(\mathsf{true}, \mathsf{0}, \mathsf{nil})$ is a well-typed basic ground term in normal form w.r.t. $\mathcal{R} \cup \mathcal{S}$.

$\mathsf{isort} :: \mathbf{List} \times \mathbf{List} \to \mathbf{List}$	$\mathsf{0} :: \mathbf{Nat}$	$\mathsf{gt} :: \mathbf{Nat} \times \mathbf{Nat} \to \mathbf{Bool}$
$\mathsf{ins} :: \mathbf{Nat} \times \mathbf{List} \to \mathbf{List}$	$\mathsf{s} :: \mathbf{Nat} \to \mathbf{Nat}$	$\mathsf{true}, \mathsf{false} :: \mathbf{Bool}$
$\mathsf{if} :: \mathbf{Bool} \times \mathbf{Nat} \times \mathbf{List} \to \mathbf{List}$	$\mathsf{nil} :: \mathbf{List}$	$\mathsf{cons} :: \mathbf{Nat} \times \mathbf{List} \to \mathbf{List}$

Definition 12 (Completely Defined). *A well-typed TRS $\mathcal{R}/\mathcal{S}$ over a many-sorted signature with types Ty is* completely defined *iff there is at least one constant for each $\tau \in Ty$ and no well-typed basic ground term in $\mathcal{R} \cup \mathcal{S}$-normal form.*

For completely defined TRSs, the transformation from TRSs to RNTSs is sound.

Theorem 13 (Soundness of Abstraction $\wr\cdot\int$). *Let $\mathcal{R}/\mathcal{S}$ be a well-typed, completely defined constructor system. Then $\mathrm{dh}(t, \xrightarrow{\mathrm{i}}_{\mathcal{R}/\mathcal{S}}) \leq \mathrm{dhw}([\![\wr t \int]\!], \to_{\wr\mathcal{R}/\mathcal{S}\int})$ holds for all well-typed ground terms t. Let $\mathcal{N}$ be a terminating variant of $\mathcal{S}$ such that $\mathcal{R}/(\mathcal{S} \cup \mathcal{N})$ is also well typed. If $\mathcal{R}/(\mathcal{S} \cup \mathcal{N})$ is completely defined, then we have $\mathrm{irc}_{\mathcal{R}/\mathcal{S}}(n) \leq \mathrm{irc}_{\wr\mathcal{R}/(\mathcal{S}\cup\mathcal{N})\int}(n)$ for all $n \in \mathbb{N}$.*

As every TRS $\mathcal{R}/\mathcal{S}$ is well typed w.r.t. *some* type assignment (e.g., the one with just a single type), the only additional restriction in Theorem 13 is that the TRS has to be completely defined. This can always be achieved by extending $\mathcal{S}$ by a suitable terminating variant $\mathcal{N}$ of $\mathcal{S}$ automatically. Based on standard algorithms to detect well-typed basic ground terms $f(\ldots)$ in $(\mathcal{R} \cup \mathcal{S})$-normal form [30,31], we add the rules $f(x_1, \ldots, x_k) \to t_f$ to $\mathcal{N}$, where again for each f, we choose some constructor ground term $t_f \in \mathcal{T}(\Sigma_c^{\mathcal{R}\cup\mathcal{S}}, \varnothing)$. As shown by Theorem 9, we have $\mathrm{dh}(t, \xrightarrow{\mathrm{i}}_{\mathcal{R}/\mathcal{S}}) \leq \mathrm{dh}(t\sigma, \xrightarrow{\mathrm{i}}_{\mathcal{R}/(\mathcal{S}\cup\mathcal{N})})$ for *any* terminating variant $\mathcal{N}$, i.e., adding such rules never decreases the derivation height. So even if $\mathcal{R}/\mathcal{S}$ is not completely defined and just $\mathcal{R}/(\mathcal{S} \cup \mathcal{N})$ is completely defined, we still have $\mathrm{irc}_{\mathcal{R}/\mathcal{S}}(n) \leq \mathrm{irc}_{\mathcal{R}/(\mathcal{S}\cup\mathcal{N})}(n) \leq \mathrm{irc}_{\wr\mathcal{R}/(\mathcal{S}\cup\mathcal{N})\wr}(n)$.

Example 14. To make the TRS of Example 2 completely defined, we add rules for all defined symbols in basic ground normal forms. In this example, the only such symbol is if*. Hence, for instance we add* $\mathsf{if}(b, x, xs) \to \mathsf{nil}$ *to* $\mathcal{S}$*. The resulting TRS* $\mathcal{S} \cup \{\mathsf{if}(b, x, xs) \to \mathsf{nil}\}$ *is clearly a terminating variant of* $\mathcal{S}$*. Hence, to analyze complexity of the insertion sort TRS, we now extend the RNTS of Example 7 by*

$$\wr\mathsf{if}(b, x, xs) \to \mathsf{nil}\wr_0 \quad = \quad \mathsf{if}(b, x, xs) \xrightarrow{0} 1 \;\; [b \geq 1 \wedge x \geq 1 \wedge xs \geq 1] \tag{10}$$

4 Analyzing the Complexity of RNTSs

Theorem 13 allows us to reduce complexity analysis of term rewriting to the analysis of RNTSs. Our RNTSs are related to *integer transition systems* (ITSs), a formalism often used to abstract programs. The main difference is that RNTSs can model procedure calls by nested function symbols $f(\ldots g(\ldots)\ldots)$ on the right-hand side of rules, whereas ITSs may allow right-hand sides like $f(\ldots) + g(\ldots)$, but no nesting of $f, g \in \Sigma$. So ITSs cannot pass the result of one function as a parameter to another function. Note that in contrast to the usual definition of ITSs, in our setting reductions can begin with any (nat-basic) terms instead of dedicated start terms, and it suffices to regard natural instead of integer numbers. (An extension to recursive transition systems on integers would be possible by measuring the size of integers by their absolute value, as in [13].)

Definition 15 (ITS). *An RNTS* $\mathcal{P}$ *over the signature* Σ *is an* ITS *iff symbols from* Σ *occur only at parallel positions in right-hand sides of* $\mathcal{P}$*. Here,* π *and* π' *are* parallel *iff* π *is not a prefix of* π' *and* π' *is not a prefix of* π*.*

Upper runtime complexity bounds for an ITS $\mathcal{P}$ can, for example, be inferred by generating ranking functions which decrease with each application of a rule from $\mathcal{P}$. Then, the ranking functions are multiplied with the weight of the rules.

However, many analysis techniques for ITSs (e.g., [1,4,13,34]) cannot handle the RNTSs generated from standard TRSs. Thus, we now introduce a new modular approach that allows us to apply existing tools for ITSs to analyze RNTSs. Our approach builds upon the idea of alternating between *runtime* and *size* analysis [13]. The key insight is to *summarize* procedures by approximating their runtime and the size of their result, and then to eliminate them from the program. In this way, our analysis decomposes the "call graph" of the RNTS into "blocks" of mutually recursive functions and exports each block of mutually recursive functions into a separate ITS. Thus, in each analysis step it suffices to analyze just an ITS instead of an RNTS. We use weakly monotonic runtime and size bounds from $\mathcal{T}(\Sigma_{\mathsf{exp}}, \mathcal{V})$ to compose them easily when analyzing nested terms.

Definition 16 (Runtime and Size Bounds). *For any terms* $t_1, \ldots, t_k$, *let* $\{x_1/t_1, \ldots, x_k/t_k\}$ *be the substitution* σ *with* $x_i\sigma = t_i$ *for* $1 \leq i \leq k$ *and* $y\sigma = y$ *for* $y \in \mathcal{V} \setminus \{x_1, \ldots, x_k\}$. *Then* $\mathsf{rt} : \Sigma \to \mathcal{T}(\Sigma_{\mathsf{exp}}, \mathcal{V}) \cup \{\omega\}$ *is a* runtime bound *for an RNTS* $\mathcal{P}$ *iff we have* $\mathrm{dhw}(f(n_1, \ldots, n_k), \to_{\mathcal{P}}) \leq [\![\mathsf{rt}(f)\,\{x_1/n_1, \ldots, x_k/n_k\}]\!]$ *for all* $n_1, \ldots, n_k \in \mathbb{N}$ *and all* $f \in \Sigma$. *Similarly,* $\mathsf{sz} : \Sigma \to \mathcal{T}(\Sigma_{\mathsf{exp}}, \mathcal{V}) \cup \{\omega\}$ *is a* size bound *for* $\mathcal{P}$ *iff* $n \leq [\![\mathsf{sz}(f)\,\{x_1/n_1, \ldots, x_k/n_k\}]\!]$ *for all* $n_1, \ldots, n_k \in \mathbb{N}$, *all* $f \in \Sigma$, *and all* $n \in \mathbb{N}$ *with* $f(n_1, \ldots, n_k) \to_{\mathcal{P}}^* n$.

Example 17. For the RNTS $\{(1'), \ldots, (9'), (10)\}$ *from Example* 14, *any function* rt *with* $\mathsf{rt}(\mathsf{isort}) \geq \lfloor \frac{x_1 - 1}{2} \rfloor \cdot x_2 + 1$, $\mathsf{rt}(\mathsf{ins}) \geq x_2$, $\mathsf{rt}(\mathsf{if}) \geq x_3 - 1$, and $\mathsf{rt}(\mathsf{gt}) \geq 0$ *is a runtime bound (recall that the* gt*-rules have weight* 0*). Similarly, any* sz *with* $\mathsf{sz}(\mathsf{isort}) \geq x_1 + x_2 - 1$, $\mathsf{sz}(\mathsf{ins}) \geq x_1 + x_2 + 1$, $\mathsf{sz}(\mathsf{if}) \geq x_2 + x_3 + 1$, $\mathsf{sz}(\mathsf{gt}) \geq 1$ *is a size bound.*

A runtime bound clearly gives rise to an upper bound on the runtime complexity.

Theorem 18 (**rt and** irc). *Let* rt *be a runtime bound for an RNTS* $\mathcal{P}$. *Then for all* $n \in \mathbb{N}$, *we have* $\mathrm{irc}_{\mathcal{P}}(n) \leq \sup\{[\![\mathsf{rt}(f)\,\{x_1/n_1, \ldots, x_k/n_k\}]\!] \mid f \in \Sigma, n_1, \ldots, n_k \in \mathbb{N}, \sum_{i=1}^{k} n_i < n\}$. *So in particular,* $\mathrm{irc}_{\mathcal{P}}(n) \in \mathcal{O}(\sum_{f \in \Sigma} [\![\mathsf{rt}(f)\,\{x_1/n, \ldots, x_k/n\}]\!])$.

Thus, a suitable runtime bound rt for the RNTS $\{(1'), \ldots, (9'), (10)\}$ yields $\mathrm{irc}(n) \in \mathcal{O}(n^2)$, cf. Example 17. In Sect. 4.2 we present a new technique to infer runtime and size bounds rt and sz automatically with existing complexity tools for ITSs. As these tools usually return only runtime bounds, Sect. 4.1 shows how they can also be used to generate size bounds.

4.1 Size Bounds as Runtime Bounds

We first present a transformation for a large class of ITSs that lets us obtain size bounds from any method that can infer runtime bounds. The transformation extends each function symbol from Σ by an additional accumulator argument. Then terms that are multiplied with the result of a function are collected in the accumulator. Terms that are added to the result are moved to the weight of the rule.

Theorem 19 (ITS Size Bounds). *Let* $\mathcal{P}$ *be an ITS whose rules are of the form* $\ell \xrightarrow{w} u + v \cdot r\,[\varphi]$ *or* $\ell \xrightarrow{w} u\,[\varphi]$ *with* $u, v \in \mathcal{T}(\Sigma_{\mathsf{exp}}, \mathcal{V})$ *and* $\mathrm{root}(r) \in \Sigma$. *Let* $\mathcal{P}_{\mathsf{size}} =$

$$\{f'(x_1, ..., x_k, z) \xrightarrow{u \cdot z} g'(t_1, ..., t_n, v \cdot z)\,[\varphi] \mid f(x_1, ..., x_k) \xrightarrow{w} u + v \cdot g(t_1, ..., t_n)\,[\varphi] \in \mathcal{P}\}$$
$$\cup \quad \{f'(x_1, ..., x_k, z) \xrightarrow{u \cdot z} 0\ [\varphi] \mid f(x_1, ..., x_k) \xrightarrow{w} u\ [\varphi] \in \mathcal{P}\}$$

for a fresh variable $z \in \mathcal{V}$. *Let* rt *be a runtime bound for* $\mathcal{P}_{\mathsf{size}}$. *Then* sz *with* $\mathsf{sz}(f) = \mathsf{rt}(f')\{x_{k+1}/1\}$ *for any* $f \in \Sigma$ *is a size bound for* $\mathcal{P}$.

Theorem 19 can be generalized to right-hand sides like $f(x) + 2 \cdot g(y)$ with $f, g \in \Sigma$, cf. [5]. However, it is not applicable if the results of function calls are multiplied on right-hand sides (e.g., $f(x) \cdot g(y)$) and our technique fails in such cases.

Example 20. To get a size bound for $\mathcal{P}^{\mathsf{gt}} = \{(7'), (8'), (9')\}$*, we construct* $\mathcal{P}^{\mathsf{gt}}_{\mathsf{size}}$:

$$\begin{array}{lll} \mathsf{gt}'(x, y, z) & \xrightarrow{z} 0 & [x = 1 \wedge \ldots] \\ \mathsf{gt}'(x', y, z) & \xrightarrow{z} 0 & [x' = 1 + x \wedge y = 1 \wedge \ldots] \\ \mathsf{gt}'(x', y', z) & \xrightarrow{0} \mathsf{gt}'(x, y, z) & [x' = 1 + x \wedge y' = 1 + y \wedge \ldots] \end{array}$$

Existing ITS tools can compute a runtime bound like $\mathsf{rt}(\mathsf{gt}') = x_3$ *for* $\mathcal{P}^{\mathsf{gt}}_{\mathsf{size}}$*. Hence, by Theorem 19 we obtain the size bound* sz *for* $\mathcal{P}^{\mathsf{gt}}$ *with* $\mathsf{sz}(\mathsf{gt}) = \mathsf{rt}(\mathsf{gt}')\{x_3/1\} = 1$.

4.2 Complexity Bounds for Recursive Programs

Now we show how complexity tools for ITSs can be used to infer runtime and size bounds for RNTSs. We first define a *call-graph* relation $\sqsupset$ to determine in which order we analyze symbols of Σ. Essentially, $f \sqsupset g$ holds iff $f(\ldots)$ rewrites to a term containing g.

Definition 21 ($\sqsupset$)**.** *For an RNTS* $\mathcal{P}$*, the* call-graph relation $\sqsupset$ *is the transitive closure of* $\{(\mathrm{root}(\ell), g) \mid \ell \xrightarrow{w} r[\varphi] \in \mathcal{P}, g \in \Sigma$ *occurs in* $r\}$*. An RNTS has* nested recursion *iff it has a rule* $\ell \xrightarrow{w} r\,[\varphi]$ *with* $\mathrm{root}(r|_\pi) \sqsupset \mathrm{root}(\ell)$ *and* $\mathrm{root}(r|_{\pi'}) \sqsupset \mathrm{root}(\ell)$ *for positions* $\pi < \pi'$*. As usual,* $\pi < \pi'$ *means that* π *is a proper prefix of* π' *(i.e., that* π' *is* strictly below π*). A symbol* $f \in \Sigma_d^{\mathcal{P}}$ *is a* bottom symbol *iff* $f \sqsupset g$ *implies* $g \sqsupset f$ *for all* $g \in \Sigma_d^{\mathcal{P}}$*. The sub-RNTS of* $\mathcal{P}$ induced *by* f *is* $\mathcal{P}^f = \{\ell \xrightarrow{w} r[\varphi] \in \mathcal{P} \mid f \sqsupseteq \mathrm{root}(\ell)\}$*, where* $\sqsupseteq$ *is the reflexive closure of* $\sqsupset$.

Example 22. For the RNTS $\mathcal{P}$ *from Examples 14 and 17, we have* $\mathsf{isort} \sqsupset \mathsf{ins} \sqsupset \mathsf{if} \sqsupset \mathsf{ins} \sqsupset \mathsf{gt}$*. The only bottom symbol is* gt*. It induces the sub-RNTS* $\mathcal{P}^{\mathsf{gt}} = \{(7'), (8'), (9')\}$*,* ins *induces* $\{(3'), \ldots, (9'), (10)\}$*, and* isort *induces the full RNTS of Example 14.*

Our approach cannot handle programs like $f(\ldots) \to f(\ldots f(\ldots) \ldots)$ with nested recursion, but such programs rarely occur in practice. To compute bounds for an RNTS $\mathcal{P}$ without nested recursion, we start with the trivial bounds $\mathsf{rt}(f) = \mathsf{sz}(f) = \omega$ for all $f \in \Sigma_d^{\mathcal{P}}$. In each step, we analyze the sub-RNTS $\mathcal{P}^f$ induced by a bottom symbol f and refine rt and sz for all defined symbols of $\mathcal{P}^f$. Afterwards we remove the rules $\mathcal{P}^f$ from $\mathcal{P}$ and continue with the next bottom symbol. By this removal of rules, the former defined symbol f becomes a constructor, and former non-bottom symbols are turned into bottom symbols.

To analyze the RNTS $\mathcal{P}^f$, Theorem 27 will transform $\mathcal{P}^f$ into two ITSs $\mathcal{P}^f_{\mathsf{sz}}$ and $\mathcal{P}^f_{\mathsf{rt},\mathsf{sz}}$ by abstracting away calls to functions which we already analyzed. Then existing tools for ITSs can be used to compute a size resp. runtime bound for $\mathcal{P}^f_{\mathsf{sz}}$ resp. $\mathcal{P}^f_{\mathsf{rt},\mathsf{sz}}$. Our overall algorithm to infer bounds for RNTSs is summarized in Algorithm 1. It clearly terminates, as every loop iteration eliminates a defined symbol (since Step 3.8 removes all rules for the currently analyzed symbol f).

When computing bounds for a bottom symbol $f \in \Sigma_d^{\mathcal{P}}$, we already know (weakly monotonic) size and runtime bounds for all constructors $g \in \Sigma_c^{\mathcal{P}}$. Hence to transform RNTSs into ITSs, *outer* calls of constructors g in terms

Algorithm 1. Computing Runtime and Size Bounds for RNTSs

1 Let $\mathsf{rt}(f) := \mathsf{sz}(f) := \omega$ for each $f \in \Sigma_d^{\mathcal{P}}$ and $\mathsf{rt}(f) := \mathsf{sz}(f) := 0$ for each $f \in \Sigma_c^{\mathcal{P}}$.
2 If $\mathcal{P}$ has nested recursion, then return rt and sz.
3 While $\mathcal{P}$ is not empty:
  3.1 Choose a bottom symbol f of $\mathcal{P}$ and let $\mathcal{P}^f$ be the sub-RNTS induced by f.
  3.2 Construct $\mathcal{P}^f_{\mathsf{sz}}$ according to Thm. 27 and $(\mathcal{P}^f_{\mathsf{sz}})_{\mathsf{size}}$ according to Thm. 19 (resp. its generalization) if possible, otherwise return rt and sz.
  3.3 Compute a runtime bound for $(\mathcal{P}^f_{\mathsf{sz}})_{\mathsf{size}}$ using existing ITS tools and let sz_f be this bound (cf. Thm. 19).
  3.4 For each $g \in \Sigma_d^{\mathcal{P}^f}$, let $\mathsf{sz}(g) := \mathsf{sz}_f(g)$.
  3.5 Construct $\mathcal{P}^f_{\mathsf{rt},\mathsf{sz}}$ according to Thm. 27.
  3.6 Compute a runtime bound rt_f for $\mathcal{P}^f_{\mathsf{rt},\mathsf{sz}}$ using existing ITS tools.
  3.7 For each $g \in \Sigma_d^{\mathcal{P}^f}$, let $\mathsf{rt}(g) := \mathsf{rt}_f(g)$.
  3.8 Let $\mathcal{P} := \mathcal{P} \setminus \mathcal{P}^f$.
4 Return rt and sz.

$g(\ldots f(\ldots)\ldots)$ can be replaced by $\mathsf{sz}(g)$. In Definition 23, while $\mathsf{sz}(t)$ replaces *all* calls to procedures $g \in \Sigma$ in t by their size bound, the *outer abstraction* $\mathfrak{a}^{\circ}_{\mathsf{sz}}(t)$ only replaces constructors $g \in \Sigma_c^{\mathcal{P}}$ by their size bound $\mathsf{sz}(g)$, provided that they do not occur below defined symbols $f \in \Sigma_d^{\mathcal{P}}$.

Definition 23 (Outer Abstraction). *Let $\mathcal{P}$ be an RNTS with the size bound* sz. *We lift* sz *to terms by defining* $\mathsf{sz}(x) = x$ *for* $x \in \mathcal{V}$ *and*

$$\mathsf{sz}(g(s_1,\ldots,s_n)) = \begin{cases} \mathsf{sz}(g)\,\{x_j/\mathsf{sz}(s_j) \mid 1 \le j \le n\} & \text{if } g \in \Sigma \\ g(\mathsf{sz}(s_1),\ldots,\mathsf{sz}(s_n)) & \text{if } g \in \Sigma_{\mathit{exp}} \end{cases}$$

The outer abstraction *of a term is defined as* $\mathfrak{a}^{\circ}_{\mathsf{sz}}(x) = x$ *for* $x \in \mathcal{V}$ *and*

$$\mathfrak{a}^{\circ}_{\mathsf{sz}}(g(s_1,\ldots,s_n)) = \begin{cases} \mathsf{sz}(g)\,\{x_j/\mathfrak{a}^{\circ}_{\mathsf{sz}}(s_j) \mid 1 \le j \le n\} & \text{if } g \in \Sigma_c^{\mathcal{P}} \\ g(\mathfrak{a}^{\circ}_{\mathsf{sz}}(s_1),\ldots,\mathfrak{a}^{\circ}_{\mathsf{sz}}(s_n)) & \text{if } g \in \Sigma_{\mathit{exp}} \\ g(s_1,\ldots,s_n) & \text{if } g \in \Sigma_d^{\mathcal{P}} \end{cases}$$

Example 24. Consider the following variant $\mathcal{R}^{\times}$ *of* `AG01/#3.16.xml` *from the TPDB*[2] *and its RNTS-counterpart* $\wr\mathcal{R}^{\times}\wr$:

$$\begin{array}{lll} \mathcal{R}^{\times}: & \wr\mathcal{R}^{\times}\wr: & \\ \mathsf{f}_+(0,y) \to y & \mathsf{f}_+(x,y) \xrightarrow{1} y & [x = 1 \land \ldots] \quad (11) \\ \mathsf{f}_+(\mathsf{s}(x),y) \to \mathsf{s}(\mathsf{f}_+(x,y)) & \mathsf{f}_+(x',y) \xrightarrow{1} 1 + \mathsf{f}_+(x,y) & [x' = x+1 \land \ldots] \quad (12) \\ \mathsf{f}_\times(0,y) \to 0 & \mathsf{f}_\times(x,y) \xrightarrow{1} 1 & [x = 1 \land \ldots] \quad (13) \\ \mathsf{f}_\times(\mathsf{s}(x),y) \to \mathsf{f}_+(\mathsf{f}_\times(x,y),y) & \mathsf{f}_\times(x',y) \xrightarrow{1} \mathsf{f}_+(\mathsf{f}_\times(x,y),y) & [x' = x+1 \land \ldots] \quad (14) \end{array}$$

[2] *Termination Problems Data Base*, the collection of examples used at the annual *Termination and Complexity Competition*, see http://termination-portal.org.

Assume that we already analyzed its only bottom symbol f_+ *and obtained* $\mathsf{sz}(\mathsf{f}_+) = x_1 + x_2$ *and* $\mathsf{rt}(\mathsf{f}_+) = x_1$. *Afterwards, (11) and (12) were removed. Now Definition 23 is used to transform the sub-RNTS* $\{(13), (14)\}$ *induced by* $\mathsf{f}_\times$ *into an* ITS. *The only rule of* $\lfloor\mathcal{R}^\times\rfloor$ *that violates the restriction of* ITSs *is (14). Thus, let (14′) result from (14) by replacing its right-hand side by* $\mathfrak{a}^{\mathsf{o}}_{\mathsf{sz}}(\mathsf{f}_+(\mathsf{f}_\times(x,y),y)) = \mathsf{sz}(\mathsf{f}_+)\,\{x_1/\mathsf{f}_\times(x,y), x_2/y\} = \mathsf{f}_\times(x,y)+y$. *Now* $\{(13), (14')\}$ *is an ITS, and together with Theorem 19, existing ITS tools can generate a size bound like* $\mathsf{sz}(\mathsf{f}_\times) = x_1 \cdot x_2$.

To finish the transformation of RNTSs to ITSs, we now handle terms like $f(\ldots g(\ldots)\ldots)$ where $f \in \Sigma_d^{\mathcal{P}}$ is the bottom symbol we are analyzing and we have an *inner* call of a constructor $g \in \Sigma_c^{\mathcal{P}}$. We would like to replace g by $\mathsf{sz}(g)$ again. However, f might behave non-monotonically (i.e., f might need *less* runtime on *greater* arguments). Therefore, we replace all inner calls $g(\ldots)$ of constructors by fresh variables x. The size bound of the replaced call $g(\ldots)$ is an upper bound for the value of x, but x can also take smaller values.

Definition 25 (Inner Abstraction). *Let* $\mathcal{P}$ *be an RNTS with size bound* sz, *t be a term, and* $\mathcal{P}os_c^{top} \subseteq \mathcal{P}os(t)$ *be the topmost positions of* $\Sigma_c^{\mathcal{P}}$*-symbols below* $\Sigma_d^{\mathcal{P}}$*-symbols in t. Thus,* $\mu \in \mathcal{P}os_c^{top}$ *iff* $\mathrm{root}(t|_\mu) \in \Sigma_c^{\mathcal{P}}$, *there exists a* $\pi < \mu$ *with* $\mathrm{root}(t|_\pi) \in \Sigma_d^{\mathcal{P}}$, *and* $\mathrm{root}(t|_{\pi'}) \in \Sigma_{\mathsf{exp}}$ *for all* $\pi < \pi' < \mu$. *For* $\mathcal{P}os_c^{top} = \{\mu_1, \ldots, \mu_k\}$, *$t$'s* inner abstraction *is* $\mathfrak{a}^{\mathsf{i}}(t) = t[x_1]_{\mu_1} \ldots [x_k]_{\mu_k}$ *where* $x_1, \ldots, x_k$ *are pairwise different fresh variables, and its* condition *is* $\psi^{\mathsf{i}}_{\mathsf{sz}}(t) = \bigwedge_{1 \le i \le k} x_i \le \mathsf{sz}(t|_{\mu_i})$.

Example 26. For the RNTS of Examples 14 and 17, we start with analyzing $\mathcal{P}^{\mathsf{gt}}$ *which yields* $\mathsf{sz}(\mathsf{gt}) = 1$ *and* $\mathsf{rt}(\mathsf{gt}) = 0$, *cf. Example 20. After removing the* gt*-rules, the new bottom symbols are* ins *and* if. *The right-hand side of Rule (4′) contains a call of* gt *below the symbol* if. *With the size bound* $\mathsf{sz}(\mathsf{gt}) = 1$, *the inner abstraction of this right-hand side is* $\mathfrak{a}^{\mathsf{i}}(\mathsf{if}(\mathsf{gt}(x,y), x, ys')) = \mathsf{if}(x_1, x, ys')$, *and the corresponding condition* $\psi^{\mathsf{i}}_{\mathsf{sz}}(\mathsf{if}(\mathsf{gt}(x,y), x, ys'))$ *is* $x_1 \le 1$, *since* $\mathsf{sz}(\mathsf{gt}(x,y)) = 1$.

Theorem 27 states how to transform RNTSs into ITSs in order to compute runtime and size bounds. Suppose that we have already analyzed the function symbols $g_1, \ldots, g_m$, that f becomes a new bottom symbol if the rules for $g_1, \ldots, g_m$ are removed, that $\mathcal{Q}$ is the sub-RNTS induced by f, and that $\mathcal{P}$ results from $\mathcal{Q}$ by deleting the rules for $g_1, \ldots, g_m$. Thus, if g_i occurs in $\mathcal{P}$, then $g_i \in \Sigma_c^{\mathcal{P}}$.

So in our leading example, we have $g_1 = \mathsf{gt}$ (i.e., all gt-rules were analyzed and removed). Thus, ins is a new bottom symbol. If we want to analyze it by Theorem 27, then $\mathcal{Q}$ contains all ins-, if-, and gt-rules and $\mathcal{P}$ just contains all ins- and if-rules.

Since we restricted ourselves to RNTSs $\mathcal{Q}$ without nested recursion, $\mathcal{P}$ has no nested defined symbols. To infer a *size* bound for the bottom symbol f of $\mathcal{P}$, we abstract away inner occurrences of g_i by $\mathfrak{a}^{\mathsf{i}}$ (e.g., gt on the right-hand side of Rule (4′) in our example), and we abstract away outer occurrences of g_i by

$\mathfrak{a}^{\mathsf{o}}_{\mathsf{sz}}$. So every right-hand side r is replaced by $\mathfrak{a}^{\mathsf{o}}_{\mathsf{sz}}(\mathfrak{a}^{\mathsf{i}}(r))$ and we add the condition $\psi^{\mathsf{i}}_{\mathsf{sz}}(r)$ which restricts the values of the fresh variables introduced by $\mathfrak{a}^{\mathsf{i}}$.

To infer *runtime* bounds, inner occurrences of g_i are also abstracted by $\mathfrak{a}^{\mathsf{i}}$, and outer occurrences of g_i are simply removed. So every right-hand side r is replaced by $\sum_{\pi \in \mathcal{P}os_d(r)} \mathfrak{a}^{\mathsf{i}}(r|_\pi)$, where $\mathcal{P}os_d(r) = \{\pi \in \mathcal{P}os(r) \mid \mathrm{root}(r|_\pi) \in \Sigma^{\mathcal{P}}_d\}$. However, we have to take into account how many computation steps would be required in the procedures g_i that were called in r. Therefore, we compute the *cost* of all calls of g_i in a rule's right-hand side and add it to the weight of the rule. To estimate the cost of a call $g_i(s_1, \ldots, s_n)$, we "apply" $\mathsf{rt}(g_i)$ to the size bounds of $s_1, \ldots, s_n$ and add the costs for evaluating $s_1, \ldots, s_n$.

Theorem 27 (Transformation of RNTSs to ITSs). *Let $\mathcal{Q}$ be an RNTS with size and runtime bounds* sz *and* rt *and let $\mathcal{P} = \mathcal{Q} \setminus (\mathcal{Q}^{g_1} \cup \ldots \cup \mathcal{Q}^{g_m})$, where $g_1, \ldots, g_m \in \Sigma$ and $\mathcal{Q}^{g_i}$ is the sub-RNTS of $\mathcal{Q}$ induced by g_i. We define*

$$\mathcal{P}_{\mathsf{sz}} \;=\; \{\, \ell \xrightarrow{w} \mathfrak{a}^{\mathsf{o}}_{\mathsf{sz}}(\mathfrak{a}^{\mathsf{i}}(r)) \; [\varphi \wedge \psi^{\mathsf{i}}_{\mathsf{sz}}(r)] \;\mid\; \ell \xrightarrow{w} r \, [\varphi] \in \mathcal{P} \,\}$$

Let sz' be a size bound for $\mathcal{P}_{\mathsf{sz}}$ where $\mathsf{sz}'(f) = \mathsf{sz}(f)$ for all $f \in \Sigma \setminus \Sigma^{\mathcal{P}}_d$. If $\mathcal{P}$ does not have nested defined symbols, then sz' is a size bound for $\mathcal{Q}$.

To obtain a runtime bound for $\mathcal{Q}$, we define an RNTS $\mathcal{P}_{\mathsf{rt},\mathsf{sz}'}$. To this end, we define the cost *of a term as $\mathfrak{c}_{\mathsf{rt},\mathsf{sz}'}(x) = 0$ for $x \in \mathcal{V}$ and*

$$\mathfrak{c}_{\mathsf{rt},\mathsf{sz}'}(g(s_1, \ldots, s_n)) = \begin{cases} \sum_{1 \le j \le n} \mathfrak{c}_{\mathsf{rt},\mathsf{sz}'}(s_j) + \mathsf{rt}(g)\, \{x_j/\mathsf{sz}'(s_j) \mid 1 \le j \le n\} & \text{if } g \in \Sigma^{\mathcal{P}}_c \\ \sum_{1 \le j \le n} \mathfrak{c}_{\mathsf{rt},\mathsf{sz}'}(s_j) & \text{otherwise} \end{cases}$$

Now $\mathcal{P}_{\mathsf{rt},\mathsf{sz}'} = \{\ell \xrightarrow{w + \mathfrak{c}_{\mathsf{rt},\mathsf{sz}'}(r)} \sum_{\pi \in \mathcal{P}os_d(r)} \mathfrak{a}^{\mathsf{i}}(r|_\pi) \;\; [\varphi \wedge \psi^{\mathsf{i}}_{\mathsf{sz}'}(r)] \;\mid\; \ell \xrightarrow{w} r\,[\varphi] \in \mathcal{P}\}$. Then every runtime bound rt' for $\mathcal{P}_{\mathsf{rt},\mathsf{sz}'}$ with $\mathsf{rt}'(f) = \mathsf{rt}(f)$ for all $f \in \Sigma \setminus \Sigma^{\mathcal{P}}_d$ is a runtime bound for $\mathcal{Q}$. Here, all occurrences of ω in $\mathcal{P}_{\mathsf{sz}}$ or $\mathcal{P}_{\mathsf{rt},\mathsf{sz}'}$ are replaced by pairwise different fresh variables.

If $\mathcal{P}$ does not have nested defined symbols, then $\mathcal{P}_{\mathsf{sz}}$ and $\mathcal{P}_{\mathsf{rt},\mathsf{sz}'}$ are ITSs and thus, they can be analyzed by existing ITS tools.

Example 28. We now finish analyzing the RNTS $\wr \mathcal{R}^{\times} \wr$ after updating sz *as in Example 24. The cost of the right-hand side of (14) is $\mathfrak{c}_{\mathsf{rt},\mathsf{sz}}(\mathsf{f}_+(\mathsf{f}_\times(x, y), y)) = \mathsf{rt}(\mathsf{f}_+)\,\{x_1/x \cdot y, x_2/y\} = x \cdot y$. So for the sub-RNTS $\mathcal{P} = \{(13), (14)\}$ induced by $\mathsf{f}_\times$, $\mathcal{P}_{\mathsf{rt},\mathsf{sz}}$ is*

$$\mathsf{f}_\times(x, y) \xrightarrow{1} 0 \;\; [x = 1 \wedge \ldots] \qquad\qquad \mathsf{f}_\times(x', y) \xrightarrow{1 + x \cdot y} \mathsf{f}_\times(x, y) \;\; [x' = x + 1 \wedge \ldots]$$

Hence, existing ITS tools like CoFloCo *[16,17] or* KoAT *[13] yield a bound like $\mathsf{rt}(\mathsf{f}_\times) = x_1^2 \cdot x_2$. So by Theorems 13 and 18 we get $\mathrm{irc}_{\mathcal{R}^\times}(n) \le \mathrm{irc}_{\wr \mathcal{R}^\times \wr}(n) \in \mathcal{O}(n^3)$.*

Example 29. To finish the analysis of the RNTS from Example 14, we continue Example 26. After we removed $\mathcal{P}^{\mathsf{gt}}$, *the new bottom symbols* ins *and* if *both induce* $\mathcal{P}^{\mathsf{ins}} = \{(3'), \ldots, (6'), (10)\}$. *Constructing* $\mathcal{P}^{\mathsf{ins}}_{\mathsf{sz}}$ *yields the rules* (3′), (5′), (6′), (10), *and*

$$\mathsf{ins}(x, ys') \xrightarrow{1} \mathsf{if}(x_1, x, ys') \; [ys' = 1 + y + ys \wedge \ldots \wedge x_1 \leq 1] \qquad (4'')$$

Existing tools like CoFloCo *or* KoAT *compute size bounds like* $1 + x_1 + x_2$ *for* ins *and* $1 + x_2 + x_3$ *for* if *using Theorem 19. After updatingsz, we construct* $\mathcal{P}^{\mathsf{ins}}_{\mathsf{rt,sz}}$ *which consists of* (4″) *and variants of* (3′), (5′), (6′), (10) *with unchanged weights (as* $\mathsf{c}_{\mathsf{rt,sz}}(\mathsf{gt}(x, y)) = \mathsf{rt}(\mathsf{gt}) = 0$). *ITS tools now infer runtime bounds like* $2 \cdot x_2$ *for* ins *and* $2 \cdot x_3$ *for* if. *After removing* ins *and* if, *we analyze the remaining RNTS* $\mathcal{P}^{\mathsf{isort}} = \{(1'), (2')\}$. *Since the right-hand side of* (2′) *contains an inner occurrence of* ins *below* isort, (2′) *is replaced by*

$$\mathsf{isort}(xs', ys) \xrightarrow{w} \mathsf{isort}(xs, ys') \; [xs' = 1 + x + xs \wedge ys' \leq 1 + x + ys \wedge \ldots]$$

where $w = 1$ *in* $\mathcal{P}^{\mathsf{isort}}_{\mathsf{sz}}$ *and* $w = 1 + \mathsf{rt}(\mathsf{ins})\{x_1/x, x_2/ys\} = 1 + 2 \cdot ys$ *in* $\mathcal{P}^{\mathsf{isort}}_{\mathsf{rt,sz}}$. *Using Theorem 19, one can now infer bounds like* $\mathsf{sz}(\mathsf{isort}) = x_1 + x_2$ *and* $\mathsf{rt}(\mathsf{isort}) = x_1^2 + 2 \cdot x_1 \cdot x_2$. *Hence, by Theorem 18 one can deduce* $\mathrm{irc}(n) \in \mathcal{O}(n^2)$.

Based on Theorem 27, we can now show the correctness of our overall analysis.

Theorem 30 (Algorithm *1* is Sound). *Let* $\mathcal{P}$ *be an RNTS and let* rt *and* sz *be the result of Algorithm 1 for* $\mathcal{P}$. *Then* rt *is a runtime bound and* sz *is a size bound for* $\mathcal{P}$.

5 Related Work, Experiments, and Conclusion

To make techniques for complexity analysis of integer programs also applicable to TRSs, we presented two main contributions: First, we showed in Sect. 3 how TRSs can be abstracted to a variant of integer transition systems (called RNTSs) and presented conditions for thc soundness of this abstraction. While abstractions from term-shaped data to numbers are common in program analysis (e.g., for proving termination), soundness of our abstraction for *complexity* of TRSs is not trivial. In [3] a related abstraction technique from first-order functional programs to a formalism corresponding to RNTSs is presented. However, there are important differences between such functional programs and term rewriting: In TRSs, one can also rewrite non-ground terms, whereas functional programming only evaluates ground expressions. Moreover, overlapping rules in TRSs may lead to non-determinism. The most challenging part in Sect. 3 is Theorem 9, i.e., showing that the step from innermost term rewriting to ground innermost rewriting is complexity preserving, even for relative rewriting. Mappings from terms to numbers were also used for complexity analysis of logic programs [15]. However, [15] operates on the logic program level, i.e., it does not translate programs to ITSs and it does not allow the application of ITS-techniques and tools.

Our second contribution (Sect. 4) is an approach to lift any technique for runtime complexity of ITSs to handle (non-nested, but otherwise *arbitrary*) recursion as well. This approach is useful for the analysis of recursive arithmetic programs in general. In particular, by combining our two main contributions we obtain a completely modular approach for the analysis of TRSs. To infer runtime bounds, we also compute size bounds, which may be useful on their own as well.

There exist several approaches that also analyze complexity by inferring both runtime and size bounds. Wegbreit [35] tries to generate closed forms for the exact runtime and size of the result of each analyzed function, whereas we estimate runtime and size by upper bounds. Hence, [35] fails whenever finding such exact closed forms automatically is infeasible. Serrano et al. [33] also compute runtime and size bounds, but in contrast to us they work on logic programs, and their approach is based on abstract interpretation. Our technique in Sect. 4 was inspired by our work on the tool KoAT [13], which composes results of alternating size and runtime complexity analyses for ITSs. In [13] we developed a "bottom-up" technique that corresponds to the approach of Sect. 4.2 when restricting it to ordinary ITSs *without (non-tail) recursion*. But in contrast to Sect. 4.2, KoAT's support for recursion is very limited, as it disregards the return values of "inner" calls. Moreover, [13] does not contain an approach like Theorem 19 in Sect. 4.1 which allows us to obtain size bounds from techniques that compute runtime bounds.

RAML [26–28] reduces the inference of resource annotated types (and hence complexity bounds) for ML programs to linear optimization. Like other techniques for functional programs, it is not directly applicable to TRSs due to the differences between ML and term rewriting.[3] Moreover, RAML has two theoretical boundaries w.r.t. modularity [26]: (A) The number of linear constraints arising from type inference grows exponentially in the size of the program. (B) To achieve context-sensitivity, functions are typed differently for different invocations. In our setting, a blow-up similar to (A) may occur within the used ITS tool, but as the program is analyzed one function at a time, this blow-up is exponential in the size of a single function instead of the whole program. To avoid (B), we analyze each function only once. However, RAML takes amortization effects into account and obtains impressive results in practice. Further leading tools for complexity analysis of programs on integers (resp. naturals) are, e.g., ABC [11], C^{4}B [14], CoFloCo [16,17], LoAT [18], Loopus [34], PUBS [1,2], Rank [4], and SPEED [23].

Finally, there are numerous techniques for automated complexity analysis of TRSs, e.g., [7,8,24,32,36]. While they also allow forms of modularity, the modularity of our approach differs substantially due to two reasons:

(1) Most previous complexity analysis techniques for TRSs are *top-down* approaches which estimate how often a rule $g(\ldots) \to \ldots$ is applied in reductions that start with terms of a certain size. So the complexity of a rule depends on

[3] See [29] for an adaption of an amortized analysis as in [27] to term rewriting. However, [29] is not automated, and it is restricted to *ground* rewriting with orthogonal rules.

the context of the whole TRS. This restricts the modularity of these approaches, since one cannot analyze g's complexity without taking the rest of the TRS into account. In contrast, we propose a *bottom-up* approach which analyzes how the complexity of any function g depends on g's inputs. Hence, one can analyze g without taking into account how g is called by other functions f.

(2) In our technique, if a function g has been analyzed, we can replace it by its size bound and do not have to regard g's rules anymore when analyzing a function f that calls g. This is possible because we use a fixed abstraction from terms to numbers. In contrast, existing approaches for TRSs cannot remove rules from the original TRS after having oriented them (with a strict order $\succ$), except for special cases. When other parts of the TRS are analyzed afterwards, these previous rules still have to be oriented weakly (with $\succsim$), since existing TRS approaches do not have any dedicated size analysis. This makes the existing approaches for TRSs less modular, but also more flexible (since they do not use a fixed abstraction from terms to numbers). In future work, we will try to improve our approach by integrating ideas from [3] which could allow us to infer and to apply multiple norms when abstracting functional programs to RNTSs.

We implemented our contributions in the tool AProVE [22] and evaluated its power on all 922 examples of the category "Runtime Complexity - Innermost Rewriting" of the *Termination and Complexity Competition 2016*.[4] Here, we excluded the 100 examples where AProVE shows $\text{irc}(n) = \omega$.

In our experiments, we consider the previous version of AProVE (AProVE '16), a version using only the techniques from this paper (AProVE RNTS), and AProVE '17 which integrates the techniques from this paper into AProVE's previous approach to analyze irc. In all these versions, AProVE pre-processes the TRS to remove rules with non-basic left-hand sides that are unreachable from basic terms, cf. [19]. AProVE RNTS uses the external tools CoFloCo, KoAT, and PUBS to compute runtime bounds for the ITSs resulting from the technique in Sect. 4. While we restricted ourselves to polynomial arithmetic for simplicity in this paper, KoAT's ability to prove exponential bounds for ITSs also enables AProVE to infer exponential upper bounds for some TRSs. Thus, the capabilities of the back-end ITS tool determine which kinds of bounds can be derived by AProVE. We also compare with TcT 3.1.0 [7], since AProVE and TcT were the most powerful complexity tools for TRSs at the *Termination and Complexity Competition 2016.*

Note that while the approach of Sect. 4 allows us to use *any* existing (or future) ITS tools for complexity analysis of RNTSs, CoFloCo can also infer complexity bounds for recursive ITSs directly, i.e., it does not require the technique in Sect. 4. To this end, CoFloCo analyzes program parts independently and uses linear invariants to compose the results. So CoFloCo's approach differs significantly from Sect. 4, which can also infer non-linear size bounds. Thus, the approach of Sect. 4 is especially suitable for examples where non-linear growth of data causes non-linear runtime. For instance, in Example 28 the quadratic size bound for $\mathsf{f}_\times$ is crucial to prove a (tight) cubic runtime bound with the technique of

[4] See http://termination-portal.org/wiki/Termination_Competition/.

Sect. 4. Consequently, CoFloCo's linear invariants are not sufficient and hence it fails for this RNTS. See [5] for a list of 17 examples with non-linear runtime where Sect. 4 was superior to all other considered techniques in our experiments. However, CoFloCo's amortized analysis often results in very precise bounds, i.e., both approaches are orthogonal. Therefore, as an alternative to Sect. 4, AProVE RNTS also uses CoFloCo to analyze the RNTSs obtained from the transformation in Sect. 3 directly.

The table on the right shows the results of our experiments. As suggested in [8], we used a timeout of 300 seconds per example (on an Intel Xeon with 4 cores at 2.33 GHz each and 16 GB of RAM). AProVE & TcT represents the former state of the art, i.e., for each example here we took the best bound found by AProVE '16 or TcT. A row "$\leq \mathcal{O}(n^k)$" means that the corresponding tools proved a bound $\leq \mathcal{O}(n^k)$ (e.g., TcT proved constant or linear upper bounds in 276 cases). Clearly, AProVE '17 is the most powerful tool, i.e., the contributions of this paper significantly improve the state of the art for complexity analysis of TRSs. This also shows that the new technique of this paper is orthogonal to the existing ones. In fact, AProVE RNTS infers better bounds than AProVE & TcT in 127 cases. In 102 of them, AProVE & TcT fails to prove any bound at all. The main reasons for this orthogonality are that on the one hand, our approaches loses precision when abstracting terms to numbers. But on the other hand, our approach allows us to apply arbitrary tools for complexity analysis of ITSs in the back-end and to benefit from their respective strengths. Moreover as mentioned above, the approach of Sect. 4 succeeds on many examples where non-linear growth of data leads to non-linear runtime, which are challenging for existing techniques.

$\mathrm{irc}_{\mathcal{R}}(n)$	TcT	AProVE RNTS	AProVE '16	AProVE & TcT	AProVE '17
$\mathcal{O}(1)$	47	43	48	53	53
$\leq \mathcal{O}(n)$	276	254	320	354	379
$\leq \mathcal{O}(n^2)$	362	366	425	463	506
$\leq \mathcal{O}(n^3)$	386	402	439	485	541
$\leq \mathcal{O}(n^{>3})$	393	412	439	491	548
$\leq EXP$	393	422	439	491	553

For further details on our experiments including a detailed comparison of AProVE RNTS and prior techniques for TRSs, to access AProVE '17 via a web interface, for improvements to increase the precision of our abstraction from TRSs to RNTSs, and for the proofs of all theorems, we refer to [5].

Acknowledgments. We thank A. Flores-Montoya for his help with CoFloCo and the anonymous reviewers for their suggestions and comments.

References

1. Albert, E., Arenas, P., Genaim, S., Puebla, G.: Closed-form upper bounds in static cost analysis. J. Autom. Reasoning **46**(2), 161–203 (2011)
2. Albert, E., Arenas, P., Genaim, S., Puebla, G., Zanardini, D.: Cost analysis of object-oriented bytecode programs. Theor. Comput. Sc. **413**(1), 142–159 (2012)

3. Albert, E., Genaim, S., Gutièrrez, R.: A transformational approach to resource analysis with typed-norms. In: Gupta, G., Peña, R. (eds.) LOPSTR 2013. LNCS, vol. 8901, pp. 38–53. Springer, Cham (2014). https://doi.org/10.1007/978-3-319-14125-1_3
4. Alias, C., Darte, A., Feautrier, P., Gonnord, L.: Multi-dimensional rankings, program termination, and complexity bounds of flowchart programs. In: Cousot, R., Martel, M. (eds.) SAS 2010. LNCS, vol. 6337, pp. 117–133. Springer, Heidelberg (2010). doi:10.1007/978-3-642-15769-1_8
5. AProVE. https://aprove-developers.github.io/trs_complexity_via_its/
6. Avanzini, M., Felgenhauer, B.: Type introduction for runtime complexity analysis. In: WST 2014, pp. 1–5 (2014). http://www.easychair.org/smart-program/VSL2014/WST-proceedings.pdf
7. Avanzini, M., Moser, G., Schaper, M.: TcT: Tyrolean complexity tool. In: Chechik, M., Raskin, J.F. (eds.) TACAS 2016. LNCS, vol. 9636, pp. 407–423. Springer, Berlin, Heidelberg (2016). https://doi.org/10.1007/978-3-662-49674-9_24
8. Avanzini, M., Moser, G.: A combination framework for complexity. Inform. Comput. **248**, 22–55 (2016)
9. Baader, F., Nipkow, T.: Term Rewriting and All That. Cambridge U. Press, Cambridge (1998)
10. Baillot, P., Dal Lago, U., Moyen, J.Y.: On quasi-interpretations, blind abstractions and implicit complexity. Math. Struct. Compt. Sci. **22**(4), 549–580 (2012)
11. Blanc, R., Henzinger, T.A., Hottelier, T., Kovàcs, L.: ABC: Algebraic bound computation for loops. In: Clarke, E.M., Voronkov, A. (eds.) LPAR 2010. LNCS, vol. 6355, pp. 103–118. Springer, Berlin, Heidelberg (2010). https://doi.org/10.1007/978-3-642-17511-4_7
12. Bonfante, G., Cichon, A., Marion, J.Y., Touzet, H.: Algorithms with polynomial interpretation termination proof. J. Funct. Program. **11**(1), 33–53 (2001)
13. Brockschmidt, M., Emmes, F., Falke, S., Fuhs, C., Giesl, J.: Analyzing runtime and size complexity of integer programs. ACM TOPLAS **38**(4), 13 (2016)
14. Carbonneaux, Q., Hoffmann, J., Shao, Z.: Compositional certified resource bounds. In: PLDI 2015, pp. 467–478 (2015)
15. Debray, S., Lin, N.: Cost analysis of logic programs. TOPLAS **15**(5), 826–875 (1993)
16. Flores-Montoya, A., Hähnle, R.: Resource analysis of complex programs with cost equations. In: Garrigue, J. (ed.) APLAS 2014. LNCS, vol. 8858, pp. 275–295. Springer, Cham (2014). https://doi.org/10.1007/978-3-319-12736-1_15
17. Flores-Montoya, A.: Upper and lower amortized cost bounds of programs expressed as cost relations. In: Fitzgerald, J., Heitmeyer, C., Gnesi, S., Philippou, A. (eds.) FM 2016. LNCS, vol. 9995, pp. 254–273. Springer, Cham (2016). https://doi.org/10.1007/978-3-319-48989-6_16
18. Frohn, F., Naaf, M., Hensel, J., Brockschmidt, M., Giesl, J.: Lower runtime bounds for integer programs. In: Olivetti, N., Tiwari, A. (eds.) IJCAR 2016. LNCS, vol. 9706, pp. 550–567. Springer, Cham (2016). https://doi.org/10.1007/978-3-319-40229-1_37
19. Frohn, F., Giesl, J.: Analyzing runtime complexity via innermost runtime complexity. In: LPAR 2017, pp. 249–268 (2017)
20. Frohn, F., Giesl, J., Hensel, J., Aschermann, C., Ströder, T.: Lower bounds for runtime complexity of term rewriting. J. Autom. Reasoning **59**(1), 121–163 (2017)
21. Fuhs, C., Giesl, J., Parting, M., Schneider-Kamp, P., Swiderski, S.: Proving termination by dep. pairs and inductive theorem proving. JAR **47**(2), 133–160 (2011)

22. Giesl, J., Aschermann, C., Brockschmidt, M., Emmes, F., Frohn, F., Fuhs, C., Hensel, J., Otto, C., Plücker, M., Schneider-Kamp, P., Ströder, T., Swiderski, S., Thiemann, R.: Analyzing program termination and complexity automatically with AProVE. J. Autom. Reasoning **58**, 3–31 (2017)
23. Gulwani, S.: SPEED: Symbolic complexity bound analysis. In: Bouajjani, A., Maler, O. (eds.) CAV 2009. LNCS, vol. 5643, pp. 51–62. Springer, Berlin, Heidelberg (2009). https://doi.org/10.1007/978-3-642-02658-4_7
24. Hirokawa, N., Moser, G.: Automated complexity analysis based on the dependency pair method. In: Armando, A., Baumgartner, P., Dowek, G. (eds.) IJCAR 2008. LNCS, vol. 5195, pp. 364–379. Springer, Berlin, Heidelberg (2008). https://doi.org/10.1007/978-3-540-71070-7_32
25. Hofbauer, D., Lautemann, C.: Termination proofs and the length of derivations. In: Dershowitz, N. (ed.) RTA 1989. LNCS, vol. 355, pp. 167–177. Springer, Heidelberg (1989). doi:10.1007/3-540-51081-8_107
26. Hoffmann, J.: Types with Potential: Polynomial Resource Bounds via Automatic Amortized Analysis. Ph.D. thesis, Ludwig-Maximilians-University Munich (2011)
27. Hoffmann, J., Aehlig, K., Hofmann, M.: Multivariate amortized resource analysis. ACM Trans. Program. Lang. Syst. **34**(3), 14 (2012)
28. Hoffmann, J., Das, A., Weng, S.C.: Towards automatic resource bound analysis for OCaml. In: POPL 2017, pp. 359–373 (2017)
29. Hofmann, M., Moser, G.: Multivariate amortised resource analysis for term rewrite systems. In: TLCA 2015, pp. 241–256 (2015)
30. Kapur, D., Narendran, P., Zhang, H.: On sufficient completeness and related properties of term rewriting systems. Acta Informatica **24**, 395–415 (1987)
31. Emmanuel, K.: Completeness in data type specifications. In: Caviness, B.F. (ed.) EUROCAL 1985. LNCS, vol. 204, pp. 348–362. Springer, Heidelberg (1985). doi:10.1007/3-540-15984-3_291
32. Noschinski, L., Emmes, F., Giesl, J.: Analyzing innermost runtime complexity of term rewriting by dependency pairs. J. Autom. Reasoning **51**(1), 27–56 (2013)
33. Serrano, A., López-García, P., Hermenegildo, M.: Resource usage analysis of logic programs via abstract interpretation using sized types. Theory Pract. Logic Program. **14**(4–5), 739–754 (2014)
34. Sinn, M., Zuleger, F., Veith, H.: Complexity and resource bound analysis of imperative programs using difference constraints. J. Autom. Reasoning **59**(1), 3–45 (2017)
35. Wegbreit, B.: Mechanical program analysis. Commun. ACM **18**, 528–539 (1975)
36. Zankl, H., Korp, M.: Modular complexity analysis for term rewriting. Logical Meth. Comput. Sci. **10**(1), 1–34 (2014)
37. Zantema, H.: Termination of term rewriting: interpretation and type elimination. J. Symbol. Comput. **17**(1), 23–50 (1994)

SAT, SMT and Automated Theorem Proving

Solving SAT and MaxSAT with a Quantum Annealer: Foundations and a Preliminary Report

Zhengbing Bian[1], Fabian Chudak[1], William Macready[1], Aidan Roy[1(✉)], Roberto Sebastiani[2], and Stefano Varotti[2]

[1] D-Wave Systems Inc., Burnaby, Canada
aroy@dwavesys.com

[2] DISI, University of Trento, Trento, Italy

Abstract. Quantum annealers (QA) are specialized quantum computers that minimize objective functions over discrete variables by physically exploiting quantum effects. Current QA platforms allow for the optimization of quadratic objectives defined over binary variables, that is, they solve quadratic unconstrained binary optimization (QUBO) problems. In the last decade, QA systems as implemented by D-Wave have scaled with Moore-like growth. Current architectures provide 2048 sparsely-connected qubits, and continued exponential growth is anticipated.

We explore the feasibility of such architectures for solving SAT and MaxSAT problems as QA systems scale. We develop techniques for effectively encoding SAT and MaxSAT into QUBO problems compatible with sparse QA architectures. We provide the theoretical foundations for this mapping, and present encoding techniques that combine offline Satisfiability and Optimization Modulo Theories with on-the-fly placement and routing. Preliminary empirical tests on a current generation 2048-qubit D-Wave system support the feasibility of the approach.

We provide details on our SMT model of the SAT-encoding problem in the hopes that further research may improve upon the scalability of this application of SMT technology. Further, these models generate hard SMT problems which may be useful as benchmarks for solvers.

1 Introduction

Quantum Annealing (QA) is a specialized form of computation that uses quantum mechanical effects to efficiently sample low-energy configurations of particular cost functions on binary variables. Currently, the largest QA system heuristically minimizes an Ising cost function given by

$$E(\underline{\mathbf{z}}) \stackrel{\text{def}}{=} \sum_{i \in V} h_i z_i + \sum_{(i,j) \in E} J_{ij} z_i z_j \tag{1}$$

$$\underset{\underline{\mathbf{z}} \in \{-1,1\}^{|V|}}{\operatorname{argmin}} \quad E(\underline{\mathbf{z}}). \tag{2}$$

where $G = (V, E)$ is an undirected graph of allowed variable interactions. Ising models are equivalent to *Quadratic Unconstrained Binary Optimization* (QUBO)

C. Dixon and M. Finger (Eds.): FroCoS 2017, LNCS 10483, pp. 153–171, 2017.
DOI: 10.1007/978-3-319-66167-4_9

problems, which use $\{0, 1\}$-valued variables rather than ± 1-valued variables. [1] The decision version of the Ising problem on most graphs G is NP-complete.

Theory suggests that quantum annealing may solve some optimization problems faster than state-of-the-art algorithms [18]. Quantum effects such as tunneling and superposition provide QA with novel mechanisms for escaping local minima, thereby potentially avoiding suboptimal solutions commonly found by classical algorithms based on bit-flip operations (such as WalkSAT). Practical QA systems are not guaranteed to return optimal solutions; however, the D-Wave processor has been shown to outperform a range of classical algorithms on certain problems designed to match its hardware structure [16,21]. These results also provide guidance about the kinds of energy landscapes on which QA is expected to perform well.

Our ultimate goal is to exploit QA as an engine for solving SAT and other NP-hard problem instances which are relatively small but hard enough to be out of the reach of state-of-the-art solvers (e.g., SAT problems coming from cryptanalysis). *SAT* is the problem of deciding the satisfiability of arbitrary formulas on atomic propositions, typically written in conjunctive normal form. *MaxSAT* is an optimization extension of SAT, in which each clause is given a positive penalty if the clause is not satisfied, and an assignment minimizing the sum of the penalties is sought.

In principle, converting SAT to optimization of an Ising cost function is straightforward. However, practical QA systems such as the D-Wave 2000Q offer sparse connectivity between variables. The connectivity graph G of current D-Wave processors is shown in Fig. 1, and is called the *Chimera* graph. Further, because the Ising model is solved on a physical, analog device, it is subject to engineering limitations. The D-Wave 2000Q system currently requires $h_i \in [-2, 2]$ and $J_{ij} \in [-1, 1]$ and there are limits on the precision to which these parameters may be specified. Parameter imprecisions act as small additive noise sources on parameter values, and arise from operating quantum mechanical systems in real-world environments. These real-world practicalities necessitate a carefully defined SAT-to-Ising encoding.

These practical constraints generate a challenging problem because the SAT encoding must be done both *effectively* (i.e., in a way that uses only the limited number of qubits and connections available within the QA architecture, while optimizing performance of the QA algorithm), and *efficiently* (i.e., using a limited computational budget for computing the encoding). In this paper, we formalize this problem and provide practical algorithms.

A direct formulation of the encoding problem results in a large system of linear inequalities over continuous- and Boolean-valued variables. This system can be effectively addressed with Satisfiability or Optimization Modulo Theory (SMT/OMT) [3,28] solvers. *Satisfiability Modulo the Theory of Linear Rational Arithmetic (SMT($\mathcal{LRA}$))* [3] is the problem of deciding the satisfiability of arbitrary formulas on atomic propositions and constraints in linear arithmetic over the rationals. *Optimization Modulo the Theory of Linear Rational Arithmetic*

[1] The transformation between $z_i \in \{-1, 1\}$ and $x_i \in \{0, 1\}$ is $z_i = 2x_i - 1$.

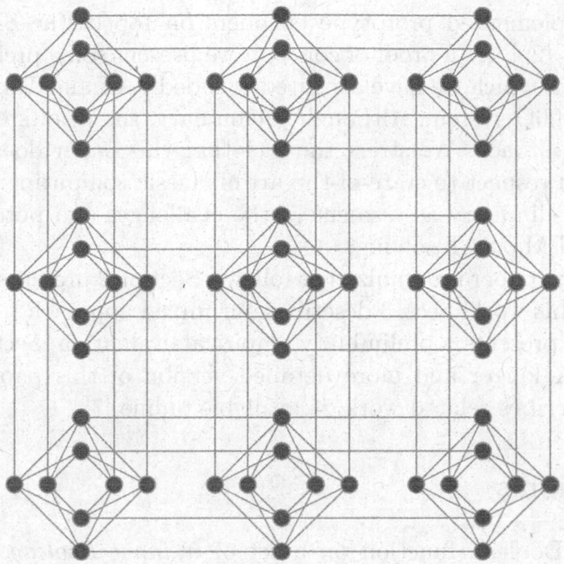

Fig. 1. Example of the Chimera topology: the hardware graph for system of 72 qubits in a 3-by-3 grid of tiles. (D-Wave 2000Q systems have 2048 qubits in a 16-by-16 grid.) This topology consists of a lattice of strongly-connected components of 8 qubits, called *tiles*. Each tile consists of a complete bipartite graph between two sets of four qubits. One set, the "vertical" set, is connected to the tiles above and below; the other set, the "horizontal" set, is connected to the tiles to the left and to the right. Notice that each qubit is connected with at most six other qubits. In other words, each variable z_i in the Ising model (1) has at most 6 non-zero J_{ij} interactions with other variables.

(OMT($\mathcal{LRA}$)) [28] extends SMT($\mathcal{LRA}$) by searching solutions which optimize some $\mathcal{LRA}$ objective(s). Efficient OMT($\mathcal{LRA}$) solvers like OPTIMATHSAT [29] allow for handling formulas with thousands of Boolean and rational variables [28].

This monolithic linear programming approach to encoding typically requires the introduction of additional ancillary Boolean variables, and the resultant SMT/OMT problem may be computationally harder than the original problem. In contrast, a large Boolean formula can be scalably converted into an Ising model by decomposing it into subformulae, converting each subformula into an Ising model (perhaps with introduction of additional fresh variables), and linking variables from different subformulae. Unfortunately, in practice this decomposition-based approach requires many auxiliary variables and connections, which are incompatible with the sparse connectivity restrictions imposed by QA architectures.

To cope with these difficulties, we propose a mixed approach, which combines (i) novel SMT/OMT-based techniques to produce off-line encodings of commonly-used Boolean subfunctions, with (ii) the usage of function instantiation and placement-and-routing techniques to combine and place on-the-fly the encoded functionalities within the QA architecture.

We have implemented prototype encoders on top of the SMT/OMT tool OPTIMATHSAT [29]. As a proof of concept, we present some preliminary empirical evaluation, in which we have executed encoded SAT and MaxSAT problems on a D-Wave 2000Q system. Although preliminary, the results confirm the feasibility of the approach. We stress the fact that this paper does not present a comparison with respect to state-of-the-art of classic computing. Rather, this is intended as a preliminary assessment of the challenges and potential of QA to impact SAT and MaxSAT solving.

The rest of the paper is organized as follows. Section 2 presents the theoretical foundations of this work; Sect. 3 describes our mixed approach to cope with this problem; Sect. 4 presents a preliminary empirical evaluation; Sect. 5 hints future developments. A longer and more detailed version of this paper, including a section that describes related work, is available online [7].

2 Foundations

Let $F(\underline{\mathbf{x}})$ be a Boolean function on a set of n *input Boolean variables* $\underline{\mathbf{x}} \stackrel{\text{def}}{=} \{x_1, ..., x_n\}$. We represent Boolean value $\bot$ with -1 and $\top$ with $+1$, so that we can assume that each $x_i \in \{-1, 1\}$. Suppose first that we have a QA system with n qubits defined on a hardware graph $G = (V, E)$, e.g., G can be any n-vertex subgraph of the Chimera graph of Fig. 1. Furthermore, assume that the state of each qubit z_i corresponds to the value of variable x_i, $i = 1, \ldots, n = |V|$. One way to determine whether $F(\underline{\mathbf{x}})$ is satisfiable using the QA system is to find an energy function as in (1) whose ground states $\underline{\mathbf{z}}$ correspond with the satisfiable assignments $\underline{\mathbf{x}}$ of $F(\underline{\mathbf{x}})$. For instance, if $F(\underline{\mathbf{x}}) \stackrel{\text{def}}{=} x_1 \oplus x_2$, since $F(\underline{\mathbf{x}}) = \top$ if and only if $x_1 + x_2 = 0$, the Ising model $(z_1 + z_2)^2$ in a graph containing 2 qubits joined by an edge has ground states $(+1, -1)$ and $(-1, +1)$, that is, the satisfiable assignments of F.

Because the energy $E(\underline{\mathbf{z}})$ in (1) is restricted to quadratic terms and graph G is typically sparse, the number of functions $F(\underline{\mathbf{x}})$ that can be solved with this approach is limited. To deal with this difficulty, we can use a larger QA system with a number of additional qubits, say h, representing *ancillary Boolean variables* (or *ancillas* for short) $\underline{\mathbf{a}} \stackrel{\text{def}}{=} \{a_1, ..., a_h\}$, so that $|V| = n + h$. A *variable placement* is a mapping of the $n+h$ input and ancillary variables into the qubits of V. Since G is not a complete graph, different variable placements will produce energy functions with different properties. We use *Ising encoding* to refer to the h_i and J_{ij} parameters in (1) that are provided to the QA hardware together with a variable placement of the variables. The *gap* of an Ising encoding is the energy difference between ground states (i.e., satisfiable assignments) and any other states (i.e., unsatisfiable assignments). An important observation from [5] is that the larger the gap the better the success rates of the QA process. The *encoding problem* for $F(\underline{\mathbf{x}})$ is to find an Ising encoding with maximum gap.

The encoding problem is typically over-constrained. In fact, the Ising model (1) has to discriminate between m satisfiable assignments and k unsatisfiable assignments, with $m+k = 2^n$, whereas the number of degrees of freedom is given by the number of the h_i and J_{ij} parameters, which in the Chimera architecture grows as $O(n+h)$.

In this section, we assume that a Boolean function $F(\underline{\mathbf{x}})$ is given and that h qubits are used for ancillary variables $\underline{\mathbf{a}}$.

2.1 Penalty Functions

Here we assume that a variable placement is given, placing $\underline{\mathbf{x}} \cup \underline{\mathbf{a}}$ into the subgraph G. Thus, we can identify each variable z_j representing the binary value of the qubit associated with the jth vertex in V with either an x_k or a_ℓ variable, writing $\underline{\mathbf{z}} = \underline{\mathbf{x}} \cup \underline{\mathbf{a}}$. Then we define *penalty function* $P_F(\underline{\mathbf{x}}, \underline{\mathbf{a}}|\underline{\boldsymbol{\theta}})$ as the Ising model:

$$P_F(\underline{\mathbf{x}}, \underline{\mathbf{a}}|\underline{\boldsymbol{\theta}}) \stackrel{\text{def}}{=} \theta_0 + \sum_{i \in V} \theta_i z_i + \sum_{(i,j) \in E} \theta_{ij} z_i z_j, \tag{3}$$

$$\text{with the property that} \quad \forall \underline{\mathbf{x}} \;\; min_{\{\underline{\mathbf{a}}\}} P_F(\underline{\mathbf{x}}, \underline{\mathbf{a}}|\underline{\boldsymbol{\theta}}) \begin{cases} = 0 & \text{if } F(\underline{\mathbf{x}}) = \top \\ \geq g_{min} & \text{if } F(\underline{\mathbf{x}}) = \bot \end{cases} \tag{4}$$

where $\theta_0 \in (-\infty, +\infty)$ ("*offset*"), $\theta_i \in [-2, 2]$ ("*biases*") and $\theta_{ij} \in [-1, 1]$ ("*couplings*"), s.t. $z_i, z_j \in \underline{\mathbf{z}}$, and $g_{min} > 0$ ("*gap*") are rational-valued parameters. Notice that a penalty function separates models from counter-models by an energy gap of at least g_{min}. We call $P_F(\underline{\mathbf{x}}, \underline{\mathbf{a}}|\underline{\boldsymbol{\theta}})$ an *exact penalty function* iff it verifies a stronger version of (4) in which the condition "$\geq g_{min}$" is substituted with "$= g_{min}$". To simplify the notation we will assume that $\theta_{ij} = 0$ when $(i, j) \notin E$, and use $P_F(\underline{\mathbf{x}}|\underline{\boldsymbol{\theta}})$ when $\underline{\mathbf{a}} = \emptyset$.

The QA hardware is used to minimize the Ising model defined by penalty function $P_F(\underline{\mathbf{x}}, \underline{\mathbf{a}}|\underline{\boldsymbol{\theta}})$. By (4), a returned value of $P_F(\underline{\mathbf{x}}, \underline{\mathbf{a}}|\underline{\boldsymbol{\theta}}) = 0$ implies that F is satisfiable. However, if $P_F(\underline{\mathbf{x}}, \underline{\mathbf{a}}|\underline{\boldsymbol{\theta}}) \geq g_{min}$, since QA does not guarantee optimality, there is still a chance that F is satisfiable. Nevertheless, the larger g_{min} is, the less likely this false negative case occurs.

The following examples show that ancillary variables are needed, even when G is a complete graph.

Example 1. The equivalence between two variables, $F(\underline{\mathbf{x}}) \stackrel{\text{def}}{=} (x_1 \leftrightarrow x_2)$, can be encoded without ancillas by means of a single coupling between two connected vertices, with zero biases: $P_F(\underline{\mathbf{x}}|\underline{\boldsymbol{\theta}}) \stackrel{\text{def}}{=} 1 - x_1 x_2$, so that $g_{min} = 2$. In fact, $P_F(\underline{\mathbf{x}}|\underline{\boldsymbol{\theta}}) = 0$ if x_1, x_2 have the same value; $P_F(\underline{\mathbf{x}}|\underline{\boldsymbol{\theta}}) = 2$ otherwise. Notice that $P_F(\underline{\mathbf{x}}|\underline{\boldsymbol{\theta}})$ is also an exact penalty function. Penalty $P_F(\underline{\mathbf{x}}|\underline{\boldsymbol{\theta}})$ is called a *chain* of length 2.

Example 2. Consider the AND function $F(\underline{\mathbf{x}}) \stackrel{\text{def}}{=} x_3 \leftrightarrow (x_1 \wedge x_2)$. If x_1, x_2, x_3 could be all connected in a 3-clique, then $F(\underline{\mathbf{x}})$ could be encoded without ancillas by setting $P_F(\underline{\mathbf{x}}|\underline{\boldsymbol{\theta}}) = \frac{3}{2} - \frac{1}{2}x_1 - \frac{1}{2}x_2 + x_3 + \frac{1}{2}x_1x_2 - x_1x_3 - x_2x_3$, so that $g_{min} = 2$. Since the Chimera graph has no cliques, so that the above AND function needs

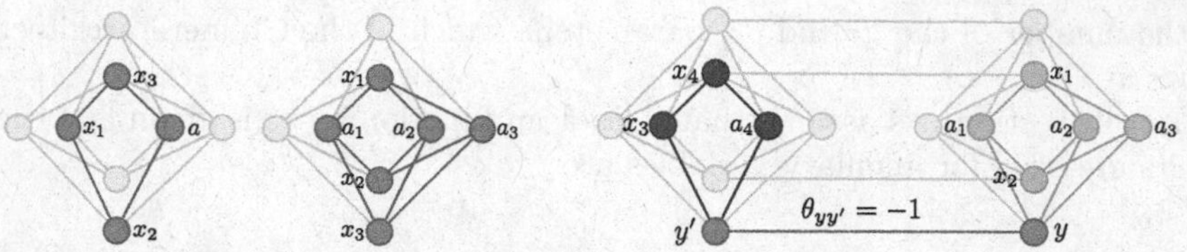

(a) $x_3 \leftrightarrow (x_1 \wedge x_2)$ with one ancilla. (b) $x_3 \leftrightarrow (x_1 \oplus x_2)$ with three ancillas. (c) $x_4 \leftrightarrow (x_3 \wedge (x_1 \oplus x_2))$ obtained by combining 2(b) and 2(a).

Fig. 2. Mappings within the Chimera graph, penalty functions use only colored edges. (c) combines (a) and (b) using chained proxy variables y, y'. The resulting penalty function is obtained by rewriting $x_4 \leftrightarrow (x_3 \wedge (x_1 \oplus x_2))$ into its equi-satisfiable formula $(x_4 \leftrightarrow (x_3 \wedge y')) \wedge (y' \leftrightarrow y) \wedge (y \leftrightarrow (x_1 \oplus x_2))$. (Color figure online)

(at least) one ancilla a to be encoded as: $P_F(\underline{\mathbf{x}}, \underline{\mathbf{a}}|\underline{\boldsymbol{\theta}}) = \frac{5}{2} - \frac{1}{2}x_1 - \frac{1}{2}x_2 + x_3 + \frac{1}{2}x_1x_2 - x_1x_3 - x_2a - x_3a$, which still has gap $g_{min} = 2$ and is embedded as in Fig. 2(a).

Example 3. Consider the XOR function $F(\underline{\mathbf{x}}) \stackrel{\text{def}}{=} x_3 \leftrightarrow (x_1 \oplus x_2)$. Even within a 3-clique, $F(\underline{\mathbf{x}})$ has no ancilla-free encoding. Within the Chimera graph, $F(\underline{\mathbf{x}})$ can be encoded with three ancillas a_1, a_2, a_3 as: $P_F(\underline{\mathbf{x}}, \underline{\mathbf{a}}|\underline{\boldsymbol{\theta}}) = 5 + x_3 + a_2 - a_3 + x_1a_1 - x_1a_2 - x_1a_3 - x_2a_1 - x_2a_2 - x_2a_3 + x_3a_2 - x_3a_3$, which has gap $g_{min} = 2$ and is embedded as in Fig. 2(b).

2.2 Properties of Penalty Functions and Problem Decomposition

After determining a variable placement, finding the values for the θs implicitly requires solving a set of equations whose size grows with the number of models of $F(\underline{\mathbf{x}})$ plus a number of inequalities whose size grows with the number of counter-models of $F(\underline{\mathbf{x}})$. Thus, the θs must satisfy a number of linear constraints that grows exponentially in n. Since the θs grow approximately as $4(n + h)$, the number of ancillary variables needed to satisfy (4) can also grow very rapidly. This seriously limits the scalability of a solution method based on (3)–(4). We address this issue by showing how to construct penalty functions by combining smaller penalty functions, albeit at the expense of a reduced gap.

The following two properties can be easily derived from the definition.

Property 1. Let $F^*(\underline{\mathbf{x}}) \stackrel{\text{def}}{=} F(x_1, ..., x_{r-1}, \neg x_r, x_{r+1}, ..., x_n)$ for some index r. Assume a variable placement of $\underline{\mathbf{x}}$ into V s.t. $P_F(\underline{\mathbf{x}}, \underline{\mathbf{a}}|\underline{\boldsymbol{\theta}})$ is a penalty function for $F(\underline{\mathbf{x}})$ of gap g_{min}. Then $P_{F^*}(\underline{\mathbf{x}}, \underline{\mathbf{a}}|\underline{\boldsymbol{\theta}}) = P_F(\underline{\mathbf{x}}, \underline{\mathbf{a}}|\underline{\boldsymbol{\theta}}^*)$, where $\underline{\boldsymbol{\theta}}^*$ is defined as follows for every $z_i, z_j \in \underline{\mathbf{x}}, \underline{\mathbf{a}}$:

$$\theta_i^* = \begin{cases} -\theta_i & \text{if } z_i = x_r \\ \theta_i & \text{otherwise;} \end{cases} \qquad \theta_{ij}^* = \begin{cases} -\theta_{ij} & \text{if } z_i = x_r \text{ or } z_j = x_r \\ \theta_{ij} & \text{otherwise.} \end{cases}$$

Notice that since the previously defined bounds over $\underline{\boldsymbol{\theta}}$ (namely $\theta_i \in [-2, 2]$ and $\theta_{ij} \in [-1, 1]$) are symmetric, if $\underline{\boldsymbol{\theta}}$ is in range then $\underline{\boldsymbol{\theta}}^*$ is as well.

Two Boolean functions that become equivalent by permuting or negating some of their variables are called *NPN-equivalent* [14]. Thus, given the penalty function for a Boolean formula, any other NPN equivalent formula can be encoded trivially by applying Property 1. Notice that checking NPN equivalence is a hard problem in theory, but it is fast in practice for small n (i.e., less than 16 [20]).

Property 2. Let $F(\underline{\mathbf{x}}) = \bigwedge_{k=1}^{K} F_k(\underline{\mathbf{x}}^k)$ be Boolean formula such that $\underline{\mathbf{x}} = \cup_k \underline{\mathbf{x}}^k$, the $\underline{\mathbf{x}}^k$s may be non-disjoint, and each sub-formula F_k has a penalty function $P_{F_k}(\underline{\mathbf{x}}^k, \underline{\mathbf{a}}^k|\underline{\boldsymbol{\theta}}^k)$ with minimum gap g_{min}^k where $\underline{\mathbf{a}} = \cup_k \underline{\mathbf{a}}^k$ and the $\underline{\mathbf{a}}^k$s are all disjoint. Given a list w_k of positive rational values such that, for every $z_i, z_j \in \underline{\mathbf{x}} \cup \bigcup_{k=1}^{K} \underline{\mathbf{a}}^k$:

$$\theta_i \stackrel{\text{def}}{=} \sum_{k=1}^{K} w_k \theta_i^k \in [-2, 2], \quad \theta_{ij} \stackrel{\text{def}}{=} \sum_{k=1}^{K} w_k \theta_{ij}^k \in [-1, 1], \tag{5}$$

then a penalty function for $F(\underline{\mathbf{x}})$ can be obtained as:

$$P_F(\underline{\mathbf{x}}, \underline{\mathbf{a}}^1 ... \underline{\mathbf{a}}^K|\underline{\boldsymbol{\theta}}) = \sum_{k=1}^{K} w_k P_{F_k}(\underline{\mathbf{x}}^k, \underline{\mathbf{a}}^k|\underline{\boldsymbol{\theta}}^k). \tag{6}$$

This new penalty function evaluates to zero if and only if all its summands do, and otherwise it is at least $g_{min} = \min_{k=1}^{K} w_k g_{min}^k$. Thus, in general, the (weighted) sum of the penalty functions of a set of formulas represents a penalty function for the conjunction of the formulas.

A formula $F(\underline{\mathbf{x}})$ can be decomposed (e.g., by a Tseitin transformation) into an equivalently-satisfiable one $F^*(\underline{\mathbf{x}}, \underline{\mathbf{y}})$:

$$F^*(\underline{\mathbf{x}}, \underline{\mathbf{y}}) \stackrel{\text{def}}{=} \bigwedge_{i=1}^{m-1} (y_i \leftrightarrow F_i(\underline{\mathbf{x}}^i, \underline{\mathbf{y}}^i)) \wedge F_m(\underline{\mathbf{x}}^m, \underline{\mathbf{y}}^m), \tag{7}$$

where the F_is are Boolean functions which decompose the original formula $F(\underline{\mathbf{x}})$, and the y_is are fresh Boolean variables each labeling the corresponding F_i. By Property 2, this allows us to decompose $F(\underline{\mathbf{x}})$ into multiple $F_i(\underline{\mathbf{x}}^i, \underline{\mathbf{y}}^i)$ that can be encoded separately and recombined. The problem is to choose Boolean functions $F_i(\underline{\mathbf{x}}^i, \underline{\mathbf{y}}^i)$ whose penalty functions are easy to compute, have a large enough gap, and whose combination keeps the gap of the penalty function for the original function as large as possible.

Summing penalty functions with shared variables may cause problems with parameter ranges: penalty functions that share terms may sum up biases or couplings resulting in out-of-range values. Using weights, Property 2 can help to mitigate this, but also it is likely that the g_{min} of the final penalty function becomes small.

We can cope with this problem by mapping shared variables into distinct qubits and then linking them together. Consider again $F(\underline{\mathbf{x}}) = \bigwedge_{k=1}^{K} F_k(\underline{\mathbf{x}}^k)$ as in Property 2. We rewrite it into its equi-satisfiable formula

$$F^*(\underline{\mathbf{x}}^*) \stackrel{\text{def}}{=} \bigwedge_{k=1}^{K} F_k(\underline{\mathbf{x}}^{k^*}) \wedge \bigwedge_{\substack{x_i \in \underline{\mathbf{x}}^k \cap \underline{\mathbf{x}}^{k'} \\ k,k' \in [1..K],\ k<k'}} ({x_i}^{k^*} \leftrightarrow {x_i}^{k'^*}) \tag{8}$$

where $\underline{\mathbf{x}}^* = \cup_k \underline{\mathbf{x}}^{k^*}$ and the $\underline{\mathbf{x}}^{k^*}$ are all disjoint. Also, as in Property 2, assume we have $P_{F_k}(\underline{\mathbf{x}}^{k^*}, \underline{\mathbf{a}}^k|\boldsymbol{\theta}^k)$ for each k with disjoint $\underline{\mathbf{a}}^k$. If there is an edge between every two copies of the same variable x_i, we can write a penalty function in the following way (using the penalty of Example 1):

$$P_{F^*}(\underline{\mathbf{x}}^*, \underline{\mathbf{a}}|\boldsymbol{\theta}) = \sum_{k=1}^{K} P_{F_k}(\underline{\mathbf{x}}^{k^*}, \underline{\mathbf{a}}^k|\boldsymbol{\theta}^k) + \sum_{\substack{x_i \in \underline{\mathbf{x}}^k \cap \underline{\mathbf{x}}^{k'} \\ k,k' \in [1..K],\ k<k}} (1 - {x_i}^{k^*} {x_i}^{k'^*}), \tag{9}$$

and the θs stay within valid range because the $\underline{\mathbf{x}}^{k^*}$s are all disjoint. Thus, we can represent a single variable x_i with a series of qubits connected by strong couplings $(1-z_i z_i')$. Figure 2(c) illustrates a simple example. Two observations are at hand. First, the gap g_{min} of $P_{F^*}(\underline{\mathbf{x}}^*, \underline{\mathbf{a}}|\boldsymbol{\theta})$ is at least $\min(\min_{k=1}^{K} w_k g_{min}^k, 2)$, since each $(1 - z_i z_i')$ penalty has a gap of 2. Second, not all copies of x_i need to be directly adjacent to obtain this bound: it suffices to use the edges of a tree connecting all copies. More generally, that tree may contain additional qubits to facilitate connectedness. A tree connecting all the copies of a variable x_i is called a *chain* and is the subject of the next section.

2.3 Embedding into Chimera Architecture

The process of representing a single variable x_i by a collection of qubits connected in chains of strong couplings is known as *embedding*, in reference to the minor embedding problem of graph theory [12,13]. More precisely, suppose we have a penalty function based on graph G (so x_i and x_j are adjacent iff $\theta_{ij} \neq 0$) and a QA hardware graph H. A *minor embedding* of G in H is a function $\Phi : V_G \rightarrow 2^{V_H}$ such that:

- for each G-vertex x_i, the subgraph induced by $\Phi(x_i)$ is connected;
- for all distinct G-vertices x_i and x_j, $\Phi(x_i)$ and $\Phi(x_j)$ are disjoint;
- for each edge (x_i, x_j) in G, there is at least one edge between $\Phi(x_i)$ and $\Phi(x_j)$.

The image $\Phi(x_i)$ of a G-vertex is a chain, and the set of qubits in a chain are constrained to be equal using $(1 - z_i z_i')$ couplings as in Fig. 2(c).

Embedding generic graphs is a computationally difficult problem [2], although certain structured problem graphs may be easily embedded in the Chimera topology [8,34] and heuristic algorithms may also be used [9]. A reasonable goal in embedding is to minimize the sizes of the chains, as quantum annealing becomes less effective as more qubits are included in chains [22].

A different approach to use QA for finding models for F, *global embedding*, is based on first finding a penalty function on a complete graph G on $n + h$ variables, and secondly, embedding G into a hardware graph H using chains (e.g., using [8]). Following [5], global embeddings usually need fewer qubits than the methods presented in this paper; however, the final gap of the penalty function obtained in this way is generally smaller and difficult to compute exactly.

3 Solving the Encoding Problem

3.1 Encoding Small Boolean Functions

Computing Penalty Functions via SMT/OMT($\mathcal{LRA}$). Given $\underline{\mathbf{x}} \stackrel{\text{def}}{=} \{x_1, ..., x_n\}$, $\underline{\mathbf{a}} \stackrel{\text{def}}{=} \{a_1, ..., a_h\}$, $F(\underline{\mathbf{x}})$ as in Sect. 2.1, a variable placement in a Chimera subgraph s.t. $\underline{\mathbf{z}} = \underline{\mathbf{x}} \cup \underline{\mathbf{a}}$, and some gap $g_{min} > 0$, the problem of finding a penalty function $P_F(\underline{\mathbf{x}}, \underline{\mathbf{a}}|\underline{\boldsymbol{\theta}})$ as in (3) reduces to solving the following SMT($\mathcal{LRA}$) problem:

$$\Phi(\underline{\boldsymbol{\theta}}) \stackrel{\text{def}}{=} \bigwedge_{z_i \in \underline{\mathbf{x}}, \underline{\mathbf{a}}} (-2 \le \theta_i) \wedge (\theta_i \le 2) \wedge \bigwedge_{\substack{z_i z_j \in \underline{\mathbf{x}}, \underline{\mathbf{a}} \\ i<j}} (-1 \le \theta_{ij}) \wedge (\theta_{ij} \le 1) \quad (10)$$

$$\wedge \bigwedge_{\{\underline{\mathbf{x}} \in \{-1,1\}^n | F(\underline{\mathbf{x}}) = \top\}} \bigvee_{\underline{\mathbf{a}} \in \{-1,1\}^h} (P_F(\underline{\mathbf{x}}, \underline{\mathbf{a}}|\underline{\boldsymbol{\theta}}) = 0) \quad (11)$$

$$\wedge \bigwedge_{\{\underline{\mathbf{x}} \in \{-1,1\}^n | F(\underline{\mathbf{x}}) = \top\}} \bigwedge_{\underline{\mathbf{a}} \in \{-1,1\}^h} (P_F(\underline{\mathbf{x}}, \underline{\mathbf{a}}|\underline{\boldsymbol{\theta}}) \ge 0) \quad (12)$$

$$\wedge \bigwedge_{\{\underline{\mathbf{x}} \in \{-1,1\}^n | F(\underline{\mathbf{x}}) = \bot\}} \bigwedge_{\underline{\mathbf{a}} \in \{-1,1\}^h} (P_F(\underline{\mathbf{x}}, \underline{\mathbf{a}}|\underline{\boldsymbol{\theta}}) \ge g_{min}). \quad (13)$$

Consequently, the problem of finding the penalty function $P_F(\underline{\mathbf{x}}, \underline{\mathbf{a}}|\underline{\boldsymbol{\theta}})$ that maximizes the gap g_{min} reduces to solving the OMT($\mathcal{LRA}$) maximization problem $\langle \Phi(\underline{\boldsymbol{\theta}}), g_{min} \rangle$.

Intuitively: (10) states the ranges of the $\underline{\boldsymbol{\theta}}$; (11) and (12) state that, for every $\underline{\mathbf{x}}$ satisfying $F(\underline{\mathbf{x}})$, $P_F(\underline{\mathbf{x}}, \underline{\mathbf{a}}|\underline{\boldsymbol{\theta}})$ must be zero for at least one "minimum" $\underline{\mathbf{a}}$ and nonnegative for all the others; (13) states that for every $\underline{\mathbf{x}}$ not satisfying $F(\underline{\mathbf{x}})$, $P_F(\underline{\mathbf{x}}, \underline{\mathbf{a}}|\underline{\boldsymbol{\theta}})$ must greater or equal than the gap. Consequently, if the values of the $\underline{\boldsymbol{\theta}}$ in $P_F(\underline{\mathbf{x}}, \underline{\mathbf{a}}|\underline{\boldsymbol{\theta}})$ satisfy $\Phi(\underline{\boldsymbol{\theta}})$, then $P_F(\underline{\mathbf{x}}, \underline{\mathbf{a}}|\underline{\boldsymbol{\theta}})$ complies with (4).

Notice that $\Phi(\underline{\boldsymbol{\theta}})$ grows exponentially with $|\underline{\mathbf{x}}| + |\underline{\mathbf{a}}|$, and no longer contains Boolean atoms. Notice also that, if $\underline{\mathbf{a}} = \emptyset$, the OMT($\mathcal{LRA}$) maximization problem $\langle \Phi(\underline{\boldsymbol{\theta}}), g_{min} \rangle$ reduces to a linear program because the disjunctions in (11) disappear.

To force $P_F(\underline{\mathbf{x}}, \underline{\mathbf{a}}|\underline{\boldsymbol{\theta}})$ to be an *exact* penalty function, we conjoin to $\Phi(\underline{\boldsymbol{\theta}})$ the following:

$$... \wedge \bigwedge_{\{\underline{\mathbf{x}} \in \{-1,1\}^n | F(\underline{\mathbf{x}}) = \bot\}} \bigvee_{\underline{\mathbf{a}} \in \{-1,1\}^h} (P_F(\underline{\mathbf{x}}, \underline{\mathbf{a}}|\underline{\boldsymbol{\theta}}) = g_{min}). \quad (14)$$

Here, (14) forces $P_F(\underline{\mathbf{x}}, \underline{\mathbf{a}}|\underline{\boldsymbol{\theta}})$ to be exactly equal to the gap for at least one "minimum" $\underline{\mathbf{a}}$. Exact penalty functions can be used to encode (weighted) MaxSAT instances. Suppose we partition a formula into the conjunction of its soft constraints C_i each of weight $w_i \geq 0$. Then for each C_i we find an *exact* penalty function of (10)–(14) for C_i imposing a gap g_i proportional to w_i, and we combine the result as in Property 2.

Improving Efficiency and Scalability Using Variable Elimination. As before, assume that the variable placement is fixed and consider the SMT/OMT($\mathcal{LRA}$) formulation (10)–(13). Notice the exponential dependency on the number of hidden variables h. For practical purposes, this typically implies a limit on h of about 10. Here, we describe an alternative formulation whose size dependence on h is $O(h2^{\mathbf{tw}})$, where **tw** is the treewidth of the subgraph of G spanned by the qubits corresponding to the ancillary variables, G_a. For the Chimera graph, even when h is as large as 32, **tw** is at most 8 and therefore still of tractable size.

The crux of the reformulation is based on the use of the variable elimination technique [15] to solve an Ising problem on G_a. This method is a form of dynamic programming, storing tables in memory describing all possible outcomes to the problem. When the treewidth is **tw**, there is a variable elimination order guaranteeing that each table contains at most $O(2^{\mathbf{tw}})$ entries. Rather than using numerical tables, our formulation replaces each of its entries with a continuous variable constrained by linear inequalities. In principle, we need to parametrically solve an Ising problem for each $\underline{\mathbf{x}} \in \{-1, 1\}^n$, generating $O(2^n h 2^{\mathbf{tw}})$ continuous variables. However, by the sequential nature of the variable elimination process, many of these continuous variables are equal, leading to a reduced (as much as an order of magnitude smaller) and strengthened SMT formulation. See [5] for more details.

Placing Variables & Computing Penalty Functions via SMT/ OMT($\mathcal{LRIA} \cup \mathcal{UF}$). The formula $\Phi(\underline{\boldsymbol{\theta}})$ in (10)–(14) can be built only after a variable placement, so that each variable $z_j \in \underline{\mathbf{x}} \cup \underline{\mathbf{a}}$ has been previously placed in some vertex $v_j \in V$. There are many such placements. For example, if $n + h = 8$ and we want to encode the penalty function into a 8-qubit Chimera tile, then we have $8! = 40320$ candidate placements. Exploiting symmetry and the automorphism group of G, one can show that most of these placements are equivalent.

Alternatively, we can combine the generation of the penalty function with an automatic variable placement by means of SMT/OMT($\mathcal{LRIA} \cup \mathcal{UF}$), $\mathcal{LRIA} \cup \mathcal{UF}$ being the combined theories of linear arithmetic over rationals and integers plus uninterpreted function symbols. This works as follows.

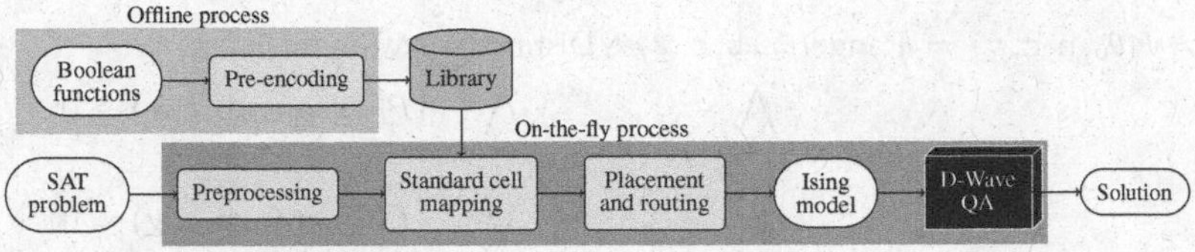

Fig. 3. Graph of the encoding process.

Suppose we want to produce the penalty function of some relatively small function (e.g., so $n + h \leq 8$, which fits into a single Chimera tile). We index the $n + h$ vertices in the set V into which we want to place the variables as $V \stackrel{\text{def}}{=} \{1, ..., n + h\}$, and we introduce a set of $n + h$ *integer* variables $\underline{\mathbf{v}} \stackrel{\text{def}}{=} \{v_1, ..., v_{n+h}\}$ s.t. each $v_j \in V$ represents (the index of) the vertex into which z_j is placed. (For example, "$v_3 = 5$" means that variable z_3 is placed in vertex #5.) Then we add the standard SMT constraint $\mathsf{Distinct}(v_1, ..., v_{n+h})$ to the formula to guarantee the injectivity of the map. Then, instead of using variables θ_i and θ_{ij} for biases and couplings, we introduce the *uninterpreted function symbols* $\mathsf{b} : V \longmapsto \mathbb{Q}$ ("bias") and $\mathsf{c} : V \times V \longmapsto \mathbb{Q}$ ("coupling"), so that we can rewrite each bias θ_j as $\mathsf{b}(v_j)$ and each coupling θ_{ij} as $\mathsf{c}(v_i, v_j)$ s.t $v_i, v_j \in [1, .., n + h]$ and $\mathsf{Distinct}(v_1, ..., v_{n+h})$.

This rewrites the SMT($\mathcal{LRA}$) problem (10)–(13) into the *SMT/OMT* ($\mathcal{LRIA} \cup \mathcal{UF}$) problem (15)–(26). Equation (19) must be used iff we need an exact penalty function. (Notice that (22) is necessary because we could have $\mathsf{c}(v_i, v_j)$ s.t. $v_i > v_j$.) By solving $\langle \Phi(\theta_0, \mathsf{b}, \mathsf{c}, \underline{\mathbf{v}}), g_{min} \rangle$ we not only find the best values of the biases b and couplers c, but also the best placement $\underline{\mathbf{v}}$ of the variables into (the indexes of) the qubits.

3.2 Encoding Larger Boolean Functions

As pointed out in Sect. 2.2, encoding large Boolean functions using the SMT formulations of the previous section is computationally intractable, so other methods must be used. One sensible approach is to pre-compute a library of encoded Boolean functions and decompose a larger Boolean function $F(\underline{\mathbf{x}})$ into a set of pre-encoded ones $\bigwedge_{k=1}^{K} F_k(\underline{\mathbf{x}}^k)$. The penalty models $P_{F_k}(\underline{\mathbf{x}}^k, \underline{\mathbf{a}}^k | \underline{\boldsymbol{\theta}}^k)$ for these pre-encoded functions may then be combined using chains as described in Sect. 2.3. This schema is shown in Fig. 3. This is not the only possible method, but it is a natural choice for SAT and constraint satisfaction problems, and in terms of QA performance it has been shown experimentally to outperform other encoding methods for certain problem classes [6]. In this section, we describe each of the stages in turn.

$$\Phi(\theta_0, \mathsf{b}, \mathsf{c}, \underline{\mathbf{v}}) \stackrel{\text{def}}{=} \mathsf{Range}(\theta_0, \mathsf{b}, \mathsf{c}, \underline{\mathbf{v}}) \wedge \mathsf{Distinct}(\underline{\mathbf{v}}) \wedge \mathsf{Graph}() \tag{15}$$

$$\wedge \bigwedge_{\{\underline{\mathbf{x}} \in \{-1,1\}^n | F(\underline{\mathbf{x}}) = \top\}} \bigwedge_{\underline{\mathbf{a}} \in \{-1,1\}^h} (P_F(\underline{\mathbf{x}}, \underline{\mathbf{a}} | \theta_0, \mathsf{b}, \mathsf{c}, \underline{\mathbf{v}}) \geq 0) \tag{16}$$

$$\wedge \bigwedge_{\{\underline{\mathbf{x}} \in \{-1,1\}^n | F(\underline{\mathbf{x}}) = \top\}} \bigvee_{\underline{\mathbf{a}} \in \{-1,1\}^h} (P_F(\underline{\mathbf{x}}, \underline{\mathbf{a}} | \theta_0, \mathsf{b}, \mathsf{c}, \underline{\mathbf{v}}) = 0) \tag{17}$$

$$\wedge \bigwedge_{\{\underline{\mathbf{x}} \in \{-1,1\}^n | F(\underline{\mathbf{x}}) = \bot\}} \bigwedge_{\underline{\mathbf{a}} \in \{-1,1\}^h} (P_F(\underline{\mathbf{x}}, \underline{\mathbf{a}} | \theta_0, \mathsf{b}, \mathsf{c}, \underline{\mathbf{v}}) \geq g_{min}) \tag{18}$$

$$\wedge \bigwedge_{\{\underline{\mathbf{x}} \in \{-1,1\}^n | F(\underline{\mathbf{x}}) = \bot\}} \bigvee_{\underline{\mathbf{a}} \in \{-1,1\}^h} (P_F(\underline{\mathbf{x}}, \underline{\mathbf{a}} | \theta_0, \mathsf{b}, \mathsf{c}, \underline{\mathbf{v}}) = g_{min}) \tag{19}$$

$$\mathsf{Range}(\theta_0, \mathsf{b}, \mathsf{c}, \underline{\mathbf{v}}) \stackrel{\text{def}}{=} \bigwedge_{1 \leq j \leq n+h} (1 \leq v_j) \wedge (v_j \leq n+h) \tag{20}$$

$$\wedge \bigwedge_{1 \leq j \leq n+h} (-2 \leq \mathsf{b}(j)) \wedge (\mathsf{b}(j) \leq 2) \tag{21}$$

$$\wedge \bigwedge_{1 \leq j \leq n+h} (\mathsf{c}(j,j) = 0) \wedge \bigwedge_{1 \leq i < j \leq n+h} (\mathsf{c}(i,j) = \mathsf{c}(j,i)) \tag{22}$$

$$\wedge \bigwedge_{1 \leq i < j \leq n+h} (-1 \leq \mathsf{c}(i,j)) \wedge (\mathsf{c}(i,j) \leq 1) \tag{23}$$

$$\mathsf{Distinct}(v_1, \ldots, v_{n+h}) \stackrel{\text{def}}{=} \bigwedge_{1 \leq i < j \leq n+h} \neg(v_i = v_j) \tag{24}$$

$$\mathsf{Graph}() \stackrel{\text{def}}{=} \wedge \bigwedge_{\substack{1 \leq i < j \leq n+h \\ \langle i,j \rangle \notin E}} (\mathsf{c}(i,j) = 0) \tag{25}$$

$$P_F(\underline{\mathbf{x}}, \underline{\mathbf{a}} | \theta_0, \mathsf{b}, \mathsf{c}, \underline{\mathbf{v}}) \stackrel{\text{def}}{=} \theta_0 + \sum_{1 \leq j \leq n+h} \mathsf{b}(v_j) \cdot z_j + \sum_{1 \leq i < j \leq n+h} \mathsf{c}(v_i, v_j) \cdot z_i \cdot z_j. \tag{26}$$

Pre-encoding. In this stage, we find effective encodings of common small Boolean functions, using the SMT methods in Sect. 3.1 or by other means, and store them in a library for later use. Finding these encodings may be computationally expensive, but this task may be performed offline ahead of time, as it is independent of the problem input, and it need only be performed once for each NPN-inequivalent Boolean function.

Preprocessing. Preprocessing, or Boolean formula minimization, consists of simplifying the input formula $F(\underline{\mathbf{x}})$ to reduce its size or complexity in terms of its graphical representation (typically and-inverter graphs). This is a well-studied problem with mature algorithms available [23, 25].

Standard cell mapping. In the standard cell mapping phase, $F(\underline{\mathbf{x}})$ is decomposed into functions $\bigwedge_{k=1}^{K} F_k(\underline{\mathbf{x}}^k)$ that are available in the library. To minimize the size of the final Ising model, K should be as small as possible. For SAT or constraint satisfaction problems, this mapping may be performed naïvely: given a set of constraints $\{F_k(\underline{\mathbf{x}}^k)\}_{k=1}^{K}$ on the variables, each $F_k(\underline{\mathbf{x}}^k)$ is found in the library (possibly combining small constraints into larger ones [5]). However, more advanced techniques have been devised in the digital logic synthesis literature. For example, *technology mapping* is the process of mapping a technology-independent circuit representation to the physical gates used in a digital circuit [17,24]. Usually technology mapping is used to reduce circuit delay and load, and performs minimization as an additional step. Delay and load do not play a role in the context of QA, but minimization is important to simplify the placement and routing phase that follows.

Placement and routing. Once $F(\underline{\mathbf{x}})$ is decomposed into functions $\bigwedge_{k=1}^{K} F_k(\underline{\mathbf{x}}^k)$ with penalty models $P_{F_k}(\underline{\mathbf{x}}^k, \underline{\mathbf{a}}^k|\underline{\boldsymbol{\theta}}^k)$, it remains to embed the entire formula onto the QA hardware as in equation (9). This process has two parts: *placement*, in which each $P_{F_k}(\underline{\mathbf{x}}^k, \underline{\mathbf{a}}^k|\underline{\boldsymbol{\theta}}^k)$ is assigned to a disjoint subgraph of the QA hardware graph; and *routing*, in which chains of qubits are built to ensure that distinct qubits x_i and x_i' representing the same variable take consistent values (using penalty functions of the form $1-x_ix_i'$). Both placement and routing are very well-studied in design of digital circuits [4]. Nevertheless, this stage is a computational bottleneck for encoding large Boolean functions.

During placement, chain lengths can be minimized by placing penalty functions that share common variables close together. Heuristic methods for doing this include simulated annealing [31], continuous optimization [10], and recursive min-cut partitioning [27]. These algorithms can be applied in the present context, but require some modification as current QA architectures do not distinguish between qubits used for penalty functions and qubits used for chains.

During routing, literals are chained together using as few qubits possible. Finding an optimal routing is NP-hard, but polynomial-time approximation algorithms exist [19]. In practice, heuristic routing algorithms scale to problem sizes much larger than current QA architectures [11,26,33].

4 Preliminary Experimental Evaluation

In this section, we offer preliminary empirical validation of the proposed methods for encoding [Max]SAT by evaluating the performance of D-Wave's 2000Q system in solving certain hard SAT and MaxSAT problems.

Remark 1. To make the results reproducible to those who have access to a D-Wave system, we have set a website [1] where the problem files, translation files and demonstration code can be accessed. We also provide contact information for D-Wave 2000Q system access.

Due to the limitations in size and connectivity of current QA systems, we require [Max]SAT problems that become difficult with few variables. To this end we modified the tool sgen [30], which has been used to generate the smallest unsolvable problems in recent SAT competitions. In particular, we modified sgen to use 2-in-4-SAT constraints instead of at-most/at-least 1-in-5-SAT constraints, as 2-in-4-SAT is particularly suitable to encoding with Ising models (see [7] for details). We generated 100 problem instances for various problem sizes up to 80 variables, the largest embeddable with current hardware. At 260 variables, these problems become unsolvable within 1000 seconds with state-of-the-art SAT solvers on standard machines [7].

Another important consideration in solving [Max]SAT instances using QA is that the QA hardware cannot be made aware of the optimality of solution; for example, QA cannot terminate when all clauses in a SAT problem are satisfied. In this way, QA hardware behaves more like an SLS [Max]SAT solver than a CDCL-based SAT solver.

Propositional Satisfiability (SAT). To solve these SAT instances using QA, we encode and embed them as in Sect. 3 and then draw a fixed number of samples at an annealing rate of 10 μs per sample. Table 1(a) shows the results from the QA hardware. The QA hardware solves almost all problems within 50 μs of anneal time, and the rates of sampling optimal solutions remain relatively stable at this scale of problem.

In order to evaluate the significance of the testbed, we solved the same problems with the UBCSAT SLS SAT solver using the best performing algorithm, namely SAPS [32]. Table 1(b) shows that the problems are nontrivial despite the small number of variables, and the run-times increase significantly with the size of the problem.

Table 1. (a) Number of problem instances (out of 100) solved by the QA hardware using 5 samples and average fraction of samples from the QA hardware that are optimal solutions. Annealing was executed at a rate of 10 μs per sample, for a total of 50 μs of anneal time per instance. Total time used by the D-Wave processor includes programming and readout; this amounts to about 150 μs per sample, plus a constant 10 ms of overhead. (b) Run-times in ms for SAT instances solved by UBCSAT using SAPS, averaged over 100 instances of each problem size. Computations were performed using an 8-core Intel® Xeon® E5-2407 CPU, at 2.20GHz.

D-Wave 2000Q		
Problem size	**# solved**	**% optimal samples**
32 vars	100	97.4
36 vars	100	96.4
40 vars	100	94.8
44 vars	100	93.8
48 vars	100	91.4
52 vars	100	93.4
56 vars	100	91.4
60 vars	100	88.2
64 vars	100	84.6
68 vars	100	84.4
72 vars	98	84.6
76 vars	99	86.6
80 vars	100	86.0

(a)

UBCSAT (SAPS)	
Problem size	**Avg time (ms)**
32 vars	0.1502
36 vars	0.2157
40 vars	0.3555
44 vars	0.5399
48 vars	0.8183
52 vars	1.1916
56 vars	1.4788
60 vars	2.2542
64 vars	3.1066
68 vars	4.8058
72 vars	6.2484
76 vars	8.2986
80 vars	12.4141

(b)

Table 2. (a) Number of problem instances (out of 100) solved by the QA hardware using 100 samples, and average fraction of samples from the QA hardware that are optimal solutions. Annealing was executed at a rate of 10 µs per sample, for a total of 1 ms of anneal time per instance. (b) Time in ms taken to find an optimal solution by various inexact weighted MaxSAT solvers, averaged over 100 MaxSAT instances of each problem size. Classical computations were performed on an Intel i7 2.90GHz × 4 processor. The solvers gw2sat, rots, and novelty are as implemented in UBCSAT [32]. All classical algorithms are performed with the optimal target weight specified; in the absence of a target weight they are much slower.

D-Wave 2000Q		
Problem size	**# solved**	**% optimal samples**
32 vars	100	78.7
36 vars	100	69
40 vars	100	60.2
44 vars	100	49.9
48 vars	100	40.4
52 vars	100	35.2
56 vars	100	24.3
60 vars	100	22.3
64 vars	99	17.6
68 vars	99	13
72 vars	98	9.6
76 vars	94	6.6
80 vars	93	4.3

(a)

MaxSAT solvers: avg time (ms)				
Problem size	**g2wsat**	**rots**	**maxwalksat**	**novelty**
32 vars	0.02	0.018	0.034	0.039
36 vars	0.025	0.022	0.043	0.06
40 vars	0.039	0.029	0.056	0.119
44 vars	0.049	0.043	0.07	0.187
48 vars	0.069	0.054	0.093	0.311
52 vars	0.122	0.075	0.115	0.687
56 vars	0.181	0.112	0.156	1.319
60 vars	0.261	0.13	0.167	1.884
64 vars	0.527	0.159	0.207	4.272
68 vars	0.652	0.21	0.27	8.739
72 vars	0.838	0.287	0.312	14.118
76 vars	1.223	0.382	0.396	18.916
80 vars	1.426	0.485	0.43	95.057

(b)

Remark 2. The results shown are not intended as a performance comparison between D-Wave's 2000Q system and UBCSAT. It is difficult to make a reasonable comparison for many reasons, including issues of specialized vs. off-the-shelf hardware, different timing mechanisms and timing granularities, and costs of encoding. Instead we aim to provide an empirical assessment of QA's potential for [Max]SAT solving, based on currently available systems.

Weighted MaxSAT sampling. One of the strengths of D-Wave's processor is its ability to rapidly sample the near-optimal solutions: current systems typically anneal at a rate of 10 µs or 20 µs per sample and are designed to take thousands of samples during each programming cycle. As a result, the first practical benefits of QA will likely come from applications which require many solutions rather than a single optimum. To demonstrate the performance of QA in this regime, we generated MaxSAT instances that have many distinct optimal solutions. These problems were generated from the 2-in-4-SAT instances described above by removing a fraction of the constraints and then adding constraints on single variables with smaller weight(details in [7]).

Table 2 summarizes the performance of the D-Wave processor in generating a single optimal MaxSAT solution, as well as the run-times for various high-

Table 3. Number of distinct optimal solutions found in 1 second by various MaxSAT solvers, averaged across 100 instances of each problem size. (a) "anneal only" accounts for only the 10 ms per sample anneal time used by the D-Wave processor. "wall-clock" accounts for all time used by the D-Wave processor, including programming and read-out. (b) Classical computations were performed as in Table 2(b).

D-Wave 2000Q		
Size	**anneal only**	**wall-clock**
32 vars	448.5	443.9
36 vars	607	579.9
40 vars	1007.9	922
44 vars	1322.6	1066.6
48 vars	1555.4	1111.8
52 vars	3229	1512.5
56 vars	2418.9	1147.4
60 vars	4015.3	1359.3
64 vars	6692.6	1339.1
68 vars	6504.2	1097.1
72 vars	3707.6	731.7
76 vars	2490.3	474.2
80 vars	1439.4	332.7

(a)

MaxSAT solvers				
Size	**g2wsat**	**rots**	**maxwalksat**	**novelty**
32 vars	448.5	448.5	448.5	448.5
36 vars	607	606.9	606.9	606.8
40 vars	1007.7	1006.3	1005.3	1005
44 vars	1313.8	1307.1	1311.7	1255.5
48 vars	1515.4	1510.7	1504.9	1320.5
52 vars	2707.5	2813	2854.6	1616.2
56 vars	2021.9	2106.2	2186.6	969.8
60 vars	2845.6	3061.7	3289	904.4
64 vars	3100	4171	4770	570.6
68 vars	2742.2	3823.3	4592.4	354.8
72 vars	1841.1	2400.2	2943.4	212.6
76 vars	1262.5	1716	2059.2	116.4
80 vars	772.2	1111.1	1363.9	66.7

(b)

performing SLS MaxSAT solvers. The QA hardware solves almost all problems within 1 ms of anneal time. (Remark 2 also applies here.)

Table 3 considers generating distinct optimal solutions. For each solver and problem size, the table indicates the number of distinct solutions found in 1 s, averaged across 100 problem instances of that size. For the smallest problems, 1 s is sufficient for all solvers to generate all solutions, while the diversity of solutions found varies widely as problem size increases. Although the D-Wave processor returns a smaller fraction of optimal solutions for MaxSAT instances than for the SAT instances, it is still effective in enumerating distinct optimal solutions because its rapid sampling rate.

5 Ongoing and Future Work

Future QA architectures will be larger and more connected, enabling more efficient encodings of larger and more difficult SAT problems. Faster and more scalable SMT-based encoding methods for small Boolean functions is currently an important direction of research. The ability to increase the number of ancillary variables can lead to larger gaps, which in turn can make QA more reliable. Among the encoding challenges presented in this paper, a few are of particular interest and relevance to SMT research:

- *Variable placement.* Methods for simultaneously placing variables and computing penalty functions are currently less scalable, and have been less studied, than those for fixed variable placements.

- *Augmenting penalty models.* For large Boolean functions, generating penalty models directly from SMT becomes difficult because the number of constraints grows much more quickly than the number of available parameters. Function decomposition and chains provide one way around this, but chains limit the resulting energy gaps. There may be other methods of recombining a decomposed function that are not so restrictive. Alternatively, it may be possible to augment an existing penalty model with additional qubits for the purposes of increasing its energy gap. SMT formulations of these problems have not yet been explored.
- *Better function decompositions.* While Boolean function decomposition and minimization are mature classical subjects, those algorithms can probably be improved by taking into consideration the specifics of the embedding (placement and routing onto a QA hardware graph) that follow them.

Furthermore, we believe the problems presented here are not only practical, but also complex enough to be used to challenge new SMT solvers. To encourage the use of these problems as SMT benchmarks, we have provided example .smt files on the website of supplementary material [1].

References

1. Experimental data, source code, and supplementary material. https://bitbucket.org/aqcsat/frocos2017
2. Adler, I., Dorn, F., Fomin, F.V., Sau, I., Thilikos, D.M.: Faster parameterized algorithms for minor containment. Theor. Comput. Sci. **412**, 7018–7028 (2011)
3. Barrett, C.W., Sebastiani, R., Seshia, S.A., Tinelli, C.: Satisfiability Modulo Theories. In: Handbook of Satisfiability (2009)
4. Betz, V., Rose, J.: Vpr: a new packing, placement and routing tool for FPGA research. In: Field Programmable Logic Workshop (1997)
5. Bian, Z., Chudak, F., Israel, R., Lackey, B., Macready, W.G., Roy A.: Discrete optimization using quantum annealing on sparse Ising models. Frontiers in Physics (2014)
6. Bian, Z., Chudak, F., Israel, R.B., Lackey, B., Macready, W.G., Roy, A.: Mapping constrained optimization problems to quantum annealing with application to fault diagnosis. In: Frontiers in ICT (2016)
7. Bian, Z., Chudak, F., Macready, W., Roy, A., Sebastiani, R., Varotti, S.: Solving SAT and MaxSAT with a Quantum Annealer: Foundations and a Preliminary Report (2017). Extended version. https://bitbucket.org/aqcsat/frocos2017/raw/HEAD/sat2ising_extended.pdf
8. Boothby, T., King, A.D., Roy, A.: Fast clique minor generation in chimera qubit connectivity graphs. Quant. Inf. Proc. **15**, 495–508 (2016)
9. Cai, J., Macready, W.G., Roy, A.: A practical heuristic for finding graph minors. arXiv preprint (2014)
10. Chan, T., Cong, J., Kong, T., Shinnerl, J.: Multilevel optimization for large-scale circuit placement. In: ICCAD (2000)
11. Chen, H.Y., Hsu, C.H., Chang Y.W.: High-performance global routing with fast overflow reduction. In: ASPDAC, January 2009

12. Choi, V.: Minor-embedding in adiabatic quantum computation: I. the parameter setting problem. Quant. Inf. Proc. **7**, 193–209 (2008)
13. Choi, V.: Minor-embedding in adiabatic quantum computation: II. minor-universal graph design. Quant. Inf. Proc. **10**, 343–353 (2011)
14. Correia, V.P., Reis A.I.: Classifying n-input boolean functions. In: VII Iberchip (2001)
15. Dechter, R.: Bucket elimination: a unifying framework for reasoning. In: Proceedings of the UAI (1996)
16. Denchev, V.S., Boixo, S., Isakov, S.V., Ding, N., Babbush, R., Smelyanskiy, V., Martinis, J., Neven, H.: What is the Computational Value of Finite-Range Tunneling? Ph.Rev.X (2016)
17. Een, N., Mishchenko, A., Sörensson, N.: Applying logic synthesis for speeding up SAT. In: Marques-Silva, J., Sakallah, K.A. (eds.) SAT 2007. LNCS, vol. 4501, pp. 272–286. Springer, Heidelberg (2007). doi:10.1007/978-3-540-72788-0_26
18. Farhi, E., Goldstone, J., Gutmann, S., Sipser, M.: Quantum computation by adiabatic evolution. arXiv preprint (2000)
19. Gester, M., Müller, D., Nieberg, T., Panten, C., Schulte, C., Vygen, J.: Bonnroute: algorithms and data structures for fast and good VLSI routing. TODAES **18**, 32 (2013)
20. Huang, Z., Wang, L., Nasikovskiy, Y., Mishchenko, A.: Fast boolean matching based on NPN classification. In: ICFPT (2013)
21. King, J., Yarkoni, S., Raymond, J., Ozfidan, I., King, A.D., Nevisi, M.M., Hilton, J.P., McGeoch, C.C.: Quantum Annealing amid Local Ruggedness and Global Frustration. arXiv preprint (2017)
22. Lanting, T., Harris, R., Johansson, J., Amin, M.H.S., Berkley, A.J., Gildert, S., Johnson, M.W., Bunyk, P., Tolkacheva, E., Ladizinsky, E., Ladizinsky, N., Oh, T., Perminov, I., Chapple, E.M., Enderud, C., Rich, C., Wilson, B., Thom, M.C., Uchaikin, S., Rose, G.: Cotunneling in pairs of coupled flux qubits. Phys. Rev. B **82**, 060512 (2010)
23. Mishchenko, A., Chatterjee, S., Brayton, R.: Dag-aware aig rewriting: a fresh look at combinational logic synthesis. In: DAC (2006)
24. Mishchenko, A., Chatterjee, S., Brayton, R., Wang, X., Kam T.: Technology mapping with boolean matching, supergates and choices (2005)
25. Mishchenko, A., Chatterjee, S., Jiang, R., Brayton, R.K.: Fraigs: a unifying representation for logic synthesis and verification. Technical report (2005)
26. Roy, J.A., Markov, I.L.: High-performance routing at the nanometer scale. TCAD **27**, 1066–1077 (2008)
27. Roy, J.A., Papa, D.A., Adya, S.N., Chan, H.H., Ng, A.N., Lu, J.F., Markov, I.L.: Capo: robust and scalable open-source min-cut floorplacer. In: ISPD (2005)
28. Sebastiani, R., Tomasi, S.: Optimization modulo theories with linear rational costs. TOCL **16**, 12 (2015)
29. Sebastiani, R., Trentin, P.: OptiMathSAT: a tool for optimization modulo theories. In: Kroening, D., Păsăreanu, C.S. (eds.) CAV 2015. LNCS, vol. 9206, pp. 447–454. Springer, Cham (2015). doi:10.1007/978-3-319-21690-4_27
30. Spence, I.: Sgen1: a generator of small but difficult satisfiability benchmarks. JEA **15**, 1–2 (2010)
31. Sun, W.-J., Sechen, C.: Efficient and effective placement for very large circuits. TCAD **14**, 349–359 (1995)

32. Tompkins, D.A.D., Hoos, H.H.: UBCSAT: an implementation and experimentation environment for SLS algorithms for SAT and MAX-SAT. In: Hoos, H.H., Mitchell, D.G. (eds.) SAT 2004. LNCS, vol. 3542, pp. 306–320. Springer, Heidelberg (2005). doi:10.1007/11527695_24
33. Xu, Y., Zhang, Y., Chu, C.: Fastroute 4.0: global router with efficient via minimization. In: ASPDAC (2009)
34. Zaribafiyan, A., Marchand, D.J.J., Rezaei, S.S.C.: Systematic and deterministic graph-minor embedding for cartesian products of graphs. CoRR (2016)

Superposition with Structural Induction

Simon Cruanes(✉)

University of Lorraine, CNRS, Inria, LORIA, 54000 Nancy, France
simon.cruanes@inria.fr

Abstract. Superposition-based provers have been successfully used to discharge proof obligations stemming from proof assistants. However, many such obligations require induction to be proved. We present a new extension of typed superposition that can perform structural induction. Several inductive goals can be attempted within a single saturation loop, by leveraging AVATAR [1]. Lemmas obtained by generalization or theory exploration can be introduced during search, used, and proved, all in the same search space. We describe an implementation and present some promising results.

1 Introduction

Superposition-based theorem provers and SMT (Satisfiability Modulo Theory) solvers have considerably improved automation in some proof assistants thanks to *hammers* [2,3]. However, because these proof assistants provide inductive datatypes, many theorems are out of reach of the automated provers, which are not able to perform inductive reasoning. Such theorems include basic properties of Peano arithmetic, reasoning about data structures such as lists and trees, manipulating syntax trees (which are often represented as a recursive datatype), etc.

Most state of the art theorem provers for first-order logic with equality are based on superposition [4–7]. However, they often lack support for types or (inductive) datatypes. Vampire [5] has recently gained some support for datatypes [8] but does not perform induction yet.

Automatic inductive provers do exist [9–11] but they are usually not complete (nor very efficient) on the classical first-order logic problems hammers rely on. INKA [10] was based on resolution, but not superposition. A recent extension to CVC4 [12] equips it with inductive reasoning, but so far no major superposition-based theorem prover has inductive capabilities. Kersani and Peltier modified Prover9 to handle induction [13], but only for natural numbers; it is unclear how their technique could be extended to arbitrary datatypes. Otter-λ [14] can use its (incomplete) higher-order unification algorithm to apply explicitly the induction principle, but it does not try to introduce any lemma nor does it handle defined functions or datatypes efficiently. Another superposition prover able to prove some inductive properties is Pirate [15, unpublished], but in its architecture each inductive property is solved in a separate saturation loop; it

C. Dixon and M. Finger (Eds.): FroCoS 2017, LNCS 10483, pp. 172–188, 2017.
DOI: 10.1007/978-3-319-66167-4_10

resembles more an inductive prover that would use a superposition prover for discharging subgoals.

In this work we propose a new architecture that permits a seamless integration of multiple induction attempts into the deduction process of a superposition prover. All the proof attempts are performed in the same saturation loop [4]. This has several advantages. First, if the problem does not actually need induction, a regular first-order proof can be obtained as usual. Second, once a particular inductive goal has been proved, it is considered as a normal first-order formula. This means it can participate in all the usual inference and simplification rules and contribute to the rest of the proof. Third, efforts are allocated to the various inductive proof attempts using the same clause selection heuristics that drive the first-order prover. This means the same elaborate heuristics can be reused for inductive proofs.

Our approach relies on a variant of superposition with polymorphic types, recursive functions, and inductive datatypes, as well as support for AVATAR [1] for reasoning by case (Sect. 3). Regular splitting without backtracking [16] could be used instead of AVATAR, but is less convenient and efficient. This richer variant of superposition treats defined functions efficiently. The prover can handle problems expressed in TIP [17] ("Thousands of Inductive Problems"). It encodes the non-first-order constructs of TIP, such as pattern matching, during a preprocessing step.

On top of this extension of superposition, we introduce a new rule to instantiate the structural induction schema and prove a property by induction (Sect. 4). Pursuing several inductive goals simultaneously is made possibly by introducing a cut rule on top of AVATAR (Sect. 5). The properties to prove by induction come from several sources: the input goal, explicit lemmas requested by the user, or subgoals needed in already ongoing proofs (Sect. 6). The numerous heuristics for guessing relevant lemmas that have been developed for decades [9,18–21] can be adapted to our framework. We also present a simple way to filter out invalid potential lemmas (Sect. 7).

To show the practical feasibility of the approach, we implemented the extensions of superposition and the inductive reasoning rules in Zipperposition, a modular prover (Sect. 8). Comparisons with CVC4 on the TIP benchmarks show that the implementation is reasonably competitive, and suggest that an implementation in E or Vampire could lead to excellent results.

2 Basic Definitions

We define some notions and notations that will be useful for the rest of the paper. An *atomic type* is a type constructor applied to 0 or more atomic types. A (polymorphic) *type* has the form $\Pi\alpha_1\ \ldots\ \alpha_n.\ (\tau_1, \ldots, \tau_k) \rightarrow \tau$ where the α_i's are *type variables* and each τ_i is an atomic type. By s, t, u, v we denote *terms*, generated from variables x, y, z and *function symbols* f, g, h. By $\overline{t}$ we denote a finite (possibly empty) sequence of terms. A term is *ground* if it contains no variable. Given a term t and a *position* p, we write $t|_p$ for the subterm of t at p.

We write $t \lhd u$ if t is a (strict) *subterm* of u, i.e. if there is a non-empty position p such that $t = u|_p$. A *substitution* is a mapping σ from variables to terms such that the set of variables $\mathrm{dom}(\sigma) \stackrel{\mathrm{def}}{=} \{x \mid x \neq x\sigma\}$ is finite. We always implicitly restrict ourselves to well-typed terms, substitutions, etc.

A *literal* is an equation $s \simeq t$ or disequation $s \not\simeq t$. Note that $\simeq$ is a logical symbol, whereas $=$ denotes syntactic equality. A proposition p is implicitly represented by $p \simeq \top$. A *clause* is a disjunction of literals, denoted by C or D. The *empty clause* is the empty disjunction, equivalent to $\bot$ (false). We sometimes view clauses as multisets of literals. Ground literals and clauses are defined in the obvious way.

We reuse some concepts from AVATAR [1]. A *boolean mapping* $[\![\cdot]\!]$ is an injective mapping from clauses (and more generally, in our case, of formulas) into the propositional literals of a SAT solver. A *clause with assertion*, or *A-clause*, is a pair of a clause C and conjunction of boolean literals Γ, called the *trail*, and noted $C \leftarrow \Gamma$. It holds in an interpretation if either C holds, or Γ does not hold. We write $\sqcap$ for boolean conjunction and $\oplus$ for exclusive disjunction.

An *inductive (data)type* is defined by a set of *constructors*, at least one of which is non-recursive — we ignore mutually recursive datatypes, which can be encoded into a single datatype. A term t is *purely inductive* if every subterm of t whose type is inductive, has the form $c(t_1, \dots, t_n)$ where c is a constructor symbol. A *constructor context* $C[\diamond]$ is a term built from constructors, function symbols of non-inductive type, and a unique occurrence of $\diamond$; *applying* the context to a term t, written $C[t]$, means replacing the occurrence of $\diamond$ by t. $C[t]$ is only defined if it is well typed. A Herbrand model is *standard* if (i) it satisfies the axioms of datatypes: exhaustiveness and disjointness of constructors; (ii) every (ground) term is equal to some purely inductive term; (iii) equivalence classes of inductive types are *acyclic*, i.e. for every non-trivial constructor context $C[\diamond]$, $t \not\simeq C[t]$ is true in the model.

We seek to establish the satisfiability of formulas in standard models. To achieve this, we will instantiate the *induction schema* over the inductive types. The induction schema for an inductive type τ is a second order formula parameterized by a variable $P : \tau \to \mathsf{bool}$, but we instantiate it into a first-order formula that will be (dis)proved by superposition.

Example 1 (Natural Numbers). The type of natural numbers, nat, is a classic inductive type whose constructors are $\{0, \mathsf{s}\}$. Its inductive values are all the natural numbers $\{0, \mathsf{s}(0), \dots, \mathsf{s}^k(0), \dots\}$. The induction schema is $\forall P : \mathsf{nat} \to \mathsf{bool}.\ P(0) \land (\forall n : \mathsf{nat}.\ P(n) \Rightarrow P(\mathsf{s}(n))) \Rightarrow \forall n.\ P(n)$.

Example 2 (Lists). The type of polymorphic lists is $\mathsf{list}(\alpha)$. Its constructors are $[]$ and $(::) : \alpha \times \mathsf{list}(\alpha) \to \mathsf{list}(\alpha)$. The purely inductive values of type $\mathsf{list}(\tau)$ are finite lists of purely inductive values of type τ. The induction schema on lists is

$$\forall \alpha.\ \forall P : \mathsf{list}(\alpha) \to \mathsf{bool}.\ P([]) \land (\forall x : \alpha\ l : \mathsf{list}(\alpha).\ P(l) \Rightarrow P(x :: l)) \Rightarrow \forall l.\ P(l)$$

3 Superposition with Recursive Functions and Datatypes

Before considering induction, we need the theorem prover to be able to handle problems that contain defined functions and datatypes. In addition, input problems can contain constructs that are outside of the realm of first-order terms, such as pattern matching and boolean conditionals ("if–then–else"). The solution we propose is multifold: (i) add some additional inference rules and simplification rules for datatypes; (ii) a notion of rewriting that does not rely on the term ordering; this is used to properly encode recursive functions; (iii) a preprocessing algorithm that removes non-first-order constructs by introducing newly defined functions and use them to encode the terms.

We adopt the notations and inference system of superposition from E [4] and AVATAR [1], and recall the following notions: an inference rule (noted with a single bar) infers the bottom clause(s) from the top clause(s); a simplification rule (with a double bar) *replaces* the top clause(s) with the bottom ones.

3.1 Recursive Functions and Rewriting

Superposition relies on a *term ordering* for orienting equations. This usually works well for first-order logic. However, recursive functions (on datatypes) are difficult to orient properly with such term orderings. Often, a rule $\forall \overline{x}.\ f(\overline{t}) \simeq u$ defining f will be oriented right-to-left because u will contain several occurrences of variables, be heavier (in KBO), etc. whereas we would like it to be oriented in the more natural left-to-right direction.

To unfold recursive functions efficiently, we translate them into rewrite rules. By construction, the left-hand side of the rewrite rules that define f is of the form $f(t_1, \ldots, t_n)$ where the t_i are generated from variables and constructors. Rules are also non-overlapping, ensuring that the resulting rewrite system is confluent: at most one rule will apply to any tuple of arguments. Rewriting is done left-to-right, regardless of the term ordering. This strategy is not complete in general,[1] but it guarantees that unfolding a function definition acts as an efficient simplification step. Recursive predicates are defined analogously, using rules of the form $l \rightsquigarrow C_i$ (rewriting a positive literal into a set of clauses) and $\neg l \rightsquigarrow \bigwedge_i C_i$ (rewriting a negative literal into a set of clauses). This sort of rewriting is known as *deduction modulo* [22] and, in our context, can be expressed as *polarized resolution* [23].

Having a well-delimited set of rules that define a function also enables the notion of argument position, defined below. This notion is useful because it provides some insight on which arguments influence the control flow of the function, and which ones are just carried around passively or serve as accumulators. In particular, it is pointless to try to perform induction on a passive argument, because the constructors at such positions cannot be eliminated.

[1] It might even induce rewriting loops in some cases where the term ordering used by superposition and the rewrite system are not compatible. In our experience this does not seem to happen often.

Definition 1 (Argument Positions). Given a function f with k arguments, defined by rules

$$f(t_{1,1},\ldots,t_{1,k}) \rightsquigarrow u_1,\ldots,f(t_{n,1},\ldots,t_{n,k}) \rightsquigarrow u_n$$

we say that each i, for $1 \leq i \leq k$, is an *argument position* of f. An argument position i is *passive* if every occurrence of f in $(u_j)_{j=1}^n$ has $t_{i,j}$ as ith argument; in other words, if f always calls itself with the same ith argument. A non-passive argument position i is an *accumulator* if every $(t_{i,j})_{j=1}^n$ is a variable; it is *primary* otherwise. Intuitively, a primary position is one that the function might examine for determining whether to recurse or not.

Example 3. (a) $+$ with the definition $0 + x \rightsquigarrow x, \mathsf{s}(x) + y \rightsquigarrow \mathsf{s}(x + y)$: the first argument is primary and the second one, passive. (b) $\leq$ defined by $(0 \leq x) \rightsquigarrow \top, (s(x) \leq 0) \rightsquigarrow \bot, (s(x) \leq s(y)) \rightsquigarrow (x \leq y)$: both positions are primary. (c) qrev with the rules $\mathsf{qrev}([], x) \rightsquigarrow x, \mathsf{qrev}(x :: y, z) \rightsquigarrow \mathsf{qrev}(y, x :: z)$: the first position is primary, the second is an accumulator.

3.2 Preprocessing the Input

Our prover can parse problems expressed in TIP [17], an extension of SMT-LIB [24] with recursive functions, polymorphism, and datatypes. However, many constructs in this language have no straightforward equivalent in a superposition prover, in which there are only clauses and first-order terms. These constructs are pattern matching, conditionals ("if–then–else"), lambda abstractions, and let-bindings; let-bindings are expanded, conditionals and pattern matches are either named, or become toplevel case distinction as a set of rewrite rules. Again, the rewrite rules generated by our encoding are terminating and confluent; they are also orthogonal to the other rewrite rules because their head symbol is a fresh constant. We show a few examples of encodings in Fig. 1.

3.3 Inference Rules for Constructors

We consider the algebra of freely generated datatypes, such as Peano numbers, lists, or binary trees. This fragment is general enough to express many classic types and data structures, yet it is reasonably simple. Other theories such as rational arithmetic can also be used (e.g. using Hierarchic superposition [25]) but no induction will be performed on variables of these types.

Even without considering induction, datatypes need dedicated inference rules to account for acyclicity; other properties such as injectivity can be accounted for by adding either rules or axioms. Some SMT solvers have decision procedures for datatypes [26–28]. Similar work exists for superposition [8,15,29]. We use a small set of rules, as presented in Fig. 2. In the rules, c and c' are distinct inductive constructors (e.g., the empty list $[]$, the successor symbol, etc.). The positive version of Acyclicity rule can also be used as a simplification when the unifier σ is trivial. These rules are sound with respect to standard models, but do not, by themselves, ensure completeness without induction.

original	encoded
(declare−datatype Nat ((z) (s Nat))) (define−fun−rec leq ((x Nat)(y Nat)) Bool (match x (**case** z true) (**case** (s x2) (match y (**case** z false) (**case** (s y2) (leq x2 y2))))))	$\forall x.\ \mathsf{leq}(z, x) \rightsquigarrow \top$ $\forall x.\ \mathsf{leq}(\mathsf{s}(x), z) \rightsquigarrow \bot$ $\forall x\ y.\ \mathsf{leq}(\mathsf{s}(x), \mathsf{s}(y)) \rightsquigarrow \mathsf{leq}(x, y)$
(define−fun pred ((x Nat)) Nat (match x (**case** z z) (**case** (s x2) x2))) (define−fun−rec fact ((x Nat)) Nat (**let** ((one (s z))) (if (leq x one) one (mult x (fact (pred x))))))	$\mathsf{pred}(z) \rightsquigarrow z$ $\forall x.\ \mathsf{pred}(\mathsf{s}(x)) \rightsquigarrow x$ $\forall x.\ \mathsf{fact}(x) \rightsquigarrow \mathsf{f}(x, \mathsf{leq}(x, \mathsf{s}(z)))$ $\forall x.\ \mathsf{f}(x, \top) \rightsquigarrow \mathsf{s}(z)$ $\forall x.\ \mathsf{f}(x, \bot) \rightsquigarrow \mathsf{mult}(x,$ $\mathsf{f}(\mathsf{pred}(x),$ $\mathsf{leq}(\mathsf{pred}(x), \mathsf{s}(z)))$ where f is fresh
(declare−fun g (Nat Nat) Nat) (define−fun h ((x Nat) (y Nat)) Bool (**let** ((g2 (lambda ((x Nat)) (g y (s x))))) (=> (= x y) (= (g2 x) (g2 y)))))	$\forall x\ y.\ \mathsf{h}(x, y) \rightsquigarrow x \simeq y \Rightarrow \mathsf{f}_2(y, x) \simeq \mathsf{f}_2(y, y)$ $\forall y\ z.\ \mathsf{f}_2(y, z) \rightsquigarrow \mathsf{g}(y, \mathsf{s}(z))$ where f_2 is fresh

Fig. 1. Encoding a few expressions and definitions

$$\frac{c(\overline{t}) \simeq c'(\overline{t'}) \vee D}{D}\ \text{Disjointness+} \qquad \frac{c(\overline{t}) \not\simeq c'(\overline{t'}) \vee D}{\top}\ \text{Disjointness-}$$

$$\frac{c(t_1, \ldots, t_n) \simeq c(t'_1, \ldots, t'_m) \vee D}{\bigwedge_{i=1}^{n} (t_i \simeq t'_i \vee D)}\ \text{Injectivity}$$

$$\frac{t \simeq C[u] \vee D \qquad t\sigma = u\sigma}{D\sigma}\ \text{Acyclicity+} \qquad \frac{t \not\simeq C[t] \vee D}{\top}\ \text{Acyclicity-}$$

where $C[\diamond]$ is a non-trivial constructor context

Fig. 2. Inference rules to deal with inductive constructors

4 Proving Formulas by Induction

Let us first look at a single proof by induction before we consider how to integrate such proofs in the superposition machinery (Sect. 5). An *inductive goal* is a closed formula $\forall x_1 \ldots x_n\ y_1 \ldots y_m.\ \bigwedge_j C_j$ where the variables x_i have inductive types and each C_j is a clause. To try and prove such a goal, we instantiate the structural induction schema over a non-empty subset of $\overline{x}$ into a first-order formula F, and try to refute $\neg F$ by the usual process of Skolemizing variables, reducing $\neg F$ to conjunctive normal form (CNF), and performing inferences until $\bot$ is deduced. We can instantiate the induction schema for a goal $\forall x_1, \ldots, x_k.\ G$ on the variables $x_1, x_2, \ldots, x_k$ ($k \geq 1$) by instantiating it on x_1 first (taking $P(x) = \forall x_2\ \ldots\ x_k.\ G$), obtaining F, and then by applying the induction principle on $x_2, \ldots, x_k$ to every occurrence of P in F.

4.1 Instantiating the Induction Schema

Before we explain how to instantiate the induction schema over a given set of variables, we must first define the notions of *inductive Skolem constant* and *coverset*.

Definition 2 (Coverset [30]). A *coverset* for an inductive type τ is a set of terms built from inductive constructors and variables $x_1, \ldots, x_n$ such that each variable x_i occurs in exactly one position, and $\forall t : \tau.\ \bigoplus_{u \in S} \exists x_1\ \ldots\ x_n.\ t \simeq u$ is valid in standard models. The terms of a coverset are distinct in any model.

Definition 3 (Inductive Skolem constant). An *inductive Skolem constant* $\mathfrak{i}$ is a Skolem constant of inductive type.

Definition 4 (Ground Coverset). A *ground coverset* $\kappa(\mathfrak{i})$ for an inductive Skolem constant $\mathfrak{i}$ is a set of ground terms obtained by replacing all variables in a coverset with fresh Skolem constants, such that $\bigoplus_{t \in \kappa(\mathfrak{i})} \mathfrak{i} \simeq t$ holds in any model. The elements of $\kappa(\mathfrak{i})$ represent all the possible "shapes" of $\mathfrak{i}$ in any model. If $t, \mathfrak{i} : \tau$ and there is some $t' \in \kappa(\mathfrak{i})$ such that $t \lhd t'$, we write $\text{sub}(t, \mathfrak{i})$. We define $\kappa_{\downarrow}(\mathfrak{i}) = \{t \in \kappa(\mathfrak{i}) \mid \exists t' \lhd t.\ \text{sub}(t', \mathfrak{i})\}$ — the set of recursive cases.

Example 4. The coversets of the type nat from Example 1 are of the form $\{0, \mathsf{s}(0), \ldots, \mathsf{s}^k(0), \mathsf{s}^{k+1}(x)\}$ for some $k \geq 0$.

Example 5. The coversets of the type $\mathsf{list}(\tau)$ from Example 2 are of the form $\{[], x_1 :: [], \ldots, x_1 :: \ldots :: x_m :: y\}$ where $m > 0$, $x_1, \ldots, x_m : \tau$, and $y : \mathsf{list}(\tau)$.

To prove an inductive goal $F \stackrel{\text{def}}{=} \forall x_1\ \ldots\ x_n\ y_1\ \ldots\ y_m.\ \bigwedge_i C_i$ by induction over variables $x_1, \ldots, x_n$, we start by skolemizing each x_i with $\mathfrak{i}_i$ and each y_j with $\mathfrak{c}_j$. Then, we map each inductive Skolem constant $\mathfrak{i}_i$ to a ground cover set $\kappa(\mathfrak{i}_i)$. Our objective is to refute the following set of clauses:

$$\begin{aligned}
&\bigcup_{t_1 \in \kappa(\mathfrak{i}_1), \ldots, t_n \in \kappa(\mathfrak{i}_n)} \left(\text{cnf}(\neg \left(\textstyle\bigwedge_i C_i[\overline{x} \mapsto \overline{t}, \overline{y} \mapsto \overline{\mathfrak{c}})]\right) \leftarrow \textstyle\prod_{j=1}^{n} [\![\mathfrak{i}_j \simeq t_j]\!]\right) \\
&\cup \bigcup_{u_1 \in \kappa_{\downarrow}(\mathfrak{i}_1), \ldots, u_n \in \kappa_{\downarrow}(\mathfrak{i}_n)} \left(\textstyle\bigcup_i \left\{\forall \overline{y}.\ C_i[\overline{x} \mapsto \overline{u}] \leftarrow \textstyle\prod_{j=1, \text{sub}(t_i, u_i)}^{n} [\![\mathfrak{i}_j \simeq t_j]\!]\right\}\right) \\
&\cup \bigcup_{j=1}^{n} \left\{\textstyle\bigoplus_{t \in \kappa(\mathfrak{i}_j)} [\![\mathfrak{i}_j \simeq t]\!]\right\}
\end{aligned}$$

The first set of clauses comes from the negation of our goal, after skolemization and case split (using a coverset to examine the possible shapes of these

Skolem constants $(\mathsf{i}_j)_j$. The second set comes from inductive hypothesis: to prove $\bot$ from $\neg(\bigwedge_i C_i)[x \mapsto n_0]$, in the case $n_0 \simeq \mathsf{s}(n_1)$, we need the hypothesis $(\bigwedge_i C_i)[x \mapsto n_1]$. The third set of boolean formulas, sent to the SAT solver, forces each Skolem constant to be equal to exactly one member of its ground coverset. We recall that $[\![\cdot]\!]$ turns a literal or clause into a propositional atom.

Example 6 (Associativity of +). Let $F \stackrel{\text{def}}{=} \forall x\ y\ z : \mathsf{nat}.\ x + (y + z) \simeq (x + y) + z$. To prove F, we perform induction on $\{x\}$, with Skolem symbols $\{\mathsf{x}_0, \mathsf{y}_0, \mathsf{z}_0\}$ and ground coverset $\kappa(\mathsf{x}_0) = \{0, \mathsf{s}(\mathsf{x}_1)\}$. The resulting clauses are:

$$
\begin{gathered}
0 + (\mathsf{y}_0 + \mathsf{z}_0) \not\simeq (0 + \mathsf{y}_0) + \mathsf{z}_0 \leftarrow [\![\mathsf{x}_0 \simeq 0]\!] \\
\mathsf{s}(\mathsf{x}_1) + (\mathsf{y}_0 + \mathsf{z}_0) \not\simeq (\mathsf{s}(\mathsf{x}_1) + \mathsf{y}_0) + \mathsf{z}_0 \leftarrow [\![\mathsf{x}_0 \simeq \mathsf{s}(\mathsf{x}_1)]\!] \\
\forall y\ z.\ \mathsf{x}_1 + (y + z) \simeq (\mathsf{x}_1 + y) + z \leftarrow [\![\mathsf{x}_0 \simeq \mathsf{s}(\mathsf{x}_1)]\!] \\
[\![\mathsf{x}_0 \simeq 0]\!] \oplus [\![\mathsf{x}_0 \simeq \mathsf{s}(\mathsf{x}_1)]\!]
\end{gathered}
$$

Now, superposition (and AVATAR) can prove $\bot$ from these clauses:

1	induction(F).base	$0 + (\mathsf{y}_0 + \mathsf{z}_0) \not\simeq (0 + \mathsf{y}_0) + \mathsf{z}_0 \leftarrow [\![\mathsf{x}_0 \simeq 0]\!]$
2	def(+)	$0 + x \simeq x$
3	rewrite(1,2)	$\mathsf{y}_0 + \mathsf{z}_0 \not\simeq \mathsf{y}_0 + \mathsf{z}_0 \leftarrow [\![\mathsf{x}_0 \simeq 0]\!]$
4	eq-res(3)	$\bot \leftarrow [\![\mathsf{x}_0 \simeq 0]\!]$
5	avatar(4)	$\neg[\![\mathsf{x}_0 \simeq 0]\!]$
6	induction(F).hyp	$\forall y\ z.\ \mathsf{x}_1 + (y + z) \simeq (\mathsf{x}_1 + y) + z \leftarrow [\![\mathsf{x}_0 \simeq \mathsf{s}(\mathsf{x}_1)]\!]$
7	induction(F).rec	$\mathsf{s}(\mathsf{x}_1) + (\mathsf{y}_0 + \mathsf{z}_0) \not\simeq (\mathsf{s}(\mathsf{x}_1) + \mathsf{y}_0) + \mathsf{z}_0 \leftarrow [\![\mathsf{x}_0 \simeq \mathsf{s}(\mathsf{x}_1)]\!]$
8	def(+)	$\mathsf{s}(x) + y \simeq \mathsf{s}(x + y)$
9	rewrite(7,8)	$\mathsf{s}(\mathsf{x}_1 + (\mathsf{y}_0 + \mathsf{z}_0)) \not\simeq \mathsf{s}((\mathsf{x}_1 + \mathsf{y}_0) + \mathsf{z}_0) \leftarrow [\![\mathsf{x}_0 \simeq \mathsf{s}(\mathsf{x}_1)]\!]$
10	sup(6,9)	$\mathsf{s}(\mathsf{x}_1 + (\mathsf{y}_0 + \mathsf{z}_0)) \not\simeq \mathsf{s}(\mathsf{x}_1 + (\mathsf{y}_0 + \mathsf{z}_0)) \leftarrow [\![\mathsf{x}_0 \simeq \mathsf{s}(\mathsf{x}_1)]\!]$
11	eq-res(10)	$\bot \leftarrow [\![\mathsf{x}_0 \simeq \mathsf{s}(\mathsf{x}_1)]\!]$
12	avatar(11)	$\neg[\![\mathsf{x}_0 \simeq \mathsf{s}(\mathsf{x}_1)]\!]$
13	induction(F).case-split	$[\![\mathsf{x}_0 \simeq 0]\!] \sqcup [\![\mathsf{x}_0 \simeq \mathsf{s}(\mathsf{x}_1)]\!]$
14	res(5,12,13)	$\bot$

The last inference is done by the SAT solver after the addition of the boolean constraints $\neg[\![\mathsf{x}_0 \simeq 0]\!]$ and $\neg[\![\mathsf{x}_0 \simeq \mathsf{s}(\mathsf{x}_1)]\!]$, establishing unsatisfiability.

Example 7 (Transitivity of $\leq$). Let $F \stackrel{\text{def}}{=} \forall x\ y\ z : \mathsf{nat}.\ x \leq y \wedge y \leq z \Rightarrow x \leq z$, where $\leq$ is defined by the rules $\{\forall x.\ 0 \leq x, \forall x.\ \neg(s(x) \leq 0), \forall x\ y.\ x \leq y \iff s(x) \leq s(y)\}$. To prove F, we perform induction on $\{x, y, z\}$, with Skolem symbols $\{\mathsf{x}_0, \mathsf{y}_0, \mathsf{z}_0\}$ and ground coversets $\kappa(\mathsf{x}_0) = \{0, \mathsf{s}(\mathsf{x}_1)\}$, $\kappa(\mathsf{y}_0) = \{0, \mathsf{s}(\mathsf{y}_1)\}$, $\kappa(\mathsf{z}_0) = \{0, \mathsf{s}(\mathsf{z}_1)\}$. We obtain the following set of clauses, which is first-order refutable:

$$
\begin{aligned}
0 \leq 0 &\leftarrow [\![\mathsf{x_0} \simeq 0]\!] \sqcap [\![\mathsf{y_0} \simeq 0]\!] \\
0 \leq 0 &\leftarrow [\![\mathsf{y_0} \simeq 0]\!] \sqcap [\![\mathsf{z_0} \simeq 0]\!] \\
\mathsf{s}(\mathsf{x_1}) \leq 0 &\leftarrow [\![\mathsf{x_0} \simeq \mathsf{s}(\mathsf{x_1})]\!] \sqcap [\![\mathsf{y_0} \simeq 0]\!] \\
\mathsf{s}(\mathsf{x_1}) \leq \mathsf{s}(\mathsf{y_1}) &\leftarrow [\![\mathsf{x_0} \simeq \mathsf{s}(\mathsf{x_1})]\!] \sqcap [\![\mathsf{y_0} \simeq \mathsf{s}(\mathsf{y_1})]\!] \\
\mathsf{s}(\mathsf{y_1}) \leq 0 &\leftarrow [\![\mathsf{y_0} \simeq \mathsf{s}(\mathsf{y_1})]\!] \sqcap [\![\mathsf{z_0} \simeq 0]\!] \\
\mathsf{s}(\mathsf{y_1}) \leq \mathsf{s}(\mathsf{z_1}) &\leftarrow [\![\mathsf{y_0} \simeq \mathsf{s}(\mathsf{y_1})]\!] \sqcap [\![\mathsf{z_0} \simeq \mathsf{s}(\mathsf{z_1})]\!] \\
\neg(0 \leq 0) &\leftarrow [\![\mathsf{x_0} \simeq 0]\!] \sqcap [\![\mathsf{z_0} \simeq 0]\!] \\
\neg(\mathsf{s}(\mathsf{x_1}) \leq 0) &\leftarrow [\![\mathsf{x_0} \simeq \mathsf{s}(\mathsf{x_1})]\!] \sqcap [\![\mathsf{z_0} \simeq 0]\!] \\
\neg(\mathsf{s}(\mathsf{x_1}) \leq \mathsf{s}(\mathsf{z_1})) &\leftarrow [\![\mathsf{x_0} \simeq \mathsf{s}(\mathsf{x_1})]\!] \sqcap [\![\mathsf{z_0} \simeq \mathsf{s}(\mathsf{z_1})]\!] \\
\neg(0 \leq \mathsf{s}(\mathsf{z_1})) &\leftarrow [\![\mathsf{x_0} \simeq 0]\!] \sqcap [\![\mathsf{z_0} \simeq \mathsf{s}(\mathsf{z_1})]\!] \\
\neg(\mathsf{x_1} \leq \mathsf{y_1}) \vee \neg(\mathsf{y_1} \leq \mathsf{z_1}) \vee (\mathsf{x_1} \leq \mathsf{z_1}) &\leftarrow [\![\mathsf{x_0} \simeq \mathsf{s}(\mathsf{x_1})]\!] \sqcap [\![\mathsf{y_0} \simeq \mathsf{s}(\mathsf{y_1})]\!] \sqcap [\![\mathsf{z_0} \simeq \mathsf{s}(\mathsf{z_1})]\!] \\
&\quad [\![\mathsf{x_0} \simeq 0]\!] \sqcup [\![\mathsf{x_0} \simeq \mathsf{s}(\mathsf{x_1})]\!] \\
&\quad [\![\mathsf{y_0} \simeq 0]\!] \sqcup [\![\mathsf{y_0} \simeq \mathsf{s}(\mathsf{y_1})]\!] \\
&\quad [\![\mathsf{z_0} \simeq 0]\!] \sqcup [\![\mathsf{z_0} \simeq \mathsf{s}(\mathsf{z_1})]\!]
\end{aligned}
$$

Remark 1. Using AVATAR for keeping track of case splits allows an inductive lemma, once proved, to become a normal axiom and participate in other proofs using the following simplifications:

$$
\frac{C \leftarrow \Gamma \sqcap a}{C \leftarrow \Gamma}\ \textsf{AvatarSimp+} \qquad \frac{C \leftarrow \Gamma \sqcap \neg a}{\top}\ \textsf{AvatarSimp-}
$$

if the SAT-solver has proved a (propagated at level 0)

4.2 Selecting the Induction Variables

We have seen how to prove an inductive goal by induction over a set of variables. But how do we know which variables to choose? Going back to the case of Example 6 (associativity of addition), there are three variables, but only the leftmost one will lead to a successful induction.

The relevant notion here is that of *primary positions* under functions (Definition 1). Here we draw inspiration from Aubin's work [21]. The heuristic is that if a variable appears in at least one *primary occurrence*, it is a candidate for induction. Let $G \stackrel{\text{def}}{=} \forall \overline{x}\, \overline{y}.\ \bigwedge_i C_i$ be an inductive goal, with variables $\overline{x}$ having an inductive type. A *primary occurrence* in G is a position p in some clause C_i such that (i) $C_i|_p$ does not occur directly under a constructor, and (ii) every non-empty prefix of p occurs either below a constructor, an uninterpreted symbol, or under a primary argument position of a defined function or predicate. Intuitively, a subterm (such as a variable on which we might do induction) is a primary occurrence in G if replacing this subterm by a constructor-headed term has a chance of making G reducible by some rewrite rule. In Example 6, the goal is $\forall x\ y\ z : \mathsf{nat}.\ x + (y + z) \simeq (x + y) + z$. Of all three variables, only x appears in primary occurrences.

Now consider Example 7, where the goal is $\forall x\ y\ z : \mathsf{nat}.\ x \leq y \wedge y \leq z \Rightarrow x \leq z$. All variables occur in primary positions, because both positions of $\leq$ are primary. However, simply replacing x with a constructor-headed term will not always suffice to reduce the (ground) goal negation; indeed $\mathsf{s}(\mathsf{x_1}) \leq \mathsf{y_0}$ and $\neg(\mathsf{s}(\mathsf{x_1}) \leq \mathsf{z_0})$ cannot be reduced. Therefore, we extend Aubin's heuristic [21].

If two variables in primary positions in the goal G occur immediately under the same defined symbol, both at primary argument positions, then we perform induction on both of them simultaneously. For Example 7 that means that we perform induction over $\{x, y, z\}$, which succeeds.

5 Performing Several Inductive Proofs with AVATAR

In practice, we need to carry out several proofs by induction. It is necessary when such a proof depends on other properties that are themselves proved by induction. One such case is nested induction: to prove $\forall x\ y.\ x + y \simeq y + x$, the lemmas $\forall x.\ x+0 \simeq x$ and $\forall x\ y.\ x+\mathsf{s}(y) \simeq \mathsf{s}(x+y)$ are required. We wish to carry out all these proofs within a single saturation loop of the superposition prover, to reuse the existing algorithms and main loop. Fortunately, AVATAR makes it easy to introduce several *lemmas* and interleaving their proof with the main saturation process. Given a (candidate) lemma F (a closed first-order formula), the clauses $\{C \leftarrow [\![\mathsf{lemma}\ F]\!] \mid C \in \mathrm{cnf}(F)\} \ \cup \ \{D \leftarrow \neg[\![\mathsf{lemma}\ F]\!] \mid D \in \mathrm{cnf}(\neg F)\}$ are added to the saturation set. This corresponds to a boolean split over $F \vee \neg F$, where the choice between F and $\neg F$ is represented by the boolean valuation of the propositional literal $[\![\mathsf{lemma}\ F]\!]$.

Definition 5 (Lemma Introduction). The *introduction rule* of a lemma F, where F is a first-order formula, is the following inference rule:

$$\frac{\top}{\bigwedge_{C\in\mathrm{cnf}(F)} C \leftarrow [\![\mathsf{lemma}\ F]\!] \\ \wedge \bigwedge_{D\in\mathrm{cnf}(\neg F)} D \leftarrow \neg[\![\mathsf{lemma}\ F]\!]}\ \mathsf{Lemma}$$

Theorem 1. *The inference rule* Lemma *is sound.*

Proof. Lemma is similar to an AVATAR boolean split on $F \vee \neg F$ using the boolean $[\![F]\!]$ (F, being closed, is either valid or unsatisfiable). Since $[\![\neg F]\!] \stackrel{\text{def}}{=} \neg[\![F]\!]$, we obtain the trivial constraint $[\![F]\!] \sqcup \neg[\![F]\!]$ and the "A-formulas" $F \leftarrow [\![F]\!]$ and $\neg F \leftarrow \neg[\![F]\!]$ that can then be reduced to CNF. In essence, Lemma is using an adaptation of AVATAR splitting to formulas of the form $F \vee \neg F$ where F is closed.

In a part of the search space, inference with A-clauses of the form $C \leftarrow [\![F]\!]$ will correspond to using the lemma F, assuming it has been proved; in another part, inferences with A-clauses of the form $D \leftarrow \neg[\![F]\!]$ will possibly lead to (conditional) proofs of F by reaching clauses of the form $\bot \leftarrow \neg[\![F]\!] \sqcap \Gamma$ (proof of F under assumptions $\neg\Gamma$).

Remark 2. (Fairness and Lemmas). Using Lemma on a non-theorem formula F does not prevent an unsatisfiable combined state from being reached. The proof of each lemma is interleaved with the rest of the saturation process. Thanks to this, it is possible to introduce several (candidate) lemmas even if they are not all true or provable. However, it might take a longer time to find a solution, because of the larger search space.

6 Finding Subgoals and Lemmas by Generalization

In this section, we examine several ways of guessing new inductive goals that are likely to help existing proof attempts progress. There is a large amount of literature dedicated to lemma guessing, either by generalizing a subgoal [9,15, 20,21] or by exploring an equational theory systematically to find formulas that *seem* to hold based on testing [12,31]. In this paper we present simple, relatively straightforward techniques that already yield good results; more sophisticated heuristics can be added on top.

Even though lemmas can either be proved on the fly by introducing a cut, or provided as axioms in the input file, they will be used in the same way in both cases. A subgoal is never generalized and replaced by a lemma; rather, we introduce a lemma which, if proved, will solve the subgoal by regular superposition.

6.1 Proving Subgoals by Induction

A superposition prover starts by reducing the input problem in CNF, in our case with some additional transformations (Sect. 3.2). A clause C containing at least one inductive Skolem constant can be negated, the constants replaced by fresh variables, resulting in an inductive goal that can be tested and then proved.

Similarly, during the course of saturation with some induction attempts, clauses of the form $C \leftarrow \neg[\![\mathsf{lemma}\ G]\!] \sqcap \Gamma$ (where G is an inductive goal) are clauses that need to be reduced to $\bot$ if G is to be proved. Again, if C contains at least one inductive Skolem constant, we can negate it, replace constants by variables, and assess the resulting goal.

More precisely, to prove a goal $\bigwedge_i C_i$ by generalizing inductive Skolem constants $\mathfrak{i}_1, \dots, \mathfrak{i}_n$ $(n \geq 1)$ occurring in the clauses C_i: (i) we replace each $\mathfrak{i}_j$ by a fresh variable x_j; (ii) we negate every literal in the C_i and swap conjunctions and disjunctions; (iii) we redistribute conjunction over disjunction to get back to a CNF. Clauses in the result are quantified over $\{x_j\}_j$ and a subset of $\biguplus_i \mathrm{freevars}(C_i)$. This generalization technique also applies to the original goal after it has been negated and reduced to CNF during preprocessing. It makes it possible to prove inductively goals that are not in CNF.

A subtlety here is that if an induction variable $\mathfrak{j}$ is a sub-case of some other constant $(\mathfrak{j} \in \kappa_{\downarrow}(\mathfrak{i}))$, there exist induction hypotheses (in other clauses) that might be needed for nested induction. In this case we also try the inductive goal where $\mathfrak{j}$ is *not* replaced by a fresh variable, and run both proof attempts simultaneously.[2]

[2] Our framework allows attempting to prove several distinct inductive goals to solve a single subgoal.

6.2 Generalizing Subgoals

An inductive goal G might not be provable by induction directly. For example, doing induction on x to prove $\forall x.\ x + (x + x) \simeq (x + x) + x$ will not succeed: in the recursive case $\mathsf{x}_0 = \mathsf{s}(\mathsf{x}_1)$, the clauses are

$$\mathsf{x}_1 + (\mathsf{x}_1 + \mathsf{x}_1) \simeq (\mathsf{x}_1 + \mathsf{x}_1) + \mathsf{x}_1$$
$$\mathsf{s}(\mathsf{x}_1) + (\mathsf{s}(\mathsf{x}_1) + \mathsf{s}(\mathsf{x}_1)) \not\simeq (\mathsf{s}(\mathsf{x}_1) + \mathsf{s}(\mathsf{x}_1)) + \mathsf{s}(\mathsf{x}_1)$$

but even after reduction, the hypothesis cannot rewrite the negative clause in any way because of successor symbols that appeared at passive positions. Following, once more, Aubin [21], we generalize *the primary occurrences* of a variable in a goal if it occurs at least twice in primary positions, and at least once in passive positions. In this way, doing inference on the primary occurrences will have better chances of succeeding. This generalization is only performed if the generalized goal still passes tests successfully (see Sect. 7).

Similarly, if a non-variable, non constructor-headed term occurs at least twice in primary positions, and is neither a variable nor constructor-headed, we can generalize it the same way.

Heuristics for guessing relevant lemmas from a goal have been developed for decades [9, 18–21] and can be adapted to our framework. For those that require to examine both the current subgoal and the induction hypothesis, more bookkeeping would be needed, because these objects live in the unstructured set of clauses, rather than in a sequent.

Remark 3. Speculating lemmas can be detrimental to the search space, by introducing many new clauses and performing arbitrary cuts. Therefore, the application of this rule must be heuristically restricted. In our implementation, we forbid deeply nested applications of generalization (beyond a small, user definable limit). Developing more advanced heuristics is however necessary.

7 Testing Conjectures Before Trying to Prove Them

Heuristics, as useful as they are, can mislead a solver into trying to prove inductive goals that are not valid. Attempting to prove an invalid goal with likely lead to a non-terminating superposition saturation on its own, draining memory and CPU resources away from the main proof effort. It pays to perform some limited amount of computation to try and rule out invalid goals.

To test a goal $G \stackrel{\text{def}}{=} \forall \overline{x}.\ \bigwedge_i C_i$, we do a limited number of saturation step, starting from $\{C_i\}_i$. Clauses from the main saturation loop can be used in inferences, emulating a *set-of-support* strategy. If $\bot$ can be derived, the goal is invalid and can be discarded. Many inductive goals, in practice, use computable (recursive) functions. Testing tools such as (Lazy) SmallCheck [32] and QuickCheck [33] are popular options for these properties; in our case, we use *narrowing* [34] because it is readily adapted to rewriting-based functions:

$$\frac{C \vee s \circ t \qquad l \rightsquigarrow r}{(C \vee s[r]_p)\sigma}\ \textsf{Narrowing} \qquad \frac{C \vee t \qquad l \rightsquigarrow \bigwedge_j D_j}{\bigwedge_j (C \vee D_j)\sigma}\ \textsf{Lit Narrowing}$$

$$\text{if } l\sigma = s|_p\sigma, \circ \in \{\simeq, \not\simeq\}, \; l \rightsquigarrow r \text{ is a rewrite rule} \qquad \text{if } l\sigma = t\sigma,\ t : \textsf{bool},\; l \rightsquigarrow \bigwedge_j D_j \text{ is a rewrite rule}$$

Fig. 3. Inference Rules Used for Testing

the resulting rules are listed in Fig. 3. In addition, not all goals contain only computable functions — some functions or predicates might only occur in axioms, not definitions — so we also need to perform the usual superposition inferences.

This mechanism for ruling out invalid goals works quite well in practice, even with a relatively small number of saturation steps. The limit on saturation steps is a trade-off between the usefulness of detecting invalid conjectures, and the time spent on each candidate lemma.

8 Implementation and Experiments

To evaluate our approach, we implemented it in a superposition prover, Zipperposition [35, chap. 3]. The prover is implemented in OCaml, available at https://github.com/c-cube/zipperposition under a permissive BSD license. Thanks to its modular architecture, many extensions of superposition have been added to it, including (as of version 1.2) integer linear arithmetic [35, chap. 4], first-class boolean terms [36], rewrite rules (used for evaluating recursive functions), a simpler version of AVATAR [1], basic support for AC symbols [4], and the inductive reasoning described in this paper. This allows the prover to solve such problems as $\forall (p : \alpha \rightarrow \textsf{bool})\ (l : \textsf{list}(\alpha)).\ \textsf{length}(l) \geq \textsf{length}(\textsf{filter}(p, l))$ by using a combination of arithmetic, booleans, and induction. The prover can parse its own native format, TPTP [37], and TIP [17].

In Fig. 4, we compare Zipperposition with two variations of CVC4[3] on TIP benchmarks.[4] The first one, CVC4, corresponds to `cvc4 --lang smt --quant-ind` to perform goal-directed induction [12]; the second one, CVC4-gen, has the additional flag `--conjecture-gen` to generate lemmas by theory exploration, like Hipspec [31]. We use https://github.com/tip-org/tools/ to convert TIP problems into SMT-LIB by removing pattern matching (which is not supported by CVC4). The classical set of IsaPlanner benchmarks [38] are included as a subset of TIP benchmarks. Solvers are given 30 s for each problem, which is a reasonable amount of time a user might wait for automatic provers in a proof assistant. The results are encouraging, since Zipperposition relies on quite simple generalization techniques.

---

[3] CVC4 1.5-prerelease r6317, see http://cvc4.cs.stanford.edu/web/ .

[4] Commit 187b71af8d920d0634b2b8b34c4ac4834b2f6a94 at https://github.com/tip-org/benchmarks.

	unsat (/86)	time (s)
Zipperposition	64	4.2
CVC4	67	1.6
CVC4-gen	73	12.4

(a) Results on the IsaPlanner problems

	unsat (/484)	time (s)
Zipperposition	139	53.2
CVC4	138	8.2
CVC4-gen	160	27.7

(b) Results for TIP benchmarks

Fig. 4. Experiments on TIP benchmarks

However, our initial aim was to extend superposition provers to do induction, while retaining their efficiency in first-order reasoning. Figure 5 shows a comparison of Zipperposition with some other provers, on TPTP 6.1, which contains 15,853 first-order problems.[5] CVC4, again, performs quite well; Prover9 is included as a base reference, and E (version 1.9) is one of the best first-order

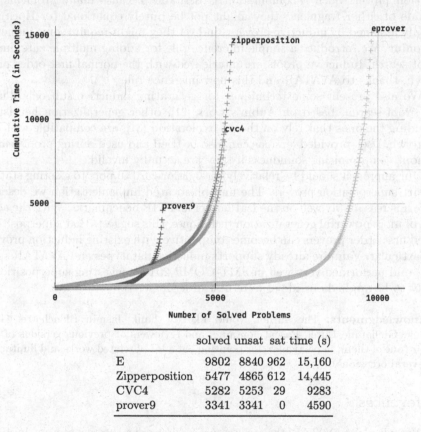

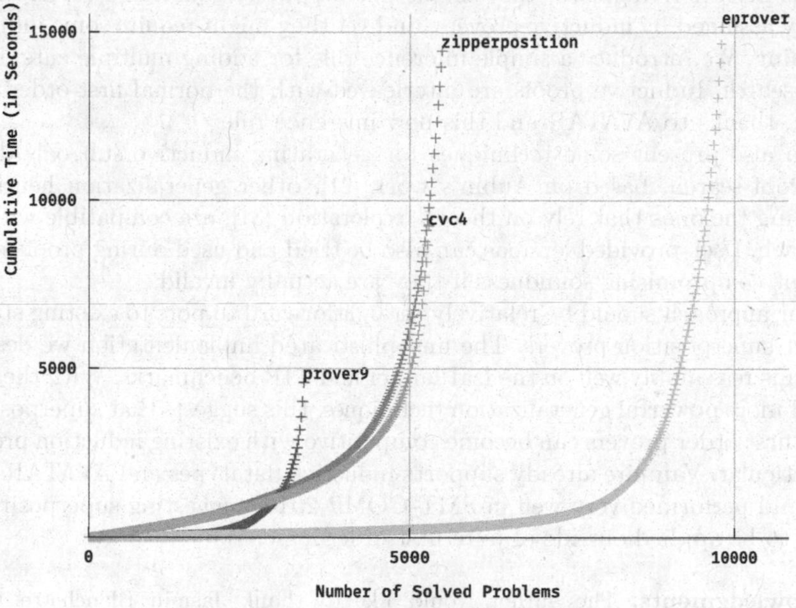

	solved	unsat	sat	time (s)
E	9802	8840	962	15,160
Zipperposition	5477	4865	612	14,445
CVC4	5282	5253	29	9283
prover9	3341	3341	0	4590

Fig. 5. Results on the first-order fragment of TPTP

[5] Experiments on TPTP were run on a 2.20 GHz Intel Xeon® CPU with 30 s timeout and a memory limit of 2 GB.

provers. This benchmark shows that Zipperposition keeps good performance on first-order problems.

It is interesting to note that CVC4 is very versatile, and can play on many boards, including first-order logic and inductive theorem proving, in addition to more traditional SMT abilities such as ground reasoning with theories such as arithmetic. We hope that superposition provers will also extend their domain of competency to tackle more expressive logics. Having diverse techniques for automated theorem proving means that portfolio approaches will work well, and will benefit from complementary strengths of the solvers.

9 Conclusion

In this work, we show a practical integration of inductive reasoning into a superposition prover. Such a combination is desirable because many problems fall outside of either fragment: they might not be purely equational (or Horn), as usually assumed by inductive provers, and yet they might require some inductive reasoning. We introduce a simple inference rule for adding multiple cuts during proof search. Inductive proofs are interleaved with the normal first-order proof search, thanks to AVATAR and this new inference rule.

We also present some techniques for generating inductive subgoals during the proof search, based on Aubin's work [21]; other generalization heuristics, including the ones that rely on theory exploration [31], are compatible with our approach. User-provided lemmas can also be tried and used during proof search, without compromising soundness if they are actually invalid.

Our approach should be relatively straightforward to port to existing state of the art superposition provers. The unsophisticated implementation we describe performs reasonably well on the IsaPlanner and TIP benchmarks. With the addition of more powerful generalization techniques, this suggests that superposition-based first-order provers can become competitive with existing induction provers. In particular, Vampire already supports inductive datatypes and AVATAR splitting, and performed very well in SMT-COMP 2016, suggesting superposition is ready to be applied outside of pure first-order logic.

Acknowledgments. The author would like to thank Jasmin Blanchette, Gilles Dowek, Guillaume Burel, Pascal Fontaine, and reviewers of previous versions of this paper (one of them, in particular, for pointing out a lot of related works and limitations in several occasions).

References

1. Voronkov, A.: AVATAR: the architecture for first-order theorem provers. In: Biere, A., Bloem, R. (eds.) CAV 2014. LNCS, vol. 8559, pp. 696–710. Springer, Cham (2014). doi:10.1007/978-3-319-08867-9_46
2. Paulson, L.C., Blanchette, J.C.: Three years of experience with Sledgehammer, a practical link between automatic and interactive theorem provers. In: Sutcliffe, G., Schulz, S., Ternovska, E. (eds.) IWIL 2010, EasyChair (2012)

3. Kaliszyk, C., Urban, J.: Learning-assisted automated reasoning with Flyspeck. J. Autom. Reason. **53**(2), 173–213 (2014)
4. Schulz, S.: E - a brainiac theorem prover. AI Commun. **15**, 111–126 (2002)
5. Riazanov, A., Voronkov, A.: Vampire 1.1 (system description). In: Goré, R., Leitsch, A., Nipkow, T. (eds.) IJCAR 2001. LNCS, vol. 2083, pp. 376–380. Springer, Heidelberg (2001). doi:10.1007/3-540-45744-5_29
6. Weidenbach, C., Schmidt, R.A., Hillenbrand, T., Rusev, R., Topic, D.: System Description: SPASS Version 3.0. In: Pfenning, F. (ed.) CADE 2007. LNCS, vol. 4603, pp. 514–520. Springer, Heidelberg (2007). doi:10.1007/978-3-540-73595-3_38
7. Bachmair, L., Ganzinger, H.: On restrictions of ordered paramodulation with simplification. In: Stickel, M.E. (ed.) CADE 1990. LNCS, vol. 449, pp. 427–441. Springer, Heidelberg (1990). doi:10.1007/3-540-52885-7_105
8. Kovács, L., Robillard, S., Voronkov, A.: Coming to terms with quantified reasoning. In: Castagna, G., Gordon, A.D. (eds.) POPL 2017, pp. 260–270. ACM (2017)
9. Kaufmann, M., Moore, J.S.: ACL2: an industrial strength version of Nqthm. In: Computer Assurance, COMPASS 1996, pp. 23–34. IEEE (1996)
10. Biundo, S., Hummel, B., Hutter, D., Walther, C.: The karlsruhe induction theorem proving system. In: Siekmann, J.H. (ed.) CADE 1986. LNCS, vol. 230, pp. 672–674. Springer, Heidelberg (1986). doi:10.1007/3-540-16780-3_132
11. Stratulat, S.: A unified view of induction reasoning for first-order logic. In: Turing-100, The Alan Turing Centenary Conference (2012)
12. Reynolds, A., Kuncak, V.: Induction for SMT solvers. In: D'Souza, D., Lal, A., Larsen, K.G. (eds.) VMCAI 2015. LNCS, vol. 8931, pp. 80–98. Springer, Heidelberg (2015). doi:10.1007/978-3-662-46081-8_5
13. Kersani, A., Peltier, N.: Combining superposition and induction: a practical realization. In: Fontaine, P., Ringeissen, C., Schmidt, R.A. (eds.) FroCoS 2013. LNCS, vol. 8152, pp. 7–22. Springer, Heidelberg (2013). doi:10.1007/978-3-642-40885-4_2
14. Beeson, M.: Otter-lambda, a Theorem-prover with Untyped Lambda-unification. In: Proceedings of the Workshop on Empirically Successful First Order Reasoning, 2nd International Joint Conference on Automated Reasoning (2004)
15. Wand, D., Weidenbach, C.: Automatic induction inside superposition (unpublished), April 2017. http://people.mpi-inf.mpg.de/dwand/datasup/d.pdf
16. Riazanov, A., Voronkov, A.: Splitting without backtracking (2001)
17. Claessen, K., Johansson, M., Rosén, D., Smallbone, N.: TIP: tons of inductive problems. In: Kerber, M., Carette, J., Kaliszyk, C., Rabe, F., Sorge, V. (eds.) CICM 2015. LNCS, vol. 9150, pp. 333–337. Springer, Cham (2015). doi:10.1007/978-3-319-20615-8_23
18. Bundy, A., Stevens, A., van Harmelen, F., Ireland, A., Smaill, A.: Rippling: a heuristic for guiding inductive proofs. Artif. Intell. **62**(2), 185–253 (1993)
19. Boyer, R.S., Moore, J.S.: A Computational Logic Handbook: Formerly Notes and Reports in Computer Science and Applied Mathematics. Elsevier, San Diego (2014)
20. Kapur, D., Subramaniam, M.: Lemma discovery in automating induction. In: McRobbie, M.A., Slaney, J.K. (eds.) CADE 1996. LNCS, vol. 1104, pp. 538–552. Springer, Heidelberg (1996). doi:10.1007/3-540-61511-3_112
21. Aubin, R.: Strategies for mechanizing structural induction. In: IJCAI (1977)
22. Dowek, G., Hardin, T., Kirchner, C.: Theorem proving modulo. J. Autom. Reason. **31**, 33–72 (2003)
23. Burel, G.: Embedding deduction modulo into a prover. In: Dawar, A., Veith, H. (eds.) CSL 2010. LNCS, vol. 6247, pp. 155–169. Springer, Heidelberg (2010). doi:10.1007/978-3-642-15205-4_15

24. Barrett, C., Fontaine, P., Tinelli, C.: The satisfiability modulo theories library (SMT-LIB) (2016). http://www.SMT-LIB.org
25. Baumgartner, P., Waldmann, U.: Hierarchic superposition with weak abstraction. In: Bonacina, M.P. (ed.) CADE 2013. LNCS, vol. 7898, pp. 39–57. Springer, Heidelberg (2013). doi:10.1007/978-3-642-38574-2_3
26. Reynolds, A., Blanchette, J.C.: A decision procedure for (Co)datatypes in SMT solvers. In: Felty, A.P., Middeldorp, A. (eds.) CADE 2015. LNCS, vol. 9195, pp. 197–213. Springer, Cham (2015). doi:10.1007/978-3-319-21401-6_13
27. Barrett, C., Shikanian, I., Tinelli, C.: An abstract decision procedure for satisfiability in the theory of inductive data types. J. Satisf. Boolean Model. Comput. **3**, 21–46 (2007)
28. de Moura, L., Bjørner, N.: Z3: an efficient SMT solver. In: Ramakrishnan, C.R., Rehof, J. (eds.) TACAS 2008. LNCS, vol. 4963, pp. 337–340. Springer, Heidelberg (2008). doi:10.1007/978-3-540-78800-3_24
29. Horbach, M., Weidenbach, C.: Superposition for fixed domains. ACM Trans. Comput. Log. (TOCL) **11**(4), 27 (2010)
30. Zhang, H., Kapur, D., Krishnamoorthy, M.S.: A mechanizable induction principle for equational specifications. In: Lusk, E., Overbeek, R. (eds.) CADE 1988. LNCS, vol. 310, pp. 162–181. Springer, Heidelberg (1988). doi:10.1007/BFb0012831
31. Claessen, K., Johansson, M., Rosén, D., Smallbone, N.: Hipspec: automating inductive proofs of program properties. In: ATx/WInG@ IJCAR (2012)
32. Runciman, C., Naylor, M., Lindblad, F.: Smallcheck and lazy smallcheck: automatic exhaustive testing for small values. ACM Sigplan Not. **44**, 37–48 (2008)
33. Claessen, K., Hughes, J.: QuickCheck: a lightweight tool for random testing of Haskell programs. ACM Sigplan Not. **46**(4), 53–64 (2011)
34. Lindblad, F.: Property directed generation of first-order test data. In: Trends in Functional Programming, pp. 105–123, Citeseer (2007)
35. Cruanes, S.: Extending superposition with integer arithmetic, structural induction, and beyond. Ph.D. thesis, École polytechnique, September 2015
36. Kotelnikov, E., Kovács, L., Reger, G., Voronkov, A.: The Vampire and the FOOL. In: Proceedings of the 5th ACM SIGPLAN Conference on Certified Programs and Proofs, pp. 37–48. ACM (2016)
37. Sutcliffe, G.: The TPTP problem library and associated infrastructure: the FOF and CNF parts, v3.5.0. J. Autom. Reason. **43**(4), 337–362 (2009)
38. Johansson, M., Dixon, L., Bundy, A.: Conjecture synthesis for inductive theories. J. Autom. Reason. **47**, 251–289 (2010)

Subtropical Satisfiability

Pascal Fontaine[1], Mizuhito Ogawa[2], Thomas Sturm[1,3(✉)], and Xuan Tung Vu[1,2]

[1] University of Lorraine, CNRS, Inria, and LORIA, Nancy, France
{Pascal.Fontaine,thomas.sturm}@loria.fr
[2] Japan Advanced Institute of Science and Technology, Nomi, Japan
{mizuhito,tungvx}@jaist.ac.jp
[3] MPI Informatics and Saarland University, Saarbrücken, Germany
sturm@mpi-inf.mpg.de

Abstract. Quantifier-free nonlinear arithmetic (QF_NRA) appears in many applications of satisfiability modulo theories solving (SMT). Accordingly, efficient reasoning for corresponding constraints in SMT theory solvers is highly relevant. We propose a new incomplete but efficient and terminating method to identify satisfiable instances. The method is derived from the subtropical method recently introduced in the context of symbolic computation for computing real zeros of single very large multivariate polynomials. Our method takes as input conjunctions of strict polynomial inequalities, which represent more than 40% of the QF_NRA section of the SMT-LIB library of benchmarks. The method takes an abstraction of polynomials as exponent vectors over the natural numbers tagged with the signs of the corresponding coefficients. It then uses, in turn, SMT to solve linear problems over the reals to heuristically find suitable points that translate back to satisfying points for the original problem. Systematic experiments on the SMT-LIB demonstrate that our method is not a sufficiently strong decision procedure by itself but a valuable heuristic to use within a portfolio of techniques.

1 Introduction

Satisfiability Modulo Theories (SMT) has been blooming in recent years, and many applications rely on SMT solvers to check the satisfiability of numerous and large formulas [2,3]. Many of those applications use arithmetic. In fact, linear arithmetic has been one of the first theories considered in SMT.

Several SMT solvers handle also non-linear arithmetic theories. To be precise, some SMT solvers now support constraints of the form $p \bowtie 0$, where $\bowtie \in \{=, \leq, <\}$ and p is a polynomial over real or integer variables. Various techniques are used to solve these constraints over reals, e.g., cylindrical algebraic decomposition (RAHD [23,24], Z3 4.3 [20]), virtual substitution (SMT-RAT [9], Z3 3.1), interval constraint propagation [4] (HySAT-II [13], dReal [17,18], RSolver [25],

The order of authors is strictly alphabetic.

C. Dixon and M. Finger (Eds.): FroCoS 2017, LNCS 10483, pp. 189–206, 2017.
DOI: 10.1007/978-3-319-66167-4_11

RealPaver [19], raSAT [28]), CORDIC (CORD [15]), and linearization (IC3-NRA-proves [8]). Bit-blasting (MiniSmt [29]) and linearization (Barcelogic [5]) can be used for integers.

We present here an incomplete but efficient method to detect the satisfiability of large conjunctions of constraints of the form $p > 0$ where p is a multivariate polynomial with strictly positive real variables. The method quickly states that the conjunction is satisfiable, or quickly returns unknown. Although seemingly restrictive, 40% of the quantifier-free non-linear real arithmetic (QF_NRA) category of the SMT-LIB is easily reducible to the considered fragment. Our method builds on a *subtropical* technique that has been found effective to find roots of very large polynomials stemming from chemistry and systems biology [12,27]. Recall that a univariate polynomial with a positive head coefficient diverges positively as x increases to infinity. Intuitively, the subtropical approach generalizes this observation to the multivariate case and thus to higher dimensions.

In Sect. 2 we recall some basic definitions and facts. In Sect. 3 we provide a short presentation of the original method [27] and give some new insights for its foundations. In Sect. 4, we extend the method to multiple polynomial constraints. We then show in Sect. 5 that satisfiability modulo linear theory is particularly adequate to check for applicability of the method. In Sect. 6, we provide experimental evidence that the method is suited as a heuristic to be used in combination with other, complete, decision procedures for non-linear arithmetic in SMT. It turns out that our method is quite fast at either detecting satisfiability or failing. In particular, it finds solutions for problems where state-of-the-art non-linear arithmetic SMT solvers time out. Finally, in Sect. 7, we summarize our contributions and results, and point at possible future research directions.

2 Basic Facts and Definitions

For $a \in \mathbb{R}$, a vector $\mathbf{x} = (x_1, \dots, x_d)$ of variables, and $\mathbf{p} = (p_1, \dots, p_d) \in \mathbb{R}^d$ we use notations $a^{\mathbf{p}} = (a^{p_1}, \dots, a^{p_d})$ and $\mathbf{x}^{\mathbf{p}} = (x_1^{p_1}, \dots, x_d^{p_d})$. The *frame* F of a multivariate polynomial $f \in \mathbb{Z}[x_1, \dots, x_d]$ in sparse distributive representation

$$f = \sum_{\mathbf{p} \in F} f_{\mathbf{p}} \mathbf{x}^{\mathbf{p}}, \quad f_{\mathbf{p}} \neq 0, \quad F \subset \mathbb{N}^d,$$

is uniquely determined, and written frame(f). It can be partitioned into a positive and a negative frame, according to the sign of $f_{\mathbf{p}}$:

$$\text{frame}^+(f) = \{\, \mathbf{p} \in \text{frame}(f) \mid f_{\mathbf{p}} > 0 \,\}, \quad \text{frame}^-(f) = \{\, \mathbf{p} \in \text{frame}(f) \mid f_{\mathbf{p}} < 0 \,\}.$$

For $\mathbf{p}$, $\mathbf{q} \in \mathbb{R}^d$ we define $\overline{\mathbf{pq}} = \{\, \lambda\mathbf{p} + (1-\lambda)\mathbf{q} \in \mathbb{R}^n \mid \lambda \in [0,1] \,\}$. Recall that $S \subseteq \mathbb{R}^d$ is *convex* if $\overline{\mathbf{pq}} \subseteq S$ for all $\mathbf{p}$, $\mathbf{q} \in S$. Furthermore, given any $S \subseteq \mathbb{R}^d$, the *convex hull* $\text{conv}(S) \subseteq \mathbb{R}^d$ is the unique inclusion-minimal convex

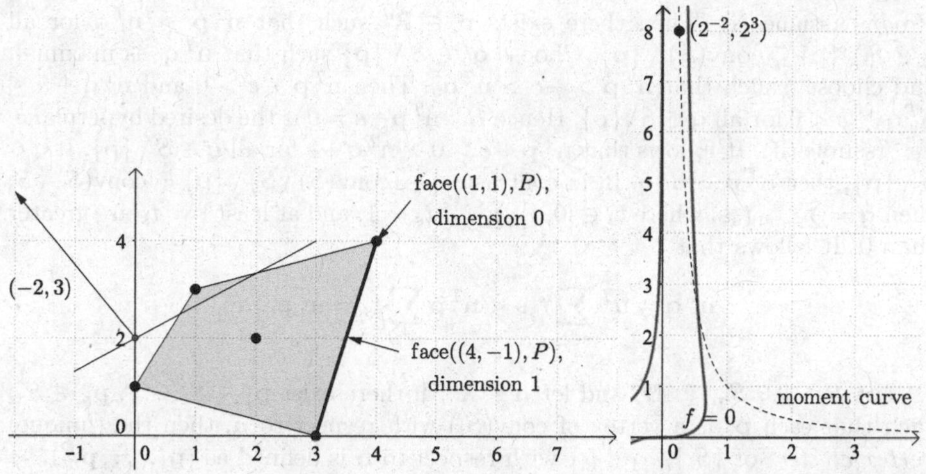

(a) The frame and the Newton polytope P of f

(b) The variety of f and the moment curve (a^{-2}, a^3)

Fig. 1. An illustration of Example 3, where $f = y + 2xy^3 - 3x^2y^2 - x^3 - 4x^4y^4$

set containing S. The *Newton polytope* of a polynomial f is the convex hull of its frame, $\mathrm{newton}(f) = \mathrm{conv}(\mathrm{frame}(f))$. Figure 1a illustrates the Newton polytope of

$$y + 2xy^3 - 3x^2y^2 - x^3 - 4x^4y^4 \in \mathbb{Z}[x, y],$$

which is the convex hull of its frame $\{(0, 1), (1, 3), (2, 2), (3, 0), (4, 4)\} \subset \mathbb{N}^2$. As a convex hull of a finite set of points, the Newton polytope is bounded and thus indeed a polytope [26].

The *face* [26] of a polytope $P \subseteq \mathbb{R}^d$ with respect to a vector $\mathbf{n} \in \mathbb{R}^d$ is

$$\mathrm{face}(\mathbf{n}, P) = \{\, \mathbf{p} \in P \mid \mathbf{n}^T\mathbf{p} \geq \mathbf{n}^T\mathbf{q} \text{ for all } \mathbf{q} \in P \,\}.$$

Faces of dimension 0 are called *vertices*. We denote by $\mathrm{V}(P)$ the set of all vertices of P. We have $\mathbf{p} \in \mathrm{V}(P)$ if and only if there exists $\mathbf{n} \in \mathbb{R}^d$ such that $\mathbf{n}^T\mathbf{p} > \mathbf{n}^T\mathbf{q}$ for all $\mathbf{q} \in P \setminus \{\mathbf{p}\}$. In Fig. 1a, $(4, 4)$ is a vertex of the Newton polytope with respect to $(1, 1)$.

It is easy to see that for finite $S \subset \mathbb{R}^d$ we have

$$\mathrm{V}(\mathrm{conv}(S)) \subseteq S \subseteq \mathrm{conv}(S). \qquad (1)$$

The following lemma gives a characterization of $\mathrm{V}(\mathrm{conv}(S))$:

Lemma 1. Let $S \subset \mathbb{R}^d$ be finite, and let $\mathbf{p} \in S$. The following are equivalent:

(i) $\mathbf{p}$ is a vertex of $\mathrm{conv}(S)$ with respect to $\mathbf{n}$.
(ii) There exists a hyperplane $H : \mathbf{n}^T\mathbf{x} + c = 0$ that strictly separates $\mathbf{p}$ from $S \setminus \{\mathbf{p}\}$, and the normal vector $\mathbf{n}$ is directed from H towards $\mathbf{p}$.

Proof. Assume (i). Then there exists $\mathbf{n} \in \mathbb{R}^d$ such that $\mathbf{n}^T\mathbf{p} > \mathbf{n}^T\mathbf{q}$ for all $\mathbf{q} \in S \setminus \{\mathbf{p}\} \subseteq \text{conv}(S) \setminus \{\mathbf{p}\}$. Choose $\mathbf{q}_0 \in S \setminus \{\mathbf{p}\}$ such that $\mathbf{n}^T\mathbf{q}_0$ is maximal, and choose c such that $\mathbf{n}^T\mathbf{p} > -c > \mathbf{n}^T\mathbf{q}_0$. Then $\mathbf{n}^T\mathbf{p} + c > 0$ and $\mathbf{n}^T\mathbf{q} + c \leq \mathbf{n}^T\mathbf{q}_0 + c < 0$ for all $\mathbf{q} \in S \setminus \{\mathbf{p}\}$. Hence $H : \mathbf{n}^T\mathbf{p} + c = 0$ is the desired hyperplane.

Assume (ii). It follows that $\mathbf{n}^T\mathbf{p} + c > 0 > \mathbf{n}^T\mathbf{q} + c$ for all $\mathbf{q} \in S \setminus \{\mathbf{p}\}$. If $\mathbf{q} \in S \setminus \{\mathbf{p}\}$, then $\mathbf{n}^T\mathbf{p} > \mathbf{n}^T\mathbf{q}$. If, in contrast, $\mathbf{q} \in (\text{conv}(S) \setminus S) \setminus \{\mathbf{p}\} = \text{conv}(S) \setminus S$, then $\mathbf{q} = \sum_{\mathbf{s} \in S} t_\mathbf{s}\mathbf{s}$, where $t_\mathbf{s} \in [0, 1]$, $\sum_{\mathbf{s} \in S} t_\mathbf{s} = 1$, and at least two $t_\mathbf{s}$ are greater than 0. It follows that

$$\mathbf{n}^T\mathbf{q} = \mathbf{n}^T \sum_{\mathbf{s} \in S} t_\mathbf{s}\mathbf{s} < \mathbf{n}^T\mathbf{p} \sum_{\mathbf{s} \in S} t_\mathbf{s} = \mathbf{n}^T\mathbf{p}. \quad \square$$

Let $S_1, \ldots, S_m \subseteq \mathbb{R}^d$, and let $\mathbf{n} \in \mathbb{R}^d$. If there exist $\mathbf{p}_1 \in S_1, \ldots, \mathbf{p}_n \in S_m$ such that each $\mathbf{p}_i$ is a vertex of $\text{conv}(S_i)$ with respect to $\mathbf{n}$, then the (unique) *vertex cluster* of $\{S_i\}_{i \in \{1,\ldots,m\}}$ with respect to $\mathbf{n}$ is defined as $(\mathbf{p}_1, \ldots, \mathbf{p}_m)$.

3 Subtropical Real Root Finding Revisited

This section improves on the original method described in [27]. It furthermore lays some theoretical foundations to better understand the limitations of the heuristic approach. The method finds real zeros with all positive coordinates of a multivariate polynomial f in three steps:

1. Evaluate $f(1, \ldots, 1)$. If this is 0, we are done. If this is greater than 0, then consider $-f$ instead of f. We may now assume that we have found $f(1, \ldots, 1) < 0$.
2. Find $\mathbf{p}$ with all positive coordinates such that $f(\mathbf{p}) > 0$.
3. Use the Intermediate Value Theorem (a continuous function with positive and negative values has a zero) to construct a root of f on the line segment $\overline{\mathbf{1p}}$.

We focus here on Step 2. Our technique builds on [27, Lemma 4], which we are going to restate now in a slightly generalized form. While the original lemma required that $\mathbf{p} \in \text{frame}(f) \setminus \{\mathbf{0}\}$, inspection of the proof shows that this limitation is not necessary:

Lemma 2. Let f be a polynomial, and let $\mathbf{p} \in \text{frame}(f)$ be a vertex of $\text{newton}(f)$ with respect to $\mathbf{n} \in \mathbb{R}^d$. Then there exists $a_0 \in \mathbb{R}^+$ such that for all $a \in \mathbb{R}^+$ with $a \geq a_0$ the following holds:

1. $|f_\mathbf{p}\, a^{\mathbf{n}^T\mathbf{p}}| > |\sum_{\mathbf{q} \in \text{frame}(f) \setminus \{\mathbf{p}\}} f_\mathbf{q}\, a^{\mathbf{n}^T\mathbf{q}}|$,
2. $\text{sign}(f(a^\mathbf{n})) = \text{sign}(f_\mathbf{p})$. $\square$

In order to find a point with all positive coordinates where $f > 0$, the original method iteratively examines each $\mathbf{p} \in \text{frame}^+(f) \setminus \{\mathbf{0}\}$ to check if it is a vertex of $\text{newton}(f)$ with respect to some $\mathbf{n} \in \mathbb{R}^d$. In the positive case, Lemma 2 guarantees for large enough $a \in \mathbb{R}^+$ that $\text{sign}(f(a^\mathbf{n})) = \text{sign}(f_\mathbf{p}) = 1$, in other words, $f(a^\mathbf{n}) > 0$.

Example 3. Consider $f = y + 2xy^3 - 3x^2y^2 - x^3 - 4x^4y^4$. Figure 1a illustrates the frame and the Newton polytope of f, of which $(1,3)$ is a vertex with respect to $(-2,3)$. Lemma 2 ensures that $f(a^{-2}, a^3)$ is strictly positive for sufficiently large positive a. For example, $f(2^{-2}, 2^3) = \frac{51193}{256}$. Figure 1b shows how the moment curve (a^{-2}, a^3) with $a \geq 2$ will not leave the sign invariant region of f that contains $(2^{-2}, 2^3)$.

An exponent vector $\mathbf{0} \in \text{frame}(f)$ corresponds to an absolute summand $f_\mathbf{0}$ in f. Its above-mentioned explicit exclusion in [27, Lemma 4] originated from the false intuition that one cannot achieve $\text{sign}(f(a^\mathbf{n})) = \text{sign}(f_\mathbf{0})$ because the monomial $f_\mathbf{0}$ is invariant under the choice of a. However, inclusion of $\mathbf{0}$ can yield a normal vector $\mathbf{n}$ which renders all other monomials small enough for $f_\mathbf{0}$ to dominate.

Given a finite set $S \subset \mathbb{R}^d$ and a point $\mathbf{p} \in S$, the original method uses linear programming to determine if $\mathbf{p}$ is a vertex of $\text{conv}(S)$ w.r.t. some vector $\mathbf{n} \in \mathbb{R}^d$. Indeed, from Lemma 1, the problem can be reduced to finding a hyperplane $H : \mathbf{n}^T\mathbf{x} + c = 0$ that strictly separates $\mathbf{p}$ from $S \setminus \{\mathbf{p}\}$ with the normal vector $\mathbf{n}$ pointing from H to $\mathbf{p}$. This is equivalent to solving the following linear problem with $d+1$ real variables $\mathbf{n}$ and c:

$$\varphi(\mathbf{p}, S, \mathbf{n}, c) \doteq \mathbf{n}^T\mathbf{p} + c > 0 \wedge \bigwedge_{\mathbf{q} \in S \setminus \{\mathbf{p}\}} \mathbf{n}^T\mathbf{q} + c < 0. \tag{2}$$

Notice that with the occurrence of a nonzero absolute summand the corresponding point $\mathbf{0}$ is generally a vertex of the Newton polytope with respect to $-\mathbf{1} = (-1, \dots, -1)$. This raises the question whether there are other special points that are certainly vertices of the Newton polytope. In fact, $\mathbf{0}$ is a lexicographic minimum in $\text{frame}(f)$, and it is not hard to see that minima and maxima with respect to lexicographic orderings are generally vertices of the Newton polytope.

We are now going to generalize that observation. A *monotonic total preorder* $\preceq \subseteq \mathbb{Z}^d \times \mathbb{Z}^d$ is defined as follows:

(i) $\mathbf{x} \preceq \mathbf{x}$ (reflexivity)
(ii) $\mathbf{x} \preceq \mathbf{y} \wedge \mathbf{y} \preceq \mathbf{z} \longrightarrow \mathbf{x} \preceq \mathbf{z}$ (transitivity)
(iii) $\mathbf{x} \preceq \mathbf{y} \longrightarrow \mathbf{x} + \mathbf{z} \preceq \mathbf{y} + \mathbf{z}$ (monotonicity)
(iv) $\mathbf{x} \preceq \mathbf{y} \vee \mathbf{y} \preceq \mathbf{x}$ (totality).

The difference to a total order is the missing anti-symmetry. As an example in $\mathbb{Z}^2$ consider $(x_1, x_2) \preceq (y_1, y_2)$ if and only if $x_1 + x_2 \leq y_1 + y_2$. Then $-2 \preceq 2$ and $2 \preceq -2$ but $-2 \neq 2$. Our definition of $\preceq$ on the extended domain $\mathbb{Z}^d$ guarantees a cancellation law $\mathbf{x} + \mathbf{z} \preceq \mathbf{y} + \mathbf{z} \longrightarrow \mathbf{x} \preceq \mathbf{y}$ also on $\mathbb{N}^d$. The following lemma follows by induction using monotonicity and cancellation:

Lemma 4. For $n \in \mathbb{N} \setminus \{0\}$ denote as usual the n-fold addition of $\mathbf{x}$ as $n \odot \mathbf{x}$. Then $\mathbf{x} \preceq \mathbf{y} \longleftrightarrow n \odot \mathbf{x} \preceq n \odot \mathbf{y}$. □

Any monotonic preorder $\preceq$ on $\mathbb{Z}^d$ can be extended to $\mathbb{Q}^d$: Using a suitable principle denominator $n \in \mathbb{N} \setminus \{0\}$ define

$$\left(\frac{x_1}{n}, \dots, \frac{x_d}{n}\right) \preceq \left(\frac{y_1}{n}, \dots, \frac{y_d}{n}\right) \quad \text{if and only if} \quad (x_1, \dots, x_d) \preceq (y_1, \dots, y_d).$$

This is well-defined.

Given $\mathbf{x} \preceq \mathbf{y}$ we have either $\mathbf{y} \not\preceq \mathbf{x}$ or $\mathbf{y} \preceq \mathbf{x}$. In the former case we say that $\mathbf{x}$ and $\mathbf{y}$ are *strictly* preordered and write $\mathbf{x} \prec \mathbf{y}$. In the latter case they are *not* strictly preordered, i.e., $\mathbf{x} \not\prec \mathbf{y}$ although we might have $\mathbf{x} \neq \mathbf{y}$. In particular, reflexivity yields $\mathbf{x} \preceq \mathbf{x}$ and hence certainly $\mathbf{x} \not\prec \mathbf{x}$.

Example 5. Lexicographic orders are monotonic total orders and thus monotonic total preorders. Hence our notion covers our discussion of the absolute summand above. Here are some further examples: For $i \in \{1, \dots, d\}$ we define $\mathbf{x} \preceq_i \mathbf{y}$ if and only if $\pi_i(\mathbf{x}) \leq \pi_i(\mathbf{y})$, where π_i denotes the i-th projection. Similarly, $\mathbf{x} \succeq_i \mathbf{y}$ if and only if $\pi_i(\mathbf{x}) \geq \pi_i(\mathbf{y})$. Next, $\mathbf{x} \preceq_\Sigma \mathbf{y}$ if and only if $\sum_i x_i \leq \sum_i y_i$. Our last example is going to be instrumental with the proof of the next theorem: Fix $\mathbf{n} \in \mathbb{R}^d$, and define for $\mathbf{p}, \mathbf{p}' \in \mathbb{Z}^d$ that $\mathbf{p} \preceq_\mathbf{n} \mathbf{p}'$ if and only if $\mathbf{n}^T \mathbf{p} \leq \mathbf{n}^T \mathbf{p}'$.

Theorem 6. *Let* $f \in \mathbb{Z}[x_1, \dots, x_d]$*, and let* $\mathbf{p} \in \operatorname{frame}(f)$*. Then the following are equivalent:*

(i) $\mathbf{p} \in \operatorname{V}(\operatorname{newton}(f))$
(ii) There exists a monotonic total preorder $\preceq$ *on* $\mathbb{Z}^d$ *such that*

$$\mathbf{p} = \max\nolimits_\preceq(\operatorname{frame}(f)).$$

Proof. Let $\mathbf{p}$ be a vertex of $\operatorname{newton}(f)$ specifically with respect to $\mathbf{n}$. By our definition of a vertex in Sect. 2, $\mathbf{p}$ is the maximum of $\operatorname{frame}(f)$ with respect to $\prec_\mathbf{n}$.

Let, vice versa, $\preceq$ be a monotonic total preorder on $\mathbb{Z}^d$, and let $\mathbf{p} = \max_\preceq(\operatorname{frame}(f))$. Shortly denote $V = \operatorname{V}(\operatorname{newton}(f))$, and assume for a contradiction that $\mathbf{p} \notin V$. Since $\mathbf{p} \in \operatorname{frame}(f) \subseteq \operatorname{newton}(f)$, we have

$$\mathbf{p} = \sum_{\mathbf{s} \in V} t_\mathbf{s} \mathbf{s}, \quad \text{where} \quad t_\mathbf{s} \in [0,1] \quad \text{and} \quad \sum_{\mathbf{s} \in V} t_\mathbf{s} = 1.$$

According to (1) in Sect. 2 we know that $V \subseteq \operatorname{frame}(f) \subseteq \operatorname{newton}(f)$. It follows that $\mathbf{s} \prec \mathbf{p}$ for all $\mathbf{s} \in V$, and using monotony we obtain

$$\mathbf{p} \prec \sum_{\mathbf{s} \in V} t_\mathbf{s} \mathbf{p} = \left(\sum_{\mathbf{s} \in V} t_\mathbf{s} \right) \mathbf{p} = \mathbf{p}.$$

On the other hand, we know that generally $\mathbf{p} \not\prec \mathbf{p}$, a contradiction. □

In Fig. 1a we have $(0,1) = \max_{\succeq_1}(\operatorname{frame}(f))$, $(3,0) = \max_{\succeq_2}(\operatorname{frame}(f))$, and $(4,4) = \max_{\preceq_1}(\operatorname{frame}(f)) = \max_{\preceq_2}(\operatorname{frame}(f))$. This shows that, besides contributing to our theoretical understanding, the theorem can be used to substantiate the efficient treatment of certain special cases in combination with other methods for identifying vertices of the Newton polytope.

Corollary 7. *Let* $f \in \mathbb{Z}[x_1, \dots, x_d]$*, and let* $\mathbf{p} \in \operatorname{frame}(f)$*. If* $p = \max(\operatorname{frame}(f))$ *or* $p = \min(\operatorname{frame}(f))$ *with respect to an admissible term order in the sense of Gröbner Basis theory [7], then* $p \in \operatorname{V}(\operatorname{newton}(f))$*.* □

It is one of our research goals to identify and characterize those polynomials where the subtropical heuristic succeeds in finding positive points. We are now going to give a necessary criterion. Let $f \in \mathbb{Z}[x_1, \ldots, x_d]$, define $\Pi(f) = \{\, \mathbf{r} \in \,]0, \infty[^d \mid f(\mathbf{r}) > 0 \,\}$, and denote by $\overline{\Pi(f)}$ its closure with respect to the natural topology. In Lemma 2, when a tends to ∞, $a^{\mathbf{n}}$ will tend to some $\mathbf{r} \in \{0, \infty\}^d$. If $\mathbf{r} = \mathbf{0}$, then $\mathbf{0} \in \overline{\Pi(f)}$. Otherwise, $\Pi(f)$ is unbounded. Consequently, for the method to succeed, Π must have at least one of those two properties. Figure 2 illustrates four scenarios: the subtropical method succeeds in the first three cases while it fails to find a point in $\Pi(f)$ in the last one. The first sub-figure presents a case where $\Pi(f)$ is unbounded. The second and third sub-figures illustrate cases where the closure of $\Pi(f)$ contains $(0, 0)$. In the fourth sub-figure where neither $\Pi(f)$ is unbounded nor its closure contains $(0, 0)$, the method cannot find any positive value of the variables for f to be positive.

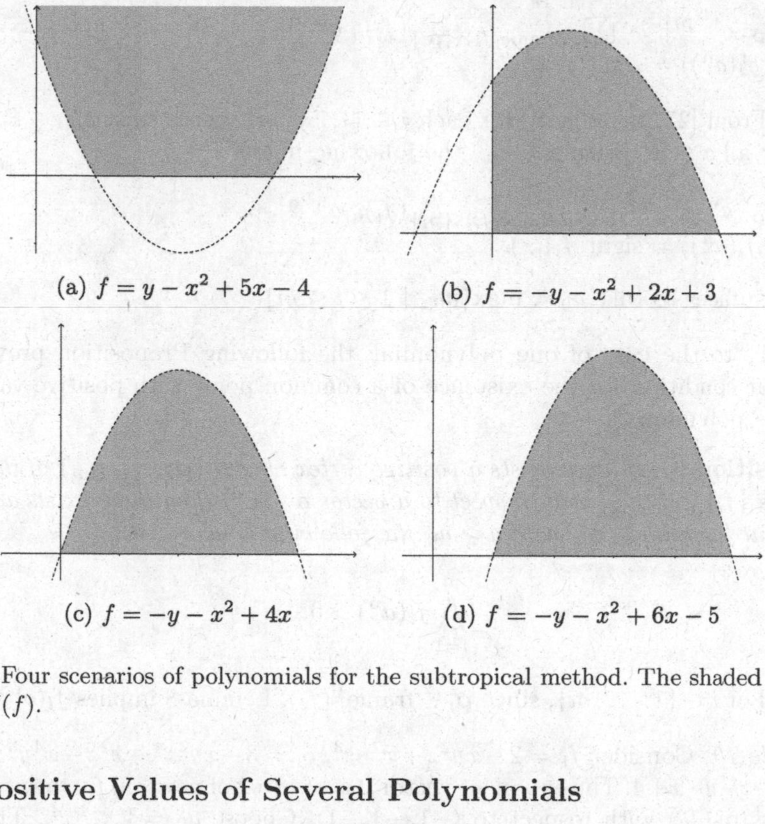

(a) $f = y - x^2 + 5x - 4$ (b) $f = -y - x^2 + 2x + 3$

(c) $f = -y - x^2 + 4x$ (d) $f = -y - x^2 + 6x - 5$

Fig. 2. Four scenarios of polynomials for the subtropical method. The shaded regions show $\Pi(f)$.

4 Positive Values of Several Polynomials

The subtropical method as presented in [27] finds zeros with all positive coordinates of one single multivariate polynomial. This requires to find a corresponding point with a positive value of the polynomial. In the sequel we restrict ourselves to this sub-task. This will allow us generalize from one polynomial to simultaneous positive values of finitely many polynomials.

4.1 A Sufficient Condition

With a single polynomial, the existence of a positive vertex of the Newton polytope guarantees the existence of positive real choices for the variables with a positive value of that polynomial. For several polynomials we introduce a more general notion: A sequence $(\mathbf{p}_1, \ldots, \mathbf{p}_m)$ is a *positive vertex cluster* of $\{f_i\}_{i\in\{1,\ldots,m\}}$ with respect to $\mathbf{n} \in \mathbb{R}^d$ if it is a vertex cluster of $\{\text{frame}(f_i)\}_{i\in\{1,\ldots,m\}}$ with respect to $\mathbf{n}$ and $\mathbf{p}_i \in \text{frame}^+(f_i)$ for all $i \in \{1, \ldots, m\}$. The existence of a positive vertex cluster will guarantee the existence of positive real choices of the variables such that all polynomials $f_1, \ldots, f_m$ are simultaneously positive. The following lemma is a corresponding generalization of Lemma 2:

Lemma 8. If there exists a vertex cluster $(\mathbf{p}_1, \ldots, \mathbf{p}_m)$ of $\{\text{frame}(f_i)\}_{i\in\{1,\ldots,m\}}$ with respect to $\mathbf{n} \in \mathbb{R}^n$, then there exists $a_0 \in \mathbb{R}^+$ such that the following holds for all $a \in \mathbb{R}^+$ with $a \geq a_0$ and all $i \in \{1, \ldots, m\}$:

1. $|(f_i)_{\mathbf{p}_i}\, a^{\mathbf{n}^T\mathbf{p}_i}| > |\sum_{\mathbf{q}\in\text{frame}(f_i)\setminus\{\mathbf{p}_i\}} (f_i)_{\mathbf{q}}\, a^{\mathbf{n}^T\mathbf{q}}|$,
2. $\text{sign}(f_i(a^{\mathbf{n}})) = \text{sign}((f_i)_{\mathbf{p}_i})$.

Proof. From [27, Lemma 4], for each $i \in \{1, \ldots, m\}$, there exist $a_{0,i} \in \mathbb{R}^+$ such that for all $a \in \mathbb{R}^+$ with $a \geq a_{0,i}$ the following holds:

1. $|(f_i)_{\mathbf{p}_i}\, a^{\mathbf{n}^T\mathbf{p}_i}| > |\sum_{\mathbf{q}\in\text{frame}(f_i)\setminus\{\mathbf{p}_i\}} (f_i)_{\mathbf{q}}\, a^{\mathbf{n}^T\mathbf{q}}|$,
2. $\text{sign}(f_i(a^n)) = \text{sign}((f_i)_{\mathbf{p}_i})$.

It now suffices to take $a_0 = \max\{a_{0,i} \mid 1 \leq i \leq m\}$. □

Similarly to the case of one polynomial, the following Proposition provides a sufficient condition for the existence of a common point with positive value for multiple polynomials.

Proposition 9. *If there exists a positive vertex cluster $(\mathbf{p}_1, \ldots, \mathbf{p}_m)$ of the polynomials $\{f_i\}_{i\in\{1,\ldots,m\}}$ with respect to a vector $\mathbf{n} \in \mathbb{R}^d$, then there exists $a_0 \in \mathbb{R}^+$ such that for all $a \in \mathbb{R}^+$ with $a \geq a_0$ the following holds:*

$$\bigwedge_{i=1}^{m} f_i(a^{\mathbf{n}}) > 0.$$

Proof. For $i \in \{1, \ldots, m\}$, since $\mathbf{p}_i \in \text{frame}^+(f_i)$, Lemma 8 implies $f_i(a^{\mathbf{n}}) > 0$.□

Example 10. Consider $f_1 = 2 - xy^2z + x^2yz^3$, $f_2 = 3 - xy^2z^4 - x^2z - x^4y^3z^3$, and $f_3 = 4 - z - y - x + 4$. The exponent vector $\mathbf{0}$ is a vertex of $\text{newton}(f_1)$, $\text{newton}(f_2)$, and $\text{newton}(f_3)$ with respect to $(-1, -1, -1)$. Choose $a_0 = 2 \in \mathbb{R}^+$. Then for all $a \in \mathbb{R}$ with $a \geq a_0$ we have $f_1(a^{-1}, a^{-1}, a^{-1}) > 0 \wedge f_2(a^{-1}, a^{-1}, a^{-1}) > 0 \wedge f_3(a^{-1}, a^{-1}, a^{-1}) > 0$. □

4.2 Existence of Positive Vertex Clusters

Given polynomials $f_1, \ldots, f_m$, Proposition 9 provides a sufficient condition, i.e. the existence of a positive vertex cluster of $\{f_i\}_{i\in\{1,\ldots,m\}}$, for the satisfiability of $\bigwedge_{i=1}^m f_i > 0$. A straightforward method to decide the existence of such a cluster is to verify whether each $(\mathbf{p}_1, \ldots, \mathbf{p}_m) \in \text{frame}^+(f_1) \times \cdots \times \text{frame}^+(f_m)$ is a positive vertex cluster by checking the satisfiability of the formula

$$\bigwedge_{i\in\{1,\ldots,m\}} \varphi(\mathbf{p}_i, \text{frame}(f_i), \mathbf{n}, c_i),$$

where φ is defined as in (2) on p.5. This is a linear problem with $d+m$ variables $\mathbf{n}$, $c_1, \ldots, c_m$. Since $\text{frame}(f_1), \ldots, \text{frame}(f_m)$ are finite, checking all m-tuples $(\mathbf{p}_1, \ldots, \mathbf{p}_m)$ will terminate, provided we rely on a complete algorithm for linear programming, such as the Simplex algorithm [10], the ellipsoid method [22], or the interior point method [21]. This provides a decision procedure for the existence of a positive vertex cluster of $\{f_i\}_{i\in\{1,\ldots,m\}}$. However, this requires checking all candidates in $\text{frame}^+(f_1) \times \cdots \times \text{frame}^+(f_m)$.

We propose to use instead state-of-the-art SMT solving techniques over linear real arithmetic to examine whether or not $\{f_i\}_{i\in\{1,\ldots,m\}}$ has a positive vertex cluster with respect to some $\mathbf{n} \in \mathbb{R}^d$. In the positive case, a solution for $\bigwedge_{i=1}^m f_i > 0$ can be constructed as $a^{\mathbf{n}}$ with a sufficiently large $a \in \mathbb{R}^+$.

To start with, we provide a characterization for the positive frame of a single polynomial to contain a vertex of the Newton polytope.

Lemma 11. Let $f \in \mathbb{Z}[\mathbf{x}]$. The following are equivalent:

(i) There exists a vertex $\mathbf{p} \in \text{frame}^+(f)$ of $\text{newton}(f) = \text{conv}(\text{frame}(f))$ with respect to $\mathbf{n} \in \mathbb{R}^d$.
(ii) There exists $\mathbf{p}' \in \text{frame}^+(f)$ such that $\mathbf{p}'$ is also a vertex of $\text{conv}(\text{frame}^-(f) \cup \{\mathbf{p}'\})$ with respect to $\mathbf{n}' \in \mathbb{R}^d$.

Proof. Assume (i). Take $\mathbf{p}' = \mathbf{p}$ and $\mathbf{n}' = \mathbf{n}$. Since $\mathbf{p}$ is a vertex of $\text{newton}(f)$ with respect to $\mathbf{n}$, $\mathbf{n}^T\mathbf{p} > \mathbf{n}^T\mathbf{p}_1$ for all $\mathbf{p}_1 \in \text{frame}(f) \setminus \{\mathbf{p}\}$. This implies that $\mathbf{n}^T\mathbf{p} > \mathbf{n}^T\mathbf{p}_1$ for all $\mathbf{p}_1 \in \text{frame}^-(f) \setminus \{\mathbf{p}\} = (\text{frame}^-(f) \cup \{\mathbf{p}\}) \setminus \{\mathbf{p}\}$. In other words, $\mathbf{p}$ is a vertex of $\text{conv}(\text{frame}^-(f) \cup \{\mathbf{p}\})$ with respect to $\mathbf{n}$.

Assume (ii). Suppose $V = \text{V}(\text{newton}(f)) \subseteq \text{frame}^-(f)$. Then, $\mathbf{p}' = \sum_{\mathbf{s}\in V} t_{\mathbf{s}}\mathbf{s}$ where $t_{\mathbf{s}} \in [0,1]$, $\sum_{\mathbf{s}\in V} t_{\mathbf{s}} = 1$. It follows that

$$\mathbf{n}'^T\mathbf{p}' = \sum_{\mathbf{s}\in V} t_{\mathbf{s}}\mathbf{n}'^T\mathbf{s} < \sum_{\mathbf{s}\in V} t_{\mathbf{s}}\mathbf{n}'^T\mathbf{p}' = \mathbf{n}'^T\mathbf{p}'\sum_{\mathbf{s}\in V} t_{\mathbf{s}} = \mathbf{n}'^T\mathbf{p}',$$

which is a contradiction. As a result, there must be some $\mathbf{p} \in \text{frame}^+(f)$ which is a vertex of $\text{newton}(f)$ with respect to some $\mathbf{n} \in \mathbb{R}^d$. □

Thus some $\mathbf{p} \in \text{frame}^+(f)$ is a vertex of the Newton polytope of a polynomial f if and only if the following formula is satisfiable:

$$\begin{aligned}
\psi(f, \mathbf{n}', c) &\doteq \bigvee_{\mathbf{p} \in \text{frame}^+(f)} \varphi\left(\mathbf{p}, \text{frame}^-(f) \cup \{\mathbf{p}\}, \mathbf{n}', c\right) \\
&\equiv \bigvee_{\mathbf{p} \in \text{frame}^+(f)} \left[\mathbf{n'}^T \mathbf{p} + c > 0 \wedge \bigwedge_{\mathbf{q} \in \text{frame}^-(f)} \mathbf{n'}^T \mathbf{q} + c < 0 \right] \\
&\equiv \left[\bigvee_{\mathbf{p} \in \text{frame}^+(f)} \mathbf{n'}^T \mathbf{p} + c > 0 \right] \wedge \left[\bigwedge_{\mathbf{p} \in \text{frame}^-(f)} \mathbf{n'}^T \mathbf{p} + c < 0 \right].
\end{aligned}$$

For the case of several polynomials, the following theorem is a direct consequence of Lemma 11.

Theorem 12. *Polynomials* $\{f_i\}_{i \in \{1,\ldots,m\}}$ *have a positive vertex cluster with respect to* $\mathbf{n} \in \mathbb{R}^d$ *if and only if* $\bigwedge_{i=1}^m \psi(f_i, \mathbf{n}, c_i)$ *is satisfiable.* □

The formula $\bigwedge_{i=1}^m \psi(f_i, \mathbf{n}, c_i)$ can be checked for satisfiability using combinations of linear programming techniques and DPLL(T) procedures [11,16], i.e., satisfiability modulo linear arithmetic on reals. Any SMT solver supporting the QF_LRA logic is suitable. In the satisfiable case $\{f_i\}_{i \in \{1,\ldots,m\}}$ has a positive vertex cluster and we can construct a solution for $\bigwedge_{i=1}^m f_i > 0$ as discussed earlier.

Example 13. Consider $f_1 = -12 + 2x^{12}y^{25}z^{49} - 31x^{13}y^{22}z^{110} - 11x^{1000}y^{500}z^{89}$ and $f_2 = -23 + 5xy^{22}z^{110} - 21x^{15}y^{20}z^{1000} + 2x^{100}y^2z^{49}$. With $\mathbf{n} = (n_1, n_2, n_3)$ this yields

$$\begin{aligned}
\psi(f_1, \mathbf{n}, c_1) &\doteq 12n_1 + 25n_2 + 49n_3 + c_1 > 0 \wedge 13n_1 + 22n_2 + 110n_3 + c_1 < 0 \\
&\quad \wedge 1000n_1 + 500n_2 + 89n_3 + c_1 < 0 \wedge c_1 < 0, \\
\psi(f_2, \mathbf{n}, c_2) &\doteq (n_1 + 22n_2 + 110n_3 + c_2 > 0 \vee 100n_1 + 2n_2 + 49n_3 + c_2 > 0) \\
&\quad \wedge 15n_1 + 20n_2 + 1000n_3 + c_2 < 0 \wedge c_2 < 0.
\end{aligned}$$

The conjunction $\psi(f_1, \mathbf{n}, c_1) \wedge \psi(f_2, \mathbf{n}, c_2)$ is satisfiable. The SMT solver CVC4 computes $\mathbf{n} = (-\frac{238834}{120461}, \frac{2672460}{1325071}, -\frac{368561}{1325071})$ and $c_1 = c_2 = -1$ as a model. Theorem 12 and Proposition 9 guarantee that there exists a large enough $a \in \mathbb{R}^+$ such that $f_1(a^\mathbf{n}) > 0 \wedge f_2(a^\mathbf{n}) > 0$. Indeed, $a = 2$ already yields $f_1(a^\mathbf{n}) \approx 16371.99$ and $f_2(a^\mathbf{n}) \approx 17707.27$. □

5 More General Solutions

So far all variables were assumed to be strictly positive, i.e., only solutions $\mathbf{x} \in \,]0, \infty[^d$ were considered. This section proposes a method for searching over $\mathbb{R}^d$ by encoding sign conditions along with the condition in Theorem 12 as a quantifier-free formula over linear real arithmetic.

Let $V = \{x_1, \dots, x_d\}$ be the set of variables. We define a *sign variant* of V as a function $\tau : V \mapsto V \cup \{-x \mid x \in V\}$ such that for each $x \in V$, $\tau(x) \in \{x, -x\}$. We write $\tau(f)$ to denote the substitution $f(\tau(x_1), \dots, \tau(x_d))$ of τ into a polynomial f. Furthermore, $\tau(a)$ denotes $(\frac{\tau(x_1)}{x_1}a, \dots, \frac{\tau(x_d)}{x_d}a)$ for $a \in \mathbb{R}$. A sequence $(\mathbf{p}_1, \dots, \mathbf{p}_m)$ is a *variant positive vertex cluster* of $\{f_i\}_{i \in \{1,\dots,m\}}$ with respect to a vector $\mathbf{n} \in \mathbb{R}^d$ and a sign variant τ if $(\mathbf{p}_1, \dots, \mathbf{p}_m)$ is a positive vertex cluster of $\{\tau(f_i)\}_{i \in \{1,\dots,m\}}$. Note that the substitution of τ into a polynomial f does not change the exponent vectors in f in terms of their exponents values, but only possibly changes signs of monomials. Given $\mathbf{p} = (p_1, \dots, p_d) \in \mathbb{N}^d$ and a sign variant τ, we define a formula $\vartheta(\mathbf{p}, \tau)$ such that it is TRUE if and only if the sign of the monomial associated with $\mathbf{p}$ is changed after applying the substitution defined by τ:

$$\vartheta(\mathbf{p}, \tau) \doteq \bigoplus_{i=1}^{d} \big(\tau(x_i) = -x_i \wedge (p_i \bmod 2 = 1)\big).$$

Note that this xor expression becomes TRUE if and only if an odd number of its operands are TRUE. Furthermore, a variable can change the sign of a monomial only when its exponent in that monomial is odd. As a result, if $\vartheta(\mathbf{p}, \tau)$ is TRUE, then applying the substitution defined by τ will change the sign of the monomial associated with $\mathbf{p}$. In conclusion, some $\mathbf{p} \in \operatorname{frame}(f)$ is in the positive frame of $\tau(f)$ if and only if one of the following mutually exclusive conditions holds:

(i) $\mathbf{p} \in \operatorname{frame}^+(f)$ and $\vartheta(\mathbf{p}, \tau) =$ FALSE
(ii) $\mathbf{p} \in \operatorname{frame}^-(f)$ and $\vartheta(\mathbf{p}, \tau) =$ TRUE.

In other words, $\mathbf{p}$ is in the positive frame of $\tau(f)$ if and only if the formula $\Theta(\mathbf{p}, f, \tau) \doteq (f_\mathbf{p} > 0 \wedge \neg\vartheta(\mathbf{p}, \tau)) \vee (f_\mathbf{p} < 0 \wedge \vartheta(\mathbf{p}, \tau))$ holds. Then, the positive and negative frames of $\tau(f)$ parameterized by τ are defined as

$$\operatorname{frame}^+(\tau(f)) = \{\, \mathbf{p} \in \operatorname{frame}(f) \mid \Theta(\mathbf{p}, f, \tau) \,\},$$
$$\operatorname{frame}^-(\tau(f)) = \{\, \mathbf{p} \in \operatorname{frame}(f) \mid \neg\Theta(\mathbf{p}, f, \tau) \,\},$$

respectively. The next lemma provides a sufficient condition for the existence of a solution in $\mathbb{R}^d$ of $\bigwedge_{i=1}^m f_i > 0$.

Lemma 14. If there exists a variant positive vertex cluster of $\{f_i\}_{i \in \{1,\dots,m\}}$ with respect to $\mathbf{n} \in \mathbb{R}^d$ and a sign variant τ, then there exists $a_0 \in \mathbb{R}^+$ such that for all $a \in \mathbb{R}^+$ with $a \geq a_0$ the following holds:

$$\bigwedge_{i=1}^{m} f_i(\tau(a)^\mathbf{n}) > 0.$$

Proof. Since $\{\tau(f_i)\}_{i \in \{1,\dots,m\}}$ has a positive vertex cluster with respect to $\mathbf{n}$, Proposition 9 guarantees that there exists $a_0 \in \mathbb{R}$ such that for all $a \in \mathbb{R}$ with $a \geq a_0$, we have $\bigwedge_{i=1}^m \tau(f_i)(a^\mathbf{n}) > 0$, or $\bigwedge_{i=1}^m f_i(\tau(a)^\mathbf{n}) > 0$. □

A variant positive vertex cluster exists if and only if there exist $\mathbf{n} \in \mathbb{R}^d$, $c_1, \ldots, c_m \in \mathbb{R}$, and a sign variant τ such that the following formula becomes TRUE:

$$\Psi(f_1, \ldots, f_m, \mathbf{n}, c_1, \ldots, c_m, \tau) \doteq \bigwedge_{i=1}^{m} \psi(\tau(f_i), \mathbf{n}, c_i),$$

where for $i \in \{1, \ldots, m\}$:

$$\begin{aligned}\psi(\tau(f_i), \mathbf{n}, c_i) &\equiv \left[\bigvee_{\mathbf{p} \in \mathrm{frame}^+(\tau(f_i))} \mathbf{n}^T\mathbf{p} + c_i > 0\right] \wedge \left[\bigwedge_{\mathbf{p} \in \mathrm{frame}^-(\tau(f_i))} \mathbf{n}^T\mathbf{p} + c_i < 0\right] \\ &\equiv \left[\bigvee_{\mathbf{p} \in \mathrm{frame}(f_i)} \Theta(\mathbf{p}, f_i, \tau) \wedge \mathbf{n}^T\mathbf{p} + c_i > 0\right] \\ &\quad \wedge \left[\bigwedge_{\mathbf{p} \in \mathrm{frame}(f_i)} \Theta(\mathbf{p}, f_i, \tau) \vee \mathbf{n}^T\mathbf{p} + c_i < 0\right].\end{aligned}$$

The sign variant τ can be encoded as d Boolean variables $b_1, \ldots, b_d$ such that b_i is TRUE if and only if $\tau(x_i) = -x_i$ for all $i \in \{1, \ldots, d\}$. Then, the formula $\Psi(f_1, \ldots, f_m, \mathbf{n}, c_1, \ldots, c_m, \tau)$ can be checked for satisfiability using an SMT solver for quantifier-free logic with linear real arithmetic.

6 Application to SMT Benchmarks

A library STROPSAT implementing Subtropical Satisfiability, is available on our web page[1]. It is integrated into veriT [6] as an incomplete theory solver for non-linear arithmetic benchmarks. We experimented on the QF_NRA category of the SMT-LIB on all benchmarks consisting of only inequalities, that is 4917 formulas out of 11601 in the whole category. The experiments thus focus on those 4917 benchmarks, comprising 3265 SAT-annotated ones, 106 UNKNOWNs, and 1546 UNSAT benchmarks. We used the SMT solver CVC4 to handle the generated linear real arithmetic formulas $\Psi(f_1, \ldots, f_m, \mathbf{n}, c_1, \ldots, c_m, \tau)$, and we ran veriT (with STROPSAT as the theory solver) against the clear winner of the SMT-COMP 2016 on the QF_NRA category, i.e., Z3 (implementing nlsat [20]), on a CX250 Cluster with Intel Xeon E5-2680v2 2.80 GHz CPUs. Each pair of benchmark and solver was run on one CPU with a timeout of 2500 s and 20 GB memory. The experimental data and the library are also available on Zenodo[2].

Since our method focuses on showing satisfiability, only brief statistics on UNSAT benchmarks are provided. Among the 1546 UNSAT benchmarks, 200 benchmarks are found unsatisfiable already by the linear arithmetic theory reasoning in veriT. For each of the remaining ones, the method quickly returns UNKNOWN within 0.002 to 0.096 s, with a total cumulative time of 18.45 s (0.014 s

[1] http://www.jaist.ac.jp/~s1520002/STROPSAT/.
[2] http://doi.org/10.5281/zenodo.817615.

on average). This clearly shows that the method can be applied with a very small overhead, upfront of another, complete or less incomplete procedure to check for unsatisfiability.

Table 1 provides the experimental results on benchmarks with SAT or UNKNOWN status, and the cumulative times. The meti-tarski family consists of small benchmarks (most of them contain 3 to 4 variables and 1 to 23 polynomials with degrees between 1 and 4). Those are proof obligations extracted from the MetiTarski project [1], where the polynomials represent approximations of elementary real functions; all of them have defined statuses. The zankl family consists of large benchmarks (large numbers of variables and polynomials but small degrees) stemming from termination proofs for term-rewriting systems [14].

Table 1. Comparison between STROPSAT and Z3 (times in seconds)

Family	STROPSAT				Z3			
	SAT	Time	UNKOWN	Time	SAT	Time	UNSAT	Time
Meti-tarski (SAT - 3220)	2359	32.37	861	10.22	**3220**	88.55	0	0
Zankl (SAT - 45)	29	3.77	16	0.59	**42**	2974.35	0	0
Zankl (UNKNOWN - 106)	**15**	2859.44	76	6291.33	14	1713.16	23	1.06

Although Z3 clearly outperforms STROPSAT in the number of solved benchmarks, the results also clearly show that our method is a useful complementing heuristic with little drawback, to be used either upfront or in portfolio with other approaches. As already said, it returns UNKNOWN quickly on UNSAT benchmarks. In particular, on all benchmarks solved by Z3 only, STROPSAT returns UNKNOWN quickly (see Fig. 4).

When both solvers can solve the same benchmark, the running time of STROPSAT is comparable with Z3 (Fig. 3). There are 11 large benchmarks (9 of them have the UNKNOWN status) that are solved by STROPSAT but time out with Z3. STROPSAT times out for only 15 problems, on which Z3 times out as well. STROPSAT provides a model for 15 UNKNOWN benchmarks, whereas Z3 times out on 9 of them. The virtual best solver (i.e. running Z3 and STROPSAT in parallel and using the quickest answer) decreases the execution time for the meti-tarski problems to 54.43 s, solves all satisfiable zankl problems in 1120 s, and 24 of the unknown ones in 4502 s.

Since the exponents of the polynomials become coefficients in the linear formulas, high degrees do not hurt our method significantly. As the SMT-LIB does not currently contain any inequality benchmarks with high degrees, our experimental results above do not demonstrate this claim. However, formulas like in Example 13 are totally within reach of our method (STROPSAT returned SAT within a second) while Z3 runs out of memory (20 GB) after 30 s for the constraint $f_1 > 0 \wedge f_2 > 0$.

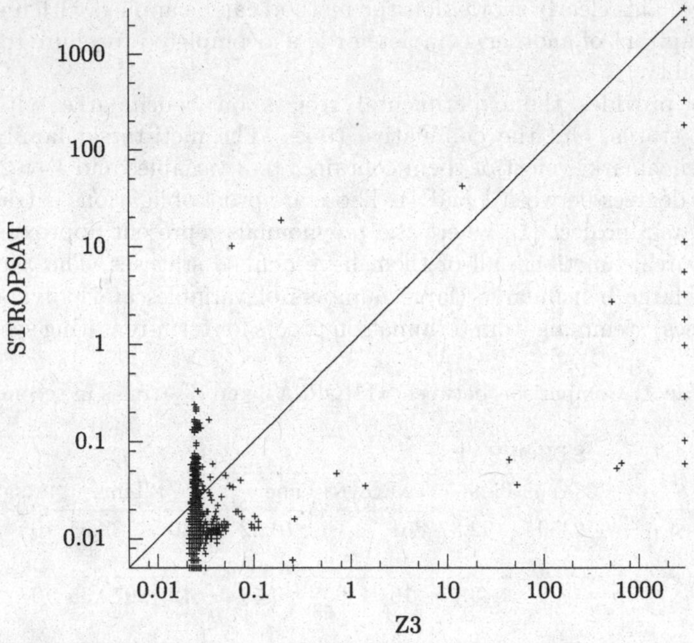

Fig. 3. STROPSAT returns SAT or timeout (2418 benchmarks, times in seconds)

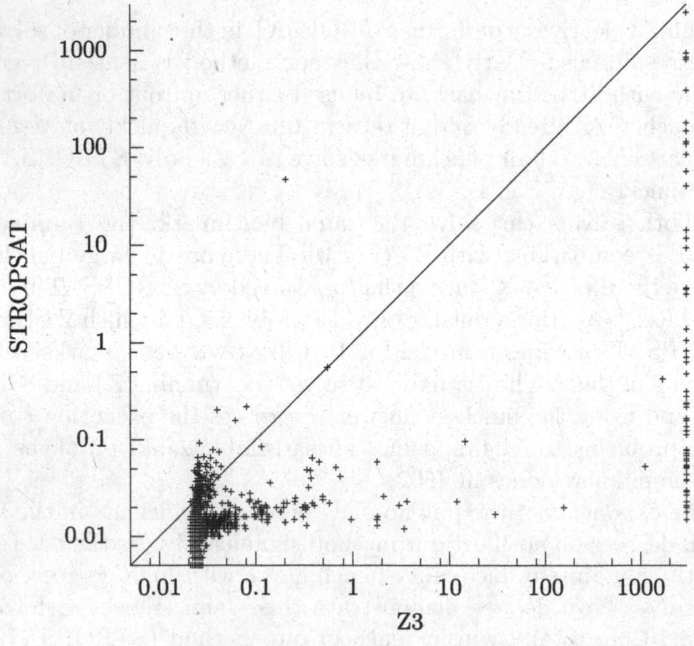

Fig. 4. STROPSAT returns UNKNOWN (2299 benchmarks, times in seconds)

7 Conclusion

We presented some extensions of a heuristic method to find simultaneous positive values of nonlinear multivariate polynomials. Our techniques turn out useful to handle SMT problems. In practice, our method is fast, either to succeed or to fail, and it succeeds where state-of-the-art solvers do not. Therefore it establishes a valuable heuristic to apply either before or in parallel with other more complete methods to deal with non-linear constraints. Since the heuristic translates a conjunction of non-linear constraints one to one into a conjunction of linear constraints, it can easily be made incremental by using an incremental linear solver.

To improve the completeness of the method, it could be helpful to not only consider vertices of Newton polytopes, but also faces. Then, the value of the coefficients and not only their sign would matter. Consider $\{\mathbf{p}_1, \mathbf{p}_2, \mathbf{p}_3\} = \text{face}(\mathbf{n}, \text{newton}(f))$, then we have $\mathbf{n}^T\mathbf{p}_1 = \mathbf{n}^T\mathbf{p}_2 = \mathbf{n}^T\mathbf{p}_3$. It is easy to see that $f_{\mathbf{p}_1}\mathbf{x}^{\mathbf{p}_1} + f_{\mathbf{p}_2}\mathbf{x}^{\mathbf{p}_2} + f_{\mathbf{p}_3}\mathbf{x}^{\mathbf{p}_3}$ will dominate the other monomials in the direction of $\mathbf{n}$. In other words, there exists $a_0 \in \mathbb{R}$ such that for all $a \in \mathbb{R}$ with $a \geq a_0$, $\text{sign}(f(a^{\mathbf{n}})) = \text{sign}(f_{\mathbf{p}_1} + f_{\mathbf{p}_2} + f_{\mathbf{p}_3})$. We leave for future work the encoding of the condition for the existence of such a face into linear formulas.

In the last paragraph of Sect. 3, we showed that, for the subtropical method to succeed, the set of values for which the considered polynomial is positive should either be unbounded, or should contain points arbitrarily near $\mathbf{0}$. We believe there is a stronger, sufficient condition, that would bring another insight to the subtropical method.

We leave for further work two interesting questions suggested by a reviewer, both concerning the case when the method is not able to assert the satisfiability of a set of literals. First, the technique could indeed be used to select, using the convex hull of the frame, some constraints most likely to be part of an unsatisfiable set; this could be used to simplify the work of the decision procedure to check unsatisfiability afterwards. Second, a careful analysis of the frame can provide information to remove some constraints in order to have a provable satisfiable set of constraints; this could be of some use for in a context of max-SMT.

Finally, on a more practical side, we would like to investigate the use of the techniques presented here for the testing phase of the raSAT loop [28], an extension the interval constraint propagation with testing and the Intermediate Value Theorem. We believe that this could lead to significant improvements in the solver, where testing is currently random.

Acknowledgments. We are grateful to the anonymous reviewers for their comments. This research has been partially supported by the ANR/DFG project SMArT (ANR-13-IS02-0001 & STU 483/2-1) and by the European Union project SC[2] (grant agreement No. 712689). The work has also received funding from the European Research Council under the European Union's Horizon 2020 research and innovation program (grant agreement No. 713999, Matryoshka). The last author would like to acknowledge the JAIST Off-Campus Research Grant for fully supporting him during his stay at LORIA, Nancy. The work has also been partially supported by the JSPS

KAKENHI Grant-in-Aid for Scientific Research(B) (15H02684) and the JSPS Core-to-Core Program (A. Advanced Research Networks).

References

1. Akbarpour, B., Paulson, L.C.: MetiTarski: an automatic theorem prover for real-valued special functions. J. Autom. Reason. **44**(3), 175–205 (2010)
2. Barrett, C., Kroening, D., Melham, T.: Problem solving for the 21st century: efficient solvers for satisfiability modulo theories. Technical Report 3, London Mathematical Society and Smith Institute for Industrial Mathematics and System Engineering Knowledge Transfer Report(2014)
3. Barrett, C., Sebastiani, R., Seshia, S.A., Tinelli, C.: Satisfiability modulo theories. In: Biere, A., Heule, M., Van Maaren, H., Walsh, T. (eds.) Handbook of Satisfiability. Frontiers in Artificial Intelligence and Applications, vol. 185, pp. 825–885. IOS Press, Amsterdam (2009)
4. Benhamou, F., Granvilliers, L.: Continuous and interval constraints. In: Rossi, F., van Beek, P., Walsh, T. (eds.) Handbook of Constraint Programming, pp. 571–604. Elsevier, New York (2006)
5. Bofill, M., Nieuwenhuis, R., Oliveras, A., Rodríguez-Carbonell, E., Rubio, A.: The barcelogic SMT solver. In: Gupta, A., Malik, S. (eds.) CAV 2008. LNCS, vol. 5123, pp. 294–298. Springer, Heidelberg (2008). doi:10.1007/978-3-540-70545-1_27
6. Bouton, T., Caminha B. de Oliveira, D., Déharbe, D., Fontaine, P.: veriT: an open, trustable and efficient SMT-solver. In: Schmidt, R.A. (ed.) CADE 2009. LNCS (LNAI), vol. 5663, pp. 151–156. Springer, Heidelberg (2009). doi:10.1007/978-3-642-02959-2_12
7. Buchberger, B.: Ein Algorithmus zum Auffinden der Basiselemente des Restklassenringes nach einem nulldimensionalen Polynomideal. Doctoral dissertation, University of Innsbruck, Austria (1965)
8. Cimatti, A., Griggio, A., Irfan, A., Roveri, M., Sebastiani, R.: Invariant checking of NRA transition systems via incremental reduction to LRA with EUF. In: Legay, A., Margaria, T. (eds.) TACAS 2017. LNCS, vol. 10205, pp. 58–75. Springer, Heidelberg (2017). doi:10.1007/978-3-662-54577-5_4
9. Corzilius, F., Loup, U., Junges, S., Ábrahám, E.: SMT-RAT: an SMT-compliant nonlinear real arithmetic toolbox. In: Cimatti, A., Sebastiani, R. (eds.) SAT 2012. LNCS, vol. 7317, pp. 442–448. Springer, Heidelberg (2012). doi:10.1007/978-3-642-31612-8_35
10. Dantzig, G.B.: Linear Programming and Extensions. Prentice University Press, Princeton (1963)
11. Dutertre, B., de Moura, L.: A fast linear-arithmetic solver for DPLL(T). In: Ball, T., Jones, R.B. (eds.) CAV 2006. LNCS, vol. 4144, pp. 81–94. Springer, Heidelberg (2006). doi:10.1007/11817963_11
12. Errami, H., Eiswirth, M., Grigoriev, D., Seiler, W.M., Sturm, T., Weber, A.: Detection of Hopf bifurcations in chemical reaction networks using convex coordinates. J. Comput. Phys. **291**, 279–302 (2015)
13. Fränzle, M., Herde, C., Teige, T., Ratschan, S., Schubert, T.: Efficient solving of large non-linear arithmetic constraint systems with complex Boolean structure. J. Satisf. Boolean Model. Comput. **1**, 209–236 (2007)

14. Fuhs, C., Giesl, J., Middeldorp, A., Schneider-Kamp, P., Thiemann, R., Zankl, H.: SAT solving for termination analysis with polynomial interpretations. In: Marques-Silva, J., Sakallah, K.A. (eds.) SAT 2007. LNCS, vol. 4501, pp. 340–354. Springer, Heidelberg (2007). doi:10.1007/978-3-540-72788-0_33
15. Ganai, M., Ivancic, F.: Efficient decision procedure for non-linear arithmetic constraints using CORDIC. In: Formal Methods in Computer-Aided Design, FMCAD 2009, pp. 61–68 (2009)
16. Ganzinger, H., Hagen, G., Nieuwenhuis, R., Oliveras, A., Tinelli, C.: DPLL(T): fast decision procedures. In: Alur, R., Peled, D.A. (eds.) CAV 2004. LNCS, vol. 3114, pp. 175–188. Springer, Heidelberg (2004). doi:10.1007/978-3-540-27813-9_14
17. Gao, S., Kong, S., Clarke, E.M.: Satisfiability modulo ODEs. In: Formal Methods in Computer-Aided Design (FMCAD) 2013, pp. 105–112 (2013)
18. Gao, S., Kong, S., Clarke, E.M.: dReal: an SMT solver for nonlinear theories over the reals. In: Bonacina, M.P. (ed.) CADE 2013. LNCS (LNAI), vol. 7898, pp. 208–214. Springer, Heidelberg (2013). doi:10.1007/978-3-642-38574-2_14
19. Granvilliers, L., Benhamou, F.: RealPaver: an interval solver using constraint satisfaction techniques. ACM Trans. Math. Softw. **32**, 138–156 (2006)
20. Jovanović, D., de Moura, L.: Solving non-linear arithmetic. In: Gramlich, B., Miller, D., Sattler, U. (eds.) IJCAR 2012. LNCS, vol. 7364, pp. 339–354. Springer, Heidelberg (2012). doi:10.1007/978-3-642-31365-3_27
21. Karmarkar, N.: A new polynomial-time algorithm for linear programming. Combinatorica **4**(4), 373–395 (1984)
22. Khachiyan, L.: Polynomial algorithms in linear programming. USSR Comput. Math. Math. Phys. **20**(1), 53–72 (1980)
23. Passmore, G.O.: Combined decision procedures for nonlinear arithmetics, real and complex. Dissertation, School of Informatics, University of Edinburgh (2011)
24. Passmore, G.O., Jackson, P.B.: Combined decision techniques for the existential theory of the reals. In: Carette, J., Dixon, L., Coen, C.S., Watt, S.M. (eds.) CICM 2009. LNCS, vol. 5625, pp. 122–137. Springer, Heidelberg (2009). doi:10.1007/978-3-642-02614-0_14
25. Ratschan, S.: Efficient solving of quantified inequality constraints over the real numbers. ACM Trans. Comput. Log. **7**, 723–748 (2006)
26. Schrijver, A.: Theory of Linear and Integer Programming. Wiley, New York (1986)
27. Sturm, T.: Subtropical real root finding. In: Proceedings of the ISSAC 2015, pp. 347–354. ACM (2015)
28. Tung, V.X., Van Khanh, T., Ogawa, M.: raSAT: an SMT solver for polynomial constraints. In: Olivetti, N., Tiwari, A. (eds.) IJCAR 2016. LNCS, vol. 9706, pp. 228–237. Springer, Cham (2016). doi:10.1007/978-3-319-40229-1_16
29. Zankl, H., Middeldorp, A.: Satisfiability of non-linear (Ir)rational arithmetic. In: Clarke, E.M., Voronkov, A. (eds.) LPAR 2010. LNCS, vol. 6355, pp. 481–500. Springer, Heidelberg (2010). doi:10.1007/978-3-642-17511-4_27

Decision Procedures, Decidability and Verification

On Solving Nominal Fixpoint Equations

Mauricio Ayala-Rincón[1(✉)], Washington de Carvalho-Segundo[1], Maribel Fernández[2], and Daniele Nantes-Sobrinho[1]

[1] Depts. de Matemática e Ciência da Computação, Universidade de Brasília, Brasília, Brazil
ayala@unb.br

[2] Department of Informatics, King's College London, London, UK

Abstract. In nominal syntax, variable binding is specified using atom-abstraction constructors, and alpha-equivalence is formalised using freshness constraints and atom swappings, which implement variable renamings. Composition of swappings gives rise to atom permutations. Algorithms to check equivalence, match and unify nominal terms have been extended to deal with terms where some operators are associative and/or commutative. In the case of nominal C-unification, problems are transformed into finite and complete families of fixpoint equations of the form $\pi.X \approx_? X$, where π is a permutation. To generate nominal C-unifiers, a technique to obtain a sound and complete set of solutions for these equations is needed. In this work we show how complete sets of solutions for nominal fixpoint problems are built and discuss efficient techniques to generate solutions based on algebraic properties of permutations.

1 Introduction

Nominal syntax is an extension of first order syntax, where terms are built using function symbols, abstractions, and two kinds of variables: atoms, which can be abstracted, and unknowns (or simply variables), which behave like first-order variables, except for the fact that they can have "suspended atom permutations", which act when the variable is instantiated by a term. Atom abstractions induce an α-equivalence relation on nominal terms, which is axiomatised using a freshness relation between atoms and terms. Nominal unification [15] is unification of nominal terms, and takes into account the α-equivalence relation. Extensions of nominal unification include equivariant unification [1,8] and nominal narrowing [5], which are useful tools in equational reasoning and confluence analysis of nominal rewriting systems [2,9].

In many application domains, function symbols have equational properties, such as associativity and commutativity, which must be taken into account during the unification process. In previous work [3], we studied α-AC-equivalence of nominal terms, and nominal C-unification [4], that is, nominal unification in

M. Ayala-Rincón—Partially supported by CNPq 307009/2013-0 and FAPDF 0193001369/2016 grants.

C. Dixon and M. Finger (Eds.): FroCoS 2017, LNCS 10483, pp. 209–226, 2017.
DOI: 10.1007/978-3-319-66167-4_12

languages with commutative operators. It is well-known that C-unification is an NP-complete problem (see Chap. 10 in [7]).

To solve nominal C-unification problems, we provided in [4] a set of simplification rules that generates, for each solvable C-unification problem, a finite set of *fixpoint problems* that are finite sets of *fixpoint equations* together with a freshness context and a substitution. Fixpoint equations have the form $\pi.X \approx_? X$, where X is a variable and π is a permutation.

Fixpoint problems are also generated in standard nominal unification algorithms, but the presence of commutative operators in the signature complicates their treatment. In nominal unification algorithms, fixpoint equations are solved simply by requiring the support of the permutation to be fresh for the variable, but that is not the only way to solve them if there are commutative operators. In [4], the correctness and completeness of the rule-based algorithm to transform a nominal C-unification problem into a finite set of fixpoint problems was formalised in Coq, and a sound method to generate solutions for fixpoint problems was given, showing that infinite independent solutions are possible for a single fixpoint equation. Thus, nominal C-unification is infinitary.

Sound and complete procedures to solve fixpoint problems modulo commutativity are needed not only within nominal-C-unification algorithms, but also in other application areas where formalisations of syntax with binders involve commutativity axioms, such as the π-calculus. For example, fixpoint problems modulo commutativity are generated when solving unification problems in extensions of the λ-calculus with recursive definitions [10].

Contribution. The main result is a sound and complete procedure to solve fixpoint problems. More specifically:

- We prove the completeness of the procedure to generate solutions for fixpoint problems described in [4]. The analysis is based on the feasibility of combinations of the atoms in the domain of permutations used in the fixpoint equations in a fixpoint problem. Solutions for these problems are built considering the combinatorial properties of atom permutations and by combining atoms using the basic elements of the nominal syntax, that is, pairs, abstractions and variables, as well as the function symbols in the signature. The variables included in these feasible combinations are new, and the atoms in the support of the permutations should be fresh for these variables. The greedy generation of complete sets of solutions for a fixpoint equation is based on the construction of the so called *extended pseudo-cycles* from permutation cycles in the algebraic representation of permutations as products of *permutation cycles.* Only permutation cycles of length (period) a power of two are considered since permutation cycles of other lengths do not generate feasible (commutative) combinations.
- Furthermore, we work out an interesting improvement that avoids the generation of feasible solutions for different fixpoint equations on the same variable. It is based on the fact that the feasible combinations for permutation cycles of the same length (a power of two) with the same domain, that are not algebraic *factors* of each other would not give rise to feasible common solutions.

Organisation. Section 2 introduces the background about nominal syntax and nominal C-unification. Section 3 proves the soundness and completeness of combinatorial solutions for fixpoint equations. Section 4 presents the improvements of the generator of solutions. Section 5 concludes the paper with future work.

2 Nominal Syntax and Nominal (α-)C-Unification

2.1 Nominal Syntax

Consider countable disjoint sets of variables $\mathcal{X} := \{X, Y, Z, \cdots\}$ and atoms $\mathcal{A} := \{a, b, c, \cdots\}$. A *permutation* π is a bijection on $\mathcal{A}$ with a finite *domain*, where the domain (i.e., the *support*) of π is the set $dom(\pi) := \{a \in \mathcal{A} \mid \pi \cdot a \neq a\}$.

We will assume as in [3] countable sets of function symbols with different equational properties such as associativity, commutativity, idempotence, etc. Function symbols have superscripts that indicate their equational properties; thus, f_k^C will denote the kth function symbol that is commutative and $f_j^{\emptyset}$ the jth function symbol without any equational property.

Definition 1 (Nominal grammar). *Nominal terms are generated by the following grammar.*

$$s, t := \langle\rangle \mid \bar{a} \mid [a]t \mid \langle s, t\rangle \mid f_k^E\, t \mid \pi.X$$

$\langle\rangle$ denotes the unit *(that is the empty tuple), $\bar{a}$ denotes an* atom term *(that is a* name *that plays the role of an object level variable), $[a]t$ denotes an* abstraction *of the atom a over the term t, $\langle s, t\rangle$ denotes a* pair, *$f_k^E\, t$ the* application *of f_k^E to t and, $\pi.X$ a* moderated *or* suspended *variable, where π is an* atom permutation.

Atom permutations are represented by finite lists of *swappings*, which are pairs of different atoms $(a\, b)$; hence, a *permutation* π has the form $(a_1\, b_1) :: \ldots :: (a_n\, b_n) :: nil$, where nil denotes the *identity* permutation.

Suspensions of the form $nil.X$ will be represented just by X. The set of variables occurring in a term t will be denoted as $Var(t)$. This notation extends to a set S of terms in the natural way: $Var(S) = \bigcup_{t \in S} Var(t)$.

A *substitution* σ is a mapping from variables to terms such that $X \neq X\sigma$ only for a finite set of variables. This set is called the *domain* of σ and is denoted by $dom(\sigma)$. For $X \in dom(\sigma)$, $X\sigma$ is called the *image* of X by σ. Define the image of σ as $im(\sigma) = \{X\sigma \mid X \in dom(\sigma)\}$. The set of variables occurring in the image of σ is then $Var(im(\sigma))$. A substitution σ with $dom(\sigma) := \{X_0, \cdots, X_n\}$ can be represented as a set of *binds* in the form $\{X_0/t_0, \cdots, X_n/t_n\}$, where for $0 \leq i \leq n$, $X_i\sigma = t_i$. We assume standard definitions for the *action* of permutations and substitutions on nominal terms (see e.g. [11,15]). Since for our purposes the algebraic combinatorial properties of permutations on atoms are relevant, in this paper atom permutations are seen as *products* of *permutation cycles* (see [12]): for instance, the nominal *swapping* permutation $(a\, b) :: (a\, c) :: (a\, d) :: (e\, f) :: (e\, g) :: nil$ is seen as the product of permutation cycles $(a\, b\, c\, d)\,(e\, f\, g)$.

2.2 The Relation $\approx_{\{\alpha,C\}}$ and Nominal $\approx_{\{\alpha,C\}}$-Unification

In [3], the relation $\approx_\alpha$ was extended to deal with associative and commutative theories. Here we will consider α-equivalence modulo commutativity, denoted $\approx_{\{\alpha,C\}}$. This means that some function symbols in our syntax are commutative.

The inference rules defining freshness and $\approx_{\{\alpha,C\}}$-equivalence are given in Figs. 1 and 2. The *difference set* between two permutations π and π' is the set of atoms where the action of π and π' differs: $ds(\pi,\pi') := \{a \in \mathcal{A} \mid \pi \cdot a \neq \pi' \cdot a\}$.

The symbols ∇ and Δ are used to denote *freshness contexts* that are sets of constraints of the form $a\#X$, meaning that the atom a is fresh in X. The domain of a freshness context $dom(\Delta)$ is the set of atoms appearing in it; $\Delta|_X$ denotes the restriction of Δ to the freshness constraints on X: $\{a\#X \mid a\#X \in \Delta\}$; $dom(\pi)\#X$ and $ds(\pi,\pi')\#X$ denote, respectively, the sets $\{a\#X \mid a \in dom(\pi)\}$ and $\{a\#X \mid a \in ds(\pi,\pi')\}$.

$$\frac{}{\nabla \vdash a\#\langle\rangle}\,(\#\langle\rangle) \quad \frac{}{\nabla \vdash a\#\overline{b}}\,(\#\,\mathbf{atom}) \quad \frac{\nabla \vdash a\#t}{\nabla \vdash a\# f_k^E\, t}\,(\#\,\mathbf{app}) \quad \frac{}{\nabla \vdash a\#[a]t}\,(\#\,\mathbf{a[a]})$$

$$\frac{\nabla \vdash a\#t}{\nabla \vdash a\#[b]t}\,(\#\,\mathbf{a[b]}) \quad \frac{(\pi^{-1}\cdot a\#X) \in \nabla}{\nabla \vdash a\#\pi.X}\,(\#\,\mathbf{var}) \quad \frac{\nabla \vdash a\#s \quad \nabla \vdash a\#t}{\nabla \vdash a\#\langle s,t\rangle}\,(\#\,\mathbf{pair})$$

Fig. 1. Rules for the relation #

$$\frac{}{\nabla \vdash \langle\rangle \approx_\alpha \langle\rangle}\,(\approx_{\{\alpha,\mathbf{C}\}}\langle\rangle) \qquad \frac{}{\nabla \vdash \overline{a} \approx_{\{\alpha,C\}} \overline{a}}\,(\approx_{\{\alpha,\mathbf{C}\}}\,\mathbf{atom})$$

$$\frac{\nabla \vdash s \approx_{\{\alpha,C\}} t}{\nabla \vdash f_k^E\, s \approx_{\{\alpha,C\}} f_k^E\, t},\ E \neq C \text{ or both } s \text{ and } t \text{ are not pairs}\ (\approx_{\{\alpha,\mathbf{C}\}}\,\mathbf{app})$$

$$\frac{\nabla \vdash s_0 \approx_{\{\alpha,C\}} t_i,\quad \nabla \vdash s_1 \approx_{\{\alpha,C\}} t_{(i+1)\,mod\,2}}{\nabla \vdash f_k^C\,\langle s_0,s_1\rangle \approx_{\{\alpha,C\}} f_k^C\,\langle t_0,t_1\rangle},\ i=0,1\ (\approx_{\{\alpha,\mathbf{C}\}}\,\mathbf{C})$$

$$\frac{\nabla \vdash s \approx_{\{\alpha,C\}} t}{\nabla \vdash [a]s \approx_{\{\alpha,C\}} [a]t}\,(\approx_{\{\alpha,\mathbf{C}\}}\,\mathbf{[aa]}) \quad \frac{\nabla \vdash s \approx_{\{\alpha,C\}} (a\,b)\cdot t \quad \nabla \vdash a\#t}{\nabla \vdash [a]s \approx_{\{\alpha,C\}} [b]t}\,(\approx_{\{\alpha,\mathbf{C}\}}\,\mathbf{[ab]})$$

$$\frac{ds(\pi,\pi')\#X \subseteq \nabla}{\nabla \vdash \pi.X \approx_{\{\alpha,C\}} \pi'.X}\,(\approx_{\{\alpha,\mathbf{C}\}}\,\mathbf{var}) \quad \frac{\nabla \vdash s_0 \approx_{\{\alpha,C\}} t_0 \quad \nabla \vdash s_1 \approx_{\{\alpha,C\}} t_1}{\nabla \vdash \langle s_0,t_0\rangle \approx_{\{\alpha,C\}} \langle s_1,t_1\rangle}\,(\approx_{\{\alpha,\mathbf{C}\}}\,\mathbf{pair})$$

Fig. 2. Rules for the relation $\approx_{\{\alpha,C\}}$

Key properties of the nominal freshness and α-equivalence relations have been extensively explored in previous works [3,6,14,15]. In [4] we also have formalised analogous properties for $\approx_{\{\alpha,C\}}$. Among them we have *freshness preservation*: If $\nabla \vdash a\#s$ and $\nabla \vdash s \approx_{\{\alpha,C\}} t$, then $\nabla \vdash a\#t$; *equivariance*: for all permutations π, if $\nabla \vdash s \approx_{\{\alpha,C\}} t$ then $\nabla \vdash \pi\cdot s \approx_{\{\alpha,C\}} \pi \cdot t$; and, *equivalence*: $\_ \vdash \_ \approx_{\{\alpha,C\}} \_$ is an equivalence relation, indeed.

Definition 2 (Nominal unification problem). *A* nominal unification problem *is a pair* $\langle \Delta, P \rangle$, *where* Δ *is a* freshness context *and* P *is a finite set of* equations *and* freshness constraints *of the form* $s \approx_? t$ *and* $a\#_?s$, *respectively, where* $\approx_?$ *is symmetric,* s *and* t *are terms and* a *is an atom. Nominal terms in the equations preserve the syntactic restriction that commutative symbols are only applied to tuples.*

A formalised sound and complete rule-based algorithm was presented in [4], that transforms a nominal unification problem, say $\langle \Delta, P \rangle$, with commutative function symbols into a finite set of fixpoint problems that consist exclusively of equations of the form $\pi.X \approx_? X$. The transformation starts from the triple $\mathcal{P} = \langle \Delta, id, P \rangle$, where *id* denotes the substitution identity, and the rules act over triples building a finite set of fixpoint problems of the form $\mathcal{Q}_i = \langle \nabla_i, \sigma_i, Q_i \rangle$, for $0 \leq i \leq n$, where for each i, ∇_i is a freshness context, σ_i a substitution, and Q_i consists only of fixpoint equations.

For ∇ and ∇' freshness contexts and σ and σ' substitutions, $\nabla' \vdash \nabla\sigma$ denotes that $\nabla' \vdash a \# X\sigma$ holds for each $(a\#X) \in \nabla$; $\nabla \vdash \sigma \approx \sigma'$ denotes that $\nabla \vdash X\sigma \approx_{\{\alpha,C\}} X\sigma'$ for all X (in $dom(\sigma) \cup dom(\sigma')$).

Definition 3 (Solution for a triple or problem). *A* solution *for a triple* $\mathcal{P} = \langle \Delta, \delta, P \rangle$ *is a pair* $\langle \nabla, \sigma \rangle$, *where the following conditions are satisfied:*

1. $\nabla \vdash \Delta\sigma$;
2. *if* $a\#_?t \in P$ *then* $\nabla \vdash a \# t\sigma$;
3. *if* $s \approx_? t \in P$ *then* $\nabla \vdash s\sigma \approx_{\{\alpha,C\}} t\sigma$;
4. *there exists* λ *such that* $\nabla \vdash \delta\lambda \approx \sigma$.

A *solution for a unification problem* $\langle \Delta, P \rangle$ is a solution for the associated triple $\langle \Delta, id, P \rangle$. The *solution set* for a problem or triple $\mathcal{P}$ is denoted by $\mathcal{U}_C(\mathcal{P})$.

Definition 4 (More general solution and complete set of solutions). *For* $\langle \nabla, \sigma \rangle$ *and* $\langle \nabla', \sigma' \rangle$ *in* $\mathcal{U}_C(\mathcal{P})$, *we say that* $\langle \nabla, \sigma \rangle$ *is* more general *than* $\langle \nabla', \sigma' \rangle$, *denoted* $\langle \nabla, \sigma \rangle \preccurlyeq \langle \nabla', \sigma' \rangle$, *if there exists a substitution* λ *satisfying* $\nabla' \vdash \sigma\lambda \approx \sigma'$ *and* $\nabla' \vdash \nabla\lambda$. *A subset* $\mathcal{V}$ *of* $\mathcal{U}_C(\mathcal{P})$ *is said to be a* complete set of solutions *of* $\mathcal{P}$ *if for all* $\langle \nabla', \sigma' \rangle \in \mathcal{U}_C(\mathcal{P})$, *there exists* $\langle \nabla, \sigma \rangle$ *in* $\mathcal{V}$ *that is more general than* $\langle \nabla', \sigma' \rangle$.

Example 1. Given the nominal unification problem $\mathcal{P} = \langle \emptyset, id, \{[a']\langle (a\,c).X \star (a\,b\,c).Y, (a\,b\,c\,d).X \rangle \approx_? [b']\langle X \star Y, X \rangle\} \rangle$, the algorithm in [4] transforms it into the fixpoint problems $\mathcal{Q}_1 = \langle \{a'\#X, a'\#Y\}, id, \{(a'\,b')(a\,c).X \approx_? X,\ (a'\,b')(a\,b\,c\,d).X \approx_? X,\ (a'\,b')(a\,b\,c).Y \approx_? Y\} \rangle$ and $\mathcal{Q}_2 = \langle \{a'\#Y, b'\#Y\}, \{X/(a\,c)(a'\,b').Y\}, \{(a\,b).Y \approx_? Y,\ (d\,c\,b\,a)(a'\,b').Y \approx_? Y\} \rangle$. These fixpoint problems are generated by considering '$\star$' to be a commutative symbol and by inversions on the permutations in the suspended variables.

The results in [4] include formalisations in Coq of theorems related with the following properties: **termination**: there are no possible infinite chains of applications of the unification transformation rules; **soundness**: for each possible transformation from $\mathcal{P}$ to $\mathcal{Q}$, one has that $\mathcal{U}_C(\mathcal{Q}) \subseteq \mathcal{U}_C(\mathcal{P})$; **unsolvability**: if $\mathcal{Q} = \langle \Delta, \sigma, Q\rangle$ cannot be simplified and Q contains non fixpoint equations or freshness constraints then $\mathcal{U}_C(\mathcal{Q}) = \emptyset$; and, **completeness**: if the unification problem $\mathcal{P} = \langle \nabla, id, P\rangle$ is transformed into the finite set of fixpoint problems $\mathcal{Q}_i$, for $1 \leq i \leq n$, then $\mathcal{U}_C(\mathcal{P}) = \bigcup_{i=1}^{n} \mathcal{U}_C(\mathcal{Q}_i)$.

Example 2 (Continuing Example 1). The unification algorithm requires a mechanism to enumerate solutions of fixpoint problems. Solutions in $\mathcal{U}(\mathcal{Q}_1)$ are built using the substitution *id* and combining solutions for the singleton fixpoint problems $\langle\{a'\#X\}, \{(a'\, b')(a\, c).X \approx_? X\}\rangle$, $\langle\{a'\#X\}, \{(a'\, b')(a\, b\, c\, d).X \approx_? X\}\rangle$ and $\langle\{a'\#Y\}, id, \{(a'\, b')(a\, b\, c).Y \approx_? Y\}\rangle$. Solutions in $\mathcal{U}(\mathcal{Q}_2)$ are built with substitution $\{X/(a\, c)(a'\, b').Y\}$ and combining solutions for the fixpoint problems $\langle\{a'\#Y, b'\#Y\}, \{(a\, b).Y \approx_? Y\}\rangle$ and $\langle\{a'\#Y, b'\#Y\}, \{(d\, c\, b\, a)(a'\, b').Y \approx_? Y\}\rangle$.

2.3 Solutions of Fixpoint Problems Through Extended Pseudo-Cycles

The set of solutions of a singleton fixpoint problem $\langle \nabla, \{\pi.X \approx_? X\}\rangle$ is built according to the recursive definition of (*unitary*) *extended pseudo-cycles* below [4]. The definition of extended pseudo-cycle given below is parametric on a set $\mathcal{X}$ of variables. In this way, we take into account the fact that this fixpoint problem could have been generated by a procedure to solve a problem $\mathcal{P}$ with a given set of variables and freshness constraints.

Definition 5 (Extended Pseudo-cycle). *Let $\pi.X \approx_? X$ and $\mathcal{X}$ a set of variables. The* extended pseudo-cycles *(for short,* epc*) κ for π relative to $\mathcal{X}$ are inductively defined from the permutation cycles of π as follows:*

1. *$\kappa = (Y)$, for any variable not occurring in $\mathcal{X}$, is an* epc *for π;*
2. *$\kappa = (\overline{a_0} \cdots \overline{a_{k-1}})$ is an* epc *for $(a_0 \;\; \cdots a_{k-1})$ a permutation cycle in π such that $k = 2^l$, for $l > 0$, called* trivial extended pseudo-cycle *of π.*
3. *$\kappa = (A_0 \,...\, A_{k-1})$, for a length $k \geq 1$, is an* epc *for π, if the following conditions are simultaneously satisfied:*
   - (a) i. *each element of κ is of the form $B_i \star B_j$, where $\star$ is a commutative function symbol in the signature, and B_i, B_j are different elements of κ', an* epc *for π; in this case, κ will be called a* first-instance extended pseudo-cycle *of κ' for π; or*
     - ii. *each element of κ is of the form $B_i \star C_j$ for any commutative symbol $\star$, where B_i and C_j are elements of κ' and κ''* epc*'s for π, which might both be the same, but κ is not a first-instance* epc *for π; or*
     - iii. *each element of κ is of the form $\langle B_i, C_j\rangle$, where B_i and C_j are elements of κ' and κ''* epc*'s for π, which might both be the same; or*
     - iv. *either each element of κ is of the form $g\, B_i$ or each element is of the form $[e]\, B_i$, where g is a non commutative function symbol in the signature and $e \notin dom(\pi)$, and each B_i is an element of κ' an* epc *for π; or*

v. each element of κ is of the form $[a_j]B_i$, where a_j are atoms in $\kappa' = (\overline{a_0} \cdots \overline{a_{k'-1}})$ a trivial epc *for π, and B_i elements of κ'' an* epc *for π; and*

(b) for $\nabla' = \cup_{Y \in Var(\kappa)}\{dom(\pi)\#Y\}$,

i. it does not hold that $\nabla' \vdash A_i \approx_{\{\alpha,C\}} A_j$ for $i \neq j$, $0 \leq i,j \leq k-1$; and

ii. for each $0 \leq i \leq k-1$ one has that $\nabla' \vdash \pi(A_i) \approx_{\{\alpha,C\}} A_{(i+1)\, mod\, k}$.

Extended pseudo-cycles built using only items 2 and 3.a.i and 3.b are called pseudo-cycles. *Extended pseudo-cycles of length $k = 1$ are called* unitary.

Remark 1. Pseudo-cycles are built just from atom terms in $dom(\pi)$ and commutative function symbols, while epc's consider all nominal syntactic elements including new variables, and also non commutative function symbols.

Example 3 (Continuing Example 2). Given the fixpoint equation $(a'\, b')(a\, b\, c\, d).X \approx_? X$. Let $\kappa = (a\, b\, c\, d)$ and $\mathcal{X} = \{X, Y\}$. Assume, $\star$ and $\oplus$ are commutative symbols, f and g non commutative symbols. The following are pseudo-cycles relative to $\mathcal{X}$: $(\overline{a}\star\overline{d}\ \ \overline{b}\star\overline{a}\ \ \overline{c}\star\overline{b}\ \ \overline{d}\star\overline{c})$, $(\overline{a}\star\overline{c}\oplus\overline{b}\star\overline{d})$, etc. The following are epc's relative to $\mathcal{X}$: $(f\langle\overline{a},\overline{b}\rangle\ \ f\langle\overline{b},\overline{c}\rangle\ \ f\langle\overline{c},\overline{d}\rangle\ \ f\langle\overline{d},\overline{a}\rangle)$, $([e]\overline{a}\star\overline{c}\ \ [e]\overline{b}\star\overline{d})$, $(g\langle f\overline{a},[e]\overline{a}\rangle\ \ g\langle f\overline{b},[e]\overline{b}\rangle\ \ g\langle f\overline{c},[e]\overline{c}\rangle\ \ g\langle f\overline{d},[e]\overline{d}\rangle)$, $(\langle t, f\langle g\langle f\overline{a},[e]\overline{b}\rangle, Z\rangle \oplus f\langle g\langle f\overline{c},[e]\overline{d}\rangle, Z\rangle\rangle \star \langle t, f\langle g\langle f\overline{b},[e]\overline{c}\rangle, Z\rangle \oplus f\langle g\langle f\overline{d},[e]\overline{a}\rangle, Z\rangle\rangle)$, etc.

A relevant aspect is that only case 3.a.i of Definition 5 allows generating epc's that might be shorter than the epc's to which this case is applied. When this is the case, the length of the generated epc is half of the original one [4].

Example 4 (Continuing Example 3). Applying case 3.a.i to the trivial epc $(\overline{a}\ \ \overline{b}\ \ \overline{c}\ \ \overline{d})$ one obtains the epc $(\overline{a}\star\overline{c}\ \ \overline{b}\star\overline{d})$.

So, unitary epc's can only be obtained from permutation cycles of length a power of two. When a unitary epc is being generated, the last application of 3.a.i transforms a length two epc of the form $(A_0\ \ A_1)$ into $(A_0 \star A_1)$. By condition 3.b.ii, $\nabla \vdash \pi(A_0) \approx_{\{\alpha,C\}} A_1$ and $\nabla \vdash \pi(A_1) \approx_{\{\alpha,C\}} A_0$. Therefore, $\nabla \vdash \pi(A_0 \star A_1) \approx_{\{\alpha,C\}} A_0 \star A_1$.

Another relevant aspect of this construction is that although, we are using the relation $\approx_{\{\alpha,C\}}$, by the class of nominal terms involved in the generation of epc's, only $\approx_C$ would be necessary, except for considerations related with the freshness constraints (on new variables); hence, the invariant 3.b.ii can be seen as $\pi(A_i) \approx_C A_{i+1}$, where $i+1$ is read modulo the length of the epc.

3 Soundness and Completeness

As in the previous section, we consider fixpoint equations of the form $\pi.X \approx_? X$ which occur in a fixpoint problem $\mathcal{Q} = \langle \Delta, \sigma, Q\rangle$ relative to a set of variables $\mathcal{X}$.

Definition 6 (Generated solutions of singleton fixpoint problems). *For Q and $\pi.X \approx_? X \in Q$ as above, the set of* generated solutions *for $\langle \Delta, \{\pi.X \approx_? X\}\rangle$, denoted as $\langle \Delta, \{\pi.X \approx_? X\}\rangle_{Sol_G}$, consists of pairs of the form $\langle \nabla, \{X/s\}\rangle$ where (s) is a unitary* epc *for π such that $\nabla \vdash dom(\Delta|_X)\#s$, where $\nabla = \Delta \cup_{Y \in Var(s)} (dom(\Delta|_X)\#Y \cup dom(\pi)\#Y)$.*

Theorem 1 (Soundness of solutions of singleton fixpoint problems). *Each $\langle \nabla, \{X/s\}\rangle$ in $\langle \Delta, \{\pi.X \approx_? X\}\rangle_{Sol_G}$ is a solution of $\langle \Delta, \{\pi.X \approx_? X\}\rangle$.*

Proof. The proof follows the lines of reasoning used for non unitary epc's. By construction, the invariant that the elements of an epc of length l, $\kappa' = (e_0 \dots e_{l-1})$, satisfy the property $\nabla' \vdash \pi(e_i) \approx_{\{\alpha,C\}} e_{i+1}$, where $i+1$ abbreviates $i+1$ modulo l, and $\nabla' = \cup_{Y \in Var(\kappa')} dom(\pi)\#Y$, holds. The only case in which the length of an epc decreases is 3.a.i. Thus, when this case applies to a binary epc, say $(s_0\ s_1)$, an unitary epc (s) is built, being this of the form $(s_0 \oplus s_1)$ for a commutative function symbol $\oplus$. Since by the invariant we have that $\nabla' \vdash \pi(s_i) \approx_{\{\alpha,C\}} s_{i+1}$, for $i = 0, 1$, we have that $\nabla' \vdash \pi(s_0 \oplus s_1) \approx_{\{\alpha,C\}} s_0 \oplus s_1$; thus, we have that $\nabla' \vdash \pi(s) \approx_{\{\alpha,C\}} s$. In further steps in the construction of epc's, new unitary epc's (t') might be built from unitary epc's (t) applying cases 3.a.ii, iii, iv and v, that, can easily be checked, preserve the property $\nabla' \vdash \pi(t') \approx_{\{\alpha,C\}} t'$, for $\nabla' = \cup_{Y \in Var(t')} dom(\pi)\#Y$, if $\nabla' \vdash \pi(t) \approx_{\{\alpha,C\}} t$, for $\nabla' = \cup_{Y \in Var(t)} dom(\pi)\#Y$. Therefore all unitary non-trivial epc's give a correct solution of the form $\langle \nabla', \{X/s\}\rangle$ of the problem $\langle \emptyset, \pi.X \approx_? X\rangle$. Hence, if in addition, we have that $\nabla' \cup \Delta \vdash dom(\Delta|_X)\#s$, then for $\nabla := \nabla' \cup \Delta$, the pair $\langle \nabla, \{X/s\}\rangle \in \langle \Delta, \{\pi.X \approx_? X\}\rangle_{Sol_G}$ is a solution of $\langle \Delta, \{\pi.X \approx_? X\}\rangle$. □

Assuming the symbols in the signature are denumerable, it is possible to enumerate the unitary epc's and thus the *generated solutions*. This can be done as usual, enumerating first all possible unitary epc's with an element of length bounded by a small natural, say twice the length of π, and using only the first $|\pi|$ symbols in the signature and atoms in $dom(\pi)$; then, this length is increased generating all extended unitary epc's with elements of length $|\pi| + 1$ and using only the first $|\pi + 1|$ symbols in the signature and atoms in $dom(\pi)$ and so on.

The following result, proved by induction in the construction of the epc's, is used in the proof of completeness of generated solutions for fixpoint problems.

Lemma 1 (Extended pseudo-cycle correspondence for π and π^2). *For $k \geq 1$, $(A_0 \cdots A_{2^k-1})$ is an* epc *for π if, and only if, there exist $(B_0 \cdots B_{2^{k-1}-1})$ and $(C_0 \cdots C_{2^{k-1}-1})$* epc*'s for π^2 with a substitution σ such that atoms in its image belong to $dom(\pi) \backslash dom(\pi^2)$, and for $0 \leq j \leq 2^{k-1} - 1$ one has $B_j\sigma \approx_{\{\alpha,C\}} A_{2j}$ and $C_j\sigma \approx_{\{\alpha,C\}} A_{2j+1}$.*

Example 5. For $(a\,b)$ and $(c\,d\,e\,f)$, permutation cycles of π, one has that (a), (b), $(c\,e)$ and $(d\,f)$ are permutation cycles of π^2, and also, $a, b \in dom(\pi) \backslash dom(\pi^2)$. Therefore, supposing that '+', '$*$' and '$\star$' are commutative function symbols, $((\overline{c} * \overline{e}) + \overline{a}) \star ((\overline{d} * \overline{f}) + \overline{b})$ and $((\overline{c} * \overline{e}) + Y) \star ((\overline{d} * \overline{f}) + Y')$ are respectively unitary epc's of π and π^2. Then:

- $\langle \Delta, \{X/((\overline{c} * \overline{e}) + \overline{a}) \star ((\overline{d} * \overline{f}) + \overline{b})\}\rangle \in \langle \Delta, \pi.X \approx_? X\rangle_{Sol_G}$ iff
- $\langle \Delta', \{X/((\overline{c} * \overline{e}) + Y) \star ((\overline{d} * \overline{f}) + Y')\}\rangle \in \langle \Delta, \pi^2.X \approx_? X\rangle_{Sol_G}$,

where $\Delta' = \Delta \cup dom(\pi^2)\#Y, Y' \cup dom(\Delta|_X)\#Y, Y'$. So the σ of Lemma 1 will be $\{Y/\overline{a}, Y'/\overline{b}\}$, so that $((\overline{c} * \overline{e}) + \overline{a}\ (\overline{d} * \overline{f}) + \overline{b})$ is an epcof π, $((\overline{c} * \overline{e}) + Y)$ and $((\overline{d} * \overline{f}) + Y')$ are epc's of π^2, with $((\overline{c} * \overline{e}) + Y)\sigma = (\overline{c} * \overline{e}) + \overline{a}$ and $((\overline{d} * \overline{f}) + Y')\sigma = (\overline{d} * \overline{f}) + \overline{b}$.

Example 6. Let $\pi = (a\ b\ c\ d\ e\ f\ g\ h)$ then $\pi^2 = (a\ c\ e\ g)(b\ d\ f\ h)$. There are solutions of $\langle \emptyset, \pi^2 \cdot X \approx_? X\rangle$ that are not solutions of $\langle \emptyset, \pi.X \approx_? X\rangle$:

- $\langle \emptyset, X/(\overline{a} \oplus \overline{e}) \oplus (\overline{c} \oplus \overline{g})\rangle, \langle \emptyset, X/(\overline{b} \star \overline{f}) \oplus (\overline{d} \star \overline{h})\rangle \in \langle \emptyset, \pi^2 \cdot X \approx_? X\rangle_{Sol_G}$;
- $\langle \emptyset, X/((\overline{a} \oplus \overline{e}) \oplus (\overline{c} \oplus \overline{g})) \oplus ((\overline{b} \star \overline{f}) \oplus (\overline{d} \star \overline{h}))\rangle \in \langle \emptyset, \pi^2 \cdot X \approx_? X\rangle_{Sol_G}$

but none of them is a solution for $\langle \emptyset, \pi.X \approx_? X\rangle$.

However there exist solutions in the intersection of both problems, for instance, $\langle \emptyset, X/((\overline{a} \oplus \overline{e}) \oplus (\overline{c} \oplus \overline{g})) * (X/(\overline{b} \oplus \overline{f}) \oplus (\overline{d} \oplus \overline{h}))\rangle$.

Theorem 2 (Completeness of solutions for singleton fixpoint problems). *Let $\langle \Delta, \{\pi.X \approx_? X\}\rangle$ be a singleton fixpoint problem with a solution $\langle \nabla, \{X/s\}\rangle$. Then there exists $\langle \nabla', \{X/t\}\rangle \in \langle \Delta, \{\pi.X \approx_? X\}\rangle_{Sol_G}$ such that $\langle \nabla', \{X/t\}\rangle \preceq \langle \nabla, \{X/s\}\rangle$.*

Proof. Since $\langle \nabla, \{X/s\}\rangle$ is a solution of the problem, it follows that $\nabla \vdash \Delta\{X/s\}$ and $\nabla \vdash \pi(s) \approx_{\{\alpha,C\}} s$. The proof is done by induction on the structure of s.
Base Case. This case will be split in two parts.

1. $s = \overline{a}$.

   The pair $\langle \nabla, \{X/\overline{a}\}\rangle$ is a solution only if $a \notin dom(\Delta|_X) \cup dom(\pi)$, then $\emptyset \vdash \pi \cdot \overline{a} = \overline{a}$. Let Y be a new variable and $\nabla' = dom(\Delta|_X)\#Y \cup dom(\pi)\#Y$, then $\langle \nabla', \{X/Y\}\rangle$ is a generated solution. Let $\sigma = \{Y/\overline{a}\}$, notice that $\nabla \vdash \nabla'\sigma$ and $Y\sigma = \overline{a}$. Therefore, $\langle \nabla', \{X/Y\}\rangle \preceq \langle \nabla, \{X/\overline{a}\}\rangle$.
2. $s = \pi'.Y$ and $dom(\pi)\#\pi'.Y$.
   Notice that $\langle \nabla, \{X/\pi'.Y\}\rangle \in \langle \Delta, \pi.X \approx_? X\rangle_{Sol_C}$ only if $\nabla \vdash dom(\Delta|_X)\#\pi'.Y, dom(\pi)\#\pi'.Y$, that is, if $\nabla \vdash (\pi')^{-1} \cdot dom(\Delta|_X)\#Y$ and $\nabla \vdash (\pi')^{-1} \cdot dom(\pi)\#Y$, so that $\Delta \cup ((\pi')^{-1} \cdot dom(\Delta|_X) \cup (\pi')^{-1} \cdot dom(\pi))\#Y \subset \nabla$.

   Let $\langle \nabla', \{X/Z\}\rangle \in \langle \Delta, \pi.X \approx_? X\rangle_{Sol_G}$ with $\nabla' = \Delta \cup dom(\pi) \cup dom(\Delta|_X)\#Z$, Consider the substitution $\sigma = \{Z/\pi'.Y\}$, then $\nabla \vdash Z\sigma \approx_{\{\alpha,C\}} \pi'.Y$ and $\nabla'\sigma = \Delta\sigma \cup (dom(\pi) \cup dom(\Delta|_X))\#Z\sigma = \Delta \cup (\pi')^{-1} \cdot dom(\pi)\#Y \cup (\pi')^{-1} \cdot dom(\Delta|_X)\#Y$, so $\nabla \vdash \nabla'\sigma$. Therefore, $\langle \nabla', \{X/Z\}\rangle \preceq \langle \nabla, \{X/\pi'.Y\}\rangle$.

Induction Step.

1. $s = \langle s_1, s_2\rangle$
   In this case $\nabla \vdash \pi(\langle s_1, s_2\rangle) \approx_{\{\alpha,C\}} \langle s_1, s_2\rangle$, that is, $\nabla \vdash \langle \pi(s_1), \pi(s_2)\rangle \approx_{\{\alpha,C\}} \langle s_1, s_2\rangle$, which implies in $\nabla \vdash \pi(s_i) \approx_{\{\alpha,C\}} s_i$, for $i = 1, 2$.

By i.h. and Definitions 5 and 6, there exist $\langle \nabla'_1, \{X/t_1\}\rangle, \langle \nabla'_2, \{X/t_2\}\rangle \in \langle \Delta, \pi \cdot X \approx_? X\rangle_{Sol_G}$ s.t. (t_1), (t_2) and $(\langle t_1, t_2\rangle)$ are unitary epc's w.r.t. π. Furthermore $\langle \nabla'_i, \{X/t_i\}\rangle \preceq \langle \nabla, \{X/s_i\}\rangle$, i.e., there exist substitutions λ_i s.t. $\nabla \vdash \nabla_i\lambda_i$ and $\nabla \vdash t_i\lambda_i \approx s_i$, for $i = 1, 2$. One can choose (t_1) and (t_2) s.t. $Var(t_1) \cap Var(t_2) = \emptyset$ and $dom(\lambda_i) \cap Var(s_j) = \emptyset$, for $i, j = 1, 2$. Then, $\nabla \vdash \langle t_1, t_2\rangle\lambda_1\lambda_2 \approx_{\{\alpha,C\}} \langle s_1, s_2\rangle$, and $\nabla \vdash (\nabla_1 \cup \nabla_2)\lambda_1\lambda_2$, that is, $\langle \nabla_1 \cup \nabla_2, \{X/\langle t_1, t_2\rangle\}\rangle \preceq \langle \nabla, \{X/\langle s_1, s_2\rangle\}\rangle$.

2. $s = fs'$
   Since $\nabla \vdash \pi \cdot fs' \approx_{\{\alpha,C\}} fs'$, it follows that $\nabla \vdash f(\pi(s')) \approx_{\{\alpha,C\}} fs'$ and therefore, $\nabla \vdash \pi(s') \approx_{\{\alpha,C\}} s'$. By i.h. and Definitions 5 and 6, there exist $\langle \nabla', \{X/t'\}\rangle \in \langle \Delta, \pi \cdot X \approx_? X\rangle_{Sol_G}$ such that (t') and (ft') are unitary epc's w.r.t. π. Furthermore $\langle \nabla', \{X/t'\}\rangle \preceq \langle \nabla, \{X/s'\}\rangle$, that is, there exist a substitution σ such that $\nabla \vdash \nabla'\sigma$ and $\nabla \vdash t'\sigma \approx_{\{\alpha,C\}} s'$, and since $\nabla \vdash ft'\sigma \approx_{\{\alpha,C\}} f(t'\sigma) \approx_{\{\alpha,C\}} fs'$ and adding f at the top of t' does not change the variables of t', therefore, $\langle \nabla', \{X/ft'\}\rangle \in \langle \Delta, \pi \cdot X \approx_? X\rangle_{Sol_G}$ and $\langle \nabla', \{X/ft'\}\rangle \preceq \langle \nabla, \{X/fs'\}\rangle$.
3. $s = [e]s'$.
   (a) $e \notin dom(\pi)$
   Since $\nabla \vdash \pi([e]s') \approx_{\{\alpha,C\}} [e]s'$, it follows that $\nabla \vdash \pi(s') \approx_{\{\alpha,C\}} s'$, i.e., $\langle \nabla, X/s'\rangle$ is a solution for $\langle \Delta, \pi \cdot X \approx_? X\rangle$. By i.h. and Definitions 5 and 6, there exist $\langle \nabla', \{X/t'\}\rangle \in \langle \Delta, \pi \cdot X \approx_? X\rangle_{Sol_G}$ such that (t') and $([e]t')$ are unitary epc's w.r.t. π. Furthermore $\langle \nabla', \{X/t'\}\rangle \preceq \langle \nabla, \{X/s'\}\rangle$, i.e., there exist a substitution σ such that $\nabla \vdash \nabla'\sigma$ and $\nabla \vdash t'\sigma \approx_{\{\alpha,C\}} s'$, therefore, $\langle \nabla', \{X/[e]t'\}\rangle \in \langle \Delta, \pi \cdot X \approx_? X\rangle_{Sol_G}$ and $\langle \nabla', \{X/[e]t'\}\rangle \preceq \langle \nabla, \{X/[e]s'\}\rangle$.
   (b) $e \in dom(\pi)$.
   By hypothesis, $\nabla \vdash \pi([e]s') \approx_{\{\alpha,C\}} [e]s'$, i.e., $\nabla \vdash [\pi \cdot e](\pi(s')) \approx_{\{\alpha,C\}} [e]s'$, and $\nabla \vdash \pi(s') \approx_{\{\alpha,C\}} (\pi \cdot e\ \ e)(s')$ only if $\nabla \vdash (\pi \cdot e)\#s'$. Notice that e occurs in s' iff $\pi \cdot e$ occurs in s'. Therefore, for $\nabla \vdash e\#s'$, it follows that $\nabla \vdash \pi(s') \approx_{\{\alpha,C\}} s'$ and the result follows by induction hypothesis.
4. $s = s_1 \oplus s_2$
   This case has two parts:

   (a) $\nabla \vdash \pi(s_1) \approx_{\{\alpha,C\}} s_1$ and $\nabla \vdash \pi(s_2) \approx_{\{\alpha,C\}} s_2$.
   By i.h. and Definitions 5 and 6, there exist $\langle \nabla'_1, \{X/t_1\}\rangle, \langle \nabla'_2, \{X/t_2\}\rangle \in \langle \Delta, \pi \cdot X \approx_? X\rangle_{Sol_G}$ s.t. (t_1), (t_2) and $(t_1 \oplus t_2)$ are unitary epc's w.r.t. π. Furthermore $\langle \nabla'_i, \{X/t_i\}\rangle \preceq \langle \nabla, \{X/s_i\}\rangle$, i.e., there exist substitutions λ_i s.t. $\nabla \vdash \nabla_i\lambda_i$ and $\nabla \vdash t_i\lambda_i \approx s_i$, for $i = 1, 2$. One can choose (t_1) and (t_2) s.t. $Var(t_1) \cap Var(t_2) = \emptyset$ and $dom(\lambda_i) \cap Var(s_j) = \emptyset$, for $i, j = 1, 2$. Then, $\nabla \vdash (t_1 \oplus t_2)\lambda_1\lambda_2 \approx_{\{\alpha,C\}} (s_1 \oplus s_2)$, and $\nabla \vdash (\nabla_1 \cup \nabla_2)\lambda_1\lambda_2$, that is, $\langle \nabla_1 \cup \nabla_2, \{X/t_1 \oplus t_2\}\rangle \preceq \langle \nabla, \{X/s_1 \oplus s_2\}\rangle$.
   (b) $\nabla \vdash \pi(s_1) \approx_{\{\alpha,C\}} s_2$ and $\nabla \vdash \pi(s_2) \approx_{\{\alpha,C\}} s_1$.
   Notice that $\nabla \vdash \pi^2(s_1) \approx_{\{\alpha,C\}} \pi(s_2) \approx_{\{\alpha,C\}} s_1$ and $\nabla \vdash \pi^2(s_2) \approx_{\{\alpha,C\}} \pi(s_1) \approx_{\{\alpha,C\}} s_2$. Therefore, $\langle \nabla, \{X/s_1\}\rangle$ and $\langle \nabla, \{X/s_2\}\rangle$ are solutions of $\langle \Delta, \pi^2.X \approx_? X\rangle$. By IH, there exist $\langle \nabla_1, \{X/t_1\}\rangle, \langle \nabla_2, \{X/t_2\}\rangle \in \langle \Delta, \pi^2 \cdot$

$X \approx_? X\rangle_{Sol_G}$ such that $\langle\nabla_i, \{X/t_i\}\rangle \preceq \langle\nabla, \{X/s_i\}\rangle$. Then there exist substitutions λ_i s.t. $\nabla \vdash \nabla_i\lambda_i$ and $\nabla \vdash t_i\lambda_i \approx_{\{\alpha,C\}} s_i$, for $i = 1, 2$.
One can choose (t_1) and (t_2) s.t. $Var(t_1) \cap Var(t_2) = \emptyset$ and $dom(\lambda_i) \cap Var(s_j) = \emptyset$, for $i, j = 1, 2$.

Therefore, $\langle\nabla_1 \cup \nabla_2, X/t_1 \oplus t_2\rangle \in \langle\Delta, \pi^2.X \approx_? X\rangle_{Sol_G}$ and $\langle\nabla_1 \cup \nabla_2, X/t_1 \oplus t_2\rangle \preceq \langle\nabla, X/s_1 \oplus s_2\rangle$, via substitution $\lambda = \lambda_1\lambda_2$.

Notice that $\nabla \vdash \pi(t_1)\lambda \approx_{\{\alpha,C\}} \pi(s_1) \approx_{\{\alpha,C\}} s_2 \approx_{\{\alpha,C\}} t_2\lambda$ and analogously, $\nabla \vdash \pi(t_2)\lambda \approx_{\{\alpha,C\}} t_1\lambda$. Hence, λ is a solution for the C-unification problem $\{\pi(t_1) =_? t_2, \pi(t_2) =_? t_1\}$. Let $\langle\nabla', \lambda'\rangle$ be a solution more general than $\langle\nabla, \lambda\rangle$ such that the atoms in the image of λ' are in $dom(\pi)\backslash dom(\pi^2)$. Since (t_1) and (t_2) are unitary epc's of π^2, it follows by Lemma 1, that $(t_1\lambda'\ t_2\lambda')$ is an epc for π. By Definition 5, $(t_1\lambda' \oplus t_2\lambda')$ is a unitary epcfor π, such that $\langle\nabla', \{X/t_1\lambda' \oplus t_2\lambda'\}\rangle \in \langle\Delta, \{\pi \cdot X \approx_? X\}\rangle_{Sol_G}$ and $\langle\nabla', \{X/t_1\lambda' \oplus t_2\lambda'\}\rangle \preceq \langle\nabla, \{X/s_1 \oplus s_2\}\rangle$. □

Remark 2. Notice that to build just a most general set of C-unifiers, without taking into account nominal equivalence, in the proof of Lemma 2 (case 4.b) and Definition 7 one can use the algorithm proposed by Siekmann [13], which provides a finite, minimal and complete set of C-unifiers.

Definition 7 (General C-matchers). *Let s_i, for $i = 1..k$, be nominal terms. A* most general C-matcher *of these terms, if it exists, is a most general C-unifier δ of the C-unification problem $\{s_i =_? Z\}_{i=1..k}$, where Z is a new variable for s_i, with $i = 1..k$.*

Remark 3. Alternatively, Definition 5 could be restricted to ground terms (by removing the first case in the construction of epc's), and then instead of computing C-matchers via C-unification, one could use an α-C-equivalence checker (for example, the one specified in [3]). This would also simplify case iv in Definition 5, since it would be sufficient to consider just one atom e' not in $dom(\pi)$.

Definition 8 (Generated solutions for a variable). *Let the fixpoint problems for X in $\mathcal{P}$ be given by $\langle\nabla, \pi_i.X \approx_? X\rangle$, for $\pi_i \in \Pi_X$, and such that $|\Pi_X| = k$. If there exist*

- *solutions $\langle\nabla_i, \{X/t_i\}\rangle \in \langle\nabla, \pi_i.X \approx_? X\rangle_{Sol_G}$ for each fixpoint problem and*
- *a most general C-matcher δ of the terms $\{t_i\}_{i=1..k}$ with X as new variable*

such that the problem $\langle\emptyset, \cup_{(a\#Y)\in\nabla''}\{a\#Y\delta\}\rangle$, where $\nabla'' := \cup_{i=1}^k \nabla_i$, has a solution $\langle\nabla', \emptyset\rangle$, then we say that $\langle\nabla', \{X/X\delta\}\rangle$ is a generated solution *for X. The set of all generated solutions is denoted by $[X]_{\mathcal{P}_G}$.*

Example 7. Let $P_i := \pi_i.X \approx_? X$, for $i = 1..3$, be fixpoint equations for $\pi_1 = (a\ b\ c\ d)$, $\pi_2 = (a\ c)$ and $\pi_3 = (b\ d)$ and suppose that $\mathcal{P} := \langle\nabla, P\rangle$ is a fixpoint problem where P_i for $i = 1..3$ are the fixpoint equations for X in P.

1. $\langle \nabla \cup a, b, c, d\#Y, \delta_1 := \{X/((a*c)*(b*d)) \oplus Y\}\rangle \in \langle \nabla, P_1\rangle_{Sol_G}$;
2. $\langle \nabla \cup a, c\#Y', Y'', \delta_2 := \{X/((a*c)*Y') \oplus Y''\}\rangle \in \langle \nabla, P_2\rangle_{Sol_G}$; and
3. $\langle \nabla \cup b, d\#Y_1', Y_1'', \delta_3 := \{X/((b*d)*Y_1') \oplus Y_1''\}\rangle \in \langle \nabla, P_3\rangle_{Sol_G}$.

Notice that $\delta = \{X/((a*c)*(b*d)) \oplus Y'', Y'/(b*d), Y_1'/(a*c), Y/Y'', Y_1''/Y''\}$ is a most general C-unifier of terms $\{t_i := X\delta_i\}$ with variable X.

According to the definition, the set of initial freshness constraints is given as $\nabla'' = \nabla \cup \{a, b, c, d\#Y, a, c\#Y', Y'', b, d\#Y_1', Y_1''\}$. Notice that $Y'' \in Var(im(\delta))$, have to satisfy the constraints on Y_1'', Y and X, that is, $a, b, c, d\#Y''$ is a new constraint on Y'', inherited from the constraints of the variables in the domain of δ. $\langle \nabla', \emptyset\rangle$ is the solution of $\langle \emptyset, \cup_{(a\#Y)\in\nabla''}\{a\#Y\delta\}\rangle$, and then it holds that $\nabla' \vdash dom(\nabla''|_Z)\#Z\delta$, for all $Z \in dom(\delta)$. Thus, $\langle \nabla', \{X/X\delta\}\rangle$ belongs to $[X]_{\mathcal{P}_G}$.

Example 8 (Continuing Example 3). Consider the singleton fixpoint problems on the variable X in $\mathcal{Q}_1$ of Examples 1 and 2 relative to the variable set $\mathcal{X} = \{X, Y\}$: $\langle \{a'\#X\}, \{Eq_1 := (a'\, b')(a\, c).X \approx_? X\}\rangle$ and $\langle \{a'\#X\}, \{Eq_2 := (a'\, b')(a\, b\, c\, d).X \approx_? X\}\rangle$. Since $a'\#X$ is in the freshness context, there is no combinatory solution with occurrences of the atoms in the permutation cycle $(a'\, b')$. For the cycles $(a\, c)$ and $(a\, b\, c\, d)$, in equations Eq_1 and Eq_2, possible solutions include, respectively:

– $\langle \nabla, \{X/(\overline{a} + \overline{c}) \star Z\}\rangle$, $\langle \nabla, \{X/(f\overline{a} + f\overline{c}) \star Z\}\rangle$, $\langle \nabla, \{X/([g]\overline{a} + [g]\overline{c}) \star Z\}\rangle$, for $\nabla = a, c, a', b'\#Z, a'\#X$;
– $\langle \nabla', \{X/(\overline{a} + \overline{c}) \star (\overline{b} + \overline{d})\}\rangle$, $\langle \nabla', \{(f\overline{a} + f\overline{c}) \star (f\overline{b} + f\overline{d})\}\rangle$, $\langle \nabla', \{([g]\overline{a} + [g]\overline{c}) \star ([g]\overline{b} + [g]\overline{d})\}\rangle$, for $\nabla' = a'\#X$.

Since the general C-matchers for pairs of these three solutions for Eq_1 and Eq_2 are respectively $\{Z/\overline{b} + \overline{d}\}$, $\{Z/f\overline{b} + f\overline{d}\}$ and $\{Z/[g]\overline{b} + [g]\overline{d}\}$, the combined solutions for both singleton fixpoint problems are those given for Eq_2.

Now, one proves that the set of solutions $[X]_{\mathcal{P}_G}$ is correct and complete.

Corollary 1 (Soundness and completeness of generated solutions for a variable). *Let $\mathcal{P} = \langle \Delta, P\rangle$ be a fixpoint problem. Any solution in $[X]_{\mathcal{P}_G}$ is a solution of each fixpoint equation for X in $\mathcal{P}$. If $\langle \nabla, \{X/s\}\rangle$ is a solution for each fixpoint equation for X in $\mathcal{P}$ then there exists $\langle \nabla', \{X/X\delta\}\rangle \in [X]_{\mathcal{P}_G}$ such that $\langle \nabla', \{X/X\delta\}\rangle \preceq \langle \nabla, \{X/s\}\rangle$.*

Proof. By Theorem 1 and Definition 6:
(Soundness) Each solution $\langle \nabla_i, \{X/t_i\}\rangle$ in $\langle \Delta, \{\pi_i.X \approx_? X\}\rangle_{Sol_G}$ is a correct solution for $\langle \Delta, \{\pi_i.X \approx_? X\}\rangle$, for $\pi_i \in \Pi_X$. Suppose $\langle \nabla', \{X/X\delta\}\rangle$ belongs to $[X]_{\mathcal{P}_G}$. Since δ is a C-unifier of terms t_i with variable X, we have that $X\delta \approx_C t_i\delta$, and also that $\nabla_i \vdash \pi(t_i) \approx_{\{\alpha,C\}} t_i$. Thus, $\nabla' \vdash \pi(t_i)\delta \approx_{\{\alpha,C\}} t_i\delta$ since by definition we also have that $\nabla' \vdash dom(\nabla|_X)\#X\delta$, because by construction for all $Y \in Var(X\delta)$, ∇' includes the freshness constraints $dom(\nabla''|_X)\#Y$ and ∇'' is an extension of ∇.
(Completeness) For $|\Pi_X| = k$, $i = 1..k$, there are $\langle \nabla_i, \{X/t_i\}\rangle \in \langle \Delta, \{\pi_i.X \approx_? X\}\rangle_{Sol_G}$, solution of $\langle \Delta, \{\pi_i.X \approx_? X\}\rangle$, such that $\langle \nabla_i, \{X/t_i\}\rangle \preceq \langle \nabla, \{X/s\}\rangle$.

Then, for each i, there exists a ∇_i s.t. $\nabla \vdash \nabla_i\lambda_i$ and $\nabla \vdash \{X/t_i\}\lambda_i \approx \{X/s\}$. One can choose each t_i in a way to satisfy $\cap_{i=1}^{k} Var(t_i) = \emptyset$, and then for $\lambda = \lambda_1 \cdots \lambda_k$ and $\nabla'' = \cup_{i=1}^{k}\nabla_i$, one also has $\nabla \vdash \nabla''\lambda$ and $\nabla \vdash \{X/t_i\}\lambda \approx \{X/s\}$.

Notice that $\langle \nabla, \lambda \rangle$ is a nominal C-unifier for the problem $\langle \nabla_i, \cup_{i=1}^{k}\{t_i \approx_? X\}\rangle$. Then, given δ, a most general C-unifier for $\{t_i =_? X\}_{i=1..k}$, it holds that there exists λ' such that $\nabla \vdash \delta\lambda' \approx \lambda$.

Let $\langle \nabla', \emptyset \rangle$ be a solution of $\langle \emptyset, \cup_{(a\#Y)\in\nabla''}\{a\#Y\delta\}\rangle$, then, by Definition 6, one has that $\langle \nabla', \{X/X\delta\}\rangle \in [X]_{\mathcal{P}_G}$, and so, since $\nabla \vdash \nabla''\lambda$, also that $\nabla \vdash \nabla''\delta\lambda'$, which is the same that $\nabla \vdash \nabla'\lambda'$. On the other hand, $X\delta \approx_C t_i\delta$ and then $\nabla \vdash s \approx_{\{\alpha,C\}} t_i\lambda \approx_{\{\alpha,C\}} t_i\delta\lambda' \approx_C X\delta\lambda'$, which implies $\nabla \vdash \{X/s\} \approx \{X/X\delta\}\lambda'$. Hence, $\langle \nabla', \{X/X\delta\}\rangle \preceq \langle \nabla, \{X/s\}\rangle$. □

Definition 9 (Generated Solutions for fixpoint problems). *Let $\mathcal{P}$ be a fixpoint problem. The set of generated solutions for $\mathcal{P}$, denoted as $[\mathcal{P}]_{Sol_G}$, is defined as the set that contains all solutions of the form*

$$\left\langle \bigcup_{X\in Var(P)} \nabla_X, \bigcup_{X\in Var(P)} \{X/s_X\} \right\rangle, \text{ where each } \langle \nabla_X, \{X/s_X\}\rangle \in [X]_{\mathcal{P}_G}.$$

Example 9 (Continuing Example 8). Consider the third singleton fixpoint problem on the variable Y in $\mathcal{Q}_1$ relative to $\mathcal{X} = \{X, Y\}$: $\langle\{a'\#Y\}, \{(a'\,b')(a\,b\,c).Y \approx_? Y\}\rangle$. There exists no possible combinatorial solution since $a'\#Y$ is in the freshness context and the length of permutation cycle $(a\,b\,c)$ is not a power of two. The only possible solution is given as $\langle a, b, c, a', b'\#Y', \{Y/Y'\}\rangle$. Hence, using the solutions in Example 8 for the fixpoint equations on X, one has the following solutions for the fixpoint problem $\mathcal{Q}_1$, where $\Delta = a', b'\#X, a, b, c, a', b'\#Y'$:

- $\langle \Delta, \{X/(\overline{a} + \overline{c}) \star (\overline{b} + \overline{d}), Y/Y'\}\rangle$
- $\langle \Delta, \{X/(f\overline{a} + f\overline{c}) \star (f\overline{b} + f\overline{d}), Y/Y'\}\rangle$
- $\langle \Delta, \{X/([g]\overline{a} + [g]\overline{c}) \star ([g]\overline{b} + [g]\overline{d}), Y/Y'\}\rangle$

A similar analysis can be done for the fixpoint problem $\mathcal{Q}_2$ in Example 1. Also, for the fixpoint equations $(a\,b).Y \approx_? Y$ and $(d\,c\,b\,a)(a'\,b').Y \approx_? Y$, the permutation cycle $(a'\,b')$ avoids any possible combinatorial solution with occurrences of the atoms a' or b'. Cycles $(a\,b)$ and $(d\,c\,b\,a)$ will allow combinatorial solutions for each of these equations, but we will see (Example 14) that they cannot be combined.

Corollary 2 (Soundness and completeness of generated solutions for fixpoint problems). *Let $\mathcal{P}$ be a fixpoint problem. Any solution in the set of solutions $[\mathcal{P}]_{Sol_G}$ is a correct solution of $\mathcal{P}$. For any $\langle \nabla, \delta\rangle$ solution of $\mathcal{P}$ there exist a pair $\langle \nabla', \sigma\rangle \in [\mathcal{P}]_{Sol_G}$ such that $\langle \nabla', \sigma\rangle \preceq \langle \nabla, \delta\rangle$.*

Proof. By Definition 9 and Corollary 1:

(Soundness) A solution of $\mathcal{P}$ is of the form $\left\langle \bigcup_{X\in Var(P)} \nabla_X, \bigcup_{X\in Var(P)}\{X/s_X\}\right\rangle$, where each $\langle \nabla_X, \{X/s_X\}\rangle \in [X]_{\mathcal{P}_G}$ is a correct solution for all fixpoint equations in $\mathcal{P}$ for the variable X, this completes the soundness proof.

(Completeness) Let $\mathcal{P} = \{\langle \Delta, \cup_{i=1}^{k}\{\pi_{i_1}.X_1 \approx_? X_1\}_{\pi_{i_1} \in \Pi_{X_1}}\}\rangle$ and $\langle \nabla, \delta \rangle$ be a solution of $\mathcal{P}$. There exist more general solutions $\langle \nabla_j, \{X_j/t_j\}\rangle \in [X_j]_{\mathcal{P}_G}$, for $j = 1, \ldots, k$; i.e., $\langle \nabla_j, \{X_j/t_j\}\rangle \preceq \langle \nabla, \delta \rangle$; hence, there is solution for $\mathcal{P}$ of the form $\langle \bigcup_j \nabla_j, \bigcup_j \{X_j/t_j\}\rangle$ is in $[\mathcal{P}]_{Sol_G}$ and $\langle \bigcup_j \nabla_j, \bigcup_j \{X_j/t_j\}\rangle \preceq \langle \nabla, \delta \rangle$. □

A greedy procedure for the generation of solutions in $[X]_{\mathcal{P}}$ proceeds as follows. Follow the construction of generated solutions in Definition 6 for each fixpoint problem $\langle \nabla, \pi_i.X \approx_? X\rangle$ in P, where $\pi_i \in \Pi_X$, as given in Lemma 1; for each generated solution $\langle \nabla', \{X/s\}\rangle$ build the freshness context $\nabla'' = \nabla' \cup \bigcup_{Y \in Var(s)} dom(\nabla|_X)\#Y \cup dom(\Pi_X)\#Y$ and check whether $\langle \nabla'', \{X/s\}\rangle$ is a solution for all $\langle \nabla, \pi_i.X \approx_? X\rangle$, for $\pi_i \in \Pi_X$. Here, $dom(\Pi_X)\#Y$ abbreviates $\cup_{\pi_i \in \Pi_X} dom(\pi_i)\#Y$.

4 Improvements in the Generation of Solutions

The greedy procedure can be improved eliminating generation of solution of non interesting permutation cycles in Π_X, according to the observations below.

In first place, notice that according to the theory of pseudo-cycles, we are interested in building solutions with atoms that occur only in permutation cycles of length a power of two in all permutations $\pi \in \Pi_X$.

In second place, notice that if there exist permutation cycles of length a power of two $\kappa_i \in \pi_i$ and $\kappa_j \in \pi_j$, for $\pi_i, \pi_j \in \Pi_X$, such that $dom(\pi_i) \cap dom(\pi_j) \neq \emptyset$, $dom(\pi_i) \backslash dom(\pi_j) \neq \emptyset$ and $dom(\pi_j) \backslash dom(\pi_i) \neq \emptyset$, then there might not be possible solutions with occurrences of atom terms in the domain of π_i and/or π_j for the fixpoint equations related with permutations π_i and π_j. The simplest example is given by permutation cycles $(a\,b)$ and $(a\,c)$. The precise relation between permutation cycles that allows for construction of solutions for all permutations in Π_X is given in the next definition.

Definition 10 (Permutation factor). *A permutation π is said to be an* n-factor *of a permutation π' whenever there exists n such that $\pi^n = \pi'$.*

Example 10. Let $\pi = (a\,b\,c\,d\,e\,f\,g\,h)$. The odd powers of π, π^1, $\pi^3 = (a\,d\,g\,b\,e\,h\,c\,f)$, $\pi^5 = (a\,f\,c\,h\,e\,b\,g\,d)$ and $\pi^7 = (a\,h\,g\,f\,e\,d\,c\,b)$ are the only factors of π.

Remark 4. For a permutation cycle κ of length 2^k, the factors corresponding to permutation cycles of the same length are exactly the permutations cycles κ^p, for p odd such that $0 < p < 2^k$; also, if λ is a p-factor of κ then λ is the q-factor of κ, where q is the minimum odd number such that $0 < q < 2^k$ and $p \cdot q = 1$ modulo 2^k. For instance, if κ is a permutation cycle of length 2^4, κ^3, κ^5, κ^7, etc., are respectively the 11- 13- and 7-factors, etc., of κ.

The key observation about permutation cycles κ and λ, of respective lengths 2^k and 2^l, for $k \geq l \geq 0$, such that, $\kappa^{2^{k-l}}$ contains a permutation cycle, say ν, that is a p-factor of λ, is that this happens if and only if regarding elements in $dom(\lambda)$, possible generated solutions from both permutation cycles coincide.

Indeed, first, notice that either $l = 0$ and then $\nu = \lambda$ or $l > 0$ and $\lambda^{2^{l-1}}$ consists of 2^{l-1} permutation cycles of length two; second, observe that if $l > 0$, then $\lambda^{2^{l-1}} = \nu^{p \cdot 2^{l-1}} = \nu^{2^{l-1}}$, since p is an odd number (such that $0 < p < 2^l$). Moreover, notice that $\kappa^{2^{k-l}}|_{dom(\lambda)} = \nu$, that implies that $\kappa^{2^{k-1}}|_{dom(\lambda)} = \nu^{2^{l-1}}$. Thus, the permutation cycles of length two generated from κ and λ, restricted to $dom(\lambda)$ are the same, which implies that commutative combinations built (according to Definition 5) regarding to the elements in $dom(\lambda)$ are the same.

Example 11. Consider $\kappa = (a\,b\,c\,d\,e\,f\,g\,h)$ and $\lambda = (a\,g\,e\,c)$. Notice that $\kappa^2 = (a\,c\,e\,g)(b\,d\,f\,h)$ and λ is a 3-factor of $\nu = (a\,c\,e\,g)$. Then $\lambda^2 = \nu^{3 \cdot 2} = \nu^2 = (a\,e)(c\,g)$. Also, notice that the unitary epc's built from λ and ν are the same.

Definition 11 (Permutation cycles in the top of Π_X). *Let Π_X be the set of permutations for fixpoint equations on the variable X in a fixpoint problem. A permutation cycle $\kappa \in \pi \in \Pi_X$ is in the top of Π_X, whenever for all atoms $a \in dom(\kappa)$ and all $\pi' \in \Pi_X$, if $a \in dom(\pi')$, and a is an element in a permutation cycle λ in π', then there exists a natural m such that the permutation cycle of the element a in π^{2^m}, say ν, is a factor of the permutation cycle λ.*

Example 12. Consider the permutations $\pi_1 = (a\,b\,c\,d\,e\,f\,g\,h)$, $\pi_2 = (a\,g\,e\,c)(b\,f)$ and $\pi_3 = (a\,e)(c\,g)(d\,h)$. The permutation cycle π_1 is in the top of the set of permutations; indeed, notice that all permutation cycles in all permutations appear as a factor in powers of two of π_1: $\pi_1^0 = (a\,b\,c\,d\,e\,f\,g\,h)$; $\pi_1^2 = (a\,c\,e\,g)(b\,d\,f\,h)$; $\pi_1^4 = (a\,e)(c\,g)(b\,f)(d\,h)$; $\pi_1^8 = (a)(e)(c)(g)(b)(f)(d)(h)$.

Theorem 3 (Atoms of interest in fixpoint problems on a variable). *Let Π_X be the set of permutations for fixpoint equations on the variable X in a fixpoint problem. Only the set of atoms in the domain of permutation cycles in the top of Π_X might occur in solutions of all fixpoint equations on X.*

Proof. Only atoms that are in permutation cycles of length a power of two in all permutations $\pi \in \Pi_X$ might occur in solutions of all fixpoint equations on X. Suppose a is an atom that only occurs in permutation cycles of length a power of two for all $\pi \in \Pi_X$ and let κ be a permutation cycle in Π_X of maximal length, say 2^k, with $a \in dom(\kappa)$. Suppose λ is a permutation cycle in ϕ, for some $\phi \in \Pi_X$, with $a \in dom(\lambda)$ and let 2^l be the length of λ. Only if λ is a factor of a permutation cycle in $\pi^{2^{k-l}}$, say ν such that $\nu^p = \lambda$, the epc's built from λ (and from κ) will maintain the invariants required, restricted to the atoms in $dom(\lambda)$, that is for an epc built from λ of the form $(A_0 \ldots A_{2^m-1})$, where $m \leq l$, $\phi(A_i) \approx_C A_{i+1}$ and $\phi^{2^{l-m}}(A_i) \approx_C A_i$, where $i+1$ reads modulo 2^m. This also holds for λ. Hence, since ν is a p-factor of λ (and also, $\pi^{2^{k-l}}|_{dom(\lambda)} = \nu$), one has that $\nu^p(A_i) \approx_C A_{i+1}$ and $\nu^{p \cdot 2^{l-m}}(A_i) \approx_C A_i$. If the epc is of length two, that is it is of the form $(A_0\,A_1)$, we have $m = 1$ and $\nu^{p \cdot 2^{l-1}}(A_i) \approx_C A_i$, for $i = 0, 1$, and since p is odd, this implies that $\nu^{2^{l-1}}(A_i) \approx_C A_i$, for $i = 0, 1$. This condition also holds for π, since $(\pi^{2^{k-l}}|_{dom(\nu)})^{2^{l-1}} = (\nu)^{2^{l-1}}$; hence, $\pi^{2^{k-1}}(A_i) = A_{i+1}$, for $i = 0, 1$. If κ is not a permutation cycle in the top of Π_X, then there exists some permutation cycle $\lambda \in \phi \in \Pi_X$, such that $a \in dom(\kappa) \cap dom(\lambda)$, 2^l is the length of λ, but the permutation cycle of length 2^l in $\kappa^{2^{k-l}}$, say ν, such that $a \in dom(\nu)$ is not a factor of λ. Thus, since $\nu^{2^{l-1}} \neq \lambda^{2^{l-1}}$ atoms in the domains of ν and λ cannot be combined uniformly to build common solutions for κ and λ (i.e., for π and ψ).

To finish we show how a common solution can be built when κ is in the top of Π_X. Suppose that (A) is a unitary epc built from λ by successive applications of case 3.a.i. of Definition 5 halving in each step the length of the epc. We have that $\lambda(A) = A$. It is possible to generate an epc for κ of the form $(A\,\kappa(A)\,\kappa^2(A)\,\ldots\,\kappa^{2^{k-l}-1}(A))$. From this epc it is possible to build a unitary epc by successive applications of case 3.a.i. of Definition 5, first obtaining $(A \star_1 \kappa^{2^{K-l-1}}(A)\;\kappa(A) \star_1 \kappa^{2^{k-l-1}+1}(A) \ldots\; \kappa^{2^{k-l-1}-1}(A) \star_1 \kappa^{2^{k-l}-1}(A))$, and so on until a unitary epc of the form $((\cdots((A \star_1 B_1) \star_2 B_2)\cdots) \star_{k-l} B_{k-l})$ is obtained where the B_i's, for $1 \leq i \leq k-l$ are adequate combinations of the terms $\kappa(A), \ldots \kappa^{2^{k-l}-1}(A)$ according to the constructions of epc's. From this epc one has the solution for $\pi.X \approx_? X$ of the form $\langle \emptyset, \{X/(\cdots((A \star_1 B_1) \star_2 B_2)\cdots) \star_{k-l} B_{k-l}\}\rangle$, where $\star_j$, for $j = 1, \ldots, l$ are commutative symbols. Using the unitary cycle (A) for λ and cases 1 and 3.a.ii of Definition 5 one can generate the unitary epc $((\cdots((A \star_1 Y_1) \star_2 Y_2)\cdots) \star_{k-l} Y_{k-l})$ which gives the solution $\langle \nabla, \{X/(\cdots((A \star_1 Y_1) \star_2 Y_2)\cdots) \star_{k-l} Y_{k-l}\}\rangle$ for λ, where $\nabla = \{dom(\lambda) \# Y_j | 1 \leq j \leq l\}$. The C-unification problem $\langle \nabla, X \approx_? (\cdots((A \star_1 B_1) \star_2 B_2)\cdots) \star_{k-l} B_{k-l}, X \approx_? (\cdots((A \star_1 Y_1) \star_2 Y_2)\cdots) \star_{k-l} Y_{k-l}\}\rangle$ unifies with solution $\langle \emptyset, \{X/(\cdots((A \star_1 B_1) \star_2 B_2)\cdots) \star_{k-l} B_{k-l}\}\rangle$ which is a common solution for π and ϕ.

Example 13 (Continuing Example 12). First, notice that the permutation cycle $\pi_1 = (a\,b\,c\,d\,e\,f\,g\,h)$ is not in the top of $(a\,d\,e\,b\,g\,h\,c\,f)$; also, π_1 is neither in the top of $(a\,b\,c\,d)$ nor in the top of $(a\,i)$. Since π_1 is not a factor of π_2, solutions generated from the epc $(\bar{a}\,\bar{d}\,\bar{e}\,\bar{b}\,\bar{g}\,\bar{h}\,\bar{c}\,\bar{f})$ might not be solutions built for π_1; for instance, consider the unitary epc built for π_2, $(((\bar{a}\star\bar{g})\diamond(\bar{e}\star\bar{c}))\oplus((\bar{d}\star\bar{h})\diamond(\bar{b}\star\bar{f}))$, which is not a solution for π_1, since not $\pi_1((\bar{a}\star\bar{g})\diamond(\bar{e}\star\bar{c})) \approx_C (\bar{d}\star\bar{h})\diamond(\bar{b}\star\bar{f})$. Also, for the epc $(\bar{a}\,\bar{b}\,\bar{c}\,\bar{d})$: the permutation cycles in π_1^2 are $(a\,c\,e\,g)$ and $(b\,d\,f\,h)$, which give different solutions. For $(\bar{a}\,\bar{i})$, the permutation cycle $(a\,e)$ in π_i^4 will produce different solutions.

Now consider solutions of fixpoint equations $\pi_i.X \approx_? X$, for $i = 1, 2, 3$, where Π_X consists of the permutations $\pi_1 = (a\,b\,c\,d\,e\,f\,g\,h)$, $\pi_2 = (a\,g\,e\,c)(b\,f)$ and $\pi_3 = (a\,e)(c\,g)(d\,h)$. In this case, we have seen (Example 12) that π_1 is a permutation cycle in the top of Π_X. Among the solutions generated for $\pi_i.X \approx_? X$, for $i = 1, 2, 3$ through epc's we have, respectively:

$\langle \nabla_1, \{X/s_1 = ((\bar{a}+\bar{e})\star(\bar{c}+\bar{g}))\oplus((\bar{b}+\bar{f})\star(\bar{d}+\bar{h})\}\rangle$,
$\langle \nabla_2, \{X/s_2 = ((\bar{a}+\bar{e})\star(\bar{c}+\bar{g}))\oplus((\bar{b}+\bar{f})\star Y\}\rangle$ and
$\langle \nabla_3, \{X/s_3 = ((\bar{a}+\bar{e})\star(\bar{c}+\bar{g}))\oplus(Z\star(\bar{d}+\bar{h})\}\rangle$,

where $\nabla_1 = \emptyset$, $\nabla_2 = \{a\#Y, b\#Y, c\#Y, e\#Y, f\#Y, g\#Y\}$ and $\nabla_3 = \{a\#Z, c\#Z, d\#Z, e\#Z, g\#Z, h\#Z\}$, and the symbols $\oplus, \star$ and $+$ are commutative. The C-unification problem $\langle \nabla_1 \cup \nabla_2 \cup \nabla_3, \{X \approx_? s_1, X \approx_? s_2, X \approx_? s_3\}\rangle$ has solution $\{X/s_1, Y/\bar{d}+\bar{h}, Z/\bar{b}+\bar{f}\}$ with the respective freshness constraints; thus, restricting this solution to the freshness constraints on X we have the common solution $\langle \emptyset, \{X/s_1\}\rangle$.

Example 14 (Continuing Example 9). As we saw in Example 9, the fixpoint equations $(a\,b).Y \approx_? Y$ and $(d\,c\,b\,a)(a'\,b').Y \approx_? Y$ in the fixpoint problem $\mathcal{Q}_2$, have no possible combinatorial solution with occurrences of the atoms a' or b'. By Theorem 3, cycles $(a\,b)$ and $(d\,c\,b\,a)$ will not give rise to possible combinatorial solutions for both fixpoint equations. Hence, there is no feasible combinatory solution for this fixpoint problem. Therefore, the unique possible solution for $\mathcal{Q}_2$ is $\langle\{a', b'\#X, a, b, c, d, a', b'\#Y\}, \{X/(a\,c)(a'\,b').Y\}\rangle$.

The greedy generation algorithm can then be improved by generating solutions only for the atoms in permutation cycles in the top of Π_X.

5 Conclusions and future work

We presented a procedure to generate solutions of fixpoint nominal C-unification problems modulo commutativity. The procedure is proved to be sound and complete. This result is relevant to provide a sound and complete procedure to generate solutions of nominal C-unification problems, which consists of an initial phase in which nominal C-unification problems are transformed into an equivalent finite set of fixpoint problems, as described in [4], and a second phase that generates a potentially infinite set of independent solutions, presented in this paper, based on combinatorial properties of permutations.

Additional improvements of the generation procedure should be investigated exhaustively, as well as possible extensions of nominal unification and matching, and nominal narrowing modulo other equational theories of interest.

References

1. Aoto, T., Kikuchi, v: A rule-based procedure for equivariant nominal unification. In: Pre-proceeding of Higher-Order Rewriting (HOR), pp. 1–5 (2016)
2. Aoto, T., Kikuchi, K.: Nominal confluence tool. In: Olivetti, N., Tiwari, A. (eds.) IJCAR 2016. LNCS (LNAI), vol. 9706, pp. 173–182. Springer, Cham (2016). doi:10.1007/978-3-319-40229-1_12
3. Ayala-Rincón, M., Carvalho-Segundo, W., Fernández, M., Nantes-Sobrinho, D.: A formalisation of nominal equivalence with associative-commutative function symbols. ENTCS **332**, 21–38 (2017). Post-proceeding of Eleventh Logical and Semantic Frameworks with Applications (LSFA)
4. Ayala-Rincón, M., Carvalho-Segundo, W., Fernández, M., Nantes-Sobrinho, D.: Nominal C-Unification. Av (2017). http://ayala.mat.unb.br/publications.html

5. Ayala-Rincón, M., Fernández, M., Nantes-Sobrinho, D.: Nominal narrowing. In: Proceedings of 1st International Conference on Formal Structures for Computation and Deduction (FSCD), vol. 52 of LIPIcs, pp. 1–16. Schloss Dagstuhl - Leibniz-Zentrum für Informatik (2016)
6. Ayala-Rincón, M., Fernández, M., Rocha-oliveira, A.C.: Completeness in PVS of a nominal unification algorithm. ENTCS **323**, 57–74 (2016)
7. Baader, F., Nipkow, T.: Term Rewriting and All That. CUP, Cambridge (1998)
8. Cheney, J.: Equivariant unification. J. Autom. Reason. **45**, 267–300 (2010)
9. Fernández, M., Gabbay, M.J.: Nominal rewriting. Inf. Comput. **205**(6), 917–965 (2007)
10. Schmidt-Schauß, M., Kutsia, T., Levy, J., Villaret, M.: Nominal unification of higher order expressions with recursive let. CoRR, abs/1608.03771 (2016)
11. Pitts, A.M.: Nominal logic, a first order theory of names and binding. Inf. Comput. **186**(2), 165–193 (2003)
12. Sagan, B.E.: The Symmetric Group: Representations, Combinatorial Algorithms, and Symmetric Functions. Graduate Texts in Mathematics, vol. 203, 2nd edn. Springer, New York (2001)
13. Siekmann, J.: Unification of commutative terms. In: Ng, E.W. (ed.) Symbolic and Algebraic Computation. LNCS, vol. 72, pp. 22–22. Springer, Heidelberg (1979). doi:10.1007/3-540-09519-5_53
14. Urban, C.: Nominal unification revisited. In: Proceedings of International Workshop on Unification (UNIF), vol. 42 of EPTCS, pp. 1–11 (2010)
15. Urban, C., Pitts, A.M., Gabbay, M.J.: Nominal unification. Theor. Comput. Sci. **323**(1–3), 473497 (2004)

Decidable Verification of Decision-Theoretic GOLOG

Jens Claßen[1(✉)] and Benjamin Zarrieß[2]

[1] Knowledge-Based Systems Group, RWTH Aachen University, Aachen, Germany
classen@kbsg.rwth-aachen.de

[2] Theoretical Computer Science, TU Dresden, Dresden, Germany
benjamin.zarriess@tu-dresden.de

Abstract. The GOLOG agent programming language is a powerful means to express high-level behaviours in terms of programs over actions defined in a Situation Calculus theory. Its variant DTGOLOG includes decision-theoretic aspects in the form of stochastic (probabilistic) actions and reward functions. In particular for physical systems such as robots, verifying that a program satisfies certain desired temporal properties is often crucial, but undecidable in general, the latter being due to the language's high expressiveness in terms of first-order quantification, range of action effects, and program constructs. Recent results for classical GOLOG show that by suitably restricting these aspects, the verification problem becomes decidable for a non-trivial fragment that retains a large degree of expressiveness. In this paper, we lift these results to the decision-theoretic case by providing an abstraction mechanism for reducing the infinite-state Markov Decision Process induced by the DTGOLOG program to a finite-state representation, which then can be fed into a state-of-the-art probabilistic model checker.

1 Introduction

When it comes to the design and programming of an autonomous agent, the GOLOG [12] family of action languages offers a powerful means to express high-level behaviours in terms of complex programs whose basic building blocks are the primitive actions described in a Situation Calculus [16] action theory. GOLOG's biggest advantage perhaps is the fact that a programmer can freely combine imperative control structures with non-deterministic constructs, leaving it to the system to resolve non-determinism in a suitable manner. Its extension DTGOLOG [2,17] includes decision-theoretic aspects in the form of stochastic (probabilistic) actions and reward functions, essentially expressing a form of (infinite-state) Markov Decisions Process (MDP) [15].

In particular when GOLOG is used to control physical robots, it is often crucial to verify a program against some specification of desired behaviour, for example in order to ensure liveness and safety properties, typically expressed by means of temporal formulas. Unfortunately, the general verification problem for GOLOG is undecidable due to the language's high expressivity in terms of first-order quantification, range of action effects, and program constructs. For this

C. Dixon and M. Finger (Eds.): FroCoS 2017, LNCS 10483, pp. 227–243, 2017.
DOI: 10.1007/978-3-319-66167-4_13

reason, there have recently been endeavours to identify restricted, but non-trivial fragments of GOLOG where verification (and hence other reasoning tasks such as projection) becomes decidable, while a great deal of expressiveness is retained. In [20] we presented one such result for a class of action theories, called acyclic, that allows for non-local effects, i.e. where actions may affect an unbounded number of objects that are not explicitly mentioned as action parameters. Decidability of verification is achieved by restricting dependencies between fluents in successor state axioms, which allows for a wide range of applications that includes the well-known briefcase domain [14].

So far, to the best of our knowledge, the verification of temporal properties of decision-theoretic GOLOG programs has not received any attention, even though in most practical applications one has to deal with uncertainty, e.g. in the form of actions failing with a certain probability and not showing the desired effects. In this paper, we lift the above mentioned decidability result on acyclic theories to the decision-theoretic case by providing an abstraction mechanism for reducing the infinite-state MDP induced by a DTGOLOG program to a finite-state representation, which then can be fed into any state-of-the-art probabilistic model checker such as PRISM [10] and STORM [4].

2 Preliminaries

2.1 The Logic $\mathcal{ES}$

We use a fragment of the first-order action logic $\mathcal{ES}$ [11], a variant of the Situation Calculus that uses modal operators instead of situation terms to express what is true after a number of actions has occurred. Not only is the syntax of $\mathcal{ES}$ in our view more readable, but its special semantics also makes proofs for many semantic properties simpler, while retaining much of the expressive power and main benefits of the original Situation Calculus. In particular, this includes the usage of *Basic Action Theories* (BATs) [16] to encode dynamic domains.

As we aim at decidability, we further have to restrict ourselves to a decidable fragment of FOL as base logic, as otherwise reasoning about theories not involving actions, programs and temporal properties would be undecidable already. For this purpose we use C^2, the *two-variable fragment of FOL with equality and counting*, an expressive fragment that subsumes most description logics.

Syntax. There are *terms* of sort *object*, *number* and *action*. Variables of sort object are denoted by symbols $x, y, \ldots$, of sort number by p, r, and of sort action by a. N_O is a countably infinite set of *object constant symbols*, N_N the countable set of rational numbers, and N_A a countably infinite set of *action function symbols* with arguments of sort object. We denote the set of all ground terms (also called *standard names*) of sort object, number and action by $\mathcal{N}_O$, $\mathcal{N}_N$, and $\mathcal{N}_A$, respectively.

Formulas are built using *fluent* predicate symbols (predicates that may vary as the result of actions) with at most two arguments of sort object, and equality, using the usual logical connectives, quantifiers, and counting quantifiers.

In addition we have the two special fluents $Prob(a_s, a_n, p)$ (taking two actions a_s, a_n and a number p as arguments), expressing that stochastic action a_s can have outcome a_n with probability p, and $Reward(r)$ (taking a number r as argument), saying that the reward in the current situation is r. Furthermore, there are two modalities for referring to future situations: $\Box\phi$ says that ϕ holds after any sequence of actions, and $[t]\phi$ means that ϕ holds after executing action t.

A formula is called *fluent formula* if it contains no $\Box$, no $[\cdot]$, no *Prob* and no *Reward* (i.e. such formulas talk about the current state of the world and do not involve dynamic or decision-theoretic aspects). A *C^2-fluent formula* is a fluent formula that contains no terms of sort action and at most two variables. A *sentence* or *closed formula* is a formula without free variables.

Semantics. A situation is a finite sequence (history) of actions. Let $\mathcal{Z} := \mathcal{N}_A^*$ be the set of all situations (including the empty sequence $\langle\rangle$) and $\mathcal{P}_F$ the set of all *primitive formulas* $F(n_1, ..., n_k)$, where F is a regular k-ary fluent with $0 \leq k \leq 2$ and the n_i are object standard names, together with all expressions of form $Prob(t_1, t_2, c_1)$ and $Reward(c_2)$, where $t_1, t_2 \in \mathcal{N}_A$ and $c_1, c_2 \in \mathcal{N}_N$. A *world* w then maps primitive formulas and situations to truth values:

$$w : \mathcal{P}_F \times \mathcal{Z} \to \{0, 1\}.$$

The set of all worlds is denoted by $\mathcal{W}$.

Definition 1 (Truth of Formulas). *Given a world $w \in \mathcal{W}$ and a closed formula ψ, we define $w \models \psi$ as $w, \langle\rangle \models \psi$, where for any $z \in \mathcal{Z}$:*

1. $w, z \models F(n_1, \ldots, n_k)$ *iff* $w[F(n_1, \ldots, n_k), z] = 1$;
2. $w, z \models (n_1 = n_2)$ *iff* n_1 *and* n_2 *are identical;*
3. $w, z \models \psi_1 \wedge \psi_2$ *iff* $w, z \models \psi_1$ *and* $w, z \models \psi_2$;
4. $w, z \models \neg\psi$ *iff* $w, z \not\models \psi$;
5. $w, z \models \forall x.\phi$ *iff* $w, z \models \phi^x_n$ *for all* $n \in \mathcal{N}_x$;
6. $w, z \models \exists^{\leq m} x.\phi$ *iff* $|\{n \in \mathcal{N}_x \mid w, z \models \phi^x_n\}| \leq m$;
7. $w, z \models \exists^{\geq m} x.\phi$ *iff* $|\{n \in \mathcal{N}_x \mid w, z \models \phi^x_n\}| \geq m$;
8. $w, z \models \Box\psi$ *iff* $w, z \cdot z' \models \psi$ *for all* $z' \in \mathcal{Z}$;
9. $w, z \models [t]\psi$ *iff* $w, z \cdot t \models \psi$.

Above, $\mathcal{N}_x$ refers to the set of all standard names of the same sort as x. Moreover ϕ^x_n denotes the result of simultaneously replacing all free occurrences of x in ϕ by n. Note that by rule 2, the unique names assumption for constants is part of our semantics. We use the notation $\boldsymbol{x}$ and $\boldsymbol{y}$ for sequences of object variables and $\boldsymbol{v}$ for a sequence of object terms. We understand $\vee$, $\exists$, $\supset$, and $\equiv$ as the usual abbreviations.

2.2 Action Theories

Definition 2 (Basic Action Theories). *A C^2-basic action theory (C^2-BAT) $\mathcal{D} = \mathcal{D}_0 \cup \mathcal{D}_{post}$ is a set of axioms that describes the dynamics of a specific application domain, where*

1. $\mathcal{D}_0$, the initial theory, *is a finite set of* C^2*-fluent sentences describing the initial state of the world;*
2. $\mathcal{D}_{post}$ *is a finite set of* successor state axioms *(SSAs), one for each fluent relevant to the application domain, incorporating Reiter's [16] solution to the frame problem to encode action effects, of the form*

$$\forall a.\forall \boldsymbol{x}.\Box\big(([a]F(\boldsymbol{x})) \equiv \gamma_F^+ \vee \big(F(\boldsymbol{x}) \wedge \neg\gamma_F^-\big)\big)$$

where the positive effect condition γ_F^+ *and* negative effect condition γ_F^- *are fluent formulas that are (possibly empty) disjunctions of formulas of the form* $\exists \boldsymbol{y}.(a = A(\boldsymbol{v}) \wedge \phi \wedge \phi')$ *such that*
   (a) $\exists \boldsymbol{y}.(a = A(\boldsymbol{v}) \wedge \phi \wedge \phi')$ *contains the free variables* $\boldsymbol{x}$ *and* a *and no other free variables;*
   (b) $A(\boldsymbol{v})$ *is an action term and* $\boldsymbol{v}$ *contains* $\boldsymbol{y}$*;*
   (c) ϕ *is a fluent formula with no terms of sort action and the number of variable symbols in it not among* $\boldsymbol{v}$ *or bound in* ϕ *is less or equal two;*
   (d) ϕ' *is a fluent formula with free variables among* $\boldsymbol{v}$*, no action terms, and at most two bound variables.*

   ϕ *is called* effect descriptor *and* ϕ' context condition.

The restrictions 2a and 2b on SSAs are without loss of generality and describe the usual syntactic form of SSAs. Intuitively, the effect descriptor ϕ defines a set of (pairs of) objects that are added to or deleted from the relational fluent F when $A(\boldsymbol{v})$ is executed. If free occurrences of variables in ϕ that appear as arguments of $A(\boldsymbol{v})$ are instantiated, condition 2c ensures definability of the (instantiated) effect descriptor in our base logic C^2. In contrast to the effect descriptor, the context condition ϕ' only tells us *whether* $A(\boldsymbol{v})$ has an effect on F, but not *which* objects are affected. Condition 2d again ensures that after instantiation of the action, the context condition is a sentence in C^2. The variables $\boldsymbol{x}$ mentioned in 2a may hence have free occurrences in ϕ but not in ϕ'.

Note that for simplicity we do not include precondition axioms, again without loss of generality: To ensure that action t only gets executed when precondition ϕ_t holds, simply precede every occurrence of t in the program expression (cf. Sect. 2.3) by a test for ϕ_t.

For representing the decision-theoretic aspects, we assume that action function symbols are subdivided into two disjoint subsets, *deterministic* actions and *stochastic* actions. We then associate every stochastic action with a probability distribution over a finite number of possible outcomes in the form of deterministic actions. Moreover, (state-based) rewards are represented by assigning numeric values to situations:

Definition 3 (Decision-Theoretic BATs). *A* C^2-decision-theoretic action theory *(*C^2*-DTBAT)* $\mathcal{DDT} = \mathcal{D} \cup \mathcal{D}_{prob} \cup \mathcal{D}_{reward}$ *extends a BAT* $\mathcal{D}$ *over deterministic actions by*

1. $\mathcal{D}_{prob}$*, an axiom of the form* $\Box Prob(a_s, a_n, p) \equiv \phi$*, where* a_s *and* a_n *are action variables,* p *is a number variable, and* ϕ *is a disjunction of formulas of the form*

$$\exists \boldsymbol{x}.\ a_s = A(\boldsymbol{x}) \wedge \bigvee_i a_n = A_i(\boldsymbol{x}_i) \wedge p = c_i,$$

where A is a stochastic action, the A_i are deterministic actions defined in $\mathcal{D}$, the $\boldsymbol{x}_i$ are contained in $\boldsymbol{x}$, and the c_i are rational constants with $0 < c_i \leq 1$ and $\sum_i c_i = 1$. Furthermore, we assume that Prob is defined to be functional in the sense that for any ground action terms t_s and t_n, there is at most one c such that $Prob(t_s, t_n, c)$.

2. *$\mathcal{D}_{reward}$, an axiom of the form $\square Reward(r) \equiv \psi$, where ψ is a fluent formula with free variable r, no terms of sort action and at most two bound variables. Reward is assumed to be partially functional, i.e. in any situation there is at most one r such that $Reward(r)$ holds.*

Example 1. Consider a warehouse domain with *shelves* holding *boxes* containing *items.* The fluent $Broken(x)$ denotes that a box or item x is currently broken, $On(x, y)$ says that box or item x is currently on shelf y, and $Contains(x, y)$ is true for a box x containing an item y.

The agent is a robot that can move a box v from shelf s to shelf s' using the action $Move(v, s, s')$. We also have actions with undesired effects: $Drop(v, s)$ stands for dropping a box v from shelf s to the ground, causing all fragile objects in it to break if there is no bubble wrap in it. Finally, $Repair(s)$ is an action by means of which the robot can repair a box or an item that is not fragile.

Figure 2 exemplarily shows the effect conditions for $Broken(x)$ and $On(x, y)$. Effect descriptors are underlined with a solid line, context conditions with a dashed line. If for example the agent were to drop the *box* in an initial situation incompletely described by the axioms in Fig. 1, everything in it will break if the box contains no bubble wrap, i.e. the BAT entails

$$\begin{aligned}&\neg\exists x\big(Contains(box, x) \wedge BubbleWrap(x)\big)\\&\quad\supset [Drop(box)]\big(\forall y. Contains(box, y) \supset Broken(y)\big).\end{aligned}$$

$MoveS(v, s, s')$ is a stochastic action that has the desired effect in 90% of the cases, but there is a 10% chance to drop v from shelf s; having the unbroken vase on shelf s_1 gives a reward of 5, while on s_2 it gives a reward of 10:

$$\begin{aligned}&\square Prob(a_s, a_n, p) \equiv \exists v, s, s'.\, a_s = MoveS(v, s, s') \wedge\\&\big(a_n = Move(v, s, s') \wedge p = 0.9 \vee\\&\ a_n = Drop(v, s) \wedge p = 0.1\big)\\&\square Reward(r) \equiv\\&\big(On(vase, s_1) \wedge \neg Broken(vase) \wedge r = 5 \vee\\&\ On(vase, s_2) \wedge \neg Broken(vase) \wedge r = 10\big)\end{aligned}$$

2.3 DTGOLOG and the Verification Problem

In a GOLOG program over ground actions we combine actions, whose effects are defined in a C^2-BAT, and tests, using a set of programming constructs to define a complex action.

$$\begin{aligned}
&On(box, s_1),\\
&\forall x \exists^{\leq 1} y. On(x, y),\\
&\forall x.(BubbleWrap(x) \supset \neg Fragile(x)),\\
&Contains(box, vase),\\
&\forall x.(Contains(box, x) \supset Fragile(x))\\
&\forall y \exists^{\leq 1} x. Contains(x, y),
\end{aligned}$$

Fig. 1. Example initial theory

$$\begin{aligned}
\gamma^{+}_{Broken} &:= \exists v, s.\big(a = Drop(v, s) \wedge \underline{On(v, s) \wedge Contains(v, x) \wedge Fragile(x)} \wedge\\
&\qquad \underline{\neg \exists y. Contains(v, y) \wedge BubbleWrap(y)}\,\big);\\
\gamma^{-}_{Broken} &:= \exists s.(a = Repair(s) \wedge \underline{s = x \wedge \neg Fragile(x)});\\
\gamma^{+}_{On} &:= \exists v, s, s'.\big(a = Move(v, s, s') \wedge \underline{y = s' \ \wedge \big(Contains(v, x) \vee x = v\big)}\big);\\
\gamma^{-}_{On} &:= \exists v, s, s'.\big(a = Move(v, s, s') \wedge \underline{y = s \ \wedge \big(Contains(v, x) \vee x = v\big)}\big) \vee\\
&\qquad \exists v, s.\big(a = Drop(v, s) \wedge \underline{y = s \wedge \big(v = x \vee Contains(v, x)\big)}\big)
\end{aligned}$$

Fig. 2. Example effect conditions

Definition 4 (Programs). *A* program expression δ *is built according to the following grammar:*

$$\delta ::= t \mid \psi? \mid \delta;\delta \mid \delta|\delta \mid \delta^*$$

A program expression can thus be a (deterministic or stochastic) ground action term t*, a* test $\psi?$ *where* ψ *is a* C^2*-fluent sentence, or constructed from sub-programs by means of* sequence $\delta;\delta$, non-deterministic choice $\delta|\delta$, *and* non-deterministic iteration δ^*. *Furthermore,* ***if*** *statements and* **while** *loops can be defined as abbreviations in terms of these constructs:*

$$\begin{aligned}
\textbf{\textit{if}}\ \phi\ \textbf{\textit{then}}\ \delta_1\ \textbf{\textit{else}}\ \delta_2\ \textbf{\textit{endIf}} &\stackrel{def}{=} [\phi?; \delta_1] \mid [\neg\phi?; \delta_2]\\
\textbf{\textit{while}}\ \phi\ \textbf{\textit{do}}\ \delta\ \textbf{\textit{endWhile}} &\stackrel{def}{=} [\phi?; \delta]^*; \neg\phi?
\end{aligned}$$

A Golog program $\mathcal{G} = (\mathcal{D}, \delta)$ *consists of a* C^2*-BAT* $\mathcal{D} = \mathcal{D}_0 \cup \mathcal{D}_{post}$ *and a program expression* δ *where all fluents occurring in* $\mathcal{D}$ *and* δ *have an SSA in* $\mathcal{D}_{post}$.

To handle termination and failure of a program we use two 0-ary fluents $Final$ *and* $Fail$ *and two 0-ary action functions* ϵ *and* $\mathfrak{f}$ *and include the SSAs* $\Box[a]Final \equiv a = \epsilon \vee Final$ *and* $\Box[a]Fail \equiv a = \mathfrak{f} \vee Fail$ *in* $\mathcal{D}_{post}$. *Furthermore, we require that* $\neg Final \in \mathcal{D}_0$ *and* $\neg Fail \in \mathcal{D}_0$*, and that the fluents* $Final$*,* $Fail$ *and actions* ϵ *and* $\mathfrak{f}$ *do not occur in* δ.

Following [3] we define the transition semantics of programs meta-theoretically. First, consider program expressions that only contain deterministic actions. A *configuration* $\langle z, \rho\rangle$ consists of a situation $z \in \mathcal{Z}$ and a program expression ρ, where z represents the actions that have already been performed, while ρ is the program that remains to be executed. Execution of a program in a world $w \in \mathcal{W}$ yields a *transition relation* $\xrightarrow{w}$ *among configurations* defined inductively over program expressions, given by the smallest set that satisfies:

1. $\langle z, t\rangle \xrightarrow{w} \langle z \cdot t, \langle\rangle\rangle$;
2. $\langle z, \delta_1; \delta_2\rangle \xrightarrow{w} \langle z \cdot t, \gamma; \delta_2\rangle$, if $\langle z, \delta_1\rangle \xrightarrow{w} \langle z \cdot t, \gamma\rangle$;
3. $\langle z, \delta_1; \delta_2\rangle \xrightarrow{w} \langle z \cdot t, \delta'\rangle$, if $\langle z, \delta_1\rangle \in \mathsf{Fin}(w)$ and $\langle z, \delta_2\rangle \xrightarrow{w} \langle z \cdot t, \delta'\rangle$;
4. $\langle z, \delta_1 | \delta_2\rangle \xrightarrow{w} \langle z \cdot t, \delta'\rangle$, if $\langle z, \delta_1\rangle \xrightarrow{w} \langle z \cdot t, \delta'\rangle$ or $\langle z, \delta_2\rangle \xrightarrow{w} \langle z \cdot t, \delta'\rangle$;
5. $\langle z, \delta^*\rangle \xrightarrow{w} \langle z \cdot t, \gamma; \delta^*\rangle$, if $\langle z, \delta\rangle \xrightarrow{w} \langle z \cdot t, \gamma\rangle$.

The set of final configurations $\mathsf{Fin}(w)$ w.r.t. a world w is defined similarly as the smallest set such that:

1. $\langle z, \psi?\rangle \in \mathsf{Fin}(w)$ if $w, z \models \psi$;
2. $\langle z, \delta_1; \delta_2\rangle \in \mathsf{Fin}(w)$ if $\langle z, \delta_1\rangle \in \mathsf{Fin}(w)$ and $\langle z, \delta_2\rangle \in \mathsf{Fin}(w)$;
3. $\langle z, \delta_1 | \delta_2\rangle \in \mathsf{Fin}(w)$ if $\langle z, \delta_1\rangle \in \mathsf{Fin}(w)$ or $\langle z, \delta_2\rangle \in \mathsf{Fin}(w)$;
4. $\langle z, \delta^*\rangle \in \mathsf{Fin}(w)$.

The set of *failing configurations* w.r.t. a world w is given by

$$\mathsf{Fail}(w) := \{\langle z, \delta\rangle \mid \langle z, \delta\rangle \notin \mathsf{Fin}(w), \text{ there is no } \langle z \cdot t, \delta'\rangle \text{ s.t. } \langle z, \delta\rangle \xrightarrow{w} \langle z \cdot t, \delta'\rangle\}.$$

We now turn to the decision-theoretic case. A DTGOLOG *program* $\mathcal{G} = (\mathcal{DDT}, \delta)$ consists of a C^2-DTBAT $\mathcal{DDT} = \mathcal{D} \cup \mathcal{D}_{\text{prob}} \cup \mathcal{D}_{\text{reward}}$ and a program expression δ that only contains stochastic actions,[1] and where all fluents occurring in $\mathcal{DDT}$ and δ have an SSA in $\mathcal{D}_{\text{post}}$. Given a world $w \in \mathcal{W}$ with $w \models \mathcal{DDT}$, execution of δ in w induces an *infinite-state MDP w.r.t.* w given by $\mathsf{M}^w_\delta = \langle \mathsf{S}, \mathsf{s}^0, \mathsf{A}, \mathsf{P}, \mathsf{R}\rangle$, where

- the (infinite) set of states S is given by $\mathsf{Reach}(w, \delta_{\mathsf{det}})$, which denotes the set of configurations reachable from $\langle\langle\rangle, \delta_{\mathsf{det}}\rangle$ via $\xrightarrow{w}$, where δ_{det} is the program obtained by replacing every stochastic action $A(\boldsymbol{v})$ in δ by the expression $(A_1(\boldsymbol{v}_1)|\cdots|A_k(\boldsymbol{v}_k))$ such that the $A_i(\boldsymbol{v}_i)$ are all deterministic actions for which
$$w, z \models Prob(A(\boldsymbol{x}), A_i(\boldsymbol{x}_i), p)^{\boldsymbol{x}}_{\boldsymbol{v}};$$
- the initial state is $\mathsf{s}^0 = \langle\langle\rangle, \delta_{\mathsf{det}}\rangle$;
- the (finite) set of actions A are all (stochastic) ground action terms occurring in δ;

[1] Note that we can always simulate a deterministic action by a stochastic one that has only one outcome.

– the transition function $\mathsf{P} : \mathsf{S} \times \mathsf{A} \times \mathsf{S} \to \mathbb{R}$ is such that

$$\mathsf{P}(\langle z,\rho\rangle, t, \langle z\cdot t',\rho'\rangle) = \begin{cases} p, & w,z \models \mathit{Prob}(t,t',p) \\ & \text{and } \langle z,\rho\rangle \xrightarrow{w} \langle z\cdot t',\rho'\rangle \\ 1, & \langle z,\rho\rangle \in \mathsf{Fin}(w),\ t=t'=\rho'=\epsilon \\ 1, & \langle z,\rho\rangle \in \mathsf{Fail}(w),\ t=t'=\rho'=\mathfrak{f} \\ 0, & \text{otherwise} \end{cases}$$

– the reward function $\mathsf{R} : \mathsf{S} \to \mathbb{R}$ is given by

$$\mathsf{R}(\langle z,\rho\rangle) = \begin{cases} r, & w,z \models \mathit{Reward}(r) \\ 0, & \text{otherwise} \end{cases}$$

In addition, final and failing configurations are absorbing states, i.e. if s is reached by ϵ, then $\mathsf{P}(\mathsf{s},\epsilon,\mathsf{s}) = 1$, and if s is reached by $\mathfrak{f}$, then $\mathsf{P}(\mathsf{s},\mathfrak{f},\mathsf{s}) = 1$.

The non-determinism on the agent's side is resolved by means of a *policy* σ, which is a mapping $\sigma : \mathsf{S} \to \mathsf{A}$ such that $\mathsf{P}(\mathsf{s},\sigma(\mathsf{s}),\mathsf{s}') > 0$ for some $\mathsf{s}' \in \mathsf{S}$. An infinite path $\pi = \mathsf{s}_0 \xrightarrow{\mathsf{a}_1} \mathsf{s}_1 \xrightarrow{\mathsf{a}_2} \cdots$ is called a *σ-path* if $\sigma(\mathsf{s}_j) = \mathsf{a}_{j+1}$ for all $j \geq 0$. The j-th state s_j of any such path is denoted by $\pi[j]$. The *set of all σ-paths* starting in s is $\mathsf{Paths}^\sigma(\mathsf{s},\mathsf{M}^w_\delta)$.

Every policy σ induces a probability space Pr^σ_{s} on the sets of infinite paths starting in s, using the cylinder set construction [8]: For any finite path prefix $\pi_{\mathsf{fin}} = \mathsf{s}_0 \xrightarrow{\mathsf{a}_1} \mathsf{s}_1 \xrightarrow{\mathsf{a}_2} \cdots \mathsf{s}_n$, we define the probability measure

$$Pr^\sigma_{\mathsf{s}_0,\mathsf{fin}} = \mathsf{P}(\mathsf{s}_0,\mathsf{a}_1,\mathsf{s}_1)\cdot\mathsf{P}(\mathsf{s}_1,\mathsf{a}_2,\mathsf{s}_2)\cdot\ldots\cdot\mathsf{P}(\mathsf{s}_{n-1},\mathsf{a}_n,\mathsf{s}_n).$$

This extends to a unique measure Pr^σ_{s}.

Definition 5 (Temporal Properties of Programs). *To express temporal properties of probabilistic systems represented by* DTGOLOG *programs, we use a probabilistic variant of* CTL *called* PRCTL *[1], which extends* PCTL *[7] with rewards. However, in place of atomic propositions, we allow for C^2-fluent sentences ψ:*

$$\Phi ::= \psi \mid \neg\Phi \mid \Phi\wedge\Phi \mid \mathbf{P}_I[\Psi] \mid \mathbf{R}_J[\Phi] \tag{1}$$

$$\Psi ::= X\Phi \mid (\Phi\, U\, \Phi) \mid (\Phi\, U^{\leq k}\, \Phi) \tag{2}$$

Above, $I \subseteq [0,1]$ and J are intervals with rational bounds. We call formulas according to (1) state formulas, *and formulas according to (2)* path formulas. *Intuitively, $\mathbf{P}_I[\Psi]$ expresses that the probability of the set of paths satisfying Ψ lies in the interval I, while $\mathbf{R}_J[\Phi]$ says that the expected reward cumulated before reaching a state that satisfies Φ is in J. Rather than providing intervals explicitly, we often use abbreviations such as $\mathbf{P}_{\geq 0.9}[\Psi]$ to denote $\mathbf{P}_{[0.9,1]}[\Psi]$, $\mathbf{P}_{=1}[\Psi]$ for $\mathbf{P}_{[1,1]}[\Psi]$, or $\mathbf{P}_{>0}[\Psi]$ for $\mathbf{P}_{]0,1]}[\Psi]$.*

$(\Phi_1\, U^{\leq k}\, \Phi_2)$ is the step-bounded *version of the until operator, expressing that Φ_2 will hold within at most k steps, where Φ_1 holds in all states before. We use*

the usual abbreviations $F\Phi$ (eventually Φ) for $(\mathit{true}\, U \Phi)$ and $G\Phi$ (globally Φ) for $\neg F \neg \Phi$, as well as their corresponding step-bounded variants.

Let Φ be a temporal state formula, M_δ^w the infinite-state MDP of a program $\mathcal{G} = (\mathcal{D}, \delta)$ w.r.t. a world w with $w \models \mathcal{DDT}$, and $\mathsf{s} = \langle z, \rho \rangle \in \mathsf{S}$. Truth of Φ in $\mathsf{M}_\delta^w, \mathsf{s}$, denoted by $\mathsf{M}_\delta^w, \mathsf{s} \models \Phi$ is defined as follows:

- $\mathsf{M}_\delta^w, \mathsf{s} \models \psi$ *iff* $w, z \models \psi$;
- $\mathsf{M}_\delta^w, \mathsf{s} \models \neg \Phi$ *iff* $\mathsf{M}_\delta^w, \mathsf{s} \not\models \Phi$;
- $\mathsf{M}_\delta^w, \mathsf{s} \models \Phi_1 \wedge \Phi_2$ *iff* $\mathsf{M}_\delta^w, \mathsf{s} \models \Phi_1$ *and* $\mathsf{M}_\delta^w, \mathsf{s} \models \Phi_1$;
- $\mathsf{M}_\delta^w, \mathsf{s} \models \mathbf{P}_I[\Psi]$ *iff for all policies* σ, $Pr_{\mathsf{s}}^\sigma(\Psi) \in I$;
- $\mathsf{M}_\delta^w, \mathsf{s} \models \mathbf{R}_J[\Phi]$ *iff for all policies* σ, $ExpRew_{\mathsf{s}}^\sigma(\Phi) \in J$,

where

$$Pr_{\mathsf{s}}^\sigma(\Psi) = Pr_{\mathsf{s}}^\sigma(\{\pi \in \mathsf{Paths}^\sigma(\mathsf{s}, \mathsf{M}_\delta^w) \mid \mathsf{M}_\delta^w, \pi \models \Psi\})$$

and $ExpRew_{\mathsf{s}}^\sigma(\Phi)$ is the expectation (wrt. measure Pr_{s}^σ) of the random variable $X_\Phi(\pi) : \mathsf{Paths}^\sigma(\mathsf{s}, \mathsf{M}_\delta^w) \rightarrow \mathbb{R}_{\geq 0}$ such that for any path $\pi = \mathsf{s}_0 \xrightarrow{\mathsf{a}_1} \mathsf{s}_1 \xrightarrow{\mathsf{a}_2} \cdots$,

$$X_\Phi(\pi) = \begin{cases} 0, & \mathsf{M}_\delta^w, \mathsf{s}_0 \models \Phi \\ \infty, & \mathsf{M}_\delta^w, \mathsf{s}_i \not\models \Phi \ \forall\, i \in \mathbb{N} \\ \sum_{i=0}^{\min\{j \,\mid\, \mathsf{M}_\delta^w, \mathsf{s}_j \models \Phi\} - 1} \mathsf{R}(\mathsf{s}_i), & \textit{otherwise} \end{cases}$$

Let Ψ be a temporal path formula, M_δ^w and $\mathsf{s} = \langle z, \rho \rangle$ as above, and $\pi \in \mathsf{Paths}^\sigma(\mathsf{s}, \mathsf{M}_\delta^w)$ for some σ. Truth of Ψ in M_δ^w, π, denoted by $\mathsf{M}_\delta^w, \pi \models \Psi$, is defined as follows:

- $\mathsf{M}_\delta^w, \pi \models X\Phi$ *iff* $\mathsf{M}_\delta^w, \pi[1] \models \Phi$;
- $\mathsf{M}_\delta^w, \pi \models (\Phi_1\, U\, \Phi_2)$ *iff* $\exists i \geq 0 : \mathsf{M}_\delta^w, \pi[i] \models \Phi_2$ *and* $\forall j, 0 \leq j < i : \mathsf{M}_\delta^w, \pi[j] \models \Phi_1$;
- $\mathsf{M}_\delta^w, \pi \models (\Phi_1\, U^{\leq k}\, \Phi_2)$ *iff* $\exists i, k \geq i \geq 0 : \mathsf{M}_\delta^w, \pi[i] \models \Phi_2$ *and* $\forall j, 0 \leq j < i : \mathsf{M}_\delta^w, \pi[j] \models \Phi_1$.

Definition 6 (Verification Problem). *A temporal state formula Φ is* valid *in a program $\mathcal{G} = (\mathcal{DDT}, \delta)$ iff for all worlds $w \in \mathcal{W}$ with $w \models \mathcal{DDT}$ it holds that $\mathsf{M}_\delta^w, \mathsf{s}^0 \models \Phi$.*

Example 2. Assume that due to the fact that the action may fail, the agent decides to simply execute the $MoveS(box, s_1, s_2)$ action repeatedly until the desired situation is reached where the unbroken vase is on shelf s_2:

$$\delta = \textbf{while}\ \neg\big(On(vase, s_2) \wedge \neg Broken(vase)\big)\ \textbf{do}\ MoveS(box, s_1, s_2)\ \textbf{endWhile}$$

Temporal properties one might want to verify for this program expression could be whether it is very likely that this can be achieved within exactly one, at least k, or an arbitrary number of steps:

$$\mathbf{P}_{\geq 0.95}[\mathsf{X}(On(vase, s_2) \wedge \neg Broken(vase))] \tag{3}$$

$$\mathbf{P}_{\geq 0.95}[\mathsf{F}^{\leq k}(On(vase, s_2) \wedge \neg Broken(vase))] \tag{4}$$

$$\mathbf{P}_{\geq 0.95}[\mathsf{F}(On(vase, s_2) \wedge \neg Broken(vase))] \tag{5}$$

3 Decidability of Verification

We first note that in general:

Theorem 1. *The verification problem for* DTGOLOG *is undecidable.*

Proof. (sketch). In [20] it is shown that given a two-counter machine M, a GOLOG program and BAT can be constructed where $\mathsf{EF}Halt$ is valid iff M halts, which is undecidable. Since regular GOLOG programs are a subset of DTGOLOG, and since the corresponding temporal property can be expressed as $\mathbf{P}_{]0,1]}[\mathsf{F}Halt]$ in PRCTL, we also get undecidability in the decision-theoretic case.

3.1 Fluent Dependencies and Acyclic Theories

One source of undecidability lies in cyclic dependencies between fluents in the effect descriptors of SSAs.

Definition 7 (Fluent Dependencies). *The* fluent dependency graph $G_{\mathcal{D}}$ *for a C^2-BAT $\mathcal{D}$ consists of a set of nodes, one for each fluent in $\mathcal{D}$. There is a directed edge (F, F') from fluent F to fluent F' iff there is a disjunct $\exists \boldsymbol{y}.(a = A(\boldsymbol{v}) \wedge \phi \wedge \phi')$ in γ_F^+ or γ_F^- such that F' occurs in the effect descriptor ϕ. We call $\mathcal{D}$* acyclic *iff $G_{\mathcal{D}}$ is acyclic. The* fluent depth *of an acyclic action theory $\mathcal{D}$, denoted by $\mathsf{fd}(\mathcal{D})$, is the length of the longest path in $G_{\mathcal{D}}$. The* fluent depth of F w.r.t. $\mathcal{D}$*, $\mathsf{fd}_{\mathcal{D}}(F)$, is the length of the longest path in $G_{\mathcal{D}}$ starting in F.*

While the BAT used in the construction for the undecidability proof has a cyclic dependency graph, the one for Example 1 is acyclic (with fluent depth 2), as shown in Fig. 3. Note that only effect descriptors are relevant. Important special cases of acyclic action theories are the *local-effect* ones [18] (corresponding to fluent depth 0) and the *context-free* [13] (fluent depth 1).

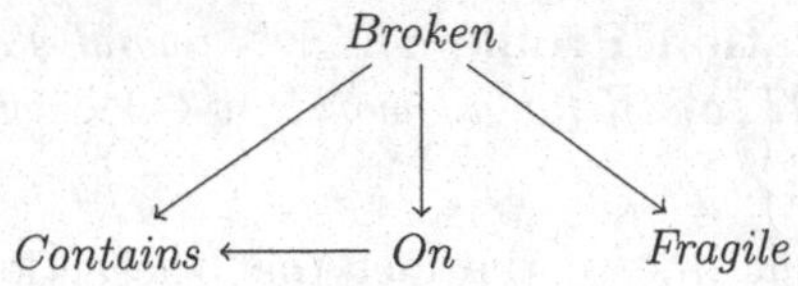

Fig. 3. Example fluent dependencies

3.2 Decidable Verification with Acyclic Theories

Let us now restrict our attention to programs over ground actions with an acyclic C^2-DTBAT $\mathcal{DDT}$. Let $\mathcal{A}$ denote the finite set of ground deterministic actions (including ϵ and $\mathfrak{f}$) occurring in δ_{det}. The goal is to construct a finite propositional abstraction of the infinite-state MDP M_δ^w with $w \models \mathcal{DDT}$. Following the construction for GOLOG programs presented in [20] and elaborated in [19], the essential part is a compact representation of effects from executing a *sequence* of such ground actions in a given world satisfying the BAT.

First we simplify SSAs as follows. If $F(\boldsymbol{x})$ is a fluent and $t \in \mathcal{A}$, the *grounding* of the SSA of F w.r.t. t is of the form

$$\square[t]F(\boldsymbol{x}) \equiv \left(\gamma_F^+\right)_t^a \vee F(\boldsymbol{x}) \wedge \neg\left(\gamma_F^-\right)_t^a.$$

The instantiated positive and negative effect conditions $\left(\gamma_F^+\right)_t^a$ and $\left(\gamma_F^-\right)_t^a$ then are each equivalent to a disjunction

$$\phi_1^{\mathsf{eff}} \wedge \phi_1^{\mathsf{con}} \vee \cdots \vee \phi_n^{\mathsf{eff}} \wedge \phi_n^{\mathsf{con}}$$

for some $n \geq 0$, where the ϕ_i^{eff} (effect descriptors) are C^2-fluent formulas with $\boldsymbol{x}$ as their only free variables, and the ϕ_i^{con} (context conditions) are C^2-fluent sentences. We often view $\left(\gamma_F^+\right)_t^a$ and $\left(\gamma_F^-\right)_t^a$ as sets and write $(\phi_i^{\mathsf{eff}}, \phi_i^{\mathsf{con}}) \in \left(\gamma_F^+\right)_t^a$ to express that the corresponding disjunct is present. An *effect function* then represents the effects of a ground action:

Definition 8 (Effects). *Let $F(\boldsymbol{x})$ be a fluent and ϕ a C^2-fluent formula with free variables $\boldsymbol{x}$, where $\boldsymbol{x}$ is empty or $\boldsymbol{x} = x$ or $\boldsymbol{x} = (x, y)$. We call the expression $\langle F^+, \phi\rangle$ a* positive effect *on F, and the expression $\langle F^-, \phi\rangle$ a* negative effect *on F. We use the notation $\langle F^\pm, \phi\rangle$ for an effect if we do not explicitly distinguish between a positive or a negative effect on F. Let $\mathcal{D}$ be a C^2-BAT, w a world with $w \models \mathcal{D}$, $z \in \mathcal{Z}$ and $t \in \mathcal{A}$. The* effects of executing t in (w, z) *are defined as:*

$$\begin{aligned}
&\mathcal{E}_{\mathcal{D}}(w, z, t) := \\
&\{\langle F^+, \phi^{\mathsf{eff}}\rangle \mid \exists(\phi^{\mathsf{eff}}, \phi^{\mathsf{con}}) \in \left(\gamma_F^+\right)_t^a \textit{ s. t. } w, z \models \phi^{\mathsf{con}}\} \cup \\
&\{\langle F^-, \phi^{\mathsf{eff}}\rangle \mid \exists(\phi^{\mathsf{eff}}, \phi^{\mathsf{con}}) \in \left(\gamma_F^-\right)_t^a \textit{ s. t. } w, z \models \phi^{\mathsf{con}}\}.
\end{aligned}$$

Intuitively, if $\langle F^+, \phi\rangle \in \mathcal{E}_{\mathcal{D}}(w, z, t)$ and $\mathbf{c}$ is an instance of ϕ *before* executing t in w, z, then $F(\mathbf{c})$ will be true *after* the execution (similar for negative effects). To accumulate effects of consecutively executed actions, we define a regression operator applied to a C^2-fluent formula given a set of effects. Without loss of generality we assume that only variable symbols x and y occur.

Definition 9 (Regression). *Let E be a set of effects and φ a C^2-fluent formula. The* regression of φ through E, *denoted by $\mathcal{R}[\mathsf{E}, \varphi]$, is a C^2-fluent formula obtained from φ by replacing each occurrence of a fluent $F(\boldsymbol{v})$ in φ by the formula*

$$F(\boldsymbol{v}) \wedge \bigwedge_{\langle F^-, \phi\rangle \in \mathsf{E}} \neg\phi_{\boldsymbol{v}}^{\boldsymbol{x}} \vee \bigvee_{\langle F^+, \phi\rangle \in \mathsf{E}} \phi_{\boldsymbol{v}}^{\boldsymbol{x}}.$$

By appropriately renaming variables in the effect descriptors ϕ it can be ensured that $\mathcal{R}[\mathsf{E}, \varphi]$ is again a C^2-fluent sentence.

The result of first executing effects E_0 and afterwards E_1 is a new set of effects $\mathsf{E}_0 \rhd \mathsf{E}_1$ given by:

$$\begin{aligned}
&\{\langle F^\pm, \mathcal{R}[\mathsf{E}_0, \varphi]\rangle \mid \langle F^\pm, \varphi\rangle \in \mathsf{E}_1\} \cup \\
&\{\langle F^+, (\varphi \wedge \bigwedge_{\langle F^-, \varphi'\rangle \in \mathsf{E}_1} \neg\mathcal{R}[\mathsf{E}_0, \varphi'])\rangle \mid \langle F^+, \varphi\rangle \in \mathsf{E}_0\} \cup \{\langle F^-, \varphi\rangle \in \mathsf{E}_0\}.
\end{aligned}$$

It can be shown that for any C^2-fluent sentence ϕ,

$$\mathcal{R}[\mathsf{E}_0, \mathcal{R}[\mathsf{E}_1, \phi]] \equiv \mathcal{R}[\mathsf{E}_0 \rhd \mathsf{E}_1, \phi].$$

Let w be a world with $w \models \mathcal{D}$. To accumulate the effects of a sequence $z = t_1 t_2 \cdots t_n \in \mathcal{A}^*$ of deterministic actions into a single set, let $z[i]$ denote the subsequence of the first $i \leq n$ elements of z. Then we set

$$\mathsf{E}_1 := \mathcal{E}_{\mathcal{D}}(w, \langle\rangle, t_1)$$
$$\mathsf{E}_i := \mathsf{E}_{i-1} \rhd \mathcal{E}_{\mathcal{D}}(w, z[i-1], t_i) \text{ for } i = 2, \ldots, n$$

and say that E_n *is generated by executing* $t_1 t_2 \cdots t_n$ *in* w. Then, for the effects E_z generated by z in w and a C^2-fluent sentence ψ, it holds that

$$w, z \models \psi \text{ iff } w, \langle\rangle \models \mathcal{R}[\mathsf{E}_z, \psi].$$

For a given DTGOLOG program $\mathcal{G} = (\mathcal{DDT}, \delta)$ with an acyclic BAT $\mathcal{D}$ and finitely many deterministic ground actions $\mathcal{A}$ occurring in δ_{det} we show that there are only finitely many possible effects that can be generated by action sequences from $\mathcal{A}$. We observe that for an effect $\langle F^{\pm}, \varphi\rangle$ on fluent F with depth $\mathsf{fd}_{\mathcal{D}}(F) = i$ all fluents occurring in φ have a depth that is strictly smaller than i. Thus, for regressing the effect descriptor φ only effects on fluents with depth strictly smaller than i are relevant. Using this argument we can define the set of all relevant effects as follows: For a fluent F the set of all positive effect descriptors for F are given by

$$\mathsf{eff}^{+}_{\mathcal{A}}(F) := \{\phi^{\mathsf{eff}} \mid (\phi^{\mathsf{eff}}, \phi^{\mathsf{con}}) \in (\gamma_F^{+})^{a}_{t} \text{ for some } t \in \mathcal{A}\},$$

and analogous for the negative effect descriptors $\mathsf{eff}^{-}_{\mathcal{A}}(F)$. For an acyclic BAT $\mathcal{D}$ and finite set of ground actions $\mathcal{A}$ the *set of all relevant effects* on all fluents with depth $\leq j$ with $j = 0, \ldots, \mathsf{fd}(\mathcal{D})$ is denoted by $\mathfrak{E}_j^{\mathcal{D},\mathcal{A}}$ and is given in Fig. 4. We define $\mathfrak{E}^{\mathcal{D},\mathcal{A}} := \mathfrak{E}_n^{\mathcal{D},\mathcal{A}}$ with $\mathsf{fd}(\mathcal{D}) = n$. For a given fluent F with $\mathsf{fd}_{\mathcal{D}}(F) = 0$ it holds that the effects on F can be described without referring to any other fluent. Consequently, all effects on F generated by a ground action sequence from $\mathcal{A}$ must be contained in $\mathfrak{E}_0^{\mathcal{D},\mathcal{A}}$. For fluents F with $\mathsf{fd}_{\mathcal{D}}(F) = i$ and $i > 0$ the fluents in the effect descriptors may also be subject to changes but have a depth strictly smaller than i. To obtain all relevant effects on F it is therefore sufficient to consider the effects in $\mathfrak{E}_{i-1}^{\mathcal{D},\mathcal{A}}$.

Lemma 1. *Let $\mathcal{D}$ and $\mathcal{A}$ be as above, $z \in \mathcal{A}^*$, $w \models \mathcal{D}$ and E_z the effects generated by executing z in w. For each $\langle F^{\pm}, \varphi\rangle \in \mathsf{E}_z$ there exists $\langle F^{\pm}, \varphi'\rangle \in \mathfrak{E}^{\mathcal{D},\mathcal{A}}$ with $\varphi \equiv \varphi'$.*

Using the finite representation of action effects we can construct a finite abstraction of the infinite-state MDP induced by a program with a C^2-DTBAT and an acyclic $\mathcal{D}$. First, we identify a finite set of *relevant C^2-fluent sentences* called *context of a program*, denoted by $\mathcal{C}(\mathcal{G})$. It consists of

$$\mathfrak{E}_0^{\mathcal{D},\mathcal{A}} := \{\langle F^-, \varphi\rangle \mid \mathsf{fd}_{\mathcal{D}}(F) = 0, \varphi \in \mathsf{eff}_{\mathcal{A}}^-(F)\} \cup \{\langle F^+, \varphi \wedge \bigwedge_{\varphi' \in X} \neg\varphi'\rangle \mid \mathsf{fd}_{\mathcal{D}}(F) = 0, \varphi \in \mathsf{eff}_{\mathcal{A}}^+(F),\, X \subseteq \mathsf{eff}_{\mathcal{A}}^-(F)\};$$

$$\mathfrak{E}_i^{\mathcal{D},\mathcal{A}} := \mathfrak{E}_{i-1}^{\mathcal{D},\mathcal{A}} \cup \{\langle F^-, \mathcal{R}[\mathsf{E}, \varphi]\rangle \mid \mathsf{fd}_{\mathcal{D}}(F) = i, \varphi \in \mathsf{eff}_{\mathcal{A}}^-(F),\, \mathsf{E} \in 2^{\mathfrak{E}_{i-1}^{\mathcal{D},\mathcal{A}}}\} \cup \{\langle F^+, \Xi\rangle \mid \mathsf{fd}_{\mathcal{D}}(F) = i, \phi \in \mathsf{eff}_{\mathcal{A}}^+(F), \mathsf{E} \in 2^{\mathfrak{E}_{i-1}^{\mathcal{D},\mathcal{A}}},\, X \subseteq \mathsf{eff}_{\mathcal{A}}^-(F) \times 2^{\mathfrak{E}_{i-1}^{\mathcal{D},\mathcal{A}}}\}$$

$$\text{with } \Xi := \big(\mathcal{R}[\mathsf{E}, \phi] \wedge \bigwedge_{(\varphi, \mathsf{E}') \in X} \neg\mathcal{R}[\mathsf{E}', \varphi]\big)$$

Fig. 4. Sets of all relevant effects with $1 \leq i \leq \mathsf{fd}(\mathcal{D})$

- all sentences in the initial theory,
- all context conditions in the instantiated SSAs,
- all instantiations ψ_c^r of the right-hand side of axiom $\mathcal{D}_{\text{reward}}$ for all occurring numeric constants c,
- all C^2-fluent subformulas in the temporal property, and
- all tests in the program.

Furthermore, the context is closed under negation.

Central for the abstraction is the notion of a *type of a world*, representing an equivalence class over $\mathcal{W}$. Intuitively, a type says which of the context axioms are satisfied initially and in all relevant future situations of that world.

Definition 10 (Types). *Let $\mathcal{G} = (\mathcal{DDT}, \delta)$ be a* DTGOLOG *program with an acyclic BAT $\mathcal{D} = \mathcal{D}_0 \cup \mathcal{D}_{post}$ w.r.t. a finite set of ground actions $\mathcal{A}$ (including ϵ and $\mathfrak{f}$). Furthermore, let $\mathcal{C}(\mathcal{G})$ be the context of $\mathcal{G}$ and $\mathfrak{E}^{\mathcal{D},\mathcal{A}}$ the set of all relevant effects. The* set of all type elements *is given by*

$$\mathsf{TE}(\mathcal{G}) := \{(\psi, \mathsf{E}) \mid \psi \in \mathcal{C}(\mathcal{G}), \mathsf{E} \subseteq \mathfrak{E}^{\mathcal{D},\mathcal{A}}\}.$$

A type w.r.t. $\mathcal{G}$ *is a set $\tau \subseteq \mathsf{TE}(\mathcal{G})$ that satisfies:*

1. *For all $\psi \in \mathcal{C}(\mathcal{G})$ and all $\mathsf{E} \subseteq \mathfrak{E}^{\mathcal{D},\mathcal{A}}$ either $(\psi, \mathsf{E}) \in \tau$ or $(\neg\psi, \mathsf{E}) \in \tau$.*
2. *There exists a world $w \in \mathcal{W}$ such that*

$$w \models \mathcal{D}_0 \cup \{\mathcal{R}[\mathsf{E}, \psi] \mid (\psi, \mathsf{E}) \in \tau\}.$$

The set of all types w.r.t. $\mathcal{G}$ *is denoted by* $\mathsf{Types}(\mathcal{G})$. *The* type of a world $w \in \mathcal{W}$ w.r.t. $\mathcal{G}$ *is given by*

$$\mathsf{type}(w) := \{(\psi, \mathsf{E}) \in \mathsf{TE}(\mathcal{G}) \mid w \models \mathcal{R}[\mathsf{E}, \psi]\}.$$

The abstraction of a world state consisting of a world $w \in \mathcal{W}$ with $w \models \mathcal{DDT}$ and an action sequence $z \in \mathcal{A}^*$ is then given by $\mathsf{type}(w)$ and the set of effects $\mathsf{E}_z \subseteq \mathfrak{E}^{\mathcal{D},\mathcal{A}}$ generated by executing z in w. Furthermore, the program only admits finitely many control states. Here we use a representation similar to the *characteristic program graphs* from [3] where nodes are the reachable subprograms $Sub(\delta)$, each of which is associated with a termination condition $\mathsf{Fin}(\delta')$, and where an edge $\delta_1 \xrightarrow{t/\psi} \delta_2$ represents a transition from δ_1 to δ_2 via action t if test condition ψ holds. Moreover, failure conditions are given by

$$\mathsf{Fail}(\delta') := \neg(\mathsf{Fin}(\delta') \vee \bigvee_{\delta' \xrightarrow{t/\psi} \delta''} \psi).$$

The abstract, finite MDP for a type τ can then be constructed using the Cartesian product of effect sets and subprograms as states, the same actions as in the original MDP, and the context formulas as labels. Formally, $\mathsf{M}^{\tau}_{\delta\,\mathsf{fin}} = \langle \mathsf{S}_{\mathsf{fin}}, \mathsf{s}^0_{\mathsf{fin}}, \mathsf{A}_{\mathsf{fin}}, \mathsf{P}_{\mathsf{fin}}, \mathsf{R}_{\mathsf{fin}}, \mathsf{L}_{\mathsf{fin}} \rangle$ consists of

- the set of states $\mathsf{S}_{\mathsf{fin}} = 2^{\mathfrak{E}^{\mathcal{D},\mathcal{A}}} \times Sub(\delta_{\mathsf{det}})$;
- the initial state $\mathsf{s}^0_{\mathsf{fin}} = \langle \emptyset, \delta_{\mathsf{det}} \rangle$;
- the set of actions $\mathsf{A}_{\mathsf{fin}} = \mathsf{A}$;
- the transition function $\mathsf{P}_{\mathsf{fin}}$ such that

$$\mathsf{P}_{\mathsf{fin}}(\langle \mathsf{E}_1, \delta_1 \rangle, t, \langle \mathsf{E}_2, \delta_2 \rangle) = \begin{cases} c, & \mathcal{D}_{\text{prob}} \models Prob(t, t', c), \\ & \delta_1 \xrightarrow{t'/\psi} \delta_2,\ (\psi, \mathsf{E}_1) \in \tau, \\ & \mathsf{E}_2 = \mathsf{E}_1 \rhd \mathcal{E}_{\mathcal{D}}(\tau, \mathsf{E}_1, t') \\ 1, & (\mathsf{Fin}(\delta_1), E_1) \in \tau,\ t = t' = \delta_2 = \epsilon \\ 1, & (\mathsf{Fail}(\delta_1), E_1) \in \tau,\ t = t' = \delta_2 = \mathfrak{f} \\ 0, & \text{otherwise} \end{cases}$$

  and all $\langle E, \epsilon \rangle$ as well as all $\langle E, \mathfrak{f} \rangle$ are absorbing states;
- the reward function $\mathsf{R}_{\mathsf{fin}}$ such that $\mathsf{R}_{\mathsf{fin}}(\langle \mathsf{E}_1, \delta_1 \rangle) = c$ iff $(\psi^{r}_{c}, \mathsf{E}_1) \in \tau$;
- and the labeling function $\mathsf{L}_{\mathsf{fin}}(\langle \mathsf{E}_1, \delta_1 \rangle) = \{\psi \in \mathcal{C}(\mathcal{G}) \mid (\psi, \mathsf{E}_1) \in \tau\}$.

We can thus regard the finitely many context formulas as atomic propositions, and hence apply propositional probabilistic model checking. The finitely many world types can be computed using a decidable consistency check in C^2, so this yields a decision procedure for the verification problem:

Theorem 2. *Let $\mathcal{G} = (\mathcal{DDT}, \delta)$ be a* DTGOLOG *program with an acyclic C^2-BAT and Φ a temporal state formula. It is decidable to verify whether Φ is valid in $\mathcal{G}$.*

Example 3. In our running example we obtain two types, one for the case that the box contains bubble wrap and one where it does not. This is due to the fact that our initial theory (Fig. 1) does not say anything about the truth of the context condition $\neg\exists y.\,Contains(box, y) \wedge BubbleWrap(y)$ for the *Drop* action in γ^{+}_{Broken} (Fig. 2).

The corresponding abstract MDPs are depicted in Figs. 5(a) and (b), respectively, where m stands for the ground action $MoveS(box, s_1, s_2)$. That is to say

Table 1. Verification results for example properties

	Φ_1	$\Phi_{\leq 1}$	$\Phi_{\leq 2}$	$\Phi_{\leq 3}$	Φ_∞
With bubble wrap	`false`	`false`	`true`	`true`	`true`
Without bubble wrap	`false`	`false`	`false`	`false`	`false`

when there is bubble wrap, a successful attempt of moving the box leads to state s_1, from where only successful termination of the program is possible, represented by entering absorbing state s_3. Should the box be dropped, state s_2 is entered, and m may be retried indefinitely until it succeeds. On the other hand, if the box does not contain any bubble wrap, the agent only has one attempt. Should it fail, absorbing state s_4 is reached, representing program failure.

We can now feed these finite MDPs into a probabilistic model checker such as STORM [4] in order to verify (the propositionalized versions of) the example properties. Table 1 shows the corresponding results, where Φ_1 stands for formula (3), $\Phi_{\leq k}$ for (4) with $k \in \{1, 2, 3\}$, and Φ_∞ for (5). None of the properties holds in both types, i.e. none is valid. We can see that in order to obtain a 95% certainty that the unbroken vase ends up on shelf s_2, we need to allow for at least two move attempts (hence bubble wrap is required). Intuitively, this is because the first one only has a 90% chance to succeed, but with two attempts we already get $0.9 + 0.1 \cdot 0.9 = 99\%$ success probability, 99.9% with three, and so on. The desired situation is thus reached eventually "almost surely", meaning with a 100% probability.

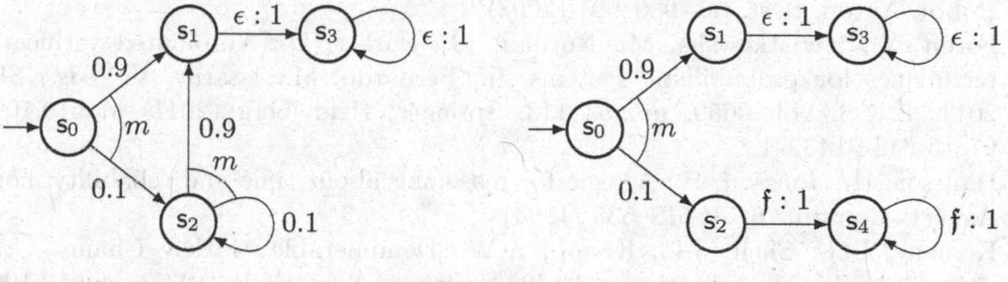

(a) with bubble wrap (b) without bubble wrap

Fig. 5. Example abstract MDPs

4 Conclusion

In this paper we lifted recent results on the decidability of verification of temporal properties of classical GOLOG programs to the decision-theoretic case. The class of acyclic theories is very expressive in the sense that it subsumes many of the popular classes, including the context-free and local-effect ones. Our result not only enables us to employ recent advances in probabilistic model checking [4,6,9] for the verification of DTGOLOG agents, variants of which have been used e.g. for controlling soccer robots [5]. Our abstraction, which can be performed as a preprocessing step, also opens the application range of methods normally working on finite MDPs to a large class of infinite-state problems.

Acknowledgments. This work was supported by the German Research Foundation (DFG) research unit FOR 1513 on Hybrid Reasoning for Intelligent Systems, project A1.

References

1. Andova, S., Hermanns, H., Katoen, J.-P.: Discrete-time rewards model-checked. In: Larsen, K.G., Niebert, P. (eds.) FORMATS 2003. LNCS, vol. 2791, pp. 88–104. Springer, Heidelberg (2004). doi:10.1007/978-3-540-40903-8_8
2. Boutilier, C., Reiter, R., Soutchanski, M., Thrun, S.: Decision-theoretic, high-level agent programming in the situation calculus. In: Kautz, H., Porter, B. (eds.) Proceedings of the Seventeenth National Conference on Artificial Intelligence (AAAI 2000), pp. 355–362. AAAI Press (2000)
3. Claßen, J., Lakemeyer, G.: A logic for non-terminating Golog programs. In: Brewka, G., Lang, J. (eds.) Proceedings of the Eleventh International Conference on the Principles of Knowledge Representation and Reasoning (KR 2008), pp. 589–599. AAAI Press (2008)
4. Dehnert, C., Junges, S., Katoen, J.P., Volk, M.: A storm is coming: a modern probabilistic model checker. In: Kuncak, V., Majumdar, R. (eds.) CAV 2017. Theoretical Computer Science and General Issues, vol. 10427, pp. 592–600. Springer, Heidelberg (2017). doi:10.1007/978-3-319-63390-9_31
5. Ferrein, A., Lakemeyer, G.: Logic-based robot control in highly dynamic domains. Robot. Auton. Syst. **56**, 980–991 (2008)
6. Forejt, V., Kwiatkowska, M., Norman, G., Parker, D.: Automated verification techniques for probabilistic systems. In: Bernardo, M., Issarny, V. (eds.) SFM 2011. LNCS, vol. 6659, pp. 53–113. Springer, Heidelberg (2011). doi:10.1007/978-3-642-21455-4_3
7. Hansson, H., Jonsson, B.: A logic for reasoning about time and reliability. Form. Aspects Comput. **6**(5), 512–535 (1994)
8. Kemeny, J.G., Snell, J.L., Knapp, A.W.: Denumerable Markov Chains. Graduate Texts in Mathematics, vol. 40. Springer, New York (1976). doi:10.1007/978-1-4684-9455-6
9. Kwiatkowska, M., Parker, D.: Advances in probabilistic model checking. In: Nipkow, T., Grumberg, O., Hauptmann, B. (eds.) Software Safety and Security - Tools for Analysis and Verification, NATO Science for Peace and Security Series - D: Information and Communication Security, vol. 33, pp. 126–151. IOS Press (2012)
10. Kwiatkowska, M., Norman, G., Parker, D.: PRISM 4.0: verification of probabilistic real-time systems. In: Gopalakrishnan, G., Qadeer, S. (eds.) CAV 2011. LNCS, vol. 6806, pp. 585–591. Springer, Heidelberg (2011). doi:10.1007/978-3-642-22110-1_47
11. Lakemeyer, G., Levesque, H.J.: A semantic characterization of a useful fragment of the situation calculus with knowledge. Artif. Intell. **175**(1), 142–164 (2010)
12. Levesque, H.J., Reiter, R., Lespérance, Y., Lin, F., Scherl, R.B.: GOLOG: a logic programming language for dynamic domains. J. Log. Program. **31**(1–3), 59–83 (1997)

13. Lin, F., Reiter, R.: How to progress a database. Artif. Intell. **92**(1–2), 131–167 (1997)
14. Pednault, E.P.D.: Synthesizing plans that contain actions with context-dependent effects. Comput. Intell. **4**, 356–372 (1988)
15. Puterman, M.L.: Markov Decision Processes: Discrete Stochastic Dynamic Programming. Wiley, New York (1994)
16. Reiter, R.: Knowledge in Action: Logical Foundations for Specifying and Implementing Dynamical Systems. MIT Press, Cambridge (2001)
17. Soutchanski, M.: An on-line decision-theoretic Golog interpreter. In: Nebel, B. (ed.) Proceedings of the Seventeenth International Joint Conference on Artificial Intelligence (IJCAI 2001), pp. 19–26. Morgan Kaufmann Publishers Inc. (2001)
18. Vassos, S., Lakemeyer, G., Levesque, H.J.: First-order strong progression for local-effect basic action theories. In: Brewka, G., Lang, J. (eds.) Proceedings of the Eleventh International Conference on the Principles of Knowledge Representation and Reasoning (KR 2008), pp. 662–672. AAAI Press (2008)
19. Zarrieß, B., Claßen, J.: Decidable verification of Golog programs over non-local effect actions. LTCS-Report 15-19, Chair of Automata Theory, TU Dresden, Dresden, Germany (2015)
20. Zarrieß, B., Claßen, J.: Decidable verification of Golog programs over non-local effect actions. In: Schuurmans, D., Wellman, M. (eds.) Proceedings of the Thirtieth AAAI Conference on Artificial Intelligence (AAAI 2016), pp. 1109–1115. AAAI Press (2016)

The Bernays–Schönfinkel–Ramsey Fragment with Bounded Difference Constraints over the Reals Is Decidable

Marco Voigt(✉)

Max Planck Institute for Informatics and Saarbrücken Graduate School of Computer Science, Saarland Informatics Campus, Saarbrücken, Germany
mvoigt@mpi-inf.mpg.de

Abstract. First-order linear real arithmetic enriched with uninterpreted predicate symbols yields an interesting modeling language. However, satisfiability of such formulas is undecidable, even if we restrict the uninterpreted predicate symbols to arity one. In order to find decidable fragments of this language, it is necessary to restrict the expressiveness of the arithmetic part. One possible path is to confine arithmetic expressions to difference constraints of the form $x - y \triangleleft c$, where $\triangleleft$ ranges over the standard relations $<, \leq, =, \neq, \geq, >$ and x, y are universally quantified. However, it is known that combining difference constraints with uninterpreted predicate symbols yields an undecidable satisfiability problem again. In this paper, it is shown that satisfiability becomes decidable if we in addition bound the ranges of universally quantified variables. As bounded intervals over the reals still comprise infinitely many values, a trivial instantiation procedure is not sufficient to solve the problem.

Keywords: Bernays–Schönfinkel–Ramsey fragment · Linear arithmetic constraints · Difference constraints · Combination of theories

1 Introduction

It has been discovered about half a century ago that linear arithmetic with additional uninterpreted predicate symbols has an undecidable satisfiability problem [15]. Even enriching Presburger arithmetic with only a single uninterpreted predicate symbol of arity one suffices to facilitate encodings of the halting problem for two-counter machines [5, 10]. These results do not change substantially when we use the reals as underlying domain instead of the integers. This means, in order to obtain a decidable subfragment of the combination of linear arithmetic with uninterpreted predicate symbols, the arithmetic part has to be restricted considerably. In this paper, two subfragments with a decidable satisfiability problem are presented. Both are based on the Bernays–Schönfinkel–Ramsey fragment (BSR) of first-order logic, which is the $\exists^*\forall^*$ prefix class. Uninterpreted constant symbols and the distinguished equality predicate are allowed,

C. Dixon and M. Finger (Eds.): FroCoS 2017, LNCS 10483, pp. 244–261, 2017.
DOI: 10.1007/978-3-319-66167-4_14

non-constant function symbols are not. The arity of uninterpreted predicate symbols is not restricted. We extend BSR in two ways and call the obtained clause fragments *BSR modulo simple linear real constraints—BSR(SLR)*—and *BSR modulo bounded difference constraints—BSR(BD)*.

The first clause class—defined in Definition 1 and treated in detail in Sect. 4—adds constraints of the form $s \triangleleft t$, $x \triangleleft t$, and $x \triangleleft y$ to BSR clauses, where x and y are real-valued variables that are implicitly universally quantified, s and t are linear arithmetic terms that are ground, and $\triangleleft$ ranges over $<, \leq, =, \neq, \geq, >$. We allow Skolem constants in the ground terms s and t. Since their value is not predetermined, they can be conceived as being existentially quantified. The constraints used in this clause fragment are similar to the kind of constraints that appear in the context of the *array property fragment* [4] and extensions thereof (see, e.g., [7,9]). The main differences are that we use the real domain in this paper instead of the integer domain, and that we allow strict inequalities and disequations between universally quantified variables. In the presence of uninterpreted function symbols, strict inequality or disequations can be used to assert that some uninterpreted function f is injective. This expressiveness prevents certain instantiation-based approaches to satisfiability checking from being applicable, e.g. the methods in [4,9]. In the context of the array property fragment, this expressiveness even leads to undecidability.

The BSR(BD) clause class—presented in Definition 2 and in Sect. 5—adds constraints of the form $x \triangleleft c$, $x \triangleleft y$ and $x - y \triangleleft c$ to BSR clauses, where x and y are real-valued variables, c could be any rational number, and $\triangleleft$ ranges over $<, \leq, =, \neq, \geq, >$ again. We refer to constraints of the form $x - y \triangleleft c$ as *difference constraints*. Already in the seventies, Pratt identified difference constraints and boolean combinations thereof as an important tool for the formalization of verification conditions [14]. Applications include the verification of timed systems and scheduling problems (see, e.g., [11] for references). As unrestricted combinations of uninterpreted predicate symbols with difference constraints lead to an undecidable satisfiability problem (once more, two-counter machines can be encoded in a simple way [17]), we have to further confine the language. Every difference constraint $x - y \triangleleft c$ has to be conjoined with four additional constraints $c_x \leq x$, $x \leq d_x$, $c_y \leq y$, $y \leq d_y$, where c_x, d_x, c_y, d_y are rationals. This restriction seems to weaken expressiveness severely. Indeed, it has to, since we aim for a decidable satisfiability problem. Yet, we show in Sect. 6 that BSR(BD) clause sets are expressive enough to formulate the reachability problem for timed automata. In [13] an encoding of the reachability problem for timed automata in *difference logic* (boolean combinations of difference constraints *without* uninterpreted predicate symbols) is given, which facilitates deciding bounded reachability, i.e. the problem of reaching a given set of states within a bounded number of transition steps. When using BSR(BD) as a modeling language, we do not have to fix an upper bound on the number of steps a priori.

The main result of the present paper is that satisfiability of finite BSR(SLR) clause sets and finite BSR(BD) clause sets is decidable, respectively (Theorems 12 and 19). The proof technique is very similar for the two fragments. It is partially based on methods from Ramsey theory, which are briefly introduced in Sect. 3. The used approach may turn out to be applicable to other fragments of BSR modulo linear real arithmetic as well. Due to space limitations, most proofs are only sketched. Detailed proofs can be found in [16].

2 Preliminaries and Notation

Hierarchic combinations of first-order logic with background theories build upon sorted logic with equality [2,3,12]. We instantiate this framework with the BSR fragment and linear arithmetic over the reals as the *base theory*. The *base sort* $\mathcal{R}$ shall always be interpreted by the reals $\mathbb{R}$. For simplicity, we restrict our considerations to a single *free sort* $\mathcal{S}$, which may be freely interpreted as some nonempty domain, as usual.

We denote by $V_{\mathcal{R}}$ a countably infinite set of base-sort variables. *Linear arithmetic (LA) terms* are build from rational constants $0, 1, \frac{1}{2}, -2, -\frac{3}{4}$, etc., the operators $+, -$, and the variables from $V_{\mathcal{R}}$. We moreover allow base-sort constant symbols whose values have to be determined by an interpretation (*Skolem constants*). They can be conceived as existentially quantified. As predicates over the reals we allow the standard relations $<, \leq, =, \neq, \geq, >$.

In order to hierarchically extend the base theory by the BSR fragment, we introduce the free sort $\mathcal{S}$, a countably infinite set $V_{\mathcal{S}}$ of *free-sort variables*, a finite set $\Omega_{\mathcal{S}}$ of *free (uninterpreted) constant symbols of sort* $\mathcal{S}$ and a finite set Π of *free predicate symbols* equipped with sort information. Note that every predicate symbol in Π has a finite, nonnegative arity and can be of a mixed sort over the two sorts $\mathcal{R}$ and $\mathcal{S}$, e.g. $P : \mathcal{R} \times \mathcal{S} \times \mathcal{R}$. We use the symbol $\approx$ to denote the built-in equality predicate on $\mathcal{S}$. To avoid confusion, we tacitly assume that no constant or predicate symbol is overloaded, i.e. they have a unique sort.

Definition 1 (BSR with simple linear real constraints—BSR(SLR)). *A* BSR(SLR) clause *has the form* $\Lambda \,\|\, \Gamma \to \Delta$, *where* Λ, Γ, Δ *are multisets of atoms satisfying the following conditions. (i) Every atom in* Λ *is an LA constraint of the form* $s \lhd t$ *or* $x \lhd t$ *or* $x \lhd y$ *where* s, t *are ground (i.e. variable-free) LA terms,* $x, y \in V_{\mathcal{R}}$, *and* $\lhd \in \{<, \leq, =, \neq, \geq, >\}$. *(ii) Every atom in* Γ *and* Δ *is either an equation* $s \approx s'$ *over free-sort variables and constant symbols, or a non-equational atom* $P(s_1, \ldots, s_m)$ *that is well sorted and where the* s_i *range over base-sort variables, free-sort variables, and free-sort constant symbols.*

Definition 2 (BSR with bounded difference constraints—BSR(BD)). *A* BSR(BD) clause *has the form* $\Lambda \,\|\, \Gamma \to \Delta$, *where the multisets* Γ, Δ *satisfy Condition (ii) of Definition 1, and every atom in* Λ *is an LA constraint of the form* $x \lhd c$, $x \lhd y$, *or* $x - y \lhd c$ *where* c *may be any rational constant (not a Skolem constant),* $x, y \in V_{\mathcal{R}}$, *and* $\lhd \in \{<, \leq, =, \neq, \geq, >\}$. *Moreover, we require that whenever* Λ *contains a constraint of the form* $x - y \lhd c$, *then* Λ *also contains constraints* $c_x \leq x$, $x \leq d_x$, $c_y \leq y$, *and* $y \leq d_y$ *with* $c_x, d_x, c_y, d_y \in \mathbb{Q}$.

We omit the empty multiset left of "$\to$" and denote it by $\Box$ right of "$\to$" (where $\Box$ at the same time stands for *falsity*). The introduced clause notation separates arithmetic constraints from the free first-order part. We use the vertical double bar "$\|$" to indicate this syntactically. Intuitively, clauses $\Lambda \,\|\, \Gamma \rightarrow \Delta$ can be read as $(\bigwedge \Lambda \wedge \bigwedge \Gamma) \rightarrow \bigvee \Delta$, i.e. the multisets Λ, Γ stand for conjunctions of atoms and Δ stands for a disjunction of atoms. Requiring the free parts Γ and Δ of clauses to not contain any base-sort terms apart from variables does not limit expressiveness. Every base-sort term $t \notin V_{\mathcal{R}}$ in the free part can safely be replaced by a fresh base-sort variable x_t when an atomic constraint $x_t = t$ is added to the constraint part of the clause (a process known as *purification* or *abstraction* [2,12]).

A *(hierarchic) interpretation* is an algebra $\mathcal{A}$ which interprets the base sort $\mathcal{R}$ as $\mathcal{R}^{\mathcal{A}} = \mathbb{R}$, assigns real values to all occurring base-sort Skolem constants and interprets all LA terms and constraints in the standard way. Moreover, $\mathcal{A}$ comprises a nonempty domain $\mathcal{S}^{\mathcal{A}}$, assigns to each free-sort constant symbol c in $\Omega_{\mathcal{S}}$ a domain element $c^{\mathcal{A}} \in \mathcal{S}^{\mathcal{A}}$, and interprets every sorted predicate symbol $P{:}\xi_1 \times \ldots \times \xi_m$ in Π by some set $P^{\mathcal{A}} \subseteq \xi_1^{\mathcal{A}} \times \ldots \times \xi_m^{\mathcal{A}}$. Summing up, $\mathcal{A}$ extends the standard model of linear arithmetic and adopts the standard approach to semantics of (sorted) first-order logics when interpreting the free part of clauses.

Given an interpretation $\mathcal{A}$ and a sort-respecting *variable assignment* β : $V_{\mathcal{R}} \cup V_{\mathcal{S}} \rightarrow \mathcal{R}^{\mathcal{A}} \cup \mathcal{S}^{\mathcal{A}}$, we write $\mathcal{A}(\beta)(s)$ to mean the *value of the term s under $\mathcal{A}$ with respect to the variable assignment β*. The variables occurring in clauses are implicitly universally quantified. Therefore, given a clause C, we call $\mathcal{A}$ a *(hierarchic) model of C*, denoted $\mathcal{A} \models C$, if and only if $\mathcal{A}, \beta \models C$ holds for every variable assignment β. For clause sets N, we write $\mathcal{A} \models N$ if and only if $\mathcal{A} \models C$ holds for every clause $C \in N$. We call a clause C (a clause set N) *satisfiable* if and only if there exists a model $\mathcal{A}$ of C (of N). Two clauses C, D (clause sets N, M) are *equisatisfiable* if and only if C (N) is satisfiable whenever D (M) is satisfiable and vice versa.

Given a BSR(SLR) or BSR(BD) clause C, we use the following notation: the set of all constant symbols occurring in C is denoted by $\text{consts}(C)$. The set $\text{bconsts}(C)$ ($\text{fconsts}(C)$) is the restriction of $\text{consts}(C)$ to base-sort (free-sort) constant symbols. We denote the set of all variables occurring in a clause C by $\text{vars}(C)$. The same notation is used for sets of clauses.

Definition 3 (Normal form of BSR(SLR) and BSR(BD) clauses). *A BSR(SLR) or BSR(BD) clause $\Lambda \,\|\, \Gamma \rightarrow \Delta$ is in* normal form *if (1) all non-ground atoms in Λ have the form $x \triangleleft c$, $x \triangleleft y$, or $x - y \triangleleft c$ where c is a rational constant or a Skolem constant, and (2) every variable that occurs in Λ also occurs in Γ or in Δ. A BSR(SLR) or BSR(BD) clause set N is in* normal form *if all clauses in N are in normal form and pairwise variable disjoint. Moreover, we assume that N contains at least one free-sort constant symbol.*

For BSR(SLR) clause sets, we pose the following additional requirement. N can be divided into two parts N_{def} and N' such that (a) every clause in N_{def} has the form $c \neq t \,\|\, \rightarrow \Box$ where c is a Skolem constant and t is some ground LA term, and (b) any ground atom $s \triangleleft t$ in any constraint part Λ in any clause $\Lambda \,\|\, \Gamma \rightarrow \Delta$ in N' is such that s and t are constants (Skolem or rational, respectively).

For every BSR(SLR) clause set N there is an equisatisfiable BSR(SLR) clause set N' in normal form, such that $N' \models N$. The same holds for BSR(BD) clause sets. Requirement (2) can be established by any procedure for eliminating existentially quantified variables in LA constraints (see, e.g., [6]). Establishing the other requirements is straightforward.

For two sets $R, Q \subseteq \mathbb{R}$ we write $R < Q$ if $r < q$ holds for all $r \in R$ and $q \in Q$. Given a real r, we denote the *integral part of* r by $\lfloor r \rfloor$, i.e. $\lfloor r \rfloor$ is the largest integer for which $\lfloor r \rfloor \leq r$. By $\text{fr}(r)$ we denote the *fractional part of* r, i.e. $\text{fr}(r) := r - \lfloor r \rfloor$. Notice that $\text{fr}(r)$ is always nonnegative, e.g. $\text{fr}(3.71) = 0.71$, whereas $\text{fr}(-3.71) = 0.29$. Given any tuple $\bar{r}$ of reals, we write $\text{fr}(\bar{r})$ to mean the corresponding tuple of fractional parts, i.e. $\text{fr}(\langle r_1, \ldots, r_\mu \rangle) := \langle \text{fr}(r_1), \ldots, \text{fr}(r_\mu) \rangle$. We use the notation $\lfloor \bar{r} \rfloor$ in a component-wise fashion as well.

We write $[k]$ to address the set $\{1, \ldots, k\}$ for any positive integer $k > 0$. Finally, $\mathcal{P}$ denotes the power set operator, i.e. for any set S, $\mathcal{P}(S)$ denotes the set of all subsets of S.

3 Basic Tools from Ramsey Theory

In this section we establish two technical results based on methods usually applied in Ramsey theory. We shall use these results later on to prove the existence of models of a particular kind for finite and satisfiable BSR(SLR) or BSR(BD) clause sets. These models meet certain uniformity conditions. In order to construct them, we rely on the existence of certain finite subsets of $\mathbb{R}$ that are used to construct prototypical tuples of reals. These finite subsets, in turn, have to behave nicely as well, since tuples that are not distinguishable by BSR(SLR) or BSR(BD) constraints are required to have certain uniformity properties.

A tuple $\langle r_1, \ldots, r_m \rangle \in \mathbb{R}^m$ is called *ascending* if $r_1 < \ldots < r_m$. A *coloring* is a mapping $\chi : S \to \mathcal{C}$ for some arbitrary set S and some finite set $\mathcal{C}$. For the most basic result of this section (Lemma 4), we consider an arbitrary coloring χ of m-tuples of real numbers and stipulate the existence of a finite subset $Q \subseteq \mathbb{R}$ of a given cardinality n such that all ascending m-tuples of elements from Q are assigned the same color by χ.

Lemma 4. *Let $n, m > 0$ be positive integers. Let $\chi : \mathbb{R}^m \to \mathcal{C}$ be some coloring. There is some positive integer $\widehat{n}$ such that for every set $R \subseteq \mathbb{R}$ with $|R| \geq \widehat{n}$—i.e. R needs to be sufficiently large— there exists a subset $Q \subseteq R$ of cardinality n such that all ascending tuples $\langle r_1, \ldots, r_m \rangle \in Q^m$ are assigned the same color by χ.*

Proof (adaptation of the proof of Ramsey's Theorem on page 7 in [8]*).* For $n < m$ the lemma is trivially satisfied, since in this case Q^m cannot contain ascending tuples. Hence, we assume $n \geq m$. In order to avoid technical difficulties when defining the sequence of elements $s_{m-1}, s_m, s_{m+1}, \ldots$ below, we assume for the rest of the proof that R is finite but sufficiently large. This assumption does not pose a restriction, as we can always consider a sufficiently large finite subset of R, if R were to be infinite.

We proceed by induction on $m \geq 1$. The base case $m = 1$ is easy, since χ can assign only finitely many colors to elements in R and thus some color must be assigned at least $\lfloor \frac{|R|}{|\mathcal{C}|} \rfloor$ times. Hence, if R contains at least $n|\mathcal{C}|$ elements, we find a uniformly colored subset Q of size n. Suppose $m > 1$. At first, we pick the $m-2$ smallest reals $s_1 < \ldots < s_{m-2}$ from R and set $S_{m-2} := R \setminus \{s_1, \ldots, s_{m-2}\}$. Thereafter, we simultaneously construct two *sufficiently long but finite* sequences $s_{m-1}, s_m, s_{m+1}, \ldots$ and $S_{m-1}, S_m, S_{m+1}, \ldots$ as follows:
Given S_i, we define s_{i+1} to be the smallest real in S_i.
Given S_i and the element s_{i+1}, we define an equivalence relation $\sim_i$ on the set $S'_i := S_i \setminus \{s_{i+1}\}$ so that $s \sim_i s'$ holds if and only if for every sequence of indices $j_1, \ldots, j_{m-1}$ with $1 \leq j_1 < \ldots < j_{m-1} \leq i+1$, we have $\chi(s_{j_1}, \ldots, s_{j_{m-1}}, s) = \chi(s_{j_1}, \ldots, s_{j_{m-1}}, s')$. This equivalence relation partitions S'_i into at most $|\mathcal{C}|^{\binom{i+1}{m-1}}$ equivalence classes. We choose one such class with largest cardinality to be S_{i+1}.

By construction of the sequence $s_1, s_2, s_3, \ldots$, we must have $\chi(s_{j_1}, \ldots, s_{j_{m-1}}, s_k) = \chi(s_{j_1}, \ldots, s_{j_{m-1}}, s_{k'})$ for every sequence of indices $j_1 < \ldots < j_{m-1}$ and all indices $k, k' \geq j_{m-1} + 1$. Please note that this covers all ascending m-tuples in $\{s_1, s_2, s_3, \ldots\}^m$ starting with $s_{j_1}, \ldots, s_{j_m - 1}$, i.e. they all share the same color. We now define a new coloring $\chi' : \{s_1, s_2, s_3, \ldots\}^{m-1} \to \mathcal{C}$ so that $\chi'(s_{j_1}, \ldots, s_{j_{m-1}}) := \chi(s_{j_1}, \ldots, s_{j_{m-1}}, s_{j_{m-1}+1})$ for every sequence of indices $j_1 < \ldots < j_{m-1}$ (in case of j_{m-1} being the index of the last element in the sequence $s_1, s_2, s_3, \ldots$, $\chi'(s_{j_1}, \ldots, s_{j_{m-1}})$ shall be an arbitrary color from $\mathcal{C}$). By induction, there exists a subset $Q \subseteq \{s_1, s_2, s_3, \ldots\}$ of cardinality n, such that every ascending $(m-1)$-tuple $\bar{r} \in Q^{m-1}$ is colored the same by χ'. The definition of χ' entails that now all ascending m-tuples $\bar{r}' \in Q^m$ are colored the same by χ. Hence, Q is the sought set. □

Based on Lemma 4, one can derive similar results for more structured ways of coloring tuples of reals. We shall employ such a structured coloring when proving that the satisfiability problem for finite BSR(SLR) clause sets is decidable. More precisely, the proof of Lemma 10 will rely on such a result. The technical details are elaborated in [16].

4 Decidability of Satisfiability for BSR(SLR) Clause Sets

For the rest of this section we fix two positive integers $m, m' > 0$ and some finite BSR(SLR) clause set N in normal form. For the sake of simplicity, we assume that all uninterpreted predicate symbols P occurring in N have the sort $P : \mathcal{S}^{m'} \times \mathcal{R}^m$. This assumption does not limit expressiveness, as the arity of a predicate symbol P can easily be increased in an (un)satisfiability-preserving way by padding the occurring atoms with additional arguments. For instance, every occurrence of atoms $P(t_1, \ldots, t_m)$ can be replaced with $P(t_1, \ldots, t_m, v, \ldots, v)$ for some fresh variable v that is added sufficiently often as argument.

Given the BSR(SLR) clause set N, every interpretation $\mathcal{A}$ induces a partition of $\mathbb{R}$ into finitely many intervals: the interpretations of all the rational and Skolem constants c occurring in N yield point intervals that are interspersed with and enclosed by open intervals.

Definition 5 ($\mathcal{A}$-induced partition of $\mathbb{R}$). *Let $\mathcal{A}$ be an interpretation and let $r_1, \ldots, r_k$ be all the values in the set $\{c^{\mathcal{A}} \mid c \in \text{bconsts}(N)\}$ in ascending order.*

By $\mathcal{J}_{\mathcal{A}}$ we denote the following partition of $\mathbb{R}$:
$$\mathcal{J}_{\mathcal{A}} := \{(-\infty, r_1), [r_1, r_1], (r_1, r_2), [r_2, r_2], \ldots, (r_{k-1}, r_k), [r_k, r_k], (r_k, +\infty)\}.$$

The idea of the following equivalence is that equivalent tuples are indistinguishable by the constraints that we allow in the BSR(SLR) clause set N.

Definition 6 ($\mathcal{J}_{\mathcal{A}}$-equivalence, $\sim_{\mathcal{J}_{\mathcal{A}}}$). *Let $\mathcal{A}$ be an interpretation and let k be a positive integer. We call two k-tuples $\bar{r}, \bar{q} \in \mathbb{R}^k$ $\mathcal{J}_{\mathcal{A}}$-equivalent if*
(i) for every $J \in \mathcal{J}_{\mathcal{A}}$ and every i, $1 \leq i \leq k$, we have $r_i \in J$ if and only if $q_i \in J$ and
(ii) for all i, j, $1 \leq i, j \leq k$ we have $r_i < r_j$ if and only if $q_i < q_j$.
The induced equivalence relation on tuples of positive length is denoted by $\sim_{\mathcal{J}_{\mathcal{A}}}$.

For every positive k the relation $\sim_{\mathcal{J}_{\mathcal{A}}}$ induces only finitely many equivalence classes on the set of all k-tuples over the reals. We intend to show that, if N is satisfiable, then there is some model $\mathcal{A}$ for N which does not distinguish between different $\mathcal{J}_{\mathcal{A}}$-equivalent tuples. First, we need some notion that reflects how the interpretation $\mathcal{A}$ treats a given tuple $\bar{r} \in \mathbb{R}^m$. This role will be taken by the coloring $\chi_{\mathcal{A}}$, which maps $\bar{r}$ to a set of expressions of the form $P\bar{a}$, where P is some predicate symbol occurring in N and $\bar{a}$ is an m'-tuple of domain elements from $\mathcal{S}^{\mathcal{A}}$. The presence of $P\bar{a}$ in the set $\chi_{\mathcal{A}}(\bar{r})$ indicates that $\mathcal{A}$ interprets P in such a way that $P^{\mathcal{A}}$ contains the pair $\langle \bar{a}, \bar{r} \rangle$. In this sense, $\chi_{\mathcal{A}}(\bar{r})$ comprises all the relevant information that $\mathcal{A}$ contains regarding the tuple $\bar{r}$.

Definition 7 ($\mathcal{A}$-coloring $\chi_{\mathcal{A}}$). *Given an interpretation $\mathcal{A}$, let $\widehat{\mathcal{S}} := \{a \in \mathcal{S}^{\mathcal{A}} \mid a = c^{\mathcal{A}}$ for some $c \in$ fconsts$(N)\}$ be the set of all domain elements assigned to free-sort constant symbols by $\mathcal{A}$. The $\mathcal{A}$-coloring of $\mathbb{R}^m$ is the mapping $\chi_{\mathcal{A}} : \mathbb{R}^m \to \mathcal{P}\{P\bar{a} \mid \bar{a} \in \widehat{\mathcal{S}}^{m'}$ and P is an uninterpreted predicate symbol in $N\}$ defined such that for every $\bar{r} \in \mathbb{R}^m$ we have $P\bar{a} \in \chi_{\mathcal{A}}(\bar{r})$ if and only if $\langle \bar{a}, \bar{r} \rangle \in P^{\mathcal{A}}$.*

Having the coloring $\chi_{\mathcal{A}}$ at hand, it is easy to formulate a uniformity property for a given interpretation $\mathcal{A}$. Two tuples $\bar{r}, \bar{r}' \in \mathbb{R}^m$ are treated *uniformly* by $\mathcal{A}$, if the colors $\chi_{\mathcal{A}}(\bar{r})$ and $\chi_{\mathcal{A}}(\bar{r}')$ agree. Put differently, $\mathcal{A}$ does not distinguish $\bar{r}$ from $\bar{r}'$.

Definition 8 ($\mathcal{J}_{\mathcal{A}}$-uniform interpretation). *An interpretation $\mathcal{A}$ is $\mathcal{J}_{\mathcal{A}}$-uniform if $\chi_{\mathcal{A}}$ colors each and every $\sim_{\mathcal{J}_{\mathcal{A}}}$-equivalence class uniformly, i.e. for all $\sim_{\mathcal{J}_{\mathcal{A}}}$-equivalent tuples $\bar{r}, \bar{r}'$ we have $\chi_{\mathcal{A}}(\bar{r}) = \chi_{\mathcal{A}}(\bar{r}')$.*

We next show that there exists a $\mathcal{J}_{\mathcal{B}}$-uniform model $\mathcal{B}$ of N, if N is satisfiable. Since such a model does not distinguish between $\mathcal{J}_{\mathcal{B}}$-equivalent m-tuples, and as there are only finitely many equivalence classes induced by $\sim_{\mathcal{J}_{\mathcal{B}}}$, only a finite amount of information is required to describe $\mathcal{B}$. This insight will give rise to a decision procedure that nondeterministically guesses how each and every equivalence class shall be treated by the uniform model.

Given some model $\mathcal{A}$ of N, the following lemma assumes the existence of certain finite sets Q_i with a fixed cardinality which are subsets of the open intervals in $\mathcal{J}_\mathcal{A}$. All $\mathcal{J}_\mathcal{A}$-equivalent m-tuples that can be constructed from the reals belonging to the Q_i are required to be colored identically by $\chi_\mathcal{A}$. The existence of the Q_i is the subject of Lemma 10.

Lemma 9. *Let λ be the maximal number of distinct base-sort variables in any single clause in N. In case of $\lambda < m$, we set $\lambda := m$. Let $\mathcal{A}$ be a model of N. Let $J_0, \ldots, J_\kappa$ be an enumeration of all open intervals in $\mathcal{J}_\mathcal{A}$ sorted in ascending order. Moreover, let $r_1, \ldots, r_\kappa$ be all reals in ascending order that define point intervals in $\mathcal{J}_\mathcal{A}$, i.e. $J_0 < [r_1, r_1] < J_1 < \ldots < [r_\kappa, r_\kappa] < J_\kappa$. Suppose we are given a collection of finite sets $Q_0, \ldots, Q_\kappa$ possessing the following properties:*
(i) $Q_i \subseteq J_i$ and $|Q_i| = \lambda$ for every i.
(ii) Let $Q := \bigcup_i Q_i \cup \{r_1, \ldots, r_\kappa\}$. For all $\mathcal{J}_\mathcal{A}$-equivalent m-tuples $\bar{q}, \bar{q}' \in Q^m$ we have $\chi_\mathcal{A}(\bar{q}) = \chi_\mathcal{A}(\bar{q}')$.
Then we can construct a model $\mathcal{B}$ of N that is $\mathcal{J}_\mathcal{B}$-uniform and that interprets the free sort $\mathcal{S}$ as a finite set.

Proof sketch.
Claim I: Let μ be a positive integer with $\mu \leq \lambda$. Every $\sim_{\mathcal{J}_\mathcal{A}}$-equivalence class over $\mathbb{R}^\mu$ contains some representative lying in Q^μ. ◊

Let $\widehat{\mathcal{S}}$ denote the set $\{a \in \mathcal{S}^\mathcal{A} \mid a = c^\mathcal{A}$ for some $c \in \text{fconsts}(N)\}$. We construct the interpretation $\mathcal{B}$ as follows: $\mathcal{S}^\mathcal{B} := \widehat{\mathcal{S}}$; $c^\mathcal{B} := c^\mathcal{A}$ for every constant symbol c; for every uninterpreted predicate symbol P and for all tuples $\bar{a} \in \widehat{\mathcal{S}}^{m'}$ and $\bar{s} \in \mathbb{R}^m$ we pick some tuple $\bar{q} \in Q^m$ with $\bar{q} \sim_{\mathcal{J}_\mathcal{A}} \bar{s}$, and we define $P^\mathcal{B}$ so that $\langle \bar{a}, \bar{s} \rangle \in P^\mathcal{B}$ if and only if $\langle \bar{a}, \bar{q} \rangle \in P^\mathcal{A}$. By construction, $\mathcal{B}$ is $\mathcal{J}_\mathcal{B}$-uniform.

It remains to show $\mathcal{B} \models N$. Consider any clause $C = \Lambda \parallel \Gamma \rightarrow \Delta$ in N and let β be any variable assignment ranging over $\mathcal{S}^\mathcal{B} \cup \mathbb{R}$. Starting from β, we derive a special variable assignment $\widehat{\beta}_C$ as follows. Let $x_1, \ldots, x_\ell$ be all base-sort variables in C. By Claim I, there is some tuple $\langle q_1, \ldots, q_\ell \rangle \in Q^\ell$ such that $\langle q_1, \ldots, q_\ell \rangle \sim_{\mathcal{J}_\mathcal{A}} \langle \beta(x_1), \ldots, \beta(x_\ell) \rangle$. We set $\widehat{\beta}_C(x_i) := q_i$ for every x_i. For all other base-sort variables, $\widehat{\beta}_C$ can be defined arbitrarily. For every free-sort variable u we set $\widehat{\beta}_C(u) := \beta(u)$.

As $\mathcal{A}$ is a model of N, we get $\mathcal{A}, \widehat{\beta}_C \models C$. By case distinction on why $\mathcal{A}, \widehat{\beta}_C \models C$ holds, one can infer $\mathcal{B}, \beta \models C$. Consequently, $\mathcal{B} \models N$. □

In order to show that uniform models always exist for satisfiable clause sets N, we still need to prove the existence of the sets Q_i mentioned in Lemma 9.

Lemma 10. *Let $\mathcal{A}$ be an interpretation. Let $r_1, \ldots, r_\kappa$ be all the reals defining point intervals in $\mathcal{J}_\mathcal{A}$ and let $J_0, \ldots, J_\kappa$ be all open intervals in $\mathcal{J}_\mathcal{A}$ such that $J_0 < [r_1, r_1] < J_1 < [r_2, r_2] < \ldots < J_{\kappa-1} < [r_\kappa, r_\kappa] < J_\kappa$. Let λ be a positive integer. There is a collection of finite sets $Q_0, \ldots, Q_\kappa$ such that Requirements (i) and (ii) of Lemma 9 are met.*

Proof sketch. We employ a more sophisticated variant of the Ramsey result stated in Lemma 4.
Claim I: There are sets $Q_0, \ldots, Q_\kappa$ satisfying Requirement (i) of Lemma 9 and the following conditions. For every Q_i, $0 \leq i \leq \kappa$, let $s_{\langle i,1\rangle}, \ldots, s_{\langle i,\lambda\rangle}$ be all the values in Q_i in ascending order. Moreover, we set $s_{\langle \kappa+i,1\rangle} := r_i$ for every i with $1 \leq i \leq \kappa$. Then, for every mapping $\varrho : [m] \to \{0, \ldots, 2\kappa\} \times [m]$ we have $\chi_{\mathcal{A}}(s_{\varrho(1)}, \ldots, s_{\varrho(m)}) = \chi_{\mathcal{A}}(s'_{\varrho(1)}, \ldots, s'_{\varrho(m)})$. $\Diamond$

One can show that for every $\sim_{\mathcal{J}_\mathcal{A}}$-equivalence class S over $\mathbb{R}^m$ there is some mapping $\varrho : [m] \to \{0, \ldots, 2\kappa\} \times [m]$ such that

(1) whenever $\varrho(i) = \langle k, \ell\rangle$ with $k > \kappa + 1$ then $\ell = 1$, and
(2) for all ascending tuples
$\bar{s}_0 = \langle s_{\langle 0,1\rangle}, \ldots, s_{\langle 0,m\rangle}\rangle \in J_0^m; \ldots; \bar{s}_\kappa = \langle s_{\langle \kappa,1\rangle}, \ldots, s_{\langle \kappa,m\rangle}\rangle \in J_\kappa^m$;
$\bar{s}_{\kappa+1} = \langle r_{\langle \kappa+1,1\rangle}\rangle = \langle r_1\rangle; \ldots; \bar{s}_{2\kappa} = \langle s_{\langle 2\kappa,1\rangle}\rangle = \langle r_\kappa\rangle$
we have $\langle s_{\varrho(1)}, \ldots, s_{\varrho(m)}\rangle \in S$, and
(3) for every tuple $\langle q_1, \ldots, q_m\rangle \in S$ there exist ascending tuples $\bar{s}_1, \ldots, \bar{s}_{2\kappa}$ defined as in (2) such that $\langle q_1, \ldots, q_m\rangle = \langle s_{\varrho(1)}, \ldots, s_{\varrho(m)}\rangle$.

Consider any $\bar{q}, \bar{q}' \in S$. By (2), $\bar{q}$ can be written into $\langle s_{\varrho(1)}, \ldots, s_{\varrho(m)}\rangle$ for appropriate values $s_{\langle k,\ell\rangle}$ and $\bar{q}'$ can be represented by $\langle s'_{\varrho(1)}, \ldots, s'_{\varrho(m)}\rangle$ for appropriate $s'_{\langle k,\ell\rangle}$. Claim I entails $\chi_{\mathcal{A}}(\bar{q}) = \chi_{\mathcal{A}}(\langle s_{\varrho(1)}, \ldots, s_{\varrho(m)}\rangle) = \chi_{\mathcal{A}}(\langle s'_{\varrho(1)}, \ldots, s'_{\varrho(m)}\rangle) = \chi_{\mathcal{A}}(\bar{q}')$. $\square$

Lemmas 9 and 10 together entail the existence of some $\mathcal{J}_\mathcal{A}$-uniform model $\mathcal{A} \models N$ with a finite free-sort domain $\mathcal{S}^\mathcal{A}$, if N is satisfiable.

Corollary 11. *If N has a model, then it has a model $\mathcal{A}$ that is $\mathcal{J}_\mathcal{A}$-uniform and that interprets the sort $\mathcal{S}$ as some finite set.*

Given any interpretation $\mathcal{A}$, the partition $\mathcal{J}_\mathcal{A}$ of the reals is determined by the rational constants in N and by the values that $\mathcal{A}$ assigns to the base-sort Skolem constants in N. Let $d_1, \ldots, d_\lambda$ be all the base-sort Skolem constants in N. If we are given some mapping $\gamma : \{d_1, \ldots, d_\lambda\} \to \mathbb{R}$, then γ induces a partition $\mathcal{J}_\gamma$, just as $\mathcal{A}$ induces $\mathcal{J}_\mathcal{A}$. We can easily verify whether N has a model $\mathcal{B}$ that is *compatible* with γ (i.e. $\mathcal{B}$ assigns the same values to $d_1, \ldots, d_\lambda$) and that is $\mathcal{J}_\mathcal{B}$-uniform. Due to the uniformity requirement, there is only a finite number of candidate interpretations that have to be checked.

Consequently, in order to show decidability of the satisfiability problem for finite BSR(SLR) clause sets in normal form, the only question that remains to be answered is whether it is sufficient to consider a finite number of assignments γ of real values to the Skolem constants in N. Recall that since N is in normal form, we can divide N into two disjoint parts N_{def} and N' such that all ground LA terms occurring in N' are either (Skolem) constants or rationals. Moreover, every clause in N_{def} constitutes a definition $c = t$ of some Skolem constant c. As far as the LA constraints occurring in N' are concerned, the most relevant information regarding the interpretation of Skolem constants is their ordering relative to one another and relative to the occurring rationals. This means, the

clauses in N' cannot distinguish two assignments γ, γ' if
(a) for every Skolem constant d_i and every rational r occurring in N' we have (a.1) $\gamma(d_i) \leq r$ if and only if $\gamma'(d_i) \leq r$, and (a.2) $\gamma(d_i) \geq r$ if and only if $\gamma'(d_i) \geq r$, and
(b) for all d_i, d_j we have that $\gamma(d_i) \leq \gamma(d_j)$ if and only if $\gamma'(d_i) \leq \gamma'(d_j)$.

This observation leads to the following nondeterministic decision procedure for finite BSR(SLR) clause sets in normal form:

(1) Nondeterministically fix a total preorder $\preceq$ (reflexive and transitive) on the set of all base-sort Skolem constants and rational constants occurring in N'. Define a clause set $N_\preceq$ that enforces $\preceq$ for base-sort Skolem constants, i.e. $N_\preceq := \{c > c' \,\|\, \to \Box \mid c \preceq c'$, either c or c' or both are Skolem constants$\}$.
(2) Check whether there is some mapping $\gamma : \{d_1, \ldots, d_\lambda\} \to \mathbb{R}$ such that γ is a solution for the clauses in $N_{\mathrm{def}} \cup N_\preceq$. (This step relies on the fact that linear arithmetic over existentially quantified variables is decidable.)
(3) If such an assignment γ exists, define an interpretation $\mathcal{B}$ as follows.
  (3.1) Nondeterministically define $\mathcal{S}^\mathcal{B}$ to be some subset of fconsts(N), i.e. use a subset of the Herbrand domain with respect to the free sort $\mathcal{S}$.
  (3.2) For every $e \in$ fconsts(N) nondeterministically pick some $a \in \mathcal{S}^\mathcal{B}$ and set $e^\mathcal{B} := a$.
  (3.3) Set $d_i^\mathcal{B} := \gamma(d_i)$ for every d_i.
  (3.4) For every uninterpreted predicate symbol P occurring in N nondeterministically define the set $P^\mathcal{B}$ in such a way that $\mathcal{B}$ is $\mathcal{J}_\mathcal{B}$-uniform.
(4) Check whether $\mathcal{B}$ is a model of N.

Theorem 12. *Satisfiability of finite BSR(SLR) clause sets is decidable.*

5 Decidability of Satisfiability for BSR(BD) Clause Sets

Similarly to the previous section, we fix some finite BSR(BD) clause set N in normal form for the rest of this section, and we assume that all uninterpreted predicate symbols P occurring in N have the sort $P : \mathcal{S}^{m'} \times \mathcal{R}^m$. Moreover, we assume that all base-sort constants in N are integers. This does not lead to a loss of generality, as we could multiply all rational constants with the least common multiple of their denominators to obtain an equisatisfiable clause set in which all base-sort constants are integers. We could even allow Skolem constants, if we added clauses stipulating that every such constant is assigned a value that is (a) an integer and (b) is bounded from above and below by some integer bounds. Dropping any of these two restrictions leads to an undecidable satisfiability problem. For the sake of simplicity, we do not consider Skolem constants in this section.

Our general approach to decidability of the satisfiability problem for finite BSR(BD) clause sets is very similar to the path taken in the previous section. Due to the nature of the LA constraints in BSR(BD) clause sets, the employed equivalence relation characterizing indistinguishable tuples has to be a different one. In fact, we use one equivalence relation $\widehat{\simeq}_\kappa$ on the unbounded space $\mathbb{R}^m$ and another equivalence relation $\simeq_\kappa$ on the subspace $(-\kappa - 1, \kappa + 1)^m$ for some positive integer κ. Our definition of the relations $\simeq_\kappa$ and $\hat{\simeq}_\kappa$ is inspired by the notion of clock equivalence used in the context of timed automata (see, e.g., [1]).

Definition 13 (bounded region equivalence $\simeq_\kappa$). *Let κ be a positive integer. We define the equivalence relation $\simeq_\kappa$ on $(-\kappa-1, \kappa+1)^m$ such that we get $\langle r_1, \ldots, r_m \rangle \simeq_\kappa \langle s_1, \ldots, s_m \rangle$ if and only if the following conditions are met:*
(i) For every i we have $\lfloor r_i \rfloor = \lfloor s_i \rfloor$, and $fr(r_i) = 0$ if and only if $fr(s_i) = 0$.
(ii) For all i, j we have $fr(r_i) \leq fr(r_j)$ if and only if $fr(s_i) \leq fr(s_j)$.

The relation $\simeq_\kappa$ induces only a finite number of equivalence classes over $(-\kappa-1, \kappa + 1)^m$. Over $\mathbb{R}^m$, on the other hand, an analogous equivalence relation $\simeq_\infty$ would lead to infinitely many equivalence classes. In order to overcome this problem and obtain an equivalence relation over $\mathbb{R}^m$ that induces only a finite number of equivalence classes, we use the following compromise.

Definition 14 (unbounded region equivalence $\hat{\simeq}_\kappa$). *Let κ be a positive integer. We define the equivalence relation $\hat{\simeq}_\kappa$ on $\mathbb{R}^m$ in such a way that $\langle r_1, \ldots, r_m \rangle \hat{\simeq}_\kappa \langle s_1, \ldots, s_m \rangle$ holds if and only if*
(i) for every i either $r_i > \kappa$ and $s_i > \kappa$, or $r_i < -\kappa$ and $s_i < -\kappa$, or the following conditions are met: (i.i) $\lfloor r_i \rfloor = \lfloor s_i \rfloor$ and (i.ii) $fr(r_i) = 0$ if and only if $fr(s_i) = 0$, and (ii) for all i, j
(ii.i) if $r_i, r_j > \kappa$ or $r_i, r_j < -\kappa$, then $r_i \leq r_j$ if and only if $s_i \leq s_j$,
(ii.ii) if $-\kappa \leq r_i, r_j \leq \kappa$, then $fr(r_i) \leq fr(r_j)$ if and only if $fr(s_i) \leq fr(s_j)$.

Obviously, the equivalence relations $\simeq_\kappa$ and $\hat{\simeq}_\kappa$ coincide on the subspace $(-\kappa, \kappa)^m$. Over $(-\kappa-1, \kappa+1)^m$ the relation $\simeq_\kappa$ constitutes a proper refinement of $\hat{\simeq}_\kappa$. Figure 1 depicts the equivalence classes induced by $\simeq_\kappa$ and $\hat{\simeq}_\kappa$ in a two-dimensional setting for $\kappa = 1$. We need both relations in our approach.

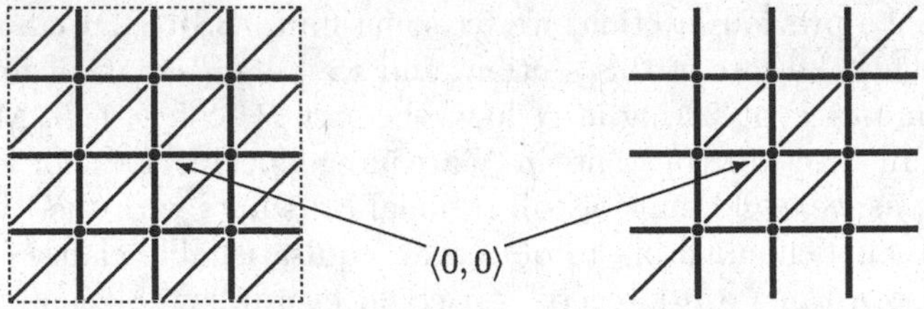

Fig. 1. Left: partition of the set $(-2, 2)^2$ induced by $\simeq_1$. Right: partition of $\mathbb{R}^2$ induced by $\hat{\simeq}_1$. Every dot, line segment, and white area represents an equivalence class.

Definition 15 ($\simeq_\kappa$-uniform and $\hat{\simeq}_\kappa$-uniform interpretations). *Let κ be a positive integer. Consider a interpretation $\mathcal{A}$. We call $\mathcal{A}$ $\simeq_\kappa$-*uniform *if its corresponding coloring $\chi_\mathcal{A}$ (cf. Definition 7) colors each $\simeq_\kappa$-equivalence class over $(-\kappa - 1, \kappa + 1)^m$ uniformly, i.e. for all tuples $\bar{q}, \bar{q}' \in (-\kappa - 1, \kappa + 1)^m$ with $\bar{q} \simeq_\kappa \bar{q}'$ we have $\chi_\mathcal{A}(\bar{q}) = \chi_\mathcal{A}(\bar{q}')$. We call $\mathcal{A}$ $\hat{\simeq}_\kappa$-*uniform *if $\chi_\mathcal{A}$ colors each $\hat{\simeq}_\kappa$-equivalence class over $\mathbb{R}^m$ uniformly.*

The parameter κ will be determined by the base-sort constant in N with the largest absolute value. If κ is defined in this way, one can show that the LA constraints occurring in N cannot distinguish between two $\widehat{\simeq}_\kappa$-equivalent m-tuples of reals. This observation is crucial for the proof of Lemma 16.

In order to prove the existence of $\widehat{\simeq}_\kappa$-uniform models for satisfiable N, we start from some model $\mathcal{A}$ of N and rely on the existence of a certain finite set $Q \subseteq [0, 1)$ of fractional parts. This set Q can be extended to a set $\widehat{Q} \subseteq (-\kappa-1, \kappa+1)$ by addition of the fractional parts in Q with integral parts k from the range $-\kappa - 1 \leq k \leq \kappa$. Hence, $\widehat{Q}$ contains $2(\kappa+1) \cdot |Q|$ reals. We assume that all $\simeq_\kappa$-equivalent tuples $\bar{s}, \bar{s}'$ from $\widehat{Q}^m$ are treated uniformly by $\mathcal{A}$. Put differently, we require $\chi_\mathcal{A}(\bar{s}) = \chi_\mathcal{A}(\bar{s}')$. We choose to formulate this requirement with respect to $\simeq_\kappa$ because of the more regular structure of its equivalence classes, which facilitates a more convenient way of invoking Lemma 4. Due to the fact that $\simeq_\kappa$ constitutes a refinement of $\widehat{\simeq}_\kappa$ on the subspace $(-\kappa - 1, \kappa + 1)^m$, and since for every $\widehat{\simeq}_\kappa$-equivalence class $\widehat{S}$ over $\mathbb{R}^m$ there is some $\simeq_\kappa$-equivalence class $S \subseteq (-\kappa - 1, \kappa + 1)^m$ such that $S \subseteq \widehat{S}$, we can use the color $\chi_\mathcal{A}(\bar{r})$ of representative m-tuples $\bar{r}$ constructed from $\widehat{Q}$ to serve as a blueprint when constructing a $\widehat{\simeq}_\kappa$-uniform model $\mathcal{B}$.

Lemma 16. *Let λ be the maximal number of distinct base-sort variables in any single clause in N; in case of $\lambda < m$, we set $\lambda := m$. Let $\mathcal{A}$ be a model of N. Let κ be the maximal absolute value of any rational occurring in N; in case this value is zero, we set $\kappa := 1$. Suppose we are given a finite set $Q \subseteq [0, 1)$ of cardinality $\lambda + 1$ such that $0 \in Q$ and for all tuples $\bar{r}, \bar{s} \in \widehat{Q}^m$, $\bar{r} \simeq_\kappa \bar{s}$ entails $\chi_\mathcal{A}(\bar{r}) = \chi_\mathcal{A}(\bar{s})$, where*

$$\widehat{Q} := \{q + k \mid q \in Q \text{ and } k \in \{-\kappa - 1, \ldots, 0, \ldots, \kappa\}\}.$$

Then we can construct a model $\mathcal{B}$ of N that is $\widehat{\simeq}_\kappa$-uniform and that interprets the free sort $\mathcal{S}$ as a finite set.

Proof sketch. The construction of $\mathcal{B}$ from $\mathcal{A}$ is similar to the construction of uniform models outlined in the proof of Lemma 9.

Claim I: Let μ be a positive integer with $\mu \leq \lambda$. For every $\widehat{\simeq}_\kappa$-equivalence class S over $\mathbb{R}^\mu$ and every $\bar{r} \in S$ there is some $\bar{q} \in S \cap \widehat{Q}^\mu$ such that $\bar{r} \widehat{\simeq}_\kappa \bar{q}$ and for all i_1, i_2, i_3 with $r_{i_1} < -\kappa$ and $r_{i_2} > \kappa$ and $-\kappa \leq r_{i_3} \leq \kappa$ we have $\mathrm{fr}(q_{i_1}) < \mathrm{fr}(q_{i_2}) < \mathrm{fr}(q_{i_3})$. ◇

Let $\widehat{\mathcal{S}}$ denote the set $\{a \in \mathcal{S}^\mathcal{A} \mid a = c^\mathcal{A}$ for some $c \in \mathrm{fconsts}(N)\}$. We construct the interpretation $\mathcal{B}$ as follows: $\mathcal{S}^\mathcal{B} := \widehat{\mathcal{S}}$; $c^\mathcal{B} := c^\mathcal{A}$ for every constant symbol c; for every uninterpreted predicate symbol P occurring in N and for all tuples $\bar{a} \in \widehat{\mathcal{S}}^{m'}$ and $\bar{r} \in \mathbb{R}^m$ we pick some tuple $\bar{q} \in \widehat{Q}^m$ in accordance with Claim I—i.e. $\bar{q}$ satisfies $\bar{r} \widehat{\simeq}_\kappa \bar{q}$—and define $P^\mathcal{B}$ in such a way that $\langle \bar{a}, \bar{r} \rangle \in P^\mathcal{B}$ if and only if $\langle \bar{a}, \bar{q} \rangle \in P^\mathcal{A}$.

Claim II: The interpretation $\mathcal{B}$ is $\widehat{\simeq}_\kappa$-uniform. ◇

It remains to show $\mathcal{B} \models N$. We use the same approach as in the proof for Lemma 9, this time based on the equivalence relation $\widehat{\simeq}_\kappa$ instead of $\sim_{\mathcal{J}_\mathcal{A}}$. □

We employ Lemma 4 to prove the existence of the set Q used in Lemma 16.

Lemma 17. *Let $\mathcal{A}$ be an interpretation and let κ, λ be positive integers with $\lambda \geq m$. There exists a finite set $Q \subseteq [0,1)$ of cardinality $\lambda + 1$ such that $0 \in Q$ and for all tuples $\bar{s}, \bar{s}' \in \widehat{Q}^m$, $\bar{s} \simeq_\kappa \bar{s}'$ entails $\chi_\mathcal{A}(\bar{s}) = \chi_\mathcal{A}(\bar{s}')$, where*

$$\widehat{Q} := \{q + k \mid q \in Q \text{ and } k \in \{-\kappa - 1, \ldots, 0, \ldots, \kappa\}\}.$$

Proof sketch. One can show that every $\simeq_\kappa$-equivalence class S over $(-\kappa-1, \kappa+1)^m$ can be represented by a pair of mappings $\varrho : [m] \to \{0, 1, \ldots, m\}$ and $\sigma : [m] \to \{-\kappa - 1, \ldots, 0, \ldots, \kappa\}$ such that

(i) for any ascending tuple $\langle r_0, r_1, \ldots, r_m \rangle \in [0,1)^{m+1}$ with $r_0 = 0$ we have $\langle r_{\varrho(1)} + \sigma(1), \ldots, r_{\varrho(m)} + \sigma(m) \rangle \in S$, and
(ii) for every tuple $\langle s_1, \ldots, s_m \rangle \in S$ there is an ascending tuple $\langle r_0, r_1, \ldots, r_m \rangle \in [0,1)^{m+1}$ with $r_0 = 0$ such that $\langle s_1, \ldots, s_m \rangle = \langle r_{\varrho(1)} + \sigma(1), \ldots, r_{\varrho(m)} + \sigma(m) \rangle$.

Having an enumeration $\langle \varrho_1, \sigma_1 \rangle, \ldots, \langle \varrho_k, \sigma_k \rangle$ of pairs of such mappings in which every $\simeq_\kappa$-equivalence class over $(-\kappa-1, \kappa+1)^m$ is represented, we construct a coloring $\widehat{\chi} : \mathbb{R}^m \to \big(\mathcal{P}\{P_i \bar{a} \mid \bar{a} \in \widehat{\mathcal{S}}^{m'} \text{ and } P_i \text{ occurs in } N\}\big)^k$ by setting

$$\begin{aligned}\widehat{\chi}(\bar{r}) := \big\langle &\chi_\mathcal{A}\big(\langle r_{\varrho_1(1)} + \sigma_1(1), \ldots, r_{\varrho_1(m)} + \sigma_1(m)\rangle\big), \\ &\ldots, \chi_\mathcal{A}\big(\langle r_{\varrho_k(1)} + \sigma_k(1), \ldots, r_{\varrho_k(m)} + \sigma_k(m)\rangle\big)\big\rangle\end{aligned}$$

for every tuple $\bar{r} = \langle r_1, \ldots, r_m \rangle \in (0,1)^m$, where we define r_0 to be 0. By virtue of Lemma 4, there is a set $Q' \subseteq (0,1)$ of cardinality λ such that all ascending tuples $\langle r_1, \ldots, r_m \rangle \in Q'^m$ are assigned the same color by χ. Then $Q := Q' \cup \{0\}$ is the sought set. □

Lemmas 16 and 17 together entail the existence of $\widehat{\simeq}_\kappa$-uniform models for finite satisfiable BSR(BD) clause sets, where κ is defined as in Lemma 16.

Corollary 18. *Let κ be defined as in Lemma 16. If N is satisfiable, then it has a model $\mathcal{A}$ that is $\widehat{\simeq}_\kappa$-uniform and that interprets the sort $\mathcal{S}$ as some finite set.*

By virtue of Corollary 18, we can devise a nondeterministic decision procedure for finite BSR(BD) clause sets N. We adapt the decision procedure for BSR(SLR) as follows. Since base-sort Skolem constants do not occur in N, Steps (1), (2), and (3.3) are skipped. Moreover, Step (3.4) has to be modified slightly. The interpretations of uninterpreted predicate symbols need to be constructed in such a way that the candidate interpretation $\mathcal{B}$ is $\widehat{\simeq}_\kappa$-uniform for $\kappa := \max\big(\{1\} \cup \{|c| \mid c \in \text{bconsts}(N)\}\big)$.

Theorem 19. *Satisfiability of finite BSR(BD) clause sets is decidable.*

6 Formalizing Reachability for Timed Automata

In this section we show that reachability for timed automata (cf. [1]) can be formalized using finite BSR(BD) clause sets. In what follows, we fix a finite sequence $\bar{x}$ of pairwise distinct *clock variables* that range over the reals. For convenience, we occasionally treat $\bar{x}$ as a set and use set notation such at $x \in \bar{x}$, $|\bar{x}|$, and $\mathcal{P}(\bar{x})$. A *clock constraint over* $\bar{x}$ is a finite conjunction of LA constraints of the form $\mathtt{true}$, $x \triangleleft c$, or $x - y \triangleleft c$, where $x, y \in \bar{x}$, c is an integer and $\triangleleft \in \{<, \leq, =, \neq, \geq, >\}$. We denote the *set of all clock constraints over* $\bar{x}$ by $\mathrm{CC}(\bar{x})$. A *timed automaton* is a tuple $\langle \mathrm{Loc}, \ell_0, \bar{x}, \langle \mathrm{inv}_\ell \rangle_{\ell \in \mathrm{Loc}}, \mathcal{T} \rangle$, where Loc is a finite set of locations; $\ell_0 \in \mathrm{Loc}$ is the initial location; $\langle \mathrm{inv}_\ell \rangle_{\ell \in \mathrm{Loc}}$ is a family of clock constraints from $\mathrm{CC}(\bar{x})$ where each inv_ℓ describes the *invariant at location* ℓ; $\mathcal{T} \subseteq \mathrm{Loc} \times \mathrm{CC}(\bar{x}) \times \mathcal{P}(\bar{x}) \times \mathrm{Loc}$ is the location transition relation within the automaton, including guards with respect to clocks and the set of clocks that are being reset when the transition is taken.

Although the control flow of a timed automaton is described by finite means, the fact that clocks can assume uncountably many values yields an infinite state space, namely, $\mathrm{Loc} \times [0, \infty)^{|\bar{x}|}$. Transitions between states fall into two categories:

delay transitions $\langle \ell, \bar{r} \rangle \hookrightarrow \langle \ell, \bar{r}' \rangle$ with $\bar{r}' = \bar{r} + t$ for some $t \geq 0$ and $[\bar{x}' \mapsto \bar{r}'] \models \mathrm{inv}_\ell[\bar{x}']$; and

location transitions $\langle \ell, \bar{r} \rangle \hookrightarrow \langle \ell', \bar{r}' \rangle$ for some $\langle \ell, g, Z, \ell' \rangle \in \mathcal{T}$ with $[\bar{x} \mapsto \bar{r}] \models g[\bar{x}]$, $\bar{r}' = \bar{r}[Z \mapsto 0]$, and $[\bar{x}' \mapsto \bar{r}'] \models \mathrm{inv}_{\ell'}[\bar{x}']$.

The operation $\bar{r}' := \bar{r} + t$ is defined by setting $r_i' := r_i + t$ for every i, and $\bar{r}' := \bar{r}[Z \mapsto 0]$ means that $r_i' = 0$ for every $x_i \in Z$ and $r_i' = r_i$ for every $x_i \notin Z$.

In [6] Fietzke and Weidenbach present an encoding of reachability for a given timed automaton $\mathbf{A}$ in terms of *first-order logic modulo linear arithmetic.*

Definition 20 (FOL(LA) encoding of a timed automaton, [6]**).** *Given a timed automaton* $\mathbf{A} := \langle \mathrm{Loc}, \ell_0, \bar{x}, \langle \mathrm{inv}_\ell \rangle_{\ell \in \mathrm{Loc}}, \mathcal{T} \rangle$, *the* FOL(LA) encoding of $\mathbf{A}$ *is the following clause set* $N_{\mathbf{A}}$, *where* Reach *is a* $(1 + |\bar{x}|)$*-ary predicate symbol:*

the initial clause $\bigwedge_{x \in \bar{x}} x = 0 \;\wedge\; \mathrm{inv}_{\ell_0}[\bar{x}] \;\|\rightarrow \mathrm{Reach}(\ell_0, \bar{x})$;

delay clauses $z \geq 0 \;\wedge\; \bigwedge_{x \in \bar{x}} x' = x + z \;\wedge\; \mathrm{inv}_\ell[\bar{x}'] \;\|\; \mathrm{Reach}(\ell, \bar{x}) \rightarrow \mathrm{Reach}(\ell, \bar{x}')$ *for every location* $\ell \in \mathrm{Loc}$;

transition clauses $g[\bar{x}] \wedge \bigwedge_{x \in Z} x' = 0 \;\wedge \bigwedge_{x \in \bar{x} \setminus Z} x' = x \;\wedge\; \mathrm{inv}_{\ell'}[\bar{x}'] \;\|\; \mathrm{Reach}(\ell, \bar{x}) \rightarrow \mathrm{Reach}(\ell', \bar{x}')$ *for every location transition* $\langle \ell, g, Z, \ell' \rangle \in \mathcal{T}$.

Corollary 4.3 in [6] states that for any model of $N_{\mathbf{A}}$, every location $\ell \in \mathrm{Loc}$, and every tuple $\bar{r} \in \mathbb{R}^{|\bar{x}|}$ we have $\mathcal{A}, [\bar{x} \mapsto \bar{r}] \models \mathrm{Reach}(\ell, \bar{x})$ if and only if $\mathbf{A}$ can reach the state $\langle \ell, \bar{r} \rangle$ from its initial configuration.

Given any clock constraint $\psi \in \mathrm{CC}(\bar{x})$ and some location ℓ, the timed automaton $\mathbf{A}$ can reach at least one of the states $\langle \ell, \bar{r} \rangle$ with $[\bar{x} \mapsto \bar{r}] \models \psi[\bar{x}]$ from its initial configuration if and only if the clause set $N_{\mathbf{A}} \cup \{\psi[\bar{x}] \,\|\, \mathrm{Reach}(\ell, \bar{x}) \rightarrow \Box\}$ is unsatisfiable (cf. Proposition 4.4 in [6]).

Next, we argue that the passage of time does not have to be formalized as a synchronous progression of all clocks. Instead, it is sufficient to require that clocks progress in such a way that their valuations do not drift apart excessively. Although this weakens the semantics slightly, reachability remains unaffected.

Lemma 21. *Consider any delay clause*
$C := \quad z \geq 0 \ \wedge \ \bigwedge_{x \in \bar{x}} x' = x + z \ \wedge \ \mathrm{inv}_\ell[\bar{x}'] \parallel \mathrm{Reach}(\ell, \bar{x}) \rightarrow \mathrm{Reach}(\ell, \bar{x}')$
that belongs to the FOL(LA) encoding of some timed automaton $\mathbf{A} := \langle \mathrm{Loc}, \ell_0, \bar{x}, \langle \mathrm{inv}_\ell \rangle_{\ell \in \mathrm{Loc}}, \mathcal{T} \rangle$. *Let* λ *be some positive integer. Let* M *be a finite clause set corresponding to the following formula*

$$\varphi := \bigwedge_{x_1, x_2 \in \bar{x}} \ \bigwedge_{-\lambda \leq k \leq \lambda} (x_1 - x_2 \leq k \ \leftrightarrow \ x_1' - x_2' \leq k) \\ \wedge \ (x_1 - x_2 \geq k \ \leftrightarrow \ x_1' - x_2' \geq k) \\ \wedge \ \bigwedge_{x \in \bar{x}} x' \geq x \ \wedge \ \mathrm{inv}_\ell[\bar{x}'] \ \parallel \ \mathrm{Reach}(\ell, \bar{x}) \rightarrow \mathrm{Reach}(\ell, \bar{x}').$$

For every $\simeq_\lambda$*-uniform interpretation* $\mathcal{A}$ *we have* $\mathcal{A}, [\bar{x} \mapsto \bar{r}, \bar{x}' \mapsto \bar{r}'] \models C$ *for all tuples* $\bar{r}, \bar{r}' \in [0, \lambda + 1)^{|\bar{x}|}$ *if and only if* $\mathcal{A}, [\bar{x} \mapsto \bar{q}, \bar{x}' \mapsto \bar{q}'] \models M$ *holds for all tuples* $\bar{q}, \bar{q}' \in [0, \lambda + 1)^{|\bar{x}|}$.

Our approach to decidability of BSR(BD)-satisfiability exploits the observation that the allowed constraints cannot distinguish between tuples from one and the same equivalence class with respect to $\widehat{\simeq}_\lambda$, which induces only a finite number of such classes. Decidability of the reachability problem for timed automata can be argued in a similar fashion, using a suitable equivalence relation on clock valuations [1]. We refer to the induced classes of indistinguishable clock valuations over $\mathbb{R}^{|\bar{x}|}$, which are induced by a given timed automaton $\mathbf{A} = \langle \mathrm{Loc}, \ell_0, \bar{x}, \langle \mathrm{inv}_\ell \rangle_{\ell \in \mathrm{Loc}}, \mathcal{T} \rangle$, as *TA regions* of $\mathbf{A}$. Figure 2 illustrates the TA regions for some

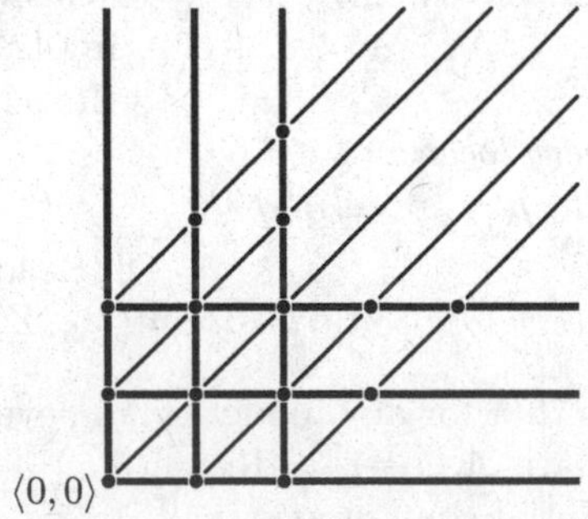

Fig. 2. Partition of the set $[0, \infty)^2$ into classes of clock valuations that cannot be distinguished by a timed automaton with two clocks in which the absolute value of integer constants occurring in location invariants and transition guards does not exceed 2. Every dot, line segment, and white area represents an equivalence class.

timed automaton with two clocks and in which all integer constants have an absolute value of at most 2. For every TA region $R \subseteq \mathbb{R}^2$ of such an automaton, there is at least one representative $\bar{r} \in R$ which lies in $[0, 5)^2$.

Let k be the maximal absolute value of any integer constant occurring in the invariants and the transition guards of **A**. Moreover, let $x_1, \ldots, x_\ell$ be the clock variables in $\bar{x}$. Consider a constraint of the form

$$\psi := x_1 - x_2 = k \wedge x_2 - x_3 = k \wedge \ldots \wedge x_{\ell-1} - x_\ell = k.$$

We observe that ψ entails $x_1 - x_\ell = (\ell - 1) \cdot k$. Of course, ψ can also be conjoined with the constraint $x_1 < -k$, say, which entails $x_\ell < -k - (\ell - 1) \cdot k$. This example illustrates that one can combine several difference constraints $x - y \triangleleft c$ over different clock variables in such a way that bounds are entailed which cannot be formulated with a single constraint $u - v \triangleleft d$ with $|d| \leq k$. However, all of these combined constraints can be equivalently represented with atomic constraints $x - y \triangleleft c$ or $x \triangleleft c$, where $|c| \leq |\bar{x}| \cdot k$.

In order to decide reachability for **A**, it is sufficient to consider a bounded subspace of $\mathbb{R}^{|\bar{x}|}$. More precisely, there exists a computable integer λ, namely $|\bar{x}| \cdot k$, such that any valuation $\bar{r}$ of **A**'s clocks can be projected to some valuation $\bar{r}' \in [0, \lambda + 1)^{|\bar{x}|}$ that **A** cannot distinguish from $\bar{r}$. In the subspace $[0, \lambda + 1)^{|\bar{x}|}$, **A**'s TA regions coincide with (finite unions of) equivalence classes with respect to $\simeq_\lambda$. In fact, the quotient $[0, \lambda+1)^{|\bar{x}|}/_{\simeq_\lambda}$ constitutes a refinement of the division of $[0, \lambda + 1)^{|\bar{x}|}$ into TA regions. Since any pair $\langle \ell, \bar{r} \rangle$ with $\bar{r} \in R$ for some TA region R is reachable if and only if all pairs $\langle \ell, \bar{r}' \rangle$ with $\bar{r} \in R$ are reachable, any minimal model $\mathcal{A}$ of the encoding $N_{\mathbf{A}}$ is $\simeq_\lambda$-uniform (where minimality of $\mathcal{A}$ refers to the minimality of the set $\text{Reach}^{\mathcal{A}}$ with respect to set inclusion). This is why Lemma 21 may focus on $\simeq_\lambda$-uniform models.

This means, given the FOL(LA) encoding $N_{\mathbf{A}}$ of **A**, we obtain a BSR(BD) encoding $N'_{\mathbf{A}}$ of reachability with respect to **A** in the following two steps:
(1) Replace every delay clause in $N_{\mathbf{A}}$ with a corresponding finite set of clauses M in accordance with Lemma 21, where we set $\lambda := |\bar{x}| \cdot k$.
(2) Conjoin the constraints $0 \leq x \wedge x < \kappa$ for $\kappa := \lambda + 1 = |\bar{x}| \cdot k + 1$ to every constraint in which a base-sort variable x occurs.
Since any $\widehat{\simeq}_{\lambda+1}$-uniform model of $N'_{\mathbf{A}}$ is $\simeq_\lambda$-uniform over the subspace $(-\lambda - 1, \lambda + 1)^{|\bar{x}|}$, Lemma 21 entails that $N'_{\mathbf{A}}$ faithfully encodes reachability for **A**.

Theorem 22. *The reachability problem for a given timed automaton can be expressed in terms of satisfiability of a finite BSR(BD) clause set.*

7 Discussion

We have shown that satisfiability for the clause fragments BSR(SLR) and BSR(BD) is decidable. Both fragments hierarchically combine the Bernays–Schönfinkel–Ramsey fragment over uninterpreted predicate symbols with restricted forms of linear arithmetic over the reals.

Since the syntax of BSR(SLR) allows only a very restricted form of arithmetic on universally quantified variables, this part of the fragment seems to reduce to the theory of (dense) orderings. Except for density, all characteristic properties of orderings (e.g. transitivity) are already definable in the non-extended BSR fragment. On the other hand, regarding existentially quantified variables—which appear in the form of Skolem constants—, BSR(SLR) allows linear arithmetic expressions without notable restrictions, as long as no universally quantified variables are involved in the arithmetic expressions, and as long as no existential quantifier lies within the scope of a universal quantifier. Unfortunately, a more liberal syntax quickly leads to undecidability, as already pointed out in Sect. 1.

With BSR(BD) we have investigated another decidable fragment that is a hierarchic combination of the Bernays–Schönfinkel–Ramsey fragment with restricted arithmetic over the reals. Since difference constraints have been of use in the analysis and verification of timed systems, the idea suggested itself that BSR(BD) may find applications in this area. Indeed, we have seen that reachability for timed automata can be expressed with BSR(BD), although not entirely in a straightforward fashion. To this end, we have slightly weakened the usual notion of synchronous progression of all clocks. Our modifications do not affect the reachability relation. It is to be expected that BSR(BD) lends itself to more sophisticated applications in the area of timed systems or other fields.

Acknowledgement. The present author is indebted to the anonymous reviewers for their constructive criticism and valuable suggestions.

References

1. Alur, R., Dill, D.L.: A theory of timed automata. Theoret. Comput. Sci. **126**(2), 183–235 (1994)
2. Bachmair, L., Ganzinger, H., Waldmann, U.: Refutational theorem proving for hierarchic first-order theories. Appl. Algebra Eng. Commun. Comput. **5**, 193–212 (1994)
3. Baumgartner, P., Waldmann, U.: Hierarchic superposition with weak abstraction. In: Bonacina, M.P. (ed.) CADE 2013. LNCS (LNAI), vol. 7898, pp. 39–57. Springer, Heidelberg (2013). doi:10.1007/978-3-642-38574-2_3
4. Bradley, A.R., Manna, Z., Sipma, H.B.: What's decidable about arrays? In: Emerson, E.A., Namjoshi, K.S. (eds.) VMCAI 2006. LNCS, vol. 3855, pp. 427–442. Springer, Heidelberg (2005). doi:10.1007/11609773_28
5. Downey, P.J.: Undecidability of Presburger arithmetic with a single monadic predicate letter. Technical report, Center for Research in Computer Technology, Harvard University (1972)
6. Fietzke, A., Weidenbach, C.: Superposition as a decision procedure for timed automata. Math. Comput. Sci. **6**(4), 409–425 (2012)
7. Ge, Y., de Moura, L.: Complete instantiation for quantified formulas in satisfiabiliby modulo theories. In: Bouajjani, A., Maler, O. (eds.) CAV 2009. LNCS, vol. 5643, pp. 306–320. Springer, Heidelberg (2009). doi:10.1007/978-3-642-02658-4_25
8. Graham, R.L., Rothschild, B.L., Spencer, J.H.: Ramsey Theory, 2nd edn. A Wiley-Interscience publication, New York (1990)
9. Horbach, M., Voigt, M., Weidenbach, C.: On the combination of the Bernays-Schönfinkel-Ramsey fragment with simple linear integer arithmetic. In: Automated Deduction (CADE-26) (to appear)

10. Horbach, M., Voigt, M., Weidenbach, C.: The universal fragment of Presburger arithmetic with unary uninterpreted predicates is undecidable. ArXiv preprint, arXiv:1703.01212 [cs.LO] (2017)
11. Kroening, D., Strichman, O.: Decision Procedures. Texts in Theoretical Computer Science. An EATCS Series, 2nd edn. Springer, Heidelberg (2016). doi:10.1007/978-3-662-50497-0
12. Kruglov, E., Weidenbach, C.: Superposition decides the first-order logic fragment over ground theories. Math. Comput. Sci. **6**(4), 427–456 (2012)
13. Niebert, P., Mahfoudh, M., Asarin, E., Bozga, M., Maler, O., Jain, N.: Verification of timed automata via satisfiability checking. In: Damm, W., Olderog, E.-R. (eds.) FTRTFT 2002. LNCS, vol. 2469, pp. 225–243. Springer, Heidelberg (2002). doi:10.1007/3-540-45739-9_15
14. Pratt, V.R.: Two Easy Theories Whose Combination is Hard. Technical report, Massachusetts Institute of Technology (1977)
15. Putnam, H.: Decidability and essential undecidability. J. Symbolic Logic **22**(1), 39–54 (1957)
16. Voigt, M.: The Bernays-Schönfinkel-Ramsey Fragment with Bounded Difference Constraints over the Reals is Decidable. ArXiv preprint, arXiv:1706.08504 [cs.LO] (2017)
17. Voigt, M., Weidenbach, C.: Bernays-Schönfinkel-Ramsey with Simple Bounds is NEXPTIME-complete. ArXiv preprint, arXiv:1501.07209 [cs.LO] (2015)

Properties and Combinations of Logic

First-Order Interpolation of Non-classical Logics Derived from Propositional Interpolation

Matthias Baaz(✉) and Anela Lolic(✉)

Institut Für Diskrete Mathematik und Geometrie 104,
Technische Universität Wien, Vienna, Austria
{baaz,anela}@logic.at

Abstract. This paper develops a general methodology to connect propositional and first-order interpolation. In fact, the existence of suitable skolemizations and of Herbrand expansions together with a propositional interpolant suffice to construct a first-order interpolant. This methodology is realized for lattice-based finitely-valued logics, the top element representing true and for (fragments of) infinitely-valued first-order Gödel logic, the logic of all linearly ordered constant domain Kripke frames.

Keywords: Proof theory · Interpolation · Lattice-based many-valued logics · Gödel logics

1 Introduction

Ever since Craig's seminal result on interpolation [8], interpolation properties have been recognized as important desiderata of logical systems. Craig interpolation has many applications in mathematics and computer science, for instance consistency proofs, model checking [18], proofs in modular specifications and modular ontologies. Recall that a logic L has *interpolation* if whenever $A \supset B$ holds in L there exists a formula I in the common language of A and B such that $A \supset I$ and $I \supset B$ both hold in L.

Propositional interpolation properties can be determined and classified with relative ease using the ground-breaking results of Maksimova cf. [12–14]. This approach is based on an algebraic analysis of the logic in question. In contrast first-order interpolation properties are notoriously hard to determine, even for logics where propositional interpolation is more or less obvious. For example it is unknown whether $G^{QF}_{[0,1]}$ (first-order infinitely-valued Gödel logic) interpolates (cf [1]) and even for MC^{QF}, the logic of constant domain Kripke frames of 3 worlds with 2 top worlds (an extension of MC), interpolation proofs are very hard cf. Ono [17]. This situation is due to the lack of an adequate algebraization of non-classical first-order logics.

C. Dixon and M. Finger (Eds.): FroCoS 2017, LNCS 10483, pp. 265–280, 2017.
DOI: 10.1007/978-3-319-66167-4_15

In this paper we present a proof theoretic methodology to reduce first-order interpolation to propositional interpolation:

$$\left.\begin{array}{r}\text{existence of suitable skolemizations } +\\ \text{existence of Herbrand expansions } +\\ \text{propositional interpolance}\end{array}\right\} \rightarrow \begin{array}{c}\text{first-order}\\ \text{interpolation.}\end{array}$$

The construction of the first-order interpolant from the propositional interpolant follows this procedure:

1. Develop a validity equivalent skolemization replacing all strong quantifiers (negative existential or positive universal quantifiers) in the valid formula $A \supset B$ to obtain the valid formula $A_1 \supset B_1$.
2. Construct a valid Herbrand expansion $A_2 \supset B_2$ for $A_1 \supset B_1$. Occurrences of $\exists x B(x)$ and $\forall x A(x)$ are replaced by suitable finite disjunctions $\bigvee B(t_i)$ and conjunctions $\bigwedge B(t_i)$, respectively.
3. Interpolate the propositionally valid formula $A_2 \supset B_2$ with the propositional interpolant I^*:
$$A_2 \supset I^* \quad \text{and} \quad I^* \supset B_2$$
are propositionally valid.
4. Reintroduce weak quantifiers to obtain valid formulas
$$A_1 \supset I^* \quad \text{and} \quad I^* \supset B_1.$$
5. Eliminate all function symbols and constants not in the common language of A_1 and B_1 by introducing suitable quantifiers in I^* (note that no Skolem functions are in the common language, therefore they are eliminated). Let I be the result.
6. I is an interpolant for $A_1 \supset B_1$. $A_1 \supset I$ and $I \supset B_1$ are skolemizations of $A \supset I$ and $I \supset B$. Therefore I is an interpolant of $A \supset B$.

We apply this methodology to lattice based finitely-valued logics and the weak quantifier and subprenex fragments of infinitely-valued first-order Gödel logic.

Note that finitely-valued first-order logics admit variants of Maehara's Lemma and therefore interpolate if all truth values are quantifier free definable [16]. For logics where not all truth-values are represented by quantifier-free formulas this argument does not hold, which explains the necessity of different interpolation arguments for e.g. $\mathrm{MC}^{\mathrm{QF}}$ (the result for $\mathrm{MC}^{\mathrm{QF}}$ is covered by our framework, cf. Example 2).

2 Lattice-Based Finitely-Valued Logics

We consider finite lattices $L = \langle W, \leq, \cup, \cap, 0, 1\rangle$ where $\cup, \cap, 0, 1$ are *supremum, infimum, minimal element, maximal element* and $0 \neq 1$, [7].

Definition 1. *A* propositional language *for* L, $\mathcal{L}^0(L, V)$, $V \subseteq W$ *is based on propositional variables* x_n, $n \in N$, *truth constants* C_v *for* $v \in V$, $\vee$, $\wedge$, $\supset$.

Definition 2. *A first-order language for L, $\mathcal{L}^1(L,V)$, $V \subseteq W$ is based on the usual first-order atoms, truth constants C_v for $v \in V$, $\vee, \wedge, \supset, \exists, \forall$.*

We write $\bot$ for C_0, $\top$ for C_1, $\neg A$ for $A \supset \bot$ if $0 \in V$.

Definition 3. $\rightarrow$: $W \times W \Rightarrow W$ *for* $L = \langle W, \leq, \cup, \cap, 0, 1\rangle$ *is an* admissible implication *iff*

$$u \rightarrow v = 1 \quad \textit{iff} \quad u \leq v,$$

$$\textit{if} \quad u \leq v, f \leq g \quad \textit{then} \quad v \rightarrow f \leq u \rightarrow g.$$

Definition 4. *The propositional logic $\boldsymbol{L}^0(L, V, \rightarrow)$ based on $\mathcal{L}^0(L,V)$, $L = \langle\ W, \leq, \cup, \cap, 0, 1\ \rangle$, $\rightarrow$ an admissible implication is defined as follows: Φ^0 is a propositional valuation iff*

1. *$\Phi^0(x) \in W$ for a propositional variable x,*
2. *$\Phi^0(C_v) = v$,*
3. *$\Phi^0(A \vee B) = \Phi^0(A) \cup \Phi^0(B)$,*
4. *$\Phi^0(A \wedge B) = \Phi^0(A) \cap \Phi^0(B)$,*
5. *$\Phi^0(A \supset B) = \Phi^0(A) \rightarrow \Phi^0(B)$.*

$$\models^0 A \textit{ iff } \forall \Phi^0 : \Phi^0(A) = 1 \quad \boldsymbol{L}(L, V, \rightarrow) = \{A \mid\ \models^0 A\}$$

we write $A_1 \ldots A_n \models^0 B$ iff for all Φ^0 $\Phi^0(A_1) = 1$ and $\ldots$ and $\Phi^0(A_n) = 1$ implies $\Phi^0(B) = 1$.

Definition 5. *The first-order logic $\boldsymbol{L}^1(L, V, \rightarrow)$ based on $\mathcal{L}^1(L,V)$, $L = \langle W, \leq, \cup, \cap, 0, 1\rangle$, $\rightarrow$ an admissible implication is defined as follows: Φ^1 is a first-order valuation into a structure $\langle D_{\Phi^1}, \Omega_{\Phi^1}\rangle$, $D_{\Phi^1} \neq \emptyset$ iff*

1. *$\Phi^1(x) \in D_{\Phi^1}$ for a variable x,*
2. *$\Phi^1(C_v) = v$,*
3. *Φ^1 is calculated for terms and other atoms according to Ω_{Φ^1}.*
4. *$\Phi^1(A \vee B) = \Phi^1(A) \cup \Phi^1(B)$,*
5. *$\Phi^1(A \wedge B) = \Phi^1(A) \cap \Phi^1(B)$,*
6. *$\Phi^1(A \supset B) = \Phi^1(A) \rightarrow \Phi^1(B)$,*
7. *$\Phi^1(\exists x A(x)) = \sup(\Phi^1(A(d) \mid d \in D_{\Phi^1})$,*
8. *$\Phi^1(\forall x A(x)) = \inf(\Phi^1(A(d)) \mid d \in D_{\Phi^1})$.*

$$\models^1 A \textit{ iff } \forall \Phi^1 : \Phi^1(A) = 1 \quad \boldsymbol{L}^1(L, V, \rightarrow) = \{A \mid\ \models^1 A\}$$

We write $A_1 \ldots A_n \models B$ iff for all Φ^1 $\Phi^1(A_1) = 1$ and $\ldots$ and $\Phi^1(A_n) = 1$ implies $\Phi^1(B) = 1$.

1 is the only value denoting truth, this justifies the chosen definitions. We omit the superscript in $\models^0$, $\models^1$ if the statement holds both for propositional and first-order logic. Quantifier-free first-order formulas can be identified with propositional formulas by identifying different atoms with different variables.

Proposition 1. *For all logics the following hold*

i. $\models A \supset A$,
ii. *If* $\models B$ *then* $\models A \supset B$,
iii. *If* $\models A \supset B$ *and* $\models C \supset D$ *then* $\models (B \supset C) \supset (A \supset D)$.

Example 1. $L = \langle \{0, 1, a\}, \leq, \cup, \cap, 0, 1\rangle$, $0 < a < 1$

$$u \to v = \begin{cases} 1 & u \leq v \\ 0 & u = 1 \text{ and } v = 0 \\ a & \text{else} \end{cases}$$

$\mathbf{L}^0(L, \{0, 1\}, \to)$ does not interpolate as

$$\models^0 (x \wedge (x \supset \bot)) \supset (y \vee (y \supset \bot))$$

does not interpolate, as the only possible interpolant is a constant with value a, as there are no common variables in the antecedent and the succedent.

$\mathbf{L}^0(L, \{0, a\}, \to)$ interpolates as all truth constants are representable, $\top$ by $\bot \supset \bot$ (c.f. Sect. 5).

Example 2. Finite propositional and constant-domain Kripke frames can be understood as lattice-based finitely valued logics: Consider upwards closed subsets $\Gamma \subseteq W$, W is the set of worlds, and order them by inclusion. A formula A is assigned the truth value Γ iff A is true at exactly the worlds in Γ.

The constant-domain intuitionistic Kripke frame $\mathcal{K}$ in Fig. 1 is represented by the lattice L in Fig. 2.

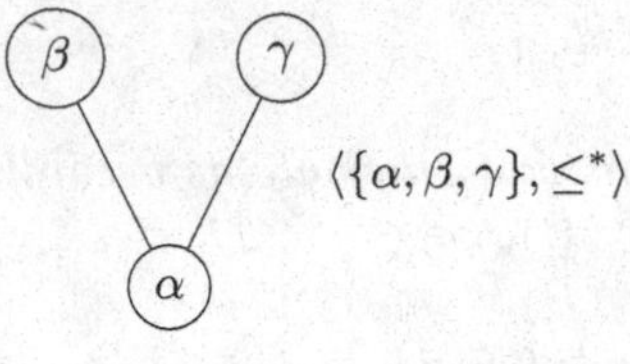

Fig. 1. Constant-domain intuitionistic Kripke frame $\mathcal{K}$.

The propositional language is given by

$$\mathcal{L}^0\left(L, \left\{\begin{pmatrix} 0 & 0 \\ & 0 \end{pmatrix}\right\}\right)$$

and the first-order language is given by

$$\mathcal{L}^1\left(L, \left\{\begin{pmatrix} 0 & 0 \\ & 0 \end{pmatrix}\right\}\right).$$

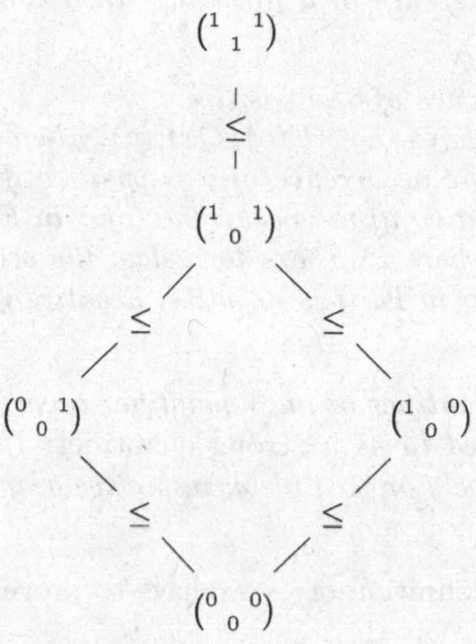

Fig. 2. Lattice L.

The admissible implication of $\mathcal{K}$ is

$$u \to v = \begin{cases} 1 & u \leq v \\ v & \text{else} \end{cases}$$

$\leq$ determines the lattice.

$$\mathrm{MC} = \mathbf{L}^0\left(L, \left\{\begin{pmatrix} 0 & & 0 \\ & 0 & \end{pmatrix}\right\}, \to\right)$$

is the set of valid propositional sentences and

$$\mathrm{MC}^{\mathrm{QF}} = \mathbf{L}^1\left(L, \left\{\begin{pmatrix} 0 & & 0 \\ & 0 & \end{pmatrix}\right\}, \to\right)$$

the set of valid first-order sentences.

Propositional interpolation is easily demonstrated for MC, one of the seven intermediate logics which admit propositional interpolation [13]. Previous proofs for the interpolation of $\mathrm{MC}^{\mathrm{QF}}$ are quite involved, [17]. In fact, in Sect. 5, Example 5 we will show that this interpolation result is a corollary of the main theorem of this paper.

Definition 6. *The occurrence of a formula* $\circ$ *in a context* $C(\circ)$ *is inductively defined as*

- $C(\circ)$ *is* $\circ$*: the occurrence of* $\circ$ *is positive,*
- $C(\circ)$ *is* $E(\circ)\Box F$, $F\Box E(\circ)$, $F \supset E(\circ)$, $QxE(\circ)$, *where* $\Box \in \{\wedge, \vee\}$, $Q \in \{\exists, \forall\}$, E, F *are formulas: the occurrence of* $\circ$ *is positive iff the occurrence of* $\circ$ *in* $E(\circ)$ *is positive, negative iff the occurrence of* $\circ$ *in* $E(\circ)$ *is negative,*
- $C(\circ)$ *is* $E(\circ) \supset F$, *where* E, F *are formulas: the occurrence of* $\circ$ *is positive iff the occurrence of* $\circ$ *in* $E(\circ)$ *is negative, negative iff the occurrence of* $\circ$ *in* $E(\circ)$ *is positive.*

Definition 7. *If a* $\forall$ *quantifier or an* $\exists$ *quantifier occurs positively or negatively, respectively, it is referred to as a* strong quantifier. *If a* $\forall$ *quantifier or an* $\exists$ *quantifier occurs negatively or positively, respectively, it is referred to as a* weak quantifier.

Due to the general definition of $\rightarrow$ we have to prove the following Lemma.

Lemma 1. *For formulas* A, B *and a corresponding context* $C(\circ)$ *it holds*

$$\text{if} \quad \models A \supset B \quad \text{then} \quad \models C(A) \supset C(B)$$

if $\circ$ *occurs positively and*

$$\text{if} \quad \models A \supset B \quad \text{then} \quad \models C(B) \supset C(A)$$

if $\circ$ *occurs negatively.*

Proof. We proof the lemma by induction on the structure of the context $C(\circ)$.

1. If $C(\circ)$ is $\circ$ or C_v, the claim holds trivially.
2. If $C(\circ)$ is $E(\circ) \wedge F$ and $\circ$ occurs positively in $E(\circ)$, then $\circ$ occurs positively in $E(\circ) \wedge F$.

$$\text{If} \quad \models A \supset B \quad \text{then} \quad \models C(A) \supset C(B)$$

as by induction hypothesis

$$\text{if} \quad \models A \supset B \quad \text{then} \quad \models E(A) \supset E(B)$$

and

$$\text{if} \quad \models E(A) \supset E(B) \quad \text{then} \quad \models E(A) \wedge F \supset E(B) \wedge F.$$

If $C(\circ)$ is $E(\circ) \wedge F$ and $\circ$ occurs negatively in $E(\circ)$, then $\circ$ occurs negatively in $E(\circ) \wedge F$.

$$\text{If} \quad \models A \supset B \quad \text{then} \quad \models C(B) \supset C(A)$$

as by induction hypothesis

$$\text{if} \quad \models A \supset B \quad \text{then} \quad \models E(B) \supset E(A)$$

and

$$\text{if} \quad \models E(B) \supset E(A) \quad \text{then} \quad \models E(B) \wedge F \supset E(A) \wedge F.$$

Analogously if $C(\circ)$ is $E \wedge F(\circ)$.

3. If $C(\circ)$ is $E(\circ) \vee F$ and $\circ$ occurs positively in $E(\circ)$, or $\circ$ occurs negatively in $E(\circ)$, similar to 2, analogously if $C(\circ)$ is $E \vee F(\circ)$.
4. If $C(\circ)$ is $E(\circ) \supset F$ and $\circ$ occurs positively in $E(\circ)$ then $\circ$ occurs negatively in $E(\circ) \supset F$.

$$\text{If} \quad \models A \supset B \quad \text{then} \quad \models C(B) \supset C(A)$$

as by induction hypothesis

$$\text{if} \quad \models A \supset B \quad \text{then} \quad \models E(A) \supset E(B).$$

The claim follows by Proposition 1.
If $C(\circ)$ is $E(\circ) \supset F$ and $\circ$ occurs negatively in $E(\circ)$ then $\circ$ occurs positively in $E(\circ) \supset F$.

$$\text{If} \quad \models A \supset B \quad \text{then} \quad \models C(A) \supset C(B)$$

as by induction hypothesis

$$\text{if} \quad \models A \supset B \quad \text{then} \quad \models E(B) \supset E(A).$$

The claim follows by Proposition 1.
If $C(\circ)$ is $E \supset F(\circ)$ and $\circ$ occurs positively in $F(\circ)$ or $\circ$ occurs negatively in $F(\circ)$ similar to 2.

5. If $C(\circ)$ is $\exists x D(\circ)$ and $\circ$ occurs positively in $D(\circ)$ then $\circ$ occurs positively in $\exists x D(\circ)$.

$$\text{If} \quad \models A \supset B \quad \text{then} \quad \models C(A) \supset C(B)$$

as by induction hypothesis

$$\text{if} \models A \supset B \quad \text{then} \quad \models D(A) \supset D(B).$$

and

$$\text{if} \quad \models D(A) \supset D(B) \quad \text{then} \quad \models \exists x D(A) \supset \exists x D(B).$$

Analogously if $C(\circ)$ is $\exists x D(\circ)$ and $\circ$ occurs negatively in $D(\circ)$.

6. If $C(\circ)$ is $\forall x D(\circ)$ and $\circ$ occurs positively in $D(\circ)$ then $\circ$ occurs positively in $\forall x D(\circ)$ similar to 5.

3 Skolemization

We use skolemization to replace strong quantifiers in valid formulas such that the original formulas can be recovered. Note that several Skolem functions for the replacement of a single quantifier are necessary to represent proper suprema and proper infima. We fix $\mathbf{L}(L, V, \rightarrow)$, $L = \langle W, \leq, \cup, \cap, 0, 1 \rangle$.

Definition 8. *Consider a formula B in a context $A(B)$. Then its skolemization $A(sk(B))$ is defined as follows:*

Replace all strong quantifier occurrences (positive occurrence of $\forall$ and negative occurrence of $\exists$) (note that no quantifiers in A bind variables in B) of the form $\exists x C(x)$ (or $\forall x C(x)$) in B by $\bigvee_{i=1}^{|W|} C(f_i(\overline{x}))$ (or $\bigwedge_{i=1}^{|W|} C(f_i(\overline{x}))$), where f_i are new function symbols and $\overline{x}$ are the weakly quantified variables of the scope.

Skolem axioms are closed sentences

$$\forall\overline{x}(\exists y A(y,\overline{x}) \supset \bigvee_{i=1}^{|W|} A(f_i(\overline{x}),\overline{x}) \quad \text{and} \quad \forall\overline{x}(\bigwedge_{i=1}^{|W|} A(f_i(\overline{x}),\overline{x}) \supset \forall y A(y,\overline{x}))$$

where f_i are new function symbols (Skolem functions).

Lemma 2. *1. If $\models^1 A(B)$ then $\models^1 A(sk(B))$.*
2. If $S_1 \dots S_k \models^1 A(sk(B))$ then $S_1 \dots S_k \models^1 A(B)$, for suitable Skolem axioms $S_1 \dots S_k$.
3. If $S_1 \dots S_k \models^1 A$, where $S_1 \dots S_k$ are Skolem axioms and A does not contain Skolem functions then $\models^1 A$.

Proof. 1. Note that

$$\text{if} \quad \models A(D) \quad \text{then} \quad \models A(D \vee D)$$

and

$$\text{if} \quad \models A(D) \quad \text{then} \quad \models A(D \wedge D).$$

Use Lemma 1 and

$$\models^1 D'(t) \supset \exists x D'(x), \quad \models^1 \forall x D'(x) \supset D'(t).$$

2. Use Lemma 1 and suitable Skolem axioms to reconstruct strong quantifiers.
3. Assume $\not\models^1 A$. As usual, we have to extend the valuation to the Skolem functions to verify the Skolem axioms. There is a valuation in $\langle D_{\Phi^1}, \Omega_{\Phi^1}\rangle$ s.t. $\Phi^1(A) \neq 1$. Using at most $|W|$ Skolem functions and AC we can always pick witnesses as values for the Skolem functions such that the first-order suprema and infima are reconstructed on the propositional level. (AC is applied to sets of objects where the corresponding truth value is taken.)

$$\sup\{\Phi^1(B(f_i(\overline{t}),\overline{t})) \mid 1 \leq i \leq |W|\} =$$
$$\sup\{\Phi^1(B(d,\overline{t}) \mid d \in D_{\Phi^1}\} = \Phi^1(\exists y B(y,\overline{t}))$$

and

$$\inf\{\Phi^1(B(f_i(\overline{t}),\overline{t})) \mid 1 \leq i \leq |W|\} =$$
$$\inf\{\Phi^1(B(d,\overline{t})) \mid d \in D_{\Phi^1}\} = \Phi^1(\forall y B(y,\overline{t})).$$

Example 3. We continue with the logic $\mathrm{MC}^{\mathrm{QF}}$ introduced in Example 2. For the given logic

$$\exists x B(x) \supset sk(\exists y \forall z C(y,z)) \equiv \exists x B(x) \supset \exists y \bigwedge_{i=1}^{5} C(y, f_i(y)).$$

4 Expansions

Expansions, first introduced in [15], are natural structures representing the instantiated variables for quantified formulas. They record the substitutions for quantifiers in an effort to recover a sound proof of the original formulation of Herbrand's Theorem. As we work with skolemized formulas, in this paper we we consider only expansions for formulas with weak quantifiers. Consequently the arguments are simplified.

In the following we assume that a constant c is present in the language and that $t_1, t_2, \ldots$ is a fixed ordering of all closed terms (terms not containing variables).

Definition 9. *A term structure is a structure $\langle D, \Omega \rangle$ such that D is the set of all closed terms.*

Proposition 2. *Let $\Phi^1(\exists x A(x)) = v$ in a term structure. Then $\Phi^1(\exists x A(x) = \Phi^1(\bigvee_{i=1}^n A(t_i))$ for some n. Analogously for $\forall x A(x)$, i.e. let $\Phi^1(\forall x A(x)) = v$ in a term structure, then $\Phi^1(\forall x A(x)) = \Phi^1(\bigwedge_{i=1}^n A(t_i))$ for some n.*

Proof. Only finitely many truth values exists, therefore there is an n such that the valuation becomes stable on $\bigvee_{i=1}^n A(t_i)$ $(\bigwedge_{i=1}^n A(t_i))$.

Definition 10. *Let E be a formula with weak quantifiers only. The n-th expansion E_n of E is obtained from E by replacing inside out all subformulas $\exists x A(x)$ $(\forall x A(x))$ by $\bigvee_{i=1}^n A(t_i)$ $(\bigwedge_{i=1}^n A(t_i))$. E_n is a Herbrand expansion iff E_n is valid. In case there are only m terms $E_{m+k} = E_m$.*

Lemma 3. *Let $\Phi^1(E) = v$ in a term structure. Then there is an n such that for all $m \geq n$ $\Phi^1(E_m) = v$.*

Proof. We apply Proposition 2 outside in to replace subformulas $\exists x\ A(x)$ $(\forall x\ A(x))$ stepwise by $\bigvee_{i=1}^n A(t_i)$ $(\bigwedge_{i=1}^n A(t_i))$ without changing the truth value. The disjunctions and conjunctions can be extended to common maximal disjunctions and conjunctions.

Theorem 1. *Let E contain only weak quantifiers. Then $\models E$ iff there is a Herbrand expansion E_n of E.*

Proof. $\Rightarrow$: Assume $\models E$ but $\not\models E_n$ for all n. Let $\Gamma_i = \{\Phi^0_{i,v} | \Phi^0_{i,v}(E_i) \neq 1\}$ and define $\Gamma = \bigcup \Gamma_i$. Note that the first index in $\Phi^0_{i,v}$ relates to the expansion level and the second index to all counter-valuations at this level. Assign a partial order $<$ to Γ by $\Phi^0_{i,v} < \Phi^0_{j,w}$ for $\Phi^0_{i,v} \in \Gamma_i$, $\Phi^0_{j,w} \in \Gamma_j$ and $i < j$ iff $\Phi^0_{i,v}$ and $\Phi^0_{j,w}$ coincide on the atoms of E_i. By König's Lemma there is an infinite branch $\Phi^0_{1,i_1} < \Phi^0_{2,i_2} < \ldots$. Define a term structure induced by an evaluation on atoms P:

$$\Phi^1(P) = \begin{cases} v & P \text{ occurs in some } E_n \text{ and } \Phi_{n,i_n}(P) = v \\ 1 & \text{else} \end{cases}$$

$\Phi^1(E) \neq 1$ by Lemma 3.

$\Leftarrow$: Use Lemma 1 and $\models A(t) \supset \exists x A(x)$ and $\models \forall x A(x) \supset A(t)$. Note that

$$\text{if} \quad \models A(D \vee D) \quad \text{then} \quad \models A(D)$$

and

$$\text{if} \quad \models A(D \wedge D) \quad \text{then} \quad \models A(D).$$

Example 4. Consider the lattice in Example 2, Fig. 2 and the term ordering $c < d$. The expansion sequence of $P(c,d,d) \supset \exists x P(c,x,d)$ is

$$E_1 = P(c,d,d) \supset P(c,c,d), E_2 = P(c,d,d) \supset P(c,c,d) \vee P(c,d,d), E_{2+k} = E_2.$$

The second formula is a Herbrand expansion.

5 The Interpolation Theorem

Theorem 2. *Interpolation holds for $\mathbf{L}^0(L, V, \rightarrow)$ iff interpolation holds for $\mathbf{L}^1(L, V, \rightarrow)$.*

Proof. $\Leftarrow$: trivial.

$\Rightarrow$: Assume $A \supset B \in \mathcal{L}(L, V)$ and $\models A \supset B$.

$$\models sk(A) \supset sk(B) \quad \text{by Lemma 2 1.}$$

Construct a Herbrand expansion $A_H \supset B_H$ of $sk(A) \supset sk(B)$ by Theorem 1. Construct the propositional interpolant I^* of $A_H \supset B_H$,

$$\models A_H \supset I^* \quad \text{and} \quad \models I^* \supset B_H.$$

Use Lemma 1 and

$$\models A(t) \supset \exists x A(x), \quad \models \forall x A(x) \supset A(t)$$

to obtain

$$\models sk(A) \supset I^* \quad \text{and} \quad \models I^* \supset sk(B)$$

Order all terms $f(t)$ in I^* by inclusion where f is not in the common language. Let $f^*(\overline{t})$ be the maximal term.

i. f^* is not in $sk(A)$. Replace $f^*(\overline{t})$ by a fresh variable x to obtain

$$\models sk(A) \supset I^*\{x/f^*(\overline{t})\}.$$

But then also

$$\models sk(A) \supset \forall x I^*\{x/f^*(\overline{t})\}$$

and

$$\models \forall x I^*\{x/f^*(\overline{t})\} \supset sk(B)$$

by

$$\models \forall x I^*\{x/f^*(\overline{t})\} \supset I^*.$$

ii. f^* is not in $sk(B)$. Replace $f^*(\bar{t})$ by a fresh variable x to obtain

$$\models I^*\{x/f^*(\bar{t})\} \supset sk(B).$$

But then also

$$\models \exists x I^*\{x/f^*(\bar{t})\} \supset sk(B)$$

and

$$\models sk(A) \supset \exists x I^*\{x/f^*(\bar{t})\}.$$

by

$$\models I^* \supset \exists x I^*\{x \backslash f^*(\bar{t})\}.$$

Repeat this procedure till all functions and constants not in the common language (among them the Skolem functions) are eliminated from the middle formula. Let I be the result. I is an interpolant of $sk(A) \supset sk(B)$. By Lemma 2 2,3 I is an interpolant of $A \supset B$. For a similar construction for classical first-order logic see Chap. 8.2 of [4].

Corollary 1. *If interpolation holds for* $\boldsymbol{L}^0(L, V, \rightarrow)$, $\models A \supset B$ *and* $A \supset B$ *contains only weak quantifiers, then there is a quantifier-free interpolant with common predicates for* $A \supset B$.

Remark 1. Corollary 1 cannot be strengthened to provide a quantifier-free interpolant with common predicate symbols and common function symbols for $A \supset B$. Consider

$$Q_\forall A(x_1, f_1(x_1), x_2, f_2(x_1, x_2), \ldots) \supset Q_\exists A(g_1, y_1, g_2(y_1), y_2, g_3(y_1, y_2), \ldots),$$

where $Q_\forall = \forall x_1 \forall x_2 \ldots$ and $Q_\exists = \exists y_1 \exists y_2 \ldots$. This is the skolemization of

$$\forall x_1 \exists x_1' \forall x_2 \ldots A(x_1, x_1', x_2, \ldots) \supset \forall x_1 \exists x_1' \forall x_2 \ldots A(x_1, x_1', x_2, \ldots),$$

where $\forall x_1 \exists x_1' \forall x_2 \exists x_2' \ldots A(x_1, x_1', x_2, x_2', \ldots)$ is the only possible interpolant modulo provable equivalence with common predicate and function symbols.

Example 5. Example 2 continued. For the given logic we calculate the interpolant for

$$\exists x(B(x) \land \forall y C(y)) \supset \exists x(A(x) \lor B(x)).$$

1. Skolemization

$$\bigvee_{i=1}^{5} (B(c_i) \land \forall y C(y)) \supset \exists x(A(x) \lor B(x)).$$

2. Herbrand expansion

$$\bigvee_{i=1}^{5} (B(c_i) \land C(c_1)) \supset \bigvee_{i=1}^{5} (A(c_i) \lor B(c_i)).$$

3. Propositional interpolant

$$\bigvee_{i=1}^{5}(B(c_i) \wedge C(c_1)) \supset \bigvee_{i=1}^{5} B(c_i) \quad \bigvee_{i=1}^{5} B(c_i) \supset \bigvee_{i=1}^{5}(A(c_i) \vee B(c_i)).$$

4. Back to the Skolem form

$$\bigvee_{i=1}^{5}(B(c_i) \wedge \forall y C(y)) \supset \bigvee_{i=1}^{5} B(c_i) \quad \bigvee_{i=1}^{5} B(c_i) \supset \exists x(A(x) \vee B(x)).$$

5. Elimination of function symbols and constants not in the common language from $\bigvee_{i=1}^{5} B(c_i)$. Result:

$$\exists z_1 \ldots \exists z_5 \bigvee B(z_i).$$

6. Use the Skolem axiom

$$\exists x(B(x) \wedge \forall y C(y)) \supset \bigvee_{i=1}^{5} B(c_i) \wedge \forall y C(y)$$

to reconstruct the original first-order form.
7. The Skolem axiom can be deleted.

Proposition 3. *Let* $L = \langle W, \leq, \cup, \cap, 0, 1 \rangle$.

i. $\boldsymbol{L}^0(L, \emptyset, \rightarrow)$ *(and therefore* $\boldsymbol{L}^1(L, \emptyset, \rightarrow)$*) never has the interpolation property.*
ii. $\boldsymbol{L}^0(L, W, \rightarrow)$ *(and therefore* $\boldsymbol{L}^1(L, W, \rightarrow)$*) always has the interpolation property.*

Proof. i. $\models^0 x \supset (y \supset y)$ and the only possible interpolant is $\top$, which is not variable-free definable.
ii. Consider $\models A(x_1, \ldots, x_n, y_1, \ldots, y_m) \supset B(y_1 \ldots y_n, z_1, \ldots z_o)$,

$$I = \bigvee_{\langle v_{i_1}, \ldots v_{i_n} \rangle \in W \times W} A(C_{v_{i_1}}, \ldots, C_{v_{i_n}}, y_1, \ldots, y_m)$$

is an interpolant as

$$\models A(x_1, \ldots, x_n, y_1, \ldots, y_m) \supset I$$

and

$$\models I \supset B(y_1 \ldots y_n, z_1, \ldots z_o)$$

by substitution.

Proposition 3 ii. makes it possible to characterize all extensions of a lattice based many-valued logic which admit first-order interpolation.

$$\text{SPECTRUM}(L, \rightarrow) = \{V \mid \mathbf{L}^1(L, V, \rightarrow) \text{ interpolates}\}.$$

Example 6. $L = \langle\{0,1\}, \leq, \cup, \cap, 0, 1\rangle$ the lattice of classical logic, $\rightarrow$ classical implication.

$$\mathrm{SPECTRUM}(L, \rightarrow) = \{\{0\}, \{1\}, \{0,1\}\}$$

This is the maximal possible spectrum by Proposition 3 *i*.

$\mathbf{L}^0(L, \{0\}, \rightarrow)$ and $\mathbf{L}^0(L, \{0,1\}, \rightarrow)$ interpolate as all truth constants are representable by closed formulas, therefore $\mathbf{L}^1(L, \{0\}, \rightarrow)$ and $\mathbf{L}^1(L, \{0,1\}, \rightarrow)$ interpolate (Craig's result, which does however not cover $\mathbf{L}^1(L, \{1\}, \rightarrow)$).

To show that $\mathbf{L}^0(L, \{1\}, \rightarrow)$ interpolates first note that in general

$$\bigvee_i E_i \supset \bigwedge_j F_j$$

interpolates iff there are interpolants

$$E_i \supset I_{ij} \quad I_{ij} \supset F_j.$$

$\bigwedge_j \bigvee_i I_{ij}$ is a suitable interpolant. Now use the value presenting transformations

$$\begin{aligned} D(A \wedge B \supset C) &\Rightarrow D(A \supset C \vee B \supset C) \\ D(A \vee B \supset C) &\Rightarrow D(A \supset C \wedge B \supset C) \\ D((A \supset B) \supset C) &\Rightarrow D(C \vee (A \wedge (B \supset C))) \\ D(x) &\Rightarrow D(\top \supset x) \end{aligned}$$

for variables x together with distributions and simplifications, to reduce the problem to

$$\bigwedge_i (u_i \supset v_i) \supset \bigvee_j (s_j \supset t_j)$$

v_i, t_j variables, u_i, s_j variables or $\top$. We assume that the succedent is not valid (otherwise $\top$ is the interpolant). So any variable occurs either in the s_j group or in the t_j group. Close the antecedents under transitivity of $\supset$. There is a common implication $u \supset v$, an interpolant (Otherwise there is a countervaluation by assigning 0 to all t_j and extending this assignment in the antecedent such that if v_i is assigned 0 also u_i is assigned 0. No s_j is assigned 0 by this procedure. Assign 1 to all other variables and derive a contradiction to the assumption, that the initial implication is valid). Therefore, $\mathbf{L}^1(L, \{1\}, \rightarrow)$ interpolates.

Example 7. n-valued Gödel logics.

Let $G_n = \langle W_n, \leq, \cup, \cap, 0, 1\rangle$, where $W_n = \{0, \frac{1}{n-1}, \ldots, \frac{n-2}{n-1}, 1\}$, $\leq$ is the natural order and $\cup, \cap, 0, 1$ are defined accordingly.

$$u \rightarrow v = \begin{cases} 1 & u \leq v \\ v & \text{else} \end{cases}$$

The first-order spectrum in the presence of $\bot$ consists of all sets of truth values $\{\bot\} \cup (\Gamma - \{\bot, \top\})$ and $\{\bot, \top\} \cup (\Gamma - \{\bot, \top\})$ such that there are no consecutive truth values v_i, v_{i+1} both not in $\Gamma - \{\bot, \top\}$ (see [6]).

6 Extensions to Infinitely-Valued Logics

We may use the described methodology to prove interpolation for (fragments of) infinitely-valued logics, as for instance Gödel logics [5]. Consider Gödel logic $\mathrm{G}^{\mathrm{QF}}_{[0,1]}$, the logic of all linearly ordered Kripke frames with constant domains. Its connectives can be interpreted as functions over the real interval $[0, 1]$ as follows: $\bot$ is the logical constant for 0, $\vee, \wedge, \exists, \forall$ are defined as *maximum*, *minimum*, *supremum*, *infimum*, respectively. $\neg A$ is an abbreviation for $A \rightarrow \bot$ and $\rightarrow$ is defined as

$$u \rightarrow v = \begin{cases} 1 & u \leq v \\ v & \text{else} \end{cases}$$

The weak quantifier fragment of $\mathrm{G}^{\mathrm{QF}}_{[0,1]}$ admits Herbrand expansions. This follows from cut-free proofs in hypersequent calculi [2]. This can be easily shown by proof transformation steps in the hypersequent calculus. Indeed, we can transform proofs by eliminating weak quantifier inferences:

i. If there is an occurrence of an $\exists$ introduction, we select all formulas A_i that correspond to this inference and eliminate the $\exists$ introduction by the use of $\bigvee_i A_i$.
ii. If there is an occurrence of a $\forall$ introduction, we select all formulas B_i that correspond to this inference and eliminate the $\forall$ introduction by the use of $\bigwedge_i B_i$.

We suppress the inference of weak quantifiers and combine the disjunctions respectively conjunctions to accommodate contractions. Propositional Gödel logic interpolates and therefore the weak quantifier fragment of $G^{QF}_{[0,1]}$ interpolates too, as no skolemization is necessary.

The fragment $A \supset B$, A, B prenex also interpolates: Skolemize as in classical logic, construct a Herbrand expansion, interpolate, go back to the Skolem form and use an immediate analogy of the 2nd ε-theorem [11] to go back to the original formulas. To illustrate the procedure, consider the following example.

Example 8.

$$\mathrm{G}^{\mathrm{QF}}_{[0,1]} \models \forall x \exists y (P(x) \wedge Q(y)) \supset \forall x \exists y (R(x) \vee P(y))$$

We skolemize as in classical logic (note that the substitution of Skolem terms is always possible).

$$\mathrm{G}^{\mathrm{QF}}_{[0,1]} \models \forall x (P(x) \wedge Q(f(x))) \supset \exists y (R(c) \vee P(y)).$$

Calculate a Herbrand expansion

$$\mathrm{G}^{\mathrm{QF}}_{[0,1]} \models P(c) \wedge Q(f(c)) \supset R(c) \vee P(c).$$

Construct a propositional interpolant

$$\mathrm{G}^{\mathrm{QF}}_{[0,1]} \models P(c) \wedge Q(f(c)) \supset P(c) \quad \mathrm{G}^{\mathrm{QF}}_{[0,1]} \models P(c) \supset R(c) \vee P(c).$$

Go back to the Skolem form

$$\mathrm{G}^{\mathrm{QF}}_{[0,1]} \models \forall x(P(x) \wedge Q(f(x))) \supset P(c) \quad \mathrm{G}^{\mathrm{QF}}_{[0,1]} \models P(c) \supset \exists x(R(c) \vee P(x)).$$

Eliminate c from the interpolant

$$\mathrm{G}^{\mathrm{QF}}_{[0,1]} \models \forall x(P(x) \wedge Q(f(x))) \supset \forall x P(x) \quad \mathrm{G}^{\mathrm{QF}}_{[0,1]} \models \forall x P(x) \supset \exists x(R(c) \vee P(x)).$$

Skolemize the interpolant in both formulas and construct a Herbrand expansion to apply the 2nd ε-Theorem to obtain

$$\mathrm{G}^{\mathrm{QF}}_{[0,1]} \models \forall x \exists y(P(x) \wedge Q(y)) \supset \forall x P(x) \quad \mathrm{G}^{\mathrm{QF}}_{[0,1]} \models \forall x P(x) \supset \forall x \exists y(R(x) \vee P(y)).$$

i. $\mathrm{G}^{\mathrm{QF}}_{[0,1]} \models P(e) \wedge Q(f(e)) \supset P(e)$: replace all Skolem terms by variables representing them.

$$\mathrm{G}^{\mathrm{QF}}_{[0,1]} \models P(x_e) \wedge Q(x_e) \supset P(x_e).$$

Infer weak quantifiers, shift and contract as much as possible, otherwise infer the strong quantifier representing a deepest Skolem term available, shift and repeat.

$$\mathrm{G}^{\mathrm{QF}}_{[0,1]} \models \exists y(P(x_e) \wedge Q(y)) \supset P(x_e)$$

$$\mathrm{G}^{\mathrm{QF}}_{[0,1]} \models \forall x \exists y(P(x) \wedge Q(y)) \supset P(x_e)$$

$$\mathrm{G}^{\mathrm{QF}}_{[0,1]} \models \forall x \exists y(P(x) \wedge Q(y)) \supset \forall x P(x)$$

ii. $\mathrm{G}^{\mathrm{QF}}_{[0,1]} \models P(c) \supset R(c) \vee P(c)$:

$$\mathrm{G}^{\mathrm{QF}}_{[0,1]} \models P(x_c) \supset R(x_c) \vee P(x_c)$$

$$\mathrm{G}^{\mathrm{QF}}_{[0,1]} \models \forall x P(x) \supset R(x_c) \vee P(x_c)$$

$$\mathrm{G}^{\mathrm{QF}}_{[0,1]} \models \forall x P(x) \supset \exists y(R(x_c) \vee P(y))$$

$$\mathrm{G}^{\mathrm{QF}}_{[0,1]} \models \forall x P(x) \supset \forall x \exists y(R(x) \vee P(y))$$

Therefore, it is possible to show interpolation for fragments of $\mathrm{G}^{\mathrm{QF}}_{[0,1]}$, however, not yet for $\mathrm{G}^{\mathrm{QF}}_{[0,1]}$. What lacks to prove interpolation for $\mathrm{G}^{\mathrm{QF}}_{[0,1]}$ is a suitable skolemization of all formulas!

7 Conclusion

Extending the notion of expansion to formulas containing strong quantifiers might be possible to cover logics which do not admit skolemization, e.g. logics based on non-constant domain Kripke frames (such notions of expansion are in the spirit of Herbrand's original proof of Herbrand's Theorem).

Another possibility is to develop unusual skolemizations e.g. based on existence assumptions [3] or on added Skolem predicates instead of Skolem functions as in [10].

The methodology of this paper can also be used to obtain negative results. First-order $S5$ does not interpolate by a well-known result of Fine [9]. As propositional $S5$ interpolates, first-order $S5$ cannot admit skolemization together with expansions in general.

Acknowledgments. Partially supported by FWF P 26976, FWF I 2671 and the Czech-Austrian project MOBILITY No. 7AMB17AT054.

References

1. Aguilera, J.P., Baaz, M.: Ten problems in Gödel logic. Soft. Comput. **21**(1), 149–152 (2017)
2. Baaz, M., Ciabattoni, A., Fermüller, C.G.: Hypersequent calculi for Gödel logics - a survey. J. Logic Comput. **13**(6), 835–861 (2003)
3. Baaz, M., Iemhoff, R.: The Skolemization of existential quantifiers in intuitionistic logic. Ann. Pure Appl. Logic **142**(1–3), 269–295 (2006)
4. Baaz, M., Leitsch, A.: Methods of Cut-Elimination, vol. 34. Springer Science & Business Media, Heidelberg (2011)
5. Baaz, M., Preining, N., Zach, R.: First-order Gödel logics. Ann. Pure Appl. Logic **147**(1), 23–47 (2007)
6. Baaz, M., Veith, H.: Interpolation in fuzzy logic. Arch. Math. Log. **38**(7), 461–489 (1999)
7. Birkhoff, G.: Lattice Theory, vol. 25. American Mathematical Society, New York (1948)
8. Craig, W.: Three uses of the Herbrand-Gentzen theorem in relating model theory and proof theory. J. Symbolic Logic **22**(03), 269–285 (1957)
9. Fine, K.: Failures of the interpolation lemma in quantified modal logic. J. Symbolic Logic **44**(02), 201–206 (1979)
10. Gödel, K.: Die Vollständigkeit der Axiome des logischen Funktionenkalküls. Monatshefte für Mathematik **37**(1), 349–360 (1930)
11. Hilbert, D., Bernays, P.: Grundlagen der Mathematik (1968)
12. Maksimova, L.: Intuitionistic logic and implicit definability. Ann. Pure Appl. Logic **105**(1–3), 83–102 (2000)
13. Maksimova, L.L.: Craig's theorem in superintuitionistic logics and amalgamable varieties of pseudo-Boolean algebras. Algebra Logic **16**(6), 427–455 (1977)
14. Maksimova, L.L.: Interpolation properties of superintuitionistic logics. Stud. Logica. **38**(4), 419–428 (1979)
15. Miller, D.A.: A compact representation of proofs. Stud. Logica. **46**(4), 347–370 (1987)
16. Miyama, T.: The interpolation theorem and Beth's theorem in many-valued logics. Mathematica Japonica **19**, 341–355 (1974)
17. Ono, H.: Model extension theorem and Craig's interpolation theorem for intermediate predicate logics. Rep. Math. Logic **15**, 41–58 (1983)
18. Vizel, Y., Weissenbacher, G., Malik, S.: Boolean satisfiability solvers and their applications in model checking. Proc. IEEE **103**(11), 2021–2035 (2015)

Finitariness of Elementary Unification in Boolean Region Connection Calculus

Philippe Balbiani[1(✉)] and Çiğdem Gencer[2,3]

[1] Institut de recherche en informatique de Toulouse, CNRS—Toulouse University, Toulouse, France
Philippe.Balbiani@irit.fr

[2] Faculty of Engineering and Natural Sciences, Sabancı University, Istanbul, Turkey

[3] Faculty of Arts and Sciences, Aydın University, Istanbul, Turkey
cigdemgencer@aydin.edu.tr

Abstract. Boolean Region Connection Calculus is a formalism for reasoning about the topological relations between regions. In this paper, we provide computability results about unifiability in Boolean Region Connection Calculus and prove that elementary unification is finitary.

Keywords: Region connection calculus · Boolean terms · Unifiability problem · Computability · Unification type

1 Introduction

The Region Connection Calculus (*RCC*) is a formalism for reasoning about the topological relations between regions [19]. With *RCC*8, a variant of *RCC* based on 8 atomic relations [6,17], knowledge is represented by means of a conjunction of disjunctions of atomic relations between variables representing regions. Given such a formula, the main task is to know whether it is consistent—an NP-complete problem [20,21]. Consisting of a combination of *RCC*8 with Boolean reasoning, *BRCC*8 is a variant of *RCC*8 in which regions are represented by Boolean terms [24]. With *BRCC*8, showing the consistency of formulas is NP-complete in arbitrary topological spaces and $PSPACE$-complete in Euclidean spaces [14–16,24]. *BRCC*8 and its multifarious variants have attracted considerable interest both for their practical applications in spatial reasoning [6,20] and for the mathematical problems they give rise to [3–5,7–9,14–16,23,24].

We are interested in supporting a new inference capability: unifiability of formulas. The unifiability problem consists, given a finite set $\{(\varphi_1(x_1,\ldots,x_n),\psi_1(x_1,\ldots,x_n)),\ldots,(\varphi_m(x_1,\ldots,x_n),\psi_m(x_1,\ldots,x_n))\}$ of pairs of formulas, in determining whether there exists Boolean terms $a_1,\ldots,a_n$ such that $\varphi_1(a_1,\ldots,a_n)\leftrightarrow\psi_1(a_1,\ldots,a_n)$, ..., $\varphi_m(a_1,\ldots,a_n)\leftrightarrow\psi_m(a_1,\ldots,a_n)$ are valid. To explain our motivation for considering unifiability, consider a finite set of pairs of *BRCC*8-formulas representing desired properties about some regions. This set may contain non-equivalent formulas that can be made equivalent by

C. Dixon and M. Finger (Eds.): FroCoS 2017, LNCS 10483, pp. 281–297, 2017.
DOI: 10.1007/978-3-319-66167-4_16

applying to them appropriate substitutions. And if one is able to find such appropriate substitutions, then one is interested to find the maximal ones. An important question is then the following: when a set of $BRCC8$-formulas is unifiable, has it a minimal complete set of unifiers? When the answer is "yes", how large is this set? See [1,2] where such question is addressed for description logics.

The section-by-section breakdown of the paper is as follows. In Sect. 2, we define the syntax of $BRCC8$. Section 3 explains our motivation for considering unification in $BRCC8$. In Sect. 4, we present the semantics of $BRCC8$. Section 5 introduces the basic ideas involved in unification. In Sect. 6, we embark on the study of specific Boolean terms: monoms and polynoms. The main result we prove there is Proposition 4. Section 7 defines equivalence relations between tuples of terms. The main results we prove there are Propositions 5 and 7. In Sect. 8, we provide computability results about unifiability in $BRCC8$. Section 9 shows that unification in $BRCC8$ is finitary. Due to lack of space, we only consider the elementary case where the considered terms do not contain free constant symbols.

2 Syntax

Now, it is time to meet the language we are working with. We adopt the standard rules for omission of the parentheses.

Let VAR be a countable set of *propositional variables* (with typical members denoted x, y, etc.). Let $(x_1, x_2, \ldots)$ be an enumeration of VAR without repetitions. The *terms* (denoted a, b, etc.) are defined as follows:

- $a ::= x \mid 0 \mid a^{\star} \mid (a \cup b)$.

The other constructs for terms (for instance, 1 and $\cap$) are defined as usual. We use the following notations for terms:

- a^0 for $a^{\star}$,
- a^1 for a.

Reading terms as regions, the constructs 0, * and $\cup$ should be regarded as the empty region, the complement operation and the union operation. As a result, the constructs 1 and $\cap$ should be regarded as the full region and the intersection operation. In the sequel, we use $a(x_1, \ldots, x_n)$ to denote a term a whose variables form a subset of $\{x_1, \ldots, x_n\}$. For all nonnegative integers n, let $TER(x_1, \ldots, x_n)$ be the set of all terms whose variables form a subset of $\{x_1, \ldots, x_n\}$. Let TER be the set of all terms and $TER(\emptyset)$ be the set of all variable-free terms.

The *formulas* (denoted φ, ψ, etc.) are defined as follows:

- $\varphi ::= P(a, b) \mid \bot \mid \neg\varphi \mid (\varphi \vee \psi)$.

Here, a and b are terms and P is one of the following 8 binary predicates corresponding to the 8 binary relations of $RCC8$:

- DC ("disconnected"),

- *EC* ("external contact"),
- *PO* ("partial overlap"),
- *TPP* ("tangential proper part"),
- *TPPI* ("inverse of *TPP*"),
- *NTPP* ("nontangential proper part"),
- *NTPPI* ("inverse of *NTPP*"),
- *EQ* ("equal").

The other constructs for formulas (for instance, $\top$ and $\wedge$) are defined as usual. We say that a formula φ is *equational* iff EQ is the only binary predicate possibly occurring in φ. In the sequel, we use $\varphi(x_1,\ldots,x_n)$ to denote a formula φ whose variables form a subset of $\{x_1,\ldots,x_n\}$. For all nonnegative integers n, let $FOR(x_1,\ldots,x_n)$ be the set of all formulas whose variables form a subset of $\{x_1,\ldots,x_n\}$. Let FOR be the set of all formulas and $FOR(\emptyset)$ be the set of all variable-free formulas. An *inference rule* is a pair of the form $\frac{\varphi}{\psi}$ where φ and ψ are formulas.

A *substitution* is a function $\sigma : VAR \longrightarrow TER$ which moves at most finitely many variables, i.e. there exists at most finitely many variables x such that $\sigma(x) \neq x$. Given a substitution σ, let $\bar{\sigma} : TER \cup FOR \longrightarrow TER \cup FOR$ be the endomorphism such that for all variables x, $\bar{\sigma}(x) = \sigma(x)$. Obviously, for all substitutions σ, τ, the function $\sigma \circ \tau$ such that for all $x \in VAR$, $(\sigma \circ \tau)(x) = \bar{\tau}(\sigma(x))$ is a substitution called the *composition* of the substitutions σ and τ.

3 Motivation for Considering Unifiability in *BRCC*8

Our motivation for considering unifiability in *BRCC*8 comes from the following three facts: *BRCC*8 is a formalism both with theoretical merits and with practical relevance; unification in Boolean algebras has attracted considerable interest; there is a wide variety of situations where unifiability problems in formalisms like *BRCC*8 arise.

*BRCC*8 is the result of the combination of *RCC*8 with Boolean reasoning. Within the context of *RCC*8, formulas would just be quantifier-free first-order formulas in a constant-free function-free language based on the 8 binary predicates of *RCC*8. For instance, $TPP(x,y) \wedge TPP(x,z) \rightarrow TPP(y,z) \vee TPP(z,y)$. By allowing to apply the 8 binary predicates of *RCC*8 not only to propositional variables but also to Boolean terms, Wolter and Zakharyaschev [24] have strictly extended their expressive capacity. For instance, in the class of all topological spaces, the *BRCC*8 formula $EQ(x \cup y, z)$ has no equivalent formula in a pure *RCC*8-based language. As well, with this enriched language, one becomes able by using the *BRCC*8 formula $DC(x, x^\star) \rightarrow EQ(x, 0) \vee EQ(x^\star, 0)$ to distinguish between connected and non-connected topological spaces.

Unification in Boolean algebras has attracted considerable interest and several algorithms for computing solutions to Boolean equations are known, some of them going back to Boole and Löwenheim. But the most important result is that unification is unitary: given an equation $a(x_1,\ldots,x_n) = b(x_1,\ldots,x_n)$, either it possesses no solution, or it possesses a single most general unifier. See [2,18] for an introduction to the unifiability problem in Boolean algebras. So, it is natural to ask whether unification in $BRCC8$ inherits the unitariness character of Boolean unification. In this paper, we refute this idea by proving that unification in $BRCC8$ is finitary.

There is a wide variety of situations where unifiability problems arise. We will explain our motivation for considering them within the context of geographical information systems. Suppose $\varphi(p_1, \ldots, p_m)$ is a formula representing our knowledge about regions denoted $p_1, \ldots, p_m$ in some geographical universe and $\psi(x_1, \ldots, x_n)$ is a formula representing a desirable property about regions denoted $x_1, \ldots, x_n$. It may happen that $\psi(x_1, \ldots, x_n)$ is not a logical consequence of $\varphi(p_1, \ldots, p_m)$ in the considered geographical universe whereas some of its instances are. Hence, one may wonder whether there are n-tuples $(a_1, \ldots, a_n)$ of terms for which the property represented by $\psi(x_1, \ldots, x_n)$ becomes a logical consequence of $\varphi(p_1, \ldots, p_m)$ in the considered geographical universe. And if one is able to decide such question, then one may be interested to obtain n-tuples $(b_1, \ldots, b_n)$ as general as possible. Central to unification theory are the questions of the computability of unifiability and the unification type. Within the context of $BRCC8$, these questions will be addressed in Sects. 8 and 9.

4 Semantics

The best way to understand the meaning of the binary predicates is by interpreting terms and formulas in topological spaces [14–16, 24]. More precisely, in a topological space (X, τ), if $Int_\tau(\cdot)$ denotes its interior operation then to each binary predicate P, one usually associates a binary relation $P^{(X,\tau)}$ on the set of all regular closed subsets of X:

- $DC^{(X,\tau)}(A, B)$ iff $A \cap B = \emptyset$,
- $EC^{(X,\tau)}(A, B)$ iff $A \cap B \neq \emptyset$ and $Int_\tau(A) \cap Int_\tau(B) = \emptyset$,
- $PO^{(X,\tau)}(A, B)$ iff $Int_\tau(A) \cap Int_\tau(B) \neq \emptyset$, $Int_\tau(A) \not\subseteq B$ and $Int_\tau(B) \not\subseteq A$,
- $TPP^{(X,\tau)}(A, B)$ iff $A \subseteq B$, $A \not\subseteq Int_\tau(B)$ and $B \not\subseteq A$,
- $TPPI^{(X,\tau)}(A, B)$ iff $B \subseteq A$, $B \not\subseteq Int_\tau(A)$ and $A \not\subseteq B$,
- $NTPP^{(X,\tau)}(A, B)$ iff $A \subseteq Int_\tau(B)$ and $B \not\subseteq A$,
- $NTPPI^{(X,\tau)}(A, B)$ iff $B \subseteq Int_\tau(A)$ and $A \not\subseteq B$,
- $EQ^{(X,\tau)}(A, B)$ iff $A = B$.

This topological semantics is considered in [14–16, 24]. Obviously, these relations are jointly exhaustive and pairwise disjoint on the set of all nonempty regular closed subsets of X. We say that a topological space (X, τ) is *indiscrete* iff $\tau = \{\emptyset, X\}$. We say that a topological space (X, τ) is *connected* iff for all $A, B \in \tau$, either $A \cap B \neq \emptyset$, or $A \cup B \neq X$.

A relational perspective is suggested by Galton [11] who introduces the notion of adjacency space. Galton's spaces are frames (W, R) where W is a nonempty set of cells and R is an adjacency relation between cells. Galton defines regions to be sets of cells. He also defines two regions A and B to be connected iff some cell in A is adjacent to some cell in B. This definition relates Galton's adjacency spaces to the relational semantics of modal logic which makes it possible to use methods from modal logic for studying region-based theories of space. The truth is that the above-mentioned topological semantics and the relational perspective suggested by Galton are equivalent [23].

In this paper, we adopt a relational perspective by interpreting terms and formulas in frames. A *frame* is a structure of the form (W, R) where W is a nonempty set (with typical members denoted s, t, etc.) and R is a reflexive and symmetric relation on W. A frame (W, R) is *indiscrete* iff $R = W \times W$. A frame (W, R) is connected iff $R^+ = W \times W$ where R^+ denotes the transitive closure of R. Let (W, R) be a frame. We associate to each binary predicate P a binary relation $P^{(W,R)}$ on 2^W as follows:

- $DC^{(W,R)}(A, B)$ iff $R \cap (A \times B) = \emptyset$,
- $EC^{(W,R)}(A, B)$ iff $R \cap (A \times B) \neq \emptyset$ and $A \cap B = \emptyset$,
- $PO^{(W,R)}(A, B)$ iff $A \cap B \neq \emptyset$, $A \not\subseteq B$ and $B \not\subseteq A$,
- $TPP^{(W,R)}(A, B)$ iff $A \subseteq B$, $R \cap (A \times (W \backslash B)) \neq \emptyset$ and $B \not\subseteq A$,
- $TPPI^{(W,R)}(A, B)$ iff $B \subseteq A$, $R \cap (B \times (W \backslash A)) \neq \emptyset$ and $A \not\subseteq B$,
- $NTPP^{(W,R)}(A, B)$ iff $R \cap (A \times (W \backslash B)) = \emptyset$ and $B \not\subseteq A$,
- $NTPPI^{(W,R)}(A, B)$ iff $R \cap (B \times (W \backslash A)) = \emptyset$ and $A \not\subseteq B$,
- $EQ^{(W,R)}(A, B)$ iff $A = B$.

This relational semantics is considered in [3–5,23]. Obviously, these binary relations are jointly exhaustive and pairwise disjoint on $2^W \backslash \{\emptyset\}$, i.e. for all nonempty subsets A, B of W, there exists exactly one binary predicate P such that $P^{(W,R)}(A, B)$. The truth is that for all binary predicates P and for all subsets A, B of W, if either $A = \emptyset$, or $B = \emptyset$ then $P^{(W,R)}(A, B)$ iff either $P = DC$, or $P = NTPP$ and $B \neq \emptyset$, or $P = NTPPI$ and $A \neq \emptyset$, or $P = EQ$ and $A = B$.

A *valuation* on W is a map $\mathcal{V}$ associating with every variable x a subset $\mathcal{V}(x)$ of W. Given a valuation $\mathcal{V}$ on W, we define

- $\bar{\mathcal{V}}(x) = \mathcal{V}(x)$,
- $\bar{\mathcal{V}}(0) = \emptyset$,
- $\bar{\mathcal{V}}(a^\star) = W \backslash \bar{\mathcal{V}}(a)$,
- $\bar{\mathcal{V}}(a \cup b) = \bar{\mathcal{V}}(a) \cup \bar{\mathcal{V}}(b)$.

Thus, every term is interpreted as a subset of W. A valuation $\mathcal{V}$ on W is *balanced* iff for all terms a, either $\bar{\mathcal{V}}(a) = \emptyset$, or $\bar{\mathcal{V}}(a) = W$, or $\bar{\mathcal{V}}(a)$ is infinite and coinfinite.

A *model* on (W, R) is a structure $\mathcal{M} = (W, R, \mathcal{V})$ where $\mathcal{V}$ is a valuation on W. The *satisfiability* of a formula φ in $\mathcal{M}$ (in symbols $\mathcal{M} \models \varphi$) is defined as follows:

- $\mathcal{M} \models P(a, b)$ iff $P^{(W,R)}(\bar{\mathcal{V}}(a), \bar{\mathcal{V}}(b))$,
- $\mathcal{M} \not\models \bot$,
- $\mathcal{M} \models \neg\varphi$ iff $\mathcal{M} \not\models \varphi$,
- $\mathcal{M} \models \varphi \vee \psi$ iff either $\mathcal{M} \models \varphi$, or $\mathcal{M} \models \psi$.

A formula φ is *valid* in (W, R) iff for all valuations $\mathcal{V}$ on W, $(W, R, \mathcal{V}) \models \varphi$. A formula φ is *satisfiable* in (W, R) iff there exists a valuation $\mathcal{V}$ on W such that $(W, R, \mathcal{V}) \models \varphi$. Let $\mathcal{C}$ be a class of frames. We say that a formula φ is $\mathcal{C}$-*valid* iff for all frames (W, R) in $\mathcal{C}$, φ is valid in (W, R). We say that a formula φ is $\mathcal{C}$-*satisfiable* iff there exists a frame (W, R) in $\mathcal{C}$ such that φ is satisfiable in (W, R). The $\mathcal{C}$ -*satisfiability problem* consists in determining whether a given formula is $\mathcal{C}$-satisfiable. We say that $\mathcal{C}$ *agrees with unions* iff for all disjoint frames $(W, R), (W', R')$ in $\mathcal{C}$, there exists a frame (W'', R'') in $\mathcal{C}$ such that $W \cup W' = W''$. Note that if $\mathcal{C}$ contains frames of arbitrary cardinality then $\mathcal{C}$ agrees with unions. We say that $\mathcal{C}$ is *determined* iff there exists a set of formulas such that $\mathcal{C}$ is the class of all frames validating each formula in that set. We say that $\mathcal{C}$ is *balanced* iff for all formulas φ, if φ is $\mathcal{C}$-satisfiable then there exists a countable frame (W, R) in $\mathcal{C}$ and there exists a balanced valuation $\mathcal{V}$ on W such that $(W, R, V) \models \varphi$.

As illustrative examples of classes of frames, let $\mathcal{C}_{all}$ denote the class of all frames, $\mathcal{C}_{ind}$ denote the class of all indiscrete frames and $\mathcal{C}_{con}$ denote the class of all connected frames. The topological counterparts of these classes are the class of all topological spaces, the class of all indiscrete spaces and the class of all connected spaces. The following formulas are $\mathcal{C}_{all}$-valid:

- $DC(x, x) \rightarrow EQ(x, 0)$,
- $DC(x, y) \rightarrow DC(y, x)$.

In an indiscrete frame (W, R), any two points are R-related. Hence, for all subsets A, B of W, if $DC^{(W,R)}(A, B)$ then either $EQ^{(W,R)}(A, \emptyset)$, or $EQ^{(W,R)}(B, \emptyset)$. Thus, the following formula is $\mathcal{C}_{ind}$-valid:

- $DC(x, y) \rightarrow EQ(x, 0) \vee EQ(y, 0)$.

In a connected frame (W, R), any two points are R^+-related. Hence, for all subsets A of W, if $DC^{(W,R)}(A, W \backslash A)$ then either $EQ^{(W,R)}(A, \emptyset)$, or $EQ^{(W,R)}(W \backslash A, \emptyset)$. Thus, the following formula is $\mathcal{C}_{con}$-valid:

- $DC(x, x^\star) \rightarrow EQ(x, 0) \vee EQ(x^\star, 0)$.

Proposition 1. *$\mathcal{C}_{all}$, $\mathcal{C}_{ind}$ and $\mathcal{C}_{con}$ agree with unions.*

Proof. By the definition of what it means for classes of frames to agree with unions.

Proposition 2. *$\mathcal{C}_{all}$, $\mathcal{C}_{ind}$ and $\mathcal{C}_{con}$ are determined.*

Proof. It suffices to note that $\mathcal{C}_{all}$ is determined by $\emptyset$, $\mathcal{C}_{ind}$ is determined by $\{DC(x, y) \rightarrow EQ(x, 0) \vee EQ(y, 0)\}$ and $\mathcal{C}_{con}$ is determined by $\{DC(x, x^\star) \rightarrow EQ(x, 0) \vee EQ(x^\star, 0)\}$.

Proposition 3. *$\mathcal{C}_{all}$, $\mathcal{C}_{ind}$ and $\mathcal{C}_{con}$ are balanced.*

Proof. By Proposition 2 and [5, Theorem 4.1], $\mathcal{C}_{all}$, $\mathcal{C}_{ind}$ and $\mathcal{C}_{con}$ admit filtration. Now, consider an arbitrary finite frame (W, R). We define the countable frame (W', R') as follows:

- $W' = W \times \mathbb{Z}$,

– for all $(s,i),(t,j) \in W'$, $(s,i)R'(t,j)$ iff sRt.

Obviously, if (W,R) is indiscrete (respectively, connected) then (W',R') is indiscrete (respectively, connected) too. Moreover, according to [4, Definition 3.1], (W,R) is a bounded morphic image of (W',R'). Thus, by [4, Proposition 3.1], for all formulas φ, if φ is satisfiable in (W,R) then there exists a balanced valuation $\mathcal{V}'$ on (W',R') such that $(W',R',\mathcal{V}') \models \varphi$. Since (W,R) was arbitrary and $\mathcal{C}_{all}$, $\mathcal{C}_{ind}$ and $\mathcal{C}_{con}$ admit filtration, therefore $\mathcal{C}_{all}$, $\mathcal{C}_{ind}$ and $\mathcal{C}_{con}$ are balanced.

As for the satisfiability problem, it is known to be NP-complete in $\mathcal{C}_{all}$ and $\mathcal{C}_{ind}$ and $PSPACE$-complete in $\mathcal{C}_{con}$ [5,14–16,24].

5 Unifiability

Let $\mathcal{C}$ be a class of frames.

We say that a substitution σ is *$\mathcal{C}$-equivalent* to a substitution τ (in symbols $\sigma \simeq_{\mathcal{C}} \tau$) iff for all variables x, $EQ(\sigma(x),\tau(x))$ is $\mathcal{C}$-valid. We say that a substitution σ is *more $\mathcal{C}$-general than* a substitution τ (in symbols $\sigma \preceq_{\mathcal{C}} \tau$) iff there exists a substitution υ such that $\sigma \circ \upsilon \simeq_{\mathcal{C}} \tau$.

We say that a finite set $\{(\varphi_1,\psi_1),\ldots,(\varphi_n,\psi_n)\}$ of pairs of formulas is *$\mathcal{C}$ -unifiable* iff there exists a substitution σ such that $\bar{\sigma}(\varphi_1) \leftrightarrow \bar{\sigma}(\psi_1)$, ..., $\bar{\sigma}(\varphi_n) \leftrightarrow \bar{\sigma}(\psi_n)$ are $\mathcal{C}$-valid. As a consequence of the classical interpretation of the constructs for formulas, this is equivalent to $\bar{\sigma}((\varphi_1 \leftrightarrow \psi_1) \wedge \ldots \wedge (\varphi_n \leftrightarrow \psi_n))$ is $\mathcal{C}$-valid. This means that we can restrict our attention to a simpler kind of unifiability problems consisting of exactly one formula. We say that a formula φ is *$\mathcal{C}$ -unifiable* iff there exists a substitution σ such that $\bar{\sigma}(\varphi)$ is $\mathcal{C}$-valid. In that case, we say that σ is a *$\mathcal{C}$-unifier* of φ. For instance, $EQ(0,x) \vee EQ(1,x)$ is unifiable in $\mathcal{C}_{all}$, $\mathcal{C}_{ind}$ and $\mathcal{C}_{con}$. As we will prove it with Proposition 15, its unifiers are the substitutions σ such that considered as a formula in Classical Propositional Logic (CPL), $\sigma(x)$ is either equivalent to 0, or equivalent to 1. The *elementary $\mathcal{C}$ -unifiability problem* consists in determining whether a given formula is $\mathcal{C}$-unifiable. See [1,2,12,13] for an introduction to the unifiability problem in modal and description logics.

We say that a set of $\mathcal{C}$-unifiers of a formula φ is *complete* iff for all $\mathcal{C}$-unifiers σ of φ, there exists a $\mathcal{C}$-unifier τ of φ in that set such that $\tau \preceq_{\mathcal{C}} \sigma$. As we will prove it with Proposition 15, the substitutions σ_0 and σ_1 such that $\sigma_0(x) = 0$, $\sigma_1(x) = 1$ and for all variables y, if $x \neq y$ then $\sigma_0(y) = y$ and $\sigma_1(y) = y$ constitute a complete set of $\mathcal{C}$-unifiers of $EQ(0,x) \vee EQ(1,x)$. An important question is: when a formula is $\mathcal{C}$-unifiable, has it a minimal complete set of $\mathcal{C}$-unifiers? When the answer is "yes", how large is this set?

We say that a $\mathcal{C}$-unifiable formula φ is *$\mathcal{C}$-nullary* iff there exists no minimal complete set of $\mathcal{C}$-unifiers of φ. We say that a $\mathcal{C}$-unifiable formula φ is *$\mathcal{C}$-infinitary* iff there exists a minimal complete set of $\mathcal{C}$-unifiers of φ but there exists no finite one. We say that a $\mathcal{C}$-unifiable formula φ is *$\mathcal{C}$-finitary* iff there exists a finite minimal complete set of $\mathcal{C}$-unifiers of φ but there exists no with cardinality 1. We say that a $\mathcal{C}$-unifiable formula φ is *$\mathcal{C}$ -unitary* iff there exists a minimal complete set of $\mathcal{C}$-unifiers of φ with cardinality 1. We say that elementary unification in $\mathcal{C}$ is *nullary* iff there exists a $\mathcal{C}$-nullary formula. We say that elementary unification in $\mathcal{C}$ is *infinitary* iff every $\mathcal{C}$-unifiable formula is either $\mathcal{C}$-infinitary, or $\mathcal{C}$-finitary, or $\mathcal{C}$-unitary and there exists a $\mathcal{C}$-infinitary formula. We say that elementary unification in $\mathcal{C}$ is *finitary* iff every $\mathcal{C}$-unifiable formula is either $\mathcal{C}$-finitary, or $\mathcal{C}$-unitary and there exists a $\mathcal{C}$-finitary formula. We say that elementary unification in $\mathcal{C}$ is *unitary* iff every $\mathcal{C}$-unifiable formula is $\mathcal{C}$-unitary. See [10] for an introduction to the unification types in logics.

An axiomatic system for $\mathcal{C}$ consists of axioms and rules. Its theorems are all formulas which can be derived from the axioms by means of the rules. See [5,23] for systems of axioms and rules characterizing validity with respect to different classes of frames. In order to make stronger an axiomatic system for $\mathcal{C}$, we can add new axioms and new rules to it. Concerning new axioms, they should always consist of $\mathcal{C}$-valid formulas. About new rules, they should always consist of rules that preserve $\mathcal{C}$-validity. We say that an inference rule $\frac{\varphi}{\psi}$ is *$\mathcal{C}$-admissible* iff for all substitutions σ, if $\sigma(\varphi)$ is $\mathcal{C}$-valid then $\sigma(\psi)$ is $\mathcal{C}$-valid. The *elementary $\mathcal{C}$-admissibility problem* consists in determining whether a given inference rule is $\mathcal{C}$-admissible. See [22] for an introduction to the admissibility problem in logics.

6 Monoms and Polynoms

Before we provide, in Sect. 8, computability results about unifiability and admissibility in $BRCC8$ and prove, in Sect. 9, that elementary unification is finitary, we introduce the notions of monom and polynom (this section) and define some equivalence relations (next section).

Let k, n be nonnegative integer and $f : \{0,1\}^k \longrightarrow \{0,1\}^n$ be a function. An *n-monom* is a term of the form

– $x_1^{\beta_1} \cap \ldots \cap x_n^{\beta_n}$

where $(\beta_1, \ldots, \beta_n) \in \{0,1\}^n$. Considering the terms $x_1^{\beta_1}$, ..., $x_n^{\beta_n}$ as literals in CPL, n-monoms are just conjunctions of literals. Considering a term a in $TER(x_1, \ldots, x_n)$ as a formula in CPL, let $mon(n, a)$ be the set of all n-monoms $x_1^{\beta_1} \cap \ldots \cap x_n^{\beta_n}$ such that a is a tautological consequence of $x_1^{\beta_1} \cap \ldots \cap x_n^{\beta_n}$. An *$n$ -polynom* is a term of the form

– $(x_1^{\beta_{11}} \cap \ldots \cap x_n^{\beta_{1n}}) \cup \ldots \cup (x_1^{\beta_{m1}} \cap \ldots \cap x_n^{\beta_{mn}})$

where m is a nonnegative integer and $(\beta_{11}, \ldots, \beta_{1n}), \ldots, (\beta_{m1}, \ldots, \beta_{mn}) \in \{0,1\}^n$. Considering the terms $x_1^{\beta_{11}} \cap \ldots \cap x_n^{\beta_{1n}}$, ..., $x_1^{\beta_{m1}} \cap \ldots \cap x_n^{\beta_{mn}}$ as conjunctions of literals in CPL, n-polynoms are just disjunctive normal forms. Note that for all terms a in $TER(x_1, \ldots, x_n)$, $\bigcup mon(n, a)$ is an n-polynom. For all positive integers i, if $i \leq n$ then let $\pi_i : \{0,1\}^n \longrightarrow \{0,1\}$ be the function such that for all $(\beta_1, \ldots, \beta_n) \in \{0,1\}^n$, $\pi_i(\beta_1, \ldots, \beta_n) = \beta_i$. For all $(\beta_1, \ldots, \beta_n) \in \{0,1\}^n$, we define

– $f^{-1}(\beta_1, \ldots, \beta_n) = \{(\alpha_1, \ldots, \alpha_k) \in \{0,1\}^k : f(\alpha_1, \ldots, \alpha_k) = (\beta_1, \ldots, \beta_n)\}$.

Obviously, for all $(\beta_1, \ldots, \beta_n) \in \{0,1\}^n$, $f^{-1}(\beta_1, \ldots, \beta_n) \subseteq \{0,1\}^k$. For all positive integers i, if $i \leq n$ then we define:

- $\Delta_i = \{(\alpha_1, \ldots, \alpha_k) \in \{0,1\}^k : \pi_i(f(\alpha_1, \ldots, \alpha_k)) = 1\}$,
- $c_i = \bigcup\{x_1^{\alpha_1} \cap \ldots \cap x_k^{\alpha_k} : (\alpha_1, \ldots, \alpha_k) \in \Delta_i\}$.

Obviously, for all positive integers i, if $i \leq n$ then $\Delta_i \subseteq \{0,1\}^k$ and c_i is a k-polynom. Note that Δ_i and c_i depend on f too. Lemma 1 is a consequence of the definition of $mon(n, a)$.

Lemma 1. *Let $a(x_1, \ldots, x_n) \in TER(x_1, \ldots, x_n)$. Considered as formulas in CPL, the terms a and $\bigcup mon(n, a)$ are equivalent.*

Proposition 4. *For all $(\beta_1, \ldots, \beta_n) \in \{0,1\}^n$, considered as formulas in CPL, the terms $\bigcup\{x_1^{\alpha_1} \cap \ldots \cap x_k^{\alpha_k} : (\alpha_1, \ldots, \alpha_k) \in f^{-1}(\beta_1, \ldots, \beta_n)\}$ and $c_1^{\beta_1} \cap \ldots \cap c_n^{\beta_n}$ are equivalent.*

Proof. Let $(\beta_1, \ldots, \beta_n) \in \{0,1\}^n$. It suffices to show that considered as formulas in CPL, for all $\theta_1, \ldots, \theta_k \in \{0,1\}$, if x_1 is interpreted by θ_1, ..., x_k is interpreted by θ_k then $\bigcup\{x_1^{\alpha_1} \cap \ldots \cap x_k^{\alpha_k} : (\alpha_1, \ldots, \alpha_k) \in f^{-1}(\beta_1, \ldots, \beta_n)\}$ is equivalent to 1 iff $c_1^{\beta_1} \cap \ldots \cap c_n^{\beta_n}$ is equivalent to 1. Let $\theta_1, \ldots, \theta_k \in \{0,1\}$. Let x_1 be interpreted by θ_1, ..., x_k be interpreted by θ_k.

Suppose $\bigcup\{x_1^{\alpha_1} \cap \ldots \cap x_k^{\alpha_k} : (\alpha_1, \ldots, \alpha_k) \in f^{-1}(\beta_1, \ldots, \beta_n)\}$ is equivalent to 1. Hence, $(\theta_1, \ldots, \theta_k) \in f^{-1}(\beta_1, \ldots, \beta_n)$. Thus, $f(\theta_1, \ldots, \theta_k) = (\beta_1, \ldots, \beta_n)$. For the sake of the contradiction, suppose $c_1^{\beta_1} \cap \ldots \cap c_n^{\beta_n}$ is equivalent to 0. Let i be a positive integer such that $i \leq n$ and $c_i^{\beta_i}$ is equivalent to 0. Since either $\beta_i = 0$, or $\beta_i = 1$, therefore we have to consider two cases. In the former case, $\beta_i = 0$ and therefore $\bigcup\{x_1^{\alpha_1} \cap \ldots \cap x_k^{\alpha_k} : (\alpha_1, \ldots, \alpha_k) \in \Delta_i\}$ is equivalent to 1. Consequently, $(\theta_1, \ldots, \theta_k) \in \Delta_i$. Hence, $\pi_i(f(\theta_1, \ldots, \theta_k)) = 1$. Since $f(\theta_1, \ldots, \theta_k) = (\beta_1, \ldots, \beta_n)$, therefore $\beta_i = 1$: a contradiction. In the latter case, $\beta_i = 1$ and therefore $\bigcup\{x_1^{\alpha_1} \cap \ldots \cap x_k^{\alpha_k} : (\alpha_1, \ldots, \alpha_k) \in \Delta_i\}$ is equivalent to 0. Thus, $(\theta_1, \ldots, \theta_k) \notin \Delta_i$. Hence, $\pi_i(f(\theta_1, \ldots, \theta_k)) = 0$. Since $f(\theta_1, \ldots, \theta_k) = (\beta_1, \ldots, \beta_n)$, therefore $\beta_i = 0$: a contradiction.

Suppose $c_1^{\beta_1} \cap \ldots \cap c_n^{\beta_n}$ is equivalent to 1. Let i be an arbitrary positive integer such that $i \leq n$. Since $c_1^{\beta_1} \cap \ldots \cap c_n^{\beta_n}$ is equivalent to 1, therefore $c_i^{\beta_i}$ is equivalent to 1. Since either $\beta_i = 0$, or $\beta_i = 1$, therefore we have to consider two cases. In the former case, $\beta_i = 0$ and therefore c_i is equivalent to 0. Hence, $(\theta_1, \ldots, \theta_k) \notin \Delta_i$. Thus, $\pi_i(f(\theta_1, \ldots, \theta_k)) = 0$. Since $\beta_i = 0$, therefore $\pi_i(f(\theta_1, \ldots, \theta_k)) = \beta_i$. In the latter case, $\beta_i = 1$ and therefore c_i is equivalent to 1. Consequently, $(\theta_1, \ldots, \theta_k) \in \Delta_i$. Hence, $\pi_i(f(\theta_1, \ldots, \theta_k)) = 1$. Since $\beta_i = 1$, therefore $\pi_i(f(\theta_1, \ldots, \theta_k)) = \beta_i$. In both cases, $\pi_i(f(\theta_1, \ldots, \theta_k)) = \beta_i$. Since i was arbitrary, therefore $f(\theta_1, \ldots, \theta_k) = (\beta_1, \ldots, \beta_n)$. Thus, $(\theta_1, \ldots, \theta_k) \in f^{-1}(\beta_1, \ldots, \beta_n)$. Consequently, $\bigcup\{x_1^{\alpha_1} \cap \ldots \cap x_k^{\alpha_k} : (\alpha_1, \ldots, \alpha_k) \in f^{-1}(\beta_1, \ldots, \beta_n)\}$ is equivalent to 1.

7 Some Equivalence Relations

Let k, n be nonnegative integers and $\mathcal{C}$ be a class of frames.

Given $(a_1, \ldots, a_n) \in TER(x_1, \ldots, x_k)^n$, we define on $\{0,1\}^k$ the equivalence relation $\sim^k_{(a_1,\ldots,a_n)}$ as follows:

- $(\alpha_1, \ldots, \alpha_k) \sim^k_{(a_1,\ldots,a_n)} (\alpha'_1, \ldots, \alpha'_k)$ iff for all positive integers i, if $i \leq n$, then $x_1^{\alpha_1} \cap \ldots \cap x_k^{\alpha_k} \in mon(k, a_i)$ iff $x_1^{\alpha'_1} \cap \ldots \cap x_k^{\alpha'_k} \in mon(k, a_i)$.

Lemma 2 is a consequence of its definition.

Lemma 2. *For all $(a_1, \ldots, a_n) \in TER(x_1, \ldots, x_k)^n$, $\sim^k_{(a_1,\ldots,a_n)}$ has at most 2^n equivalence classes on $\{0,1\}^k$.*

Let $f : \{0,1\}^k \longrightarrow \{0,1\}^n$ be a function such that for all $(\alpha_1, \ldots, \alpha_k), (\alpha'_1, \ldots, \alpha'_k) \in \{0,1\}^k$, if $f(\alpha_1, \ldots, \alpha_k) = f(\alpha'_1, \ldots, \alpha'_k)$ then $(\alpha_1, \ldots, \alpha_k) \sim^k_{(a_1,\ldots,a_n)} (\alpha'_1, \ldots, \alpha'_k)$. By means of the function f, we define the n-tuple $(b_1, \ldots, b_n)$ of n-polynoms as follows:

- $b_i = \bigcup\{x_1^{\beta_1} \cap \ldots \cap x_n^{\beta_n} : x_1^{\alpha_1} \cap \ldots \cap x_k^{\alpha_k} \in mon(k, a_i)$ and $f(\alpha_1, \ldots, \alpha_k) = (\beta_1, \ldots, \beta_n)\}$.

We say that $(b_1, \ldots, b_n)$ is the n-tuple of n-polynoms *properly obtained* from the given n-tuple $(a_1, \ldots, a_n)$ in $TER(x_1, \ldots, x_k)^n$ with respect to (k, n). Lemma 3 is a consequence of its definition.

Lemma 3. *Let $(a_1, \ldots, a_n)$ be an n-tuple in $TER(x_1, \ldots, x_k)^n$ and $(b_1, \ldots, b_n)$ be an n-tuple of n-polynoms. Let W be a nonempty set. If $(b_1, \ldots, b_n)$ is properly obtained from $(a_1, \ldots, a_n)$ with respect to (k, n) then for all valuations $\mathcal{V}$ on W, there exists a valuation $\mathcal{V}'$ on W such that for all positive integers i, if $i \leq n$, then $\bar{\mathcal{V}}(a_i) = \bar{\mathcal{V}}'(b_i)$ and for all valuations $\mathcal{V}$ on W, there exists a valuation $\mathcal{V}'$ on W such that for all positive integers i, if $i \leq n$, then $\bar{\mathcal{V}}(b_i) = \bar{\mathcal{V}}'(a_i)$.*

For all $(\beta_1, \ldots, \beta_n) \in \{0,1\}^n$, let $f^{-1}(\beta_1, \ldots, \beta_n)$ be as in Sect. 6. For all positive integers i, if $i \leq n$ then let Δ_i and c_i be as in Sect. 6. Let v be the substitution such that

- for all positive integers i, if $i \leq n$ then $v(x_i) = c_i$,
- for all variables y, if $y \notin \{x_1, \ldots, x_n\}$ then $v(y) = y$.

Proposition 5. *For all positive integers i, if $i \leq n$ then considered as formulas in CPL, the terms a_i and $\bar{v}(b_i)$ are equivalent.*

Proof. Let i be a positive integer such that $i \leq n$. Considered as formulas in CPL, the following terms are equivalent:

1. $\bar{v}(b_i)$.
2. $\bigcup\{c_1^{\beta_1} \cap \ldots \cap c_n^{\beta_n} : x_1^{\alpha_1} \cap \ldots \cap x_k^{\alpha_k} \in mon(k, a_i)$ and $f(\alpha_1, \ldots, \alpha_k) = (\beta_1, \ldots, \beta_n)\}$.

3. $\bigcup\{\bigcup\{x_1^{\alpha'_1} \cap \ldots \cap x_k^{\alpha'_k} : (\alpha'_1, \ldots, \alpha'_k) \in f^{-1}(\beta_1, \ldots, \beta_n)\} : x_1^{\alpha_1} \cap \ldots \cap x_k^{\alpha_k} \in mon(k, a_i)$ and $f(\alpha_1, \ldots, \alpha_k) = (\beta_1, \ldots, \beta_n)\}$.
4. $\bigcup\{x_1^{\alpha'_1} \cap \ldots \cap x_k^{\alpha'_k} : (\alpha'_1, \ldots, \alpha'_k) \in f^{-1}(\beta_1, \ldots, \beta_n), x_1^{\alpha_1} \cap \ldots \cap x_k^{\alpha_k} \in mon(k, a_i)$ and $f(\alpha_1, \ldots, \alpha_k) = (\beta_1, \ldots, \beta_n)\}$.
5. $\bigcup\{x_1^{\alpha'_1} \cap \ldots \cap x_k^{\alpha'_k} : x_1^{\alpha_1} \cap \ldots \cap x_k^{\alpha_k} \in mon(k, a_i)$ and $f(\alpha'_1, \ldots, \alpha'_k) = f(\alpha_1, \ldots, \alpha_k)\}$.
6. $\bigcup mon(k, a_i)$.
7. a_i.

The equivalence between 1 and 2 is a consequence of the definition of υ; the equivalence between 2 and 3 is a consequence of Proposition 4; the equivalences between 3, 4 and 5 are consequences of simple set-theoretic properties; the equivalence between 5 and 6 is a consequence of the definition of $\sim^k_{(a_1,\ldots,a_n)}$ and the fact that for all $(\alpha_1, \ldots, \alpha_k), (\alpha'_1, \ldots, \alpha'_k) \in \{0,1\}^k$, if $f(\alpha_1, \ldots, \alpha_k) = f(\alpha'_1, \ldots, \alpha'_k)$ then $(\alpha_1, \ldots, \alpha_k) \sim^k_{(a_1,\ldots,a_n)} (\alpha'_1, \ldots, \alpha'_k)$; the equivalence between 6 and 7 is a consequence of Lemma 1.

We define on $FOR(x_1, \ldots, x_n)$ the equivalence relation $\equiv^n_{\mathcal{C}}$ as follows:

- $\varphi \equiv^n_{\mathcal{C}} \psi$ iff $\varphi \leftrightarrow \psi$ is $\mathcal{C}$-valid.

Proposition 6. *$\equiv^n_{\mathcal{C}}$ has finitely many equivalence classes on $FOR(x_1, \ldots, x_n)$.*

Proof. Each formula φ in $FOR(x_1, \ldots, x_n)$ is a combination of formulas of the form $P(a, b)$ where a and b are terms in $TER(x_1, \ldots, x_n)$ and P is one of the 8 binary predicates of $RCC8$. Hence, $\equiv^n_{\mathcal{C}}$ has finitely many equivalence classes on $FOR(x_1, \ldots, x_n)$.

Let A_n be the set of all n-tuples of terms. Note that n-tuples of terms in A_n may contain occurrences of variables outside $\{x_1, \ldots, x_n\}$. Given a model $(W, R, \mathcal{V})$ on a frame in $\mathcal{C}$ and $(a_1, \ldots, a_n) \in A_n$, let $\Phi^{(W,R,\mathcal{V})}_{(a_1,\ldots,a_n)}$ be the set of all equational formulas $\varphi(x_1, \ldots, x_n)$ in $FOR(x_1, \ldots, x_n)$ such that $(W, R, \mathcal{V}) \models \varphi(a_1, \ldots, a_n)$. Consider a complete list of representatives for each equivalence class on $\Phi^{(W,R,\mathcal{V})}_{(a_1,\ldots,a_n)}$ modulo $\equiv^n_{\mathcal{C}}$ and let $\varphi^{(W,R,\mathcal{V})}_{(a_1,\ldots,a_n)}(x_1, \ldots, x_n)$ be their conjunction.

We define on A_n the equivalence relation $\cong^n_{\mathcal{C}}$ as follows:

- $(a_1, \ldots, a_n) \cong^n_{\mathcal{C}} (b_1, \ldots, b_n)$ iff for all formulas $\varphi(x_1, \ldots, x_n)$ in $FOR(x_1, \ldots, x_n)$, $\varphi(a_1, \ldots, a_n)$ is $\mathcal{C}$-valid iff $\varphi(b_1, \ldots, b_n)$ is $\mathcal{C}$-valid.

Now, we define on A_n the equivalence relation $\simeq^n_{\mathcal{C}}$ as follows:

- $(a_1, \ldots, a_n) \simeq^n_{\mathcal{C}} (b_1, \ldots, b_n)$ iff for all equational formulas $\varphi(x_1, \ldots, x_n)$ in $FOR(x_1, \ldots, x_n)$, $\varphi(a_1, \ldots, a_n)$ is $\mathcal{C}$-valid iff $\varphi(b_1, \ldots, b_n)$ is $\mathcal{C}$-valid.

Obviously, $\cong^n_{\mathcal{C}}$ is finer than $\simeq^n_{\mathcal{C}}$. Lemma 4 is a consequence of Proposition 6; Lemma 5 is a consequence of Lemma 4; Lemma 6 is a consequence of the definition of $\simeq^n_{\mathcal{C}}$ and Lemma 3; Lemma 7 is a consequence of Lemma 6; Lemma 8 is a consequence of the definition of $\varphi^{(W,R,\mathcal{V})}_{(a_1,\ldots,a_n)}(x_1, \ldots, x_n)$.

Lemma 4. *$\cong^n_{\mathcal{C}}$ has finitely many equivalence classes on A_n.*

Lemma 5. *$\simeq^n_{\mathcal{C}}$ has finitely many equivalence classes on A_n.*

Lemma 6. *Let $(a_1, \ldots, a_n)$ be an n-tuple in $TER(x_1, \ldots, x_k)^n$ and $(b_1, \ldots, b_n)$ be an n-tuple of n-polynoms. If $(b_1, \ldots, b_n)$ is properly obtained from $(a_1, \ldots, a_n)$ with respect to (k, n) then $(a_1, \ldots, a_n) \simeq^n_{\mathcal{C}} (b_1, \ldots, b_n)$.*

Lemma 7. *$TER(x_1, \ldots, x_n)^n$ constitutes a complete set of representatives for each equivalence class on A_n modulo $\simeq^n_{\mathcal{C}}$.*

Lemma 8. *Let $(W, R, \mathcal{V})$ be a model on a frame in $\mathcal{C}$ and $(a_1, \ldots, a_n) \in A_n$. $(W, R, \mathcal{V}) \models \varphi^{(W,R,\mathcal{V})}_{(a_1,\ldots,a_n)}(a_1, \ldots, a_n)$.*

Proposition 7. *If $\mathcal{C}$ is balanced then for all $(a_1, \ldots, a_n), (b_1, \ldots, b_n) \in A_n$, if $(a_1, \ldots, a_n) \simeq^n_{\mathcal{C}} (b_1, \ldots, b_n)$ then $(a_1, \ldots, a_n) \cong^n_{\mathcal{C}} (b_1, \ldots, b_n)$.*

Proof. Suppose $\mathcal{C}$ is balanced. Let $(a_1, \ldots, a_n), (b_1, \ldots, b_n) \in A_n$ be such that $(a_1, \ldots, a_n) \simeq^n_{\mathcal{C}} (b_1, \ldots, b_n)$ and $(a_1, \ldots, a_n) \not\cong^n_{\mathcal{C}} (b_1, \ldots, b_n)$. Let $\varphi(x_1, \ldots, x_n)$ be a formula in $FOR(x_1, \ldots, x_n)$ such that $\varphi(a_1, \ldots, a_n)$ is $\mathcal{C}$-valid not-iff $\varphi(b_1, \ldots, b_n)$ is $\mathcal{C}$-valid. Without loss of generality, let us assume that $\varphi(a_1, \ldots, a_n)$ is $\mathcal{C}$-valid and $\varphi(b_1, \ldots, b_n)$ is not $\mathcal{C}$-valid. Since $\mathcal{C}$ is balanced, therefore let $(W, R, \mathcal{V})$ be a balanced model on a countable frame in $\mathcal{C}$ such that $(W, R, \mathcal{V}) \not\models \varphi(b_1, \ldots, b_n)$. By Lemma 8, $(W, R, \mathcal{V}) \models \varphi^{(W,R,\mathcal{V})}_{(b_1,\ldots,b_n)}(b_1, \ldots, b_n)$. Hence, $\neg\varphi^{(W,R,\mathcal{V})}_{(b_1,\ldots,b_n)}(b_1, \ldots, b_n)$ is not $\mathcal{C}$-valid. Since $(a_1, \ldots, a_n) \simeq^n_{\mathcal{C}} (b_1, \ldots, b_n)$, therefore $\neg\varphi^{(W,R,\mathcal{V})}_{(b_1,\ldots,b_n)}(a_1, \ldots, a_n)$ is not $\mathcal{C}$-valid. Since $\mathcal{C}$ is balanced, therefore let $(W', R', \mathcal{V}')$ be a balanced model on a countable frame in $\mathcal{C}$ such that $(W', R', \mathcal{V}') \models \varphi^{(W,R,\mathcal{V})}_{(b_1,\ldots,b_n)}(a_1, \ldots, a_n)$. Now, consider $(\beta_1, \ldots, \beta_n) \in \{0,1\}^n$. If $\bar{\mathcal{V}}(b_1^{\beta_1} \cap \ldots \cap b_n^{\beta_n}) = \emptyset$ then $(W, R, \mathcal{V}) \models EQ(b_1^{\beta_1} \cap \ldots \cap b_n^{\beta_n}, 0)$. Thus, $\varphi^{(W,R,\mathcal{V})}_{(b_1,\ldots,b_n)}(x_1, \ldots, x_n) \to EQ(x_1^{\beta_1} \cap \ldots \cap x_n^{\beta_n}, 0)$ is $\mathcal{C}$-valid. Since $(W', R', \mathcal{V}') \models \varphi^{(W,R,\mathcal{V})}_{(b_1,\ldots,b_n)}(a_1, \ldots, a_n)$, therefore $(W', R', \mathcal{V}') \models EQ(a_1^{\beta_1} \cap \ldots \cap a_n^{\beta_n}, 0)$. Consequently, $\bar{\mathcal{V}}'(a_1^{\beta_1} \cap \ldots \cap a_n^{\beta_n}) = \emptyset$. Similarly, the reader may easily verify that if $\bar{\mathcal{V}}(b_1^{\beta_1} \cap \ldots \cap b_n^{\beta_n}) = W$ then $\bar{\mathcal{V}}'(a_1^{\beta_1} \cap \ldots \cap a_n^{\beta_n}) = W'$ and if $\bar{\mathcal{V}}(b_1^{\beta_1} \cap \ldots \cap b_n^{\beta_n})$ is infinite and coinfinite then $\bar{\mathcal{V}}'(a_1^{\beta_1} \cap \ldots \cap a_n^{\beta_n})$ is infinite and coinfinite. In all cases, there exists a bijection $g_{(\beta_1,\ldots,\beta_n)}$ from $\bar{\mathcal{V}}(b_1^{\beta_1} \cap \ldots \cap b_n^{\beta_n})$ to $\bar{\mathcal{V}}'(a_1^{\beta_1} \cap \ldots \cap a_n^{\beta_n})$. Let g be the union of all $g_{(\beta_1,\ldots,\beta_n)}$ when $(\beta_1, \ldots, \beta_n)$ describes $\{0,1\}^n$. The reader may easily verify that g is a bijection from W to W' such that for all $u \in W$ and for all $(\beta_1, \ldots, \beta_n) \in \{0,1\}^n$, $u \in \bar{\mathcal{V}}(b_1^{\beta_1} \cap \ldots \cap b_n^{\beta_n})$ iff $g(u) \in \bar{\mathcal{V}}'(a_1^{\beta_1} \cap \ldots \cap a_n^{\beta_n})$. Let R'_g be the binary relation on W' defined by $u' R'_g v'$ iff $g^{-1}(u') R g^{-1}(v')$. Obviously, g is an isomorphism from (W, R) to (W', R'_g). Since $\varphi(a_1, \ldots, a_n)$ is $\mathcal{C}$-valid, therefore $(W', R'_g, \mathcal{V}') \models \varphi(a_1, \ldots, a_n)$. Hence, $(W, R, \mathcal{V}) \models \varphi(b_1, \ldots, b_n)$: a contradiction.

8 Computability of Unifiability

Let $\mathcal{C}$ be a class of frames. Lemma 9 is a consequence of the definitions in Sect. 4.

Lemma 9

1. *For all $a \in TER(\emptyset)$, either $EQ(a, 0)$ is $\mathcal{C}$-valid, or $EQ(a, 1)$ is $\mathcal{C}$-valid. Moreover, the formula in $\{EQ(a, 0), EQ(a, 1)\}$ that is $\mathcal{C}$-valid can be computed in linear time.*
2. *For all $a, b \in TER(\emptyset)$, either $DC(a, b)$ is $\mathcal{C}$-valid, or $EQ(a, b)$ is $\mathcal{C}$-valid. Moreover, the formula in $\{DC(a, b), EQ(a, b)\}$ that is $\mathcal{C}$-valid can be computed in linear time.*

Lemma 10 is a consequence of the definition of unifiability.

Lemma 10. *For all formulas $\varphi(x_1, \ldots, x_n)$, φ is $\mathcal{C}$-unifiable iff there exists $a_1, \ldots, a_n \in TER(\emptyset)$ such that $\varphi(a_1, \ldots, a_n)$ is $\mathcal{C}$-valid.*

Proposition 8. *The elementary $\mathcal{C}$-unifiability problem is in NP.*

Proof. By Lemmas 9 and 10, for all formulas $\varphi(x_1, \ldots, x_n)$, $\varphi(x_1, \ldots, x_n)$ is $\mathcal{C}$-unifiable iff there exists $a_1, \ldots, a_n \in \{0, 1\}$ such that $\varphi(a_1, \ldots, a_n)$ is $\mathcal{C}$-valid. Obviously, this can be decided in polynomial time.

Proposition 9. *Let $a(x_1, \ldots, x_n)$ be a term. $EQ(a(x_1, \ldots, x_n), 1)$ is $\mathcal{C}$-unifiable iff considered as a formula in CPL, $a(x_1, \ldots, x_n)$ is satisfiable.*

Proof. Suppose considered as a formula in CPL, $a(x_1, \ldots, x_n)$ is satisfiable. Let $b_1, \ldots, b_n$ in $\{0,1\}$ be such that $a(b_1, \ldots, b_n)$ is a tautology. Hence, $EQ(a(b_1, \ldots, b_n), 1)$ is $\mathcal{C}$-valid. Thus, $EQ(a(x_1, \ldots, x_n), 1)$ is $\mathcal{C}$-unifiable.

Suppose $EQ(a(x_1, \ldots, x_n), 1)$ is $\mathcal{C}$-unifiable. By Lemmas 9 and 10, let $b_1, \ldots, b_n$ in $\{0, 1\}$ be such that $EQ(a(b_1, \ldots, b_n), 1)$ is $\mathcal{C}$-valid. Consequently, $a(b_1, \ldots, b_n)$ is a tautology. Hence, considered as a formula in CPL, $a(x_1, \ldots, x_n)$ is satisfiable.

Proposition 10. *The elementary $\mathcal{C}$-unifiability problem is NP-hard.*

Proof. By Proposition 9 and the NP-hardness of the satisfiability problem of formulas in CPL.

It follows from Propositions 8 and 10 that

Proposition 11. *The elementary unifiability problem in $\mathcal{C}_{all}$, $\mathcal{C}_{ind}$ and $\mathcal{C}_{con}$ is NP-complete.*

In other respect,

Proposition 12. *Let A be a complexity class. If $\mathcal{C}$ is balanced and the $\mathcal{C}$-satisfiability problem is in A then the elementary $\mathcal{C}$-admissibility problem is in $coNEXP^A$.*

Proof. Suppose $\mathcal{C}$ is balanced and the $\mathcal{C}$-satisfiability problem is in A. By Lemma 7 and Proposition 7, for all inference rules $\frac{\varphi(x_1,\ldots,x_n)}{\psi(x_1,\ldots,x_n)}$, $\frac{\varphi(x_1,\ldots,x_n)}{\psi(x_1,\ldots,x_n)}$ is not $\mathcal{C}$-admissible iff there exists $(b_1,\ldots,b_n) \in TER(x_1,\ldots,x_n)^n$ such that $\neg\varphi(b_1,\ldots,b_n)$ is not $\mathcal{C}$-satisfiable and $\neg\psi(b_1,\ldots,b_n)$ is $\mathcal{C}$-satisfiable. Obviously, this can be decided in exponential time with oracle in A.

Since the satisfiability problem in $\mathcal{C}_{all}$ and $\mathcal{C}_{ind}$ is in NP and the satisfiability problem in $\mathcal{C}_{con}$ is in $PSPACE$, it follows from Propositions 3 and 12 that

Proposition 13. *The elementary admissibility problem in* $\mathcal{C}_{all}$ *and* $\mathcal{C}_{ind}$ *is in* $coNEXP^{NP}$ *and the elementary admissibility problem in* $\mathcal{C}_{con}$ *is in* $coNEXP^{PSPACE}$.

Still, we do not know whether the elementary $\mathcal{C}$-admissibility problem is in co$NEXP$. We conjecture that in $\mathcal{C}_{all}$, $\mathcal{C}_{ind}$ and $\mathcal{C}_{con}$, it is co$NEXP$-complete

9 Unification Type

Let $\mathcal{C}$ be a class of frames.

Proposition 14. *If* $\mathcal{C}$ *agrees with unions then* $EQ(0,x) \vee EQ(1,x)$ *is not* $\mathcal{C}$*-unitary.*

Proof. Suppose $\mathcal{C}$ agrees with unions and $EQ(0,x) \vee EQ(1,x)$ is $\mathcal{C}$-unitary. Let σ_0 and σ_1 be substitutions such that $\sigma_0(x) = 0$ and $\sigma_1(x) = 1$. Obviously, σ_0 and σ_1 are $\mathcal{C}$-unifiers of $EQ(0,x) \vee EQ(1,x)$. Since $EQ(0,x) \vee EQ(1,x)$ is $\mathcal{C}$-unitary, therefore let τ be a $\mathcal{C}$-unifier of $EQ(0,x) \vee EQ(1,x)$ such that $\tau \preceq_{\mathcal{C}} \sigma_0$ and $\tau \preceq_{\mathcal{C}} \sigma_1$. Let μ,ν be substitutions such that $\tau \circ \mu \simeq_{\mathcal{C}} \sigma_0$ and $\tau \circ \nu \simeq_{\mathcal{C}} \sigma_1$. Hence, $EQ(\bar{\mu}(\tau(x)),0)$ is $\mathcal{C}$-valid and $EQ(\bar{\nu}(\tau(x)),1)$ is $\mathcal{C}$-valid. Thus, neither $EQ(0,\tau(x))$ is $\mathcal{C}$-valid, nor $EQ(1,\tau(x))$ is $\mathcal{C}$-valid. Let (W,R) and (W',R') be disjoint frames in $\mathcal{C}$, $\mathcal{V}$ be a valuation on W and $\mathcal{V}'$ be a valuation on W' such that neither $\bar{\mathcal{V}}(\tau(x)) = \emptyset$, nor $\bar{\mathcal{V}}'(\tau(x)) = W'$. Since $\mathcal{C}$ agrees with unions, therefore let (W'',R'') be a frame in $\mathcal{C}$ such that $W \cup W' = W''$. Let $\mathcal{V}''$ be the valuation on W'' such that for all variables z, $\mathcal{V}''(z) = \mathcal{V}(z) \cup \mathcal{V}'(z)$. Obviously, for all terms a, $\bar{\mathcal{V}}''(a) = \bar{\mathcal{V}}(a) \cup \bar{\mathcal{V}}'(a)$. Since neither $\bar{\mathcal{V}}(\tau(x)) = \emptyset$, nor $\bar{\mathcal{V}}'(\tau(x)) = W'$, therefore neither $\bar{\mathcal{V}}''(\tau(x)) = \emptyset$, nor $\bar{\mathcal{V}}''(\tau(x)) = W''$. Consequently, τ is not a $\mathcal{C}$-unifier of $EQ(0,x) \vee EQ(1,x)$: a contradiction.

Proposition 15. *If* $\mathcal{C}$ *agrees with unions then the substitutions* σ_0 *and* σ_1 *such that* $\sigma_0(x) = 0$, $\sigma_1(x) = 1$ *and for all variables* y, *if* $x \neq y$ *then* $\sigma_0(y) = y$ *and* $\sigma_1(y) = y$ *constitute a complete set of* $\mathcal{C}$*-unifiers of* $EQ(0,x) \vee EQ(1,x)$. *Moreover,* $EQ(0,x) \vee EQ(1,x)$ *is* $\mathcal{C}$*-finitary.*

Proof. Suppose $\mathcal{C}$ agrees with unions. Hence, by Proposition 14, $EQ(0,x) \vee EQ(1,x)$ is not $\mathcal{C}$-unitary. Obviously, σ_0 and σ_1 are $\mathcal{C}$-unifiers of $EQ(0,x) \vee EQ(1,x)$. Let τ be an arbitrary $\mathcal{C}$-unifier of $EQ(0,x) \vee EQ(1,x)$ such that neither $\sigma_0 \preceq_{\mathcal{C}} \tau$, nor $\sigma_1 \preceq_{\mathcal{C}} \tau$. Thus, neither $EQ(0,\tau(x))$ is $\mathcal{C}$-valid, nor $EQ(1,\tau(x))$

is $\mathcal{C}$-valid. Following the same line of reasoning as in the proof of Proposition 14, we conclude τ is not a $\mathcal{C}$-unifier of $EQ(0,x) \vee EQ(1,x)$: a contradiction. Since τ was arbitrary, therefore σ_0 and σ_1 constitute a complete set of $\mathcal{C}$-unifiers of $EQ(0,x) \vee EQ(1,x)$. Consequently, $EQ(0,x) \vee EQ(1,x)$ is either $\mathcal{C}$-unitary, or $\mathcal{C}$-finitary. Since $EQ(0,x) \vee EQ(1,x)$ is not $\mathcal{C}$-unitary, therefore $EQ(0,x) \vee EQ(1,x)$ is $\mathcal{C}$-finitary.

Proposition 16. *If $\mathcal{C}$ is balanced then elementary unification in $\mathcal{C}$ is either finitary, or unitary. Moreover, if $\mathcal{C}$ agrees with unions then elementary unification in $\mathcal{C}$ is finitary.*

Proof. Suppose $\mathcal{C}$ is balanced. Let $\varphi(x_1, \ldots, x_n)$ be an arbitrary $\mathcal{C}$-unifiable formula. Let σ be an arbitrary substitution such that $\bar{\sigma}(\varphi)$ is $\mathcal{C}$-valid. Without loss of generality, we can assume that for all variables y, if $y \notin \{x_1, \ldots, x_n\}$ then $\sigma(y) = y$. Let k be a nonnegative integer and $(a_1, \ldots, a_n) \in TER(x_1, \ldots, x_k)^n$ be such that for all positive integers i, if $i \leq n$ then $\sigma(x_i) = a_i$. Since $\bar{\sigma}(\varphi)$ is $\mathcal{C}$-valid, therefore $\varphi(a_1, \ldots, a_n)$ is $\mathcal{C}$-valid. Let $\sim^k_{(a_1,\ldots,a_n)}$, $f\colon \{0,1\}^k \longrightarrow \{0,1\}^n$ and $(b_1, \ldots, b_n)$ be as in Sect. 7. By Lemma 6, $(a_1, \ldots, a_n) \simeq^n_{\mathcal{C}} (b_1, \ldots, b_n)$. Since $\mathcal{C}$ is balanced, therefore by Proposition 7, $(a_1, \ldots, a_n) \cong^n_{\mathcal{C}} (b_1, \ldots, b_n)$. Let τ be the substitution such that for all positive integers i, if $i \leq n$ then $\tau(x_i) = b_i$ and for all variables y, if $y \notin \{x_1, \ldots, x_n\}$ then $\tau(y) = y$. Note that $(\tau(x_1), \ldots, \tau(x_n)) \in TER(x_1, \ldots, x_n)^n$. Moreover, since $\varphi(a_1, \ldots, a_n)$ is $\mathcal{C}$-valid and $(a_1, \ldots, a_n) \cong^n_{\mathcal{C}} (b_1, \ldots, b_n)$, therefore $\varphi(b_1, \ldots, b_n)$ is $\mathcal{C}$-valid. Hence, τ is a $\mathcal{C}$-unifier of φ. For all positive integers i, if $i \leq n$ then let Δ_i and c_i be as in Sect. 6. Let υ be as in Sect. 7. By Proposition 5, for all positive integers i, if $i \leq n$ then considered as formulas in CPL, the terms a_i and $\bar{\upsilon}(b_i)$ are equivalent. Thus, for all positive integers i, if $i \leq n$ then $EQ(\bar{\upsilon}(\tau(x_i)), \sigma(x_i))$ is $\mathcal{C}$-valid. Consequently, $\tau \circ \upsilon \simeq_{\mathcal{C}} \sigma$. Hence, $\tau \preceq_{\mathcal{C}} \sigma$. Since σ was arbitrary and $(\tau(x_1), \ldots, \tau(x_n)) \in TER(x_1, \ldots, x_n)^n$, therefore φ is either $\mathcal{C}$-finitary, or $\mathcal{C}$-unitary. Since φ was arbitrary, therefore elementary unification in $\mathcal{C}$ is either finitary, or unitary. Now, suppose $\mathcal{C}$ agrees with unions. By Proposition 15, elementary unification in $\mathcal{C}$ is not unitary. Since elementary unification in $\mathcal{C}$ is either finitary, or unitary, therefore elementary unification in $\mathcal{C}$ is finitary.

It follows from the above discussion that elementary unification in $\mathcal{C}_{all}$, $\mathcal{C}_{ind}$ and $\mathcal{C}_{con}$ is finitary.

10 Conclusion

Much remains to be done. For example, what becomes of the computability of unifiability and admissibility when the language is extended by the connectedness predicate considered in [14,16]? What becomes of the unification type? And when the language is interpreted in different Euclidean spaces as in [15,16]? In other respect, it remains to see how decision procedures for unifiability and admissibility can be used to improve the performance of algorithms that handle the satisfiability problem. Finally, one may as well consider these questions when the language is extended by a set of propositional constants (denoted p, q, etc.). In this case: **(i)** the unifiability problem is to determine, given a formula $\varphi(p_1, \ldots, p_m, x_1, \ldots, x_n)$, whether there exists terms $a_1, \ldots, a_n$ such that $\varphi(p_1, \ldots, p_m, a_1, \ldots, a_n)$ is valid; **(ii)** the admissibility problem is to determine, given an inference rule $\frac{\varphi(p_1, \ldots, p_m, x_1, \ldots, x_n)}{\psi(p_1, \ldots, p_m, x_1, \ldots, x_n)}$, whether for all terms $a_1, \ldots, a_n$, if $\varphi(p_1, \ldots, p_m, a_1, \ldots, a_n)$ is valid then $\psi(p_1, \ldots, p_m, a_1, \ldots, a_n)$ is valid. We conjecture that in $\mathcal{C}_{all}$, $\mathcal{C}_{ind}$ and $\mathcal{C}_{con}$, unification with constants is $NEXP$-complete but still finitary.

Acknowledgements. We make a point of thanking Joseph Boudou, Yannick Chevalier and Tinko Tinchev who contributed to the development of the work we present today.

References

1. Baader, F., Borgwardt, S., Morawska, B.: Extending unification in $\mathcal{EL}$ towards general TBoxes. In: Principles of Knowledge Representation and Reasoning, pp. 568–572. AAAI Press (2012)
2. Baader, F., Ghilardi, S.: Unification in modal and description logics. Logic J. IGPL **19**, 705–730 (2011)
3. Balbiani, P., Tinchev, T.: Boolean logics with relations. J. Logic Algebr. Program. **79**, 707–721 (2010)
4. Balbiani, P., Tinchev, T.: Definability and canonicity for Boolean logic with a binary relation. Fundamenta Informaticæ **129**, 301–327 (2014)
5. Balbiani, P., Tinchev, T., Vakarelov, D.: Modal logics for region-based theories of space. Fundamenta Informaticæ **81**, 29–82 (2007)
6. Cohn, A., Renz, J.: Qualitative spatial representation and reasoning. In: Handbook of Knowledge Representation, pp. 551–596. Elsevier (2008)
7. Dimov, G., Vakarelov, D.: Contact algebras and region-based theory of space: a proximity approach – I. Fundamenta Informaticæ **74**, 209–249 (2006)
8. Dimov, G., Vakarelov, D.: Contact algebras and region-based theory of space: proximity approach – II. Fundamenta Informaticæ **74**, 251–282 (2006)
9. Düntsch, I., Winter, M.: A representation theorem for Boolean contact algebras. Theor. Comput. Sci. **347**, 498–512 (2005)
10. Dzik, W.: Unification Types in Logic. Wydawnicto Uniwersytetu Slaskiego (2007)
11. Galton, A.: Qualitative Spatial Change. Oxford University Press, Oxford (2000)
12. Gencer, Ç., de Jongh, D.: Unifiability in extensions of $K4$. Logic J. IGPL **17**, 159–172 (2009)
13. Ghilardi, S.: Best solving modal equations. Ann. Pure Appl. Logic **102**, 183–198 (2000)
14. Kontchakov, R., Pratt-Hartmann, I., Wolter, F., Zakharyaschev, M.: Spatial logics with connectedness predicates. Logical Methods Comput. Sci. **6**, 1–43 (2010)
15. Kontchakov, R., Pratt-Hartmann, I., Zakharyaschev, M.: Interpreting topological logics over Euclidean spaces. In: Proceedings of the Twelfth International Conference on the Principles of Knowledge Representation and Reasoning, pp. 534–544. AAAI Press (2010)
16. Kontchakov, R., Nenov, Y., Pratt-Hartmann, I., Zakharyaschev, M.: Topological logics with connectedness over Euclidean spaces. ACM Trans. Comput. Logic **14**, 1–13 (2013)

17. Li, S., Ying, M.: Region connection calculus: its model and composition table. Artif. Intell. **145**, 121–146 (2003)
18. Martin, U., Nipkow, T.: Boolean unification – the story so far. J. Symbol. Comput. **7**, 275–293 (1989)
19. Randell, D., Cui, Z., Cohn, A.: A spatial logic based on regions and connection. In: Proceedings of the Third International Conference on Principles of Knowledge Representation and Reasoning, pp. 165–176. Morgan Kaufman (1992)
20. Renz, J.: Qualitative Spatial Reasoning with Topological Information. Lecture Notes in Artificial Intelligence, vol. 2293. Springer, Heidelberg (2002). doi:10.1007/3-540-70736-0
21. Renz, J., Nebel, B.: On the complexity of qualitative spatial reasoning: a maximal tractable fragment of the region connection calculus. Artif. Intell. **108**, 69–123 (1999)
22. Rybakov, V.: Admissibility of Logical Inference Rules. Elsevier, Amsterdam (1997)
23. Vakarelov, D.: Region-based theory of space: algebras of regions, representation theory, and logics. In: Gabbay, D.M., Zakharyaschev, M., Goncharov, S.S. (eds.) Mathematical Problems from Applied Logic II. International Mathematical Series, vol. 5. Springer, New York (2007). doi:10.1007/978-0-387-69245-6_6
24. Wolter, F., Zakharyaschev, M.: Spatio-temporal representation and reasoning based on *RCC*-8. In: Proceedings of the Seventh International Conference on Principles of Knowledge Representation and Reasoning, pp. 3–14. Morgan Kaufmann (2000)

Merging Fragments of Classical Logic

Carlos Caleiro[1], Sérgio Marcelino[1], and João Marcos[2](✉)

[1] Departament of Mathematics, IST, Universidade de Lisboa, Lisbon, Portugal
{ccal,smarcel}@math.tecnico.ulisboa.pt
[2] Lo.L.I.T.A. and DIMAp, UFRN, Natal, Brazil
jmarcos@dimap.ufrn.br

Abstract. We investigate the possibility of extending the non-functionally complete logic of a collection of Boolean connectives by the addition of further Boolean connectives that make the resulting set of connectives functionally complete. More precisely, we will be interested in checking whether an axiomatization for Classical Propositional Logic may be produced by merging Hilbert-style calculi for two disjoint incomplete fragments of it. We will prove that the answer to that problem is a negative one, unless one of the components includes only top-like connectives.

1 Introduction

Hilbert-style calculi are arguably the most widespread way of defining logics, and simultaneously the least studied one, from the metalogical viewpoint. This is mostly due to the fact that proofs in Hilbert-style calculi are hard to obtain and systematize, in contrast with other proof formalisms such as sequent calculi and their well developed proof-theory, and semantic approaches involving algebraic or relational structures. Still, Hilbert-style calculi are most directly associated with the fundamental notion of logic as a consequence operation and are thus worth studying. Furthermore, merging together Hilbert-style calculi for given logics in order to build a combined logic precisely captures the mechanism for combining logics known as *fibring*, yielding the least logic on the joint language that extends the logics given as input [2]. Fibring fares well with respect to two basic guiding principles one may consider, conservativity and interaction. In contrast, despite their better behaved compositional character, alternative approaches based for instance on sequent calculi are prone to emerging interactions and breaches in conservativity (see, for instance, the *collapsing problem* [3]).

In this paper, as an application of recent results about fibred logics, we investigate the modular construction of Hilbert-style calculi for classical logic.

This research was done under the scope of R&D Unit 50008, financed by the applicable financial framework (FCT/MEC through national funds and when applicable co-funded by FEDER/PT2020), and is part of the MoSH initiative of SQIG at Instituto de Telecomunicações. Sérgio Marcelino acknowledges the FCT postdoc grant SFRH/BPD/76513/2011. João Marcos acknowledges partial support by CNPq and by the Humboldt Foundation.

C. Dixon and M. Finger (Eds.): FroCoS 2017, LNCS 10483, pp. 298–315, 2017.
DOI: 10.1007/978-3-319-66167-4_17

Take, for instance, implication and negation. Together, they form a functionally complete set of connectives. However, all suitable axiomatizations of classical logic we have seen include at least one axiom/rule where implication and negation interact. Rautenberg's general method for axiomatizing fragments of classical logic [9], which explores the structure of Post's lattice [5,8], further confirms the intuition about the essential role of interaction axioms/rules, that one may have drawn from any experience with axiomatizations of classical logic. Additionally, such expectation is consistent with a careful analysis of the characterization of the complexity of different fragments of classical logic and their associated satisfiability problems [10,12], namely in the light of recent results on the decidability and complexity of fibred logics [6]. The question we wish to give a definitive answer to, here, is precisely this: is it possible to recover classical logic by fibring two disjoint fragments of it? We will show that the recovery is successful iff one of the logics represents a fragment of classical logic consisting only of top-like connectives (i.e., connectives that only produce theorems, for whichever arguments received as input), while the other results in a functionally complete set of connectives with the addition of $\top$.

The paper is organized as follows. In Sect. 2, we overview basic notions of logic, including Hilbert calculi and logical matrices, and introduce helpful notation. In Sect. 3 we carefully review the mechanism for fibring logics, as well as some general results about disjoint fibring that shall be necessary next. Our main results, analyzing the merging of disjoint fragments of classical logic, are obtained in Sect. 4. We conclude, in Sect. 5, with a brief discussion of further work. To the best of our knowledge, Proposition 1 (Sect. 3) and all the characterization results in Sect. 4 are new.

2 Preliminaries

2.1 Logics in Abstract

In what follows, a *signature* Σ is an indexed set $\{\Sigma^{(k)}\}_{k\in\mathbb{N}}$, where each $\Sigma^{(k)}$ is a collection of k-place *connectives*. Given a signature Σ and a (disjoint) set P of *sentential variables*, we denote by $L_\Sigma(P)$ the absolutely free Σ-algebra generated by P, also known as *the language generated by P over Σ*. The objects in $L_\Sigma(P)$ are called *formulas*, and a formula is called *compound* in case it belongs to $L_\Sigma(P)\backslash P$, that is, in case it contains some connective. We will sometimes use $\mathsf{head}(C)$ to refer to the main connective in a compound formula C, and say that a formula C is *Σ-headed* if $\mathsf{head}(C) \in \Sigma$. Furthermore, we will use $\mathsf{sbf}(C)$ to refer to the set of subformulas of C, and use $\mathsf{var}(C)$ to refer to the set of sentential variables occurring in C; the definitions of sbf and var are extended to sets of formulas in the obvious way. Given a formula C such that $\mathsf{var}(C) \subseteq \{p_1, \dots, p_k\}$, it is sometimes convenient to take it as inducing a *k-ary term function* $\varphi = \lambda p_1 \dots p_k.C$ such that $\varphi(p_1, \dots, p_k) = C$, over which we will employ essentially the same terminology used to talk about connectives and formulas therewith constructed —in particular, a k-ary term function is induced by a formula generated by k distinct sentential variables over a k-place connective.

In such cases we will also say that the corresponding term functions are *allowed by* the underlying language and *expressed by* the corresponding logic. We will often employ the appellations *nullary* for 0-ary and *singulary* for 1-ary term functions (or for the connectives that induce them). Given signatures $\Sigma \subseteq \Sigma'$ and sets $P \subseteq P'$ of sentential variables, a *substitution* is a structure-preserving mapping over the corresponding sets of formulas, namely a function $\sigma : P \longrightarrow L_{\Sigma'}(P')$ which extends uniquely to a homomorphism $\sigma^\star : L_\Sigma(P) \longrightarrow L_{\Sigma'}(P')$ by setting $\sigma^\star(©(C_1,\ldots,C_k)) := ©(\sigma^\star(C_1),\ldots,\sigma^\star(C_k))$ for every $© \in \Sigma^{(k)}$. We shall refer to $\sigma^\star(C)$ more simply as C^σ. The latter notation is extended in the natural way to sets of formulas: given $\Pi \subseteq L_\Sigma(P)$, Π^σ denotes $\{C^\sigma : C \in \Pi\}$.

A *logic* $\mathcal{L}$ over the language $L_\Sigma(P)$ is here a structure $\langle L_\Sigma(P), \vdash\rangle$ equipped with a so-called *consequence relation* $\vdash \subseteq \mathsf{Pow}(L_\Sigma(P)) \times L_\Sigma(P)$ respecting **(R)** $\Gamma \cup \{C\} \vdash C$; **(M)** if $\Gamma \vdash C$ then $\Gamma \cup \Delta \vdash C$; **(T)** if $\Gamma \vdash D$ for every $D \in \Delta$ and $\Gamma \cup \Delta \vdash C$, then $\Gamma \vdash C$; and **(SI)** if $\Gamma \vdash C$ then $\Gamma^\sigma \vdash C^\sigma$ for any substitution $\sigma : P \longrightarrow L_\Sigma(P)$. Any assertion in the form $\Pi \vdash E$ will be called a *consecution*, and may be read as 'E follows from Π (according to $\mathcal{L}$)'; whenever $\langle \Pi, E\rangle \in \vdash$ one may say that $\mathcal{L}$ *sanctions* $\Pi \vdash E$. Henceforth, union operations and braces will be omitted from consecutions, and the reader will be trusted to appropriately supply them in order to make the expressions well-typed.

Given two logics $\mathcal{L} = \langle L_\Sigma(P), \vdash\rangle$ and $\mathcal{L}' = \langle L_{\Sigma'}(P'), \vdash'\rangle$, we say that $\mathcal{L}'$ *extends* $\mathcal{L}$ in case $P \subseteq P'$, $\Sigma \subseteq \Sigma'$ and $\vdash \subseteq \vdash'$. In case $\Gamma \vdash C$ iff $\Gamma \vdash' C$, for every $\Gamma \cup \{C\} \subseteq L_\Sigma(P)$, we say that the extension is *conservative*. So, in a conservative extension no new consecutions are added in the 'reduced language' $L_\Sigma(P)$ by the 'bigger' logic $\mathcal{L}'$ to those sanctioned by the 'smaller' logic $\mathcal{L}$. Fixed $\mathcal{L} = \langle L_\Sigma(P), \vdash\rangle$, and given $\Sigma \subseteq \Sigma'$ and $P \subseteq P'$, let Sbst collect all the substitutions $\sigma : P \longrightarrow L_{\Sigma'}(P')$. We say that a formula B of $L_{\Sigma'}(P')$ is a *substitution instance* of a formula A of $L_\Sigma(P)$ if there is a substitution $\sigma \in \mathsf{Sbst}$ such that $A^\sigma = B$. A *natural conservative extension induced by* $\mathcal{L}$ is given by the logic $\mathcal{L}' = \langle L_{\Sigma'}(P'), \vdash'\rangle$ equipped by the smallest substitution-invariant consequence relation preserving the consecutions of $\mathcal{L}$ inside the extended language, that is, such that $\Gamma \vdash' C$ iff there is some $\Delta \cup \{D\} \subseteq L_\Sigma(P)$ and some $\sigma \in \mathsf{Sbst}$ such that $\Delta \vdash D$, where $\Delta^\sigma = \Gamma$ and $D^\sigma = C$. In what follows, when we simply enrich the signature and the set of sentential variables, we shall not distinguish between a given logic and its natural conservative extension.

Two formulas C and D of a logic $\mathcal{L} = \langle L_\Sigma(P), \vdash\rangle$ are said to be *logically equivalent according to* $\mathcal{L}$ if $C \vdash D$ and $D \vdash C$; two sets of formulas Γ and Δ are said to be logically equivalent according to $\mathcal{L}$ if each formula from each one of these sets may correctly be said to follow from the other set of formulas (notation: $\Gamma \dashv\vdash_\mathcal{L} \Delta$). We call the set of formulas $\Gamma \subseteq L_\Sigma(P)$ *trivial* (*according to* $\mathcal{L}$) if $\Gamma \dashv\vdash_\mathcal{L} L_\Sigma(P)$. We will say that the logic $\mathcal{L}$ is *consistent* if its consequence relation $\vdash$ does not sanction all possible consecutions over a given language, that is, if there is some set of formulas $\Pi \cup \{E\}$ such that $\Pi \nvdash E$, in other words, if $\mathcal{L}$ contains some non-trivial set of formulas Π; we call a logic *inconsistent* if it fails to be consistent. We say that a set of formulas Π in $\mathcal{L} = \langle L_\Sigma(P), \vdash\rangle$ is $\vdash$*-explosive* in case $\Pi^\sigma \vdash E$ for every substitution $\sigma : P \longrightarrow L_\Sigma(P)$ and every formula E. Obviously, an inconsistent logic $\mathcal{L}$ is one in which the empty set of formulas is $\vdash$-explosive.

Fixed a denumerable set of sentential variables P and a non-empty signature Σ, let $\mathsf{conn} = \bigcup \Sigma$. To simplify notation, whenever the context eliminates any risk of ambiguity, we will sometimes refer to $L_\Sigma(P)$ more simply as L_{conn}. For instance, given the 2-place connective $\wedge$, in writing $L_\wedge$ we refer to the language generated by P using solely the connective $\wedge$, and similarly for the 2-place connective $\vee$ and the language $L_\vee$. Taking the union of the corresponding signatures, in writing $L_{\wedge\vee}$ we refer to the *mixed language* whose formulas may be built using exclusively the connectives $\wedge$ and $\vee$.

Example 1. For an illustration involving some familiar connectives, a logic $\mathcal{L} = \langle L_\Sigma(P), \vdash\rangle$ will be said to be ©-*classical* if, for every set of formulas $\Gamma \cup \{A, B, C\}$ in its language (see, for instance, [4]):

[$© = \top \in \Sigma^{(0)}$] $\Gamma, \top \vdash C$ implies $\Gamma \vdash C$
[$© = \bot \in \Sigma^{(0)}$] $\Gamma \vdash \bot$ implies $\Gamma \vdash C$
[$© = \neg \in \Sigma^{(1)}$] (i) $A, \neg A \vdash C$; and (ii) $\Gamma, A \vdash C$ and $\Gamma, \neg A \vdash C$ imply $\Gamma \vdash C$
[$© = \wedge \in \Sigma^{(2)}$] $\Gamma, A \wedge B \vdash C$ iff $\Gamma, A, B \vdash C$
[$© = \vee \in \Sigma^{(2)}$] $\Gamma, A \vee B \vdash C$ iff $\Gamma, A \vdash C$ and $\Gamma, B \vdash C$
[$© = \to \in \Sigma^{(2)}$] (i) $A, A \to B \vdash B$; (ii) $\Gamma, A \to B \vdash C$ implies $\Gamma, B \vdash C$; and (iii) $\Gamma, A \vdash C$ and $\Gamma, A \to B \vdash C$ implies $\Gamma \vdash C$

Other classical connectives may also be given appropriate abstract characterizations, 'upon demand'. If the logic $\mathcal{L}_{\mathsf{conn}} = \langle L_{\mathsf{conn}}, \vdash\rangle$ is ©-classical for every $© \in \mathsf{conn}$, we call it *the logic of classical* conn and denote it by $\mathcal{B}_{\mathsf{conn}}$. △

Let φ be some k-ary term function expressed by the logic $\mathcal{L} = \langle L_\Sigma(P), \vdash\rangle$. If $\varphi(p_1, \ldots, p_k) \vdash p_j$ for some $1 \leq j \leq k$, we say that φ *is projective over its j-th component.* Such term function is called a *projection-conjunction* if it is logically equivalent to its set of projective components, i.e., if there is some $J \subseteq \{1, 2, \ldots, k\}$ such that (i) $\varphi(p_1, \ldots, p_k) \vdash p_j$ for every $j \in J$ and (ii) $\{p_j : j \in J\} \vdash \varphi(p_1, \ldots, p_k)$. In case $\varphi(p_1, \ldots, p_k) \vdash p_{k+1}$, we say that φ is *bottom-like.* We will call φ *top-like* if $\vdash \varphi(p_1, \ldots, p_k)$; do note that the latter is a particular case of projection-conjunction (take $J = \varnothing$). Classical conjunction is another particular case of projection-conjunction (take $n = 2$ and $J = \{1, 2\}$); its singulary version (take $n = 1$ and $J = \{1\}$) corresponds to the so-called *affirmation connective.* A term function that is neither top-like nor bottom-like will here be called *significant*; if in addition it is not a projection-conjunction, we will call it *very significant*; in each case, connectives shall inherit the corresponding terminology from the term functions that they induce. Note that being not very significant means being either bottom-like or a projection-conjunction.

2.2 Hilbert-Style Proof Systems

One of the standard ways of presenting a logic is through the so-called 'axiomatic approach'. We call *Hilbert calculus* over the language $L_\Sigma(P)$ any structure $\mathcal{H} = \langle L_\Sigma(P), \mathsf{R}\rangle$, *presented by* a set of *inference rules* $\mathsf{R} \subseteq \mathsf{Pow}(L_\Sigma(P)) \times L_\Sigma(P)$.

An inference rule $\circledR = \langle \Delta, D \rangle \in \mathsf{R}$ is said to have *premises* Δ and *conclusion* D, and is often represented in tree-format by writing $\frac{\Delta}{D}\circledR$, or $\frac{D_1\ \ldots\ D_n}{D}\circledR$ when $\Delta = \{D_1, \ldots, D_n\}$, or $\frac{}{D}\circledR$ in case $\Delta = \varnothing$. The latter type of rule, with an empty set of premises, is called *axiom*.

Fix in what follows a Hilbert calculus presentation $\mathcal{H} = \langle L_\Sigma(P), \mathsf{R} \rangle$, and consider signatures $\Sigma \subseteq \Sigma'$ and sets $P \subseteq P'$ of sentential variables, with the corresponding collection Sbst of substitutions from $L_\Sigma(P)$ into $L_{\Sigma'}(P')$. Given formulas $\Gamma \cup \{C\} \subseteq L_{\Sigma'}(P')$, a *rule application allowing to infer* C *from* Γ *according to* $\mathcal{H}$ corresponds to a pair $\langle \circledR, \sigma \rangle$ such that $\frac{\Delta}{D}\circledR$ is in R and $\sigma \in \mathsf{Sbst}$, while $\Delta^\sigma = \Gamma$ and $D^\sigma = C$. Such rule applications are often annotated with the names of the corresponding rules being applied. In case $\Delta = \varnothing$ we may also refer to the corresponding rule application as an *instance of an axiom*. As usual, an $\mathcal{H}$*-derivation of* C *from* Γ is a tree $\mathcal{T}$ with the following features: (i) all nodes are labelled with substitution instances of formulas of $L_\Sigma(P)$; (ii) the root is labelled with C; (iii) the existing leaves are all labelled with formulas from Γ; (iv) all non-leaf nodes are labelled with instances of axioms, or with premises from Γ, or with formulas inferred by rule applications from the formulas labelling the roots of certain subtrees of $\mathcal{T}$, using the inference rules R of $\mathcal{H}$. It is not hard to see that $\mathcal{H}$ induces a logic $\mathcal{L}_\mathcal{H} = \langle L_{\Sigma'}(P'), \vdash_\mathsf{R} \rangle$ by setting $\Gamma \vdash_\mathsf{R} C$ iff there is some $\mathcal{H}$-derivation of C from Γ; indeed, we may safely leave to the reader the task of verifying that postulates (**R**), (**M**), (**T**) and (**SI**) are all respected by $\vdash_\mathsf{R}$. We shall say that a logic $\mathcal{L} = \langle L_\Sigma(P), \vdash \rangle$ is *characterized by a Hilbert calculus* $\mathcal{H} = \langle L_\Sigma(P), \mathsf{R} \rangle$ iff $\vdash\, = \,\vdash_\mathsf{R}$.

Example 2. We revisit the well-known connectives of classical logic whose inferential behaviors were described in Example 1. What follows are the rules of appropriate Hilbert calculi for the logics $\mathcal{L}_© = \langle L_©, \vdash_{\mathsf{R}_©} \rangle$, where $p, q, r \in P$:

$$[© = \top]\quad \frac{}{\top}\,\mathsf{t1}$$

$$[© = \bot]\quad \frac{\bot}{p}\,\mathsf{b1}$$

$$[© = \neg]\quad \frac{p}{\neg\neg p}\,\mathsf{n1} \qquad \frac{\neg\neg p}{p}\,\mathsf{n2} \qquad \frac{p \qquad \neg p}{q}\,\mathsf{n3}$$

$$[© = \wedge]\quad \frac{p \wedge q}{p}\,\mathsf{c1} \qquad \frac{p \wedge q}{q}\,\mathsf{c2} \qquad \frac{p \qquad q}{p \wedge q}\,\mathsf{c3}$$

$$[© = \vee]\quad \frac{p}{p \vee q}\,\mathsf{d1} \qquad \frac{p \vee p}{p}\,\mathsf{d2} \qquad \frac{p \vee q}{q \vee p}\,\mathsf{d3} \qquad \frac{p \vee (q \vee r)}{(p \vee q) \vee r}\,\mathsf{d4}$$

$$[© = \rightarrow]\quad \frac{}{p \rightarrow (q \rightarrow p)}\,\mathsf{i1} \qquad \frac{}{(p \rightarrow (q \rightarrow r)) \rightarrow ((p \rightarrow q) \rightarrow (p \rightarrow r))}\,\mathsf{i2} \qquad \frac{}{((p \rightarrow q) \rightarrow p) \rightarrow p}\,\mathsf{i3} \qquad \frac{p \qquad p \rightarrow q}{q}\,\mathsf{i4}$$

Of course, other classical connectives can also be axiomatized. For instance, the bi-implication $\leftrightarrow$ defined by the term function $\lambda pq.(p \to q) \wedge (q \to p)$ may be presented by:

$$[© = \leftrightarrow]\quad \frac{}{(p \leftrightarrow (q \leftrightarrow r)) \leftrightarrow ((p \leftrightarrow q) \leftrightarrow r)}\,\mathsf{e1} \qquad \frac{}{((p \leftrightarrow r) \leftrightarrow (q \leftrightarrow p)) \leftrightarrow (r \leftrightarrow q)}\,\mathsf{e2} \qquad \frac{p \qquad p \leftrightarrow q}{q}\,\mathsf{e3}$$

△

2.3 Matrix Semantics

Another standard way of presenting a logic is through 'model-theoretic semantics'. A *matrix semantics* $\mathcal{M}$ over the language $L_\Sigma(P)$ is a collection of logical matrices over $L_\Sigma(P)$, where by a *logical matrix* LM over $L_\Sigma(P)$ we mean a structure $\mathsf{LM} = \langle \mathsf{V}, \mathsf{D}, \mathsf{C} \rangle$ in which the set V is said to contain *truth-values*, each truth-value in $\mathsf{D} \subseteq \mathsf{V}$ is called *designated*, and for each $© \in \Sigma^{(k)}$ there is in C a k-ary *interpretation* mapping $\widetilde{©}$ over V. A *valuation* over a logical matrix LM is any mapping $v : L_\Sigma(P) \longrightarrow \mathsf{V}$ such that $v(©(C_1, \ldots, C_k)) = \widetilde{©}(v(C_1), \ldots, v(C_k))$ for every $© \in \Sigma^{(k)}$. We denote by $\mathcal{V}_{\mathsf{LM}}$ the set of all valuations over LM, and say that the valuation v over LM *satisfies* a formula $C \in L_\Sigma(P)$ if $v(C) \in \mathsf{D}$. Note that a valuation might be thought more simply as a mapping $v : P \longrightarrow \mathsf{V}$, given that there is a unique extension of v as a homomorphism from $L_\Sigma(P)$ into the similar algebra having V as carrier and having each symbol $© \in \Sigma^{(k)}$ interpreted as the k-ary operator $\widetilde{©} : \mathsf{V}^k \longrightarrow \mathsf{V}$. Analogously, each k-ary term function $\lambda p_1 \ldots p_k.\varphi$ over $L_\Sigma(P)$ is interpreted by a logical matrix LM in the natural way as a k-ary operator $\widetilde{\varphi} : \mathsf{V}^k \longrightarrow \mathsf{V}$. We shall call $\mathcal{C}^\Sigma_{\mathsf{LM}}$ the collection of all term functions compositionally derived over Σ and interpreted through LM; in the literature on Universal Algebra, $\mathcal{C}^\Sigma_{\mathsf{LM}}$ is known as the *clone* of operations definable by term functions allowed by the signature Σ, under the interpretation provided by LM.

Given a valuation $v : L_\Sigma(P) \longrightarrow \mathsf{V}$, where the truth-values $\mathsf{D} \subseteq \mathsf{V}$ are taken as designated, and given formulas $\Gamma \cup \{C\} \subseteq L_\Sigma(P)$, we say that C *follows from* Γ *according to* v (notation: $\Gamma \vdash_v C$) iff it is not the case that v simultaneously satisfies all formulas in Γ while failing to satisfy C. We extend the definition to a set $\mathcal{V}$ of valuations by setting $\Gamma \vdash_{\mathcal{V}} C$ iff $\Gamma \vdash_v C$ for every $v \in \mathcal{V}$, that is, $\vdash_{\mathcal{V}} = \bigcap_{v \in \mathcal{V}} (\vdash_v)$. On its turn, a matrix semantics $\mathcal{M}$ defines a consequence relation $\vdash_{\mathcal{M}}$ by setting $\Gamma \vdash_{\mathcal{M}} C$ iff $\Gamma \vdash_{\mathcal{V}_{\mathsf{LM}}} C$ for every $\mathsf{LM} \in \mathcal{M}$, that is, $\vdash_{\mathcal{M}} = \bigcap_{\mathsf{LM} \in \mathcal{M}} (\vdash_{\mathcal{V}_{\mathsf{LM}}})$. If we set $\mathcal{V}_{\mathcal{M}} := \bigcup_{\mathsf{LM} \in \mathcal{M}} (\mathcal{V}_{\mathsf{LM}})$, it should be clear that $\vdash_{\mathcal{M}} = \vdash_{\mathcal{V}_{\mathcal{M}}}$. We shall say that a logic $\mathcal{L} = \langle L_\Sigma(P), \vdash \rangle$ is *characterized by a matrix semantics* $\mathcal{M}$ iff $\vdash = \vdash_{\mathcal{M}}$. To make precise what we mean herefrom by a 'fragment' of a given logic, given a subsignature $\Sigma' \subseteq \Sigma$, a *sublogic* $\mathcal{L}'$ of $\mathcal{L}$ is a logic $\mathcal{L}' = \langle L_{\Sigma'}(P), \vdash' \rangle$ characterized by a matrix semantics $\mathcal{M}'$ such that the interpretation $\widetilde{©}$ of the connective $©$ is the same at both $\mathcal{M}$ and $\mathcal{M}'$, for every $© \in \Sigma'$ and every $\mathsf{LM} \in \mathcal{M}'$. It is not hard to see that $\mathcal{L}$ will in this case consist in a conservative extension of $\mathcal{L}'$. There are well-known results in the literature to the effect that any logic whose consequence relation satisfies (**R**), (**M**), (**T**) and (**SI**) may be characterized by a matrix semantics [13].

Example 3. We now revisit yet again the connectives of classical logic that received our attention at Examples 1 and 2. Let $\mathsf{V} = \{0, 1\}$ and $\mathsf{D} = \{1\}$. Given a logical matrix $\langle \mathsf{V}, \mathsf{D}, \mathsf{C} \rangle$, we will call it $©$-*Boolean* if:

[$© = \top$] $\widetilde{\top} = 1$
[$© = \bot$] $\widetilde{\bot} = 0$
[$© = \neg$] (i) $\widetilde{\neg}(1) = 0$; and (ii) $\widetilde{\neg}(0) = 1$
[$© = \wedge$] (i) $\widetilde{\wedge}(1, 1) = 1$; and (ii) $\widetilde{\wedge}(x, y) = 0$ otherwise
[$© = \vee$] (i) $\widetilde{\vee}(0, 0) = 0$; and (ii) $\widetilde{\vee}(x, y) = 1$ otherwise
[$© = \to$] (i) $\widetilde{\to}(1, 0) = 0$; and (ii) $\widetilde{\to}(x, y) = 1$ otherwise
[$© = \leftrightarrow$] (i) $\widetilde{\leftrightarrow}(x, y) = 1$ if $x = y$; and (ii) $\widetilde{\leftrightarrow}(x, y) = 0$ otherwise

It is not difficult to show that, if $\mathcal{M}$ is a collection of ©-Boolean logical matrices, the logic $\mathcal{L}_{©} = \langle L_{©}, \vdash_{\mathcal{M}} \rangle$ is ©-classical. Conversely, every ©-classical logic may be characterized by a single ©-Boolean logical matrix.

We take the chance to introduce a few other connectives that will be useful later on. These connectives may be primitive in some sublogics of classical logic, but can also be defined by term functions involving the previously mentioned connectives, as follows:

$$\begin{aligned}
\not\to &:= \lambda pq.\neg(p \to q) \\
+ &:= \lambda pq.(p \wedge \neg q) \vee (q \wedge \neg p) \\
\text{IF} &:= \lambda pqr.(p \to q) \wedge (\neg p \to r) \\
T_0^n &:= \lambda p_1 \dots p_n.\top, \text{ for } n \geq 0 \\
T_n^n &:= \lambda p_1 \dots p_n.p_1 \wedge \dots \wedge p_n, \text{ for } n > 0 \\
T_k^n &:= \lambda p_1 \dots p_n.(p_1 \wedge T_{k-1}^{n-1}(p_2, \dots, p_n)) \vee T_k^{n-1}(p_2, \dots, p_n), \text{ for } n > k > 0
\end{aligned}$$

Note that a logical matrix containing such connectives is ©-Boolean if:

[© $= \not\to$] (i) $\widetilde{\not\to}(1,0) = 1$; and (ii) $\widetilde{\not\to}(x,y) = 0$ otherwise

[© $= +$] (i) $\widetilde{+}(x,y) = 0$ if $x = y$; and (ii) $\widetilde{+}(x,y) = 1$ otherwise

[© $=$ IF] (i) $\widetilde{\text{IF}}(1,y,z) = y$; and (ii) $\widetilde{\text{IF}}(0,y,z) = z$ △

[© $= T_k^n$] (i) $\widetilde{T_k^n}(x_1, \dots, x_n) = 0$ if $\mathsf{Size}(\{i : x_i = 1\}) < k$;
and (ii) $\widetilde{T_k^n}(x_1, \dots, x_n) = 1$ otherwise

In what follows we shall use the expression *two-valued logic* to refer to any logic characterized by the logical matrix $\{\mathsf{V}_2, \mathsf{D}_2, \mathsf{C}\}$, where $\mathsf{V}_2 = \{0,1\}$ and $\mathsf{D}_2 = \{1\}$, and use the expression *Boolean connectives* to refer to the corresponding 2-valued interpretation of the symbols in Σ (see Example 3). From this perspective, whenever we deal with a two-valued logic whose language is expressive enough, modulo its interpretation through a matrix semantics, to allow for all operators of a Boolean algebra BA over V_2 to be compositionally derived, we will say that we are dealing with *classical logic*. Alternatively, whenever the underlying signature turns out to be of lesser importance, one might say that classical logic is the two-valued logic that corresponds to the clone $\mathcal{C}_{\mathsf{BA}}$ containing all operations over V_2. Due to such level of expressiveness, classical logic is said thus to be *functionally complete* (*over* V_2). On those grounds, it follows that all two-valued logics may be said to be sublogics of classical logic. The paper [9] shows how to provide a Hilbert calculus presentation for any proper two-valued sublogic of classical logic.

Emil Post's characterization of functional completeness for classical logic [5,8] is very informative. First of all, it tells us that there are exactly five maximal functionally incomplete clones (i.e., co-atoms in Post's lattice), namely:

$$\mathbb{P}_0 = \mathcal{C}_{\mathsf{BA}}^{\vee\not\to} \qquad \mathbb{P}_1 = \mathcal{C}_{\mathsf{BA}}^{\wedge\to} \qquad \mathbb{A} = \mathcal{C}_{\mathsf{BA}}^{\leftrightarrow\bot} \qquad \mathbb{M} = \mathcal{C}_{\mathsf{BA}}^{\wedge\vee\top\bot} \qquad \mathbb{D} = \mathcal{C}_{\mathsf{BA}}^{T_2^3\neg}$$

The Boolean top-like connectives form the clone $\mathbb{UP}_1 = \mathcal{C}_{\mathsf{BA}}^{\top}$. As it will be useful later on, we mention that an analysis of Post's lattice also reveals that there are also a number of clones which are maximal with respect to $\top$, i.e., functionally incomplete clones that become functionally complete by the mere addition of the nullary connective $\top$ (or actually any other connective from $\mathbb{UP}_1$). In terms of the Post's lattice, the clones whose join with $\mathbb{UP}_1$ result in $\mathcal{C}_{\mathsf{BA}}$ are:

$$\mathbb{D} \qquad \mathbb{T}_0^\infty = \mathcal{C}_{\mathsf{BA}}^{\not\to} \qquad \mathbb{T}_0^n = \mathcal{C}_{\mathsf{BA}}^{T_n^{n+1}\not\to} \text{ (for } n \in \mathbb{N})$$

It is worth noting that $\mathbb{T}_0^1 = \mathbb{P}_0$.

If a logic turns out to be characterized by a single logical matrix with a finite set of truth-values, a 'tabular' decision procedure is associable to its consequence relation based on the fact that the valuations over a finite number of sentential variables may be divided into a finite number of equivalence classes, and one may then simply do an exhaustive check for satisfaction whenever a finite number of formulas is involved in a given consecution. More generally, we will say that a logic $\mathcal{L}$ is *locally tabular* if the relation of logical equivalence $\dashv\vdash_{\mathcal{L}}$ partitions the language $L_\Sigma(\{p_1,\ldots,p_k\})$, freely generated by the signature Σ over a finite set of sentential variables, into a finite number of equivalence classes. It is clear that all two-valued sublogics of classical logic are locally tabular. On the same line, it should be equally clear that any logic that fails to be locally tabular cannot be characterized by a logical matrix with a finite set of truth-values.

3 Combining Logics

Given two logics $\mathcal{L}_a = \langle L_{\Sigma_a}(P), \vdash_a\rangle$ and $\mathcal{L}_b = \langle L_{\Sigma_b}(P), \vdash_b\rangle$, their *fibring* is defined as the smallest logic $\mathcal{L}_a \bullet \mathcal{L}_b = \langle L_{a\bullet b}(P), \vdash_{a\bullet b}\rangle$, where $L_{a\bullet b}(P) = L_{\Sigma_a\cup\Sigma_b}(P)$, and where $\vdash_a \subseteq \vdash_{a\bullet b}$ and $\vdash_b \subseteq \vdash_{a\bullet b}$, that is, it consists in the smallest logic over the joint signature that extends both logics given as input. Typically, one could expect the combined logic $\mathcal{L}_a \bullet \mathcal{L}_b$ to *conservatively* extend both $\mathcal{L}_a$ and $\mathcal{L}_b$. That is not always possible, though (consider for instance the combination of a consistent logic with an inconsistent logic). A full characterization of the combinations of logics through disjoint fibring that yield conservative extensions of both input logics may be found at [7]. The fibring of two logics is called *disjoint* (or *unconstrained*) if their signatures are disjoint. A neat characterization of fibring is given by way of Hilbert calculi: Given $\vdash_a = \vdash_{\mathsf{R}_a}$ and $\vdash_b = \vdash_{\mathsf{R}_b}$, where R_a and R_b are sets of inference rules, we may set $\mathsf{R}_{a\bullet b} := \mathsf{R}_a \cup \mathsf{R}_b$ and then note that $\mathcal{L}_a \bullet \mathcal{L}_b = \langle L_{a\bullet b}(P), \vdash_{\mathsf{R}_{a\bullet b}}\rangle$.

Insofar as a logic may be said to codify inferential practices used in reasoning, the (conservative) combination of two logics should not only allow one to faithfully recover the original forms of reasoning sanctioned by each ingredient logic over the respective underlying language, but should also allow the same forms of reasoning —and no more— to obtain over the mixed language. Hence, it is natural to think that each of the ingredient logics cannot see past the connectives belonging to the other ingredient logic —the latter connectives look like 'monoliths' whose internal structure is inaccessible from the outside.

To put things more formally, given signatures $\Sigma \subseteq \Sigma'$ and given a formula $C \in L_{\Sigma'}(P)$, we call *Σ-monoliths* the largest subformulas of C whose heads belong to $\Sigma'\backslash\Sigma$. Accordingly, the set $\mathsf{mon}_\Sigma(C) \subseteq \mathsf{sbf}(C)$ of all Σ-monoliths of C is defined by setting:

$$\mathsf{mon}_\Sigma(C) := \begin{cases} \varnothing & \text{if } C \in P, \\ \bigcup_{i=1}^{k} \mathsf{mon}_\Sigma(C_i) & \text{if } C = \copyright(C_1, \ldots, C_k) \text{ and } \copyright \in \Sigma^{(k)}, \\ \{C\} & \text{otherwise.} \end{cases}$$

This definition may be extended to sets of formulas in the usual way, by setting $\mathsf{mon}_\Sigma(\Gamma) := \bigcup_{C\in\Gamma} \mathsf{mon}_\Sigma(C)$. Note, in particular, that $\mathsf{mon}_\Sigma(\Gamma) = \varnothing$ if $\Gamma \subseteq L_\Sigma(P)$. From the viewpoint of the signature Σ, monoliths may be seen as 'skeletal' (sentential) variables that represent formulas of $L_{\Sigma'}(P)$ whose inner structure cannot be taken advantage of. In what follows, let $X^{\Sigma'} := \{x_D : D \in L_{\Sigma'}(P)\}$ be a set of fresh symbols for sentential variables. Given $C \in L_{\Sigma'}(P)$, in order to represent the *Σ-skeleton of C* we define the function $\mathsf{sk}_\Sigma : L_{\Sigma'}(P) \longrightarrow L_{\Sigma'}(P \cup X^{\Sigma'})$ by setting:

$$\mathsf{sk}_\Sigma(C) := \begin{cases} C & \text{if } C \in P, \\ \copyright(\mathsf{sk}_\Sigma(C_1), \ldots, \mathsf{sk}_\Sigma(C_k)) & \text{if } C = \copyright(C_1, \ldots, C_k) \text{ and } \copyright \in \Sigma^{(k)}, \\ x_C, & \text{otherwise.} \end{cases}$$

Clearly, a skeletal variable x_D is only really useful in case $\mathsf{head}(D) \in \Sigma' \backslash \Sigma$.

Example 4. Recall from Example 2 the inference rules characterizing the logic $\mathcal{B}_\wedge$ of classical conjunction and the logic $\mathcal{B}_\vee$ of classical disjunction. As in Example 1, we let $\mathcal{B}_{\wedge\vee}$ refer to a logic that is at once $\wedge$-classical and $\vee$-classical, and contains no other primitive connectives besides $\wedge$ and $\vee$. Consider now the fibred logic $\mathcal{L}_{\wedge\bullet\vee} := \mathcal{B}_\wedge \bullet \mathcal{B}_\vee$. It should be clear that $\vdash_{\wedge\bullet\vee} \subseteq \vdash_{\wedge\vee}$. It is easy to see now that $p \wedge (p \vee q) \dashv\vdash_{\wedge\bullet\vee} p$ (a logical realization of an absorption law of lattice theory). Indeed, a one-step derivation $\mathcal{D}_1$ of p from $p \wedge (p \vee q)$ in $\mathcal{L}_{\wedge\bullet\vee}$ is obtained simply by an application of rule c1 to $p \wedge (p \vee q)$, and a two-step derivation $\mathcal{D}_2$ of $p \wedge (p \vee q)$ from p in $\mathcal{L}_{\wedge\bullet\vee}$ is obtained by the application of rule d1 to p to obtain $p \vee q$, followed by an application of c3 to p and $p \vee q$ to obtain $p \wedge (p \vee q)$. Note that $\mathsf{mon}_{\Sigma_\wedge}(p \wedge (p \vee q)) = \{p \vee q\}$ and $\mathsf{mon}_{\Sigma_\vee}(p \wedge (p \vee q)) = \{p \wedge (p \vee q)\}$, and note also that $\mathsf{sk}_{\Sigma_\wedge}(p \wedge (p \vee q)) = p \wedge x_{p\vee q}$ and $\mathsf{sk}_{\Sigma_\vee}(p \wedge (p \vee q)) = x_{p\wedge(p\vee q)}$. This means that from the viewpoint of $\mathcal{B}_\wedge$ the step of $\mathcal{D}_2$ in which the foreign rule d1 is used is seen as a 'mysterious' passage from p to a new sentential variable $x_{p\vee q}$ taken *ex nihilo* as an extra hypothesis in the derivation, and from the viewpoint of $\mathcal{B}_\vee$ the step of $\mathcal{D}_2$ in which the foreign rule c3 is used is seen as the spontaneous introduction of an extra hypothesis $x_{p\wedge(p\vee q)}$. At our next example we will however show that the dual absorption law, represented by $p \vee (p \wedge q) \dashv\vdash_{\wedge\bullet\vee} p$, does not hold, even though the corresponding equivalence holds good over all Boolean algebras. This will prove that $\vdash_{\wedge\vee} \not\subseteq \vdash_{\wedge\bullet\vee}$, and thus $\mathcal{B}_{\wedge\vee} \not\subseteq \mathcal{B}_\wedge \bullet \mathcal{B}_\vee$. △

Remark 1. In a natural conservative extension, where the syntax of a logic is extended with new connectives but no further inference power is added, it is clear that formulas headed by the newly added connectives are treated as monoliths. Hence, the following result from [6] applies: Given $\mathcal{L} = \langle L_\Sigma(P), \vdash\rangle$, $\Sigma \subseteq \Sigma'$ and $\Delta \cup \{C, D\} \subseteq L_{\Sigma'}(P)$ we have $\Delta \vdash D$ if and only if $\mathsf{sk}_\Sigma(\Delta) \vdash \mathsf{sk}_\Sigma(D)$. △

We will present next a fundamental result from [6] that fully describes disjoint mixed reasoning in $\mathcal{L}_a \bullet \mathcal{L}_b$, viz. by identifying the consecutions sanctioned by such combined logic with the help of appropriate consecutions sanctioned by its ingredient logics $\mathcal{L}_a$ and $\mathcal{L}_b$. Given that consecutions in $\vdash_{a\bullet b}$ are justified by alternations of consecutions sanctioned by $\vdash_a$ and consecutions sanctioned by $\vdash_b$, given a set of mixed formulas $\Delta \subseteq L_{a\bullet b}$, we define the *saturation* $\mathsf{S}_{a\bullet b}(\Delta)$ of Δ as $\bigcup_{n\in\mathbb{N}} \mathsf{S}^n_{a\bullet b}(\Delta)$, where $\mathsf{S}^0_{a\bullet b}(\Delta) := \Delta$ and $\mathsf{S}^{n+1}_{a\bullet b}(\Delta) := \{D \in \mathsf{sbf}(\Delta) : \mathsf{S}^n_{a\bullet b}(\Delta) \vdash_a D$ or $\mathsf{S}^n_{a\bullet b}(\Delta) \vdash_b D\}$. In addition, given a set of mixed formulas $\Delta \cup \{D\} \subseteq L_{a\bullet b}$, we abbreviate by $\mathsf{M}^i_{a\bullet b}(\Delta, D)$ the set of Σ_i-monoliths $\{C \in \mathsf{mon}_{\Sigma_i}(D) : \Delta \vdash_{a\bullet b} C\}$, for each $i \in \{a, b\}$. Such ancillary notation helps us stating:

Theorem 1. *Let $\mathcal{L}_a$ and $\mathcal{L}_b$ be two logics, each one characterizable by a single logical matrix. If $\mathcal{L}_a$ and $\mathcal{L}_b$ have disjoint signatures, the consecutions in the fibred logic $\mathcal{L}_{a\bullet b}$ are such that $\Gamma \vdash_{a\bullet b} C$ iff the following condition holds good:* ($\mathbf{Z}^a$) $\mathsf{S}_{a\bullet b}(\Gamma), \mathsf{M}^a_{a\bullet b}(\Gamma, C) \vdash_a C$ *or* $\mathsf{S}_{a\bullet b}(\Gamma)$ *is* $\vdash_b$*-explosive.*

Note that the roles of a and b may be exchanged in the above theorem, given that the fibring operation is obviously commutative, so we might talk accordingly of a corresponding condition ($\mathbf{Z}^b$), in case it turns out to be more convenient. The original formulation of this result in [6] was based on a slightly more sophisticated notion of saturation, which reduces to the above one in particular when the logics involved in the combination are characterizable by means of a truth-functional semantics (i.e., a matrix semantics involving a single logical matrix), as it is indeed the case for all sublogics of classical logic.

Example 5. Set $a = \wedge$ and $b = \vee$, $E = p\vee(p\wedge q)$, and let $\Gamma = \{E\}$ and $C = p$. Note that (i) $\mathsf{sbf}(\Gamma) = \{p, q, p\wedge q, p\vee(p\wedge q)\}$. Moreover, it is clear that (ii) $\mathsf{mon}_{\Sigma_a}(p) = \mathsf{mon}_{\Sigma_b}(p) = \varnothing$, given that $p \in P$, thus $\mathsf{M}^a_{a\bullet b}(\Gamma, C) = \mathsf{M}^b_{a\bullet b}(\Gamma, C) = \varnothing$. We know by the base case of the definition of S that (iii) $\mathsf{S}^0_{a\bullet b}(\Gamma) = \Gamma$. Let us now show that $\mathsf{S}^1_{a\bullet b}(\Gamma) = \Gamma$, from which it follows that $\mathsf{S}_{a\bullet b}(\Gamma) = \Gamma$. We shall be freely making use of item (a) of Remark 1. Note first, by ($\mathbf{R}$), that we obviously have $\Gamma \vdash_c E$, for $c \in \{a, b\}$, and note also that (iv) $\mathsf{sk}_{\Sigma_a}(E) = x_E$, (v) $\mathsf{sk}_{\Sigma_b}(E) = p \vee x_{p\wedge q}$, (vi) $\mathsf{sk}_{\Sigma_a}(p\wedge q) = p\wedge q$, (vii) $\mathsf{sk}_{\Sigma_b}(p\wedge q) = x_{p\wedge q}$ and (viii) $\mathsf{sk}_{\Sigma_c}(r) = r$ when $r \in \{p, q\}$, for $c \in \{a, b\}$. To see that $\mathsf{S}^0_{a\bullet b}(\Gamma) \nvdash_c D$ for every $D \in \mathsf{sbf}(\Gamma)\backslash\{E\}$ in case c is a it suffices to invoke (i), (iii), (iv), (vi) and (viii), and set a valuation v such that $v(x_E) := 1$ and $v(p) = v(q) := 0$; in case c is b it suffices to invoke (i), (iii), (v), (vii) and (viii), and one may even reuse the previous valuation v, just adding the extra requirement that $v(x_{p\wedge q}) := 0$. It thus follows from the recursive case of the definition of S that $\mathsf{S}^1_{a\bullet b}(\Gamma) = \Gamma$. It is easy to see, with the help of (iv) and (v), that $\mathsf{S}_{a\bullet b}(\Gamma) = \{E\}$ is neither $\vdash_a$-explosive nor $\vdash_b$-explosive. Therefore, according to condition ($\mathbf{Z}^c$) in Theorem 1, to check whether $\Gamma \vdash_{a\bullet b} C$ one may in this case simply check whether $\Gamma \vdash_a C$ or $\Gamma \vdash_b C$. From the preceding argument about $\mathsf{S}^0_{a\bullet b}(\Gamma)$ we already know that the answer is negative in both cases. We conclude that $p\vee(p\wedge q) \nvdash_{a\bullet b} p$, thus indeed the fragment of classical logic with conjunction and disjunction as sole primitive connectives must be a non-conservative extension of the fibring of the logic of classical conjunction with the logic of classical disjunction, as we had announced at the end of Example 4. △

The following is the first useful new result of this paper, establishing that conservativity is preserved by disjoint fibring, here proved for the (slightly simpler) case where each logic is characterized by a single logical matrix.

Proposition 1. *Let $\mathcal{L}_a$ and $\mathcal{L}_b$ be logics with disjoint signatures, each characterizable by means of a single logical matrix. If $\mathcal{L}_a$ and $\mathcal{L}_b$ conservatively extend logics $\mathcal{L}_1$ and $\mathcal{L}_2$, respectively, then $\mathcal{L}_a \bullet \mathcal{L}_b$ also conservatively extends $\mathcal{L}_1 \bullet \mathcal{L}_2$.*

Proof. Let Σ_a, Σ_b, Σ_1 and Σ_2, be the signatures of, respectively, $\mathcal{L}_a$, $\mathcal{L}_b$, $\mathcal{L}_1$ and $\mathcal{L}_2$. Fix $\Gamma \cup \{C\} \subseteq L_{\Sigma_1 \cup \Sigma_2}(P)$. From Theorem 1 we may conclude that: (a) $\Gamma \vdash_{a \bullet b} C$ if and only if either $\mathsf{S}_{a\bullet b}(\Gamma), \mathsf{M}^a_{a\bullet b}(\Gamma, C) \vdash_a C$, or $\mathsf{S}_{a\bullet b}(\Gamma)$ is $\vdash_b$-explosive; (b) $\Gamma \vdash_{1 \bullet 2} C$ if and only if either $\mathsf{S}_{1\bullet 2}(\Gamma), \mathsf{M}^1_{1\bullet 2}(\Gamma, C) \vdash_1 C$, or $\mathsf{S}_{1\bullet 2}(\Gamma)$ is $\vdash_2$-explosive. Now, from the fact that $\mathsf{S}^n_{a\bullet b}(\Gamma) \cup \mathsf{S}^n_{1\bullet 2}(\Gamma) \subseteq L_{\Sigma_1 \cup \Sigma_2}(P)$, for all $n \in \mathbb{N}$, together with the assumptions that $\mathcal{L}_a$ conservatively extends $\mathcal{L}_1$ and $\mathcal{L}_b$ conservatively extends $\mathcal{L}_2$ we conclude that $\mathsf{S}_{a\bullet b}(\Gamma) = \mathsf{S}_{1\bullet 2}(\Gamma)$. The assumption about conservative extension also guarantees that (c) $\mathsf{S}_{a\bullet b}(\Gamma)$ is $\vdash_b$-explosive if and only if $\mathsf{S}_{1\bullet 2}(\Gamma)$ is $\vdash_2$-explosive.

We prove, by induction on the structure of C, that (d) $\Gamma \vdash_{a\bullet b} C$ if and only if $\Gamma \vdash_{1\bullet 2} C$. If C is a sentential variable then $\mathsf{M}^a_{a\bullet b}(\Gamma, C) \subseteq \mathsf{mon}_{\Sigma_a}(C) = \varnothing$ and, also, $\mathsf{M}^1_{1\bullet 2}(\Gamma, C) \subseteq \mathsf{mon}_{\Sigma_1}(C) = \varnothing$. We note that (d) then follows from (a), (b) and (c). For the induction step, let C be compound. From the inductive hypothesis we conclude that $\mathsf{M}^a_{a\bullet b}(\Gamma, C) = \mathsf{M}^1_{1\bullet 2}(\Gamma, C)$. Hence, again from (a), (b) and (c), we note that (d) follows. □

4 Merging Fragments

This section studies the expressivity of logics obtained by fibring disjoint fragments of classical logic. We start by analyzing the cases in which combining disjoint sublogics of classical logic still yields a sublogic of classical logic.

Proposition 2. *Let $©_1$ be a Boolean connective and $©_2$ be top-like. We then have that $\mathcal{B}_{©_1} \bullet \mathcal{B}_{©_2} = \mathcal{B}_{©_1 ©_2}$.*

Proof. By assumption, $©_2$ is top-like, hence: ($\star$) for any given set of formulas Δ, we have $\Delta \vdash_{©_2} \psi$ iff $\psi \in \Delta$ or $\mathsf{head}(\psi) = ©_2$. Let us prove that $\Gamma \vdash_{©_1 ©_2} \varphi$ iff $\Gamma \vdash_{©_1 \bullet ©_2} \varphi$. By Theorem 1, we know that $\Gamma \vdash_{©_1 \bullet ©_2} \varphi$ iff $\mathsf{S}_{©_1\bullet ©_2}(\Gamma), \mathsf{M}^{©_1}_{©_1\bullet ©_2}(\Gamma, \varphi) \vdash_{©_1} \varphi$ or $\mathsf{S}_{©_1\bullet ©_2}(\Gamma)$ is $\vdash_{©_2}$-explosive. By ($\star$) it follows that if $\mathsf{S}_{©_1\bullet ©_2}(\Gamma)$ is $\vdash_{©_2}$-explosive then $\mathsf{S}_{©_1\bullet ©_2}(\Gamma)$ must contain all the sentential variables and $\{©_1\}$-headed formulas. Furthermore, $\mathsf{mon}_{©_2}(\mathsf{sbf}(\Gamma)) \subseteq \mathsf{S}_{©_1\bullet ©_2}(\Gamma)$ and $\mathsf{M}^{©_1}_{©_1\bullet ©_2}(\Gamma, \varphi) = \mathsf{mon}_{©_2}(\varphi)$. Therefore, $\Gamma \vdash_{©_1\bullet ©_2} \varphi$ iff $\mathsf{S}_{©_1\bullet ©_2}(\Gamma), \mathsf{M}^{©_1}_{©_1\bullet ©_2}(\Gamma, \varphi) \vdash_{©_1} \varphi$. Moreover, $\mathsf{S}_{©_1\bullet ©_2}(\Gamma) = \{\psi \in \mathsf{sbf}(\Gamma) : \Gamma, \mathsf{mon}_{©_1}(\Gamma) \vdash_{©_1} \psi\}$. We may then finally conclude that $\Gamma \vdash_{©_1\bullet ©_2} \varphi$ iff $\Gamma, \mathsf{mon}_{©_1}(\Gamma \cup \{\varphi\}) \vdash_{©_1} \varphi$ iff $\Gamma \vdash_{©_1 ©_2} \varphi$. □

Example 6. $\mathcal{B}_{\not\to} \bullet \mathcal{B}_{\top} = \mathcal{B}_{\not\to\top}$ yields full classical logic, as the set $\{\not\to, \top\}$ is functionally complete. △

Proposition 3. *Let* $©_1$ *and* $©_2$ *be Boolean connectives neither of which are very significant. Then,* $\mathcal{B}_{©_1} \bullet \mathcal{B}_{©_2} = \mathcal{B}_{©_1 ©_2}$.

Proof. There are three possible combinations, either **(a)** both connectives are conjunction-projections, or **(b)** both are bottom-like, or **(c)** one connective is bottom-like and the other is a conjunction-projection.

[Case **(a)**] Let J_1 and J_2 be the sets of indices corresponding respectively to the projective components of $©_1$ and of $©_2$. For each $\psi \in L_{©_1©_2}(P)$ let us define $P_\psi \subseteq P$ recursively, in the following way: $P_\psi := \{\psi\}$ if $\psi \in P$ and $P_{©_i(\psi_1,\ldots,\psi_k)} := \bigcup_{a \in J_i} P_{\psi_a}$ for $i \in \{1,2\}$. We claim that ψ is equivalent to P_ψ both according to $\mathcal{B}_{©_1} \bullet \mathcal{B}_{©_2}$ and according to $\mathcal{B}_{©_1©_2}$. Let us prove this by induction on the structure of ψ. For the base case, let ψ be a sentential variable, and note that ψ is equivalent to itself. If ψ is a nullary connective $©_i$, for some $i \in \{1,2\}$ (and therefore $©_i$ is top-like), then $©_i$ is equivalent to $P_{©_i}$ (namely, the empty set). For the inductive step, consider $\psi = ©_i(\psi_1, \cdots, \psi_{k_i})$ where k_i is the arity of $©_i$. Using the fact that $©_i$ is a projection-conjunction we have that $©_i$ is equivalent to $\{\psi_a : a \in J_i\}$. By induction hypothesis, each ψ_a is equivalent to P_{ψ_a}, hence ψ is equivalent to $\bigcup_{a\in J_i} P_{\psi_a}$. Finally, for a set of sentential variables $B \cup \{b\}$ we clearly have that $B \vdash_{©_1 \bullet ©_2} b$ iff $B \vdash_{©_1©_2} b$ iff $b \in B$. So, the logics are equal.

[Case **(b)**] This is similar to the previous case. Let $\psi \in L_{©_1©_2}(P)$. We now define A_ψ recursively in the following way: $A_\psi := \{\psi\}$ if $\psi \in P$ or $\mathsf{head}(\psi) = ©_2$, and $A_{©_1(\psi_1,\ldots,\psi_k)} := \bigcup_{a\in J_1} A_{\psi_a}$. Again, it is not hard to check that in both $\mathcal{B}_{©_1} \bullet \mathcal{B}_{©_2}$ and $\mathcal{B}_{©_1©_2}$ we have that ψ is equivalent to A_ψ. Moreover, given $B \cup \{b\} \subseteq P \cup \{\psi : \mathsf{head}(\psi) = ©_2\}$ we clearly have that $B \vdash_{©_1 \bullet ©_2} b$ iff $B \vdash_{©_1©_2} b$ iff $b \in B$ or there is $\psi \in B$ such that $\mathsf{head}(\psi) = ©_2$.

[Case **(c)**] It should be clear that according to both $\mathcal{B}_{©_1} \bullet \mathcal{B}_{©_2}$ and $\mathcal{B}_{©_1©_2}$ we may conclude that φ follows from Γ iff either $\varphi \in \Gamma$ or there is $\psi \in \Gamma$ such that $\psi \notin P$. □

Proposition 4. *For any set of Boolean connectives* $\mathsf{conn} \subseteq \mathcal{C}_{\mathsf{BA}}^{\leftrightarrow}$, *we have that* $\mathcal{B}_{\mathsf{conn}} \bullet \mathcal{B}_{\bot} = \mathcal{B}_{\mathsf{conn}\cup\{\bot\}}$.

Proof. We first show that $\mathcal{B}_{\leftrightarrow} \bullet \mathcal{B}_{\bot} = \mathcal{B}_{\leftrightarrow\bot}$. As $\mathcal{B}_{\bot}$ is axiomatized by just the single rule $\frac{\bot}{p}$, it easily follows that (a) $\Gamma \vdash_{\leftrightarrow\bullet\bot} C$ iff $\Gamma \vdash_{\leftrightarrow} \bot$ or $\Gamma \vdash_{\leftrightarrow} C$. By [4, Exercise 7.31.3(iii)], we note that (b) for every $\Gamma \cup \{B, C\} \subseteq L_{\leftrightarrow}(P)$ we have that $\Gamma, B \vdash_{\leftrightarrow} C$ iff $\Gamma \vdash_{\leftrightarrow} C$ or $\Gamma \vdash_{\leftrightarrow} B \leftrightarrow C$. Note in addition that (c) $\vdash_{\leftrightarrow} B \leftrightarrow ((B \leftrightarrow A) \leftrightarrow A)$. Now, if $\Gamma \nvdash_{\leftrightarrow\bullet\bot} A$ then by (a) we have that $\Gamma \nvdash_{\leftrightarrow} A$ and $\Gamma \nvdash_{\leftrightarrow} \bot$. Further, using (b) and (c), it follows also that $\Gamma, A \leftrightarrow \bot \nvdash_{\leftrightarrow} A$ and $\Gamma, A \leftrightarrow \bot \nvdash_{\leftrightarrow} \bot$. Now, a straightforward use of the Lindenbaum-Asser lemma shows that there exists a $\vdash_{\leftrightarrow}$-theory T extending $\Gamma \cup \{A \leftrightarrow \bot\}$ which is maximal relative to A. Obviously $\bot \notin T$, and $\mathcal{B}_{\leftrightarrow} \bullet \mathcal{B}_{\bot} = \mathcal{B}_{\leftrightarrow\bot}$ then follows from the completeness of the axiomatization of $\mathcal{B}_{\leftrightarrow}$. From this, given $\mathsf{conn} \subseteq \mathcal{C}_{\mathsf{BA}}^{\leftrightarrow}$, we conclude with the help of Proposition 1 that $\mathcal{B}_{\mathsf{conn}} \bullet \mathcal{B}_{\bot} = \mathcal{B}_{\mathsf{conn}\bot}$. □

Example 7. For every connective © expressed by the logic of classical bi-implication, e.g. $© \in \{\leftrightarrow, \lambda pqr.p + q + r\}$, we have that $\mathcal{B}_{©} \bullet \mathcal{B}_{\perp} = \mathcal{B}_{©\perp}$. △

We now analyze the cases in which combining disjoint sublogics of classical logic results in a logic strictly weaker than the logic of the corresponding classical mixed language.

Remark 2. A detailed analysis of Post's lattice tells us that every clone $\mathcal{C}^{\Sigma}_{\mathsf{BA}}$ that contains the Boolean function of a very significant connective (i.e., $\mathcal{C}^{\Sigma}_{\mathsf{BA}} \not\subseteq \mathcal{C}^{\wedge\top\perp}_{\mathsf{BA}}$) must contain the Boolean function associated to at least one of the following connectives: $\neg$, $\to$, $\leftrightarrow$, $\not\to$, $+$, IF, T^{n+1}_n (for $n \in \mathbb{N}$), T^{n+1}_2 (for $n \in \mathbb{N}$), $\lambda pqr.p \vee (q \wedge r)$, $\lambda pqr.p \vee (q + r)$, $\lambda pqr.p \wedge (q \vee r)$, $\lambda pqr.p \wedge (q \to r)$, $\lambda pqr.p + q + r$. △

Lemma 1. *Let* conn *be a family of Boolean connectives, and assume that* $\mathcal{B}_{\mathsf{conn}}$ *expresses at least one among the connectives in Remark 2, distinct from* $\leftrightarrow$ *and* $\lambda pqr.p + q + r$. *Then* $\mathcal{B}_{\mathsf{conn}} \bullet \mathcal{B}_{\perp} \subsetneq \mathcal{B}_{\mathsf{conn}\cup\{\perp\}}$.

Proof. Let © be one of the above Boolean connectives. We show that there are $\Gamma \cup \{C\} \subseteq L_{©}(P)$ and $\sigma : P \longrightarrow P \cup \{\top\}$ such that $\Gamma^{\sigma} \vdash_{©\perp} C^{\sigma}$ yet $\Gamma^{\sigma} \nvdash_{©\bullet\perp} C^{\sigma}$, thus concluding that $\mathcal{B}_{©} \bullet \mathcal{B}_{\perp} \subsetneq \mathcal{B}_{©\perp}$. Hence, by applying Proposition 1, we obtain that $\mathcal{B}_{\mathsf{conn}} \bullet \mathcal{B}_{\perp} \subsetneq \mathcal{B}_{\mathsf{conn}\cup\{\perp\}}$ for conn in the conditions of the statement.

We will explain two cases in detail, and for the remaining cases we just present the relevant formulas Γ^{σ} and C^{σ}, as the rest of the reasoning is analogous.

[Case $© = \neg$] Set $\Gamma := \varnothing$ and $C^{\sigma} := \neg\perp$. We have that $\vdash_{©\perp} \neg\perp$. However, since $\nvdash_{©} \neg(x_{\perp})$ and $\mathsf{S}_{©\bullet\perp}(\Gamma) = \varnothing$ is not $\vdash_{\perp}$-explosive, we conclude that $\nvdash_{©\bullet\perp} \neg(\perp)$ by Theorem 1.

[Case $© = \vee$] Set $\Gamma^{\sigma} := \{\perp \vee q\}$ and $C^{\sigma} := q$. We have that $\perp \vee q \vdash_{©\perp} q$. However, since $x_{\perp} \vee q \nvdash_{©} q$ and $\mathsf{S}_{©\bullet\perp}(\{\varphi(x_{\perp}, q)\}) = \{\varphi(x_{\perp}, q)\}$ is not $\vdash_{\perp}$-explosive, we conclude that $\perp \vee q \nvdash_{©\bullet\perp} q$ by Theorem 1.

[Case $© = +$] Set $\Gamma^{\sigma} := \{\perp + q\}$ and $C^{\sigma} := q$.

[Case $© = \to$] Set $\Gamma^{\sigma} := \varnothing$ and $C^{\sigma} := \perp \to q$.

[Case $© = \not\to$] let $\Gamma^{\sigma} := \{p\}$ and $C^{\sigma} := p \not\to \perp$.

[Case $© = \lambda pqr.p\vee(q+r)$] Set $\Gamma^{\sigma} := \{\perp\vee(q+\perp)\}$ and $C^{\sigma} := q$.

[Case $© = \lambda pqr.p\wedge(q\to r)$] Set $\Gamma^{\sigma} := \{p\}$ and $C^{\sigma} := p\wedge(\perp\to r)$.

[Case $© = \lambda pqr.p\wedge(q\vee r)$] Set $\Gamma^{\sigma} := \{p\wedge(\perp\vee r)\}$ and $C^{\sigma} := r$.

[Case $© = \lambda pqr.p\vee(q\wedge r)$] Set $\Gamma^{\sigma} := \{\perp\vee(q\wedge r)\}$ and $C^{\sigma} := q$.

[Case $© =$ IF] Set $\Gamma^{\sigma} := \{\text{IF}(\perp, q, r)\}$ and $C^{\sigma} := r$.

[Case $© = T^{k+1}_k$] Set $\Gamma^{\sigma} := \{T^{k+1}_k(p, \ldots, p, q, \perp)\}$ and $C^{\sigma} := q$.

[Case $© = T^{k+1}_2$] Set $\Gamma^{\sigma} := \{T^{k+1}_2(p, p, \perp, \ldots, \perp)\}$ and $C^{\sigma} := p$. □

Corollary 1. *Let* © $\notin \mathcal{C}_{\mathsf{BA}}^{\leftrightarrow}$ *be some very significant Boolean connective. Then,* $\mathcal{B}_{©} \bullet \mathcal{B}_{\bot} \subsetneq \mathcal{B}_{©\bot}$.

Proof. Note, by Remark 2 and the fact that both $\leftrightarrow$ and $\lambda pqr.p+q+r$ belong to $\mathcal{C}_{\mathsf{BA}}^{\leftrightarrow}$, that © fulfills the conditions of application of Lemma 1. □

Example 8. For every connective © among $\neg$, $\rightarrow$, $\not\leftarrow$, $+$, IF, T_n^{n+1} (for $n \in \mathbb{N}$), T_2^{n+1} (for $n \in \mathbb{N}$), $\lambda pqr.p \vee (q \wedge r)$, $\lambda pqr.p \vee (q + r)$, $\lambda pqr.p \wedge (q \vee r)$, and $\lambda pqr.p \wedge (q \rightarrow r)$, we have that $\mathcal{B}_{©} \bullet \mathcal{B}_{\bot} \subsetneq \mathcal{B}_{©\bot}$. △

Remark 3. On a two-valued logic: (i) sentential variables are always significant, every nullary connective is either top-like or bottom-like; (ii) top-like term functions are always assigned the value 1 and bottom-like term functions are always assigned the value 0; (iii) significant singulary term functions all behave semantically either as Boolean affirmation or as Boolean negation. △

Lemma 2. *The logic of a significant Boolean k-place connective © expresses some 1-ary significant compound term function.*

Proof. Let φ denote the singulary term function induced by the formula $©(\overline{p})$ obtained by substituting a fixed sentential variable p at all argument positions of $©(p_1, \ldots, p_k)$. If φ is significant, we are done. Otherwise, there are two cases to consider.

For the first case, suppose that φ is top-like. Thus, given that © is significant and the logic is two-valued, we know from Remark 3(ii), in particular, that there must be some valuation v such that $v(©(p_1, \ldots, p_k)) = 0$. Set $I := \{i : v(p_i) = 1\}$, and define the substitution σ by $\sigma(p_j) := \varphi(p)$ if $j \in I$, and $\sigma(p_j) := p$ otherwise. Let ψ denote the new singulary term function induced by $(©(p_1, \ldots, p_k))^\sigma$. On the one hand, choosing a valuation v' such that $v'(p) = 0$ we may immediately conclude that $v'(\psi(p)) = v(©(p_1, \ldots, p_k)) = 0$. On the other hand, choosing v'' such that $v''(p) = 1$ we see that $v''(\sigma(p_j)) = 1$ for every $1 \leq j \leq k$. We conclude $v''(\psi(p)) = v''(©(\overline{p})) = v''(\varphi(p))$, thus $v''(\psi(p)) = 1$, for φ was supposed in the present case to be top-like. It follows that $\psi(p)$ is indeed equivalent here to the sentential variable p.

For the remaining case, where we suppose that φ is bottom-like, it suffices to set $I := \{i : v(p_i) = 0\}$ and then reason analogously. In both the latter cases our task is seen to have been accomplished in view of Remark 3(i). □

Lemma 3. *Let* $\mathcal{L} = \langle L_\Sigma(P), \vdash \rangle$ *be a two-valued logic whose language allows a very significant k-ary term function* φ, *let I be the set of indices that identify the projective components of* φ, *and let* σ *be some substitution such that* $\sigma(p_i) = p_i$, *for* $i \in I$, *and* $\sigma(p_i) = p_{k+i}$, *for* $i \notin I$. *Then,* $\varphi(p_1, \ldots, p_k) \not\vdash (\varphi(p_1, \ldots, p_k))^\sigma$.

Proof. By the assumption that φ is very significant, we know that this term function is not a projection-conjunction. Thus, given that $I \subsetneq \{1, \ldots, k\}$ is the exact set of indices such that $\varphi(p_1, \ldots, p_k) \vdash p_i$, for every $i \in I$, we conclude that $\{p_i : i \in I\} \not\vdash \varphi(p_1, \ldots, p_k)$. There must be, then, some valuation v over $\{0, 1\}$ such that $v(p_i) = 1$, for every $i \in I$, while $v(\varphi(p_1, \ldots, p_k)) = 0$.

From the assumption about significance we also learn that φ is not bottom-like, thus, in view of two-valuedness and the Remark 3(ii), we know that there must be some valuation v' such that $v'(\varphi(p_1,\ldots,p_k)) = 1$. Using the assumption that $\varphi(p_1,\ldots,p_k) \vdash p_i$ for every $i \in I$ one may conclude that $v'(p_i) = v(p_i) = 1$ for every $i \in I$. Our final step to obtain a counter-model to witness $\varphi(p_1,\ldots,p_k) \not\vdash (\varphi(p_1,\ldots,p_k))^\sigma$ is to glue together the two latter valuations by considering a valuation v'' such that $v''(p_j) = v'(p_j)$ for $1 \leq j \leq k$ (satisfying thus the premise) and such that $v''(p_j) = v(p_j)$ for $j > k$ (allowing for the conclusion to be falsified). □

Proposition 5. *The fibring $\mathcal{B}_{©_1} \bullet \mathcal{B}_{©_2}$ of the logic of a very significant classical connective $©_1$ and the logic of a non-top-like Boolean connective $©_2$ distinct from $\bot$ fails to be locally tabular, and therefore $\mathcal{B}_{©_1} \bullet \mathcal{B}_{©_2} \subsetneq \mathcal{B}_{©_1 ©_2}$.*

Proof. We want to build over $\Sigma_1 \cup \Sigma_2$, on a finite number of sentential variables, an infinite family $\{©_m\}_{m \in \mathbb{N}}$ of syntactically distinct formulas that are pairwise inequivalent according to $\mathcal{B}_{©_1} \bullet \mathcal{B}_{©_2}$.

In case $©_2$ is significant we know from Lemma 2 that we can count on a singulary significant term function ψ_0 allowed by $L_{©_2}(\{p\}) \backslash P$. Set, in this case, $\psi_{n+1} := \psi_0 \circ \psi_n$. Given the assumption that $\mathcal{B}_{©_2}$ is a two-valued logic, in view of Remark 3(iii) it should be clear that no such ψ_{n+1} can be top-like. To the same effect, in case $©_2$ is bottom-like, just consider any enumeration $\{\psi_m\}_{m \in \mathbb{N}}$ of the singulary term functions allowed by $L_{©_2}(\{p\}) \backslash P$. In both cases we see then how to build a family of syntactically distinct $\{©_2\}$-headed singulary term functions, and these will be used below to build a certain convenient family of ($\{©_1\}$-headed) formulas in the mixed language.

In what follows we abbreviate $©_1(p_1, p_2, \ldots, p_{k_1})$ to C. We may assume, without loss of generality, that there is some $j < k_1$ such that $C \vdash_{©_1} p_i$ for every $i \leq j$ and $C \not\vdash_{©_1} p_i$ otherwise. Let σ_n, for each $n > 0$, denote a substitution such that $\sigma_n(p_i) = p_i$, for $i \leq j$, and $\sigma_n(p_i) = \psi_{n \times i}(p)$ otherwise. We claim that $C^{\sigma_a} \not\vdash_{©_1 \bullet ©_2} C^{\sigma_b}$, for every $a \neq b$.

To check the claim, first note that, for each $a > 0$, we have $\mathsf{S}_{©_1 \bullet ©_2}(\{C^{\sigma_a}\}) = \{C^{\sigma_a}\} \cup \{p_i : i \leq j\}$. From the fact that C is a significant term function, it follows that $\mathsf{S}_{©_1 \bullet ©_2}(\{C^{\sigma_a}\})$ is neither $\vdash_{©_1}$-explosive nor $\vdash_{©_2}$-explosive. For arbitrary $b > 0$, since $\mathsf{mon}_{\Sigma_2}(\psi_b(p)) = \varnothing$, we have $\mathsf{M}^2_{©_1 \bullet ©_2}(\{C^{\sigma_a}\}, \psi_b(p)) = \varnothing$. Therefore, using Theorem 1 we may conclude that $C^{\sigma_a} \not\vdash_{©_1 \bullet ©_2} \psi_b(p)$ and, given that $\mathsf{mon}_{\Sigma_1}(C^{\sigma_b}) \subseteq \{\psi_k(p) : k \in \mathbb{N}\}$, it also follows that $\mathsf{M}^1_{©_1 \bullet ©_2}(\{C^{\sigma_a}\}, C^{\sigma_b}) = \varnothing$. Note, in addition, for each $n > 0$, that $\mathsf{sk}_{\Sigma_1}(C) = C^{\sigma'_n}$, where $\sigma'_n(p_i) := p_i$ for $i \in I$, and $\sigma'_n(p_i) := x_{\psi_{n \times i}}$ for $i \notin I$. Therefore, given that $©_1$ is very significant, using Remark 1 and Lemma 3 we conclude at last, for every $a \neq b$, that C^{σ_b} does not follow from C^{σ_a} according to $\mathcal{B}_{©_1} \bullet \mathcal{B}_{©_2}$. The latter combined logic, thus, fails to be locally tabular. As a consequence, given that all two-valued logics are locally tabular we see that $\mathcal{B}_{©_1} \bullet \mathcal{B}_{©_2}$ cannot coincide with $\mathcal{B}_{©_1 ©_2}$. □

Example 9. If $©_1$ and $©_2$ are among the Boolean connectives mentioned in Remark 2 then we have that $\mathcal{B}_{©_1} \bullet \mathcal{B}_{©_2} \subsetneq \mathcal{B}_{©_1 ©_2}$. △

The following theorem makes use of the previous results to capture the exact circumstances in which the logic that merges the axiomatizations of two classical connectives coincides with the logic of these Boolean connectives.

Theorem 2. *Consider the logic* $\mathcal{B}_{©_1}$ *of the classical connective* $©_1$ *and the logic* $\mathcal{B}_{©_2}$ *of the distinct classical connective* $©_2$*. Then,* $\mathcal{B}_{©_1} \bullet \mathcal{B}_{©_2} = \mathcal{B}_{©_1 ©_2}$ *iff* *<u>either</u>:*

(**a**) *at least one among* $©_1$ *and* $©_2$ *is top-like,* *<u>or</u>*
(**b**) *neither* $©_1$ *nor* $©_2$ *are very significant,* *<u>or</u>*
(**c**) $©_1 \in \mathcal{C}_{\mathsf{BA}}^{\leftrightarrow}$ *and* $©_2 = \bot$ *(or* $©_1 = \bot$ *and* $©_2 \in \mathcal{C}_{\mathsf{BA}}^{\leftrightarrow}$*).*

Proof. The direction from right to left follows from Propositions 2 to 4. The other direction follows from Corollary 1 and Proposition 5. □

We can finally obtain the envisaged characterization result:

Theorem 3. *Let* conn_1 *and* conn_2 *be non-functionally complete disjoint sets of connectives such that* $\mathsf{conn} = \mathsf{conn}_1 \cup \mathsf{conn}_2$ *is functionally complete. The disjoint fibring of the classical logics of* conn_1 *and* conn_2 *is classical iff* $\mathcal{C}_{\mathsf{BA}}^{\mathsf{conn}_i} \in \{\mathbb{D}, \mathbb{T}_0^{\infty}\} \cup \{\mathbb{T}_0^k : k \in \mathbb{N}\}$ *and* $\mathcal{C}_{\mathsf{BA}}^{\mathsf{conn}_j} = \mathbb{UP}_1$*, for some* $i \in \{1,2\}$ *and* $j = 3 - i$*.*

Proof. Note that if $\mathcal{C}_{\mathsf{BA}}^{\mathsf{conn}_i} \in \{\mathbb{D}, \mathbb{T}_0^{\infty}\} \cup \{\mathbb{T}_0^k : k \in \mathbb{N}\}$ and $\mathcal{C}_{\mathsf{BA}}^{\mathsf{conn}_j} = \mathbb{UP}_1$, for $i \neq j \in \{1,2\}$, then we have that conn is functionally complete. For the right to left implication, it suffices to invoke Proposition 1 and item (**a**) of Theorem 2.

As for the converse implication, let us assume that $\mathcal{B}_{\mathsf{conn}_1} \bullet \mathcal{B}_{\mathsf{conn}_2} = \mathcal{B}_{\mathsf{conn}}$. Using Proposition 1, we know that for every pair of connectives $©_1 \in \mathsf{conn}_1$ and $©_2 \in \mathsf{conn}_2$ one of the items (**a**), (**b**) or (**c**) of Theorem 2 must hold. If (**a**) holds in all cases, then, without loss of generality, $\mathcal{C}_{\mathsf{BA}}^{\mathsf{conn}_j} = \mathbb{UP}_1$. This, given the functional completeness of conn, implies that $\mathcal{C}_{\mathsf{BA}}^{\mathsf{conn}_i} \in \{\mathbb{D}, \mathbb{T}_0^{\infty}\} \cup \{\mathbb{T}_0^k : k \in \mathbb{N}\}$. Otherwise, we would have $\mathcal{C}_{\mathsf{BA}}^{\mathsf{conn}_i}$ and $\mathcal{C}_{\mathsf{BA}}^{\mathsf{conn}_j}$ both distinct from $\mathbb{UP}_1$, and items (**b**) or (**c**) of Theorem 2 would have to hold in all the remaining cases. If (**b**) holds in all the remaining cases then we would conclude that $\mathsf{conn}_i \cup \mathsf{conn}_j$ contains only connectives that are not very significant, and that would contradict the functional completeness of conn. Thence, without loss of generality, we could say that $\mathcal{C}_{\mathsf{BA}}^{\mathsf{conn}_i}$ contains very significant connectives, and item (**c**) of Theorem 2 would have to hold in those cases. But this would mean that $\mathcal{C}_{\mathsf{BA}}^{\mathsf{conn}_i} \subseteq \mathcal{C}_{\mathsf{BA}}^{\leftrightarrow\wedge\top\bot} = \mathcal{C}_{\mathsf{BA}}^{\leftrightarrow\wedge\bot}$ and $\mathcal{C}_{\mathsf{BA}}^{\mathsf{conn}_j} \subseteq \mathcal{C}_{\mathsf{BA}}^{\top\bot}$. Note, however, that neither $\wedge$ nor $\bot$ can coexist in $\mathcal{C}_{\mathsf{BA}}^{\mathsf{conn}_i}$ with $\leftrightarrow$, or the underlying logic would express some very significant connective not expressible using only $\leftrightarrow$. We are therefore led to conclude that $\mathcal{C}_{\mathsf{BA}}^{\mathsf{conn}_i} \subseteq \mathcal{C}_{\mathsf{BA}}^{\leftrightarrow}$ and $\mathcal{C}_{\mathsf{BA}}^{\mathsf{conn}_j} \subseteq \mathcal{C}_{\mathsf{BA}}^{\top\bot}$. But this is impossible, as we would then have $\mathcal{C}_{\mathsf{BA}}^{\mathsf{conn}} \subseteq \mathbb{A}$, contradicting the functional completeness of conn. □

5 Closing Remarks

In the present paper, we have investigated and fully characterized the situations when merging two disjoint fragments of classical logic still results in a fragment of classical logic. As a by-product, we showed that recovering full classical logic in such a manner can only be done when one of the logics is a fragment of classical logic consisting exclusively of top-like connectives, while the other forms a functionally complete set of connectives with the addition of $\top$. Our results take full advantage of the characterization of Post's lattice, and may be seen as an application of recent developments concerning fibred logics. Though our conclusions cannot be seen as a total surprise, we are not aware of any other result of this kind. Some unexpected situations do pop up, like the fact that $\mathcal{B}_{\leftrightarrow} \bullet \mathcal{B}_{\perp} = \mathcal{B}_{\leftrightarrow\perp}$, or the fact that $\mathcal{B}_{\not\to} \bullet \mathcal{B}_{\top}$ and $\mathcal{B}_{\vee+} \bullet \mathcal{B}_{\top}$ both yield full classical logic. The latter two combinations are particularly enlightening, given that according to [6] the complexity of disjoint fibring is only polynomially worse than the complexity of the component logics, and we know from [1] that the decision problems for $\mathcal{B}_{\not\to}$ or $\mathcal{B}_{\vee+}$ are both **co-NP-complete**, as in full classical logic. As a matter of fact, some of the results we obtained may alternatively be established as consequences of the complexity result in [6] together with the conjecture that $\mathbf{P} \neq \mathbf{NP}$. In fact, for disjoint sets of Boolean connectives conn_1 and conn_2 such that $\mathsf{conn}_1 \cup \mathsf{conn}_2$ is functionally complete, if the decision problems for $\mathcal{B}_{\mathsf{conn}_1}$ and for $\mathcal{B}_{\mathsf{conn}_2}$ are both in **P** then clearly $\mathcal{B}_{\mathsf{conn}_1} \bullet \mathcal{B}_{\mathsf{conn}_2} \neq \mathcal{B}_{\mathsf{conn}_1 \cup \mathsf{conn}_2}$. However, the techniques we use here do not depend on $\mathbf{P} \neq \mathbf{NP}$ and allow us to solve also the cases in which the complexity of the components is already in **co-NP**, for which the complexity result in [6] offers no hints.

Similar studies could certainly be pursued concerning logics other than classical. However, even for the classical case there are some thought-provoking unsettled questions. Concretely, we would like to devise semantical counterparts for all the combinations that do not yield fragments of classical logic, namely those covered by Proposition 5. So far, we can be sure that such semantic counterparts cannot be provided by a single finite logical matrix. Additionally, we would like to link the cases yielding fragments of classical logic (as covered by the conditions listed in Theorem 2) to properties of the multiple-conclusion consequence relations [11] pertaining to such connectives.

References

1. Beyesrdorff, O., Meier, A., Thomas, M., Vollmer, H.: The complexity of propositional implication. Inf. Process. Lett. **109**, 1071–1077 (2009)
2. Caleiro, C., Carnielli, W., Rasga, J., Sernadas, C.: Fibring of logics as a universal construction. In: Gabbay, D., Guenthner, F. (eds.) Handbook of Philosophical Logic, vol. 13, 2nd edn, pp. 123–187. Kluwer, Dordrecht (2005)
3. Caleiro, C., Ramos, J.: From fibring to cryptofibring: a solution to the collapsing problem. Logica Universalis **1**(1), 71–92 (2007)
4. Humberstone, L.: The Connectives. MIT Press, Cambridge (2011)
5. Lau, D.: Function Algebras on Finite Sets: Basic Course on Many-Valued Logic and Clone Theory. Springer, New York (2006). doi:10.1007/3-540-36023-9
6. Marcelino, S., Caleiro, C.: Decidability and complexity of fibred logics without shared connectives. Logic J. IGPL **24**(5), 673–707 (2016)
7. Marcelino, S., Caleiro, C.: On the characterization of fibred logics, with applications to conservativity and finite-valuedness. J. Logic Comput. (2016). doi:10.1093/logcom/exw023

8. Post, E.L.: On the Two-Valued Iterative Systems of Mathematical Logic. Princeton University Press, Princeton (1941)
9. Rautenberg, W.: 2-element matrices. Studia Logica **40**(4), 315–353 (1981)
10. Reith, S., Vollmer, H.: Optimal satisfiability for propositional calculi and constraint satisfaction problems. Inf. Comput. **186**(1), 1–19 (2003)
11. Shoesmith, D., Smiley, T.: Multiple-Conclusion Logic. Cambridge University Press, Cambridge (1978)
12. Sistla, A.P., Clarke, E.M.: The complexity of propositional linear temporal logics. J. ACM **32**(3), 733–749 (1985)
13. Wójcicki, R.: Theory of Logical Calculi. Kluwer, Dordrecht (1988)

Interpolation, Amalgamation and Combination (The Non-disjoint Signatures Case)

Silvio Ghilardi and Alessandro Gianola(✉)

Dipartimento di Matematica, Università degli Studi di Milano, Milan, Italy
alessandro.gianola93@gmail.com

Abstract. In this paper, we study the conditions under which existence of interpolants (for quantifier-free formulae) is modular, in the sense that it can be transferred from two first-order theories T_1, T_2 to their combination $T_1 \cup T_2$. We generalize to the non-disjoint signatures case the results from [3]. As a surprising application, we relate the Horn combinability criterion of this paper to superamalgamability conditions known from propositional logic and we use this fact to derive old and new results concerning fusions transfer of interpolation properties in modal logic.

1 Introduction

Craig's interpolation theorem [5] applies to first order formulae and states that whenever the formula $\phi \to \psi$ is valid, then it is possible to find a formula θ such that (i) $\phi \to \theta$ is valid; (ii) $\theta \to \psi$ is valid, and (iii) θ is defined over the common symbols of ϕ and ψ. Interpolation theory has a long tradition in non-classical logics (see for instance the seminal papers by L.L. Maksimova [12,13]) and has been recently introduced also in verification, after the work of McMillan (see, e.g., [15]). Intuitively, the interpolant θ can be seen as an over-approximation of ϕ with respect to ψ: thus, for example, in the abstraction-refinement phase of software model checking [10], interpolants are used to compute increasingly precise over-approximations of the set of reachable states.

Of particular importance for verification techniques are those algorithms capable of computing *quantifier-free* interpolants in presence of some background theory. This is so because several symbolic verification problems are formalized by representing sets of states and transitions as quantifier-free formulae. Unfortunately, Craig's interpolation theorem does not guarantee that it is always possible to compute quantifier-free interpolants when reasoning *modulo a first-order theory*: in fact, for certain first-order theories, it is known that quantifiers must occur in interpolants of quantifier-free formulae [11]. Even when quantifier-free interpolants exist for single theories, this might not be anymore the case when considering their combinations (see e.g. Example 3.5 below). Since verification techniques frequently require to reason in combinations of theories, methods to modularly combine available interpolation algorithms are indeed desirable.

The study of the modularity property of quantifier-free interpolation was first started in [27], where the disjoint signatures convex case was solved; in [3] - the

C. Dixon and M. Finger (Eds.): FroCoS 2017, LNCS 10483, pp. 316–332, 2017.
DOI: 10.1007/978-3-319-66167-4_18

journal version of [2] - the non-convex (still disjoint) case was also thoroughly investigated. The analysis in [3] is large-spectrum: combinability of quantifier-free interpolation is first semantically analyzed (where it is related to strong sub-amalgamability), then it is syntactically characterized and finally suitable combination algorithms are designed.

This paper intends to be a first contribution for an extension to the non-disjoint signatures case. Given the complexity of the problem, we shall limit to semantic investigations, leaving for future research the subsequent, algorithmically oriented aspects. However, we show that our semantic techniques can be quite effective in practice: in fact, we show how to use them in order to establish that some theories combining integers and common datatypes (lists, trees, etc.) indeed enjoy quantifier-free interpolation. In addition, we employ our results in order to get interesting information concerning the transfer of interpolation properties to the fusion of modal logics: in fact, not only we show how to obtain Wolter's interpolation fusion transfer theorem [26] for normal modal logics, but we also identify a modular interpolation property for the non-normal case.

In attacking combination problems for non-disjoint signatures, we follow the model-theoretic approach successfully employed in [6,9,17–20]; this approach relies on the notion of T_0-compatibility, in order to identify modular conditions for combinability. The reason why this approach works can roughly be explained as follows. In combining a model of a theory T_1 with a model of a theory T_2, one needs to produce a superstructure of both of them: in such a superstructure, additional constraints in the shared subsignature might turn out to be satisfied and T_0-compatibility is meant to keep satisfiability of constraints in superstructures under control inside T_1 and T_2. This is because T_0-compatibility refers to model-completeness and model-completeness is the appropriate technique [4] to talk about satisfiability of quantifier-free formulae in extended structures.

The paper is organized as follows: in Sect. 2, we introduce notations and basic ingredients from the literature; in Sect. 3 we obtain a first general result (Theorem 3.2) and show how to use it in examples taken from verification theories. In the final Sect. 4, we apply our results to modal logic (Corollary 4.3 and Theorem 4.7); the proofs of the results from this last section require some algebraic logic background, so they are moved to the (online available from authors' web page) manuscript [7] for space reasons.

2 Formal Preliminaries

We adopt the usual first-order syntactic notions of signature, term, atom, (ground) formula, sentence, and so on. Let Σ be a first-order signature; we assume the binary equality predicate symbol '=' to be added to any signature (so, if $\Sigma = \emptyset$, then Σ just contains equality). The signature obtained from Σ by adding it a set $\underline{a}$ of new constants (i.e., 0-ary function symbols) is denoted by $\Sigma^{\underline{a}}$. A *positive clause* is a disjunction of atoms. A *constraint* is a conjunction of literals. A formula is *quantifier-free* (or open) iff it does not contain quantifiers. A *Σ-theory* T is a set of sentences (called the axioms of T) in the signature Σ and it is *universal* iff it has universal closures of open formulae as axioms.

We also assume the usual first-order notion of interpretation and truth of a formula, with the proviso that the equality predicate $=$ is always interpreted as the identity relation. We let $\bot$ denote a ground formula which is true in no structure. A formula φ is *satisfiable* in $\mathcal{M}$ iff its *existential* closure is true in $\mathcal{M}$. A Σ-structure $\mathcal{M}$ is a *model* of a Σ-theory T (in symbols $\mathcal{M} \models T$) iff all the sentences of T are true in $\mathcal{M}$. If φ is a formula, $T \models \varphi$ ('*φ is a logical consequence of T*') means that the universal closure of φ is true in all the models of T. T is *consistent* iff it has a model, i.e., if $T \not\models \bot$. A sentence φ is T-consistent iff $T \cup \{\varphi\}$ is consistent. A Σ-theory T is *complete* iff for every Σ-sentence φ, either φ or $\neg\varphi$ is a logical consequence of T. T admits *quantifier elimination* iff for every formula $\varphi(\underline{x})$ there is a quantifier-free formula $\varphi'(\underline{x})$ such that $T \models \varphi(\underline{x}) \leftrightarrow \varphi'(\underline{x})$ (notations like $\varphi(\underline{x})$ mean that φ has free variables only among the tuple $\underline{x}$).

If $\Sigma_0 \subseteq \Sigma$ is a subsignature of Σ and if $\mathcal{M}$ is a Σ-structure, the Σ_0-*reduct* of $\mathcal{M}$ is the Σ_0-structure $\mathcal{M}_{|\Sigma_0}$ obtained from $\mathcal{M}$ by forgetting the interpretation of function and predicate symbols from $\Sigma \setminus \Sigma_0$. A Σ-*homomorphism* (or, simply, a homomorphism) between two Σ-structures $\mathcal{M}$ and $\mathcal{N}$ is any mapping $\mu : |\mathcal{M}| \longrightarrow |\mathcal{N}|$ among the support sets $|\mathcal{M}|$ of $\mathcal{M}$ and $|\mathcal{N}|$ of $\mathcal{N}$ satisfying the condition

$$\mathcal{M} \models \varphi \quad \Rightarrow \quad \mathcal{N} \models \varphi \tag{1}$$

for all $\Sigma^{|\mathcal{M}|}$-atoms φ (here $\mathcal{M}$ is regarded as a $\Sigma^{|\mathcal{M}|}$-structure, by interpreting each additional constant $a \in |\mathcal{M}|$ into itself and $\mathcal{N}$ is regarded as a $\Sigma^{|\mathcal{M}|}$-structure by interpreting each additional constant $a \in |\mathcal{M}|$ into $\mu(a)$). In case condition (1) holds for all $\Sigma^{|\mathcal{M}|}$-literals, the homomorphism μ is said to be an *embedding* and if it holds for all first order formulae, the embedding μ is said to be *elementary.* If $\mu : \mathcal{M} \longrightarrow \mathcal{N}$ is an embedding which is just the identity inclusion $|\mathcal{M}| \subseteq |\mathcal{N}|$, we say that $\mathcal{M}$ is a *substructure* of $\mathcal{N}$ or that $\mathcal{N}$ is an *extension* of $\mathcal{M}$. A Σ-structure $\mathcal{M}$ is said to be *generated by* a set X included in its support $|\mathcal{M}|$ iff there are no proper substructures of $\mathcal{M}$ including X.

Given a signature Σ and a Σ-structure $\mathcal{A}$, we indicate with $\Delta_\Sigma(\mathcal{A})$ the *diagram* of $\mathcal{A}$: this is the set of sentences obtained by first expanding Σ with a fresh constant $\bar{a}$ for every element a from $|\mathcal{A}|$ and then taking the set of ground $\Sigma^{|\mathcal{A}|}$-literals which are true in $\mathcal{A}$ (under the natural expanded interpretation mapping $\bar{a}$ to a).

Finally, we point out that all the above definitions can be extended in a natural way to many-sorted signatures (we shall use many-sorted theories in some examples).

2.1 Model Completion and T_0-compatibility

We recall a standard notion in Model Theory, namely the notion of a *model completion* of a first order theory [4] (we limit the definition to universal theories, because we shall use only this case):

Definition 2.1. *Let T_0 be a universal Σ-theory and let $T_0^\star \supseteq T_0$ be a further Σ-theory; we say that $T_0^\star$ is a model completion of T_0 iff:* (i) *every model of T_0*

can be embedded into a model of $T_0^\star$; (ii) *for every model* $\mathcal{M}$ *of* T_0, *we have that* $T_0^\star \cup \Delta_\Sigma(\mathcal{M})$ *is a complete theory in the signature* $\Sigma^{|\mathcal{M}|}$.

Being T_0 universal, condition (ii) is equivalent to the fact that $T_0^\star$ *has quantifier elimination*; we recall also that the model completion $T_0^\star$ of a theory T_0 is unique, if it exists (see [4] for these results and for examples).

We also recall the concept of T_0-compatibility [6,9], which is crucial for our combination technique.

Definition 2.2. *Let* T *be a theory in the signature* Σ *and let* T_0 *be a universal theory in a subsignature* $\Sigma_0 \subseteq \Sigma$. *We say that* T *is* T_0-compatible *iff* $T_0 \subseteq T$ *and there is a* Σ_0*-theory* $T_0^\star$ *such that:*

(i) $T_0 \subseteq T_0^\star$;
(ii) $T_0^\star$ *is a model completion of* T_0;
(iii) *every model of* T *can be embedded, as a* Σ*-structure, into a model of* $T \cup T_0^\star$.

Notice that if T_0 is the empty theory over the empty signature, then T_0^* is the theory axiomatizing an infinite domain, and the requirement of T_0-compatibility is equivalent to the stably infinite requirement of the Nelson-Oppen schema [16, 24] (in the sense that T is T_0-compatible iff it is stably infinite). We remind that a theory T is stably infinite iff every T-satisfiable quantifier-free formula (from the signature of T) is satisfiable in an infinite model of T. By compactness, it is possible to show that T is stably infinite iff every model of T embeds into an infinite one.

We shall see many examples of T_0-compatible theories (for various T_0) during the paper, here we just underline that T_0-compatibility is a modular condition. The following result is proved in [6] (as Proposition 4.4):

Proposition 2.3. *Let* T_1 *be a* Σ_1*-theory and let* T_2 *be a* Σ_2*-theory; suppose they are both compatible with respect to a* Σ_0*-theory* T_0 *(where* $\Sigma_0 := \Sigma_1 \cap \Sigma_2$*). Then* $T_1 \cup T_2$ *is* T_0*-compatible too.*

2.2 Interpolation and Amalgamation

We say that a theory T *has quantifier-free interpolation* iff the following hold, for every pair of quantifier free formulae $\varphi(\underline{x}, \underline{y}), \psi(\underline{y}, \underline{z})$: if $T \models \varphi(\underline{x}, \underline{y}) \to \psi(\underline{y}, \underline{z})$, then there exists a quantifier-free formula $\theta(\underline{y})$ such that $T \models \varphi(\underline{x}, \underline{y}) \to \theta(\underline{y})$ and $T \models \theta(\underline{y}) \to \psi(\underline{y}, \underline{z})$. We underline that the requirement that θ is quantifier-free is essential: in general such a $\theta(\underline{y})$ exists by the Craig interpolation theorem, but it is not quantifier-free even if φ, ψ are such.[1] Quantifier-free interpolation property can be semantically characterized using the following notions, introduced in [1,3]:

[1] Notice that in the above definition free function and predicate symbols (not already present in the signature Σ of T) are not allowed; allowing them (and requiring that only shared symbols occur in the interpolant θ) produces a different stronger definition, which is nevertheless reducible to quantifier-free interpolation in the combination with the theory of equality with uninterpreted function symbols (see [3]).

Definition 2.4. *A theory T has the* sub-amalgamation property *iff, for given models $\mathcal{M}_1$ and $\mathcal{M}_2$ of T sharing a common substructure $\mathcal{A}$, there exists a further model $\mathcal{M}$ of T endowed with embeddings $\mu_1 : \mathcal{M}_1 \longrightarrow \mathcal{M}$ and $\mu_2 : \mathcal{M}_2 \longrightarrow \mathcal{M}$ whose restrictions to the support of $\mathcal{A}$ coincide. The triple $(\mathcal{M}, \mu_1, \mu_2)$ (or, by abuse, $\mathcal{M}$ itself) is said to be a T-*sub-amalgama *of $\mathcal{M}_1, \mathcal{M}_2, \mathcal{A}$.*

Definition 2.5. *A theory T has the* strong sub-amalgamation property *if the T-sub-amalgama $(\mathcal{M}, \mu_1, \mu_2)$ of $\mathcal{M}_1, \mathcal{M}_2, \mathcal{A}$ can be chosen so as to satisfy the following additional condition: if for some m_1, m_2 we have $\mu_1(m_1) = \mu_2(m_2)$, then there exists an element a in $|\mathcal{A}|$ such that $m_1 = a = m_2$.*

If T is universal, then every substructure of a model of T is itself a model of T: in these cases, we shall drop the prefix sub- and directly speak of 'amalgamability', 'strong amalgamability' and 'T-amalgama'. The following fact is proved in [3], as Theorem 3.3:

Theorem 2.6. *A theory T has the sub-amalgamation property iff it admits quantifier-free interpolants.*

3 Conditions for Combination

The main result from [3] says that if T_1, T_2 have disjoint signatures, are both stably infinite and both enjoy the strong sub-amalgamation property, then the combined theory $T_1 \cup T_2$ also has the strong sub-amalgamation property[2] (and so it has quantifier-free interpolation).

In this paper, we try to extend the above results to the non-disjoint signatures case. The idea, already shown to be fruitful for combined satisfiability problems in [6], is to use T_0-compatibility as the proper generalization of stable infiniteness.

We shall first obtain a rather abstract sufficient condition for transfer of quantifier-free interpolation property to combined theories; nevertheless, we show that such sufficient condition generalizes the disjoint signatures result from [3] and is powerful enough to establish the quantifier-free interpolation property for some natural combined theories arising in verification. Then we move to the case in which the shared theory T_0 is Horn and obtain as a corollary a specialized result which is quite effective in modal logic applications.

3.1 Sub-amalgamation Schemata

Let T_0, T be theories in their respective signatures Σ_0, Σ such that $\Sigma_0 \subseteq \Sigma$, T_0 is universal and $T_0 \subseteq T$. If $\mathcal{M}_1$ and $\mathcal{M}_2$ are Σ-models of T with a common substructure $\mathcal{A}$, we call the triple $(\mathcal{M}_1, \mathcal{M}_2, \mathcal{A})$ a *T-fork* (or, simply, a *fork*).

[2] It is possible to characterize syntactically strong sub-amalgamability in terms of a suitable 'equality interpolating' condition [3]. That sub-amalgamability needs to be strenghtened to strong sub-amalgamability in order to get positive combination results is demonstrated by converse facts also proved in [3].

The *sub-amalgamation schema* $\sigma^T_{T_0}$ (of T over T_0) is the following function, associating sets of T_0-amalgama with T-forks:[3]

$$\sigma^T_{T_0}[(\mathcal{M}_1, \mathcal{M}_2, \mathcal{A})] := \left\{ \begin{array}{l} \text{the set of all } (\mathcal{B}, \nu_1, \nu_2) \text{ s.t.} \\ (i)\ (\mathcal{B}, \nu_1, \nu_2) \text{ is a } T_0\text{-amalgama of the } \Sigma_0\text{-reducts of} \\ \qquad \mathcal{M}_1 \text{ and } \mathcal{M}_2 \text{ over the } \Sigma_0\text{-reduct of } \mathcal{A}; \\ (ii)\ \mathcal{B} \text{ is generated, as } \Sigma_0\text{-structure, by the union of} \\ \qquad \text{the images of } \nu_1 \text{ and } \nu_2; \\ (iii)\ (\mathcal{B}, \nu_1, \nu_2) \text{ is embeddable in the } \Sigma_0\text{-reduct of a} \\ \qquad T\text{-sub-amalgama of the fork } (\mathcal{M}_1, \mathcal{M}_2, \mathcal{A}). \end{array} \right\}$$

Condition (iii) means that there is a T-sub-amalgama $(\mathcal{M}, \mu_1, \mu_2)$ such that $\mathcal{B}$ is a Σ_0-substructure of $\mathcal{M}$ and that μ_1, μ_2 coincide with ν_1, ν_2 on their domains.

Condition (ii) ensures that, disregarding isomorphic copies, $\sigma^T_{T_0}[(\mathcal{M}_1, \mathcal{M}_2, \mathcal{A})]$ is a set and not a proper class. Recall that T_0 is universal, so that substructures of models of T_0 are also models of T_0. This ensures that the following Proposition trivially holds:

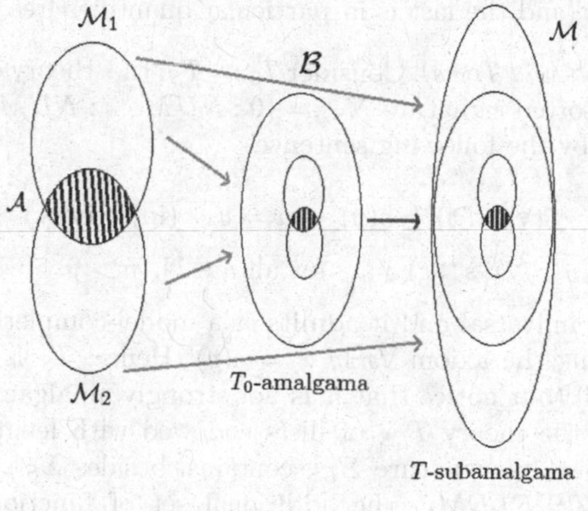

Proposition 3.1. *T is sub-amalgamable iff $\sigma^T_{T_0}$ is not empty (i.e. iff we have that $\sigma^T_{T_0}[(\mathcal{M}_1, \mathcal{M}_2, \mathcal{A})] \neq \emptyset$, for all forks $(\mathcal{M}_1, \mathcal{M}_2, \mathcal{A})$).*

One side of the inclusion of the following Theorem is also immediate; for the other one, T_0-compatibility is needed (we shall prove the theorem in Subsect. 3.2 below).

Theorem 3.2. *Let T_1 and T_2 be two theories in their respective signatures Σ_1, Σ_2; assume that they are both T_0-compatible, where T_0 is a universal theory*

[3] It is not difficult to realize (using well-known Löwenheim-Skolem theorems [4]) that one can get all the results in the paper by limiting this definition to forks among structures whose cardinality is bounded by the cardinality of set of the formulae in our signatures (signatures are finite or countable in all practical cases).

in the signature $\Sigma_0 := \Sigma_1 \cap \Sigma_2$. *The following hold for the amalgamation schema of* $T_1 \cup T_2$ *over* T_0*:*

$$\sigma_{T_0}^{T_1 \cup T_2}[(\mathcal{M}_1, \mathcal{M}_2, \mathcal{A})] = \sigma_{T_0}^{T_1}[(\mathcal{M}_1, \mathcal{M}_2, \mathcal{A})_{|\Sigma_1}] \cap \sigma_{T_0}^{T_2}[(\mathcal{M}_1, \mathcal{M}_2, \mathcal{A})_{|\Sigma_2}]$$

for every $(T_1 \cup T_2)$*-fork* $(\mathcal{M}_1, \mathcal{M}_2, \mathcal{A})$ *(here, with* $(\mathcal{M}_1, \mathcal{M}_2, \mathcal{A})_{|\Sigma_i}$ *we indicate the* T_i*-fork obtained by taking reducts to the signature* Σ_i*).*

Despite its abstract formulation, Theorem 3.2 is powerful enough to imply the main disjoint signatures result of [3] and also to work out interesting examples.

Example 3.3. (The disjoint signature case). Let S_0, S_1, S_2 be sets such that $S_0 \subseteq S_1, S_0 \subseteq S_2$; the amalgamated sum $S_1 +_{S_0} S_2$ of S_1, S_2 over S_0 is just the set-theoretic union $S_1 \cup S_2$ in which elements from $S_1 \setminus S_0$ are renamed away so as to be different from the elements of $S_2 \setminus S_0$. With this terminology, a theory T is strongly sub-amalgamable iff its sub-amalgamation schema over the empty theory T_0 is such that $\sigma_{T_0}^{T}[(\mathcal{M}_1, \mathcal{M}_2, \mathcal{A})]$ always contains the amalgamated sum of the supports of $\mathcal{M}_1, \mathcal{M}_2$ over the support of $\mathcal{A}$. Thus, Theorem 3.2 says in particular that if T_1, T_2 are both stably infinite and strongly sub-amalgamable, then so is $T_1 \cup T_2$ (and the last is in particular quantifier-free interpolating).

Example 3.4 (Lists and Trees). Consider $T_0 := T_S$, the 'theory of increment' [20]; T_S has the monosorted signature $\Sigma_S := \{0 : NUM,\ s : NUM \longrightarrow NUM\}$ and it is axiomatized by the following sentences:

$$\forall x \forall y\ s(x) = s(y) \rightarrow x = y \qquad \text{(injectivity)}$$
$$\forall x\ s^n(x) \neq x \quad \text{for all } n \in \mathbb{N},\ n > 0$$

This theory is universal and it admits as a model-completion T_S^* the theory obtained by adding the axiom $\forall x \exists y\ x = s(y)$. Hence, T_S is amalgamable for general reasons [4] (but notice that it is not strongly amalgamable).

Now consider the theory T_{LS} of 'lists endowed with length' [20]. This is a many-sorted theory; its signature Σ_{LS} contains, besides Σ_S-symbols, the additional sorts $LISTS, ELEM_L$, the additional set of function symbols $\{nil : LISTS,\ car : LISTS \longrightarrow ELEM_L,\ cdr : LISTS \longrightarrow LISTS,\ cons : ELEM_L \times LISTS \longrightarrow LISTS,\ l : LISTS \longrightarrow NUM\}$ and a single unary relation symbol $atom : LISTS$. The axioms of T_{LS} are the following:

1. $car(cons(x, y)) = x$	5. $\neg atom(x) \rightarrow cons(car(x), cdr(x)) = x$
2. $cdr(cons(x, y)) = y$	6. $\neg atom(cons(x, y))$
3. $l(nil) = 0$	7. $atom(nil)$
4. $l(cons(x, y)) = s(l(y))$	

This theory is T_S-compatible [20]; below, we show that *every* T_S-amalgama of the T_S-reducts of two models of T_{LS} (sharing a common submodel) can be embedded in a T_{LS}-amalgama (since T_{LS} is universal we can speak of amalgams instead of sub-amalgams).

Let a T_{LS}-fork $(\mathcal{M}_1, \mathcal{M}_2, \mathcal{A})$ be given and let $\mathcal{B}$ be any amalgam of the T_S-reducts of $\mathcal{M}_1, \mathcal{M}_2$. We sketch the definition of a T_{LS}-amalgam $\mathcal{M}$ of the fork (based on $\mathcal{B}$). The support $NUM^{\mathcal{M}}$ is the support of $\mathcal{B}$ and $ELEM_L^{\mathcal{M}_1} \cup ELEM_L^{\mathcal{M}_2}$ is the support of $ELEM_L^{\mathcal{M}}$. It remains to define $LISTS^{\mathcal{M}}$;[4] we take $LISTS^{\mathcal{M}}$ to be the union of $LISTS^{\mathcal{M}_1}$, $LISTS^{\mathcal{M}_2}$ and of LT, where LT is the set containing the pairs (x, l), with $x \in LIST^{\mathcal{M}_{3-j}} \setminus LIST^{\mathcal{M}_j}$ and l a finite list of elements from $ELEM_L^{\mathcal{M}_1} \cup ELEM_L^{\mathcal{M}_2}$ which begins with an element in $ELEM_L^{\mathcal{M}_j}$ $(j = 1, 2)$. In other words, an element in LT has the form:

$$(x, (e_1, e_2, ..., e_n))$$

where (1) $j = 1, 2$; (2) e_1 is in $ELEM_L^{\mathcal{M}_j}$; (3) x is in $LISTS^{\mathcal{M}_{3-j}}$; and (4) e_i $(i > 1)$ is in $ELEM_L^{\mathcal{M}_1} \cup ELEM_L^{\mathcal{M}_2}$. Σ_{LS}-operations and relations can be defined in the obvious way so that axioms 1–7 above hold and so that the inclusions $\mathcal{M}_1 \subseteq \mathcal{M}$ and $\mathcal{M}_2 \subseteq \mathcal{M}$ are embeddings.

Let us now consider the theory T_{BS} of binary trees endowed with size functions [20]. This is also a many-sorted theory: its signature Σ_{BS} has the symbols of the signature Σ_S of the theory of increment plus the set of function symbols $\{null : TREES,\ bin : ELEM_T \times TREES \times TREES \longrightarrow TREES,\ l_L : TREES \longrightarrow NUM,\ l_R : TREES \longrightarrow NUM\}$. The axioms of T_{LS} are the following:

1. $l_L(null) = 0$
2. $l_R(null) = 0$
3. $l_L(bin(e, t_1, t_2)) = s(l_L(t_1))$
4. $l_R(bin(e, t_1, t_2)) = s(l_R(t_2))$

It can be showed that this theory is T_S-compatible [20]. By arguments similar to those we employed for T_{LS}, it is possible to show that *every* T_S-amalgama of the T_S-reducts of two models of T_{BS} (sharing a common submodel) can be embedded in a T_{BS}-amalgama.

In conclusion, by (the multi-sorted version of) Theorem 3.2 we get that for every $(T_{LS} \cup T_{BS})$-fork $(\mathcal{M}_1, \mathcal{M}_2, \mathcal{A})$, the amalgamation schema for this fork $\sigma_{T_S}^{T_{LS} \cup T_{BS}}[(\mathcal{M}_1, \mathcal{M}_2, \mathcal{A})]$, being equal to the intersection of $\sigma_{T_S}^{T_{LS}}[(\mathcal{M}_1, \mathcal{M}_2, \mathcal{A})_{|\Sigma_{LS}}]$ and of $\sigma_{T_S}^{T_{BS}}[(\mathcal{M}_1, \mathcal{M}_2, \mathcal{A})_{|\Sigma_{BS}}]$, contains all the amalgams of the Σ_S-reduced fork $(\mathcal{M}_1, \mathcal{M}_2, \mathcal{A})_{|\Sigma_S}$ and hence it is trivially not empty. This guarantees that $T_{LS} \cup T_{BS}$ has quantifier-free interpolation by Proposition 3.1.

Example 3.5 (Where combined quantifier-free interpolation fails). Let T_0 be the theory of linear orders (its signature Σ_0 has just a binary relation symbol $<$ and the axioms of T_0 say that $<$ is irreflexive, transitive and satisfies the trichotomy condition $x < y \vee x = y \vee y < x$). This is a universal theory and admits a model completion T_0^*, which is the theory of dense linear orders without endpoints [4]; it is easily seen also that T_0 is strongly sub-amalgamable. We consider the signature Σ_1 of linear orders endowed with an extra unary relation symbol P and we let let T_1 be the theory obtained by adding to T_0 the following axiom:

$$\forall x \forall y\ (P(x) \wedge \neg P(y) \rightarrow x < y)$$

[4] We can freely assume that $ELEM_L^{\mathcal{M}_1} \cap ELEM_L^{\mathcal{M}_2} = ELEM_L^{\mathcal{A}}$ and $LIST^{\mathcal{M}_1} \cap LIST^{\mathcal{M}_2} = LIST^{\mathcal{A}}$.

It is not difficult to see that T_1 is T_0-compatible and also strongly-sub-amalgamable. We shall be interested in the combination of T_1 with a partially renamed copy of itself: this is the $\Sigma_2 := \Sigma_0 \cup \{Q\}$-theory T_2 axiomatized by the axioms of T_0 and

$$\forall x \forall y \ (Q(x) \wedge \neg Q(y) \to x < y)$$

Quantifier-free interpolation fails in $T_1 \cup T_2$, because sub-amalgamability fails: to see this fact, just consider a fork $(\mathcal{M}_1, \mathcal{M}_2, \mathcal{A})$ such that there exists an element $a \in |\mathcal{M}_1| \setminus |\mathcal{A}|$ which satisfies $P \wedge \neg Q$ and another element $b \in |\mathcal{M}_2| \setminus |\mathcal{A}|$ that satisfies Q and $\neg P$. Notice that we have $\sigma_{T_0}^{T_1}[(\mathcal{M}_1, \mathcal{M}_2, \mathcal{A})_{|\Sigma_1}] \cap \sigma_{T_0}^{T_2}[(\mathcal{M}_1, \mathcal{M}_2, \mathcal{A})_{|\Sigma_2}] = \emptyset$ although both $\sigma_{T_0}^{T_i}[(\mathcal{M}_1, \mathcal{M}_2, \mathcal{A})_{|\Sigma_i}]$ are not empty (the sub-amalgamation schemata here 'do not match').

3.2 Proof of Theorem 3.2

This subsection is entirely devoted to the proof of Theorem 3.2. We begin by recalling some standard results from model theory and by introducing some preliminary lemmata. The following easy fact is proved in [3], as Lemma 3.7:

Lemma 3.6. *Let Σ_1, Σ_2 be two signatures and $\mathcal{A}$ be a $\Sigma_1 \cup \Sigma_2$-structure; then $\Delta_{\Sigma_1 \cup \Sigma_2}(\mathcal{A})$ is logically equivalent to $\Delta_{\Sigma_1}(\mathcal{A}) \cup \Delta_{\Sigma_2}(\mathcal{A})$.*

An easy but nevertheless important basic result, called *Robinson Diagram Lemma* [4], says that, given any Σ-structure $\mathcal{B}$, the embeddings $\mu : \mathcal{A} \longrightarrow \mathcal{B}$ are in bijective correspondence with expansions of $\mathcal{B}$ to $\Sigma^{|\mathcal{A}|}$-structures which are models of $\Delta_\Sigma(\mathcal{A})$. The expansions and the embeddings are related in the obvious way: $\bar{a}$ is interpreted as $\mu(a)$.

The following Lemma is proved using this property of diagrams:

Lemma 3.7. *Let T_0, T be theories in their respective signatures Σ_0, Σ such that $\Sigma_0 \subseteq \Sigma$ and $T_0 \subseteq T$; let $(\mathcal{M}_1, \mathcal{M}_2, \mathcal{A})$ be a T-fork. For a T_0-amalgam $(\mathcal{B}, \nu_1, \nu_2)$ the following conditions are equivalent (we suppose that the support of $\mathcal{B}$ is disjoint from the supports of $\mathcal{M}_1, \mathcal{M}_2$):*

(i) $(\mathcal{B}, \nu_1, \nu_2) \in \sigma_{T_0}^{T}[(\mathcal{M}_1, \mathcal{M}_2, \mathcal{A})]$;
(ii) *the following theory* $(*)$ *is consistent*

$$\begin{aligned} &T \cup \Delta_\Sigma(\mathcal{M}_1) \cup \Delta_\Sigma(\mathcal{M}_2) \cup \Delta_{\Sigma_0}(\mathcal{B}) \cup \\ &\cup \{\bar{a}_1 = \bar{b} \parallel b \in |\mathcal{B}|, a_1 \in |\mathcal{M}_1|, \nu_1(a_1) = b\} \cup \\ &\{\bar{a}_2 = \bar{b} \parallel b \in |\mathcal{B}|, a_2 \in |\mathcal{M}_2|, \nu_2(a_2) = b\}. \end{aligned}$$

Furthermore, in case T is T_0-compatible, we can equivalently put $T \cup T_0^\star$ instead of T in the theory $(*)$ *mentioned in* (ii) *above.*

Proof. By the above mentioned property of diagrams, the consistency of $(*)$ means that there is a model $\mathcal{N} \models T$ and there are three embeddings

$$\mu_1 : \mathcal{M}_1 \longrightarrow \mathcal{N}, \quad \mu_2 : \mathcal{M}_2 \longrightarrow \mathcal{N}, \quad \nu : \mathcal{B} \longrightarrow \mathcal{N}$$

(the last one is a Σ_0-embedding, the first two are Σ-embeddings) such that $\nu \circ \nu_1 = \mu_1$ and $\nu \circ \nu_2 = \mu_2$. Since μ_1, μ_2 agree on the support of $\mathcal{A}$, the triple $(\mathcal{N}, \mu_1, \mu_2)$ is a T-sub-amalgam of the fork. To make $\mathcal{B}$ a substructure of $\mathcal{N}$, it is sufficient to make a renaming of the elements in the image of ν (so that ν becomes an inclusion). Thus consistency of $(*)$ means precisely that $(\mathcal{B}, \nu_1, \nu_2) \in \sigma^T_{T_0}[(\mathcal{M}_1, \mathcal{M}_2, \mathcal{A})]$.

Since, by T_0-compatibility, every model of T can be embedded into a model of $T \cup T^*$, the consistency of $(*)$ is the same of the consistency of $T^\star \cup (*)$. ⊣

We need a further result from model theory to be found in textbooks like [4]; it can be seen as a combination result 'ante litteram':

Lemma 3.8. *[Joint Consistency] Let Θ_1, Θ_2 be two signatures and let $\Theta_0 := \Theta_1 \cap \Theta_2$; suppose that the Θ_1-theory U_1 and the Θ_2-theory U_2 are both consistent and that there is a Θ_0-theory U_0 which is complete and included both in U_1 and in U_2. Then, $U_1 \cup U_2$ is also consistent.*

Proof. There are basically two proofs of this result, one by Craig's interpolation Theorem and another one by a double chain argument. The interested reader is referred to [4]. ⊣

We can now *prove Theorem* 3.2; the Theorem concerns theories T_1, T_2 (in their respective signatures Σ_1, Σ_2) which are both T_0-compatible with respect to a universal theory T_0 in the shared signature $\Sigma_0 := \Sigma_1 \cap \Sigma_2$.

Fix a $T_1 \cup T_2$-fork $(\mathcal{M}_1, \mathcal{M}_2, \mathcal{A})$. On one side, it is evident that if $(\mathcal{B}, \nu_1, \nu_2)$ belongs to $\sigma^{T_1 \cup T_2}_{T_0}[(\mathcal{M}_1, \mathcal{M}_2, \mathcal{A})]$, then it also belongs to $\sigma^{T_1}_{T_0}[(\mathcal{M}_1, \mathcal{M}_2, \mathcal{A})_{|\Sigma_1}] \cap \sigma^{T_2}_{T_0}[(\mathcal{M}_1, \mathcal{M}_2, \mathcal{A})_{|\Sigma_2}]$.

Vice versa, suppose that $(\mathcal{B}, \nu_1, \nu_2)$ belongs to $\sigma^{T_1}_{T_0}[(\mathcal{M}_1, \mathcal{M}_2, \mathcal{A})_{|\Sigma_1}]$ and to $\sigma^{T_2}_{T_0}[(\mathcal{M}_1, \mathcal{M}_2, \mathcal{A})_{|\Sigma_2}]$; in order to show that it belongs to $\sigma^{T_1 \cup T_2}_{T_0}[(\mathcal{M}_1, \mathcal{M}_2, \mathcal{A})]$, in view of Lemmas 3.6 and 3.7 (recall also Proposition 2.3), we need to show that the following theory (let us call it U) is consistent:

$$\begin{aligned}
&T_1 \cup T_2 \cup T_0^\star \cup \Delta_{\Sigma_1}(\mathcal{M}_1) \cup \Delta_{\Sigma_1}(\mathcal{M}_2) \cup \Delta_{\Sigma_0}(\mathcal{B}) \cup \\
&\cup \Delta_{\Sigma_2}(\mathcal{M}_1) \cup \Delta_{\Sigma_2}(\mathcal{M}_2) \cup \\
&\cup \{\bar{a}_1 = \bar{b} \parallel b \in |\mathcal{B}|, a_1 \in |\mathcal{M}_1|, \nu_1(a_1) = b\} \cup \\
&\{\bar{a}_2 = \bar{b} \parallel b \in |\mathcal{B}|, a_2 \in |\mathcal{M}_2|, \nu_2(a_2) = b\}.
\end{aligned}$$

The idea is to use Robinson Joint Consistency Lemma 3.8 and split U as $U_1 \cup U_2$. Now U is a theory in the signature $\Sigma_1 \cup \Sigma_2 \cup |\mathcal{M}_1| \cup |\mathcal{M}_2| \cup |\mathcal{B}|$; we let (for $i = 1, 2$) U_i be the following theory in the signature $\Sigma_i \cup |\mathcal{M}_1| \cup |\mathcal{M}_2| \cup |\mathcal{B}|$:

$$\begin{aligned}
&T_i \cup T_0^\star \cup \Delta_{\Sigma_i}(\mathcal{M}_1) \cup \Delta_{\Sigma_i}(\mathcal{M}_2) \cup \Delta_{\Sigma_0}(\mathcal{B}) \cup \\
&\cup \{\bar{a}_1 = \bar{b} \parallel b \in |\mathcal{B}|, a_1 \in |\mathcal{M}_1|, \nu_1(a_1) = b\} \cup \\
&\{\bar{a}_2 = \bar{b} \parallel b \in |\mathcal{B}|, a_2 \in |\mathcal{M}_2|, \nu_2(a_2) = b\}.
\end{aligned}$$

Notice that U_i is consistent by Lemma 3.7 because our assumption is that $(\mathcal{B}, \nu_1, \nu_2)$ belongs to $\sigma_{T_0}^{T_i}[(\mathcal{M}_1, \mathcal{M}_2, \mathcal{A})_{|\Sigma_i}]$. We now only have to identify a complete theory U_0 included in $U_1 \cap U_2$. The shared signature of U_1 and U_2 is $\Sigma_0 \cup |\mathcal{M}_1| \cup |\mathcal{M}_2| \cup |\mathcal{B}|$ and we take as U_0 the theory

$$
\begin{aligned}
&T_0^\star \cup \Delta_{\Sigma_0}(\mathcal{M}_1) \cup \Delta_{\Sigma_0}(\mathcal{M}_2) \cup \Delta_{\Sigma_0}(\mathcal{B}) \cup \\
&\cup \{\bar{a}_1 = \bar{b} \parallel b \in |\mathcal{B}|, a_1 \in |\mathcal{M}_1|, \nu_1(a_1) = b\} \cup \\
&\{\bar{a}_2 = \bar{b} \parallel b \in |\mathcal{B}|, a_2 \in |\mathcal{M}_2|, \nu_2(a_2) = b\}.
\end{aligned}
$$

By the definition of a model-completion ($T_0^\star$ is a model-completion of T_0), we know that $T_0^\star \cup \Delta_{\Sigma_0}(\mathcal{B})$ is a complete theory in the signature $\Sigma_0 \cup |\mathcal{B}|$. Now it is sufficient to observe that every $\Sigma_0 \cup |\mathcal{M}_1| \cup |\mathcal{M}_2| \cup |\mathcal{B}|$-sentence is equivalent, modulo $U_0 \supseteq T_0^\star \cup \Delta_{\Sigma_0}(\mathcal{B})$, to a $\Sigma_0 \cup |\mathcal{B}|$-sentence: this is clear because U_0 contains the sentences

$$
\begin{aligned}
&\{\bar{a}_1 = \bar{b} \parallel b \in |\mathcal{B}|, a_1 \in |\mathcal{M}_1|, \nu_1(a_1) = b\} \cup \\
&\{\bar{a}_2 = \bar{b} \parallel b \in |\mathcal{B}|, a_2 \in |\mathcal{M}_2|, \nu_2(a_2) = b\}.
\end{aligned}
$$

which can be used to eliminate the constants from $|\mathcal{M}_1| \cup |\mathcal{M}_2|$. ⊣

3.3 When the Shared Theory is Horn

Theorem 3.2 gives modular information to determine the combined sub-amalgamation schema, but it is not a modular result itself. In fact, a modular result should identify a condition C on a single (standing alone) theory such that whenever T_1, T_2 satisfy C, then $T_1 \cup T_2$ is sub-amalgamable and also satisfies C. To get a modular sufficient condition, we need to specialize our framework. In doing that, we are still guided by what happens in the disjoint signatures case. Although we feel that suitable conditions could be identified without Horn hypotheses, we prefer to assume that the shared theory is universal Horn to get simpler statements of our results below.

Recall that a Σ-theory T is *universal Horn* iff it can be axiomatized via Horn clauses (i.e. via formulae of the form $A_1 \wedge \cdots \wedge A_n \to B$, where the A_i are atoms and B is either an atom or $\bot$). In universal Horn theories, it is possible to show that if amalgamation holds, then there is always a minimal amalgama, as stated in the following fact (which is basically due to the universal property of pushouts, see [7] for a proof):

Proposition 3.9. *Let T be a universal Horn theory having the amalgamation property; given a T-fork $(\mathcal{M}_1, \mathcal{M}_2, \mathcal{A})$, there exists a T-amalgam $(\mathcal{M}, \mu_1, \mu_2)$ of $\mathcal{M}_1$ and $\mathcal{M}_2$ over $\mathcal{A}$ such that for every other T-amalgam $(\mathcal{M}', \mu_1', \mu_2')$ there is a unique homomorphism $\nu : \mathcal{M} \longrightarrow \mathcal{M}'$ such that $\nu \circ \mu_i = \mu_i'$ $(i = 1, 2)$.*

We call the amalgam mentioned in the above Proposition (which is unique up to isomorphism) the *minimal T-amalgam* of the T-fork $(\mathcal{M}_1, \mathcal{M}_2, \mathcal{A})$; the homomorphism ν (which needs not to be an embedding) is called the *comparison homomorphism*.

Let now T be a Σ-theory and let $T_0 \subseteq T$ be a universal Horn Σ_0-theory having the amalgamation property (with $\Sigma_0 \subseteq \Sigma$). We say that T is T_0*-strongly sub-amalgamable* if the sub-amalgamation schema $\sigma_{T_0}^{T}$ always contains the minimal T_0-amalgama (meaning that for every T-fork $(\mathcal{M}_1, \mathcal{M}_2, \mathcal{A})$, we have that the minimal T_0-amalgama of $(\mathcal{M}_1, \mathcal{M}_2, \mathcal{A})$ belongs to $\sigma_{T_0}^{T}[(\mathcal{M}_1, \mathcal{M}_2, \mathcal{A})]$). Notice that, whenever T_0 is the empty theory in the empty signature, being T_0-strongly sub-amalgamable is the same as being strongly sub-amalgamable.

Theorem 3.2 immediately implies the following:

Theorem 3.10. *If T_1, T_2 are both T_0-compatible and T_0-strongly sub-amalgamable (over an amalgamable universal Horn theory T_0 in their common subsignature Σ_0), then so it is $T_1 \cup T_2$.*

Proof. Since T_1 and T_2 are T_0-strongly sub-amalgamable, their sub-amalgamation schemata $\sigma_{T_0}^{T_i}$ $(i = 1, 2)$ always contain minimal T_0-amalgamas. By Theorem 3.2 (T_1 and T_2 are also T_0-compatible), this implies that for every $T_1 \cup T_2$-fork $(\mathcal{M}_1, \mathcal{M}_2, \mathcal{A})$, the minimal amalgama $\mathcal{B}$ of $(\mathcal{M}_1, \mathcal{M}_2, \mathcal{A})_{|\Sigma_0}$ belongs to the set $\sigma_{T_0}^{T_1 \cup T_2}[(\mathcal{M}_1, \mathcal{M}_2, \mathcal{A})]$. Using Proposition 2.3, we conclude that also $T_1 \cup T_2$ is T_0-compatible and T_0-strongly sub-amalgamable. ⊣

4 Applications to Modal Logic

Theorem 3.10 (obtained as a generalization of the analogous result from [3] for the disjoint signatures case) has surprising applications to modal logic. To get such applications, we need to reformulate it in the case of Boolean algebras with operators: the reformulation needs a further Theorem, showing that T_0-strong sub-amalgamability, in case T_0 is the theory of Boolean algebras, is nothing but the superamalgamability property known from algebraic logic. Let us recall the last property and state the Theorem we are still missing. For space reasons, all proofs in this section are deferred to [7].

In the following, we let BA be the theory of Boolean algebras; a *BAO-equational theory*[5] is any theory T whose signature extends the signature of Boolean algebras and whose axioms are all equations and include the Boolean algebra axioms. In [7] we shall recall in detail how BAO-equational theories are related to modal propositional logics via Lindenbaum constructions. The *fusion* of two BAO-equational theories T_1 and T_2 is just their combination $T_1 \cup T_2$ (when speaking of the fusion of T_1 and T_2, we assume that T_1 and T_2 share only the Boolean algebras operations and no other symbol).

The following Proposition is proved in [6] (proof is reported in [7]):

Proposition 4.1. *Every BAO-equational theory is BA-compatible.*

We say that a BAO-equational theory T has the *superamalgamation* property iff for every T-fork $(\mathcal{M}_1, \mathcal{M}_2, \mathcal{A})$ there exists a T-amalgam $(\mathcal{M}, \mu_1, \mu_2)$ such that

[5] BAO stands for 'Boolean algebras with operators'.

for every $a_1 \in |\mathcal{M}_1|, a_2 \in |\mathcal{M}_2|$ such that $\mu_1(a_1) \leq \mu_2(a_2)$ there exists $a_0 \in |\mathcal{A}|$ such that $a_1 \leq a_0$ holds in $\mathcal{M}_1$ and $a_0 \leq a_2$ holds in $\mathcal{M}_2$.[6]

We can now state our second main result (see [7] for the proof):

Theorem 4.2. *A BAO-equational theory T has the superamalgamation property iff it is BA-strongly amalgamable.*

As an immediate consequence, from Theorem 3.10, we get:

Corollary 4.3. *If two BAO-equational theories T_1 and T_2 both have the superamalgamability property, so does their fusion.*

4.1 Superamalgamability and Interpolation in Propositional Logic

Corollary 4.3 immediately implies Wolter's result [26] on fusion transfer of Craig interpolation property for normal modal logics and says something new for non-normal modal logics too. To see all this, we only need to recall some background from propositional logic. For simplicity, we deal only with unary modalities (and, consequently, we shall consider only BAO-theories whose non-Boolean symbols are unary function symbols), however we point out that the extension to n-ary modalities is straightforward.

A *modal signature* Σ_M is a set of unary operation symbols; from Σ_M, propositional *modal formulae* are built using countably many propositional variables, the operation symbols in Σ_M, the Boolean connectives $\cap, \cup, \sim$ and the constants 1 for truth and 0 for falsity. We use the letters $x, x_1, \ldots, y, y_1, \ldots$ to denote propositional variables and the letters $t, t_1, \ldots, u, u_1, \ldots$ to denote propositional formulae; $t \Rightarrow u$ and $t \Leftrightarrow u$ are abbreviations for $(\sim t) \cup u$ and for $(t \Rightarrow u) \cap (u \Rightarrow t)$, respectively. We use notations like $t(\underline{x})$ (resp. $\Gamma(\underline{x})$) to say that the modal formula t (the set of modal formulae Γ) is built up from a set of propositional variables included in the tuple $\underline{x}$.

The following definition is taken from [21], pp. 8–9:

Definition 4.4. *A* classical modal logic *L based on a modal signature Σ_M is a set of modal formulae that*

(i) *contains all classical propositional tautologies;*
(ii) *is closed under uniform substitution of propositional variables by propositional formulae;*
(iii) *is closed under the modus ponens rule ('from t and $t \Rightarrow u$ infer u');*
(iv) *is closed under the replacement rules, which are specified as follows. We have one such rule for each $o \in \Sigma_M$, namely:*

$$\frac{t \Leftrightarrow u}{o(t) \Leftrightarrow o(u)}$$

[6] We recall that in every Boolean algebra (more generally, in every semilattice) $x \leq y$ is defined as $x \cap y = x$, where $\cap$ is the meet operation.

A classical modal logic L is said to be normal *iff for every modal operator $o \in \Sigma_M$, L contains the modal formulae $o(1)$ and $o(y \Rightarrow z) \Rightarrow (o(y) \Rightarrow o(z))$.*

Since classical modal logics (based on a given modal signature) are closed under intersections, it makes sense to speak of the least classical modal logic $[S]$ containing a certain set of propositional formulae S. If $L = [S]$, we say that S is a set of *axiom schemata* for L.

If L_1 is a classical modal logic over the modal signature Σ_M^1 and L_2 is a classical modal logic over the modal signature Σ_M^2 and $\Sigma_M^1 \cap \Sigma_M^2 = \emptyset$, the *fusion* $L_1 \oplus L_2$ is the modal logic $[L_1 \cup L_2]$ over the modal signature $\Sigma_M^1 \cup \Sigma_M^2$.

Given a modal logic L, a set of modal formulae Γ and a modal formula t, the *global consequence relation* $\Gamma \vdash_L t$ holds iff there is a finite list of modal formulae $t_0, \ldots, t_n$ such that: (i) t_n is t; (ii) each t_i is either a member of L or a member of Γ or is obtained from previous members of the list by applying one of the two inference rules from Definition 4.4 (i.e. modus ponens and replacement).

Global consequence relation should be contrasted with *local consequence relation*, to be indicated with $\vdash_L \Gamma \Rightarrow t$: this holds iff there are $g_1, \ldots, g_n \in \Gamma$ such that $\bigcap_{i=1}^n g_i \Rightarrow t$ belongs to L. If Γ consists of a single modal formula g, below we write $g \vdash_L t$ and $\vdash_L g \Rightarrow t$ instead of $\{g\} \vdash_L t$ and of $\vdash_L \{g\} \Rightarrow t$.

In case L is normal, one can reduce the global consequence relation to the local one: in fact, it is not difficult to see by induction that the following fact ('deduction theorem') holds:

$$\Gamma \vdash_L t \quad \text{iff} \quad \vdash_L o\Gamma \Rightarrow t$$

where $o\Gamma$ is some finite set of modal formulae (depending on t) obtained from Γ by prefixing a string of modal operators (i.e. elements of $o\Gamma$ are modal formulae of the kind $o_1(o_2 \cdots o_n(g) \cdots)$, for $g \in \Gamma$ and $n \geq 0$, $o_1, \ldots, o_n \in \Sigma_M$).

Due to the presence of local and global consequence relations, we can formulate two different versions of the Craig's interpolation theorem:

Definition 4.5. *Let L be a classical modal logic in a modal signature Σ_M.*

(i) *We say that L enjoys the* local *interpolation property iff whenever we have $\vdash_L t_1(\underline{x}, \underline{y}) \Rightarrow t_2(\underline{x}, \underline{z})$ for two modal formulae t_1, t_2, then there is a modal formula $u(\underline{x})$ such that $\vdash_L t_1 \Rightarrow u$ and $\vdash_L u \Rightarrow t_2$.*
(ii) *We say that L enjoys the* global *interpolation property iff whenever we have $t_1(\underline{x}, \underline{y}) \vdash_L t_2(\underline{x}, \underline{z})$ for two modal formulae t_1, t_2, then there is a modal formula $u(\underline{x})$ such that $t_1 \vdash_L u$ and $u \vdash_L t_2$.*

For *normal* modal logics, in view of the above deduction theorem, it is easy to see that the local interpolation property implies the global one (but it is not equivalent to it, see [13]). In the non-normal case, there is no deduction theorem available, so that in order to have an interpolation property encompassing both the local and the global versions, it seems that a different notion needs to be introduced. This is what we are doing now.

Given a modal logic L and two sets of modal formulae $\Gamma_1(\underline{x}, \underline{y}), \Gamma_2(\underline{x}, \underline{z})$, let us call an $\underline{x}$-*residue chain* a tuple of modal formulae $C(\underline{x}) = g_1(\underline{x}), \ldots, g_k(\underline{x})$

such that we have $\Gamma_1 \cup \{g_1, \dots, g_{2i}\} \vdash_L g_{2i+1}$ and $\Gamma_2 \cup \{g_1, \dots, g_{2j-1}\} \vdash_L g_{2j}$, for all i such that $0 \leq 2i < n$ and for all j such that $0 < 2j \leq n$.

Definition 4.6. *Let L be a classical modal logic in a modal signature Σ_M.*

(iii) *We say that L enjoys the* comprehensive *interpolation property iff whenever we have $\Gamma_1(\underline{x}, \underline{y}), \Gamma_2(\underline{x}, \underline{z}) \vdash_L t_1(\underline{x}, \underline{y}) \Rightarrow t_2(\underline{x}, \underline{z})$ for two modal formulae t_1, t_2 and for two finite sets of modal formulae Γ_1, Γ_2, there are an $\underline{x}$-residue chain $C(\underline{x})$ and a modal formula $u(\underline{x})$ such that we have $\Gamma_1, C \vdash_L t_1 \Rightarrow u$ and $\Gamma_2, C \vdash_L u \Rightarrow t_2$.*

Notice that the comprehensive interpolation property implies both the local and the global interpolation properties; moreover, in the normal case, via deduction theorem, it is easily seen that the comprehensive interpolation property is equivalent to the local interpolation property. Our final result, giving an extension of Wolter's result [26] to non-normal case, is the following:

Theorem 4.7. *If the modal logics L_1 and L_2 both have the comprehensive interpolation property, so does their fusion $L_1 \oplus L_2$.*

The proof of the above Theorem is reported in [7] for space reasons; in fact, it requires some background, but only routine work. The idea is the following. One first recall that classical modal logics are in bijective correspondence with BAO-equational theories. Under this correspondence, in the normal case, global interpolation property coincides with quantifier-free interpolation (alias amalgamation property) and local interpolation property coincides with superamalgamability [13] (see [8] for a proof operating in a general context). Using similar techniques as in the above mentioned papers, in the non-normal general case, we show that *the comprehensive interpolation property coincides with superamalgamability*. Now it is sufficient to apply Corollary 4.3.

5 Conclusions and Future Work

In this paper we considered the problem of transferring the quantifier-free interpolation property from two theories to their union, in the case where the two theories share symbols other than pure equality.

We are not aware of previous papers attacking this problem. One should however mention a series of papers (e.g. [22, 23, 25]) analyzing the problem of transferring, in a hierarchical way, interpolation properties to theory extensions. This problem is related to ours, but it is different because there interpolation is assumed to hold for a basic theory T_0 and conditions on super-theories $T \supseteq T_0$ are analyzed in order to be able to extend interpolation to them. In our case, we are given interpolation properties for component theories T_1, T_2 and we are asked for modular conditions in order to transfer the property to $T_1 \cup T_2$.

To this aim, we obtained a sufficient condition (Theorem 3.2) in terms of sub-amalgamation schemata; we used such result to get a modular condition in case the shared theory is universal Horn (Theorem 3.10). For equational theories extending the theory of Boolean algebras, this modular condition turns out to be equivalent to the superamalgamability condition known from algebraic logic [14]. Thus, our results immediately imply the fusion transfer of local interpolation property [26] for classical normal modal logics. In the general non-normal case, the modularity of superamalgamability can be translated into a fusion transfer result for a new kind of interpolation property (which we called 'comprehensive interpolation property').

Still, many problems need to be faced by future research. Our combinability conditions should be characterizable from a syntactic point of view and, from such syntactic characterizations, we expect to be able to design concrete combined interpolation algorithms. Concerning modal logic, besides the old question about modularity of local interpolation property in the non-normal case, new questions arise concerning the status of the new comprehensive interpolation property: is it really stronger than other forms of interpolation property (e.g. than the local one)? Are there different ways of specifying it? Is it modular also for modal logics on a non-classical basis?

Acknowledgements. The first author was supported by the GNSAGA group of INdAM (Istituto Nazionale di Alta Matematica).

References

1. Bacsich, P.D.: Amalgamation properties and interpolation theorems for equational theories. Algebra Universalis **5**, 45–55 (1975)
2. Bruttomesso, R., Ghilardi, S., Ranise, S.: From strong amalgamability to modularity of quantifier-free interpolation. In: Gramlich, B., Miller, D., Sattler, U. (eds.) IJCAR 2012. LNCS (LNAI), vol. 7364, pp. 118–133. Springer, Heidelberg (2012). doi:10.1007/978-3-642-31365-3_12
3. Bruttomesso, R., Ghilardi, S., Ranise, S.: Quantifier-free interpolation in combinations of equality interpolating theories. ACM Trans. Comput. Log. **15**(1), 5:1–5:34 (2014)
4. Chang, C.-C., Keisler, J.H.: Model Theory, 3rd edn. North-Holland, Amsterdam-London (1990)
5. Craig, W.: Three uses of the Herbrand-Gentzen theorem in relating model theory and proof theory. J. Symb. Log. **22**, 269–285 (1957)
6. Ghilardi, S.: Model theoretic methods in combined constraint satisfiability. J. Autom. Reasoning **33**(3–4), 221–249 (2004)
7. Ghilardi, S., Gianola, A.: Interpolation, amalgamation and combination (extended version). Technical report (2017)
8. Ghilardi, S., Meloni, G.C.: Modal logics with n-ary connectives. Z. Math. Logik Grundlag. Math. **36**(3), 193–215 (1990)
9. Ghilardi, S., Nicolini, E., Zucchelli, D.: A comprehensive framework for combined decision procedures. ACM Trans. Comput. Logic **9**(2), 1–54 (2008)
10. Henzinger, T., McMillan, K.L., Jhala, R., Majumdar, R.: Abstractions from Proofs. In: POPL, pp. 232–244 (2004)
11. Kapur, D., Majumdar, R., Zarba, C.: Interpolation for data structures. In: SIGSOFT'06/FSE-14, pp. 105–116 (2006)

12. Maksimova, L.L.: Craig's theorem in superintuitionistic logics and amalgamable varieties. Algebra i Logika **16**(6), 643–681, 741 (1977)
13. Maksimova, L.L.: Interpolation theorems in modal logics and amalgamable varieties of topological Boolean algebras. Algebra i Logika **18**(5), 556–586, 632 (1979)
14. Maksimova, L.L.: Interpolation theorems in modal logics. Sufficient conditions. Algebra i Logika **19**(2), 194–213, 250–251 (1980)
15. McMillan, K.: Applications of craig interpolation to model checking. In: Marcinkowski, J., Tarlecki, A. (eds.) CSL 2004. LNCS, vol. 3210, pp. 22–23. Springer, Heidelberg (2004). doi:10.1007/978-3-540-30124-0_3
16. Nelson, G., Oppen, D.C.: Simplification by cooperating decision procedures. ACM Trans. Programm. Lang. Syst. **1**(2), 245–257 (1979)
17. Nicolini, E., Ringeissen, C., Rusinowitch, M.: Combinable extensions of abelian groups. In: Schmidt, R.A. (ed.) CADE 2009. LNCS (LNAI), vol. 5663, pp. 51–66. Springer, Heidelberg (2009). doi:10.1007/978-3-642-02959-2_4
18. Nicolini, E., Ringeissen, C., Rusinowitch, M.: Data structures with arithmetic constraints: a non-disjoint combination. In: Ghilardi, S., Sebastiani, R. (eds.) FroCoS 2009. LNCS (LNAI), vol. 5749, pp. 319–334. Springer, Heidelberg (2009). doi:10.1007/978-3-642-04222-5_20
19. Nicolini, E., Ringeissen, C., Rusinowitch, M.: Satisfiability procedures for combination of theories sharing integer offsets. In: Kowalewski, S., Philippou, A. (eds.) TACAS 2009. LNCS, vol. 5505, pp. 428–442. Springer, Heidelberg (2009). doi:10.1007/978-3-642-00768-2_35
20. Nicolini, E., Ringeissen, C., Rusinowitch, M.: Combining satisfiability procedures for unions of theories with a shared counting operator. Fundam. Inform. **105**(1–2), 163–187 (2010)
21. Segerberg, K.: An Essay in Classical Modal Logic, Filosofiska Studier, vol. 13. Uppsala Universitet (1971)
22. Sofronie-Stokkermans, V.: Interpolation in local theory extensions. Logical Methods Comput. Sci. **4**(4), 1–31 (2008)
23. Sofronie-Stokkermans, V.: On interpolation and symbol elimination in theory extensions. In: Olivetti, N., Tiwari, A. (eds.) IJCAR 2016. LNCS (LNAI), vol. 9706, pp. 273–289. Springer, Cham (2016). doi:10.1007/978-3-319-40229-1_19
24. Tinelli, C., Harandi, M.T.: A new correctness proof of the Nelson-Oppen combination procedure. In: Proceedings of FroCoS 1996, Applied Logic, pp. 103–120. Kluwer Academic Publishers (1996)
25. Totla, N., Wies, T.: Complete instantiation-based interpolation. J. Autom. Reasoning **57**(1), 37–65 (2016)
26. Wolter, F.: Fusions of modal logics revisited. In Advances in Modal Logic, vol. 1 (Berlin, 1996), CSLI Lecture Notes, pp. 361–379 (1998)
27. Yorsh, G., Musuvathi, M.: A combination method for generating interpolants. In: Nieuwenhuis, R. (ed.) CADE 2005. LNCS, vol. 3632, pp. 353–368. Springer, Heidelberg (2005). doi:10.1007/11532231_26

The Boolean Solution Problem from the Perspective of Predicate Logic

Christoph Wernhard(✉)

Technische Universität Dresden, Dresden, Germany
info@christophwernhard.com

Abstract. Finding solution values for unknowns in Boolean equations was a principal reasoning mode in the *Algebra of Logic* of the 19th century. Schröder investigated it as *Auflösungsproblem* (*solution problem*). It is closely related to the modern notion of Boolean unification. Today it is commonly presented in an algebraic setting, but seems potentially useful also in knowledge representation based on predicate logic. We show that it can be modeled on the basis of first-order logic extended by second-order quantification. A wealth of classical results transfers, foundations for algorithms unfold, and connections with second-order quantifier elimination and Craig interpolation show up.

1 Introduction

Finding solution values for unknowns in Boolean equations was a principal reasoning mode in the *Algebra of Logic* of the 19th century. Schröder [27] investigated it as *Auflösungsproblem* (*solution problem*). It is closely related to the modern notion of Boolean unification. For a given formula that contains unknowns formulas are sought such that after substituting the unknowns with them the given formula becomes valid or, dually, unsatisfiable. Of interest are also most general solutions, condensed representations of all solution substitutions. A central technique there is the *method of successive eliminations*, which traces back to Boole. Schröder investigated *reproductive solutions* as most general solutions, anticipating the concept of *most general unifier*. A comprehensive modern formalization based on this material, along with historic remarks, is presented by Rudeanu [23] in the framework of Boolean algebra. In automated reasoning variants of these techniques have been considered mainly in the late 80s and early 90s with the motivation to enrich Prolog and constraint processing by Boolean unification with respect to propositional formulas handled as terms [8,15,16,20–22]. An early implementation based on [23] has been also described in [29]. An implementation with BDDs of the algorithm from [8] is reported in [9]. The Π_2^P-completeness of Boolean unification with constants was proven only later in [15,16] and seemingly independently in [2]. Schröder's results were developed further by Löwenheim [18,19]. A generalization of Boole's method beyond propositional logic to relational monadic formulas has been presented by Behmann in the early 1950s [5,6]. Recently the complexity of Boolean unification in a predicate logic setting has been investigated for some formula classes, in particular for

C. Dixon and M. Finger (Eds.): FroCoS 2017, LNCS 10483, pp. 333–350, 2017.
DOI: 10.1007/978-3-319-66167-4_19

quantifier-free first-order formulas [12]. A brief discussion of Boolean reasoning in comparison with predicate logic can be found in [7].

Here we remodel the solution problem formally along with basic classical results and some new generalizations in the framework of first-order logic extended by second-order quantification. The main thesis of this work is that it is possible and useful to apply second-order quantification consequently throughout the formalization. What otherwise would require meta-level notation is then expressed just with formulas. As will be shown, classical results can be reproduced in this framework in a way such that applicability beyond propositional logic, possible algorithmic variations, as well as connections with second-order quantifier elimination and Craig interpolation become visible. As demonstrated in [30], the foundations developed here are adequate as basis for adaptions of further classical material, notably reproductive solutions, and for further studies such as the investigation of certain special cases for which constructive solution methods are available and a generalization of the solution problem where vocabulary restrictions are taken into account.

The envisaged application scenario is to let solving "solution problems", or Boolean equation solving, on the basis of predicate logic join reasoning modes like second-order quantifier elimination (or "semantic forgetting"), Craig interpolation and abduction to support the mechanized reasoning about relationships between theories and the extraction or synthesis of subtheories with given properties. On the practical side, the aim is to relate it to reasoning techniques such as Craig interpolation on the basis of first-order provers, SAT and QBF solving, and second-order quantifier elimination based on resolution [14] and the Ackermann approach [11]. Numerous applications of Boolean equation solving in various fields are summarized in [24, Chap. 14]. Applications in automated theorem proving and proof compression are mentioned in [12, Sect. 7]. The prevention of certain redundancies has been described as application of (concept) unification in description logics [4]. In [30] the synthesis of definitional equivalences is sketched as an application.

The rest of the paper is structured as follows: Notation, in particular for substitution in formulas, is introduced in Sect. 2. In Sect. 3 a formalization of the solution problem is presented and related to different points of view. Section 4 is concerned with abstract properties of and algorithmic approaches to solution problems with several unknowns. Conditions under which solutions exist are discussed in Sect. 5. Section 6 closes the paper with concluding remarks.

2 Notation and Preliminaries

2.1 Notational Conventions

We consider formulas in first-order logic extended by second-order quantification upon predicates. They are constructed from atoms, constant operators $\top$, $\bot$, the unary operator $\neg$, binary operators $\land, \lor$ and quantifiers $\forall, \exists$ with their usual meaning. Further binary operators $\rightarrow, \leftarrow, \leftrightarrow$, as well as n-ary versions of $\land$ and $\lor$ can be understood as meta-level notation. The operators $\land$ and $\lor$ bind stronger than $\rightarrow$, $\leftarrow$ and $\leftrightarrow$. The scope of $\neg$, the quantifiers, and the n-ary connectives is the immediate subformula to the right. A subformula occurrence has in a given formula *positive (negative) polarity* if it is in the scope of an even (odd) number of negations.

A *vocabulary* is a set of *symbols*, that is, predicate symbols (briefly *predicates*), function symbols (briefly *functions*) and *individual symbols*. (Individual symbols are not partitioned into variables and constants. Thus, an individual symbol is – like a predicate – considered as variable if and only if it is bound by a quantifier.) The arity of a predicate or function s is denoted by $\mathsf{arity}(s)$. The set of symbols that occur *free* in a formula F is denoted by $\mathsf{free}(F)$. Symbols not present in the formulas and other items under discussion are called *fresh*. We write $F \models G$ for *F entails G*; $\models F$ for *F is valid*; and $F \equiv G$ for *F is equivalent to G*, that is, *$F \models G$ and $G \models F$*.

We write *sequences* of symbols, of terms and of formulas by juxtaposition. Their length is assumed to be finite. The empty sequence is written ϵ. A sequence with length 1 is not distinguished from its sole member. In contexts where a set is expected, a sequence stands for the set of its members. Atoms are written in the form $p(\boldsymbol{t})$, where $\boldsymbol{t}$ is a sequence of terms whose length is the arity of the predicate p. Atoms of the form $p(\epsilon)$, that is, with a nullary predicate p, are written also as p. For a sequence of *fresh* symbols we assume that its members are distinct. A sequence $p_1 \ldots p_n$ of predicates is said to *match* another sequence $q_1 \ldots q_m$ if and only if $n = m$ and for all $i \in \{1, \ldots, n\}$ it holds that $\mathsf{arity}(p_i) = \mathsf{arity}(q_i)$. If $\boldsymbol{s} = s_1 \ldots s_n$ is a sequence of symbols, then $\forall \boldsymbol{s}$ stands for $\forall s_1 \ldots \forall s_n$ and $\exists \boldsymbol{s}$ for $\exists s_1 \ldots \exists s_n$.

As explained below, in certain contexts the individual symbols in the set $\mathcal{X} = \{x_i \mid i \geq 1\}$ play a special role. For example in the following shorthands for a predicate p, a formula F and $\boldsymbol{x} = x_1 \ldots x_{\mathsf{arity}(p)}$: $p \Leftrightarrow F$ stands for $\forall \boldsymbol{x}\, (p(\boldsymbol{x}) \leftrightarrow F)$; $p \not\Leftrightarrow F$ for $\neg(p \Leftrightarrow F)$; $p \Rightarrow F$ for $\forall \boldsymbol{x}\, (p(\boldsymbol{x}) \rightarrow F)$; and $p \Leftarrow F$ for $\forall \boldsymbol{x}\, (p(\boldsymbol{x}) \leftarrow F)$.

2.2 Substitution with Terms and Formulas

To express systematic substitution of individual symbols and predicates concisely we use the following notation:

- *$F(\boldsymbol{c})$ and $F(\boldsymbol{t})$ – Notational Context for Substitution of Individual Symbols.* Let $\boldsymbol{c} = c_1 \ldots c_n$ be a sequence of distinct individual symbols. We write F as $F(\boldsymbol{c})$ to declare that for a sequence $\boldsymbol{t} = t_1 \ldots t_n$ of terms the expression $F(\boldsymbol{t})$ denotes F with, for $i \in \{1, \ldots, n\}$, all free occurrences of c_i replaced by t_i.
- *$F[\boldsymbol{p}]$, $F[\boldsymbol{G}]$ and $F[\boldsymbol{q}]$ – Notational Context for Substitution of Predicates.* Let $\boldsymbol{p} = p_1 \ldots p_n$ be a sequence of distinct predicates and let F be a formula. We write F as $F[\boldsymbol{p}]$ to declare the following:
  - For a sequence $\boldsymbol{G} = G_1(x_1 \ldots x_{\mathsf{arity}(p_1)}) \ldots G_n(x_1 \ldots x_{\mathsf{arity}(p_n)})$ of formulas the expression $F[\boldsymbol{G}]$ denotes F with, for $i \in \{1, \ldots, n\}$, each atom occurrence $p_i(t_1 \ldots t_{\mathsf{arity}(p_i)})$ where p_i is free in F replaced by $G_i(t_1 \ldots t_{\mathsf{arity}(p_i)})$.
  - For a sequence $\boldsymbol{q} = q_1 \ldots q_n$ of predicates that matches $\boldsymbol{p}$ the expression $F[\boldsymbol{q}]$ denotes F with, for $i \in \{1, \ldots, n\}$, each free occurrence of p_i replaced by q_i.

  • The above notation $F[\boldsymbol{S}]$, where $\boldsymbol{S}$ is a sequence of formulas or of predicates, is generalized to allow also p_i at the ith position of $\boldsymbol{S}$, for example $F[G_1 \ldots G_{i-1} p_i \ldots p_n]$. The formula $F[\boldsymbol{S}]$ then denotes F with only those predicates p_i with $i \in \{1, \ldots, n\}$ that are not present at the ith position in $\boldsymbol{S}$ replaced by the ith component of $\boldsymbol{S}$ as described above (in the example only $p_1, \ldots, p_{i-1}$ would be replaced).

- $\boldsymbol{F}[\boldsymbol{p}]$ – *Notational Context for Substitution in a Sequence of Formulas.* If $\boldsymbol{F} = F_1 \ldots F_n$ is a sequence of formulas, then $\boldsymbol{F}[\boldsymbol{p}]$ declares that $\boldsymbol{F}[\boldsymbol{S}]$, where $\boldsymbol{S}$ is a sequence with the same length as $\boldsymbol{p}$, is to be understood as the sequence $F_1[\boldsymbol{S}] \ldots F_n[\boldsymbol{S}]$ with the meaning of the members as described above.

In the above notation for substitution of predicates by formulas the members $x_1, \ldots, x_{\mathsf{arity}(p)}$ of $\mathcal{X}$ play a special role: $F[\boldsymbol{G}]$ can be alternatively considered as obtained by replacing predicates p_i with λ-expressions $\lambda x_1 \ldots \lambda x_{\mathsf{arity}(p_i)}.G_i$ followed by β-conversion. The shorthand $p \Leftrightarrow F$ can be correspondingly considered as $p \leftrightarrow \lambda x_1 \ldots \lambda x_{\mathsf{arity}(p)}.G$. The following property *substitutible* specifies preconditions for meaningful simultaneous substitution of formulas for predicates:

Definition 1 ($\mathsf{SUBST}(\boldsymbol{G}, \boldsymbol{p}, F)$ – **Substitutible Sequence of Formulas).** A sequence $\boldsymbol{G} = G_1 \ldots G_m$ of formulas is called *substitutible for* a sequence $\boldsymbol{p} = p_1 \ldots p_n$ of distinct predicates *in* a formula F, written $\mathsf{SUBST}(\boldsymbol{G}, \boldsymbol{p}, F)$, if and only if $m = n$ and for all $i \in \{1, \ldots, n\}$ it holds that (1.) No free occurrence of p_i in F is in the scope of a quantifier occurrence that binds a member of $\mathsf{free}(G_i)$; (2.) $\mathsf{free}(G_i) \cap \boldsymbol{p} = \emptyset$; and (3.) $\mathsf{free}(G_i) \cap \{x_j \mid j > \mathsf{arity}(p_i)\} = \emptyset$.

The following propositions demonstrate the introduced notation for formula substitution. It is well known that terms can be "pulled out of" and "pushed in to" atoms, justified by the equivalences $p(t_1 \ldots t_n) \equiv \exists x_1 \ldots \exists x_n \, (p(x_1 \ldots x_n) \land \bigwedge_{i=1}^{n} x_i = t_i) \equiv \forall x_1 \ldots \forall x_n \, (p(x_1 \ldots x_n) \lor \bigvee_{i=1}^{n} x_i \neq t_i)$, which hold if no member of $\{x_1, \ldots, x_n\}$ does occur in the terms $t_1, \ldots, t_n$. Analogously, substitutible subformulas can be "pulled out of" and "pushed in to" formulas:

Proposition 2 (Pulling-Out and Pushing-In of Subformulas). *Let $\boldsymbol{G} = G_1 \ldots G_n$ be a sequence of formulas, let $\boldsymbol{p} = p_1 \ldots p_n$ be a sequence of distinct predicates and let $F = F[\boldsymbol{p}]$ be a formula such that $\mathsf{SUBST}(\boldsymbol{G}, \boldsymbol{p}, F)$. Then*

(i) $F[\boldsymbol{G}] \equiv \exists \boldsymbol{p} \, (F \land \bigwedge_{i=1}^{n} (p_i \Leftrightarrow G_i)) \equiv \forall \boldsymbol{p} \, (F \lor \bigvee_{i=1}^{n} (p_i \not\Leftrightarrow G_i))$.
(ii) $\forall \boldsymbol{p} \, F \models F[\boldsymbol{G}] \models \exists \boldsymbol{p} \, F$.

Ackermann's Lemma [1] can be applied in certain cases to *eliminate* second-order quantifiers, that is, to compute for a given second-order formula an equivalent first-order formula. It plays an important role in many modern methods for elimination and semantic forgetting – see, e.g., [10,11,13,17,26,31]:

Proposition 3 (Ackermann's Lemma, Positive Version). *Let F, G be formulas and let p be a predicate such that $\mathsf{SUBST}(G, p, F)$, $p \notin \mathsf{free}(G)$ and all free occurrences of p in F have negative polarity. Then $\exists p \, ((p \Leftarrow G) \land F[p]) \equiv F[G]$.*

3 The Solution Problem from Different Angles

3.1 Basic Formal Modeling

Our formal modeling of the Boolean solution problem is based on two concepts, *solution problem* and *particular solution*:

Definition 4 ($F[\boldsymbol{p}]$ – Solution Problem (SP), Unary Solution Problem (1-SP)). *A solution problem (SP) $F[\boldsymbol{p}]$ is a pair of a formula F and a sequence $\boldsymbol{p}$ of distinct predicates. The members of $\boldsymbol{p}$ are called the unknowns of the SP. The length of $\boldsymbol{p}$ is called the arity of the SP. A SP with arity 1 is also called unary solution problem (1-SP).*

The notation $F[\boldsymbol{p}]$ for solution problems establishes as a "side effect" a context for specifying substitutions of $\boldsymbol{p}$ in F by formulas as specified in Sect. 2.2.

Definition 5 (Particular Solution). *A particular solution (briefly solution) of a SP $F[\boldsymbol{p}]$ is defined as a sequence $\boldsymbol{G}$ of formulas such that $\mathsf{SUBST}(\boldsymbol{G}, \boldsymbol{p}, F)$ and $\models F[\boldsymbol{G}]$.*

The property $\mathsf{SUBST}(\boldsymbol{G}, \boldsymbol{p}, F)$ in this definition implies that no member of $\boldsymbol{p}$ occurs free in a solution. Of course, *particular solution* can also be defined on the basis of unsatisfiability instead of validity, justified by the equivalence of $\models F[\boldsymbol{G}]$ and $\neg F[\boldsymbol{G}] \models \bot$. The variant based on validity has been chosen here because then the associated second-order quantifications are existential, matching the usual presentation of elimination techniques.

Solution problem and *solution* as defined here provide abstractions of computational problems in a technical sense that would be suitable, e.g., for complexity analysis. Problems in the latter sense can be obtained by fixing involved formula and predicate classes. The abstract notions are adequate to develop much of the material on the "Boolean solution problem" shown here and in [30]. On occasion, however, we consider restrictions, in particular to propositional and to first-order formulas, as well as to nullary predicates. As shown in [30, Sect. 6], further variants of *solution*, general representations of several particular solutions, can be introduced on the basis of the notions defined here.

Example 6 (A Solution Problem and its Particular Solutions). As an example of a solution problem consider $F[p_1 p_2]$ where

$$F = \forall x\,(a(x) \rightarrow b(x)) \rightarrow \\ (\forall x\,(p_1(x) \rightarrow p_2(x)) \land \forall x\,(a(x) \rightarrow p_2(x)) \land \forall x\,(p_2(x) \rightarrow b(x))).$$

The intuition is that the antecedent $\forall x\,(a(x) \rightarrow b(x))$ specifies the "background theory", and w.r.t. that theory the unknown p_1 is "stronger" than the other unknown p_2, which is also "between" a and b. Examples of solutions are: $a(x_1)a(x_1)$; $a(x_1)b(x_1)$; $\bot a(x_1)$; $b(x_1)b(x_1)$; and $(a(x_1) \land b(x_1))(a(x_1) \lor b(x_1))$. No solutions are for example $b(x_1)a(x_1)$; $a(x_1)\bot$; and all members of $\{\top, \bot\} \times \{\top, \bot\}$.

Assuming a countable vocabulary, the set of valid first-order formulas is recursively enumerable. It follows that for an n-ary SP $F[\boldsymbol{p}]$ where F is first-order the set of those of its particular solutions that are sequences of first-order formulas is also recursively enumerable: An n-ary sequence $\boldsymbol{G}$ of well-formed first-order formulas that satisfies the syntactic restriction $\mathsf{SUBST}(\boldsymbol{G}, \boldsymbol{p}, F)$ is a solution of $F[\boldsymbol{p}]$ if and only if $F[\boldsymbol{G}]$ is valid.

In the following subsections further views on the solution problem will be discussed: as unification or equation solving, as a special case of second-order quantifier elimination, and as related to determining definientia and interpolants.

3.2 View as Unification

Because $\models F[\boldsymbol{G}]$ if and only if $F[\boldsymbol{G}] \equiv \top$, a particular solution of $F[\boldsymbol{p}]$ can be seen as a unifier of the two formulas $F[\boldsymbol{p}]$ and $\top$ modulo logical equivalence as equational theory. From the perspective of unification the two formulas appear as terms, the members of $\boldsymbol{p}$ play the role of variables and the other predicates play the role of constants.

Vice versa, a unifier of two formulas can be seen as a particular solution, justified by the equivalence of $L[\boldsymbol{G}] \equiv R[\boldsymbol{G}]$ and $\models (L \leftrightarrow R)[\boldsymbol{G}]$, which holds for sequences $\boldsymbol{G}$ and $\boldsymbol{p}$ of formulas and predicates, respectively, and formulas $L = L[\boldsymbol{p}], R = R[\boldsymbol{p}], (L \leftrightarrow R) = (L \leftrightarrow R)[\boldsymbol{p}]$ such that $\mathsf{SUBST}(\boldsymbol{G}, \boldsymbol{p}, L)$ and $\mathsf{SUBST}(\boldsymbol{G}, \boldsymbol{p}, R)$. This view of formula unification can be generalized to sets with a finite cardinality k of equivalences, since *for all* $i \in \{1, \ldots, k\}$ *it holds that* $L_i \equiv R_i$ can be expressed as $\models \bigwedge_{i=1}^{k} (L_i \leftrightarrow R_i)$.

An exact correspondence between solving a solution problem $F[p_1 \ldots p_n]$ where F is a propositional formula with $\vee, \wedge, \neg, \bot, \top$ as logic operators and E-unification with constants in the theory of Boolean algebra (with the mentioned logic operators as signature) applied to $F =_E \top$ can be established: Unknowns $p_1, \ldots, p_n$ correspond to variables and propositional atoms in F correspond to constants. A particular solution $G_1 \ldots G_n$ corresponds to a unifier $\{p_1 \leftarrow G_1, \ldots, p_n \leftarrow G_n\}$ that is a ground substitution. The restriction to ground substitutions is due to the requirement that unknowns do not occur in solutions. General solutions [30, Sect. 6] are expressed with further special parameter atoms, different from the unknowns. These correspond to fresh variables in unifiers.

A generalization of Boolean unification to predicate logic with various specific problems characterized by the involved formula classes has been investigated in [12]. The material presented here and in [30] is largely orthogonal to that work, but a technique from [12] has been adapted to more general cases in [30, Sect. 7.3].

3.3 View as Construction of Elimination Witnesses

Another view on the solution problem is related to eliminating second-order quantifiers by replacing the quantified predicates with "witness formulas".

Definition 7 (ELIM-Witness). Let $\boldsymbol{p} = p_1 \dots p_n$ be a sequence of distinct predicates. An *ELIM-witness of* $\boldsymbol{p}$ *in* a formula $\exists \boldsymbol{p}\, F[\boldsymbol{p}]$ is defined as a sequence $\boldsymbol{G}$ of formulas such that $\mathsf{SUBST}(\boldsymbol{G}, \boldsymbol{p}, F)$ and $\exists \boldsymbol{p}\, F[\boldsymbol{p}] \equiv F[\boldsymbol{G}]$.

The condition $\exists \boldsymbol{p}\, F[\boldsymbol{p}] \equiv F[\boldsymbol{G}]$ in this definition is equivalent to $\models \neg F[\boldsymbol{p}] \lor F[\boldsymbol{G}]$. If $F[\boldsymbol{p}]$ and the considered $\boldsymbol{G}$ are first-order, then finding an ELIM-witness is second-order quantifier elimination on a first-order argument formula, restricted by the condition that the result is of the form $F[\boldsymbol{G}]$. Differently from the general case of second-order quantifier elimination on first-order arguments, the set of formulas for which elimination succeeds and, for a given formula, the set of its elimination results, are then recursively enumerable. Some well-known elimination methods yield ELIM-witnesses, for example rewriting a formula that matches the left side of Ackermann's Lemma (Proposition 3) with its right side, which becomes evident when considering that the right side $F[G]$ is equivalent to $\forall x_1 \dots \forall x_{\mathsf{arity}(p)}\, (G \leftarrow G) \land F[G]$. Finding particular solutions and finding ELIM-witnesses can be expressed in terms of each other:

Proposition 8 (Solutions and ELIM-Witnesses). *Let* $F[\boldsymbol{p}]$ *be SP and let* $\boldsymbol{G}$ *be a sequence of formulas. Then:*

(i) $\boldsymbol{G}$ *is an ELIM-witness of* $\boldsymbol{p}$ *in* $\exists \boldsymbol{p}\, F$ *if and only if* $\boldsymbol{G}$ *is a solution of the SP* $(\neg F[\boldsymbol{q}] \lor F)[\boldsymbol{p}]$*, where* $\boldsymbol{q}$ *is a sequence of fresh predicates matching* $\boldsymbol{p}$*.*
(ii) $\boldsymbol{G}$ *is a solution of* $F[\boldsymbol{p}]$ *if and only if* $\boldsymbol{G}$ *is an ELIM-witness of* $\boldsymbol{p}$ *in* $\exists \boldsymbol{p}\, F$ *and it holds that* $\models \exists \boldsymbol{p}\, F$*.*

Proof (Sketch). Assume $\mathsf{SUBST}(\boldsymbol{G}, \boldsymbol{p}, F)$. (Proposition 8i) Follows since $\exists \boldsymbol{p}\, F[\boldsymbol{p}] \equiv F[\boldsymbol{G}]$ iff $\exists \boldsymbol{p}\, F[\boldsymbol{p}] \models F[\boldsymbol{G}]$ iff $F[\boldsymbol{p}] \models F[\boldsymbol{G}]$ iff $\models \neg F[\boldsymbol{q}] \lor F[\boldsymbol{G}]$. (Proposition 8ii) Left-To-Right: Follows since $\models F[\boldsymbol{G}]$ implies $\models \exists \boldsymbol{p}\, F[\boldsymbol{p}]$ and $\models F[\boldsymbol{G}]$, which implies $\exists \boldsymbol{p}\, F[\boldsymbol{p}] \equiv \top \equiv F[\boldsymbol{G}]$. Right-to-left: Follows since $\exists \boldsymbol{p}\, F[\boldsymbol{p}] \equiv F[\boldsymbol{G}]$ and $\models \exists \boldsymbol{p}\, F[\boldsymbol{p}]$ together imply $\models F[\boldsymbol{G}]$. □

3.4 View as Related to Definientia and Interpolants

The following proposition shows a further view on the solution problem that relates it to definitions of the unknown predicates:

Proposition 9 (Solution as Entailed by a Definition). *A sequence* $\boldsymbol{G} = G_1 \dots G_n$ *of formulas is a particular solution of a SP* $F[\boldsymbol{p} = p_1 \dots p_n]$ *if and only if* $\mathsf{SUBST}(\boldsymbol{G}, \boldsymbol{p}, F)$ *and* $\bigwedge_{i=1}^{n} (p_i \Leftrightarrow G_i) \models F$*.*

Proof. Follows from the definition of *particular solution* and Proposition 2i. □

In the special case where $F[p]$ is a 1-SP with a *nullary* unknown p, the characterization of a solution G according to Proposition 9 can be expressed with an entailment where a definition of the unknown p appears on the right instead of the left side: If p is nullary, then $\neg(p \Leftrightarrow G) \equiv p \Leftrightarrow \neg G$. Thus, the statement $p \Leftrightarrow G \models F$ is for nullary p equivalent to

$$\neg F \models p \Leftrightarrow \neg G. \tag{i}$$

The second condition of the characterization of *solution* according to Proposition 9, that is, $\mathsf{SUBST}(G, p, F)$, holds if it is assumed that p is not in $\mathsf{free}(G)$, that $\mathsf{free}(G) \subseteq \mathsf{free}(F)$ and that no member of $\mathsf{free}(F)$ is bound by a quantifier occurrence in F. A solution is then characterized as negated definiens of p in the negation of F. Another way to express (i) along with the condition that G is semantically independent from p is as follows:

$$\exists p\,(\neg F \land \neg p) \models G \models \neg\exists p\,(\neg F \land p). \tag{ii}$$

The second-order quantifiers upon the nullary p can be eliminated, yielding the following equivalent statement:

$$\neg F[\bot] \models G \models F[\top]. \tag{iii}$$

Solutions G then appear as the formulas in a range, between $\neg F[\bot]$ and $F[\top]$. This view is reflected in [23, Theorem 2.2], which goes back to work by Schröder. If F is first-order, then Craig interpolation can be applied to compute formulas G that also meet the requirements $\mathsf{free}(G) \subseteq \mathsf{free}(F)$ and $p \notin \mathsf{free}(F)$ to ensure $\mathsf{SUBST}(G, p, F)$. Further connections to Craig interpolation are discussed in [30, Sect. 7].

4 The Method of Successive Eliminations – Abstracted

4.1 Reducing n-ary to 1-ary Solution Problems

The *method of successive eliminations* to solve an n-ary solution problem by reducing it to unary solution problems is attributed to Boole and has been formally described in a modern algebraic setting in [23, Chap. 2, Sect. 4]. It has been rediscovered in the context of Boolean unification in the late 1980s, notably with [8]. Rudeanu notes in [23, p. 72] that variants described by several authors in the 19th century are discussed by Schröder [27, vol. 1, Sects. 26 and 27]. To research and compare all variants up to now seems to be a major undertaking on its own. Our aim is here to provide a foundation to derive and analyze related methods. The following proposition formally states the core property underlying the method in a way that, compared to the Boolean algebra version in [23, Chap. 2, Sect. 4], is more abstract in several aspects: Second-order quantification upon predicates that represent unknowns plays the role of meta-level shorthands that encode expansions; no commitment to a particular formula class is made, thus the proposition applies to second-order formulas with first-order and propositional formulas as special cases; it is not specified how solutions of the arising unary solution problems are constructed; and it is not specified how intermediate second-order formulas (that occur also for inputs without second-order quantifiers) are handled. The algorithm descriptions in the following subsections show different possibilities to instantiate these abstracted aspects.

Proposition 10 (Characterization of Solution Underlying the Method of Successive Eliminations). *Let $F[\mathbf{p} = p_1 \ldots p_n]$ be a SP and let $\mathbf{G} = G_1 \ldots G_n$ be a sequence of formulas. Then the following statements are equivalent:*

(a) $\boldsymbol{G}$ *is a solution of* $F[\boldsymbol{p}]$.
(b) For $i \in \{1, \ldots, n\}$: G_i *is a solution of the 1-SP*

$$(\exists p_{i+1} \ldots \exists p_n\, F[G_1 \ldots G_{i-1} p_i \ldots p_n])[p_i]$$

such that $\mathsf{free}(G_i) \cap \boldsymbol{p} = \emptyset$.

Proof. Left-to-right: From (a) it follows that $\models F[\boldsymbol{G}]$. Hence, for all $i \in \{1, \ldots, n\}$ by Proposition 2ii it follows that

$$\models \exists p_{i+1} \ldots \exists p_n\, F[G_1 \ldots G_i p_{i+1} \ldots p_n].$$

From (a) it also follows that $\mathsf{SUBST}(\boldsymbol{G}, \boldsymbol{p}, F)$. This implies that for all $i \in \{1, \ldots, n\}$ it holds that

$$\mathsf{SUBST}(G_i, p_i, \exists p_{i+1} \ldots \exists p_n\, F[G_1 \ldots G_{i-1} p_i \ldots p_n]) \text{ and } \mathsf{free}(G_i) \cap \boldsymbol{p} = \emptyset.$$

We thus have derived for all $i \in \{1, \ldots, n\}$ the two properties that characterize G_i as a solution of the 1-SP as stated in (b).

Right-to-left: From (b) it follows that G_n is a solution of the 1-SP

$$(F[G_1 \ldots G_{n-1} p_n])[p_n].$$

Hence, by the characteristics of *solution* it follows that $\models F[G_1 \ldots G_n]$. The property $\mathsf{SUBST}(\boldsymbol{G}, \boldsymbol{p}, F)$ can be derived from $\mathsf{free}(\boldsymbol{G}) \cap \boldsymbol{p} = \emptyset$ and the fact that for all $i \in \{1, \ldots, n\}$ it holds that $\mathsf{SUBST}(G_i, p_i, (\exists p_{i+1} \ldots \exists p_n\, F[G_1 \ldots G_{i-1} p_i \ldots p_n]))$. The properties $\models F[G_1 \ldots G_n]$ and $\mathsf{SUBST}(\boldsymbol{G}, \boldsymbol{p}, F)$ characterize $\boldsymbol{G}$ as a solution of the SP $F[\boldsymbol{p}]$. ◻

This proposition states an equivalence between the solutions of an n-ary SP and the solutions of n 1-SPs. These 1-SPs are on formulas with an existential second-order prefix. The following gives an example of this decomposition:

Example 11 (Reducing an n-ary Solution Problem to Unary Solution Problems). Consider the SP $F[p_1 p_2]$ of Example 6. The 1-SP with unknown p_1 according to Proposition 10 is

$$(\exists p_2\, F[p_1 p_2])[p_1],$$

whose formula is, by second-order quantifier elimination, equivalent to $\forall x\, (a(x) \rightarrow b(x)) \rightarrow \forall x\, (p_1(x) \rightarrow b(x))$. Take $a(x_1)$ as solution G_1 of that 1-SP. The 1-SP with unknown p_2 according to Proposition 10 is

$$(F[G_1 p_2])[p_2].$$

Its formula is then, by replacing p_1 in F as specified in Example 6 with a and removing the duplicate conjunct obtained then, equivalent to

$$\forall x\, (a(x) \rightarrow b(x)) \rightarrow (\forall x\, (a(x) \rightarrow p_2(x)) \land \forall x\, (p_2(x) \rightarrow b(x))).$$

A solution of that second 1-SP is, for example, $b(x_1)$, yielding the pair $a(x_1) b(x_1)$ as solution of the originally considered SP $F[p_1 p_2]$.

4.2 Solving on the Basis of Second-Order Formulas

The following algorithm to compute particular solutions is an immediate transfer of Proposition 10. Actually, it is more an "algorithm template", since it is parameterized with a method to compute 1-SPs and covers a nondeterministic as well as a deterministic variant:

Algorithm 12 (SOLVE-ON-SECOND-ORDER). *Let $\mathcal{F}$ be a class of formulas and let 1-SOLVE be a nondeterministic or a deterministic algorithm that outputs for 1-SPs of the form $(\exists p_1 \ldots \exists p_n\, F[p])[p]$ with $F \in \mathcal{F}$ solutions G such that* $\mathsf{free}(G) \cap \{p_1, \ldots, p_n\} = \emptyset$ *and $F[G] \in \mathcal{F}$.*
INPUT: *A SP $F[p_1 \ldots p_n]$, where $F \in \mathcal{F}$, that has a solution.*
METHOD: *For $i := 1$ to n do: Assign to G_i an output of 1-SOLVE applied to the 1-SP $(\exists p_{i+1} \ldots \exists p_n\, F[G_1 \ldots G_{i-1} p_i \ldots p_n])[p_i]$.*
OUTPUT: *The sequence $G_1 \ldots G_n$ of formulas, which is a particular solution of $F[p_1 \ldots p_n]$.*

The solution components G_i are successively assigned to some solution of the 1-SP given in Proposition 10, on the basis of the previously assigned components $G_1 \ldots G_{i-1}$. Even if the formula F of the input problem does not involve second-order quantification, these 1-SPs are on second-order formulas with an existential prefix $\exists p_{i+1} \ldots \exists p_n$ upon the yet "unprocessed" unknowns.

The algorithm comes in a nondeterministic and a deterministic variant, just depending on whether *1-SOLVE* is instantiated by a nondeterministic or a deterministic algorithm. Thus, in the nondeterministic variant the nondeterminism of *1-SOLVE* is the only source of nondeterminism. With Proposition 10 it can be verified that if a nondeterministic *1-SOLVE* is "complete" in the sense that for each solution there is an execution path that leads to the output of that solution, then also SOLVE-ON-SECOND-ORDER based on it enjoys that property, with respect to the n-ary solutions $G_1 \ldots G_n$.

For the deterministic variant, from Proposition 10 it follows that if *1-SOLVE* is "complete" in the sense that it outputs some solution whenever a solution exists, then, given that $F[p_1 \ldots p_n]$ has a solution, which is ensured by the specification of the input, also SOLVE-ON-SECOND-ORDER outputs some solution $G_1 \ldots G_n$.

This method applies *1-SOLVE* to existential second-order formulas, which prompts some issues for future research: As indicated in Sect. 3.4 (and elaborated in [30, Sect. 7]) Craig interpolation can in certain cases be applied to compute solutions of 1-SPs. Can QBF solvers, perhaps those that encode QBF into predicate logic [28], be utilized to compute Craig interpolants? Can it be useful to allow second-order quantifiers in solution formulas because they make these smaller and can be passed between different calls to *1-SOLVE*?

As shown in [30, Sect. 6], if *1-SOLVE* is a method that outputs so-called *reproductive* solutions, that is, most general solutions that represent all particular solutions, then also SOLVE-ON-SECOND-ORDER outputs reproductive solutions. Thus, there are two ways to obtain representations of all particular solutions whose comparison might be potentially interesting: A deterministic method that outputs a single reproductive solution and the nondeterministic method with an execution path to each particular solution.

4.3 Solving with the Method of Successive Eliminations

The *method of successive eliminations* in a narrower sense is applied in a Boolean algebra setting that corresponds to propositional logic and outputs reproductive solutions. The consideration of reproductive solutions belongs to the classical material on Boolean reasoning [19,23,27] and is modeled in the present framework in [30, Sect. 6]. Compared to SOLVE-ON-SECOND-ORDER, the method handles the second-order quantification by eliminating quantifiers one-by-one, inside-out, with a specific method and applies a specific method to solve 1-SPs, which actually yields reproductive solutions. These incorporated methods apply to propositional input formulas (and to first-order input formulas if the unknowns are nullary). Second-order quantifiers are eliminated by rewriting with the equivalence $\exists p\, F[p] \equiv F[\top] \vee F[\bot]$. As solution of an 1-SP $F[p]$ the formula $(\neg F[\bot] \wedge t) \vee (F[\top] \wedge \neg t)$ is taken, where t is a fresh nullary predicate that is considered specially. The intuition is that particular solutions are obtained by replacing t with arbitrary formulas in which p does not occur (see [30, Sect. 6] for a more in-depth discussion).

The following algorithm is an iterative presentation of the *method of successive eliminations*, also called *Boole's method*, in the variant due to [8]. The presentation in [22, Sect. 3.1], where apparently minor corrections compared to [8] have been made, has been taken here as technical basis. We stay in the validity-based setting, whereas [8,22,23] use the unsatisfiability-based setting. Also differently from [8,22] we do not make use of the *xor* operator.

Algorithm 13 (SOLVE-SUCC-ELIM).
INPUT: *A SP* $F[p_1 \ldots p_n]$*, where* F *is propositional, that has a solution and a sequence* $t_1 \ldots t_n$ *of fresh nullary predicates.*
METHOD:

1. *Initialize* $F_n[p_1 \ldots p_n]$ *with* F.
2. *For* $i := n$ *to* 1 *do: Assign to* $F_{i-1}[p_1 \ldots, p_{i-1}]$ *the formula* $F_i[p_1 \ldots p_{i-1} \top] \vee F_i[p_1 \ldots p_{i-1} \bot]$.
3. *For* $i := 1$ *to* n *do: Assign to* G_i *the formula* $(\neg F_i[G_1 \ldots G_{i-1} \bot] \wedge t_i) \vee (F_i[G_1 \ldots G_{i-1} \top] \wedge \neg t_i)$.

OUTPUT: *The sequence* $G_1 \ldots G_n$ *of formulas, which is a reproductive solution of* $F[p_1 \ldots p_n]$ *with respect to the special predicates* $t_1 \ldots t_n$.

The formula assigned to F_{i-1} in step (2.) is the result of eliminating $\exists p_i$ in $\exists p_i\, F_i[p_1 \ldots p_i]$ and the formula assigned to G_i in step (3.) is the reproductive solution of the 1-SP $(F_i[G_1 \ldots G_{i-1} p_i])[p_i]$, obtained with the respective incorporated methods indicated above. The recursion in the presentations of [8,22] is translated here into two iterations that proceed in opposite directions: First, existential quantifiers of $\exists p_1 \ldots \exists p_n\, F$ are eliminated inside-out and the intermediate results, which do not involve second-order quantifiers, are stored. Solutions of 1-SPs are computed in the second phase on the basis of the stored formulas.

In this presentation it is easy to identify two "hooks" where it is possible to plug-in alternate methods that produce other outputs or apply to further formula classes: In step (2.) the elimination method and in step (3.) the method to determine solutions of 1-SPs. If the plugged-in method to compute 1-SPs outputs particular solutions, then SOLVE-SUCC-ELIM computes particular instead of reproductive solutions.

4.4 Solving by Inside-Out Witness Construction

Like SOLVE-SUCC-ELIM, the following algorithm eliminates second-order quantifiers one-by-one, inside-out, avoiding intermediate formulas with existential second-order prefixes of length greater than 1, which arise with SOLVE-ON-SECOND-ORDER. In contrast to SOLVE-SUCC-ELIM, it performs elimination by the computation of ELIM-witnesses.

Algorithm 14 (SOLVE-BY-WITNESESS)**.** *Let $\mathcal{F}$ be a class of formulas and ELIM-WITNESS be an algorithm that computes for formulas $F \in \mathcal{F}$ and predicates p an ELIM-witness G of p in $\exists p\, F[p]$ such that $F[G] \in \mathcal{F}$.*
INPUT: *A SP $F[p_1 \ldots p_n]$, where $F \in \mathcal{F}$, that has a solution.*
METHOD: *For $i := n$ to 1 do:*

1. *Assign to $G_i[p_1 \ldots p_{i-1}]$ the output of ELIM-WITNESS applied to*

$$\exists p_i\, F[p_1 \ldots p_i G_{i+1} \ldots G_n].$$

2. *For $j := n$ to $i+1$ do: Re-assign to $G_j[p_1 \ldots p_{i-1}]$ the formula $G_j[p_1 \ldots p_{i-1} G_i]$.*

OUTPUT: *: The sequence $G_1 \ldots G_n$ of formulas, which provides a particular solution of $F[p_1 \ldots p_n]$.*

Step (2.) in the algorithm expresses that a new value is assigned to G_j and that G_j can be designated by $G_j[p_1 \ldots p_{i-1}]$, justified because the new value does not contain free occurrences of $p_i, \ldots, p_n$. In step (1.) the respective current values of $G_{i+1} \ldots G_n$ are used to instantiate F. It is not hard to see from the specification of the algorithm that for input $F[\boldsymbol{p}]$ and output $\boldsymbol{G}$ it holds that $\exists \boldsymbol{p}\, F \equiv F[\boldsymbol{G}]$ and that SUBST$(\boldsymbol{G}, \boldsymbol{p}, F)$. By Proposition 8ii, $\boldsymbol{G}$ is then a solution if $\models \exists \boldsymbol{p}\, F$. This holds indeed if $F[\boldsymbol{p}]$ has a solution, as shown below with Proposition 15.

If *ELIM-WITNESS* is "complete" in the sense that it computes an elimination witness for all input formulas in $\mathcal{F}$, then SOLVE-BY-WITNESESS outputs a solution. Whether all solutions of the input SP can be obtained as outputs for different execution paths of a nondeterministic version of SOLVE-BY-WITNESESS obtained through a nondeterministic *ELIM-WITNESS*, in analogy to the nondeterministic variant of SOLVE-ON-SECOND-ORDER, appears to be an open problem.

5 Existence of Solutions

5.1 Conditions for the Existence of Solutions

We now turn to the question under which conditions there exists a solution of a given SP, or, in the terminology of [23], the SP is *consistent*. A necessary condition is easy to see:

Proposition 15 (Necessary Condition for the Existence of a Solution). *If a SP $F[\boldsymbol{p}]$ has a solution, then it holds that* $\models \exists \boldsymbol{p}\, F$.

Proof. Follows from the definition of *particular solution* and Proposition 2ii. □

Under certain presumptions that hold for propositional logic this condition is also sufficient. To express these abstractly we use the following concept:

Definition 16 (SOL-Witnessed Formula Class). A formula class $\mathcal{F}$ is called *SOL-switnessed for* a predicate class $\mathcal{P}$ if and only if for all $p \in \mathcal{P}$ and $F[p] \in \mathcal{F}$ the following statements are equivalent:

(a) $\models \exists p\, F$.
(b) There exists a solution G of the 1-SP $F[p]$ such that $F[G] \in \mathcal{F}$.

Since the right-to-left direction of that equivalence holds in general, the left-to-right direction alone would provide an alternate characterization. The class of propositional formulas is SOL-witnessed (for the class of nullary predicates). This follows since in propositional logic it holds that

$$\exists p\, F[p] \equiv F[F[\top]], \tag{iv}$$

which can be derived in the following steps: $F[F[\top]] \equiv \exists p\, (F[p] \wedge (p \leftrightarrow F[\top])) \equiv (F[\top] \wedge (\top \leftrightarrow F[\top])) \vee (F[\bot] \wedge (\bot \leftrightarrow F[\top])) \equiv F[\top] \vee F[\bot] \equiv \exists p\, F[p]$.

The following definition adds closedness under existential second-order quantification to the notion of *SOL-witnessed*, to allow the application on 1-SPs matching with item (b) in Proposition 10:

Definition 17 (MSE-SOL-Witnessed Formula Class). A formula class $\mathcal{F}$ is called *MSE-SOL-witnessed* for a predicate class $\mathcal{P}$ if and only if it is SOL-witnessed for $\mathcal{P}$ and for all sequences $\boldsymbol{p}$ of predicates in $\mathcal{P}$ and $F \in \mathcal{F}$ it holds that $\exists \boldsymbol{p}\, F \in \mathcal{F}$.

The class of existential QBFs (formulas of the form $\exists \boldsymbol{p}\, F$ where F is propositional) is MSE-SOL-witnessed (like the more general class of QBFs – second-order formulas with only nullary predicates). Another example is the class of first-order formulas extended by second-order quantification upon nullary predicates, which is MSE-SOL-witnessed for the class of nullary predicates. The following proposition can be seen as expressing an invariant of the method of successive eliminations that holds for formulas in an MSE-SOL-witnessed class:

Proposition 18 (Solution Existence Lemma). *Let $\mathcal{F}$ be a formula class that is MSE-SOL-witnessed for predicate class $\mathcal{P}$. Let $F[\boldsymbol{p} = p_1 \ldots p_n] \in \mathcal{F}$ with $\boldsymbol{p} \in \mathcal{P}^n$. If $\models \exists \boldsymbol{p}\, F[\boldsymbol{p}]$, then for all $i \in \{0, \ldots, n\}$ there exists a sequence $G_1 \ldots G_i$ of formulas such that $\mathsf{free}(G_1 \ldots G_i) \cap \boldsymbol{p} = \emptyset$, $\mathsf{SUBST}(G_1 \ldots G_i, p_1 \ldots p_i, F)$, $\models \exists p_{i+1} \ldots \exists p_n F[G_1 \ldots G_i p_{i+1} \ldots p_n]$ and $\exists p_{i+1} \ldots \exists p_n F[G_1 \ldots G_i p_{i+1} \ldots p_n] \in \mathcal{F}$.*

Proof. By induction on the length i of the sequence $G_1 \ldots G_i$. The conclusion of the proposition holds for the base case $i = 0$: The statement $\mathsf{SUBST}(\epsilon, \epsilon, F)$ holds trivially, $\models \exists \boldsymbol{p}\, F$ is given as precondition, and $\exists \boldsymbol{p}\, F \in \mathcal{F}$ follows from $F \in \mathcal{F}$. For the induction step, assume that the conclusion of the proposition holds for some $i \in \{0, \ldots n-1\}$. That is, $\mathsf{SUBST}(G_1 \ldots G_i, p_1 \ldots p_i, F)$, $\models \exists \boldsymbol{p}\, F[G_1 \ldots G_i p_{i+1} \ldots p_n]$ and $\exists \boldsymbol{p}\, F[G_1 \ldots G_i p_{i+1} \ldots p_n] \in \mathcal{F}$. Since $\mathcal{F}$ is witnessed for $\mathcal{P}$ and $p_{i+1} \in \mathcal{P}$ it follows that there exists a solution G_{i+1} of the 1-SP $(\exists \boldsymbol{p}\, F[G_1 \ldots G_i p_{i+1} \ldots p_n])[p_{i+1}]$ such that $(\exists \boldsymbol{p}\, F[G_1 \ldots G_{i+1} p_{i+2} \ldots p_n]) \in \mathcal{F}$. From the characteristics of *solution* it follows that $\models \exists \boldsymbol{p}\, F[G_1 \ldots G_{i+1} p_{i+2} \ldots p_n])$ and $\mathsf{SUBST}(G_{i+1}, p_{i+1}, \exists \boldsymbol{p}\, F[G_1 \ldots G_{i+1} p_{i+2} \ldots p_n])$. In the latter statement the quantifier $\exists \boldsymbol{p}$ ensures that $\mathsf{free}(G_{i+1}) \cap \boldsymbol{p} = \emptyset$. With the induction hypothesis $\mathsf{SUBST}(G_1 \ldots G_i, p_1 \ldots p_i, F)$ it follows that $\mathsf{SUBST}(G_1 \ldots G_{i+1}, p_1 \ldots p_{i+1}, F)$, which completes the proof of the induction step. (The existential quantification is here upon $\boldsymbol{p}$, not just $p_{i+1} \ldots p_n$, to ensure that no members of $\boldsymbol{p}$ at all occur as free symbols in the solutions.) □

A sufficient and necessary condition for the existence of a solution of formulas in MSE-SOL-witnessed classes now follows from Propositions 15 and 18:

Proposition 19 (Existence of a Solution). *Let $\mathcal{F}$ be a formula class that is MSE-SOL-witnessed on predicate class $\mathcal{P}$. Then for all $F[\boldsymbol{p}] \in \mathcal{F}$ where the members of $\boldsymbol{p}$ are in $\mathcal{P}$ the following statements are equivalent:*

(a) $\models \exists \boldsymbol{p}\, F$.
(b) There exists a solution $\boldsymbol{G}$ of the SP $F[\boldsymbol{p}]$ such that $F[\boldsymbol{G}] \in \mathcal{F}$.

Proof. Follows from Propositions 15 and 18. □

From that proposition it is easy to see that for SPs with propositional formulas the complexity of determining the existence of a solution is the same as the complexity of deciding validity of existential QBFs, as proven in [2,15,16], that is, Π_2^P-completeness: By Proposition 19, an SP $F[\boldsymbol{p}]$ where F is propositional has a solution if and only if the existential QBF $\exists \boldsymbol{p}\, F[\boldsymbol{p}]$ is valid and, vice versa, an arbitrary existential QBF $\exists \boldsymbol{p}\, F[\boldsymbol{p}]$ (where F is quantifier-free) is valid if and only if the SP $F[\boldsymbol{p}]$ has a solution.

5.2 Characterization of SOL-Witnessed in Terms of ELIM-Witness

The following proposition shows that under a minor syntactic precondition on formula classes, *SOL-witnessed* can also be characterized in terms of *ELIM-witness* instead of *solution* as in Definition 16:

Proposition 20 (SOL-Witnessed in Terms of ELIM-Witness). *Let $\mathcal{F}$ be a class of formulas that satisfies the following properties: For all $F[p] \in \mathcal{F}$ and predicates q with the same arity of p it holds that $F[p] \lor \neg F[q] \in \mathcal{F}$, and for all $F \lor G \in \mathcal{F}$ it holds that $F \in \mathcal{F}$. The class $\mathcal{F}$ is SOL-witnessed for a predicate class $\mathcal{P}$ if and only if for all $p \in \mathcal{P}$ and $F[p] \in \mathcal{F}$ there exists an ELIM-witness G of p in $F[p]$ such that $F[G] \in \mathcal{F}$.*

Proof. Left-to-right: Assume that $\mathcal{F}$ is meets the specified closedness conditions and is SOL-witnessed for $\mathcal{P}$, $p \in \mathcal{P}$ and $F[p] \in \mathcal{F}$. Let q be a fresh predicate with the arity of p. The obviously true statement $\models \exists p\, F[p] \lor \neg \exists p\, F[p]$ is equivalent to $\models \exists p\, F[p] \lor \neg F[q]$ and thus to $\models \exists p\, (F[p] \lor \neg F[q])$. By the closedness properties of $\mathcal{F}$ it holds that $F[p] \lor \neg F[q] \in \mathcal{F}$. Since $\mathcal{F}$ is SOL-witnessed for $\mathcal{P}$ it thus follows from Definition 16 that there exists a solution G of the SP $(F[p] \lor \neg F[q])[p]$ such that $(F[G] \lor \neg F[q]) \in \mathcal{F}$, and, by the closedness properties, also $F[G] \in \mathcal{F}$. From the definition of *solution* it follows that $\models F[G] \lor \neg F[q]$, which is equivalent to $\exists p\, F[p] \equiv F[G]$, and also that $\mathsf{SUBST}(G, p, F[G] \lor \neg F[q])$, which implies $\mathsf{SUBST}(G, p, F[G])$. Thus G is an SO-witness of p in $F[p]$ such that $F[G] \in \mathcal{F}$. Right-to-left: Easy to see from Proposition 8ii. □

5.3 The Elimination Result as Precondition of Solution Existence

Proposition 19 makes an interesting relationship between the existence of a solution and second-order quantifier elimination apparent that has been pointed out by Schröder [27, vol. 1, Sect. 21] and Behmann [5], and is briefly reflected in [23, p. 62]: The formula $\exists \mathbf{p}\, F$ is valid if and only if the result of eliminating the existential second-order prefix (called *Resultante* by Schröder [27, vol. 1, Sect. 21]) is valid. If it is not valid, then, by Proposition 19, the SP $F[\mathbf{p}]$ has no solution, however, in that case the elimination result represents the *unique (modulo equivalence) weakest precondition under which the SP would have a solution.* The following proposition shows a way to make this precise:

Proposition 21 (The Elimination Result is the Unique Weakest Precondition of Solution Existence). *Let $\mathcal{F}$ be a formula class and let $\mathcal{P}$ be a predicate class such that $\mathcal{F}$ is MSE-SOL-witnessed on $\mathcal{P}$. Let $F[\mathbf{p}]$ be a solution problem where $F \in \mathcal{F}$ and all members of $\mathbf{p}$ are in $\mathcal{P}$. Let A be a formula such that $(A \rightarrow F) \in \mathcal{F}$, $A \equiv \exists \mathbf{p}\, F$, and no member of $\mathbf{p}$ does occur in A. Then*

(i) The SP $(A \rightarrow F)[\mathbf{p}]$ has a solution.
(ii) If B is a formula such that $(B \rightarrow F) \in \mathcal{F}$, no member of $\mathbf{p}$ occurs in B, and the SP $(B \rightarrow F)[\mathbf{p}]$ has a solution, then $B \models A$.

Proof. (Proposition 19i) From the specification of A it follows that $\models A \rightarrow \exists \mathbf{p} F$ and thus $\models \exists \mathbf{p}\, (A \rightarrow F)$. Hence, by Proposition 19, the SP $(A \rightarrow F)[\mathbf{p}]$ has a solution. (Proposition 19ii) Let B be a formula such that the left side of holds. With Proposition 19 it follows that $\models B \rightarrow \exists \mathbf{p} F$. Hence $B \models \exists \mathbf{p} F$. Hence $B \models A$. □

The following example illustrates Proposition 21:

Example 22 (Elimination Result as Precondition for Solvability). Consider the SP $F[p_1 p_2]$ where

$$F = \forall x\,(p_1(x) \rightarrow p_2(x)) \wedge \forall x\,(a(x) \rightarrow p_2(x)) \wedge \forall x\,(p_2(x) \rightarrow b(x)).$$

Its formula is the consequent of the SP considered in Example 6. Since $\exists p_1 \exists p_2\, F \equiv \forall x\,(a(x) \rightarrow b(x)) \not\equiv \top$, from Proposition 19 it follows that $F[p_1 p_2]$ has no solution. If, however, the elimination result $\forall x\,(a(x) \rightarrow b(x))$ is added as an antecedent to F, then the resulting SP, which is the SP of Example 6, has a solution.

6 Conclusion

The *solution problem* and second-order quantifier *elimination* were interrelated tools in the early mathematical logic. Today elimination has entered automatization with applications in the computation of circumscription, in modal logics, and for semantic forgetting and modularizing knowledge bases, in particular for description logics. Since the solution problem on the basis of first-order logic is, like first-order validity, recursively enumerable there seems some hope to adapt techniques from first-order theorem proving.

The paper makes the relevant scenario accessible from the perspective of predicate logic and theorem proving. Together with the consideration of most general solutions in [30] it shows that a wealth of classical material on Boolean equation solving can be transferred to predicate logic. Some essential diverging points crystallize, like the constructability of witness formulas for quantified predicates. An abstracted version of the core property underlying the classical method of successive eliminations provides a foundation for systematizing and generalizing algorithms that reduce n-ary solution problems to unary solution problems.

Beyond the presented core framework there seem to be many results from different communities that are potentially relevant for further investigation. This includes the vast amount of techniques for equation solving on the basis of Boolean algebra and its variants, developed over the last 150 years. For description logics there are several results on concept unification, e.g., [3,4]. Variants of Craig interpolation such as disjunctive interpolation [25] share with the solution problem at least the objective to find substitution formulas such that the overall formula becomes valid (or, dually, unsatisfiable).

First steps towards constructive methods for the solution problem that apply to special cases of first-order inputs are described in [30], including methods based on Craig interpolation and on an elimination technique from [12]. The possible characterization of *solution* by an entailment also brings up the question whether Skolemization and Herbrand's theorem justify some "instance-based" technique for computing solutions that succeeds on large enough quantifier expansions.

Acknowledgments. The author thanks anonymous reviewers for their helpful comments. This work was supported by DFG grant WE 5641/1-1.

References

1. Ackermann, W.: Untersuchungen über das Eliminationsproblem der mathematischen Logik. Math. Ann. **110**, 390–413 (1935)
2. Baader, F.: On the complexity of Boolean unification. Inf. Process. Lett. **67**(4), 215–220 (1998)
3. Baader, F., Morawska, B.: Unification in the description logic $\mathcal{EL}$. Log. Methods Comput. Sci. **6**(3), 1–31 (2010)
4. Baader, F., Narendran, P.: Unification of concept terms in description logics. J. Symb. Comput. **31**, 277–305 (2001)
5. Behmann, H.: Das Auflösungsproblem in der Klassenlogik. Archiv für Philosophie **4**(1), 97–109 (1950). (First of two parts, also published in Archiv für mathematische Logik und Grundlagenforschung, 1.1 (1950), pp. 17–29)
6. Behmann, H.: Das Auflösungsproblem in der Klassenlogik. Archiv für Philosophie **4**(2), 193–211 (1951). (Second of two parts, also published in Archiv für mathematische Logik und Grundlagenforschung, 1.2 (1951), pp. 33–51)
7. Brown, F.M.: Boolean Reasoning, 2nd edn. Dover Publications, Mineola (2003)
8. Büttner, W., Simonis, H.: Embedding Boolean expressions into logic programming. J. Symb. Comput. **4**(2), 191–205 (1987)
9. Carlsson, M.: Boolean constraints in SICStus Prolog. Technical report SICS T91:09, Swedish Institute of Computer Science, Kista (1991)
10. Conradie, W., Goranko, V., Vakarelov, D.: Algorithmic correspondence and completeness in modal logic. I. The core algorithm SQEMA. LMCS **2**(1:5), 1–26 (2006)
11. Doherty, P., Łukaszewicz, W., Szałas, A.: Computing circumscription revisited: a reduction algorithm. J. Autom. Reason. **18**(3), 297–338 (1997)
12. Eberhard, S., Hetzl, S., Weller, D.: Boolean unification with predicates. J. Log. Comput. **27**(1), 109–128 (2017)
13. Gabbay, D.M., Schmidt, R.A., Szałas, A.: Second-Order Quantifier Elimination: Foundations, Computational Aspects and Applications. College Publications, London (2008)
14. Gabbay, D., Ohlbach, H.J.: Quantifier elimination in second-order predicate logic. In: KR 1992, pp. 425–435. Morgan Kaufmann (1992)
15. Kanellakis, P.C., Kuper, G.M., Revesz, P.Z.: Constraint query languages. In: PODS 1990, pp. 299–313. ACM Press (1990)
16. Kanellakis, P.C., Kuper, G.M., Revesz, P.Z.: Constraint query languages. J. Comput. Syst. Sci. **51**(1), 26–52 (1995)
17. Koopmann, P., Schmidt, R.A.: Uniform interpolation of $\mathcal{ALC}$-ontologies using fixpoints. In: Fontaine, P., Ringeissen, C., Schmidt, R.A. (eds.) FroCoS 2013. LNCS, vol. 8152, pp. 87–102. Springer, Heidelberg (2013). doi:10.1007/978-3-642-40885-4_7
18. Löwenheim, L.: Über das Auflösungsproblem im logischen Klassenkalkül. In: Sitzungsberichte der Berliner Mathematischen Gesellschaft, vol. 7, pp. 89–94. Teubner (1908)
19. Löwenheim, L.: Über die Auflösung von Gleichungen im logischen Gebietekalkül. Math. Ann. **68**, 169–207 (1910)
20. Martin, U., Nipkow, T.: Unification in Boolean rings. In: Siekmann, J.H. (ed.) CADE 1986. LNCS, vol. 230, pp. 506–513. Springer, Heidelberg (1986). doi:10.1007/3-540-16780-3_115
21. Martin, U., Nipkow, T.: Unification in Boolean rings. J. Autom. Reason. **4**(4), 381–396 (1988)

22. Martin, U., Nipkow, T.: Boolean unification - the story so far. J. Symb. Comput. **7**, 275–293 (1989)
23. Rudeanu, S.: Boolean Functions and Equations. Elsevier, Amsterdam (1974)
24. Rudeanu, S.: Lattice Functions and Equations. Springer, London (2001). doi:10.1007/978-1-4471-0241-0
25. Rümmer, P., Hojjat, H., Kuncak, V.: Disjunctive interpolants for Horn-clause verification. In: Sharygina, N., Veith, H. (eds.) CAV 2013. LNCS, vol. 8044, pp. 347–363. Springer, Heidelberg (2013). doi:10.1007/978-3-642-39799-8_24
26. Schmidt, R.A.: The Ackermann approach for modal logic, correspondence theory and second-order reduction. J. Appl. Log. **10**(1), 52–74 (2012)
27. Schröder, E.: Vorlesungen über die Algebra der Logik. Teubner (vol. 1, 1890; vol. 2, pt. 1, 1891; vol. 2, pt. 2, 1905; vol. 3, 1895)
28. Seidl, M., Lonsing, F., Biere, A.: bf2epr: a tool for generating EPR formulas from QBF. In: PAAR-2012. EPiC, vol. 21, pp. 139–148 (2012)
29. Sofronie, V.: Formula-handling computer solution of Boolean equations. I. Ring equations. Bull. EATCS **37**, 181–186 (1989)
30. Wernhard, C.: The Boolean solution problem from the perspective of predicate logic - extended version. Technical report KRR 17-01, TU Dresden (2017)
31. Zhao, Y., Schmidt, R.A.: Concept forgetting in $\mathcal{ALCOI}$-ontologies using an Ackermann approach. In: Arenas, M., et al. (eds.) ISWC 2015. LNCS, vol. 9366, pp. 587–602. Springer, Cham (2015). doi:10.1007/978-3-319-25007-6_34

Author Index

Printed in the United States
By Bookmasters